ENCYCLOPAEDIA OF
MOUNTAINEERING

Also by WALT UNSWORTH

The English Outcrops
North Face
The High Fells of Lakeland
Peaks, Passes and Glaciers
Everest
This Climbing Game
Classic Walks of the World
Savage Snows

Fiction

The Devil's Mill
Whistling Clough
Grimsdyke

British Library Cataloguing in Publication Data

Unsworth, Walt
    Encyclopaedia of Mountaineering.–
    2Rev.ed
    I. Title
    796.5

    ISBN 0–340–57744–4

Published by Hodder and Stoughton,
a division of Hodder and Stoughton Ltd,
Mill Road, Dunton Green, Sevenoaks, Kent TN13 2YA
Editorial Office: 47 Bedford Square, London WC1B 3DP

Photoset by Rowland Phototypesetting Ltd, Bury St Edmunds, Suffolk
Printed in Great Britain by St Edmundsbury Press Ltd,
Bury St Edmunds, Suffolk

ENCYCLOPAEDIA OF
MOUNTAINEERING
Walt Unsworth

Hodder & Stoughton
LONDON SYDNEY AUCKLAND

Acknowledgements

My thanks are due to the many authors, past and present, upon whose work I have freely drawn in compiling this encyclopaedia. I am similarly indebted to numerous magazines and journals, British, American and European.

Many climbers gave me information, advice and encouragement either for the original edition of this work or subsequent ones, including: Nat Allen, Allan Austin, Mike Banks, John Barry, Paul Bauer, John Baxter, Bill Birkett, Barry Bishop, Peter Biven, Allan Blackshaw, Pete Bland, Chris Bonington, Mick Burke, John Cleare, John Cousins, A. D. M. Cox, Peter Crew, John Cunningham, John Dawes, Henry Day, Ed Douglas, Xavier Eguskitza, Nick Estcourt, Peter Evans, Ken Falconer, Mick Fowler, Dennis Gray, Alfred Gregory, Peter Habeler, Peter Harding, Charles Houston, Tony Howard, Dr P. Hurley, Ron James, Pat Littlejohn, Sir Arnold Lunn, Ian McNaught-Davis, Jerry Moffatt, Tony Moulam, Bill Murray, Hideki Nagata, Paul Nunn, Roger Payne, Fred Piggott, Doug Scott, Malcolm Slesser, Tony Streather, Jeremy Talbot, Mike Walford, Derek Walker, Ivan Waller, Michael Ward, Mike Westmacott, Fritz Wiessner, Ken Wilson and Alfred Zurcher. Mrs Diana Penny and Mrs Audrey Salkeld also provided useful information and my thanks are due to them. Sadly, the hand of time has removed a number of these friends from us.

WALT UNSWORTH
Milnthorpe 1992

How to Use This Book

An encyclopaedia, while it must be all-embracing, must also have certain limitations. The chief of these is depth: important topics cannot be followed to their ultimate conclusions (some require, and have, books to themselves) yet enough information must be given to form a broad picture. This book does just that, and where necessary, references are added so that the topic may be pursued further (see below). Less important topics receive only a sentence or two. Another limitation is continuity: mountaineering, like life itself, continues even as the book is being written and produced. There is bound to be a time lag between events and public knowledge of those events, but there is also an imposed time lag while the significance of the events is assessed. The scope of the work itself also imposes limitations on the compiler: whilst every effort has been made to use the best available references it has not been possible to cross-check every detail.

Although the entries are strictly alphabetical, the subject matter divides itself into four major areas: places, people, techniques and equipment, and miscellanea. A few notes about each of these will not be out of place since they will help the reader to understand the scope and limitations of the book.

Places

The entries cover all the important mountain areas of the world and many of the lesser ones. An entry may be under the country concerned (e.g. Australia) or if it is one of the great ranges – Alps, Andes, Himalaya – under the range. Thus 'Dolomites' will be found as a subsection under 'Alps' and 'Yosemite' under 'United States'. English regions are treated similarly – all the Yorkshire crags will be found in subsections of Yorkshire, and so on.

Some particular peaks or crags are so famous that they deserve their own separate entry – the Matterhorn, for example.

Most regional entries have a note about climbing guidebooks available. The following abbreviations are used:

A.A.C.	American Alpine Club
A.C.	Alpine Club
B.M.C.	British Mountaineering Council
C.C.	Climbers Club
C.M.C.	Cleveland Mountaineering Club
C.O.	Cordee
C.P.	Cicerone
F.R.C.C.	Fell & Rock Climbing Club
N.M.C.	Northumbrian Mountaineering Club
S.M.C.	Scottish Mountaineering Club
S.W.M.C.	South Wales Mountaineering Club
W.C.P.	West Col/Gaston West Col
Y.M.C.	Yorkshire Mountaineering Club

People

This heading covers the largest number of entries – over 400 – and was the most difficult to compile. A climber can only be judged in the context of his own time and many of the pioneers who figure in the book would not have gained entry had they lived at a later date. But the matter is further complicated by the fact that many are enshrined in books and climbing lore and for this reason alone require a mention. The nearer we come to modern times the more good climbers there are, but the standard of entry gets tougher! There are so many top rank modern climbers that it is not possible to mention them all. The selection is there to argue over! However, where a climber does not have an entry to himself his name could well appear in connection with particular mountains. Wherever possible all entries give full names and dates, except where a climber has preferred to give only his commonly accepted, usually abbreviated, first name. The net has been cast fairly wide but in an English-language publication it is inevitable that many of the climbers will be British or American – about half in fact. However, the number of Japanese entries has been increased and the European ones substantially so since the last edition.

Techniques and Equipment

The encyclopaedia is not an instructional textbook, but sufficient information is given to enable the layman or climber to grasp the technique involved or the purpose of any particular piece of equipment. Colloquial expressions have been included where appropriate because climbing does have a special jargon. Due attention has also been given to trends where these are apparent.

Miscellanea

Mountaineering has common ground with many broader subjects, such as geography, geology, physics and so on. In general, phenomena from these subjects are only included where they have a specific bearing on the sport – glaciers being an obvious example. Under this heading, too, comes a host of other 'fringe' topics including ethical and philosophical considerations.

References

It would double the size of this book to list the thousands of references consulted during compilation. However, books and journals are quoted where it is felt that a fuller explanation would be especially helpful. Climbers' own books are listed with date of publication. Cross-references are indicated thus: ◊ (see), ◊◊ (see also).

Corrections and Additions

The author would welcome, via the publisher, any factual corrections or suggested additions to the encyclopaedia for possible inclusion in future editions. Such notes should give the exact source: publication and date, author and page number.

'If a man can climb, and in safety, rocks that others will not attempt or cannot scale, he is an exceptional rock-climber; and may be no more. If he can quickly judge the right line and thread his way unerringly and without hesitation through an unknown intricate ice-fall, if he is an unfailing judge of snow and ice, he is a snow craftsman of the first rank; but it may end there. Combine these qualities, add power, resource and courage that rises under the stress of bad weather or in times of difficulty or danger, and he becomes a great mountaineer.'

C. T. DENT

A

Abalakov, Vitali Mikhailovich (1906–86) An outstanding Soviet mountaineer, often regarded as the 'father' of Russian climbing. Abalakov made some early scrambles on the Krasnojarsk Pillars as a boy (1915) but his serious climbing began in 1931 with the first Soviet ascent of Dychtau. Then came (in the Caucasus):

1932 Bezingi Ridge traverse Gestola–Shkhara
1947 P. Schurovski, N W Face
      Shkhelda, second W Summit by Face
1948 Tomashek–Muller Route, Shkhara followed by traverse to Gestola
1949 Koshtantau–Dychtau traverse
1950 Shkhelda, third W Summit by Face
1951 Chanchahi, N Face
      Ullutauchana
1953 P. Schurovski, N E Face
1954 Dychtau, N Face

Important first ascents in the greater ranges are:

Altai – Belukha from N, Iiktu (1933)
Pamirs – P. Lenin from N (1934), P. Trapezia (1935), P.XIX Party Congress (1952), Musdzhilga–Sandal traverse (1955), P. Voroshilov (1959), P. Dserzhinski–P. Lenin–P.XIX Party Congress traverse (1960)
Turkestan – Oloviannaja stena (1934)
Tian Shan – P. Pobeda (1956)

While descending from Khan Tengri in the Tian Shan in 1936 he lost several fingers and toes from frostbite which stopped him climbing for ten years.

Abalakov was ten times champion of the U.S.S.R. in mountaineering and leader of 12 high-altitude expeditions. He has done considerable work on equipment development both in climbing and other sports, and is a member of the U.I.A.A. Commissions on Safety and Belaying. Honoured Master of Mountaineering, 1935; Honoured Master of Sport, 1943; Honoured Trainer of the U.S.S.R. in Mountaineering, 1957.

Wrote: *The Fundamentals of Mountaineering* (German and Japanese editions amongst others, but no English version).

Abney, Sir William de Wiveleslie (1843–1920) Trained in the Royal Engineers, where he held rank of Captain until he retired in 1881, Abney was one of the foremost pioneers in the development of photographic science, especially the dry-plate process. Elected F.R.S. in 1876 and Rumford Medallist for his photographic researches (1883). K.C.B. in 1900. He was for many years science adviser to the Board of Education and was the author of many works on photography.

He seems to have little climbing to his credit but is well known for his magnificent series of portraits of the early Alpine guides published in ◊ Cunningham and Abney's *Pioneers of the Alps* (1887).

Abominable snowman   The abominable snowman, or yeti, is a creature said to live in the high Himalaya and associated ranges such as the Pamirs. One seen on the Fedchenko Glacier in the Pamirs was said to be thick-set with unusually long forearms, walking on its hind legs and bent slightly forwards. It wore no clothing and was covered in thick reddish-grey hair. Several Sherpas claim to have seen yeti, and various expeditions have seen yeti tracks in the snow.

According to the Sherpas there are two types of yeti: the 'little yeti' which eats men, and the 'big yeti' which eats yaks. Yeti have been seen eating frogs in the Dudh Kosi valley.

There have been several yeti-hunting expeditions but all have failed to find the creature. Other mythological creatures include the big foot and sasquatch of North America and the hualapichi (snow ghost) of the Cordillera Real of Bolivia.

The classic essay on the yeti is Appendix B of *Mount Everest 1938* by H. W. Tilman.

Abraham brothers   George Dixon Abraham (1872–1965) and Ashley Perry Abraham (1876–1951) were two Keswick brothers who played an important part in establishing rock-climbing as a sport in Britain. Well known for their association with O. G. ◊ Jones, they were also innovators in their own right.

They began climbing about 1890 but their early routes were gullies of little account (Sandbed Ghyll, 1890; Dollywaggon Gully, 1894; Bridge Gully, 1895; Iron Crag Chimney, 1896 – all in the Lake District). At Christmas, 1895, they met Jones and began climbing with him in 1896 (Jones' Direct from Deep Ghyll, 1896; Walker's Gully, 1899 – Ashley did not take part; Pisgah Buttress, 1898, and several famous Welsh climbs, including North Buttress, Terrace Wall Variant and Milestone Buttress, all on Tryfan, 1899). (See below.)

During this period, but without Jones, they visited Skye (1896), climbed Bowfell Links (1897), Mouse Ghyll (1897) and the Keswick Brothers' Climb on Scafell (1897). Only the last achieved fame.

After Jones' death in 1899 the brothers continued to make new climbs with other partners, such as Phillipson, Harland, Barton and ◊ Puttrell. In the Lakes these were: New West, Pillar (1901), Shamrock Buttress, Pillar (1902), and their eponymous routes on A and B Buttresses, Dow Crag (1903). In Scotland, with Puttrell, they climbed Church Door Buttress, Bidean, and the Direct ascent of Crowberry Ridge, where Abraham's Ledge is named in their honour. They made some other minor routes, too, and George returned to Glencoe later the same year on his honeymoon and with his wife climbed Winifred's Pinnacle, Aonach Dubh, and Lady's Gully, Buachaille Etive Mor. In 1905 they climbed the celebrated Monolith Crack of the Gribin Facet in Wales.

Ashley visited Skye with H. Harland in 1906 and 1907 making half a dozen new climbs, of which Cioch Direct is best known. George revisited Skye as late as 1920 and made a couple of new routes. The brothers climbed extensively in the Alps but seemed content to repeat existing climbs.

The brothers were professional photographers and as such the first to popularize climbing. They agreed to illustrate Jones' book on the Lakes in return for action shots of the master which they sold in their Keswick shop. A heavy plate camera was their constant companion and many of their climbs were undertaken with photographs in mind and, later, guidebooks (for instance on the Welsh tour of 1899 and Ashley's Skye tour of 1907). This professionalism aroused considerable antagonism from the older establish-ment climbers: they were accused of tilting the camera!

After Jones' death they took up writing and publishing guidebooks:

Rock Climbing in the English Lake District, Jones (revised) 2nd and 3rd ed.
Rock Climbing in North Wales, G. D. and A. P. Abraham.
Rock Climbing in Skye, A. P. Abraham.
The Complete Mountaineer, G. D. Abraham.
British Mountain Climbs, G. D. Abraham.
Mountain Adventures at Home and Abroad, G. D. Abraham.
Swiss Mountain Climbs, G. D. Abraham.
On Alpine Heights and British Crags, G. D. Abraham.
First Steps to Climbing, G. D. Abraham.

British Mountain Climbs ran to six main editions (1908–48), and was enormously influential in the development of the sport.

George was always the leader on the brothers' climbs together. They have been credited with the invention of ◊ belaying.

See A. Hankinson, *Camera on the Crags*.

Abruzzi, Duke of the (1873–1933) Luigi Amadeo Giuseppe, grandson of King Victor Emmanuel II of Italy. Abruzzi was in the tradition of wealthy Italian explorer-climbers. Vittorio ◊ Sella, the photographer, was another, and he accompanied Abruzzi on several expeditions. The expeditions were large, well organized and equipped with the best Italian guides.
They were:

1897   Alaska. The first ascent of Mt St Elias. The expedition was planned after an expedition to Nanga Parbat was prevented by plague in India.
1899   Attempt to reach the North Pole. Abruzzi lost two fingers in an accident and the leadership of the final push devolved upon U. Gagni, who reached Lat. 86° 34′ N – the furthest north reached at the time (1900). Several lives were lost and the expedition was an epic of endurance.
1906   Ruwenzori. The expedition climbed all the main peaks (all first ascents) and mapped the area.
1909   Karakoram. An attempt on K2 was foiled at 6,640 m on the Abruzzi Ridge. Reached 7,500 m on Chogolisa – the highest point reached at that date.
1928–9 Exploration of the Uebi Shebeli River in Ethiopia–Eritrea.

In the First World War the Duke was C.I.C. of the Italian Fleet and of the Allied Adriatic fleets. In 1919 he began work on the Eritrean colony which was to be his final life's work and to which, in the end, he returned to die.

Abruzzi had been a good climber in his early days: he did the Zmutt on the Matterhorn with Mummery and Collie, and made several first ascents. The Pic Luigi Amadeo in the Mt Blanc Range is named in his honour.

Abseil (G.) (Fr.:rappel) A rapid method of descent using the rope to slide down. Both the French and German terms are used by British climbers, but the German is more common. Common slang: to 'ab'. Note also 'abseiling' (G. *abseilen*).

Abseiling is commonly done using a doubled rope hanging from an abseil point, which may be a tree, rock spike or peg. The climber slides down the rope, using friction to control his descent, until he reaches a stance. When all the party have abseiled to the stance, the rope is pulled down and the next

Abseiling, on the Jagigrat near Saas Fee. (*W.U.*)

abseil commenced, and so on to the bottom of the climb. On many Continental peaks there are permanent abseil pegs (for example in the Dolomites) to make descent quicker.

Abseiling down ice is also common. It is done from a screw or ice peg. It can also be done from an ice 'mushroom' or 'bollard' – a substantial pinnacle of ice cut out by the ice axe – but this is not popular.

Abseiling may also be necessary during the course of a climb, especially on a ridge with many gendarmes, e.g. the Jagigrat. On some routes a diagonal abseil is made to change lines, but only on higher-grade climbs. A free abseil is one where the climber does not touch the rock, e.g. from an overhang.

Abseiling is a necessary part of climbing technique but it needs to be learnt on small outcrops first and always with the protection of a safety rope. Done carelessly it is highly dangerous and there have been numerous fatalities. There are several ways of using the rope to gain the necessary friction. The original method, known as the 'classic abseil', passes the rope between the legs, then across the front of the body and over the opposite shoulder. One hand lightly holds the rope in front, the other hand holds the rope behind – the latter is the controlling hand. The climber leans out from the cliff, backwards, until he is able to walk backwards down the rock, the speed of descent being controlled by the rear hand. By moving this forward, friction is increased and descent slowed. It is possible to stop still if necessary. The climber is actually sitting in the rope and it is this which enables him to leave the rock altogether, e.g. at an overhang, yet continue his descent.

The classic method is uncomfortable and there are numerous alternatives using slings, krabs, abseil bars, etc., but the most common nowadays is the figure-of-8♢ descender.

When a lot of abseils are expected, e.g. in the Dolomites, a special abseil rope is carried. This may be 100 m in length, but can be thinner than climbing rope – 9 mm is satisfactory.

The chief dangers of abseiling are: insecure abseil points, e.g. loose pegs;

unsatisfactory abseil points, e.g. allowing the rope to ride off; insufficient rope to reach the desired stance; and incorrect or careless technique. Where a lot of overhangs are involved the climber should always carry ♢ prusiks so that if the abseil ends away from the rock he can climb back up the rope to safety and try a different abseil. For this reason, too, it is worth putting a knot in the end of the rope.

Abseiling is nowadays sometimes practised as a sub-sport. There are various fancy ways of doing it, including a sensational one facing outwards.

Abseil loop   Where an abseil rope might jam when pulling it down, things can be eased by using a sling and krab. A sling alone is not satisfactory because when pulled down the friction of nylon on nylon can cause heat which damages the rope's sheath and can melt the sling. On a long continuous abseil the sling and krab have to be abandoned. Because this is expensive it was once the fashion to carry hemp slings and thread the rope directly through the sling.

Accidents   There is an old mountaineering saying that accidents most often happen in the easy places; meaning that when the obvious difficulties have been overcome, a relaxation of vigilance can be fatal. This is actually borne out by the statistics, both in the U.K. and the Alps. The commonest cause of accident is a simple slip resulting in a fall, but imperfect technique is often to blame, as is inadequate equipment. These are especially lethal if allied to poor weather. Unavoidable accidents are sometimes caused by falling rocks or lightning. Heart attacks claim a number of victims – in 1987 they accounted for 36 per cent of all fatalities in the hills of England and Wales.

Common mistakes leading to accidents include: inadequate footwear, lack of ice axe and crampons in ice/snow conditions, lack of a helmet in rock/ice climbing.

As more people use the hills in Britain accidents increase:

Year	Accidents	Fatalities
1957	57	12 (21%)
1968	221	30 (14%)
1986	474	69 (15%)

Not all accidents involve death and injury: of 700 people involved in rescue incidents in England and Wales in 1987, 50 were killed, 165 were seriously hurt and 219 had minor injuries – the rest were just lost or in need of other help.

The most frequent injuries are to the legs (30 per cent) and the head (14 per cent). Twenty-two per cent of head injuries are fatal – a figure only exceeded by heart attacks, where 50 per cent are fatal.

Apart from skiing in Europe, most accidents happen to hillwalkers, both at home and abroad: 45 per cent in England and Wales, 23 per cent in Austria, for example, in 1985. Rock-climbing accounted for only 6 per cent and 4 per cent respectively. But in the Alps, skiing accounts for far more accidents than any other activity.

ACCIDENT PROCEDURE
Two-man party: make the victim as comfortable as possible, ensuring that he cannot fall further. Take careful note of his position and mark it with a bright garment, rope, etc. Go for help to the nearest telephone, dial 999 and ask for Police (Coastguard for sea cliffs).
Larger party: if the party is inexperienced make sure that the uninjured members are conducted to safe ground. Someone should be left with the

victim and a messenger sent to contact the Police as above. He should have written instructions (if possible) stating the precise location of the accident, including name of route and pitch if a climb, injuries and time of accident. See *Mountain & Cave Rescue* and the *SMC Journal*, both annually, for British rescue and accident statistics.

Acclimatization   The adaptation of the human body to the rarefied air at high altitudes. The process is a slow one, especially for the really big mountains of the Himalaya, where acclimatization can take from four to six weeks. During acclimatization the following physiological changes take place: breathing becomes deeper and faster, and often irregular (Cheyne-Stokes respiration); heartbeat speed and force is increased; blood thickens because the red cells multiply and the plasma becomes less.

Acclimatization can affect climbers even in the Alps and other relatively low mountains: two or three days should be spent on lower peaks before attempting anything high, though acclimatization is a very personal thing and some people are scarcely affected at all. At its worst it produces mountain sickness, manifested by headaches, sleeplessness and nausea.

At higher altitudes, lack of acclimatization can cause pulmonary oedema or cerebral oedema. Water is not passed at the usual rate and accumulates as fluid on the lungs or the brain. The treatment is oxygen via a face mask and a diuretic drug to make the patient pass water. Evacuation to a lower altitude is urgent and only then will the patient revive – otherwise oedema is rapidly fatal. (◊ Mountain sickness.)

À cheval   A method of climbing a rib or arête in which the climber places one foot on either side of the arête and grips the crest with his hands. He then moves up in a series of frog-like hops. The Americans call it rib-riding. The technique is not common in Britain. The Black Rocks, Derbyshire, is well known as a place where it is used.

In the Alps some narrow arêtes are taken by sitting astride them for a few moves and this is also called à cheval.

Achille Ratti (1857–1939)   A Catholic priest later to become Pope Pius XI. As a young man he was an enthusiastic mountaineer, climbing mainly in the Monte Rosa area. The Achille Ratti climbing club is named in his honour.

His book, *Climbs on Alpine Peaks* was translated into English, 1926.

Aconcagua (6,960 m)   The highest peak in South America and in the western world, Aconcagua dominates the Central Andes of Argentina. There are two summits: North (6,960 m) and South (6,028 m). The Ordinary Route (N N E Face) begins at Puente del Inca and rises via the huts at Plaza de Mulas, Plantamura (two huts) and Indepencia, to the summit of N peak. By 1965 there had been over 50 ascents, but no fewer than 36 lives had been lost in attempts. The mountain has sudden severe storms when winds reach 160 m.p.h. and the temperature can drop to -45°C. The name comes from the local native word *Kon-kawa* (snowy mountain).

In 1883 P. ◊ Güssfeldt attempted the mountain from the N, with only local help – his guide, ◊ Burgener, being ill. With virtually no equipment he reached a height of about 6,600 m. Another attempt was less successful. In 1897, the Fitzgerald Expedition attempted the peak. The leader gave up about 500 m short of the top, but the guide, Matthias ◊ Zurbriggen, reached the N summit on 14 January – a first ascent. A month later S. Vines and N. Lanti also reached the summit. 1897 and 1898 saw two incredible attempts by a German party helped by Chilean miners. Using Güssfeldt's route they reached a height of about 6,500 m. In 1898, ◊ Conway deliberately stopped some 15 m short of the summit. He later claimed that he did not wish to embarrass Fitzgerald by doing in a week what it had taken the latter months to achieve! Other notable ascents include:

1934   E Face, first ascent – K. Narkievicz-Jodko, St. Dazynski, W. Ostrowski, S. Osiecki
1940   First woman's ascent – Adriana Link and party
1947   S Summit, first ascent – T. Kopp, L. Herold
1951   Güssfeldt's route completed – W. Foerster, L. Krahl, E. Maier
1953   W Face–S Ridge, first ascent – F. Ibanez, Mr and Mrs F. Marmillod, F. Grajales
1953   First winter ascent – E. Huerta, F. Godoy, H. Vasalla
1954   S S E Face, first ascent – R. Ferlet's Expedition
1965   W Face, first ascent – G. Mason, T. Hill, R. Mackey
1966   S Face of S Summit, first ascent – F. Moravec's Expedition

Ferlet's expedition of 1954 is reckoned one of the greatest feats in Andean climbing. (See A. J. 60.)

Several dogs have been to the top of Aconcagua – almost certainly the canine height record.

Adams Reilly, Anthony Miles William (1836–85) Irish artist noted for making the first reliable map of the Mont Blanc area, begun in 1863 and published two years later. In 1864 he was with Whymper on many of the first ascents in the area, and they had intended to attempt the Matterhorn together but Whymper was recalled to England.

Agassiz, Jean-Louis Rudolphe (1807–73) A Swiss–American naturalist, professor at Neuchâtel and later Harvard. His life-long study was actually fishes, but in 1836 he began a study of ◊ glaciers, which is the foundation of modern glaciology. His work was published as *Études sur les glaciers*, 1840. He kept a hut on the Aar Glacier known as the Hôtel des Neuchâtelois from which he carried out the study. He made an early ascent of the Jungfrau. The Agassizhorn and Agassizjoch in the Bernese Alps are named after him as are Mount Agassiz and Col Agassiz in the Sierra Nevada of California. There is an Agassiz glacier on Mt St Elias in the Yukon.

Agostini, Father Alberto De (1883–1960) A Patagonian missionary who played a large part in the exploration of Tierra del Fuego. Reached the highest point of the Martial Mountains, c. 1,400 m, and in 1913 the difficult rock summit of Monte Olivia (1,270 m) above Ushuaia, with the guides Abele and Agostino Pession.

He failed to reach the summit of Sarmiento (2,404 m) despite two attempts. No more attempts were made on it for 41 years but Agostini lived to see the summit reached by C. Mauri and C. Maffei in 1956.

Aid climbing Climbing which relies on aids such as pegs, bolts and étriers to overcome a problem. It may be that the rock (or ice) overhangs too much for natural balance, or that there is a deficiency of holds. A climb may have a few aided moves, or a few pitches, or may be entirely aided from start to finish. The majority of climbs, of course, have no aid climbing whatsoever and are known as 'free climbs', if a distinction has to be made between the two. A number of originally aid climbs have later been done free.

Left, Ashley (*left*) and George Abraham; right, aid climbing: Royal Robbins demonstrates the single-rope technique in Yosemite. (*A. Greenbank*)

On rock, aid climbing involves the planting of pegs in cracks and moving up on the pegs by means of ◊ étriers. By using karabiners, the pegs can also serve as ◊ runners and thus, if the pegs are well planted, the leader of an aid climb is well protected. It is possible to belay by sitting in the étriers and belaying to a peg, and even to bivouac using special hammocks slung between pegs (e.g. on some of the long Yosemite routes). Where the rock has no cracks, ◊ bolts may be used. Bolts are often left in place and in the Alps pegs are too, though it is considered more ethical for the last man to remove the pegs if possible.

On aided ice-climbs, ice pegs or (more usual) ice screws are used to support the étriers. Aided ice-climbs are generally fairly short (e.g. overcoming a sérac barrier).

There are single- and double-rope techniques for aided climbing. In the former the rope is used only for protection. The climber keeps himself in balance when planting a peg by means of a short loop called a ◊ cow's tail. In double-rope technique he may also use a cow's tail but he can be kept in position by the second man pulling on the rope. Once another peg is placed above, the rope can be passed through a karabiner on this peg and tension gained from above. The climber instructs his second in this and it is useful to have two differently coloured ropes, e.g. 'slack on white, pull on red'. There are many variations on this, usually aimed at saving time and energy, for aid climbing is both slow and tiring. A considerable amount of gear may need to be carried on a long route.

The opportunity for its misuse is apparent and still provokes occasional comment. The term 'mechanized climbing' is totally obsolete and 'peg climbing' or 'artificial climbing' little used today.

Aiguille du Dru (3,754 m) An outlier of the Verte massif in the Mont Blanc range, overlooking the Mer de Glace. Seen from ◊ Montenvers it presents one of the most startling pictures in the Alps – a gigantic obelisk.

There are two tops, known as the Grand and Petit Dru (3,733 m), and one speaks of 'the Drus'. The great modern climbs for which the mountain is famous lie on the flanks of the Petit Dru.

The first ascent was that of C. T. Dent and J. Walker with A. Burgener and K. Maurer, 1878 – Dent's 19th attempt on the peak. The Petit Dru was first climbed by the guides J. E. Charlet-Stratton, P. Payot and F. Folliguet, in 1879. The first traverse, Petit–Grand (the usual way), was by E. Giraud with – J. Ravanel and A. Comte, 1903, and the first winter ascent and traverse was by the two guides A. Charlet and C. Dévouassoud, in 1928.

The three modern classics are: N Face (P. Allain, R. Leininger, 1935) after it had previously been descended by abseil by A. Roch and R. Gréloz (1932); the W Face (L. Berardini, A. Dagory, M. Laine, G. Magnone, 1952) – climbed in two stages separated by 11 days and thus provoking criticism; the Bonatti Pillar, climbed solo by Walter Bonatti in five days, 1955; one of the epics of modern climbing (see Bonatti, *On the Heights*). The Americans Hemming and Robbins made a direct start to the W Face in 1962 and Harlin and Robbins made another in 1965. Both are very hard.

Ainslie, Charles (1820–63) Original Member of the A.C. With Hudson, Kennedy and the Smyths he made the first guideless ascent of Mont Blanc, 1855.

Alaska Alaska contains the highest mountain in North America: ◊ Mt McKinley (6,194 m) and Mt Logan (6,050 m). The latter is actually just in Canada, making it the highest Canadian peak.

Other principal ranges are the Chugach Mountains, Wrangell Mountains, Mackenzie Mountains and Brooks Range. The climbing on all these peaks is virtually expeditionary because of the weather conditions and remoteness. Some of the world's biggest glaciers are in this region. Climbers usually fly in to base camp. The most popular ascent is McKinley, done frequently these days. McKinley is often referred to by its native name, Denali.

1 Aleutian Range; 2 Alaska Range; 3 Brooks Range; 4 Chugach Mountains; 5 Wrangell Mountains; 6 St. Elias Mountains; 7 Fairweather Range; 8 Coast Mountains

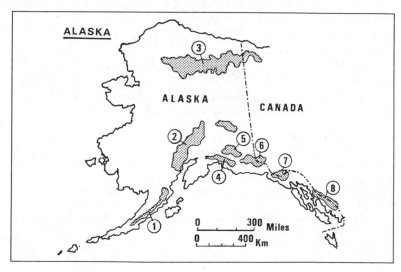

Some of the lesser peaks offer great technical climbing, with huge rock walls which have been compared with those of Patagonia. The Moose's Tooth (3,150 m) and Kichatna Spires (2,739 m) near McKinley, and Kate's Needle (3,049 m) and similar spires on the British Columbia border, are noteworthy. There are multi-day climbs of Gr VI.

ALASKA RANGE

Mt McKinley (6,194 m) – H. Stuck, H. Karstens, R. Tatum, W. Harper, 1913
Mt Foraker (5,304 m) – C. Houston, T. G. Brown, G. Waterson, 1934
Mt Hunter (4,442 m) – F. Beckey, H. Meybohm, H. Harrer, 1954
Mt Hayes (4,188 m) – Mr & Mrs B. Washburn, S. Hendricks, B. Ferris, W. Shand, 1942
Mt Deborah (3,822 m) – F. Beckey, H. Meybohm, H. Harrer, 1954

YUKON

Mt Logan (6,050 m) – A. H. MacCarthy, H. Lambart, W. Foster, L. Lindsay, N. Reade, A. Carpe, 1925
Mt St Elias (5,489 m) – Duke of the Abruzzi, 1897
Mt Fairweather (4,670 m) – A. Carpe, T. Moore, 1931

Albert I, King of the Belgians (1875–1934) A noted mountaineer who died as a result of an abseiling accident in the Ardennes. Though the King had climbed a number of the higher Alpine peaks (Matterhorn, Monte Rosa, Eiger), his special interest was in rock-climbing and his favourite area was the Dolomites, where he climbed most of the hardest routes of the day. Before his accession to the throne he and his wife, Princess Elisabeth, had climbed together many times and made the first ascent of the N E Ridge of Piz Carale. In the Kaisergebirge he made some of the hardest climbs of the day on the steep faces of the Fleischbank, Predigstuhl and Totenkirchl. Though he climbed with guides, the King was often leader on the climbs.

Allain, Pierre (b. 1904) A French climber, trained on the rocks of Fontainebleau, who became one of the leading guides of the inter-war years. Climbing usually with J. and R. Leininger, he made numerous routes, amongst which are:

1933   S W Ridge of Fou
1935   E Face, Dent du Caiman
       N Face of the Dru
1936   E Ridge of Dent du Crocodile

He later became an equipment designer and manufacturer – the well-known ◊ P.A. rock boot was a revolutionary addition to climbing gear.

Allen, Nat (b. 1928) A founder member of the Rock and Ice Club and the Alpine Climbing Group. In the former, particularly, he played an important role and was partner to Joe ◊ Brown and ◊ Whillans on numerous occasions, among which might be mentioned the first ascents of Llithrig and the E Buttress Girdle of Clogwyn Du'r Arddu, and Erosion Grooves, Carreg Wastad.

In the Peak District, Allen made forty new gritstone climbs and two new limestone climbs before 1951, and many more since then. His limestone climbs are mainly in the Manifold Valley and Dovedale and his best-known gritstone climbs are at Froggatt (Allen's Slab, etc.). He has also made new routes in Pembroke, Swanage and on Cader Idris (Route II, Slanting Gully Grooves). Allen is a leading authority on Peak District climbing.

Allmen, Hilti von (1935–66)   A Swiss guide who climbed a number of north faces and made the first winter ascent of the ◊ Matterhorn Nordwand, with Paul Etter, 3–4 February 1962. He died in an avalanche near St Moritz.

Almer, Christian (1826–98)   Possibly the greatest of the early Alpine guides; his only possible equal being Melchior ◊ Anderegg. Almer took part in the celebrated ascent of the Wetterhorn from Grindelwald by Sir Alfred ◊ Wills and thereafter climbed with many of the leading amateurs including ◊ Moore, ◊ Whymper, ◊ Hornby and Philpott, and ◊ Coolidge. He climbed with Coolidge almost exclusively from 1868 to 1884, but during a winter ascent of Jungfrau (1884) he lost several toes from frostbite and was incapacitated for a couple of seasons. He seems to have been fully active again by 1890, but his place as Coolidge's chief guide had by then been taken by his son, Christian Almer II.

He made numerous first ascents in the Oberland and was with Whymper during the famous seasons of 1864 and 1865, though he did not take part in the ◊ Matterhorn ascent. His experience ranged from end to end of the Alps – Dachstein in Austria (1866) to the Maritime Alps (1879). His favourite peak was always the Wetterhorn and he made a Golden Wedding anniversary ascent with his wife in 1896 – he was 70 and his wife, who accompanied him, was 71. He climbed it again in 1897.

Almer was at the centre of two famous climbing controversies. One, known as 'Almer's leap', concerned an illustration by Whymper in *Scrambles* showing Almer making a daring leap across a break in the ridge of the Écrins: this led to a classic controversy between Whymper and Coolidge over whether the incident took place. The other was the publication by ◊ Abney and ◊ Cunningham of a facsimile of Almer's *Führerbuch* (1897) which was deeply resented by many climbers.

Almer had five sons: Ulrich (b. 1849), Christian (b. 1859), Hans (b. 1861), Rudolf (b. 1864) and Peter (b. 1869). They all became first-class guides, Ulrich (who died in 1940) being especially notable. He accompanied his father on many expeditions and he also led Cockin on the first ascent of Ushba in the Caucasus, 1888.

Alp   The grassy pastures below the snowline in the Alps but above the valley and the place where the animals are taken to feed in the summer months. Adopted in error by the early travellers who thought it referred to the whole mountain, hence the Alps. In the Eastern Alps an alp is known as an *alm*.

Alpenstock   A long wooden pole fitted with a spike at the lower end and used as a sort of 'third leg' on glaciers and snow slopes by the pioneers. Frequently seen in early alpine engravings. It was supplanted by the ◊ ice axe and had virtually disappeared by the 1870s.

Alpine Climbing Group   A British club, founded in the early 1950s, to raise the standard of post-war British alpinism and to provide guidebooks for the major areas of the Alps. In 1957 they published *Selected Climbs in the Range of Mont Blanc*. Their publishing interests were later assumed by the Alpine Club with whom the A.C.G. formed an alliance. It remains an élitist group of young climbers comparable with the French G.H.M.

Alpine Club   The idea of a club to cater for Alpine climbers was first mooted by William Mathews in a letter to F. J. A. Hort at the end of 1856 or early 1857. It was revived at a meeting between the Mathews and Kennedy in the Hasli Tal, 4 August 1857, and first seriously discussed at the Mathews' house, The Leasowes, Worcestershire, on 6 November 1857, when a list of prospective members was drawn up. The first meeting was at Ashley's Hotel, Henrietta Street, Covent Garden, on 22 December 1857 when only 11 members turned up. An attempt to turn it into an élitist group – by electing only members who had ascended 13,000 ft peaks – was defeated. A second meeting was held in the same hotel on 19 January 1858 when the rules were revised for approval at the next meeting, 3 February, when E. S. Kennedy was elected Vice-President and Hinchcliff, Hon. Secretary. The post of President was not filled until 31 March, when John Ball was elected. All those who had joined the Club on or before 19 January were designated Original Members.

The initial idea was that the Club should be of a social nature, but this soon changed and the first lecture was given by ◊ Ormsby in February 1860.

A detailed history of the Club can be gleaned from the numerous volumes of the ◊ *Alpine Journal* published since 1863, and a general summary in the centennial volume, 1957. Until the 1920s its influence in world mountaineering was considerable, but it declined somewhat when it failed to take account of changing conditions and attitudes to the sport, as shown by Continental climbers. In recent years it has recovered, and now holds a respected position in world climbing circles.

An applicant for membership must be over 21 and be proposed and seconded by two members. Letters of support may come from other members. He is elected by the Committee. Technical qualifications are not high – roughly several Alpine seasons (or other high ranges) with at least 20 good peaks to the applicant's credit. Candidates need not be British, but until May 1974 only male members were admitted.

ALPINE CLUB, PRESIDENTS OF THE

1858 J. Ball	1905 G. F. Browne	1953 E. S. Herbert
1861 E. S. Kennedy	1908 H. Woolley	1956 H. C. J. Hunt
1864 A. Wills	1911 W. E. Davidson	1959 G. I. Finch
1866 L. Stephen	1914 W. Pickford	1962 T. H. Somervell
1869 W. Mathews	1917 J. P. Farrar	1965 E. E. Shipton
1872 W. Longman	1920 J. N. Collie	1968 R. C. Evans
1875 T. W. Hinchcliff	1923 C. G. Bruce	1971 A. D. M. Cox
1878 C. E. Mathews	1926 G. H. Morse	1974 J. L. Longland
1881 T. G. Bonney	1929 C. Wilson	1977 P. Lloyd
1884 F. C. Grove	1932 J. J. Withers	1980 J. H. Emlyn Jones
1887 C. T. Dent	1935 J. L. Strutt	1983 Lord Chorley
1890 H. Walker	1938 C. Schuster	1986 A. K. Rawlinson
1893 D. W. Freshfield	1941 G. W. Young	1987 G. C. Band
1896 C. Pilkington	1944 L. S. Amery	1990 H. R. A. Streather
1899 J. Bryce	1947 T. G. Longstaff	
1902 W. M. Conway	1950 C. A. Elliott	

Sir Anthony Rawlinson was killed on Crib Goch, Wales on 22 February 1986. He was the only President to die in office and the only one to be killed in a mountain accident. Vice President Lady Evans assumed the Presidency until the election of George Band.

Alpine clubs Following the formation of the ◊ Alpine Club, similar institutions sprang up in many parts of the world. On the Continent the principal clubs adopted a wider policy of membership and this is still the case, so that clubs such as the Austrian, Swiss and French, for example, have thousands of members, divided into regional sections. The clubs own and maintain an elaborate system of huts for the use of which members pay reduced fees. Reciprocal rights exist.

Following upon the establishment of the British Alpine Club (1857) came:

1862 Austria	1883 Belgium
1863 Switzerland, Italy	1885 Sweden
1868 Norway	1891 New Zealand, South Africa
1869 Germany	1902 Russia, Holland, United States
1874 France	1906 Canada, Japan
1878 Spain	

Not all these clubs began on a national basis, but they eventually acquired it. They are not all called 'Alpine Club'.

The Russian A.C. no longer exists. It is interesting to note that a local Alpine Club was founded in Williamstown, U.S.A., as early as 1863. (◊ Climbing Clubs.)

Alpine fashion   (a) In rope management it refers to the simultaneous movement of a roped party over snow or easy rocks. Protection can be got by a direct ◊ belay over a rock or an embedded ice axe. It is an attempt to combine speed with safety and is frequently used in the Alps.
(b) In high-altitude mountaineering it refers to climbing a big peak as if it were Alpine i.e. without pre-placed camps, supplementary oxygen or ◊ fixed ropes.

Alpine Journal   The premier mountaineering journal, published by the ◊ Alpine Club.

A collection of papers first appeared in volume form in 1859 and was called *Peaks, Passes and Glaciers*. It was edited by John ◊ Ball and the idea was to disseminate information about the relatively unknown parts of the Alps. Two further volumes of *Peaks, Passes and Glaciers* were issued in 1862, edited by E. S. ◊ Kennedy, and regular publication with the title *Alpine Journal* (quarterly) began in March 1863 under the editorship of H. B. ◊ George. It is now issued annually in volume form. The journal has always concerned itself with world rather than just Alpine climbing.

There are five index volumes:
Vols I–XV (includes *PPG* i–iii) 1859–91
Vols 16–38 1891–1926
Vols 39–58 1927–52
Vols 59–73 1953–68
Vols 74–92 1969–87

Alpine start   In the Alps it is usual to start a climb very early in the morning so as to obtain the best snow conditions. The actual time depends upon the route: 4 a.m. is common, but it may be any time between midnight and 6 a.m.

Alpinism   Sometimes used to denote climbing which involves snow and ice at fairly high altitudes – as in the Alps. Perhaps a corruption of the French *alpinisme*.

Alps, the (Fr.: Les Alpes; G.: Die Alpen; It.: Le Alpi)   The best-known range of high mountains in the world. The Alps stretch from the Mediterra-

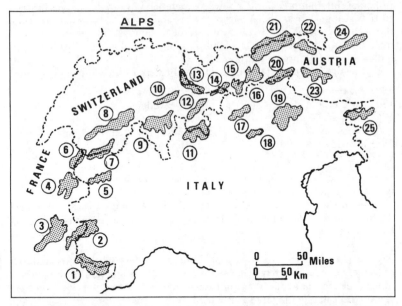

1 Maritime Alps; 2 Cottian Alps; 3 Dauphiné; 4 Graian Alps (Tarentaise); 5 Graian Alps (Cogne); 6 Chain of Mont Blanc; 7 Pennine Alp; 8 Bernese Alps; 9 Lepontine Alps; 10 Tödi Range; 11 Bernina Alps; 12 Albula Group; 13 Rhätikon; 14 Silvretta; 15 Ötztal Alps; 16 Stubai Alps; 17 Ortler Alps; 18 Lombard Alps; 19 Dolomites; 20 Zillertal Alps; 21 Bavarian Alps; 22 Karwendel-Kaisergebirge; 23 Tauern Alps; 24 Salzburg Alps; 25 Julian Alps.

nean hinterland near Nice in an immense arc to the environs of Ljubljana in Yugoslavia and Vienna in Austria. In general terms they form a natural border between Italy and her neighbours France, Switzerland, Austria and Yugoslavia and for much of the distance a political border too.

Within this overall picture the internal structure is complex with several important groups of mountains lying off the main watershed, particularly the Bernese Alps. There are, too, important flanking ranges known as the Pre-Alps (e.g. the Jura). While the main range tends to be igneous (granite, etc.) the outliers tend to be limestones (including the Bernese Alps). In all of these regions, mountaineering is actively practised.

The accepted classification of the range for mountaineering was put forward by ₵ Coolidge, though the extension of the sport, particularly in rock-climbing, has led to minor modifications (see below). Coolidge laid down three principal divisions: I – Western Alps (Col de Tenda to Simplon); II – Central Alps (Simplon to Reschen Scheideck and Stelvio); III – Eastern Alps (Reschen Scheideck to Radstatter Tauern). In common parlance climbers speak of 'the Alps', meaning the first two, and 'the Eastern Alps' meaning the last.

The highest mountain is Mont Blanc (4,807 m) and there are 52 mountains of 4,000 m, 64 counting multiple summits (Collomb, 1971) – but it is not always easy to determine these. All but one – Piz Bernina – are in the Western and Central Alps. There are hundreds of summits between 3,500 m and 4,000 m. Much of the range is under permanent ice and snow and there are numerous glaciers, the longest being the Great Aletsch, 13·75 miles long. Most glaciers are in retreat and there are marked differences between conditions now and in the pioneering days.

The complex variety of the range means that climbing of every kind and every standard is common. There are innumerable hotels, guest houses, mountain huts and bivouac huts throughout, as well as ancillary services such as guides, rescue teams and mountain transport of all kinds. Many centres today exist primarily for the skiing and tourist industries but it is still possible to find areas which are relatively unknown.

The great peaks and glaciers were of no interest to the native population before visitors arrived. The word *alp* (Eastern Alps: *alm*) refers to the lower hill pastures and was mistakenly adopted by visitors to refer to the whole mountain. Similarly the word *mont*, or *monte*, originally meant a pass (e.g. Monte Moro), which was the only feature of high mountains useful to the natives. Some of the famous passes were certainly known to the Romans and possibly earlier.

Wills' ascent of the Wetterhorn in 1854 is often taken to be the start of mountaineering as a sport, but Coolidge lists 132 peaks ascended before that date (including the Wetterhorn itself). ◊ Mont Blanc was climbed in 1786 (by M. G. ◊ Paccard and J. ◊ Balmat). Preceding the ascent of Mont Blanc were:

1358 Rochemelon	1770 Buet
1492 Mont Aiguille	1778 Triglav
before 1654 W Karwendelspitze	1779 Mont Velan
before 1694 Mont Tabor	1782 Scopi
before 1742 Scesaplana	1784 Aig. and Dôme du Goûter
1744 Titlis	Dent du Midi
c. 1762 Ankogel	

These were isolated events. The first real explorers of the high Alps were H. B. ◊ de Saussure and the monk, ◊ Placidus à Spescha, in the late eighteenth century. Considerable exploration (and ascents) took place before 1854, but from then until the ascent of the ◊ Matterhorn in 1865 is known as the Golden Age, the conquest of great peaks, though La Meije was not climbed until 1877. From 1865 to 1914 was the Silver Age, during which the route rather than the peak became important, with many difficult ridges and 'smaller' peaks being climbed (e.g. the Drus). Since the First World War, increasingly difficult routes, especially on the faces, have been followed, with an increase in winter ascents of great difficulty.

The Divisions and Groups of the Alps (based on Coolidge) DIVISIONS: I – Western Alps; II – Central Alps; III – Eastern Alps

I WESTERN ALPS

Ligurian Alps The western extremity of the Alps immediately beyond the Col de Tende, though not accepted as such by Coolidge. Collomb points out correctly (1971) that these hills must belong to the Alps or Appenines and fit more logically into the former. Coolidge left them out because they do not have the characteristics of the Alps: they are largely wooded and though there are a few rock faces, they are of little interest to the climber. The highest summit is Mt Marguareis (2,659 m).

Maritime Alps The main Alpine chain between the Col de Tende and the Col de Larche, considered by Coolidge to be the beginning of the Alps at the western end, though the Ligurian Alps are now included. The nearness of the Mediterranean (the mountains are scarcely 40 km from Nice) and relative lack of height make permanent snow and ice scarce, though there is a little.

Generally rock peaks which offer ridge and face climbs. The area has been compared with Skye. The highest summit is Punta dell'Argentera (3,297 m) and the best centre is St Martin.

Cottian Alps The main range between the Col de l'Argentière and Mont Cenis, and east of the Col du Galibier (west of this is the more important ⟡ Dauphiné Alps). The area is quite vast but has little to offer to climbers, only Monte Viso (3,841 m), the highest summit, being of any interest. (First ascent: W. Mathews and party, 1861.)

Dauphiné Alps A westerly extension of the Cottian Alps, entirely in France, and the most important climbing area between Mont Blanc and the Mediterranean. The principal centres are La Grave, La Bérarde and Ailefroide.

The landscape of the Dauphiné is starkly barren and the peaks are jagged and rocky. Snow- and ice-climbing is relatively unimportant though there are plenty of glaciers and snowfields. The highest summit is the Barre des Écrins (4,101 m) and the Dôme de Neige des Écrins is 4,015 m. Many of the peaks show a remarkable uniformity of height between 3,500 m and 3,800 m – 'a forest of peaks', extremely impressive. Other famous peaks, among many, are: La Meije (3,983 m), Ailefroide (3,954 m), Mt Pelvoux (3,946 m), Pic Sans Nom (3,914 m), Le Râteau (3,809 m), Les Bans (3,669 m) and Aigs. d'Arves (3,510 m). The latter is north of the main group, in the Grandes Rousses massif.

One would hesitate to recommend the area to novices though there are climbs of all grades. The traverse of La Meije (Gibson, U. Almer and Boss, 1891) is the traditional classic of the area; one of the finest traverses in the Alps. The South Face Direct of the same peak (Allain, Leininger, Vernet, 1934) is another fine route. The rock of the Dauphiné is not always good.

The area was always one of the most remote and backward regions of the Alps (⟡ Whymper, Moore etc.). Though Mont Pelvoux was climbed as early as 1848 (V. Puiseux), the Écrins was not climbed until the Moore–Whymper expedition of 1864. The Meije was the last of the really big Alpine peaks to be climbed (E. Boileau de Castelnau with P. Gaspard and son, 1877). Many of the peaks were not climbed until the last quarter of the century, and some minor ones not until the first quarter of this century. (See Whymper, *Scrambles*; Moore, *The Alps in 1864*; and J. Boell, *High Heaven*.) Numerous huts serve the area.

Graian Alps A large area of the Alps stretching from the Cottians in the south to the Mont Blanc group in the north. The Graians form three principal ranges, roughly parallel, running N–S. These are the Central Graians, the West Graians (Tarentaise), and the East Graians (Mountains of Cogne).

The Central Graians are relatively unfrequented and the mountains easy. The highest is Pte de Charbonnel (3,750 m). Rochemelon (3,538 m) was the first known ascent in the Alps (1,358 m). The West Graians (known also as Tarentaise or Vanoise) are noted for their beauty. The highest peak is Grande Casse (3,852 m) and though most peaks are easy, the Aig. de Vanoise (2,790 m) offers good rock-climbing. Pralognan and Val d'Isère are the best centres.

The Eastern Graians are probably the most popular of these mountains, more so since the Mt Blanc Tunnel has made them fairly accessible to Chamonix. The centre is Cogne, near Aosta, and the highest peak is Gran Paradiso (4,061 m) one of the easiest of the big Alpine peaks. Other well-known mountains are Herbetet (3,778 m) and Grivola (3,969 m). Harder climbs are on the ridge which includes the Roccia Viva and Tour du Grand St Pierre. There are several huts and bivouac huts.

Mont Blanc Group The principal range between the Col de la Seigne and the

Grand Col Ferret in the Western Alps. The mountains run south-west to north-east and are limited on the northern side by the vale of Chamonix and on the southern by the Val Veni and Val Ferret. In practical terms they are limited to the west by the Val Montjoie (Col du Bonhomme) and in the east by the Swiss Val Ferret. In area they do not compare with many other Alpine groups, but their importance to Alpinism is unquestionable.

The mountains are divided between France, Italy and Switzerland, the borders meeting at the summit of Mont Dolent (3,820 m) near the Col Ferret. Most of the area is in France. There are 25 tops of over 4,000 m, of which the highest is ◊ Mont Blanc, 4,807 m, the highest summit in Western Europe. The area is heavily glaciated and the rock (granite) runs to superb pinnacles (*aiguilles* = needles) giving fine climbing of all standards. The snow- and ice-climbing is equally good and varied and the region is immensely popular.

◊ Chamonix is by far the most important centre, and connects by rack railway with Montenvers, a hotel complex on an alp above the Mer de Glace and an important starting point for expeditions. On the Italian side, Cour-mayeur is the best centre. The two villages are connected by the Mont Blanc Tunnel (road only) and by a téléphérique system. There are several other villages, as well as téléphériques, etc. There are numerous huts.

The presence of the highest mountain in the Alps, and the intensive development of climbing in this area, means that every important peak, and almost every climb, is redolent of history. Only a broad picture can be given here:

The earliest attempts were on Mt Blanc itself and culminated in the first ascent by Dr M. G. Paccard and J. Balmat, 8 August 1786. Tourist ascents followed. The ascent of other peaks followed the general pattern of Alpine pioneering in which the highest peaks were the general goal. Typical is the first ascent of the Aig. Verte (E. Whymper with C. Almer, F. Biner, 1865).

Towards the end of the nineteenth century the aiguilles assumed import-ance as rock-climbing skills increased: Aig. du Grépon (A. F. Mummery with A. Burgener and B. Venetz, 1881), Aig. du Grand Dru (C. T. Dent, J. Walker with A. Burgener, K. Maurer, 1878). First ascents of the numerous aiguilles continued well into this century.

The first ascent of the Brenva Ridge (G. S. Mathews, A. W. Moore, F. and H. Walker, with J. and M. Anderegg, 1865) was outstanding for its time. The other great ridges were then climbed at intervals well into the present century, for example, the Hirondelles Ridge of Grandes Jorasses (G. Gaia, S. Matteoda, F. Ravelli, G. A. Rivetti with A. Rey, A. Chenoz, 1927).

The decade prior to the Second World War saw attempts on various N Faces and include the first ascent of the N Face of the Dru (P. Allain, R. Leininger, 1935) and the Walker Spur of Grandes Jorasses (R. Cassin, G. Esposito, U. Tizzoni, 1938).

Between the wars, too, came the development of the Brenva Face, begin-ning with Sentinelle Rouge (T. G. Brown, F. S. Smythe, 1927).

Of the numerous hard post-war climbs, one might pick out the Bonatti Pillar of the Dru (W. Bonatti, 1955) and Central Pillar of Frêney (C. Bonington, I. Clough, D. Whillans, J. Dlugosz, 1961) as particularly inter-esting. (◊◊ Mer de Glace; Chamonix Aiguilles; Mont Blanc; Aig. du Dru; Gr. Jorasses.)

Haute Savoie Alps   The large area between the Lake of Geneva and the Chamonix valley. The principal summits are those of the Dents du Midi, above Champery (highest top: 3,257 m). Above the Chamonix valley, the Aigs. Rouges are popular viewpoints (highest top: 2,965 m), easily reached by cablecar to Le Brévent (2,526 m). There are also considerable rock-climbs on the Aig. Rouges. A little further north Le Buet (3,099 m) is also a popular viewpoint.

The area also provides limestone climbing of quality. Best known are the crags of Mont Salève (about 120 m high), immediately south of Geneva. At Sallanches there is the Croix de Fer which gives two miles of cliff some 200–250 m in height and there are numerous crags in the region of Annecy. Plenty of scope for exploration.

Pennine Alps   The main range of the Alps from the Grand Col Ferret in the west to the Simplon Pass in the east. It is one of the largest Alpine groups and it has a greater number of 4,000 m peaks than any other – 42 tops exceed this height. Dufourspitze of Monte Rosa is the highest (4,634 m) and is the third highest mountain in the Alps. The ◊ Matterhorn is unquestionably the best-known peak.

The Swiss–Italian frontier follows the main range. Long valleys run down on the north and south flanks of this, those on the north (Swiss) side to the deep trench of the Rhône, those on the south (Italian) side to the Aosta valley or, in the east, the Lombardy plains. Between the valleys are ranges of high peaks, though on the south these are of little importance. On the north, these lateral valleys and ranges are of great importance to the climber. From west to east the valleys and ranges are:

Val d'Entremont (principal centre: Bourg St Pierre), Combin group
Val de Bagne (Fionnay), Cheilon group
Val d'Hérens (Arolla), Dent Blanche group
Val d'Anniviers (Zinal), Les Diablons
Turtmanntal (Meiden), Weisshorn range
Mattertal (Zermatt), Mischabel group
Saastal (Saas Fee), Weissmies group
Simplon Pass

By far the most important centre is ◊ Zermatt, followed by Saas Fee and Arolla. The others are of interest only for certain peaks. On the Italian side of the main range only Macugnaga in Valle Anzasca and Breuil in Valtournanche are of importance. There are numerous huts throughout the district.

The climbing here is more akin to that of the Oberland than it is to that of Chamonix. There are rock-climbs, but these do not seriously compare with those of the aiguilles nor is the rock as good. There are plenty of long, mixed climbs and of all standards. There are numerous glaciers, the longest being the Gorner Glacier (11 km, with the Grenz feeder).

With the exception of the Combin group, Lagginhorn and Weissmies, all the 4,000 m peaks are accessible from Zermatt, a fact which made it the pre-eminent mountaineering centre of pioneer days. All the important big peaks were climbed by the 1860s, leaving only the lower peaks and the more obscure ones such as Dürrenhorn (1879). Outstanding during this period was ◊ Whymper's struggle for the Matterhorn. There followed the great ridge climbs, exampled by:

1879   Zmutt Ridge, Matterhorn – A. F. Mummery with A. Burgener, J. Petrus, A. Gentinetta
1882   Viereselsgrat, Dent Blanche – J. S. Anderson, G. P. Baker with U. Almer, A. Pollinger
1887   Teufelsgrat, Täschhorn – Mr and Mrs Mummery with A. Burgener, F. Andermatten
1889   Ferpecle Arête, Dent Blanche – W. Gröbli with A. Pollinger
1895   Schaligrat, Weisshorn – E. Broome, with J. M. Biner, A. Imboden

1901 Rothorngrat, Zinal Rothorn – C. R. Gross with R. Taugwalder
1911 Furggengrat, Matterhorn – M. Piacenza with J. J. Carrel, J. Gaspard

However, some great face climbs were also being done at this time, for example:

1872 Marinelli Couloir, Monte Rosa – R. and W. M. Pendlebury, C. Taylor, with F. Imseng, G. Spechtenhauser, G. Oberto
1890 N E Face, Lyskamm – L. Norman-Neruda with C. Klucker, J. Reinstadler
1906 S W Face, Täschhorn – V. J. E. Ryan with F. and J. Lochmatter, G. W. Young with J. Knubel

The latter climb is still one of the most difficult and dangerous in the Alps. In the years following the First World War there were still hard ridges and faces to climb:

1923 Gracey Route, Mont Collon – Miss L. Gracey with M. and M. Pralong
1925 Bouquetins Traverse – I. A. Richards with J. Georges
     N Face, Dent d'Hérens – W. Welzenbach, E. Allwein
1928 N N W Ridge, Dent Blanche – Mr and Mrs Richards with J. and A. Georges
1931 N Face, Matterhorn – F. and T. Schmid
1938 N Face, Mt Blanc de Cheilon – L. Steinauer, W. Gorter

Outstanding post-war achievements have been solo and winter ascents of these and similar routes. The greatest new route is Bonatti's N Face Direct on the Matterhorn, done by Bonatti solo, in winter (1965).

II CENTRAL ALPS

Bernese Alps A range of high mountains extending from Lake Geneva to the Lake of Lucerne, bounded in the south, for the most part, by the upper Rhône, and in the north by the valley of the Aare (Interlaken, etc.). It can be divided naturally into three sections: West Bernese Alps, Central Bernese Alps (the Oberland proper), and East Bernese Alps. The division between the first two is the Gemmi Pass and between the last two, the Grimsel Pass. A good deal of the Bernese Alps are not, paradoxically, in the Canton Berne but in Valais (principally), Vaud, Fribourg, Uri, Unterwalden and Lucerne.

From a mountaineering point of view the Western section is of the least interest. The highest summit is Wildhorn (3,248 m) and two other peaks of note are Wildstrubel (3,242 m) and Les Diablerets (3,210 m). The climbing is generally easy, though the Argentine (2,422 m) offers rock climbs of quality. Various huts.

The Eastern section is both more complex and more interesting, and is split into a northern and southern portion by the Susten Pass. North of the pass the principal centre is Engelberg and the highest peak is Titlis (3,239 m). Other peaks of interest include Uri Rotstock (2,928 m) and the little-known Fünffingerstöck–Spannort range. The limestone of the region gives good rock-climbing, Gross Schlossberg etc., and is easily accessible.

South of the Susten Pass rises the Sustenhorn (3,504 m) group which provides easy snow climbs (centre: Stein) and south of that again is the more difficult Dammastock (3,630 m) group offering good rock climbs (centre: Furka Pass). At the extreme east end of the area is the famous ◊ Salbitschijen.

The central region of the Bernese Alps is known, not altogether accurately, as the Oberland. It is a heavily glaciated region of high peaks (Gr. Aletsch glacier 22 km the longest in the Alps): nine peaks exceed 4,000 m. The principal centre is ◊ Grindelwald but this is not convenient for outlying peaks. ◊ Kandersteg, Lötschental, the upper Rhône valley and Grimsel are all useful in this respect. There is an important rail-car link between Kandersteg and Lötschental and hence to the Rhône valley.

The climbing is mainly mixed snow/rock of all standards including some famous ridges and faces. The highest peak is Finsteraarhorn (4,274 m), first climbed in 1812 by A. Volker, J. Bortis and A. Abbühl. The Hangendgletscherhorn (1788), Sparrhorn (1800), Rottalhorn (c. 1811) and Jungfrau (1811) were climbed earlier. The Wetterhorn (3,701 m) was first climbed in 1844 by M. Bannholzer and J. Jaun, but ◊ Wills' famous ascent of 1854 led to the Golden Age of alpinism. The most famous peak of modern times is undoubtedly the ◊ Eiger (3,970 m). Notable routes include:

1865	Guggi route, Jungfrau – H. B. George, Sir G. Young, with C. Almer, A. Baumann, U. Almer
1866	Nollen Route, Mönch – E. von Fellenberg with C. Michel, P. Egger
1883	Andersongrat, Gr. Schreckhorn – J. S. Anderson, G. P. Baker with U. Almer, A. Pollinger
1899	Galletgrat, Doldenhorn – J. Gallet, with J. Kalbermatten, A. Muller
1904	N E Face, Finsteraarhorn – G. Hasler with F. Amatter
1909	Unterbächhorn–Nesthorn Traverse – G. W. Young, G. L. Mallory, D. Robertson
1911	N E Ridge, Jungfrau – A. Weber with A. Schlunegger
1914	Rote Zähne Ridge, Gspaltenhorn – G. W. Young, S. W. Herford, with J. Knubel, H. Brantschen
1921	Mönch Nordwand – H. Lauper, M. Liniger
	Mittelegi Ridge, Eiger – Yuko Maki with F. Amatter, F. Steuri, S. Brawand
1925	Aletschhorn Nordwand – E. Blanchet with A. Rübi, K. Mooser
1932	Grosshorn Nordwand – W. Welzenbach, A. Drexel, H. Rudy, E. Schultze
	N W Face, Gletscherhorn – same party
	Lauper Route, Eiger – H. Lauper, A. Zurcher with J. Knübel, A. Graven
1938	Schneehorn Nordwand – I. and J. Taguchi with S. Brawand, C. Kaufmann
	Eigerwand – H. Harrer, F. Kasparek, A. Heckmair, W. Vorg
1966	Eigerwand Direct (winter) – J. Lehne, G. Strobel, D. Haston, S. Hupfauer, R. Votteler

As a contrast to the main area the valley of Rosenlaui in the north-east of the group offers high-grade rock-climbing on the Engelhörner and there is a famous rock traverse on the Lobhörner, above Lauterbrunnen.

In most of the Bernese Alps the rock is limestone, but there is also some gneiss. There are numerous huts.

Lepontine Alps A vast area of mountains between the Simplon and Splügen passes, south of the Furka–Oberalp line and north of the Italian lakes. It is bisected, N–S, by the popular St Gotthard Pass. The eastern part is sometimes known as the Adula Alps. It is an area of low peaks suited to mountain walking and is very beautiful, though little frequented. The chief peaks are Monte Leone (3,553 m), Blinnenhorn (3,370 m), Basodino (3,273 m) – all in the W – and Rheinwaldhorn (3,402 m) in the Adula. A good deal of rock-climbing exploration could be done, especially in Val Maggia.

Tödi Range A range of mountains extending from Göschenan in the west to Sargans in the east and forming the north flank of the upper Vorder Rhine.

The highest point is Tödi (3,620 m), but other peaks of interest include Oberalpstock (3,328 m) and Bifertenstock (3,425 m). The peaks are generally easy but there is considerable rock-climbing of high quality. Several huts. The Glärnisch (2,914 m), further north, is a similar but lower area.

North-East Switzerland A division of the Alps invented by Coolidge to account for a number of outlying peaks of some interest. These are (from west to east): Gr. Mythen (1,899 m), the Glärnisch (2,914 m), the Churfirsten (Kurfürsten) (2,306 m) and the Säntis (2,502 m). These are limestone Alps offering rock-climbs of all grades, and all are readily accessible. The Säntis is of startling appearance.

Bernina Alps An important group of mountains on the Swiss–Italian border rising above the international resorts of St Moritz and Pontresina. It includes Bernina proper and the adjacent ◊ Bregaglia Alps. The highest summit is Piz Bernina (4,049 m) – the only 4,000 m summit outside the Western Alps. Other well-known peaks are Piz Palu (3,905 m), Piz Zupo (3,996 m), Piz Argient (3,945 m), Crast' Aguzza (3,869 m), Piz Morteratsch (3,751 m), Piz Tschierva (3,546 m), Piz Scerscen (3,971 m), Piz Roseg (3,937 m) and Piz Corvatsch (3,451 m). All are popular and there are climbs of all grades in the region, both rock and ice. There are several huts.

The first ascent of Piz Bernina was by J. Coaz with J. and L. R. Tscharner, 1850. Other notable ascents include:

1866	Spallagrat, Piz Bernina – F. F. Tuckett, F. Brown, C. Almer, F. Andermatten
1872	Güssfeldtsattel – P. Güssfeldt, H. Grass, P. Jenny, C. Capat (traverse)
1876	Middlemoregrat, Piz Roseg – H. Cordier, T. Middlemore, J. Jaun, K. Maurer
1877	Piz Scerscen – P. Güssfeldt, H. Grass, C. Capat
1878	Biancograt, Piz Bernina – P. Güssfeldt, H. Grass, J. Gross
1887	Eisnase, Piz Scerscen – P. Güssfeldt, E. Rey, J. B. Aymonod (in descent)
	Bumillergrat, Piz Palu – H. Bumiller, M. Schocher, J. Gross, C. Schnitzler
1890	N E Wall, Piz Bernina – L. Norman-Neruda, C. Klucker
	Neruda Route, Piz Scerscen – L. Norman-Neruda, C. Klucker

Christian ◊ Klucker was the outstanding climber of the region and one of the most famous guides in the Alps.

Bregaglia A very popular area of sharp granite peaks on the Swiss–Italian border above the Val Bregaglia between Chiavenna and the Maloja Pass. Promontogno is a popular centre.

Though the total area is fairly small the region divides naturally into three major cirques (on the northern, popular side). From west to east these are: the Sciora Cirque (Val Bondasca), the Albigna Cirque and the Forno Cirque. All contain good climbs, especially in the middle and upper grades of difficulty. Best-known is the Sciora Cirque, which contains the famous Piz Badile (3,308 m) (N E Face: Cassin, Esposito, Ratti, Molteni and Valseschi, 1937).

Albula Alps The mountains on the N side of the Engadine from the Splügenpass to the Flüela Pass. It is bisected N–S by the Chur–Silvaplana road (Julier Pass). The highest summit is the Piz Kesch (3,418 m). Other peaks of interest are the Piz Vadret (3,229 m) and Alplihorn (3,006 m). These are in the eastern part of the group, but in the centre, above Tinizong, rise the interesting group of the 'Bergun Dolomites': Piz Ela (3,338 m), Das Tinzenhorn (3,172 m) and Piz Michel (Mitgel) (3,159 m).

The area is surrounded by famous ski resorts: St Moritz, Davos, Arosa, Lenzerheide.

Silvretta Alps A range of mountains on the Austro–Swiss border, north of the Unter Engadine valley. The highest summit is the Fluchthorn (3,403 m). The climbing is mostly easy, but the peaks are shapely. The range continues N W to the Rätikon Group (Schesaplana, 2,967 m) and N E to the Samnaun Group (Vesispitze, 3,116 m), both of which offer considerable rock-climbing.

III EASTERN ALPS (CENTRAL RANGES)

Ortler Alps A fine group of mountains south of the ◊ Otztal Alps and separated from them by the Unter Vintschgau valley. The mountains, though now in Italy, were once Austrian and so carry dual German and Italian names. The highest summit is Ortles (Ortler) (3,899 m) but Gran Zebru (Königspitze) (3,859 m) is more impressive. There are climbs of all grades and the region is particularly good for steep ice-climbs. Numerous huts. Trafoi is perhaps the best centre.

Otztal Alps A popular group of mountains on the Austro–Italian border south of the Inn at Imst. The highest peak is Wildspitze (3,772 m). Much of the area offers easy ascents but with large snow-fields and glaciers. There are many huts and hut-touring is popular. Harder climbs (mostly rock) are found in the Kaunergrat. The chief centres are Solden, Vent, Obergurgl and Mittelberg.

Stubai Alps A popular area in Tyrol between the Otztal mountains in the west and the Zillertal mountains in the east. Penetrated by the long and beautiful Stubaital where Fulpmes and Neustift are centres. The factory at Fulpmes has given the district's name to a famous make of climbing equipment.

The mountains are mostly easy and hut-to-hut touring is popular. The highest summit is Zuckerhutl (3,505 m). On the eastern fringes of the area there are some interesting rock peaks of which mention might be made: Pflerscher Tribulaun (3,096 m), Serles (2,718 m) and the Kalkogels.

Zillertal Alps A range of mountains on the Austro–Italian border between the Stubai and Venediger groups. Penetrated by the long valley of Zillertal where Mayrhofen is an international tourist centre. The peaks here are more difficult than in the neighbouring areas, and include rock-climbs as well as ice-climbs. The highest summit is Hochfeiler (3,510 m) which has a notable N Face.

Venediger–Glockner Groups A group of mountains in East Tyrol, which includes Gross Glockner (3,797 m), the highest peak in Austria. The highest of the Venediger group is the Gross Venediger (3,674 m). The peaks are mostly easy.

Radstatter Tauern The east end of the Alps by Coolidge's definition; a small group of peaks between Badgastein and the Radstatter Tauern Pass. The highest point is the Hochalmspitze (3,350 m) but the best-known peak is Ankogel (3,246 m). Hafnereck (3,061 m) is the most easterly snow peak in the Alps.

NORTHERN RANGES (KALKALPEN)

Between Bludenz in the west and Vienna in the east there are numerous groups of limestone mountains forming an unbroken chain. West of Salzburg they are contained in an area roughly north of the Inn and south of Munich, forming the boundary between Austria and Bavaria, and for this reason are sometimes known as the Bavarian Alps. East of Salzburg they are less easily defined but may be considered to be immediately south of the Salzburg–Vienna autobahn, and limited by the Enns valley.

This eastern half is beyond the Radstatter Tauern Pass, which Coolidge defined as the eastern limit of the Alps, but such a limit is not defensible when it excludes mountains such as Dachstein, almost 3,000 m high. Only Vienna will serve as the true eastern limit.

Within these limits there are dozens of mountain groups, highly complex in arrangement. They are mostly fairly small, well confined in area. All have the familiar look of limestone – sharp peaks, steep crags and airy ridges – and though there is some permanent ice and snow on the higher groups, it is of little consequence to the climber. They are predominantly mountains for the rock-climber and hill-scrambler; it is a common misconception that only hard rock-climbs exist. Huts are numerous and the whole area is very popular with Austro–German climbers.

The highest peak is the Parseierspitze (3,040 m) in the Lechtaler Alps, near Landeck. The famous Zugspitze (2,963 m) in the Wetterstein is frequently claimed as the highest mountain in Germany, though in fact it is on the German–Austrian border: the highest peak completely in Germany is Watzmann (2,713 m), near Berchtesgaden.

Lechtaler Alps   A long range of limestone mountains between the Lechtal and Inn. There is no one centre and to reach one side of the range from the other involves a lengthy car journey. The highest peak is the Parseierspitze (3,040 m). Other peaks of interest are: Wetterspitze (2,898 m), Freispitze (2,887 m), Platteinspitze (2,639 m) and Heiterwand (2,638 m).

Allgauer Alps   Part of the Northern Tyrolese Alps forming the border between Tyrol and Bavaria. There are really two parts: the Allgauer Voralpen and the Allgauer proper, separated by the long valley wherein lies the ski resort of Obersdorf, the principal centre. The very long Lechtal separates the Allgauer and ◊ Lechtaler Alps.

The highest summit is Grosser Krottenkoff (2,657 m). Other peaks of interest include the Mädelegabel (2,649 m), the Höfats (2,258 m) and the Hochvogel (2,594 m), all typically steep limestone. There is an interesting sub-group, the Tannheimer, just south of Fussen (Kellenspitze, or Köllespitze, 2,240 m).

Wetterstein Gebirge   A small but important group of limestone mountains on the Austro–German border, immediately south of the ski resort of Garmisch-Partenkirchen. The highest summit is the Zugspitze (2,963 m), easily reached by cable car. Other interesting peaks include: Grosser Waxenstein (2,277 m), Alpspitze (2,628 m) and Partenkirchner Dreitorspitze (2,634 m). Several huts.

Mieminger Kette   A small group of limestone mountains between the Fern Pass and Telfs in the Tyrol. Highest point is the Griesspitze (2,739 m). Ehrwald is the best centre.

Karwendelgebirge   An important group of limestone peaks between the Inn valley and Mittenwald, on the Austro–German border. As they rise immediately above Innsbruck (the Nordkette range) they give that town its celebrated background, and Hafelekar (2,334 m) can be reached by cable car.

There are four main ranges running east to west with deep valleys between, and crossing from north to south can be difficult. Scharnitz is perhaps the best general centre and there are several huts, of which the Falken Hutte, with its views of Laliderer, is best known.

The peaks are typical of the North Tyrol ranges, with ridges and steep walls, but the climbs are generally longer than those of, say, the Kaiser or

Wetterstein. The highest point is the Birkkar Spitze (2,756 m) but others of interest include: Kaltwasserkarspitze (2,733 m), Lamsenspitze (2,508 m), Grosser Bettelwurf (2,727 m) and Lalidererspitze (2,594 m). The area is famous for its steep walls, best known being the Lalidererwand (M. and G. Mayer with A. Dibona and L. Rizzi, 1911).

Kaisergebirge (Wilder Kaiser) A small and compact group of limestone peaks immediately east of Kufstein, Tyrol. The highest peak is Elmauer Halt (2,344 m), but despite the general lack of height and small area, the Kaiser are among the most important of the North Tyrolese Alps. The peaks are sharp and there are enormous limestone walls, all of attraction to the climber, including:

Fleischbank E Face – H. Dulfer, W. Schaarschmidt, 1912
Predigstuhl N Ridge – H. Matejak, 1908
Totenkirchl W Face – H. Dulfer and W. von Redwitz, 1913

There are several huts and the area is very accessible and very popular.

Berchtesgadener Alps A region of limestone Alps extending south from the famous resort of Berchtesgaden. With the exception of Watzmann (2,713 m) the peaks are fairly undistinguished, though the area is extremely beautiful. The Watzmann is the highest peak entirely in Germany: first ascent – Stanig, Beck and Von Buch, 1799 or 1801. The mountain has a tremendous E Face above the Königsee, with several routes up it.

Dachstein Group An important group of limestone mountains south of Bad Ischl in Austria. The highest peak is Dachstein (2,996 m). Other interesting peaks include Grosser Bischofsmütze (2,455 m) and the Torstein (2,947 m). The northern part of the group is known as the Gosaukamm and is noted for spectacular scenery. There are a number of famous caves in the area. The best centre is Hallstadt.

Totes Gebirge A region of limestone mountains east of Bad Ischl in Austria. The highest peak is Grosser Priel (2,514 m). Several huts, and the region is readily accessible.

Niedere Tauern Used here to indicate the mountains of Steiermark, north of Klagenfurt and Graz, and east of the Radstatter Tauern Pass. The area is composed of numerous small groups, and the highest peak is Hochgolling (2,863 m) in the Schladminger Tauern. There is much rock-climbing and scrambling, and interesting peaks include the Hochtor (2,365 m), Kleine Buchstein (1,994 m) and Pfaffenstein (1,871 m).

SOUTHERN RANGES

Dolomites A remarkable area of rocky peaks in the north-east corner of Italy in what was, until 1918, the Austrian South Tyrol. The political change has meant that most peaks and villages have both German and Italian names. The principal peaks lie south of Brunico and east of the Adige valley (Trento) and do, in fact, cross the border into Austria with the lesser-known Lienzer Dolomites. An important sub-group, the Brenta Dolomites, lies west of the Adige, adjacent to the Adamello-Presanella Alps.

The highest peak of the Dolomites is Marmolata (3,342 m), but it is the steep walls and towers, and the unusual rock, which attract climbers and height is of less importance here than almost anywhere else in the Alps. There are rock climbs of all standards, including the highest, and the area is extremely popular.

No one centre is ideal for all the peaks, but for those on the east, Cortina d'Ampezzo offers good communications and for the west, Canazei is a favourite base. For the Brenta group, Pinzolo or Madonna di Campiglio are suitable. There are numerous huts.

LIST OF ALPINE 4,000 M PEAKS

(Summits and other eminences indicated)

4,807 m Mont Blanc	4,153 m Bishorn
4,748 m Mont Blanc de Courmayeur	4,122 m Aig. Verte (two tops)
	4,114 m Aigs. du Diable (two tops)
4,634 m Monte Rosa (ten tops)	4,107 m Aig. Blanche de Peuterey
4,545 m Dom	4,102 m Grande Rocheuse
4,527 m Lyskamm (two tops)	4,101 m Barre des Écrins
4,505 m Weisshorn	4,099 m Mönch
4,491 m Taschhorn	4,091 m Pollux
4,477 m Matterhorn (two tops)	4,078 m Schreckhorn
4,469 m Picco Luigi Amadeo	4,069 m Mont Brouillard
4,465 m Mont Maudit	4,063 m Obergabelhorn
4,357 m Dent Blanche	4,061 m Gran Paradiso
4,327 m Nadelhorn	4,052 m Aig. de Bionnassay
4,314 m Grand Combin (four tops)	4,049 m Gr. Fiescherhorn
4,304 m Dôme du Goûter	4,049 m Piz Bernina
4,294 m Lenzspitze	4,043 m Gr. Grünhorn
4,274 m Finsteraarhorn	4,042 m Lauteraarhorn
4,248 m Mont Blanc de Tacul	4,035 m Dürrenhorn
4,241 m Stecknadelhorn	4,035 m Aig. du Jardin
4,226 m Castor	4,029 m Allalinhorn
4,221 m Zinal Rothorn	4,025 m Hinter Fiescherhorn
4,219 m Hohberghorn	4,023 m Weissmies
4,208 m Grandes Jorasses (five tops)	4,015 m Dôme de Rochefort
	4,013 m Punta Baretti
4,206 m Alphubel	4,013 m Aig. du Géant
4,199 m Rimpfischhorn	4,010 m Lagginhorn
4,195 m Aletschhorn	4,001 m Aig. du Rochefort
4,190 m Strahlhorn	4,000 m Les Droites
4,171 m Dent d'Hérens	(Next highest, Fletschhorn
4,165 m Breithorn (three tops)	3,996 m)
4,158 m Jungfrau	

By far the largest number of the above are in the ◇ Pennine Alps.

The first ascent of a Dolomite peak was that of Monte Pelmo by John Ball in 1857. Of the many hard climbs, most famous is that of the Cima Grande N Face (E. Comici, A. and J. Dimai, 1933).

Lombard Alps   The southern limits of the Alps between Como and Trento, south of the Bernina–Ortles massifs and north of the Milan–Verona motor-way. It includes the lakes of Como, Iseo, Idro and Garda and is easily accessible from the towns of northern Italy. The area lies entirely within the Italian borders.

The name is one of convenience invented by ◇ Ball and taken up by Coolidge (cf. N E Switzerland) to describe several disparate groups. The highest peaks are those of the Presanella–Adamello groups: Adamello (3,554 m), Cima Presanella (3,556 m), Caré Alto (3,462 m). This is a snowy region with wild glens, but the climbing is mostly easy. There are several huts and the best centre is Pinzolo.

Immediately to the east of these rise the Brenta ◊ Dolomites, a complete contrast in form.

West of the Aprica Pass lie the Bergamesque Alps whose highest peak is Pizzo di Coca (3,052 m). It is an area for mountain walking, though in the extreme west, above Lecco, lies the Grigna.

Julian Alps A group of limestone mountains on the Jugoslav–Italian borders. The chief summit is Triglav (2,863 m), whose N Face has a number of good climbs, though the ordinary ascent is easy. Other good peaks are Jalovec (2,643 m), Skrlatica (2,738 m) and Canin (2,587 m). There are many others. Bohinjska Bistrica is a well-known tourist village central to the area, but other good centres are Kranjska Gora, Mojstrana and Jesenice. Numerous huts for climbers.

GUIDEBOOKS There are numerous walkers' guides but these are not listed. All guides by A.C., W.C.P. or C.P.

The Western Alps:
Brailsford, *Ecrins Massif*.
Collomb, *Ecrins Park: Dauphiné Alps*. Walking/climbing.
Collomb, *Graians East: Gran Paradiso National Park*.
Collomb/O'Connor, *Mont Blanc Range* – Vol. 1. Mont Blanc.
Griffin, *Mont Blanc Range* – Vol. 3. Triolet, Drus, Argentiere.
Griffin, *Mont Blanc Range* – Vol. 1 (1990). Col de la Berangere–Col du
    Geant–Col de Talefre. (Mt Blanc, Jorasses, etc.)
Collomb, *Pennine Alps West*. Gd. Dents, Collon, Gd. Combin, etc.
Collomb, *Pennine Alps Central*. Monte Rosa, Matterhorn, etc.
Collomb, *Pennine Alps East*. Saas and Mischabel Chains.
Collomb, *Vanoise Park*. Tarentaise & Haute Maurienne.
Roberts, *High Level Route*. Chamonix–Zermatt–Saas.
    Ski-mountaineering, with summer route supplement.
Collomb, *Mercantour Park: Maritime Alps*. Walking/climbing.

Central Alps:
Anderson, *Mittel Switzerland*. Lepontine–Ticino–Adula Alps. Pilot guide.
Collomb, *Bernese Alps Central*. Blumlisalp, Jungfrau, Nesthorn,
    Aletsch, etc.
Talbot, *Central Switzerland*. Grimsel, Furka, Susten.
Collomb, *Bernina Alps*. Palu–Bernina–Roseg–Sella–Fora, etc.
Collomb, *Bregaglia East*. Forno–Allievi–Albigna–Disgrazia.
Collomb, *Bregaglia West*. Sciora–Cengalo–Badile–Trubinasca.

Eastern Alps:
Roberts, *Stubai Alps*.
Unsworth, *Otztal Alps*.
Roberts, *Glockner Region*.
Roberts, *Zillertal Alps*.
Talbot, *Kaisergebirge*.
Anderson, *Karwendel*.
Anderson, *Brenta Dolomites*. Scramblers' Guide.
Collomb, *Julian Alps*. Walking/climbing.
Davies, *Via Ferrata: Scrambles in the Dolomites*.
Werner, *Klettersteig: Scrambles in the Northern Limestone Alps*.
Churcher, *Italian Rock*. Selected Northern Italy.
Dinoia/Casari, *Classic Climbs in the Dolomites*.

Altai Mountains   The High Altai Mountains cover an area of 300 × 300 km just inside Siberia on the Chinese and Mongolian borders. The range continues into Outer Mongolia another 1,000 km. The highest peak is Belukha (E peak – 4,506 m, W peak – 4,460 m) first explored by Sapozhnikov in nine expeditions between 1895 and 1911. In 1914 the E peak was climbed by B. V. and M. V. Tronov via the Katun Glacier and the saddle between the E and W Faces. The W summit was climbed in 1936. In 1938 Abalakov's party traversed the Delone Ridge (Gr 4a) and in 1953 thorough exploration by Kazakov crossed the Delone Pass and found the now usual route from the north. The peak has a very fine north face with two routes (1984), Gr 5a, 5b.

Other peaks are P. XX Let Oktabrya (4,167 m), P. 50 Let K.P.S.S. (4,000 m), and P. Sapozhnikov (3,950 m).

Amery, Leopold Charles Maurice Stennet (1873–1955)   Statesman, Cabinet Minister and keen mountaineer who climbed in many parts of the world. In 1929 he made the first ascent of the mountain in Canada which bears his name. President of the A.C. 1944–7 during which the A.C. led in the formation of the ◊ British Mountaineering Council. Wrote two books of his climbing experiences: *Days of Fresh Air* (1939) and *In the Rain and the Sun* (1946).

Ames, Edward Levi (1832–92)   Original Member of the A.C. In 1856 he made the first ascent of the Fletschhorn and Allalinhorn.

Anderegg, Jakob (1827–78)   Cousin and contemporary of the great Melchior ◊ Anderegg, whose reputation long overshadowed him. Much more daring than Melchior, to whom he proved a perfect foil, though they did not always climb together. It was Jakob who led the ice arête of the Old Brenva on the first ascent when Melchior might have retreated.

Jakob took part in many first ascents of famous mountains and climbs:

1864	Balmhorn; Jungfrau by the Rottal; W Peak of Lyskamm; Zinal Rothorn
1865	Piz Roseg; Obergabelhorn; Pigne d'Arolla; Old Brenva
1866	Piz Palu (Central and W Peaks)
1869	Gspaltenhorn; Midi by N E arête
1870	Aig. de Trélatête (N Peak)
1872	Studerhorn (N E arête and W Face); Grand Paradis (new route)
1875	Monte della Disgrazia by S E arête
1876	Aig. du Plat; Le Rateau by S and E arêtes; Grd Flambeau; Finsteraarhorn by S E arête; Aig. Verte from Argentière Glacier; Les Courtes from Argentière Glacier
1877	Le Plaret.

Many of his later climbs were done with Henri ◊ Cordier, who was killed in a foolish accident on the glacier after the Plaret climb. During the Verte ascent Jakob was soaked and this led to recurring illnesses from which he never recovered.

Anderegg, Melchior (1828–1912)   Born near Meiringen, Melchior, as he was always known, became one of the greatest of all the early guides – his career only equalled by that of Christian ◊ Almer. Though he had done some guiding before 1855, the year he was 'discovered' by ◊ Hinchcliff, his principal occupation was wood-carving. He was expert at this; some later work was exhibited in London galleries.

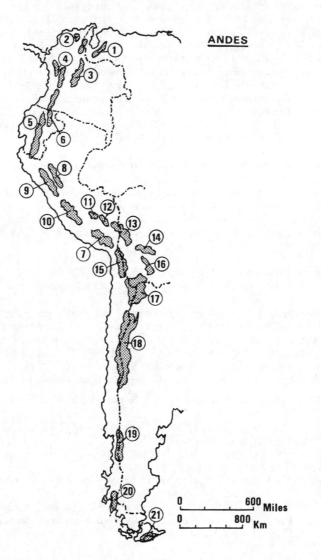

ANDES

VENEZUELA: **1** Sierra Nevada de Merida. COLOMBIA: **2** Sierra Nevada de Santa Marta; **3** Sierra Nevada de Cocuy; **4** Cord. Central. ECUADOR: **5** Cord. Occidental; **6** Cord. Oriental. PERU: **7** Cord. Occidental; **8** Cord. Blanca; **9** Cord. Huayhuash; **10** Cord. Vilcabamba; **11** Cord. Veronica de Urubamba; **12** Cord. Vilcanota; **13** Nudo de Apolobamba. BOLIVIA: **14** Cord. de Quinza Cruz/Cochabamba; **15** Cord. Occidental; **16** Cord. Real; **17** Puna de Atacama. CHILE/ARGENTINA: **18** Aconcagua Region; **19** Lakes District; **20** Patagonia; **21** Tierra del Fuego

His principal climbs include the first ascents of Rimpfischhorn, Mont Blanc by the Bosses Ridge (1859), Monte della Disgrazia (1862), Dent d'Hérens, Parrotspitze of Monte Rosa (1863), Mont Blanc by the Brenva Face (1865), Mont Mallet (1871). He climbed with many of the leading amateurs but especially ◊ Stephen and later, the ◊ Walkers.

A big, genial, intelligent man, Melchior is credited with many famous quotes, amongst which are: 'We must go back – we cannot reach the summit in less than five or six hours' (on seeing a winter Snowdon from Crib Goch. They reached it in 1 hr 5 min.).

On looking out over the rooftops of London, Stephen said, 'That is not so fine a view as we have seen together from Mont Blanc.' 'Ah, sir, it is far finer,' Melchior replied.

On observing the Zmutt Ridge from the Dent Blanche: 'It goes – but I'm not going.'

Melchior was guest of honour at an A.C. Winter Dinner in 1894. He was married and had a large family, of whom Andreas, his second son, became a noted guide. He was one of the few early guides to die comparatively affluent.

Andermatten, Franz (1823–83) One of the earliest of the Saastal guides who made the first ascent of the Strahlhorn (1854), Lagginhorn (1856), and Nadelhorn (1858). His most famous expedition was with Dent, Burgener, Imseng and Passingham on the first ascent of Zinal Rothorn from Zermatt (1872).

Anderson, John Stafford (1851–1930) Brother-in-law of G. P. ◊ Baker with whom he frequently climbed in the Alps. Anderson made several important new climbs among which the following were outstanding: the Viereselsgrat of the Dent Blanche (1882), so called after his chief guide, Ulrich Almer, commented '*Wir sind vier Esel!*' ('We are four asses!'), the Andersongrat of the Schreckhorn (1883) and the first E–W traverse of the Breithorn (1884).

Andes, the A long mountain system (6,500 km) running down the western side of the South American continent, from Caracas in Venezuela to Cape Horn. Within this vast range there are peaks of almost every size and shape ranging from the great volcanoes such as Cotopaxi and Chimborazo, through the ice-draped peaks of the Cordillera Blanca, to the stark rock obelisks of Patagonia. Some, even quite high ones, are easy to climb and were certainly ascended by the native Indians before the coming of the white man. Others are extremely difficult and provide some of the hardest rock- and ice-climbs in the world. The highest peak is ◊ Aconcagua, 6,960 m (the highest peak in the western hemisphere) (M. ◊ Zurbriggen, solo, 1898).

The earliest attempts on the mountains were made in the north, where the peaks are lower. A Conquistador is credited with the ascent of Pichincha (4,791 m) as early as 1582. This was repeated by Bouguer and Condamine between 1736 and 1744, who also climbed Corazón, a similar peak. Humboldt climbed Pichincha in 1802 and tried Chimborazo, but was defeated. The huge volcanoes were prime targets for the early expeditions: Cotopaxi (5,897 m) was climbed by A. Escobar and W. Reiss in 1872 and ◊ Whymper climbed Chimborazo (6,267 m) in 1880. Sievers and Engel began climbing in the Sierra Mérida of the extreme north in 1885 and 1887, but the big guns were now turned on Aconcagua in the south. Güssfeldt (1882–3) failed twice and it was E. A. Fitzgerald's guide, M. Zurbriggen, who succeeded (1898). Conway's expedition climbed Aconcagua and also Illimani (6,462 m), though an attempt on Sarmiento in Tierra del Fuego (1898) failed.

A number of expeditions followed, especially German, and built up to a climax in the 1930s. In 1932, P. Borcher's party climbed the South Peak of Huascarán (6,768 m) and four other peaks of about 6,000 m. After the war, exploration and climbing in the Andes rivalled that of the Himalayas for intensity. All the larger peaks were ascended: an outstanding feat being that of L. Terray's party on Chacaraju, 1956. Further south, in Patagonia, Terray and G. Magnone climbed Fitzroy (3,375 m) in 1952, and Bonington and Whillans climbed the Central Tower of Paine in 1963. Despite the large number of expeditions, the range of the Andes is so vast that there is still plenty of scope for exploration and new ascents.

From north to south the Andes comprise the following ranges. The list has been simplified somewhat (for extensive detail see J. Neate, *Mountaineering in the Andes*).

VENEZUELA

Sierra de Norte
Sierra de Santo Domingo
Sierra Nevada de Mérida   The highest part of the Venezuelan Andes, rising above the town of Mérida, from which there is a cable railway to the Pico Espejo (4,765 m). The climbs are short and many are easy. The highest is Pico Bolivar at 4,979 m (F. Weiss, 1936. Claimed by H. Burgoin, 1934, but disputed). Only six peaks are above the snow line, which is approximately 4,500 m.

COLOMBIA

Sierra Nevada de Santa Marta   An isolated offshoot of the Eastern Cordillera of Colombia, and claimed to be the highest coastal range of mountains in the world. Opinion is divided as to whether they form part of the Andes, but they are usually counted as such. They were first explored by T. Cabot in 1930, but not visited by climbing parties until 1939.

The peaks run west to east and extend about 20 miles. There are three main groups: the Western Group, with the highest peaks; the Eastern Group, with some fine ice mountains; and the rocky group near the head of the Cabaca Valley. All the main peaks have been climbed, but the group is very accessible and the climbing very good. The best season is January to March.

West Group

Pico Colon (5,775 m) – A. Bakewell, W. A. Wood, A. Praolini, 1939
Pico Bolivar (5,775 m) – G. Pichler, E. Praolini, E. Kraus, 1939
Pico Simmons (5,660 m) – Mr and Mrs F. Marmillod, 1943
Pico Santander (5,600 m) – A. Gansser, 1943

East Group

La Reina (5,535 m) – P. Petzoldt, Mrs E. Cowles, Miss E. Knowlton, 1941
Pico Ojeda (5,490 m) – Petzoldt party, 1941

Cabaca Group

El Guardian (5,285 m) – Petzoldt party, 1941
There are numerous other peaks of over 5,000 m in the area.

Cordillera Oriental (Cocuy)   A small section of the Andes some 500 km north-east of Bogota in Columbia and near the town of Cocuy. Heavy rain and mists hide the peaks for much of the time (January is the best month for climbing) and they were unknown until 1910. They have been compared with ▷ Ruwenzori.

Most of the peaks are about 5,000 m, the highest being Alto Ritacuba at 5,493 m (C. Cuénet, A. Gansser, 1942). The range extends for about 12 miles and all the important summits have been reached.

Cordillera Central   Said to resemble the mountains of East Africa. Several active volcanos including Nevado del Ruiz (5,237 m) which erupted in 1985 killing 22,000 people. Highest peak is Nevado de Huila (c.5,350 m) (Kraus, Drees, Hüblitz, 1944). Best climbing is on the steep Nevado de Tolima (c.5,160 m) (Golay 1923 – but disputed. Climbed by locals 1926).

ECUADOR

Cordilleras Oriental and Occidental   These two parallel chains lie east and west of a long valley known as the Avenue of the Volcanoes. Some of the volcanoes are still active: Sangay (5,320 m), Tungurahua (5,005 m), Reventador (3,485 m) and Cotopaxi (5,897 m), the highest active volcano in the world. Ecuador was the scene of Whymper's great expedition of 1880.

The volcanoes, especially Chimborazo and Cotopaxi, make popular ascents, but the best climbing is probably on Altar (5,319 m). There are huts and climbing clubs.

C. Oriental

Cotopaxi, 5,897 m – W. Reiss, A. M. Escobar, 1872
Cayambe, 5,789 m – Whymper's party, 1880
Antisana, 5,705 m – Whymper's party, 1880
Altar, 5,319 m – M. Tremonti's party, 1963
Tungurahua, 5,005 m – W. Reiss, A. Stubel, 1873
Quilindana, 4,898 m – Italian party, 1953
Sangay, 5,320 m – R. & T. Moore, W. Austin, L. Thorne, 1929

C. Occidental

Chimborazo, 6,267 m – Whymper's party, 1880
Illiniza, 5,261 m – J. A. & L. Carrel, 1880
Carihuairazo, 5,028 m – Whymper's party, 1880
Cotocachi, 4,939 m – Whymper's party, 1880
Pinchincha, 4,791 m – T. Orteguerra, 1582 (Humboldt's party, 1802)
Llanganate Range   Hermoso, 4,639 m, first ascent 1941.
There are several other isolated peaks in Ecuador; little interest.

PERU

Peru is the most important region of the Andes, much developed in post-war years. There are 20 or more groups of which the following are the most important.

Cordillera Blanca   The best-known region of the Peruvian Andes, intensively developed in recent years. The region has everything in its favour: easy access from Lima, good weather from May to mid-August, some of the most beautiful-looking peaks in the world, which, at the same time, offer some of the hardest ice-climbs known. Unfortunately, the area was subjected to a tremendous earthquake in 1970, which devastated Huaras and other villages, and affected Huascarán. Fifteen Czech and one Chilean climber were killed in the disaster.

Huascarán is the highest peak, with two summits:

N, 6,655 m – Miss A. Peck, G. zum Taugwald, T. Taugwalder, 1908
S, 6,768 m – Borchers' Expedition, 1932

Various other routes have since been made on the mountain.

Borchers' Expedition also accounted for many of the other highest peaks of the region including the N peak of Huandoy (6,395 m). Three lesser peaks claimed particular attention because of their beauty and difficulty: Chacaraju (6,113 m), Alpamayo (5,945 m) and Nevado Cayesh (5,721 m).

1956   Chacaraju W peak – L. Terray, M. Davaille, C. Gaudin, R. Jenny, M. Martin, R. Sennelier, P. Souriac
1957   Alpamayo – G. Hauser's expedition
1960   Nevado Cayesh – Ryan, Crawford, Stewart
1963   Chacaraju E peak – L. Terray, G. Magnone, L. Dubost, P. Gendre, J. Soubis

The Cordillera Blanca remains the most popular part of the Andes for expeditions. A detailed guidebook is *Yuraq Janka* by J. F. Ricker.
Cordillera Huayhuash (Pronounced 'Way-wash')   South of the ⟡ Cordillera Blanca, Peru. The range has some of the finest and most difficult mountains of the Andes. It is notorious for avalanches, bad cornices and the disease *verruga peruana*. The best base is Chiquian, from which the range can be reached in two days.
The first peak climbed was Nevada Suila (6,352 m) by E. Schneider and A. Awerzger in 1936. Outstanding climbs include:

Yerupaja, 6,634 m – Harrah and Maxwell, 1950
Jirishanca, 6,126 m – T. Egger, S. Jungmeier, 1957
Rondoy, 5,883 m – V. Walsh, P. Farrell, P. Bebbington, C. Powell, D. Condict, G. Sadler, 1963

Yerupaja has received much attention. It was traversed by Adcock's party in 1968, and the S Face was climbed by Dix and Jones in the same year. The developments within this area have been intense.
Cordillera Vilcabamba   An attractive range of mountains attainable from Cuzco, Peru. The peaks are big and icy, often showing the typical flutings of this part of the Andes. All the highest peaks have been climbed but there are many others and some parts of the area are little known. Amongst the highest peaks are:

Salcantay, 6,271 m – G. I. Bell, F. D. Ayres, D. Michael, W. V. G. Matthews, M. de C. Kogan, B. Pierre, 1952
Pumasillo, 6,070 m – H. Carslake, J. H. Longland, 1957
Sacsarayoc, 5,996 m – P. Farrell (solo), 1963

The Pumasillo ascent was repeated later by other members of the team. (See *The Puma's Claw*, by S. Clark.)
The Cordillera Veronica de Urubamba, on the other side of the Urubamba River, is sometimes taken as part of the Vilcabamba range. The main peak is the fine Nevado Veronica, 5,822 m (Egeler, de Booy, 1956).
Cordillera Vilcanota   A group of mountains some 110 km from Cuzco, Peru, the highest of which is Ausangate (6,384 m), climbed by a German party under H. Harrer in 1953. The same party climbed six other high peaks. The peaks are icy, well-shaped and easy of access. There are no unclimbed summits.

BOLIVIA

Cordillera Real   The Andes of N W Bolivia, stretching 160 km north-west to south-east, and quite near La Paz, the capital. The range stretches from Illampu (6,362 m) in the north to Illimani (6,462 m) in the south and forms a spectacular background to the high and arid Altiplano with Lake Titicaca. The range offers some of the best ice-climbing in the Andes. Little in the way of rock-climbing except the striking obelisk of Tiquimani (5,590 m).

The largest concentration of high peaks and the most glaciers are in the Sorata Group in the north of the range. Notable peaks include:

Ancohuma, 6,388 m – R. Dienst, A. Schultze, 1919
Illampu, 6,362 m – E. Hein, A. Horeschowsky, H. Hortnagel, H. Pfann, 1928
Haukaña, 6,249 m – probably the Hein party, 1928
Pico del Norte, 6,030 m – Hein party, 1928
Numerous other peaks over 5,500 m.

Between the Sorata Group and Illimani are various groups with many peaks in the 5,500–6,000 m range. Notable are:

Chearoco, 6,127 m – A. Horeschowsky, H. Hortnagel, 1928
Cacca Aca, 6,094 m – R. Dienst, A. Schultze, 1919
Chachacomani, 6,074 m – G. Buccholtz party, 1945
Condoriri, 5,656 m – W. Kuhm, 1941 (probably)

Illimani has three summits. The S and highest summit was climbed by M. Conway, A. Macquignaz and L. Pellisier in 1898. The N Summit, just a few feet lower, by H. Ertl and G. Schröder in 1950.
Cordillera Apolobamba A group of peaks on the Peruvian–Bolivian border. Most of them are between 5,000 and 6,000 m. The highest is Chaupi Orco (6,100 m), a snow-dome climbed by a German expedition in 1958.

Cordillera Munecas
Cordillera de Quinza Cruz
Cordillera de Santa Vera Cruz
Cordillera de Cocapata
Cordillera Occidental This range includes the highest summit in Bolivia: Sajama, 6,542 m – J. Prem, P. Ghiglione, 1939.

CHILE/ARGENTINA

Cordillera Central This cordillera is some 320 km long and the Chile–Argentine border runs along the crest. The highest peak in the Western Hemisphere is here: ◊ Aconcagua (6,960 m), which is in Argentina. In Chile the highest point is the second highest of the range, Ojos del Salado (6,885 m). In 1956 a Chilean military expedition erroneously measured this peak as 7,048 m, which caused considerable geographical consternation until it was correctly remeasured by an American team later the same year.

The mountains are easily accessible to a large population so climbing is well developed with huts, clubs etc. There is considerable skiing during a 5 month season and rock-climbing on the Cortaderas, near Santiago and the Paradones (Tall Walls) and Punzones (Piercing Spires); said to be some of the best rock-climbing in South America.

Aconcagua, 6,960 m – M. Zurbriggen, solo, 1897
Ojos del Salado, 6,885 m – J. Wojsznis, J. Szczepanski, 1937
Tupungato, 6,550 m – S. Vines, M. Zurbriggen, 1897
Juncal, 6,110 m – F. Reichart, R. Helbing, D. Beiza, 1910

There are many more peaks over 6,000 m, some of which are very easy ascents and were certainly climbed by local Indians centuries ago, e.g. Llullaillaco (6,723 m).
Patagonia The southernmost part of South America, from the Rio Negro to the Magellan Straits. In the west of this area, the Andes continue for about

1,600 km. Unlike the ranges further north, the peaks here are broken into more individual groups. The top half of the range, from Rio Negro to Lago Buenos Aires, consists of forested country with several volcanoes, including El Tronador (3,430 m), and, a little further south, groups of glaciated peaks rising to about 2,500 m. The area is little explored.

The chief mountaineering interest has centred on the southern half of the range, approximately from Lago Buenos Aires to Punta Arenas, and especially on the great Heilo Continental – an ice-cap extending from Lat. 46°S to 52°S and divided into two parts by the Canal Baker, an inlet which cuts into the range to the depth of 100 miles. The division gives rise to the North Patagonian Ice-cap (Heilo Patagonico Norte) and South Patagonian Ice-cap (Heilo Sur). The Chile–Argentine border threads a circuitous route through this country, most of the ice-caps being in Chile, but the important Fitzroy Group being in Argentina. The eastern (Argentine) side is open country but the western side is wet and forested and the coast is deeply indented with fjords. The ice-caps reach sea level in various places. Throughout the range, the weather is notoriously bad.

The Heilo Norte was crossed by Shipton's party in 1963–4 and the highest peak in Patagonia (Monte San Valentin, 4,058 m), near the northern extremity of the ice-cap, was climbed by O. Meiling's party in 1952. The area is difficult of access and there remains plenty of exploration and climbing for future expeditions.

The Heilo Sur is much longer than its northern counterpart. The crossing of the ice-cap was attempted by F. Reichart in 1916 and 1933, but the first successful crossing was by W. Tilman in 1956. He left his boat, *Mischief*, in Calvo Fjord, and traversed to Lago Argentino and back. The length of the ice-cap was traversed by Shipton's party in 1960–1. There are numerous peaks on the ice-cap but the most famous groups are just to the east: the Fitzroy Group, between Lagos San Martin and Viedma, and the Paine Group, about 160 km further south. These two groups, though the peaks are not particularly high, offer some of the most difficult climbing in the world. Notable ascents include:

Fitzroy Group (also: FitzRoy, Chalten)
Cerro Fitzroy, 3,375 m – C. Magnone, L. Terray, 1952
Fitzroy Super Couloir – J. L. Fonrouge, C. Comesana, 1964
Aig. Poincenot, 2,900 m – D. Whillans, F. Cochrane, 1962
Cerro Torre, 3,020 m – C. Maestri, T. Egger, 1959 (disputed)

Paine Group
Paine Grande, 3,050 m – W. Bonatti, T. Gobbi, 1957
Central Tower, 2,460 m – C. Bonington, D. Whillans, 1963
The Fortress, 2,755 m – G. Hibberd, D. Nicol, J. Gregory, 1968
The Shield, 2,450 m – M. Dotti, M. Curnis, 1968
Tierra del Fuego 'The Land of Fire' – an island at the southern tip of South America, the notorious Cape Horn. Despite a relative lack of height the peaks are ice-draped, often to sea level and the weather is bad.

In 1898 Martin ◊ Conway made an abortive attempt on Sarmiento, the so-called 'Wiesshorn of Chile', which has twin peaks East and West of 2,184 m. The East Peak was climbed by C. Mauri and C. Mattei in 1956, but the West does not seem to have had a successful ascent. Conway climbed a peak of 1,120 m since named after him, but most of the early ascents were by Fr De ◊ Agostini, a local priest.

The highest peaks are in the Darwin Range and the highest summit, Darwin I, now Mt Shipton, was climbed by Shipton's expedition in 1962.

GUIDEBOOKS
Pecher & Schmiemann, *The Southern Cordillera Real.*
Rachowiecki, *Climbing and Hiking in Equador.*
Ricker, *Yuraq Janka.* Cordilleras Blanca and Rosko.
Beaud, *The Peruvian Andes.* Cordillera Blanca, Cordillera Huayhuash.

Andinismo A word used in South America to mean Andean climbing: a local variation on alpinism.

Andrews, Arthur Westlake (1868–1959) A. W. Andrews first visited Snowdonia in 1889 or 1890, but it was not until he returned in 1901 that he met J. M. A. Thomson and shared with him, Eckenstein and a few others the early exploration of ◊ Lliwedd. Central Chimney (1908) is perhaps his best-known route. With Thomson he compiled *The Climbs on Lliwedd* (1909), the first pocket guide to a British crag.

In 1902 he began climbing at Wicca and Bosigran in ◊ Cornwall and for over 30 years was alone in the development of Cornish climbing. The early routes on all the major cliffs are his – his sister usually acting as second. With E. C. Pyatt he edited *Cornwall, A Climber's Guide* (1950).

Andrews was of independent means, a scholar and notable athlete. He was an international miler and in 1900 reached the semi-finals of the Men's Singles at Wimbledon.

Angeville, Henriette d' (1794–1871) The second woman to ascend ◊ Mt Blanc, in 1838, 29 years after ◊ Maria Paradis. Sometimes called 'The Bride of Mt Blanc', she was a spinster who loved Mt Blanc because she had nothing else to love, according to one woman historian! She was said to have attempted the mountain for the publicity, in order to spite George Sand, who was a rival for drawing room gossip.

Anglesey An island off the coast of North Wales which has the huge sea cliffs of ◊ Gogarth, first climbed by Martin Boysen and Baz Ingle in 1964 with two routes, Gogarth and Shag Rock. Rapid development followed with leading parts played by Peter ◊ Crew, Ingle, Dave Alcock and Joe ◊ Brown. In 1966 it was the scene of a T.V. spectacular. Ed Ward-Drummond put up Strand in 1967, T. Rex and Afreet Street in 1969, The Moon in 1971 (amongst other climbs) but undoubtedly his most popular route is A Dream of White Horses, done with Dave Pearce in 1968.

Almost every British climber of note took part in the developments during the 1960s and 1970s. All the climbs are VS and above – usually well above. The rock is igneous, variable but generally sound.

There are also climbs on Holyhead Mountain and Quarry, and some smaller crags.

Annapurna (8,091 m) The Annapurna Himal lies on the eastern side of the Gandaki Section of the Nepal Himalaya. There are four principal summits:

Annapurna I	8,091 m	1950
Annapurna II	7,937 m	1960
Annapurna III	7,555 m	1961
Annapurna IV	7,524 m	1955

Annapurna I was the first 8,000 m peak in the world to be climbed. M. Herzog led a French expedition which first attempted Dhaulagiri then changed to Annapurna almost at the last moment. Herzog and Lachenal reached the summit at 2 p.m., 3 June 1950. Both were badly frostbitten and the French retreat from the mountain was epic. (See *Annapurna*, by M. Herzog.)

Annapurna II was climbed by Bonington and Grant; Annapurna III by Kholi, Gyatso and Sonam Girmi; Annapurna IV by Biller, Steinmetz and Wellenkamp.

In 1970, Bonington returned with an expedition to attempt the S Face of the mountain and D. Whillans, D. Haston reached the summit. Though not the first Himalayan face climb it was the most difficult to date and brought Alpine thinking to the Himalaya – a sign of the development of Himalayan climbing. (See *Annapurna South Face*, by C. Bonington.)

Anorak An Eskimo word for a wind-proof smock which is pulled over one's head. Made of Ventile, or similar material, anoraks were the universal climbing garment from the 1930s to the 1960s after which they tended to be replaced by shell clothing and more adaptable jackets. Rarely seen today.

Antarctica The vast Antarctic continent is covered with an ice sheet which attains a maximum depth of 4,275 m. The principal mountain ranges are in the west where the Transantarctic Range stretches from Victoria Land to the Filchner Ice Shelf. It is at its highest near the Ross Ice Shelf, where there are many peaks of 4,000 m, including the highest, Mt Kirkpatrick (4,511 m).

West of this the continent narrows into the Antarctic Peninsula or Lesser Antarctica, where there are several mountain groups, including the Ellsworth Mountains. Here is the highest peak on the continent, Vinson Massif (5,140 m), first climbed by W. Long, P. Schoening, B. Corbet, and J. Evans of N. B. Clinch's 1966 A.A.C. Expedition. Corbet and Evans also climbed Mt Turee (4,965 m). The A.A.C. party climbed several other peaks in the area. Other mountains have been climbed by surveyors and scientists but there are a great many still unclimbed and probably unexplored.

Ardennes Wooded limestone hills on the Franco–Belgian border; popular with tourists. The chief centre is Dinant. There are limestone crags of considerable interest, particularly those at Freyr on the Meuse between Dinant and Givet. The crags are about 140 m in height and have numerous climbs.
GUIDEBOOK Hart, *German & Belgian Rock Climbs*.

Arolla A small hamlet at the head of the Val d'Hérens (Switzerland) which has always been a popular centre with British climbers (Larden etc.). The principal peaks are Dent Blanche, Mont Blanc de Cheilon, Mont Collon, Ruinette, L'Évêque, Grand Cornier and Pigne d'Arolla, but there are many lesser peaks noted for their rock-climbs.
GUIDEBOOK Collomb, *Pennine Alps West* (A.C.).

Aschenbrenner, Peter (b. 1902) A climber from Tyrol who made many fine climbs, particularly on limestone ranges. Best known is the Asche–Lucke Route, E Face of Fleischbank (with H. Lucke, 1930).

In 1932 Aschenbrenner joined Merkl's expedition to ◊ Nanga Parbat, during which he succeeded in climbing Rakhiot Peak (7,074 m) with Kunigk, and in reaching Camp V (6,196 m) before retiring with frostbite. He returned to the mountain in 1934 and with Schneider reached 7,850 m, the highest point reached by the expedition, before taking part in, and surviving, the terrible retreat. After the war he was in charge of the climbing on the successful Herrligkoffer Expedition to Nanga Parbat, when H. Buhl reached the summit (1953).

Atlas Mountains A range of high mountains extending along the North African coast from Tunis in the east to Ifni in the west. The highest peak is Toubkal (4,165 m). Of the various groups, the most important are found in Morocco – the coastal Rif; the Middle Atlas, on the northern slopes of which lie Fez and Meknes; the High Atlas dominating the town of Marrakesh; and the Anti Atlas. Only the High Atlas have been climbed to any large degree and even here, the Toubkal massif has had the major share of attention. There are several huts.

In summer the mountains are arid, but conditions are better in spring, or, as a number of parties have recently found, winter. Long ridge traverses give the best climbing, though there are some face and buttress routes. The rock can be poor.

GUIDEBOOK Smith, *The Atlas Mountains* (C.P.).

Auckenthaler, Matthias (1906–36) An Innsbruck chimney-sweep who put up some of the hardest rock-climbs in the Eastern Alps between the wars. Best known is the original route up the Laliderer Nordwand (Gr 6 inf) with H. Schmidhuber, 1932. He died from a rockfall below the Schusselkarspitze.

Austin, John Allan (b. 1934) A leading British rock-climber of the post-war years with several hundred new routes to his credit, especially, but not entirely, in the Pennines and Lake District.

His early gritstone routes (with R. B. Evans) include High Street, Ilkley (1956), the Shelf, Crookrise (1957), Western Front, Almscliff (1958), and the Wall of Horrors, Almscliff (1961). With Evans and Fuller at this time (1957) he did Nightshade, Poisoned Glen (one of the best of Irish climbs), and in 1960, Astra, Langdale (Metcalfe and Roberts). Later climbs include Hanging Slab, Sgurr Mhic Coinnich, and Haste Not Direct, White Ghyll (both 1971).

It is perhaps Austin's development of Yorkshire limestone which has been most significant: and especially the free lead of Scorpio at Malham in 1959. Austin has always been a purist when it comes to aid climbing and his example has done much to make limestone shake off its early reputation as being purely for such climbs.

Australia, climbing in The highest mountain in Australia is Mount Kosciusko (2,230 m) in the Snowy Mountains, New South Wales. Most other peaks are in the 900–1,500 m range. Rock-climbing has been extensively developed since the 1950s and there are now routes of 300 m or more and all standards of difficulty. Development has mainly centred on those rocks nearest to the big cities of the south-east coast such as Glasshouse Mountains, Frog Buttress, Wurrumbungles, Blue Mountains, Booroomba Rocks, Mt Buffalo, Grampians, Mt Arapiles.

Other developments have taken place in Tasmania, especially on Frenchman's Cap and Federation Peak. Frenchman's Cap has a 360 m E Face, reputedly the finest crag in Australia, but access is very difficult. There are sea-stacks, too, off Tasmania, including the remarkable Totem Pole, 60 m high and 3.5 m square. Ball's Pyramid is a 550 m sea-stack, 120 km off the east coast. Both stacks have been climbed.

GUIDEBOOK *Mt Arapiles – A Rockclimbers' Handbook*.

Avalanche The sliding away of surface material from a mountain, especially snow. One also speaks of ice avalanches, such as are caused by falling ◊ séracs, and rock avalanches, caused by chutes of stones in a couloir. Earth avalanches, of loose wet soil, are not unknown. In all cases the word implies considerable volume and force.

Given the correct conditions, snow will avalanche at a very shallow angle and presents considerable danger to the climber and skier. The phenomenon is quite common in Britain as well as in greater mountain areas: people have been killed by snow avalanches in the Pennines, Lake District and Scotland within recent years. In Britain it is recommended that no snow-climb (especially gully routes) should be done for three days after a heavy fall of new snow. There is no sure way of testing whether a slope will avalanche or not: the old idea of throwing a heavy stone on to the slope seems of doubtful value.

Some areas of the Alps are known to be avalanche-prone at certain times of the year or even times of day, and these should be avoided. These are usually indicated in the guidebooks.

The following types of avalanche are common:

Wet-snow avalanche – snow and water flow down the hillside in a compact mass. Often thaw conditions.
Powder-snow avalanche – loose powder snow, unable to stick to the underlying snow-ice (because it is too cold), rolls down in great billowing clouds.
Slab avalanche – a surface layer of snow, compacted by wind, cracks off and slides down, unable to stick to loose snow underneath.

Avalanches often push before them a huge mass of air, the avalanche wind, which can do more damage than the snow. The force is incredible and can flatten whole forests.

In the Alps, winter protection against avalanches includes the building of walls and barriers, and the firing of various bombs to precipitate snow masses which are growing too large. There is little an individual can do if caught in an avalanche, though a swimming action is advocated to try and keep near the surface. Some skiers are now equipped with electronic bleepers which will give their location if they are buried by an avalanche. (See *The Avalanche Enigma*, by C. Fraser.)

B

Backhouse, John Henry (1844–69) A companion of ◊ Freshfield and ◊ Tuckett in 1865, making with them the first ascent of the Grosser Mösele and the first crossing of the popular Mittelberg Joch (Ötztal).

Backing off Abandoning a climb in the early stages or even before it is properly commenced, either because of the weather or because of second thoughts.

Backing up A method of climbing a ◊ chimney by placing one's back against one side wall and one's feet, or knees (depending on the width of the chimney) against the other. Movement is made by pushing up with the hands against the back wall (it can help to bring one foot back against the same wall) and then moving the feet up. Rather strenuous, but offers good resting positions. Sometimes called 'back and foot' (or 'knee') or 'chimneying'.

Back rope A rope manoeuvre to see a second man across a difficult traverse. A ◊ runner is put at the start of the traverse and a second rope run through this. The leader then takes in the normal rope and pays out the back rope as the second advances. At the end of the traverse the second man unties from the back rope and pulls it in. The runner has to be abandoned unless it can be flicked off. If only one rope is available, the second can use it as a back rope and clip himself over it with a karabiner.

Baffin Island A huge island lying between Greenland and the Hudson Bay. In the south it is deeply indented by the Cumberland Sound, the northern edge of which reaches the Arctic Circle. The Cumberland Peninsula, between the Sound and Baffin Bay, contains the highest peaks (Tête Blanche, 2,156 m, climbed 1953). The most spectacular peak is Mt Asgard (2,011 m) which has twin plateau tops divided by a brèche and surrounded by steep walls (first ascent, Swiss expedition, 1953). Scott's party (1971) climbed a number of new peaks and some big walls – the latter are one of the chief attractions of Baffin Island. The rock is granite.

Baillie, Rusty (b. 1940) Climbing instructor born in Rhodesia and educated at Cape Town University. His early climbs included many on Table Mt and new routes on Mt Kenya (1961). In 1964 he made a traverse of Mt Kenya (Pt Pigott–Pt John) with T. P. Philips. With Haston he made the second British ascent of the Eigerwand (1963), and with Bonington, Harlin and Robertson the first ascent of the Right Hand Pillar of Brouillard (1965). In the following year he made the first ascent of the Old Man of Hoy with Patey and Bonington and in 1967 the first ascent of the N Wall of Søndre Trolltind in Norway (with J. Amatt).

He became an instructor in the U.S.A. for several years during which he took part in the first ascent of Dragon Route on the Painted Wall of Gunnison Black Canyon (823 m). He returned to Britain to become Deputy Director at Glenmore Lodge. He now lives in Canada.

Baillie-Grohman, William Adolf (1851–1921) A remarkably adventurous Anglo-Austrian who made the first winter ascent of Gross Glockner (1875) and made early explorations of the limestone Alps of Tyrol, especially the Karwendel (1872–4). He opened up the Kootenay River area of British Columbia, where he lived for 11 years and was one of the first to explore the Selkirk Range (1882–93).

Baillie-Grohman's chief interest was game hunting and he wrote many books on the subject. His sporting library of over 4,000 items was bought by the Library of Congress, Washington, D.C., in 1919. From 1893 until his death he lived in the Tyrol.

Baker, Ernest Albert (1869–1941) Along with ◊ Puttrell, one of the founders of outcrop climbing in the ◊ Peak District. Also took part in the first ascent of Crowberry Ridge, Buachaille Etive Mor, in 1900, with the ◊ Abrahams and Puttrell, and Ben Nuis Chimney on Arran, 1901, with Puttrell and Oppenheimer.

His failure on High Tor Gully and the subsequent success of Puttrell led to a rift between them and the break-up of the Kyndwr Club they had founded.

Baker was Director of the University of London School of Librarianship and a prolific author, though his mountaineering books tended to reflect an egotistical personality. His best-known book is *Moors, Crags and Caves of the High Peak* (1903).

Baker, George Percival (1856–1951) Baker is a typical example of those turn-of-the-century climbers who were wealthy enough to make expeditions to the more obscure ranges. He climbed Ararat, and visited Norway, Caucasus, the Canadian Rockies (first ascents Mt Gordon and Mt Sarbach with ◊ Collie 1897), Greece and Crete. He also climbed in Skye and was with ◊ Solly on the first ascent of the Eagle's Nest Ridge in the Lake District.

Balfour, Francis Maitland (1851–82) A brilliant young biologist who was elected F.R.S. at the age of 26 and for whom a special Chair was created at Cambridge when he was 29. He climbed for two years (1880 and 1881) with his brother, F. W. Balfour, during which time they made the first ascent of the lower summit of the Grépon (Pic Balfour) (1881). In July of 1882 he attempted the unclimbed Aig. Blanche de Peuterey with his guide, J. Petrus, and both were killed. The accident was never satisfactorily explained.

Balfour's death was the first of three notable fatalities in the Alps in 1882; the others were W. Penhall with the guide, A. Maurer (killed on the Wetterhorn), and W. E. Gabbett with the guides J. M. Lochmatter and his son (killed on the Dent Blanche). These three accidents caused Queen Victoria to inquire of Gladstone whether she should speak out against mountaineering. He advised against it.

Ball, John (1818–89) Irish politician and naturalist and first president of the A.C. 1858–60.

Ball first visited the Alps in 1827. From Chamonix he climbed up to Montenvers and he also ascended the Salève: experiences which were to have a profound effect on his whole life. From 1840 until his death, scarcely a year passed without his visiting the Alps. He made the first ascent of Pelmo in 1857; the first major Dolomite peak to be climbed. His other first ascents were minor affairs and he gained his chief satisfaction in exploring the valleys and passes. His knowledge of the whole range resulted in the publication of the famous *Ball's Alpine Guides*, the first real Alpine guidebooks (*The Western*

Henry Barber (*J. Tullis*)　　　　　Jacques Balmat

Alps, 1863; *The Central Alps*, 1864; *The Eastern Alps*, 1868).

It was Ball's suggestion to ◊ Longman that there should be an annual volume devoted to the interests of Alpine travellers, which resulted in the first volume of *Peaks, Passes and Glaciers* in 1859. Ball was its editor, and the book was the forerunner of the ◊ *Alpine Journal*.

His travels extended to several other mountain regions besides the Alps: notably the Atlas and Andes. He figured prominently in the great glacier controversies of the mid-nineteenth century.

Balmat, Auguste (1808–62)　A notable Chamonix guide, renowned for his devotion to duty and high intellectual ability. He was a great-nephew of Jacques Balmat (see next entry) but a man of very different character, totally oblivious of wealth or fame.

His career came to prominence in 1842–3 when he was employed by Forbes on glacier work. He was with ◊ Wills on the latter's famous ascent of the Wetterhorn in 1854 and with Wills and ◊ Tyndall on Mont Blanc in 1858, during which he suffered severe frostbite owing to his burying thermometers in the snow with his bare hands when he realized the digging implement had been forgotten. For his devotion to science on this occasion the Royal Society awarded him a special recognition of 25 guineas, which he took in the form of a camera. In the following year, 1859, he spent 20 hours on the summit with Tyndall.

Wills nursed him through his final painful illness and he died, impoverished in all but spirit, at the Eagle's Nest.

Balmat, Jacques (1762–1834)　A crystal and chamois hunter of Chamonix who was with ◊ Paccard on the first ascent of Mont Blanc in 1786. Earlier in the year Balmat had been with other local men as high as the present position of the Vallot hut, but with Paccard a new route was chosen and it seems certain it was Paccard's choosing. Indeed, evidence suggests that Balmat wished to give up the attempt. It was ◊ Bourrit, jealous of Paccard, who suggested that Balmat was the prime leader of the ascent, thus starting a controversy which lasted more than 150 years. Bourrit's work was unfortunately given further credence by Alexandre Dumas, who interviewed Balmat in 1832 – the story could not be contradicted since Paccard had been dead five years.

Balmat made four further ascents, as a guide, including one with Maria Paradis, a servant from Chamonix, and the first woman to climb the mountain. He gradually gave up climbing and became a gold prospector. He was killed in 1834 while prospecting in the mountains, possibly by foul play. See *The First Ascent of Mont Blanc*, by T. G. Brown and G. R. de Beer.

Banks, Michael Edward Borg (b. 1922)   Began climbing in the Commandos, where for many years he was a climbing instructor. This and his Alpine climbs he distilled into *Commando Climber* (1955), one of the most popular climbing books of the day. He has since climbed in many parts of the world and in 1958 attained the summit of Rakaposhi (7,788 m) with ◊ T. Patey. Awarded M.B.E.

Barber, Henry (b. 1953)   An American climber from Boston, famous during the late 1970s as 'Hot Henry'. Barber is an expert solo climber and one who has climbed in many parts of the world, his forte being technical climbing rather than expeditioning. In 1976 he took part in a classic climbing film *Sea Cliff Climbing*, with a dramatic crux as he solos Strand, a hard climb on ◊ Gogarth. In January 1978 his partner, Rob Taylor, suffered a broken ankle on ◊ Kilimanjaro and the ensuing retreat and rescue was both dramatic and acrimonious.

See *On Edge – The Life & Climbs of Henry Barber* by Chip Lee.

Barford, John Edward Quintus (1914–47)   Best known as the compiler of the Penguin book *Climbing in Britain* (1946) which helped to popularize the sport after the war. He was the first secretary of the British Mountain Council. A fine rock-climber, he produced, with J. M. ◊ Edwards, the interim guide to Clogwyn Du'r Arddu and, on his own, to the Three Cliffs. Barford was killed by a stonefall in the Dauphiné.

Barlow, Frederick Thomas Pratt (1843–93)   Made a number of minor new routes in the Alps including N E arête of Grivola and first English ascent of Grand Paradis from Cogne (1872); Monte Rosa from the Grenzsattel (1874); S E arête of Disgrazia (1875).

Bar National, Chamonix   Known as the 'Bar Nash', though its proper name is the National Bar. Stands at the corner of the Place Jacques Balmat, near the Post Office. The bar was the favourite meeting place for climbers, especially British and American, during the fifties and sixties and figures in various accounts of that period. A sympathetic owner and relative cheapness were its main attractions. Still patronized by climbers, though less exclusively.

Barrington, Richard Manliffe (?–1915)   Well known for his descriptions of St Kilda, where in 1883 he made the first ascent of Stack na Biorrach by an outsider. He also tried to land on Rockall (1896) but failed. Barrington had a number of Alpine seasons and was an Original Member of the Climbers' Club. His brother, C. Barrington, made the first ascent of the Eiger in 1858.

Barry, John (b. 1944) Climber, writer and raconteur who once commanded the Arctic Warfare Unit of the Royal Marines (1974–6) and was Director of Plas y Brenin from 1978–85.

Amongst his first ascents in Britain are the rock-climbs Raging Bull, E4 (Fairhead, 1985) and Camelot, E3 (Carn Boel, 1982), and the ice-climbs Smith's Gully, V (Creag Meaghaidh, 1985), Devil's Appendix, V (Clogwyn y Geifr, 1985) and Central Ice Fall, V (Craig Rhaeadr, 1987).

In the Alps, with D. Nicholls, Barry put up a number of new lines on the north faces of Morgenhorn, Leschaux and Dent Blanche, as well as the N E Face of Gletscherhorn and the Bowie Couloir of Mt Cook in New Zealand. All these were TD or harder. The N Face of Gaskajiekkelakka in Arctic Norway, a first ascent, was as hard to climb as to pronounce – ED, V.

In 1971 he made the first ascent of Menthosa in the Himalaya and in 1986 he was joint leader with ◊ Rouse of the British expedition to ◊ K2, which was caught up in the terrible events of that year on the mountain.

His writing began in various journals, then in 1983 he wrote part of *Cold Climbs* with Wilson and Alcock. In 1985 came an autobiographical book *The Great Climbing Adventure*, followed by various technical books. He also wrote an account of the K2 tragedy *K2: Savage Mountain, Savage Summer* (1987). He was also producer of two TV programmes, *Conquer the Arctic* (1989–91).

Barth, Hermann von (1845–76) A Munich lawyer who was one of the founders of German climbing. He made numerous ascents in the Tyrol and Bavaria between 1867 and 1873.

Base Camp The principal depot of an expedition, placed near the foot of their objective. All the materials and men required come to the Base Camp and on a large expedition there may well be a Base Camp Manager to see to the complex arrangements. In certain cases (e.g. Everest S W Face) there may be an Advanced Base Camp, if the first Base Camp cannot be pitched near enough to launch an assault.

Bauer, Paul (b. 1896) German climber of the inter-war years. Made first ascents of the Schönanger Nordwand, Wetterstein and the Kasselerspitze Nordgrat, Zillertal Alps in the 1920s, then led an expedition to the Caucasus in 1928 in which he made the first ascents of Tschumurtscherantau (4,304 m), Katuintau N Face (4,900 m) and Adischtau (4,968 m), and took part in the first ascent of Shkhara N Peak, N Face (5,184 m), though he did not reach the summit. The expedition was important in that the techniques of the Germans helped the development of the sport in Russia.

In 1929 Bauer led a reconnaissance of Kangchenjunga in which Allwein and Krause reached 7,400 m. He returned to the peak in 1931, when Hartmann and Wien reached 7,700 m, but Schaller was killed.

The terrible disaster of ◊ Nanga Parbat in 1934 destroyed the core of experience of Himalayan climbing in Germany, and Bauer was principally responsible for its rebirth. In 1936 he led a party to Sikkim during which expedition Wien and Gottner reached the summit of Siniolchu (6,888 m). Simvu (6,544 m) N W peak, was also climbed. The second great Nanga Parbat disaster of 1937 (Wien's expedition) led to Bauer taking command of another attempt in 1938, but without success, though there were no casualties.

Baumann, John (1848–90 or 91)   An enterprising climber who made the first ascent of the Aig. de Talèfre (1879) and a new route on the Lauteraarhorn (1881). He made the second ascents of some of the hardest climbs of his day, including the Dru, the Plan, W Ridge of Dent d'Hèrens and Zmutt arête of Matterhorn. He also made unsuccessful attempts on the Mittelegi ridge of Eiger and the N Face of Aig. du Plan. Baumann died in mysterious circumstances in South Africa.

Beckey, Fred (b. 1923)   One of the most prolific climbers in the USA, with many fine first ascents to his name, often on high, remote peaks. He was the chief explorer of the (◊ USA) Cascades, for which he wrote three classic guidebooks. His finest Cascades route is probably NE Buttress of Mt Slesse, done with S. Marts and E. Bjornstad in 1963. His explorations have since ranged widely from ◊ Alaska to the desert regions of the South West.

Beckey first came to attention with the second ascent of the fearsome (◊ Canada) Mt Waddington, done with his brother Helmy in 1942 when he was 19 and his brother 16. Four years later came the ascent of the (◊ Canada) Devil's Thumb E Ridge; a highly technical climb in a remote area done in bad weather. With Heinrich ◊ Harrer and H. Meybohm he climbed the E Ridge of Deborah in Alaska and Mt Hunter (both 1954). With H. Mather he climbed the E face of Snowpatch Spire in the (◊ Canada) Bugaboos, 1959. In 1957 he discovered the popular Squamish Chief and made the first route there, but perhaps one of his greatest achievements was the first ascent, with Y. Chouinard and D. Doody of the N Face of Mt Edith Cavell in 1961 – a climb of Eigerwand proportions and difficulty.

To list all his routes is not possible here – he did 25 new climbs in 1963 alone! He has been criticised for using siege tactics on some routes in the 50's and 60's, before more rigorous ethics became universal, but Beckey remains a seminal figure in American climbing; a legend after the fashion of ◊ Whillans or Batso ◊ Harding. (See *Challenge of the North Cascades*, F. Beckey, 1969)

Beetham, Bentley (1886–1963)   A schoolmaster from Barnard Castle, noted for his development of climbing in Borrowdale, Lake District. Beetham was, in fact, a good all-round mountaineer and was a member of the 1924 Everest expedition, though illness prevented him going beyond Camp III.

With Frankland, Beetham made the second ascent of Central Buttress, Scafell, and then, almost accidentally, they together re-opened Borrowdale climbing by first ascents in 1921 of Woden's Face (Bowderstones) and Troutdale Ridge (Black Crag), and finally, in 1922, Brown Slabs Arête (Shepherd's Crag).

Beetham investigated the other neglected crags of the valley, at first desultorily, then with more vigour, putting up some 50 new routes. Many of these were of poor quality but the following are notable and popular: Brown Slabs Ordinary (1946), Crack (1947), Direct (1948), Chamonix (1946), Little Chamonix (1946), Crescendo (1948), Shepherd's Chimney (1946), Monolith Crack (1947), Devil's Wedge (1948), Donkey's Ears (1947). (All these are on Shepherd's Crag, his most notable 'discovery'.)

On Raven Crag he made Pedestal Wall (1940), Corvus (1950), Corax (1950), and Summit Route (1951). Again, this opened out the crag considerably.

It was Beetham's idea of stringing individual pitches together to make a climb which helped in the post-war reappraisal of the sport. He himself took the idea to extremes, however, and his later reputation tended to suffer in consequence.

An authority on ornithology, he wrote several books on that subject.

Belay   The device and technique employed by a climber to safeguard the party from the effects of a fall by one of its members. Also the verb, 'to belay', the act of using a belay. Belays are of four main types: (1) direct belay, (2) static belay or anchor, (3) dynamic belay, (4) running belay or runner (⟡ Runner).

Direct belay   On rock, the climber doing the belaying takes a firm stance and simply passes the rope over a convenient spike of rock, or through a piton, and draws it in as the second man climbs towards him. Used a lot in Alpine climbing when the going is fairly easy and speed is desirable, but its use in steep rock-climbing ended long ago. It is far from secure. In snow-climbing a direct belay is often made round an axe shaft firmly planted into the snow – again, for speed. On ice slopes, direct belays can be made round the axe pick driven into the ice or even round crampons stamped hard in. Both may be regarded as extreme measures to be avoided if possible.

Static belay   The basic belay normally used in steep climbing. Its purpose is literally to anchor the party to the rock face or ice slope. All members of a party, except the one actually climbing, should be belayed. A static belay consists of a loop from the climber's harness passed over a spike, round a tree, or attached to a piton. Whatever the anchor point, it should be firm – even large boulders have been known to move under shock loading. The loop should not be able to ride off or be pulled off in the event of a fall. It is normal practice to use a separate loop (a belay loop) for static belays. It should be nylon rope or tape at least equal in breaking strain to the main rope. In some cases, where the anchor points are not good, two or three belays might be arranged, but this is not common. The main rope itself can be used to arrange a belay.

On ice a static belay can be arranged using an ice peg or ice screw as anchor point, placed above a stance cut in the ice. On snow, an axe driven well in can serve as an anchor or use can be made of a ⟡ 'dead man'.

Dynamic belay   This refers to the way the rope is handled when paying out or taking in. It is common nowadays to use a belaying device which does not depend on body friction but on friction between the device – such as a Sticht plate or Figure 8 descender – to effect an arrest. The device is attached to the belayer's harness.

The old methods of body friction – the shoulder belay and waist belay – are not recommended as they can be injurious to hands and clothing.

Bell, Gertrude Lothian (1868–1926)   Noted Arabian explorer and archaeologist who, at the turn of the century, was also a considerable climber. With Ulrich Führer as guide she made the first systematic exploration of the Engelhörner in 1901 and 1902. Gertrude's Peak is named after her. In 1902 she made the first traverse Lauteraarhorn–Schreckhorn. In the same year she made a dramatic attempt on the N E Face of Finsteraarhorn, lasting 57 hours, with retreat in a blizzard.

Miss Bell was an incredibly tough lady: after interviewing an Arab chief, the latter is said to have remarked, 'And this is one of their women! Allah, what must their men be like?'

Bennen, Johann Joseph (1824–64)   A guide from the upper Rhine valley whose brief but brilliant career has long been the subject of controversy amongst Alpine historians. He came to general notice after ◊ Tyndall hired him for the Finsteraarhorn in 1858, and he it was who led Tyndall on the first ascent of Weisshorn (1861). He also made three attempts on the Matterhorn and it could be argued that Bennen's lack of consistency caused Tyndall to lose that great prize. It may also have contributed to his own death on the Haut de Cry in February 1864 during a winter ascent of that minor peak. Against his own expressed judgement he allowed himself to be talked into crossing a dangerous couloir and was overwhelmed by an avalanche.

His correct name was Benet, and it is not clear why he was universally known as Bennen.

Ben Nevis (1,344 m)   The highest mountain in Britain. With Carn Dearg (1,221 m) and Carn Mor Dearg (1,223 m) it forms a fine horseshoe enclosing the Coire Leis and the upper Allt a Mhuilinn glen, the entrance to which is to the north-west. The actual summit is a small plateau.

The nearest village is Fort William, at the entrance to Glen Nevis, but nearer climbing accommodation includes the Youth Hostel in Glen Nevis, the Steall Hut (Upper Glen Nevis) and the finely situated Charles Inglis Clark Hut in the Allt a Mhuilinn.

The tourist path to the summit begins at Achintee Farm (or the Youth Hostel) in Glen Nevis and follows an old pony track constructed for the former Observatory (1883–1904). It leads easily to the summit without incident. The classic circuit of the horseshoe is airy and dangerous in mists: there have been numerous fatalities here.

The Glen Nevis side of the mountain is grass slopes cut by several deep gullies and various outcrops, of which Polldubh Crags offer the best climbing. The principal climbing, however, is on the N Faces of Carn Dearg and Ben Nevis, overlooking the Allt a Mhuilinn where the crags stretch for 3 km and reach a height of 600 m (Tower Ridge).

In winter the crags of Carn Dearg and Ben Nevis form one of the major snow- and ice-climbing areas of Britain and though there are routes of all standards, they can only be recommended to experienced mountaineers. The mountain has a bad winter record of accidents.

Though the Hopkinsons had visited Ben Nevis in 1892 it was Collie's visit of 1894 which resulted in the first ascent of Tower Ridge that began the mountain's popularity with climbers. A summary of important first ascents is given below:

1892	N E Buttress – Hopkinson brothers. Tower Ridge (descent) – Hopkinson brothers
1894	Tower Ridge – Collie, Solly, Collier
1895	Castle Ridge – Collie, Naismith, Thomson, Travers
1897	Gardyloo Gully (winter) – Hastings, Haskett Smith
1901	Observatory Ridge – Raeburn (solo)
1902	Observatory Buttress – Raeburn (solo)
	Glover's Chimney – Glover, Dr and Mrs Inglis Clark
1938	Green Gully (winter) – Bell, Henson, Morsley, Small
1946	The Crack – Carsten, McGuinness
1954	Sassenach – Brown, Whillans
1956	Centurion – Whillans, Downes
1957	Cresta (winter) – Patey, Lovat, Nicol
	Zero Gully (winter) – MacInnes, Nicol, Patey
1959	The Bat – Haston, Smith
	Point Five Gully (winter) – Alexander, Clough, Pipes, Shaw

1962   Torro – McLean, Smith, Gordon
1964   King Kong – Robertson, Harper, Graham
1965   The Curtain (winter) – Knight, Bathgate
1970   Torro – freed at E2,5c by Nicholson & Fulton
1977   Titan's Wall – freed at E3,6a by Fowler & Thomas
1983   Agrippa E5,6b – Whillance, Anderson

GUIDEBOOKS Marshall, *Ben Nevis* (S.M.C.); Kimber, *Winter Climbs Ben Nevis & Glencoe* (C.P.).

Ben Nevis Race   An annual race from the New Town Park, Claggan, to the summit of Ben Nevis and back – approximately 14 km with a vertical interval of 1,340 m. The winner receives the MacFarlane Trophy, a gold medal and £10, and there are numerous other awards.

The race began in 1895, when it was won by W. Swan of Fort William in 2 hr 41 min., but only became an annual event in 1951, since when it has attracted leading entries from all over Britain. Though the race is confined to men, the course has been run by women (K. Connochie, aged 16, 3 hr 2 min., 1955). The usual winner's time is under 2 hr.

From 1951 to 1970 the starting point was the King George V Playing Fields, Fort William. The present starting point makes the run about 1½ miles shorter. The old course record is held by Peter Hall, who in 1964 clocked 1 hr 38 min. 30 sec.

Berg heil!   A familiar greeting in the mountains of Austria and the German border when parties reach the summit. Nowadays a little archaic, according to one authority the greeting was said to have originated in 1881 on the summit of Olperer in the Zillertal range, when August von Bohm so greeted the ◊ Zsigmondy brothers and ◊ Purtscheller, but the incident was more likely to be on the adjacent peak called Fussstein, where they all made the first ascent of the S W Face that year.

Bergschrund (Fr.: rimaye)   The crevasse between the glacier proper and the upper snows (*névé*). They may be negligible or formidable and can vary from season to season. Double and triple bergschrunds are quite common. Where the upper lip is much higher than the lower a bergschrund will have to be climbed by ice techniques, even, in extreme conditions, artificial techniques. In descent, in such cases, an abseil is necessary.

Bergsteigeressen   In Austrian and German ◊ huts the guardian must provide, amongst a sometimes extensive menu, a simple dish which is inexpensive. This is known as *Bergsteigeressen*, 'climber's food'.

Bibliography   The standard bibliography for English language mountaineering books is J. Neate, *Mountaineering Literature* (C.P.) (1986). This first appeared as *Mountaineering and its Literature* in 1978 and this first edition is still a valuable reference work because it links the books to areas and peaks.

Bich family   An Italian family of guides from the Val Tournanche, closely linked with the ◊ Matterhorn. Jean Baptiste Bich (1822–1903) was sometimes called Bardolet and was with J.-A. ◊ Carrel on the second ascent of the Matterhorn, 1865; the first of the Italian Ridge: 'Man cannot do anything more difficult than that,' said Carrel in response to Whymper's question whether he had ever climbed anything more difficult. He is not to be confused with Jean Baptiste Bich (1837–1909) who was with ◊ Lord Wentworth and Emile ◊ Rey on the first ascent of the Aiguille Noire de Peuterey, 1877. Maurizio Bich (1895–1936) was with E. Benedetti and Louis Carrel on the second ascent of the Furggen Ridge (1930) of the Matterhorn and the first ascent of the South Face (1931). The same party was joined by G. Mazzotti, Lucien Carrel and Antoine Gaspard on the first ascent of the difficult East Face of the Matterhorn, 1932. He was killed by an avalanche. Jean Bich (b. 1916) was the first Italian guide to climb the Matterhorn Nordwand (1961).

Birkbeck, John, Sen. (1817–90)   Yorkshire banker who was both climber and potholer: forerunner of the Slingsby group in this respect. In 1847 he made the first descent of Alum Pot with Metcalfe and in 1872 he made the first attempt on Gaping Ghyll, reaching a depth of 190 ft (Birkbeck's Ledge).

In 1855 he was with Hudson, Stevenson and the Smyths on the first ascent of Monte Rosa. In 1858 he crossed the Mönchjoch and in 1860 took part in the first ascent of the Col de Triolet. He was an Original Member of the A.C.

His son, also called John (1842–92), made one of the earliest attempts on the Dru and an early ascent of the Weisshorn. In 1864 made the first traverse of the Dôme de Goûter with Adams Reilly. His initiation to climbing was unfortunate: he had a sliding fall of almost 550m from the Col de Miage (1861), losing most of the skin from his back and legs and suffering severe shock. His remarkable recovery can be attributed to the speed of his rescue by his companions: Hudson, Tuckett, Stephen and Anderegg. In 1874 he made the first double traverse of the Matterhorn—Breuil back to Breuil in 19 hours.

Birkett, Robert James (b. 1915)   A Lakeland climber active in the immediate pre-war and post-war years, Jim Birkett made 45 new routes, mostly in the harder grades. He had a fine eye for a line and most of the routes are now classics.

His activity extended to many crags and mention might be made of Tophet Grooves, Gable (1940); F Route, Gimmer (1941); and Leopard's Crawl, Dow (1947). His contributions to three crags are outstanding: E Buttress, Scafell; Castle Rock, Thirlmere; and White Ghyll.

His first big new route was May Day Climb, E Buttress (1938). Though he used pegs for protection, it was a very hard climb for the time. Other E Buttress routes are the Girdle (1938) and Gremlin Groove (1945). He also put up Great Central Route on Esk Buttress (1945) among several others.

Birkett's ascent of Overhanging Bastion, Castle Rock (1939), with C. R. Wilson and L. Muscroft created a sensation at the time. It was followed by Zig Zag in the same year, May Day Cracks in 1947 and, finally, Harlot's Face in 1949. This was the first extreme-grade climb in Lakeland. A number of his easier climbs on this crag have also become popular.

In 1945 he climbed Hollin Groove in White Ghyll: not the first climb in the Ghyll, but it was Birkett's subsequent climbs that helped make the Ghyll popular: White Ghyll Wall (1946), Slip Knot (1947), Haste Not (1948), Perhaps Not (1948) and Do Not (1949).

Birkett's influence on Lakeland climbing cannot be overestimated.

His son, Bill Birkett, is a well-known mountaineering photo-journalist.

Bishop, Barry Chapman (b. 1932)   A leading American mountaineer and geographer who made the first ascent of the W Buttress of Mt McKinley (6,193 m) in 1951 and the first ascent of Ama Dablam (6,856 m) in 1961. The latter was a winter ascent.

On 22 May 1963, Bishop, with L. G. Jerstad, reached the summit of Mt Everest. They climbed the South Ridge and beat Hornbein and Unsoeld by a few hours – the latter traversing the mountain, west–south. The two parties met on the descent. (See *Everest – The West Ridge*, by T. F. Hornbein.)

As a geographer Bishop has done much research in Nepal and various arctic zones. He works for the National Geographic Society.

Biven, Peter Harvey (1935–76)   An outstanding rock-climber of the post-war years, who, with his partner, Trevor Peck, was one of the few people to match the achievements of the Rock and Ice Club on outcrops. Amongst his early first ascents are:

1953   Original Route, Matlock High Tor
1955   Moyer's Buttress, Gardom's Edge. Suicide Wall, Bosigran
1956   Phantom, Bosigran. Congo Corner, Stanage. Eye of Faith, Gardom's Edge
1958   Central Wall, Malham Cove

In all, Biven made some 300 new ascents. He was one of the earliest practitioners in Britain of aided climbing. He developed Millstone Edge as a gritstone peg-climbing quarry, though this was only as practice for the larger peg climbs of the Alps. He later played a considerable part in the development of Chudleigh and the Devon sea cliffs.

In the Alps, Biven made the first ascents of the North Face of Valette and North Face of Aig. de la Vanoise, in the Vanoise, and of the Westwand of Predigstuhl in the Kaisergebirge, all in 1956. He also made the first British ascent of the North Face of Piz Ligoncio in the Bregaglia.

He was the compiler of guidebooks to *Cornwall* (Vol. 1), 1968, and *Devon* (with P. Littlejohn), 1970. Died in a belaying accident in the Avon Gorge.

Bivouac   Spending the night in the open on a mountain. Many long Alpine climbs demand one or more bivouacs for which the climbers go prepared, but climbers are sometimes delayed and forced to bivouac unexpectedly.

In a normal bivouac the climbers will search for some suitable ledge before dark and prepare to sit out the night. It is usual, unless the ledge is extremely wide, to tie off rucksacks and gear to belays such as pegs, and for each person to be similarly belayed. The stove, pots and food are placed accessibly, as constant brewing-up is a feature of bivouacs. All available clothing is usually worn including long johns and ◊ duvet gear. It may or may not be feasible to lie down, but some sleep is generally possible. In any case, boots are usually removed and put in the rucksack, which is then used as a short form of sleeping bag. Some climbers carry pied d'éléphants, which are short duvet bags designed for this purpose. The 'bivvy sac', once in vogue, is no longer popular and if the night is very cold the protection of a large plastic bag can be employed instead.

Where several bivouacs are intended, or where the weather seems doubtful, a special bivouac tent can be carried. If the bivouac is to be on very steep rock, without ledges, bivouac hammocks can be used slung from pegs.

An involuntary bivouac can be a serious matter if the climbers are unprepared, particularly in bad weather or winter. The main aim is to keep out of the wind and conserve body heat. The emergency plastic bag should be carried at all times. In winter it may be necessary to dig a snow hole or make an igloo.

Bivouac hut   A small hut made of wood, metal or plastic usually with 3–12 places which can be found in the Alps in situations where a larger ◊ hut is unwarranted because of the demand or in airy positions where a larger hut would be impractical. Examples are on the East Face of Watzmann and the Frontier Ridge of Mt Blanc. Bivouac huts are not guardianed.

The Solvay Hut on the Matterhorn and the Vallot Hut on Mt Blanc are in a sense bivouac huts though their use is restricted to emergencies.

Black ice   Thin water ice so transparent that the underlying rock shows through, giving it a dark hue. Extremely tough and 'rubbery' – very difficult to cut with an ice axe.

Blackshaw, Alan (b. 1933)   One of the leaders of the post-war British resurgence in Alpine climbing. He visited the Caucasus in 1958 and Greenland in 1960. In 1972 he took part in the British Alpine Ski Traverse and the following year in a ski traverse of Lapland. President of the B.M.C. in 1973–6.

From 1968 to 1970, Blackshaw was Editor of the *Alpine Journal*, but is best known for his book, *Mountaineering* (1965) – regarded at the time as the climber's 'bible'.

Blaikie, Thomas (1750–1838)   A Scottish plant hunter who visited the Alps in 1775. He visited the Jura, Chablais, Oberland and Diablerets and had a hair-raising escapade on Salève. He was the first Briton to cross the Gemmi Pass from the Rhône to Kandersteg.

His greatest claim to fame, however, rests on his brief acquaintance with the young M.-G. ◊ Paccard with whom he explored the approaches to Mont Blanc and visited le Jardin – almost certainly the first time this had been done by other than crystal seekers. He also made the second British ascent of Brévent, a few weeks after Col. Hervey of the Royal Marines.

Blaikie lived in France through the Revolution and kept a diary, rediscovered and published in 1931. See T. Blaikie, *Diary of a Scotch Gardener*.

Blanchet, Émile Robert (1877–1943)   A Swiss climber with a long record of difficult Alpine ascents. Between the wars, often with the guide Kaspar Mooser, Blanchet was responsible for some extraordinary climbs on the big faces, the best known being a variant on the E Face of the Zinal Rothorn (1932). Blanchet and Mooser also reconnoitred the Matterhorn N Face but rejected the route later climbed by the Schmids. Unfortunately, most of Blanchet and Mooser's routes lack the quality of the great face climbs done by other climbers of the period. In private life Blanchet was a pianist.

Blodig, Karl (1859–1956)   One of the earliest advocates of guideless Alpine climbing and a companion of ◊ Purtscheller. Climbed often with British climbers: H. O. Jones, Young, Eckenstein, Compton, etc. He made a number of first ascents but is most notable as being the first to climb all the then known 4,000 m peaks in the Alps (1911). He added to the list as new heights were discovered, including the Gd. Rocheuse and Aig. du Jardin, which he climbed solo at the age of 73. Wrote *Die Viertausender der Alpen*. In private life Blodig was a dentist from Bregenz.

Blond, Mrs Aubrey Le (1861–1934)   One of the most skilful of the early women climbers, slightly built but strong. She climbed in every part of the Alps, but particularly the Bernina. Though she employed some of the best

Peter Boardman (*C. Bonington*) Jean-Marc Boivin (*B. Cropper*)

guides of the day she made occasional guideless climbs and even 'all women' climbs – almost unheard of. She was one of the founders and first President of the Ladies' Alpine Club.

Mrs Le Blond wrote *High Alps in Winter* (1883), *High Life and Towers of Silence* (1886), *My Home in the Alps* (1892), *Hints on Snow Photography* (1894), *True Tales of Mountain Adventure* (1903), *Story of an Alpine Winter* (novel) (1907), *Mountaineering in the Land of the Midnight Sun* (1908) and *Day In and Day Out* (1929).

Boardman, Peter David (1950–82) Boardman began climbing as a Stockport schoolboy and soon built up an impressive list of Alpine ascents including N Face of the W Shoulder, Pic Sans Nom (second ascent), S Face direct, Sialouze; N W Face, Olan and the Welzenbach routes on the N Faces of Lauterbrunnen, Breithorn and Nesthorn.

His first expedition was in 1972 to the Hindu Kush where he climbed five new routes, including two big face climbs: N Face, Koh-i-Khaiik and N Face, Koh-i-Mondi. In 1974 he made the first ascent of S Face of Mt Dan Beard in Alaska.

In 1975 he was made National Officer of the ◊ B.M.C. and that same year went on the ◊ Bonington expedition to the S W Face of ◊ Everest, where, with Sherpa Pertemba, he made the second ascent, following the success of ◊ Scott and ◊ Haston. On their return they were surprised to see Mick ◊ Burke making his way up solo. They waited for him on the S Peak in worsening conditions, but he did not return and Boardman and his companion had a difficult retreat to Camp VI.

The following year, 1976, he teamed up with Joe ◊ Tasker who was to become his boon companion and together they did the difficult W Wall of Changabang (6,864 m). In 1978 he took over as Principal at Leysin mountaineering school following the death of Haston and went with Bonington on the unsuccessful K2 attempt. Later in 1978 he was in New Guinea to climb

Carstensz Pyramid (4,883 m). In 1979 he climbed ◊ Kangchenjunga (8,597 m) by the N Ridge, a first ascent and done without oxygen, and the W Ridge of Gauri Sankar (7,145 m). In 1980 he made another unsuccessful attempt on K2, but in the following year was with the successful party to make the first ascent of Kongur (7,719 m).

Peter Boardman and Joe Tasker disappeared whilst attempting the un-climbed N E Ridge of Everest in 1982.

Shortly before his death Boardman had established himself as a very fine mountain writer, as had his friend Tasker. To commemorate them, the ◊ Boardman–Tasker Award for mountain literature was established.

His books are *The Shining Mountain* (1978) and *Sacred Summits* (1982).

Boardman–Tasker Award　A literary prize instituted in memory of Peter ◊ Boardman and Joe ◊ Tasker who died on Everest in 1982. The award is a cash prize given annually for an outstanding work of mountain literature published during the previous 12 months. A permanent committee appoints three judges each year. The work must be in English and the judges can, at their discretion, withhold the prize – as, indeed, they did in the inaugural year of 1983.

Boccalatte, Gabriele Gallo (1907–38)　A fine Italian climber who made hard new routes in the Mont Blanc massif and the Dolomites. He was in the party that climbed the Aig. du Diable Couloir of Mont Blanc du Tacul in 1930, and he climbed the N Face of Mont Gruetta in 1937. He is best remembered for the climbs done with Mme Nina Pietrasanta (later his wife): Boccalatte Pillar of Mont Blanc du Tacul (1936) and the W Face of Aig. Noire de Peuterey (1935). He also paid a visit to the Andes. He was killed attempting the S W Face of the Triolet in 1938.

Bohren, Peter (1822–82)　One of the early Oberland guides who was with ◊ Wills on the Wetterhorn in 1854. He was a very small man, meticulous and intelligent. He figures in many of the early accounts of climbs written by the pioneers and was called 'die Gletscher-Wolf'. It was Bohren who was responsible for the well-known remark: 'Herr, you are master in the valley: I am master here', made when one of his employers questioned his judgement during a climb.

Boileau de Castelnau, Henri Emmanuel (1857–1923)　A distinguished French climber noted for his first ascents in the Dauphiné Alps. These include Aig. d'Olan (1876) and all four summits of the Pelvoux traversed for the first time (1877).

After two previous attempts, he finally succeeded in making the first ascent of the Meije (15–17 August 1877).

Boivin, Jean-Marc (1951–90)　A professional adventurer who devoted his life to the mountains. As well as climbing, he was an expert at hang-gliding, para-pente and free fall. Later he took up BASE jumping, including a jump from the Grand Capucin. He successfully completed a jump from the 900 m Angel Falls cliff in Venezuela, but was killed trying to repeat it.

Boivin's ascents include solos of the Peuterey Ridge Integrale, the Eiger North Face and the Pilier d'Angle. He was an enthusiast for linking routes in the Alps, often climbing solo. He held the world record height for para-pente – from the summit of Masherbrum II in 1985 and from Everest in 1988 (11 minutes down to Camp 2).

Bolts   Expansion bolts are sometimes used in aid climbing to overcome blank sections of rock or in hard 'free' climbing for protection. They can be bought in kit form from climbing shops.

Systems vary – some bolts are self-drilling – but basically a hole is drilled in the rock and the bolt, with a hanger to which a karabiner can be attached, is inserted. It is essential to place the bolt properly by drilling deep enough and preferably using a stainless steel bolt which will last.

Hangers were called golos or fishplates in the 1960s when bolts were first used in Britain, but those names seem to have died.

Bolting is avoided whenever possible, not only because of the labour involved but also on ethical grounds. The use and misuse of bolts is a matter of fierce debate and many climbers are wholeheartedly opposed to their use in any circumstances, others claim they have led to rising standards. Bolts have been 'chopped', i.e. removed, in anger – though also because rising standards have made them no longer necessary on some routes.

Bonatti, Walter (b. 1930)   An Italian alpinist born in Bergamo, who has become one of the world's greatest mountaineers. His Alpine achievements are probably without compare. He became a professional guide in 1954 and has lived at Courmayeur since 1957.

Among many of his new or outstanding climbs in the Alps might be mentioned:

1951   E Face of the Grand Capucin (with L. Ghigo), first ascent
1955   S W Pillar of the Dru (Bonatti Pillar), solo, first ascent
1957   Eckpfeiler Buttress, Mont Blanc (with T. Gobbi), first ascent
1959   Pilastro Rosso, Mont Blanc (with A. Oggioni), first ascent
          Route Major, Mont Blanc, first solo ascent
1965   Matterhorn Nordwand Direct, solo, first ascent.

This selection shows Bonatti to be a master of all techniques, from the artificial climbing on the Capucin to the difficult mixed terrain of the Matterhorn Nordwand.

In 1954 he was with the Italian party that made the first ascent of K2, the second highest mountain in the world, but not in the summit assault. In 1958 he returned to the Himalaya and with C. Mauri reached the summit of Gasherbrum IV (first ascent).

Earlier in the same year, 1958, he visited Patagonia. Though he failed on ◊ Cerro Torre he made, with Mauri, the first ascent of Cerro Moreno (3,536 m) and then a complete traverse of the Cerro Adela group – five summits in a single push. He returned to S. America in 1961 and climbed Nevado Ninashanca (5,639 m), Cerro Parin Nord (5,166 m) and Rondoy Nord (5,821 m), all first ascents.

Bonatti's career has not been without tragedy and controversy. In the winter of 1956 he and S. Gheser climbed the Brenva Ridge with J. Vincendon and F. Henry. The parties became separated and Vincendon and Henry died in a blizzard. In 1961, only he, R. Gallieni and P. Mazeaud survived a terrible retreat from the Central Pillar of Frêney in a blizzard during which four of their companions died.

His books are *On the Heights* (1964), *The Great Days* (1974) and *Magic of Mont Blanc* (1985).

Bonington, Christian John Storey (b. 1934)   One of the best-known British climbers of the present era, with numerous new ascents in Britain, the Alps and elsewhere to his credit. Bonington first came to prominence with his

first winter ascent of Raven's Gully on Buachaille Etive Mor in 1953 (with H.
◊ MacInnes) and with some hard first routes on the cliffs of the Avon Gorge in
the late fifties. In the sixties he was putting up some hard Lakeland routes,
among them: The Medlar (with M. Boysen) and Totalitarian, both on Raven
Crag, Thirlmere, and The Last Laugh, Castle Rock.

Bonington's first Alpine season was 1957 when, with MacInnes, he made a
half-hearted attempt on the Eigerwand. In the following year they made the
first British ascent of the Bonatti Pillar of the Dru. In 1959, with Gunn Clark,
he made the first British ascent of the Cima Grande Direct. In 1961, with
Whillans, he again attempted the Eigerwand, but frustrated by weather they
went to Chamonix, where, with ◊ Clough and Dlugosz, he made the first
ascent of the Central Pillar of Frêney, then regarded as the greatest unsolved
problem in the Alps. In 1962 with Whillans, he took part in the rescue of Nally
from the Eigerwand, and later in the same year made the first British ascent of
the Eigerwand with Clough. He has made several other first ascents in the
Alps, with Brown, Patey and others.

Commissioned into the Army in 1956, Bonington spent five years in the
forces before taking up a position as a trainee manager with Unilever, but his
increasing involvement with expeditions decided him to resign, and in 1962
he became a full-time writer and photographer. He established himself in this
with his photographic coverage of the Eiger Direct climb in 1966. A number
of exciting projects followed, including the first descent of the Blue Nile
(1968).

Bonington's first Himalayan expedition was in 1960 when he reached the
summit of Annapurna II (7,937 m) with R. Grant. In 1961 he reached the
summit of Nuptse (7,833 m). In 1963, with Whillans, he reached the summit
of the Central Tower of Paine in Patagonia. He did not join another
expedition for seven years, but in 1970 he organized the immensely successful
expedition to climb the S Face of Annapurna: the most important Himalayan
face climb to that date.

There followed a series of expeditions which established him as one of the
world's leading mountaineers (all Himalaya/Karakoram except where
shown):

Year	Peak	Comment
1971	Mooses Tooth, E Face, Alaska	Beaten by weather
1972	Everest, S W Face	Reached Rock Band
1973	Brammah, S Ridge	1st asc. with Estcourt
1974	Changabang, E Ridge	1st asc. with 5 others
1975	Everest, S W Face	1st asc. by Haston and Scott
1976	Pt 20,309, N Face	Defeated at 2/3 height
1977	Ogre, W Ridge	1st asc. with Scott
1978	K2, West Face	Estcourt killed in avalanche
1980	Kongur group, Kun Lun	Recce: 1st asc. 2 minor peaks
1981	Kongur, W Ridge	1st asc. with 3 others
1982	Everest, N E Ridge	Boardman and Tasker killed
1983	Shivling S W, S E Ridge	1st asc. with J. Fotheringham
1983	Mt Vinson, Antarctica	1st British asc., solo
1984	Kurun Koh, W Ridge	Defeated by weather
1985	Everest, S E Ridge	Reached summit
1987	Menlungtse, S W Buttress	Defeated by weather
1988	Menlungtse, W Ridge	1st asc. W Peak, Fanshawe, Hinkes

Several expeditions were marred by tragedy. Ian ◊ Clough was killed by an

Chris Bonington on Great Gable (*Border TV*)

avalanche on Annapurna, as was Nick ◊ Estcourt on ◊ K2. Burke disappeared on Everest in 1975 as did ◊ Tasker and ◊ Boardman in 1982. Tony Tighe died in the Everest ice-fall in 1972.

Numerous honours have been awarded to Bonington, including a C.B.E. in 1976. A dozen books record his life and expeditions, summed up in *Mountaineer – Thirty Years Climbing on the World's Highest Peaks* (1989).

Bonney, Rev. Thomas George (1833–1923) Distinguished geologist and theologian and an indefatigable Alpine traveller, almost rivalling ◊ Ball. Bonney climbed many of the Alpine giants and made the first English attempt on Pelvoux (1860). Most of his later travels were of a geological nature. Wrote several books on the Alps and geology.

Boots From an early date climbers recognized that the ordinary industrial boot or shooting boots were not the best models for climbing. Special boots were made from the 1870s at least, judging by early advertisements – 'James A. Carter, Alpine Bootmaker'. Carter's boots appear to have been fitted with a stiffening shank. A bellows tongue is mentioned about 1890 as being desirable.

Boots were nailed at first with hobs then later with specially designed ◊ nails such as clinkers and tricounis. Clinkers were soft and allowed the rock to bite into them; tricounis were hard steel and bit into the rock. In the nineteenth century clinkers were obtainable from the village blacksmith at Grindelwald for 6 shillings a set, including spares. Tricounis were invented on the Continent just prior to 1914, but the old clinker was often still preferred. There was also a variety of special patent nails: Hill's, Mummery, Brigham etc., but none were universally popular.

Nails lingered on until the 1960s – they had advantages on steep slippery ground or snow-ice – but were displaced by the cleated rubber sole invented by ◊ Vibram SpA. of Italy.

Three types of modern boot can be identified:

Walking boots   Lightweight boots were developed in the 1970s and soon displaced the old heavy mountaineering boots. They are flexible and something like the old *kletterschuhe* in appearance, but designed for walking. Some are more waterproof than others. Useful for fell-walking tours or crag approaches, though some climbers prefer trainers for the latter.

Mountaineering boots   Leather boots are still available but the current fashion is for plastic boots with separate inners. The latter can be varied to suit conditions. The boots have a deep rubber rand which helps with friction on rock and of course, rubber-cleated soles. The soles are stiffened to take crampons and allow good front-pointing technique.

Rock-climbing boots   A purely rock-climbing boot of canvas uppers and felt or cord soles appeared in the Eastern Alps early on, where they were known as *scarpetti* or *kletterschuhe*. In Britain rock-climbing, when not done in boots, was usually done in cheap thin-soled plimsolls.

The *kletterschuhe* ('klets') became essentially a lightweight boot with a thinner Vibram sole, stiffened with a steel or plastic shank. These soon gave way to the canvas boot with smooth, narrow and very stiff soles developed by the French climber Pierre Allain and known as P.A.s.

Now generally referred to as friction boots, the P.A. has spawned many similar models. Most innovative in recent years has been the development of special rubbers for the soles – the so-called 'sticky soles'. There is now almost a division of rock-climbing boots into two specialized types: those whose design best suits them for edging, i.e. the use of small, sharp holds, and those best designed for smearing, i.e. friction climbing. Most boots are, of necessity, something of a compromise.

Botterill, Fred (?–1920)   A Yorkshire gritstone climber who made some outstanding Lake District climbs, notably Botterill's Slab, Scafell (1903), and the Northwest Climb, Pillar Rock (1906). One of the first to bring gritstone standards to other areas, he retired from climbing in 1909 after an accident on Eagle's Nest Ridge, Gable, in which his leader was killed.

Bottoming   A term used to mean that a piton has reached the back of a crack before its blade is fully home. Either a shorter piton or a tie-off is used.

Bouldering   Climbing boulder problems; a common game amongst climbers. The problems are on small rocks and are highly technical, often gymnastic. No ropes are used and a fall or jump-off is not generally serious. Bouldering is almost a sub-sport; some rock-climbers do little else.

Many climbing areas have boulder problems. One of the most comprehensive areas is Fontainebleau, near Paris, where there are dozens of sandstone boulders laced with problems of varying degrees of difficulty.

Bourdillon, Thomas Duncan (1924–56)   The leading spirit in the British post-war Alpine climbing renaissance whose ascent with Nicol of the N Face of the Dru in 1950 showed the way for others. Was on the expedition to Cho Oyu (1952) and Everest (1951) with ◊ Shipton and took part in the first assault on the summit, with ◊ Evans, during the 1953 expedition. He was professionally a physicist and, with his father, developed the oxygen apparatus used on the 1953 expedition. Bourdillon was killed climbing the Jagihorn, Oberland.

Bourrit, Marc-Théodore (1739–1819)   Precentor of Geneva Cathedral, self-styled 'Indefatigable Bourrit'. One of the early explorers of the Alps, contemporary and rival of de ◊ Saussure. Bourrit was a painter, writer and climber – all of which he did badly. He climbed the Buet in 1775 and explored many of the almost unknown valleys and glaciers of the Central Alps. In 1766 he visited Chamonix and heard about de Saussure's offer of a reward for a first ascent of Mont Blanc. Bourrit changed the apathy with which news of the award had been greeted into enthusiasm, though it took him several years to do it – the first attempt by guides was not until 1775. He made an attempt himself in 1783 with Paccard, but retreated feebly, much to Paccard's disgust. He tried again in 1784 but again withdrew, though his guides reached the Dôme du Goûter. The following year he tried again with de Saussure and failed. When Paccard and Balmat reached the summit in 1786 Bourrit became insanely jealous and published a libellous document about Paccard which was, unfortunately, widely distributed and began the long controversy over the motives and origins of the first ascent (◊ Paccard). Bourrit never managed to climb the mountain (see *The First Ascent of Mont Blanc*, by T. G. Brown and G. R. de Beer).

Bowdler, Thomas (1754–1825)   Well known as the man who tried to expurgate Shakespeare and other texts ('to bowdlerize'). Bowdler was also an Alpine traveller who, in 1779, made the first crossing of the Col de la Vanoise (Graians). He was the first Englishman to climb the Buet (also 1779) – he held the height record for an Englishman for eight years until Beaufoy climbed Mont Blanc – and the first Englishman to take an interest in Mont Blanc by offering a reward of five guineas to any guides who succeeded in reaching the summit.

Bowen, Cecil Hubert (1864–1956)   One of the pioneers of British rock-climbing who, in 1893, took part in the first ascent of the Arrowhead Ridge on Gable, Lake District. His best known ascents were with ◊ Jones, whom he seconded on the first ascent of Kern Knotts Crack (1897). They also made the first ascent of C Gully on the Screes (1897) and the second of Eagle's Nest Direct, Gable.

Bowen made the first traverse of the Gletscherhorn (1908) and several new climbs in Norway.

Bradby, Edward Hugh Folkwine (1866–1947)   The third member of a famous trio, ◊ Wicks, ◊ Wilson and Bradby, who made a number of fine climbs at Chamonix during the turn of the century. In private life a solicitor.

Braithwaite, Paul (b. 1947)   Began climbing at the age of 16 on his local moors around Oldham. Though his chief interest is in Alpine and expedition climbing he has nevertheless put up some 25 new routes in Britain including, for example, Scansor on Stob Coire nan Lochan, and Cumbrian on Esk Buttress. In the Alps he made the first British ascent of Croz Spur of the Grandes Jorasses (1969). Visited Baffin Island in 1972 and 1973, during which he made the first ascent of Asgard E Pillar (1972). In 1974 he made first ascents of Pt Innominata in Patagonia and the S E Spur of Pic Lenin in the Pamirs. As a member of the 1975 S W Face expedition to Everest he partnered Nick Estcourt on the first ascent of the Rock Band – the key to the climb.

Brandler, Lothar (b. 1936)   Best known for his two outstanding routes of 1958: Nordwand direct on Grosser Zinne, with Hasse, Lehne and Löw, and Rotwand–Sudwestwand with Hasse. Brandler is a film cameraman.

Breathable fabrics The major problem with using waterproof material for shell clothing is that body moisture (perspiration) condenses on the inside, trapped by the impermeability and leaving the wearer as wet as ever.

The first partial solution was developed for pilots during the war, and called Ventile. It is a cotton of very fine weave made from long staple Egyptian yarn. Extraordinarily warm and windproof, Ventile still allows the body to breathe. It is less satisfactory as a waterproof, when the breathability is reduced. Some mountaineers still prefer it to modern materials.

The first successful breathable material of the modern kind was Gore-tex, developed in the U.S. in the 1970s by W. L. Gore and Associates. Gore-tex is a plastic film, 0.001 inches thick made of polytetrafluorethylene (P.T.F.E.), which has some nine billion tiny pores to the square inch. These pores will let molecules of water vapour pass through but not the larger water drops; thus body vapour can pass out but rain can't pass in.

The material is not strong enough to use on its own and so a sandwich is made in which it is bonded between two layers of conventional material like nylon. Tests show that this laminate is about as breathable as Ventile, transmitting 4,800 g per m² per 24h as against 4,900 for the older cloth. It is, however, much more waterproof, withstanding 65 psi against Ventile's 2 psi.

Other breathable materials and coatings have been developed in recent years. All breathable materials function less well in heavy humidity and personal metabolism also plays a part: some people generate perspiration at too great a rate for the material to handle.

Breuil (Breuil-Cervinia) Ski resort beneath the Italian slopes of the ◊ Matterhorn separated from Zermatt by the Théodule Pass (cable cars etc.). The scene of ◊ Whymper's famous attempts on the mountain.

Bridge, Alfred William (1902–71) Alf Bridge was a partner of ◊ Kirkus and one of the best-known climbers of the thirties. In 1932 he seconded Kirkus on Curving Crack and the Direct Finish to the E Buttress, Clogwyn Du'r Arddu. He was a Manchester man who had done a great deal of Pennine bog trotting and many climbs on gritstone. He perfected a method of controlled falling by which he could drop thirty feet without injury. Bridge was a somewhat controversial personality.

Bridging A method of climbing a wide ◊ chimney by using left hand and foot on one side wall and right hand and foot on the other. The term 'straddling' is obsolescent.

Bristow, Lily Family friend of Mummery and his wife, Lily Bristow probably began climbing with them some time between 1883 and 1891, though this is not certain. She sprang to fame in 1892 when, with Miss Pasteur, she accompanied Mummery and his companions on a traverse of the Charmoz (first ascent by women). In 1893 she accompanied Mummery, Slingsby, Collie and Hastings on the Petit Dru, Zinal Rothorn, Italian Ridge of the Matterhorn and the traverse of the Grépon. It was only the second time the Grépon had been traversed and Miss Bristow's performance led to Mummery's famous phrase, 'an easy day for a lady'.

In 1894 she climbed with the guides Pollinger and Zurbriggen and made the first descent ever of the Zmutt Ridge.

Her exact relationship with Mummery remains vague, but she did not climb with him in 1894 and, with Mummery's death in 1895, she seems to have given up climbing altogether.

British Mountaineering Council (B.M.C.) The advisory body of British mountaineering, composed of elected representatives of member clubs which form the Committee of Management. The Patron is Lord ◊ Hunt and there are the usual elected officers served by a small professional secretariat, of whom the General Secretary is chief. The Mountaineering Council of Scotland looks after the interests of Scottish clubs, though Scottish clubs may also join the B.M.C. and some do. Irish Clubs belong to the Federation of Mountaineering Clubs of Ireland.

The B.M.C. represents Britain at the ◊ Union Internationale des Associations d'Alpinisme (U.I.A.A.), the international regulatory body of mountaineering. Through the Mountain Leadership Training Board (M.L.T.B.) it oversees training in this country; a right only won after a hard political struggle with educationists in the 1970s over the Hunt Report.

The B.M.C. concerns itself with a wide range of interests: access, Peak District guidebooks and other publications, two huts in Scotland, technical matters regarding equipment, and the general well-being of the sport. It is grant-aided by the Sports Council but also supports itself with a profitable insurance agency.

The B.M.C. was formed in 1944, principally through the work of G. W. ◊ Young and was originally composed of representatives from 30 clubs, mostly of long foundation. There are now over 200 clubs and organizations involved as well as thousands of individual members.

Broadrick, Richard Wilfred (1872–1903) The best known of three Windermere brothers who were pioneer rock-climbers in the Lakes. Broadrick's Crack, Dow Crag, is perhaps the best-known climb (1902). Broadrick was a good alpinist also, making the first traverse of the Aig. Sans Nom and attempting the Mer de Glace face of Charmoz, only failing 200 ft from the summit (1901).

On 21 September 1903, Broadrick, with H. Jupp, A. E. W. Garrett and S. Ridsdale, attempted to reach Hopkinson's Cairn from Lord's Rake – an outstanding climbing problem of the day, on Scafell. Broadrick gave up the lead to Garrett, who subsequently slipped; the party was pulled from the rock and killed.

Brocherel family A family of guides from Courmayeur. Guiseppe (b. 1864) was with Sir H. Mackinder on the first ascent of ◊ Mt Kenya. The two brothers, Alexis and Henry Brocherel were in the Himalaya with ◊ Longstaff. Alexis (1874–1927) was with ◊ Blodig on the first ascent of the Brouillard Ridge whilst Henry (1879–1945) took part in the famous ascent of the Grépon Mer de Glace Face by Young's party in 1911.

Brocken spectre A phenomenon seen in mountains when there is a low cloud base with clear sky above. In the early morning the low-slanting rays of the sun throw a shadow of the peaks, and climbers, upon the clouds below. The shadow is enormously magnified. The name comes from the Brocken Mountains of Germany where the phenomenon is said to be common.

Broome, Edward Alfred (1846–1920) One of the most remarkable climbers of his day; a man utterly devoted to the mountains. Though he did not visit the Alps until he was 40, Broome took at once to the sport of climbing, helped by good guides (particularly J. M. Biner) and a strong constitution. He was a formidable walker.

Broome concentrated on the most difficult expeditions of the time, particularly at Zermatt, Chamonix and the Dolomites. He made a number of first ascents including the first complete traverse from the Triftjoch of the Rothorngrat (1903). His most famous expedition was, however, the first ascent of the Schalligrat on Weisshorn (1895).

In his 67th year he traversed the Nordend of Monte Rosa, from Macugnaga (Brioschi Route), and the year before he died, 1919, he traversed the Charmoz. He was then 75.

Broome died at Zermatt in 1920 and is buried there.

Brown, Joe (b. 1930) One of the greatest mountaineers Britain has ever produced, whose achievements stretch from the outcrops of Derbyshire to the Himalaya. His influence on rock-climbing, in particular, has been profound.

Brown and his companions from the Valkyrie Club, and later the Rock and Ice Club, played a leading part in the gritstone campaign that swept Stanage and elsewhere from 1949 onwards. In 1952 he formed a partnership with ◊ Whillans which for a few years was the strongest ever seen in Britain. Their list of climbs in Derbyshire, Wales and elsewhere is formidable, and all at the highest standards.

Brown's first major new route in Wales was Hangover (Grochan), which he did in 1951 with R. Greenall, M. T. Sorrel, and F. Ashton. Other notable early ascents (among many – see guidebooks for full details) were:

1951   The Boulder (Clogwyn Du'r Arddu) (rest unable to follow)
      Cemetery Gates (Cromlech) – D. Whillans
      Cenotaph Corner (Cromlech) – D. Belshaw
      Diglyph (Clogwyn Du'r Arddu) – M. T. Sorrel
      Vember (Clogwyn Du'r Arddu) – D. Whillans
1952   (All on Clogwyn Du'r Arddu) Octo – Sorrel and Belshaw
      The Spillikin – Whillans and J. N. Allen
      Pinnacle Flake – Whillans (alt. leads)
      Llithrig – Allen
      The Corner – Allen and Belshaw
1953   Surplomb (Grochan) – Whillans (alt. leads)
      Subsidiary Groove (Cyrn Las) – Whillans (alt. leads)
      The Grooves (Cyrn Las) – D. Cowan, E. Price
      E Buttress Girdle (Clogwyn du'r Arddu) – Allen and Whillans

It must be remembered that at this time and for some time afterwards, Brown was also putting up new routes on gritstone and limestone. In 1953 visits to the Lake District resulted in Laugh Not (White Ghyll) and Dovedale Groove (Dove Crag) and a visit to Ben Nevis in 1954 brought about Sassenach (with Whillans). In the same summer, with Whillans, came the first British ascent of the W Face of the Dru and the Brown–Whillans Route on the Blaitière – easily the hardest British rock-climb in the Alps to that date. In 1955, with G. Band, Brown reached the summit of Kangchenjunga, the third highest mountain in the world. In 1956 he reached the summit of the Mustagh Tower in the Karakoram.

This can be taken as the close of the opening phase of Brown's career, and the most remarkable. With Whillans, particularly, he set new standards wherever he went.

In the early sixties Brown investigated the 'new' Welsh crags such as Tremadoc and Hylldrem, where mention might be made, respectively, of Vector (1960) and Hardd (1960) (amongst others), but it was not until 1966 that he was persuaded to look at the great sea cliff of Gogarth in Anglesey where he was to create dozens of new routes including the sensational Spider's

Joe Brown   Walter Bonatti (*S. Ashton*)

Web (1968). In 1962 he visited Russia and climbed Mt Communism. He was in the Andes in 1970, Roraima, Venezuela in 1973, Karakoram in 1975. Various expeditions since then.

Brown has appeared in various films and television climbing broadcasts. He was a property repairer until 1961 when he joined the staff of White Hall Outdoor Pursuits Centre, where he stayed until 1965. In 1965 he opened an equipment shop in Llanberis. His autobiography, *The Hard Years*, was published in 1967.

Brown, Thomas Graham (1882–1965)   One of the most important British mountaineers of the inter-war years; famous for his work on the Brenva face of Mont Blanc.

Brown began climbing late in life. He was over 30 when he made his first climb (on Pillar, Lake District) and 42 when he first climbed in the Alps. He was primarily a discoverer with a superb eye for a line: the technical climbing, and leading, he left to others.

After a minor route in Eskdale, Brown's first innovation was the opening up of Boat Howe on Kirkfell as a climbing area. In 1925, with Basterfield, he made four routes on this previously neglected crag and four more the next year with Hazard. Convinced that the great face of the Brenva on Mont Blanc had not been exploited to the full he set out to examine its possibilities in 1927. Bad weather delayed matters but late in the season he teamed up with ◊ Smythe, who wished to do a variant on the Old Brenva Route. Brown wished to do what is now Route Major, and a compromise was reached by making a route between the two lines – Red Sentinel. The following year (1928) they climbed Route Major: one of the most important climbs in the Alps. In 1933 Brown returned with guides Graven and ◊ Knubel and climbed the Via della Pera, completing a trio of hard routes which transformed the Brenva Face as a climbing area.

Brown went to the Himalaya twice: Nanda Devi (1936) and Masherbrum

(1938) reaching heights in excess of 6,000 m on each occasion. His other new routes in the Alps are: S S W Buttress of Les Courtes (1927), E Face of Mont Brouillard, traverse of Col Maudit (1932), traverse of summit ridge of l'Ailefroide, N Face of Les Bans (1933), traverse of Dent Blanche from W to E (1935). In 1934 he visited Alaska and climbed Mt Foraker.

His book, *Brenva* (1944), is a modern classic. He was Professor of Physiology, University of Wales, from 1920 to 1947.

Browne, Frederic Augustus Yeats (1837–1925) Made the second ascent of Grandes Jorasses (1868) and a number of new ascents with ◊ Tuckett. Yeats Brown was on the fringe of the Matterhorn tragedy in 1865: he climbed Mont Blanc the same day as Hudson and Hadow, and after completing the High Level Route to Zermatt, met the first party of guides who were looking for the victims of the disaster. He then made a solo climb on the Riffelhorn, and it was in trying to emulate this that Knyvett Wilson was killed the same day, thus increasing the general outrage which the Matterhorn affair had aroused.

Browne, Thomas Lloyd Murray (1838–1900) Made the first ascents of Dreieckhorn and Ebnefluh in 1868. With his brother, W. R. Browne, he also made the first English ascent of Glittertind, Norway, and the first ascent of Uledalstind. The two brothers were amongst the first to draw attention to Scafell Crag (1869) and Lliwedd (1872). They attempted the latter, but failed.

Bruce, Charles Granville (1866–1939) One of the great pioneers of Himalayan climbing. His climbing came about through his commission in the 5th Gurkha Rifles: it seemed logical to him that troops stationed in the Himalayan foothills should become proficient mountaineers and his regiment acquitted itself so well in the various border wars that 'mountain scouts' became valued. They were even, at Bruce's suggestion, allowed to wear shorts – the first ever in the British Army. Some of the Gurkhas he trained became good climbers, notably Harkabir Thapa, Goman Singh, Raghobir and Karbir. The latter traversed the Alps with Conway in 1894, Harkabir was loaned to Col. Stewart for surveys in the Pamirs, whilst Goman Singh and Raghobir perished with ◊ Mummery on Nanga Parbat.

Apart from the training climbs done with his men, Bruce joined Conway's ◊ Karakoram Expedition (1892) and was one of the main reasons for its success. He was with ◊ Younghusband in Chitral, and in 1895 with the Mummery party on Nanga Parbat, though he was taken ill and had to leave before the final tragedy. In 1898 he reconnoitred the Nun Kun massif. In 1907 after permission to attempt Everest was refused he joined ◊ Longstaff and ◊ Mumm in the Nanda Devi area where Longstaff, two Swiss guides and Karbir made the first ascent of Trisul. They also reconnoitred Kamet.

Bruce was wounded during the First World War but was chosen to lead the 1922 and 1924 ◊ Mt Everest expeditions. It was he who suggested Sherpas as porters.

Bruce was immensely strong and had a legendary sense of humour. He attained General rank, received many honours from geographical and other societies, and was President of the A.C. 1923–6. He wrote four books: *Twenty Years in the Himalaya* (1910), *Kulu and Lahoul* (1914), *Assault on Mount Everest, 1922* (1923) and *Himalayan Wanderer* (1934).

Brulle, Henri (1854–1936) French lawyer noted for his many first ascents in the Pyrenees, particularly around Gavarnie. He made the first traverse of the great Gavarnie Cirque (1881). Brulle climbed in the Alps occasionally: he was the first to climb the Meije in a single day (1883). He visited the Lake District twice, climbing a number of the standard routes.

Bryce, James (1838–1922) Distinguished lawyer and politician best known for the Bryce Report on Secondary Education, 1895. In 1884 he introduced the Access to Mountains (Scotland) Bill, but was defeated. Bryce was a keen mountaineer and he never missed an opportunity to climb during his extensive travels. Ambassador to Washington (1907–12); visited every State. President of the A.C. 1899–1901. Created Viscount, 1914.

Buachaille Etive Mor (Stob Dearg, 1,022 m) A fine mountain standing at the eastern entrance to ◊ Glencoe, Scotland. The peak is invariably called by climbers 'the Buachaille'.

The N Face is a complex series of buttresses and gullies all of which give fine climbs, summer and winter, of all grades. Notable ascents include:

1894 Collie's Climb – Collie, Solly, Collier
1900 Crowberry Ridge Direct – Abraham brothers, Puttrell, Baker
1910 Crowberry Gully – Greig, Raeburn, Cumming, Menzies
ditto winter 1936 – MacKenzie, Russell, Hamilton, Dunn
1929 N Face – Bell, Harrison
1936 Agag's Groove – Hamilton, Anderson, Small
1937 Raven's Gully – Nimlin and party
1953 Raven's Gully (winter) – MacInnes, Bonington
1958 Carnivore – Cunningham, Noon
1980 The Risk Business E5,6a – Whillance, Botterill, Parker
1986 Uncertain Emotions E6 – Cuthbertson
1986 Fated Path E7 – Livingstone

Buchan, John (Lord Tweedsmuir) (1875–1940) Noted author of the Richard Hannay stories and others. Climbed extensively in Scotland and in the Alps around the turn of the century, as well as South Africa and Canada. Climbing incidents and mountains are found in many of his stories.

Buhl, Hermann (1924–57) One of the best-known post-war Austrian climbers, noted for his winter ascents and solo ascents of difficult routes in the Dolomites and elsewhere. In 1953 Buhl reached the summit of Nanga Parbat alone – the first ascent. In 1957 he fell through a cornice while descending Chogolisa and was killed. Autobiography: *Nanga Parbat Pilgrimage* (1956).

Bullock, Guy Henry (1887–1956) School companion of ◊ Mallory and one of ◊ Irving's 'recruits'. Bullock went on the first Everest expedition (1921) and with Mallory discovered the North Col. (◊ Mount Everest.)

Bumiller, Hans (1864–1912) Bumiller was a 23-year-old student when he embarked on his great adventure. Choosing the best guides in Pontresina, Martin Schochter, Johann Gross and Christian Schnitzler, he successfully attempted the steep North Pillar of the Central Peak of Piz Palu (1 September 1887). The hardest route on the mountain, the Bumillergrat had less than 10 ascents in the next 50 years. Now graded D, IV.

Burgener, Alexander (1846–1910) One of the most outstanding guides of the late nineteenth century, noted for his association with great climbers and explorers such as Dent, Mummery, Déchy, Güssfeldt, von Kuffner and others. He came from Eisten in Saas, where the rock peaks of the area gave him a good ground in rock-climbing – then becoming a necessary art in climbing, since the big snow peaks were all conquered. He began as a chamois hunter – and kept this up all his life. Burgener undoubtedly brought prestige to the Saas valley and was, indirectly, responsible for popularizing the modern resort of Saas Fee.

Amongst his many great climbs might be mentioned:

1870	Lenzspitze, first ascent – Dent, F. Burgener
1871	Portjengrat, first ascent – Dent, F. Burgener
1878	Grand Dru, first ascent – Dent, Walker, Maurer
1879	Matterhorn, Zmutt first ascent – Mummery, Gentinetta, Petrus
1880	Col du Lion, first traverse – Mummery
	Grands Charmoz, first ascent – Mummery, Venetz
1881	Verte, Charpoua Face, first ascent – Mummery
	Grépon, first ascent – Mummery, Venetz
1887	Mont Maudit, Frontier Ridge, first ascent – von Kuffner, Furrer, a porter
	Täschhorn, Teufelsgrat, first ascent – Mummery, Mrs Mummery, Andermatten

Burgener visited the Caucasus with Déchy (1884) and Dent (1886) and went to S. America with Güssfeldt in 1882. A big, hearty man with a caustic tongue, he was killed by an avalanche near the Bergli Hut in the Oberland.

Burke, Mick (1941–75) Noted British alpinist who made the second ascent of the Robbins–Hemming route on the W Face of the Dru, a new route on the N Face of the Aig. du Midi, winter ascents of the Gervasutti Couloir of Mont Blanc du Tacul, and in 1967, first British winter ascent of the Matterhorn Nordwand. In 1968 he made the first British ascent of the Nose of ◊ El Capitan, Yosemite, and in 1972 took part in the British ski traverse of the Alps.

Burke took part in a number of outstanding expeditions including Cerro Torre (1968), Annapurna S Face (1970) and the S W Face of Everest (1972). He also visited Baffin Island and, as a cameraman, helped Bonington on the Eiger Direct epic (1966).

Burke was a cameraman and climber on the 1975 Everest S W Face Expedition. From Camp VI he took part in the second summit assault with Boysen, Boardman and Pertemba. Boysen's equipment became defective and he was forced to turn back. Burke elected to continue alone, following the other pair who had gone on ahead. They met near the S Summit and Boardman and Pertemba, who were returning, waited whilst Burke continued to the top. A storm came down and Burke failed to reappear. It is likely that he reached the summit of Everest and fell from the ridge on the descent in the storm.

Burton, Sir Richard Francis (1831–90) One of the foremost explorers of the nineteenth century, particularly famous for his African discoveries in search of the source of the Nile. Mountain climbing was not one of his principal activities but he did make the first ascent of Cameroon Peak (4,070 m). (With G. Mann, 1861.)

Buttress A rocky protuberance from a mountain side *or* the rock mass between two gullies (but if narrow this may be called a ridge). They are usually named: North Buttress, Central Buttress, Bilberry Buttress, etc. The majority of British rock-climbs are buttress climbs.

Buxton, Edward North (1840–1924) A wealthy London brewer whose brief climbing career lasted only six years, after which he turned to big game hunting. Two of his brothers were also climbers for a brief period.

Buxton took part in some important first ascents including that of Nord End (Monte Rosa) in 1861. In 1864 he made the first ascents of Monte Cristallo, Königsspitze, and the west summit of Lyskamm. In his last season, 1865, he made the first ascent of Aig. de Bionnassay. His brother, H. E. Buxton, accompanied him on his 1864 climbs.

Byne, Eric (1911–69) A Midlands climber who began climbing on gritstone in 1928, and besides taking part in the discoveries of that time, developed a passionate interest in the history of climbing and walking in the Peak District. He accumulated material which formed the basis of the first gritstone series guidebooks, of which he was editor (*Climbs on Gritstone*, 1948 on). Byne compiled some of them himself, and helped with others. He also compiled *A Climbing Guide to Brassington Rocks* (1950), but his best-known work is *High Peak* (1966), which he wrote with G. Sutton.

C

Cagoule A windproof outer garment, like a hooded smock, which, with overtrousers, forms shell clothing. Originally made of polyurethane they offered some protection from rain but suffered from body condensation. Nowadays they are frequently made of one of the ◊ breathable fabrics.

Cairn A pile of stones used for marking the summit of a mountain, or even some minor eminence. Can be large and elaborately constructed. Cairns are also used to mark out routes where paths are not obvious – in the Alps, way-marks consisting of splashes of paint are often used instead.

Cairney, Maud (1893–1939) A doctor who, with the guide T. Theytaz, made the first descent of the N Face of Lo Besso (1927), the first winter ascent of Obergabelhorn from Mountet (1927) and the first ascent of the N Face of Dent Blanche (1928).

Calanques A series of sea-cliffs on the French Mediterranean coast, near Marseilles, and popular with climbers. The rock is limestone.

Calhoun-Grissom, Kitty (b. 1960) An outstanding American mountaineer from North Carolina with many ascents throughout the world. Began climbing on local rocks then gained alpine experience in Colorado and Wyoming Rockies in winter. In 1985 she climbed the Cassin Route on McKinley and the following year the South Face of Chacaraju. In 1986 she also made her first Himalayan visit, climbing Thelay-Sagar. In 1987 she led a lightweight expedition on a successful ascent of Dhaulagiri (8,167 m) and in 1991 climbed Makalu (8,463 m) – 7th and 5th highest peaks in the world.

Camping mat (karrimat) A rectangle of cellular foam plastic, very light and easily carried, invaluable as ground insulation when camping or bivouacking.

Canada, climbing in The highest mountain in Canada is Mt Logan (6,050 m) in the Yukon (◊ Alaska). Though there is some rock-climbing done in eastern Canada, by far the most important mountains and climbing takes place in the west. Here there are three ranges from west to east:
The Coast Ranges of British Columbia
The Interior Ranges of British Columbia
The Rocky Mountains

THE COAST RANGES

Mt Waddington (3,994 m) is the best-known peak and lies in the central area of the Coast Ranges. It was first seen by Capt. R. Bishop of the Canadian Geological Survey in 1922 but his report was lost and the peak was re-discovered four years later by Don and Phyllis Munday. It was named Mystery Mountain. In 1927 the Mundays reached the N W Summit. The final summit was reached by F. Weissner and W. House in 1936. During the thirties the peak was renamed Waddington in memory of a construction engineer whose crew was massacred by Indians in the area in 1893.

Waddington is a striking mountain of great pinnacled ridges – perhaps one of the finest on the continent.

Further north, The Devil's Thumb (2,767 m) is a difficult mountain to climb, or even reach. First ascent by F. Beckey, R. Craig and C. Schmidtke, 1946.

In the south, above the port of Squamish, just north of Vancouver, is the steep granite cliff, 425 m high, called Squamish Chief. Hard rock-climbs, free and aided, of which the first was Grand Wall (J. Baldwin, E. Cooper, 1961). The climbing has been compared with ◊ Yosemite.

THE INTERIOR RANGES

There are three major ranges, from west to east: Monashees, Selkirks and Purcells, the last two of importance.

Selkirk Range Among the most important and accessible of the Canadian mountain ranges, lying beyond the first crest line of the Rockies proper, in the big bend of the Columbia River. It was designated Glacier National Park, 1886.

Being west of the Rockies the Selkirks attract more rainfall and so have plenty of glaciation and, at lower levels, dense forest. Valleys are steep-sided and narrow and the large single peaks, characteristic of the Rockies further east, do not occur here. Instead there are interlocking ridges making for complex terrain – 'a rugged vigorous appeal', according to one of the pioneers.

The Selkirks were the first peaks to attract climbers in the Canadian west. In 1884 it was visited by the Rev. H. Swanzy and R. M. ◊ Barrington and their enthusiasm brought the Rev. W. S. ◊ Green in 1888 and the ◊ Topham brothers. Access was made easy by the new Canadian Pacific Railroad which established a hotel, ◊ Glacier House, at the foot of the Rogers Pass. Green and Swanzy made the first ascent of Mt Bonney (3,050 m) in that year, the first technical climb done in Canada.

Mt Sir Donald (3,297 m), known as 'the Matterhorn of the Selkirks' was climbed by C. Sulzer and E. Huber in 1890. The highest peak is Mt Sir Sandford climbed by E. Holway, H. Palmer, R. Aemmer, E. Feuz Jr, in 1912.

Purcell Range The highest peak is Mt Farnham (3,457 m) climbed by Mr and Mrs A. MacCarthy with Conrad Kain in 1914, but the most popular mountains in the Purcells are the dramatic group known as the Bugaboos; granite spires on the Bugaboo Creek near the town of Parson. They give some of the finest rock-climbing on the continent.

Rising sheer from their surrounding glaciers the spires are startling. The three main groups are Howser Spires (North Tower 3,399 m, South Tower 3,307 m), Bugaboo Spire (3,176 m) and Snowpatch Spire (3,063 m). These are all adjacent to the Warren Glacier in the south of the group. Other fine peaks lie a little further north-west, including Mt Conrad (3,252 m), named after Conrad ◊ Kain who first explored the area in 1910.

Bugaboo Spire was climbed by Kain with Mr and Mrs A. MacCarthy and J. Vincent by its South Ridge in 1916 – claimed by Kain to be the hardest climb of his career (today's grade is 5.4). In the same year Kain climbed the North Tower of the Howser Spires. The celebrated East Ridge of Bugaboo Spire was climbed by J. Turner, D. Isles, D. Sykes and D. Craft, 1958, the East Face by Gran and Cooper in 1961.

The South Tower of Howser was climbed in 1941 by L. Anderson, H. Beckey, L. Boyer and T. Campbell, whilst the East Ridge, another classic,

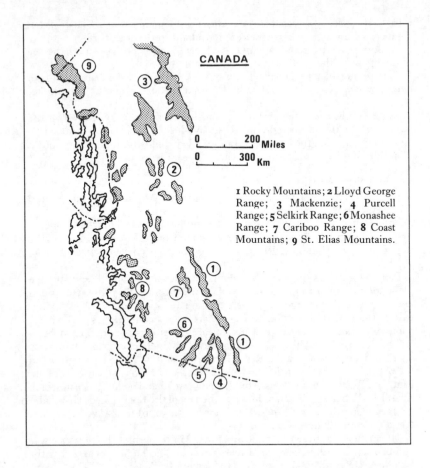

CANADA

0 ____200 Miles
0 ____300 Km

1 Rocky Mountains; 2 Lloyd George Range; 3 Mackenzie; 4 Purcell Range; 5 Selkirk Range; 6 Monashee Range; 7 Cariboo Range; 8 Coast Mountains; 9 St. Elias Mountains.

was done by F. Beckey and Yvon Chouinard in 1961 who also did the West Face. The North Face and the traverse of the Howser Spires was done by Rayson, Lang, Chouinard, and Thompkins in 1965. Snowpatch Spire was climbed by J. Arnold and R. Bedayn in 1940 by the South Ridge, now a popular hard climb.

THE CANADIAN ROCKIES

The Canadian Rockies extend for a thousand miles north-west from the U.S. border. They are bounded by the deep Rocky Mountain Trench on the west and the prairies on the east. The parts best known to climbers lie in the south of the range, from Mt Joffre to Mt Robson, where all the big mountains are to be found. The total length is about 720 km from the U.S. border to Mt Sir Alexander and the distance is conveniently divided into three according to the railway passes: between the northern peaks and central peaks is the Yellowhead Pass and Canadian National Railroad; between the central peaks and southern peaks is the Kicking Horse Pass, with the Canadian Pacific Railroad. The C.P.R. played a prominent part in the development of the Rockies and B.C. Ranges by inviting ▷ Whymper to explore them and by making hotel bases at Lake Louise, near Kicking Horse, and Glacier.

There are some 750 peaks of 2,750 m and 47 peaks of 3,400 m; four in the north, 29 in the central section and 14 in the south. Most of the range is covered by National or Provincial Parks.

Northern Group   The northernmost peak of interest is Mt Sir Alexander (3,274 m) climbed in 1929 by Miss H. I. Buck, A. J. Gilmour and N. D. Waffl. The peak is 130 km north of ◊ Mt Robson (3,954 m), the highest peak in the Canadian Rockies, first climbed by W. Foster, A. ◊ MacCarthy and C. ◊ Kain in 1913.

Robson is called Yuh-hai-has-kun by the Indians, which describes its striped appearance due to the layers of sedimentary rock, a feature of the range in general. There are no easy ways to its summit.

Central Group   This area contains the vast Columbia Icefield where 13 of the 29 highest peaks are located. Highest is Mt Columbia (3,747 m). There is a ski traverse of the range in winter. When David Douglas (of fir tree fame) climbed Mt Brown (2,791 m) in 1827 it was the first ascent above the snow line in the Canadian Rockies.

Southern Group   The pride of the group is undoubtedly Mt Assiniboine (3,618 m), the 'Matterhorn of the Rockies', first climbed in 1901 by ◊ Outram. Like half of the really high peaks, it is in the Lake Louise area. Mt Temple (3,547 m) was the first peak in the Canadian Rockies over 3,400 m to be climbed – S. Allen's party, 1894.

The first expeditions were those of the Appalachian Club of the U.S.A. in the 1890s. In 1896 Phillip Abbot of the club was killed whilst attempting Mt Lefroy (3,423 m) – the first climbing fatality in North America. The ubiquitous W. S. ◊ Green also visited the peaks but it was not until the coming of the railroad and in particular the opening of the Lake Louise area that climbing flourished. Alpine guides were imported and played a part in many of the first ascents: famous ones included Conrad Kain, Edward Feuz, Peter Sarbach and the Kaufmann brothers. Whymper visited the area in 1901, 1904 and 1909 but did little of note. Much exploration and early climbing was done by Norman ◊ Collie, Charles ◊ Fay, Hugh ◊ Stutfield and Hermann ◊ Woolley on various visits around the turn of the century, though pride of place must go to the concentrated and successful campaign of James ◊ Outram, who in 1902 climbed Mt Alexandra (3,418 m), Mt Bryce (3,507 m), Mt Lyell (3,511 m), Mt Forbes (3,628 m) and Mt Columbia (3,747 m). He had climbed Assiniboine the previous summer!

From 1908 the chief goal became Mt Robson; finally climbed by MacCarthy, Foster and Kain in 1913. It is interesting that Mt Alberta (3,619 m) was climbed by a Japanese party in 1925; the first overseas expedition by Japanese climbers. It is a particularly difficult mountain and has had relatively few ascents.

GUIDEBOOKS

Fairley, *A Guide to Climbing and Hiking in S W British Columbia*.

Boles, *Rocky Mountains of Canada, South*.

Kruszyna/Putnam, *Rocky Mountains of Canada, North*.

Kruszyna/Putnam, *Climber's Guide to the Interior Ranges of British Columbia*.

Patton/Robinson, *The Canadian Rockies Trail Guide*.

Cannon stone   An obsolete name for a rock splinter jammed in a chimney and sticking out like a gun barrel. There is a well-known one in Gwynne's Chimney, Pavey Ark.

Capstone   A ◊ chockstone on top of a chimney or gully. Common on gritstone crags.

Carpe, Allen (1894–1932) An American electrical engineer trained in Germany where he first learned to climb. Explored the Selkirks, Cariboos and Rockies, making several first ascents. In 1925 he took part in the first ascent of Mt Logan; in 1930, with A. M. Taylor and T. Moore, the first ascent of Mt Bona; and finally, in 1931, with Moore he reached the summit of Mt Fairweather.

Carr, Ellis (1852–1930) One of the leaders of the second wave of guideless climbing in the Alps which began about 1890. With Morse and ◊ Wicks he made the first ascent of the Pic Sans Nom (Verte) (1890), and with Wilson and the ◊ Pasteur family the first ascent of L'Évêque (Verte) (1892).

He seems to have met Mummery in 1891, when they did some climbs together, and he was with Mummery and Slingsby on the dramatic attempt on the North Face of the Plan (1892). Carr's description of this climb, 'Two Days on an Ice Slope' (*A.J.* 16), is one of the great classics of climbing literature.

Carr climbed in many parts of the Alps, the Lake District and Skye. He took part in the second ascent of the N Climb, Pillar Rock, when he is reputed to have invented the Hand Traverse of the Nose Pitch (1891).

Carr had considerable talents as musician and artist. His sketches illustrated ◊ Haskett Smith's *Climbing in the British Isles*. He was descended from the biscuit-making family of the same name and was a director of Peek Frean.

Carrel, Jean-Antoine (1829–90) One of the chief protagonists in the Matterhorn drama which ended with the first ascent of the mountain by ◊ Whymper in 1865.

Carrel was a stonemason and one-time soldier (hence his nickname, *Bersagliere*) who lived at Breuil, below the Italian slopes of the Matterhorn. Accompanied by other villagers he made his first reconnaissances in 1858–9 reaching a height of a little over 12,500 ft on the Italian Ridge. Between then and 1865 he took part in most of the attempts on the mountain, as guide, with climbers such as ◊ Whymper, ◊ Tyndall, ◊ Hawkins and ◊ MacDonald. The highest point reached was with Tyndall, Bennen and three other guides or porters in 1862, to a point called Pic Tyndall, a little below the final summit.

Carrel was an intense patriot, and there is little doubt that he wanted the mountain climbed by Italians, but whether in that fateful July of 1865 he actually double-crossed Whymper, as the latter implied, is a subject which many mountain historians have tried to unravel. Whymper found that Carrel had set out for the peak with a party of Italian climbers and in a fit of pique he left Breuil for Zermatt, from where the first ascent·was made. From the summit of the Matterhorn Whymper was able to see Carrel's party still climbing up the Italian Ridge so he threw down rocks to attract their attention. Carrel at once turned back, but he returned the next day and on 18 July he and J. B. Bich made the first ascent of the Italian Ridge and second of the mountain.

Whymper had a strange kinship with Carrel. He forgave him his 'treachery' and climbed the Matterhorn with him in 1874. Carrel was also one of Whymper's guides on the Andes expedition of 1879–80.

Carrel died of exhaustion during a retreat from the Italian Ridge in a snow-storm, with the climber Sinigaglia. He left a wife and three children. A memorial marks the place where he died.

Cassin, Riccardo (b. 1909) An Italian climber from Lecco; one of the finest mountaineers of the present century. Cassin's career falls into two parts: pre-war and post-war.

Riccardo Cassin   Norman Collie

He began rock-climbing in the ◊ Grigna in 1928 with other local youths, and they formed themselves into the 'New Italy Climbing Group'. He paid his first visit to the Dolomites in 1932 and at once began doing the hardest climbs and making new routes. His greatest Dolomite success was the first ascent of the N Face of Cima Ovest (1935). He followed this in 1937 with the N E Face of Piz Badile – for long regarded as one of the most daring climbs in the Alps, but now one of the most popular of the harder rock-climbs. Beset by storms, Cassin, Ratti and Esposito, with two Como climbers, Valsecchi and Molseni, spent three days on the face before reaching the summit. Unfortunately, the two Como men died of exhaustion.

In 1938 came Cassin's finest ascent: the Walker Spur of the Grandes Jorasses which he did with Esposito and Tizzoni, 4 to 6 August. It was Cassin's first visit to the Mont Blanc area and his first sight of the Jorasses! It remains one of the greatest climbs in the Alps; it is very popular.

Although he holds instructors' certificates in both climbing and skiing, Cassin never became a guide. He worked first as a mechanic and then manager at an electrical engineering works in Lecco. During the war he became a partisan and was wounded. After the war he established a factory making climbing equipment.

Cassin has led a number of successful expeditions:

1958   Gasherbrum IV (Himalaya)
1961   S Face of Mount McKinley (Alaska)
1969   W Face of Jirishanca (Peru)

He repeated the N E Face of Badile when he was 62.

Caucasus A range of high mountains extending between the Black Sea in the west and the Caspian Sea in the east, some 950 km in length. The Caucasus is bounded by Georgia and Azerbaijan to the south and various small republics to the north. It is a geographical boundary between Europe and Asia, and as such may be regarded as the highest mountains in Europe. The highest peak is Elbruz (5,633 m) and the Central Caucasus average some 1,000 m higher than their Alpine counterparts.

The range is divided into three natural divisions: Western Caucasus, Central Caucasus and Eastern Caucasus. All of these contain high peaks. The weather, which can often be poor, is wetter in the west than the east. The snowline is higher than in the Alps and the glaciers smaller.

Western Caucasus Reaches as far as the Klukhor Pass. The best climbing is in the eastern part of the section. The highest peak is Dombai-ulgen (4,047 m) (Schuster and Fischer, 1914).

Other important peaks include:

Juguturlyuchat 3,921 m	Ertsog 3,867 m
Bu-ulgen 3,913 m	Dottakh-kaya 3,864 m
Aksaut 3,910 m	and several others over 3,500 m
Kara-kaya 3,896 m	

Central Caucasus From the Klukhor Pass to the Krestovy Pass. This section contains the highest peaks and is by far the most popular with climbers, especially in the Bezingi valley – a vast cwm of immense, jagged peaks. The so-called Bezingi Wall is 1,800 m high and 13 km long, with many hard climbs. There are many other fine peaks, away from Bezingi, notably Shkhelda (4,360 m) and Ushba and, of course, the easily climbed extinct volcano of Elbruz (Freshfield, Moore, Tucker, 1868 to the lower E Summit – though possibly climbed by surveyors in 1829). The principal peaks (highest summit only – some have two) are:

Elbruz 5,633 m	Jimarai-khokh 4,778 m
Dychtau* 5,203 m	Ushba 4,710 m
Kasbek 5,047 m	Ullu-auz* 4,679 m
Koshtantau* 5,144 m	Khrumkol* 4,675 m
Jangitau* 5,051 m	Adai-khokh 4,646 m
Shkhara* 5,201 m	Tikhtengen 4,610 m
Katuintau* 4,985 m	*Peaks in the Benzingi region
Pik Rustaveli* 4,960 m	There are many more peaks of less
Mishirgi* 4,922 m	than 4,500 m
Kunjum-Mishirgi* 4,880 m	
Gestola* 4,860 m	
Tetnuld* 4,853 m	

Eastern Caucasus East of the Krestovy Pass. Rather drier than the other areas. The peaks tend to be more separated, and are generally of little interest to climbers. The highest peak is Tebulos-mta (4,494 m) and there are several more over 4,000 m.

Apart from survey work, climbing in the Caucasus began with the visit of Freshfield, Moore and Tucker in 1868 when they explored the entire range and climbed Elbruz and Kasbek. Moore, with Gardiner, Grove and Walker returned in 1874 and climbed the W (higher) Summit of Elbruz. In 1884, de Déchy paid the first of his seven visits to the range (1884–1902). During this period, too, many British climbers visited the range. There were nine expeditions between 1868 and Mummery's of 1888.

Notable ascents include:

Left, the Caucasus: Shkelda from the W Face of Ushba (*M. Fowler*); right, Cerro Torre (*L. Dickinson*)

1888	Dychtau – Mummery
	Shkhara, Jangitau, Ushba N – Cockin
1903	Ushba S – Schultze
1936	Shkelda N Face – Vorg
	Ushba W Face
1937	Tetnuld N Face – Hodgkin
	Ushba South NE Face
1938	Dychtau to Koshtantau
	traverse – Abalakov

Some of the nineteenth century names for Caucasian peaks were later swapped around, which is confusing.

Old name	Present name
Dych-tau	Koshtan-tau
Koshtan-tau	Shkhara
Guluku	Dych-tau
Koshtan-tau	Dych-tau (alternative)
Adish-tau (Saddle Peak)	Katuin-tau
Tetnuld	Gestola
Totonal	Tetnuld

Since the pioneer days, ascents have concentrated on the two aspects of climbing for which the Caucasus is admirably suited, that is long ridge traverses, often of several days, and steep face climbs. The first British party to do one of the classic traverses was MacInnes and Ritchie on Shkhelda, 1961. It took nine days. Others have done new face climbs, and repeated some of the Russian routes.

Centre Internationale de Secours Alpins (C.I.S.A.L.P.) Located at Geneva. A bureau supplying information about rescue services in the Alps. It does not initiate or co-ordinate rescues itself.

Centrist and ex-centrist One of the great feuds of the Alpine Club in the latter years of the nineteenth century was between those who believed in living at a centre such as Zermatt and climbing the peaks round about (a centrist) and those who believed in moving from valley to valley, crossing cols and peaks *en route* (ex-centrist). ◊ Davidson was a typical centrist, known as 'King of the Rifel' where he stayed season after season, whilst ◊ Conway was the archetypal ex-centrist. Indeed, his 'Alps from end to end' (1894) was done to prove his point.

Cerro Torre (3,128 m) A spectacular rock spire in the FitzRoy Group of the Patagonian Andes. In view of the prevailing bad weather, one of the most difficult climbs in the world. Three routes, with some variations, have been attempted: the E and W Faces, and the S E Ridge.
  In 1958, W. Bonatti and C. Mauri made an attempt on the W Face and C. Maestri on the E Face. Both failed, but in 1959 Maestri returned with T. Egger and C. Fava and climbed the E Face from the N Col. Maestri and Egger reached the summit but on the descent Egger was killed by an ice avalanche. Maestri's ascent has been disputed.
  In 1968 a strong British party attempted the S E Ridge but failed after 600 m as did Argentinian and Japanese groups. In 1970 Mauri returned to the W Face but also failed.
  During the winter (July) of 1970, Maestri returned for an attack on the S E Ridge, made some progress, then returned a few months later to complete the route (C. Maestri, C. Claus, E. Alimonta). The ascent caused a sensation because Maestri used a compressed air drill for bolting his route. The method has been vigorously attacked as unethical and equally vigorously defended by Maestri.
  In 1971–2 two further expeditions, one Spanish, one British, failed to climb the S E Ridge by more conventional methods.
  Finally, in 1974 C. Ferrari, D. Chiappa, M. Conti, and G. Negri reached the summit by the W Face and S W Ridge.

Cesen, Tomo (b. 1959) Born in Kranj in Slovenia, this Yugoslavian mountaineer is considered by many to be the spiritual heir of Buhl, Bonatti and Messner. In a period when there are many exceptionally gifted climbers, Cesen stands out by his ability to move the sport forward in dramatic ways.
  He began climbing at 14 and rose through the rigid East European club system until he was ranked as 'alpinist', at 18. From 1980–5 he climbed increasingly difficult routes, often solo and in fast times.
  In 1979 he did a new route on the S Face of Alpamayo in Peru. The next few seasons saw the N Face of Pik Kommunizma (7,482 m) in the Pamirs and the first ascent of the N Face of Yalung Kang (8,505 m) – the fifth highest summit in the world. These exploits made him one of the élite Yugoslav 'international' mountaineers, with a small state grant.
  In the winter of 1986 he linked the Eiger Nordwand, Grandes Jorasses (Shroud) and Matterhorn Nordwand into a continuous expedition, done in a week, solo. The following summer he soloed Broad Peak (8,047 m) in 19 hours, but retreated from high up on the face of K2, thus avoiding the storm which killed so many others on the peak that year.
  Extremely difficult winter routes in the Alps followed, including No Siesta,

1987 (N Face Jorasses, 1,200 m, 6b/A2, 90° ice); Modern Times, 1989 (S Face Marmolata, 800 m, 6b/c) done in 7 hours and the second ascent of the Gabarrou–Long Route on the Red Pillar of Brouillard (1989).

In the summer of 1989 he made the astonishing solo ascent of the N Face of Jannu (7,710 m). The climb involved 2,800 m on a face of 70°–90° with rock pitches of 6b/A2. He completed it in 23 hours.

In 1990 Cesen tackled the S Face of Lhotse, which had been the goal of many leading climbers and where Kukuczka and Jaeger had met their deaths. Climbing solo Cesen completed the route, up and down, in 62 hours.

Chalet Austria   A sort of shepherds' hut on the Plan de l'Aiguille to Montenvers track, near Chamonix, frequently used by impecunious climbers as a base and very famous in this respect, featuring in numerous climbing stories.

Chalk   High-standard rock-climbers benefit from dusting their fingers with light magnesium carbonate. It helps maintain grip on small holds when sweat or dampness makes them difficult. Chalk disfigures the rock and there has been some criticism on environmental grounds – not to mention ethical grounds, since chalk-marked holds are easily visible and reduce the problem of route finding. Advocates claim the chalk washes off in the rain, and certainly its use is widespread on harder routes.

The chalk is carried in a special chalkbag fastened to the waist. It is designed to allow ease of access ('dipping') and it is lined with pile fibre to distribute the chalk to the fingers.

Chalk, climbing on   The unreliable nature of this rock has prevented it from becoming popular though routes have been done. In pioneering days it was sometimes used as practice for step-cutting, which says something for its consistency, but it was also climbed on by ◊ Crowley. More recently some hard routes have been put up on the Dover cliffs by Mick ◊ Fowler and others.

Chamonix   A valley limiting the northern flanks of the Mont Blanc range, France. It includes the villages of Le Tour, Montroc, Argentière, Les Praz, Les Bossons and Les Houches as well as the principal village of Chamonix–Mont Blanc. There are good road and rail connections with Geneva and, via the Cols Forclaz and Montets, with Martigny. The Mont Blanc Tunnel connects the valley with Italy. The highest cable car in Europe rises from Chamonix to the summit of the Aig. du Midi (3,842 m) – it also continues across the Vallée Blanche to Italy.

Chamonix gained early fame as the starting point for ascending Mont Blanc and with the spread of alpinism became a serious rival to Zermatt. It is unquestionably the leading centre for modern alpinism. (◊◊ Mont Blanc; Mont Blanc Group; Chamonix Aiguilles.)

Chamonix Aiguilles, the   A range of shapely peaks (*aiguilles* = needles) on the southern side of the Chamonix valley and separating that valley from the Mer de Glace and the Vallée Blanche. The range extends in an arc from the Aig. du Midi in the south-west to the Aig. de l'M in the north-east. On the Chamonix side it is bounded by a curious high plateau generally known as the Plan de l'Aiguille, reached by cable car from the village, or from Montenvers, or by various paths. All the climbs on the Chamonix side start from the Plan de l'Aiguille. On the Mer de Glace side climbs are started from ◊ Montenvers, the Requin Hut, the Envers Hut or the Tour Rouge Bivouac Hut.

The peaks are very popular with rock-climbers because of the excellent granite and there are all standards of climbs. There are also some notable ice-climbs, for example the N Face of the Plan. The glaciers, though small, are often steep and can be difficult. The summit of Aig. du Midi can be reached by cable car from Chamonix or Entrèves (Italy). It is the highest cable car station in Europe.

The first complete traverse of all the peaks from Charmoz to Plan was done by Mme d'Albertas with A. Ottoz in 1939. Parts had been done before and it has since been extended from l'M to Mt Blanc. A list of peaks and their first ascents is given below. Other outstanding climbs include:

1906   Ryan–Lochmatter Route, Plan – V. J. E. Ryan with F. and J. Lochmatter
       N W Ridge, Blaitière – V. J. E. Ryan with F. and J. Lochmatter
1911   Mer de Glace Face, Grépon – H. O. Jones, R. Todhunter, G. W. Young with J. Knubel, H. Brocherel
1913   Mayer–Dibona Route, Requin – G. Mayer with A. Dibona
1924   N Face, Plan – J. Lagarde, J. de Lépiney, H. de Ségogne
1936   E Ridge, Crocodile – P. Allain, J. and R. Leininger
1941   Frendo Spur, Midi – E. Frendo, R. Rionda
1947   N Ridge, Peigne – F. Aubert, J. C. Martin, J. C. Ménégaux, M. Schatz
1954   W Face, Blaitière – J. Brown, D. Whillans
1956   Rébuffat Route, Midi – G. Rébuffat, M. Baquet
1963   S Face, Fou – T. Frost, J. Harlin, G. Hemming, S. Fulton
1973   First solo traverse l'M to Plan – N. Jaeger
1983   SE Face Grand Capucin, Flagrante Delire – J. M. Boivin, M. Piola

List of the Aiguilles, Midi–Charmoz, and first ascents:

Aig. du Midi (3,842 m) – F. de Bouillé with J. A. Devouassoud, A. and J. Simond, 1856
Aig. du Plan (3,672 m) – J. Eccles with M. and A. Payot, 1871

Peigne–Requin branches of Plan:
Aig. du Peigne (3,192 m) – J. Liégard, R. O'Gorman with J. Ravanel, J. Couttet, 1906
Aig. des Pélerins (3,318 m) – A. Brun, R. O'Gorman with J. Ravanel, E. Charlet, 1905
Aig. des Deux Aigles (3,487 m) – H. E. Beaujard, J. Simond, 1905
Pain de Sucre (3,607 m) – G. Mayer, A. Dibona, 1913
Dent du Requin (3,422 m) – G. Hastings, A. F. Mummery, J. N. Collie, W. C. Slingsby, 1893
Capucin du Requin (3,047 m) – V. Hugonnet with A. Couttet, M. Bozon, E. Ravanel, 1927

Main Chain:
Dent du Crocodile (3,640 m) – E. Fontaine with J. Ravanel, E. Charlet, 1904
Dent du Caiman (3,554 m) – E. Fontaine with J. Ravanel, L. Tournier, 1905
Pt de Lépiney (3,249 m) – J. and T. de Lépiney, 1920
Aig. du Fou (3,501 m) – E. Fontaine with J. and J. Ravanel, 1901
Aig. des Ciseaux (3,497 m) – Mme Berthelot with J. and E. Ravanel, 1906
Aig. de Blaitière (3,522 m) – E. R. Whitwell with C. and J. Lauener, 1874
Aig. du Grépon (3,482 m) – A. F. Mummery with A. Burgener, B. Venetz, 1881

Aig. des Grands Charmoz (3,444 m) – H. Dunod, P. Vignon with F. Simond,
    F. Folliguet, G. Simond, J. Desailloux, 1885
Aig. des Petits Charmoz (2,867 m) – J. A. Hutchinson, 1880
Aig. de l'M (2,844 m)
Pointe Albert (2,816 m)
    It should be noted that many other peaks in the area are called Aiguille, but
are not part of this particular chain.
GUIDEBOOK *Mont Blanc Range* (3 vols., A.C.). (◊ Mont Blanc Group.)

Channel Islands, climbs in   A few climbs have been done in Guernsey but
the rock is not good and climbing is discouraged because of the tourism. The
best prospects are in Jersey, where there has been considerable development
on the sea cliffs near Grosnez in the north of the island. Sark also has
prospects – the island has been almost completely girdled and it was here that
Shadbolt in 1912 suggested that limpets might make portable holds. The idea
did not work.
GUIDEBOOK Smith/Hill, *Jersey and Guernsey*.

Chapman, Frederick Spencer (1907–71)   Traveller, mountaineer,
guerilla leader and writer, Spencer Chapman led a life of adventure seldom
equalled in this century. An orphan, Chapman was brought up in the Lake
District and at Sedbergh School, where he gained a love of the fells. He later
came under the influence of men such as Winthrop ◊ Young and ◊ Wakefield.
    Helped by the latter he attempted the ◊ Lake District Fell Record in 1931
and set the incredible standard of 130 miles and 33,000 ft, but took 25 hours
and therefore failed to qualify for the record.
    He was in Greenland 1930–1, 1932, and 1934, for which he gained the
Polar Medal. 1936 saw him in Sikkim first with Marco Pallis and then
Harrison (Fluted Peak, 7,000 m). From there he joined an official mission to
Lhasa. In the following year (1937) with Crawford and three Sherpas he
attempted the unknown mountain Chomolhari (7,314 m). Chapman and
Pasang Dawa Lama reached the summit.
    Trained as a Commando during the War he conducted a single-handed
campaign against the Japanese in Malaya, which lasted three and a half years,
during which he was captured and escaped. He recounted these adventures in
his best-known book, *The Jungle is Neutral*. Other works are: *Northern
Lights*, *Watkins' Last Expedition*, *Lhasa the Holy City*, *Living Dangerously*
and *Lightest Africa*. His biography, *Helvellyn to Himalaya*, was published in
1940.
    A schoolmaster by profession, Chapman became first organizing secretary
of the Outward Bound Trust after the War. He was later head of various
schools and finally a college warden at Reading, where he died by his own
hand.

Charlet, Armand (1900–75)   Noted French guide who made the first
traverse of the Aigs. du Diable in 1928, first winter traverse of the Drus and
numerous other new climbs. His well-known remark about attempts on the N
Face of the Grandes Jorasses in the 1930s is often quoted: '*C'est pas
d'alpinisme, ça, c'est la guerre*' ('This isn't alpinism, it's war'). From 1945 to
1955 he was technical director of the École Nationale de Ski et d'Alpinisme at
Chamonix.

Chimborazo (6,267 m)   Famous volcano in the Cordillera Occidental of
Ecuador. An attempt was made on it by the explorer Alexander von Hum-

boldt in 1802 who reached a height of about 5,500 m. It was first climbed by Whymper with the guides J. A. and L. Carrel (1880) and repeated by Whymper a few months later. From 1745 to 1818, Chimborazo was thought to be the highest mountain in the world.

Chimney   A vertical fissure in a rock face, wider than a ◊ crack but narrower than a ◊ gully. Generally, one can get the body into a chimney but touch the sides easily. Often climbed by ◊ backing-up or ◊ bridging but some are pure squirms. May contain ◊ chockstones. A 'chimney sweep' is an obsolete derogatory term for a rock-climber.

China and Chinese Asia, climbing in   With the relaxation of political restraints in recent years the mountains of China and Chinese Asia have become much better known to Western mountaineers. Nevertheless, this huge area is still not properly explored. Unclimbed peaks abound and there may yet be unrecorded mountains of considerable size.

In China proper the two highest mountains are Minya Konka (7,556 m) and Amne Machin (6,282 m), in the provinces of Szechwan and Tsinghai respectively. Minya Konka was climbed by the remarkable American expedition of Richard Burdsall, Arthur Emmons, Terris Moore and Jack Young in 1932. Burdsall and Moore reached the summit via the N W Ridge. Amne Machin also fell to Americans – G. ◊ Rowell, H. Knutsen and K. Schmitz, via the N E ridge, in 1981. The ascent by a Chinese party in 1960 was later discovered not to have reached the real summit.

In greater China, including Tibet, many of the ranges are little known. Recent surveys by the Chinese have tended to downgrade them in height to below 7,000 m, though they are still considerable peaks. Perhaps the most fascinating are the virtually unknown Dupleix Mountains where Purog Kangri (Mt Dupleix) is given as 6,929 m. No ascents are known. Another remote peak is Ulugh Muztagh (6,987 m) climbed by Chinese in a Sino–U.S. expedition in 1985.

Better known peaks include:

Peak	Range	m	Asc	Nation
Shisha Pangma	Himalaya	8,046	1964	China
Namcha Barwa	Himalaya	7,782	?1	
Gurla Mandhata	Himalaya	7,728	1985	China/Japan
Kongur	Kun Lun	7,719	1981	U.K.
Kongur Tiube	Kun Lun	7,595	1956	China/ U.S.S.R.
Muztagh Ata	Kun Lun	7,546	1956	China/ U.S.S.R.
Muztagh Ata North	Kun Lun	7,427	1981	Japan
Kailas	Himalaya	6,714	?2	
Muztagh (K5)	Kun Lun	6,710	?3	
Bogdo Ola	Tien Shan	5,445	1981	Japan

1. At present (1990) and discounting subsidiary tops of greater peaks, Namcha Barwa is the highest unclimbed mountain in the world.
2. Kailas is a holy mountain.
3. W. H. Johnson's ascent of K5 in 1865 is now discounted.

The above list of high mountains is by no means complete. In addition there are many lesser mountain areas often with small but sharp peaks and large cliffs. The well-known karst scenery of Kweilin (Guilin) is one such – it is also an area of considerable caving potential. Mention might be made also of the famous nine sacred mountains, each with its monastery:

Peak	Province	Religion
T'ai-shan	Shantung	Taoist
Heng-shan	Shansi	Taoist
Sung-shan	Honan	Taoist
Heng-shan	Hunan	Taoist
Hua-shan	Shensi	Taoist
Wu-t'ai-shan	Shansi	Buddhist
P'u-t'o-shan	Chekiang	Buddhist
Chiu-hua-shan	Anhwei	Buddhist
Omei-shan	Szechwan	Buddhist

The monasteries are often in dramatic situations reached by airy scrambles.

Chinese mountaineering began in June 1955 when the All China Federation of Trade Unions sent four men, Xu Jing, Shi Xiu, Yang Deyuan and Zhou Zeng, to the Caucasus as guests of the Soviets to learn about climbing. The instructors were E. A. Beletskij and S. A. Ugalov and the aim was to prepare for a joint Sino–Soviet ascent of Muztagata which took place in 1956. The proposed Sino–Soviet ascent of Everest did not take place because of a political break between the two countries but the Chinese climbed the mountain on their own in 1960 – the third ascent and first from the north.

The country became increasingly open to foreign climbers during the 1980s, either as joint expeditions with the Chinese or without them, though either way the Chinese exact a hefty price for the privilege.

Large expeditions are the norm for the Chinese, but there is some indication of rock-climbing being taken up as a sport.

Chockstone A stone jammed in a crack. It can vary from pebble size to an enormous boulder jammed across a gully (hence 'chockstone pitch').

Chockstones can be used for ◊ belays or ◊ runners. Originally the rope was untied, threaded behind the chockstone, and retied on the climber – a somewhat hazardous procedure, eliminated by the use of slings and karabiners. The idea of deliberately placing stones in cracks to act as chocks was conceived by Morley Wood during the first ascent of Pigott's Climb, Clogwyn Du'r Arddu, 1927 and it has been used from time to time since. It was logical that in the 1950s reamed out steel ◊ nuts, with slings ready threaded, were used instead and these in turn developed into commercially produced chocks. Chocks were the start of modern protection; the word is obsolescent now, 'nuts' being generally preferred.

Choss Colloquialism to describe a climb which is loose, dirty, covered in herbage etc. 'A chossy climb' or 'the place is full of choss'. Possibly from chaos.

Classic A much misused and almost indefinable term used to describe certain climbs, both in Britain and abroad. A classic climb need not be particularly difficult (e.g. Bowfell Buttress) but it must have a good line and offer stimulating situations at its own level of difficulty. Many are older climbs, but not all; Fool's Paradise in Borrowdale, for example, is one which is not. Neither are all old climbs classics.

A variant is the term 'the route of the crag', meaning the most obvious challenge. Not necessarily classic – some crags have no classic lines.

Cleare, John (b. 1936) An outstanding British mountain photographer of the post-war era and an experienced climber in his own right, with new summer and winter routes to his credit including Magical Mystery Tour, Torbay, 1967 and Traverse of the Gods, Swanage, 1963. He was with Bonington and Greenbank on the first ascent of Coronation Street, Cheddar, in 1965 – the first climb done specifically for T.V. Besides a number of new routes in the Alps he has also made new routes in several other parts of the world. He led the British Himalchuli expedition, 1978 and the American Muztagh Ata ski expedition, 1982. Muztagh Ata (7,546 m) is the highest peak to be climbed on ski.

Cleare has made major ski traverses elsewhere and also river-rafting trips.

He has worked extensively in T.V., including the famous Old Man of Hoy broadcast (B.B.C., 1967). As a film consultant he was on Everest in 1971 with the international team, doing high-altitude film work, and he worked on Clint Eastwood's *The Eiger Sanction* (1974). His film *The Climbers* won the Trento Prize (35 mm) in 1971.

He is the author of numerous books and his work has appeared in magazines in many parts of the world. He is a regular lecturer on his work and travels.

Climbing breeches Knee-length breeches leave the lower part of the legs unencumbered and are commonly used for all types of climbing. They are usually made of a tough, warm material (e.g. 'moleskin') with double thickness at the seat and sometimes the knees. They fasten at the knee with buckles or Velcro and the pockets also have fastenings to prevent things falling out during climbing. A hammer loop or pocket is usually incorporated. In fitting, it is important to ensure there is plenty of freedom for leg movement at the knees and crutch. Braces make the best support, but are currently out of favour.

At present rock-climbing fashion dictates multicoloured Lycra tights, influenced no doubt by climbing walls and competition climbing.

Climbing clubs The term is taken here to mean a club which is not the national 'Alpine club', though it may be national (or international) in membership, and may well have members who are at the top of the sport. Clubs may be based on a geographical area or on some sectional basis, for example, a university. A few clubs are based on élitist principles e.g. G.H.M. (France), A.C.G. (Britain). In Russia, climbing clubs are usually sections of a greater sporting club (e.g. Moscow Locomotive) belonging to a trade union.

Many university clubs are of old foundation. Examples are: Oxford Alpine Club (1875, later reorganized), Akad. A.C., Zurich (1896), Techniker A.C., Graz (1873), Akad. A.C., Innsbruck (1893).

Local clubs were even earlier, though few of the originals remain: Williamstown Alpine Club, U.S.A. (1863), Society Ramond, France (1865), Leipziger A.V., Germany (1869), Club Jurassien, Switzerland (1865). There were many more.

The earliest U.S. climbing clubs still extant are the Appalachian Mountain Club (1876) and the Sierra Club (1892).

The earliest known 'climbing club' in Britain was the Highland Mountain Club of Lochgoilhead (1815) which held a meet every Midsummer Day to climb some local hill and celebrate the fact in true Highland fashion! Other early clubs (all Scottish) were The Gaiter Club (1849), The Cobbler Club (1866), The Dundee Institution Club (1879), Dundee Rambling Club (1886), The Cairngorm Club (1889) and the Scottish Mountaineering Club (1889).

Apart from Scotland and the Oxford Club already mentioned, the earliest

British club was the Manchester Zweigverein (1889) – Manchester members of the Austrian A.C. The first club based on a home tradition was the Yorkshire Ramblers Club (1892). This club, the Scottish Mountaineering Club and the Cairngorm Club are still functioning.

The other 'senior' clubs are: Climbers' Club (1898), Rucksack Club (1902), Wayfarers' Club, Fell and Rock Climbing Club and Derbyshire Pennine Club (all 1906).

A number of other clubs were formed before the Second World War and a great many after it: there are now several hundred clubs in Britain. Unlike the 'senior' clubs which often have a membership of hundreds and to which entry is by election, many of the newer clubs are small and demand nothing in the way of entry, except a fee. The most famous post-war club is the ◊ Rock and Ice Club, formed by J. Brown and his companions in the 1950s. In Scotland the best-known club is the ◊ Creag Dhu, founded in 1930.

Many clubs own one or more mountain ◊ huts, usually restricted to members, though there are reciprocal rights with other clubs. Some clubs publish guidebooks.

Climbing helmet   The greatest proportion of serious climbing accidents involve head injuries. Helmets are designed to reduce this risk in two ways: (a) they protect the head in the event of a fall; and (b) they protect the head from falling debris.

They are made of fibre-glass and have firm chin fastenings – it is essential the latter should not come apart in the event of a fall. The more recent helmets tend to extend some way down the back of the neck and give further protection. Helmets were introduced in the 1950s but only achieved popularity in the 1960s.

Despite the protection afforded by a helmet many climbers refuse to wear one on rock-climbs, claiming it upsets the balance. One suspects fashion and false pride have much to do with it, too.

Climbing wall   A wall in which bricks have been removed and various projections added in order to simulate a rock face. Often built as one end of a sports hall, for indoor practice in climbing. Useful for teaching techniques. There are several varieties, including outdoor walls, towers and wooden models known as climbing frames – some of which are semi-portable.

In more recent years climbing walls have become more sophisticated in design. It is possible to purchase various types of holds and bolt them on to a suitable frame. Climbing competitions are held on specially designed and transportable walls.

Clogwyn Du'r Arddu   One of the most important climbing crags in Britain; the scene of many of the major post-war climbs.

The crag rises above Lyn Arddu in the Snowdon massif and is very conspicuous from the ◊ Snowdon railway, the track of which is probably the most convenient approach. Most conspicuous of all are the huge East and West Buttresses. The former is a set of steep walls comprising a triangular face, the upper part of which is known as the Pinnacle, whilst the other is a remarkable series of steeply tilted slabs. They are separated by the Eastern Terrace, a convenient way down from the climbs. To the left of East Buttress is the large somewhat shapeless mass of the Far East Buttress and beyond that again the small Far Far East Buttress. To the right of West Buttress and separated from it by the steep Western Terrace lies The Steep Band and then a considerable area of less formidable rock. The crag is impressively steep, and big. Though there are a few easier climbs, these are of little importance. The chief routes, the majority, are 'Very Severe' or harder. The crag is affectionately known as Cloggy.

The first climb was Deep Chimney by P. S. Thompson in 1905 and there followed a scattering of minor routes in the next few years, though nobody was bold enough to attack the main bastions until 1927, when Pigott's climb was made on the East Buttress (Pigott, Wood, Henshaw, Burton). Longland's climb on the West Buttress came the following year (1928, Longland, Pigott, Smythe, Eversden, Wood). ◊ Kirkus then began his campaign (1930–2) to be followed by ◊ Brown and ◊ Whillans in the 1950s, and Crew and Ingle in the 1960s. These were sustained efforts, but many other climbers played a part in the crag's development.

Almost every climb on Cloggy is of some significance; the following is merely representative of the best and most favoured following Pigott's and Longland's:

1930	Great Slab – Kirkus, Macphee
1931	Pedestal Crack – Kirkus, Macphee
1932	Birthday Crack – Kirkus, Linnell, Pallis
	Curving Crack – Kirkus, Bridge, Linnell, Hargreaves, Dyson
1933	Narrow Slab – Linnell, Pigott, Holliday, Roberts
1941	Bow Shaped Slab – Edwards, Cooper, Parkinson
1945	The Sheaf – Campbell, Cox
1951	Diglyph – Brown, Sorrell
	Vember – Brown, Whillans
	The Boulder – Brown (rest unable to follow)
1952	The Black Cleft – Brown, Whillans
	Pinnacle Flake – Brown, Whillans
	Spillikin – Brown, Whillans
	Bloody Slab (Red Slab) – Streetly (rest unable to follow)
	Llithrig – Brown, Allen
	The Corner – Brown, Allen, Belshaw
1953	East Buttress Girdle – Brown, Allen, Whillans
1955	Slanting Slab – Whillans, Betts
	Woubits – Whillans, Brown
1956	The White Slab – Moseley, J. Smith
1957	The Mostest – J. Brown (rest unable to follow)
	November – Brown, J. Smith
1958	The Shrike – J. Brown, H. Smith, J. Smith
1959	Woubits Left Hand – Brown, Boysen
	The Troach – Banner, Wilson
1961	Pinnacle Girdle – Soper, Crew
1962	The Great Wall – Crew (second did not follow)
1978	A Midsummer Night's Dream 36,6a – Whillance, Armstrong
1979	The Axe E4,6a – Littlejohn, King
1983	Master's Wall, E7 – Moffatt, Williams (supersedes Great Wall)
1986	Indian Face, E9 – Dawes, Miles (supersedes Master's Wall)

GUIDEBOOK Sharp, *Clogwyn Du'r Arddu* (C.C.).

Clough, Ian Stewart (1937–70)

One of the most popular figures in British post-war climbing; a professional mountaineer of distinction.

Clough began climbing as a youth on his native Yorkshire gritstone. He developed rapidly and under the influence of ◊ MacInnes he also became a first-rate snow- and ice-climber. After National Service in the R.A.F. Mountain Rescue he became a tutor for the ◊ Mountaineering Association

Ian Clough (*R. R. Butchart*)   Michel Croz

and later founded (in association with MacInnes) the Glencoe School of Mountaineering.

He made numerous first ascents, especially in the remoter parts of Scotland, but his work on Ben Nevis is perhaps most notable. He opened up the 'Little Brenva' face (1958–9), made several rock routes and the first winter ascent of Point Five Gully (1959).

His first visit to the Alps was in 1953 when he climbed Wildstrubel. He later climbed many of the Gr. VI courses and in 1962 traversed the whole of the Chamonix Aiguilles (first British traverse). In the same year with Bonington, Whillans and Dlugosz he made the first ascent of the Central Pillar of Frêney. The following summer (1962) with Bonington, he made the first British ascent of the Eigerwand.

He made two expeditions to Patagonia: 1963, first ascent of the Central Tower of Paine; 1967–8, leader of the Fortress expedition, though not himself one of the summit party. He made an unsuccessful attempt on Gauri Sankar in the Himalaya in 1964, and in 1970 returned to the Himalaya as a member of the successful Annapurna S Face expedition. The expedition was virtually over when Clough was caught by an ice avalanche and killed instantly.

Cobbler, the (Ben Arthur) (881 m)   A craggy summit at the head of Loch Long, Arrochar, Scotland. There are three tops: South Peak (also called The Cobbler's Daughter, Jean or The Cobbler's Last); Central Peak (The Cobbler), North Peak (The Cobbler's Wife). There are climbs of all standards and the district is popular with Scottish climbers.

GUIDEBOOK Crocket/Walker, *A Climbers' Guide to Arran, Arrochar & the Southern Highlands*.

Cockin, John Garforth (1846–1900) One of the most active of the early explorers of Caucasus which he visited in 1888, 1890, 1893 and 1896. He made a number of first ascents including the second summits of Janga and Ushba. Most notable, perhaps, was the first ascent of Shkhara (1888).

Cockin was a keen guideless climber. He had made a solo ascent of the Weisshorn in 1889, but was killed on that mountain in 1900 while trying a solo descent when the party he was with were in route-finding difficulties.

Coiling a rope Climbing ropes are invariably carried coiled. Unless the coiling is properly done the rope will kink badly and may not uncoil easily when it is required. In Britain the chief coil used is the shoulder coil. In this, one end of the rope is held in the left hand and a length of rope equal to the arms extended is pulled out across the body. The right-hand point is then transferred to the left hand (making a loop) and the process repeated until almost all the rope is coiled. Enough is left to make the shoulder knot. Another popular way of doing this is to coil the rope by boot and knee – but note that a hand must be placed between rope and knee. It is finished with a shoulder knot as before.

A different way of coiling is used for a long rope or abseil rope. The rope is doubled and coiled as before, but it is finished by wrapping the two ends round the top of the coils and threading them through to make a 'dolly'. The rope is tied to the climber's back and waist. Climbing ropes are stored away coiled when not in use.

Col (Fr.) (E.: saddle; G.: Joch; W.: bwlch; Ga.: bealach; It.: colle) A dip in a ridge, usually between two peaks. May be deep and wide enough to carry a motor road (e.g. Col de Forclaz) or it may be a mere dip in a high and icy skyline (e.g. Col d'Hérens). The way across a col is known as a ◊ pass. Narrow cols are known as gaps (Fr.: brèche; G.: Scharte).

Coleman, Edmund Thomas (c. 1823–92) Made the first ascent of the Dômes de Miage (1858). He later went to America for several years during which he made the first ascent of Mt Baker in the Cascades on his third attempt (1868). He was a companion of General Stevens on the latter's first ascent of Mt Rainier in 1870, but got separated from the main party and did not reach the top.

Coleman was an artist. He was a member of the original committee of the A.C.

Collie, John Norman (1859–1942) One of the greatest mountaineers of the turn of the century, whose activities profoundly affected climbing from Britain to the Himalaya. He began climbing in Skye in 1887 and 1888 with the local guide, John Mackenzie, when they climbed every peak except Sgurr Coire an Lochan. In 1890 they began a systematic survey of the Cuillins (the O. S. maps being unreliable) and each man has a peak named after him – Sgurr MhicCoinnich (Mackenzie's Peak) and Sgurr Thormaid (Norman's Peak). In 1891 they made the first crossing of the Thearlaich–Dubh Gap (with King), thus completing the ridge as a route. They also ascended Sgurr Coire an Lochan, the last summit to be attained in Britain. In 1899 Collie photographed the Cioch, though he and Mackenzie did not visit this popular pinnacle until seven years later. Skye was always Collie's first love; he retired to the island and is buried there, next to Mackenzie, in Struan churchyard.

He was a prolific climber in other areas of Britain. Most famous is his ascent of Moss Ghyll, Scafell, in 1892, when he cut a hold in the rock with an ice axe

– the celebrated Collie Step. During the Easter of 1894 with ◊ Collier, ◊ Solly and ◊ Hastings he made the first rock-climb on Buachaille Etive Mor and the first ascent of the Tower Ridge, Ben Nevis. This campaign is generally accepted as one which marked the beginning of climbing on the Scottish mainland.

In the Alps he was one of the select band climbing with ◊ Mummery. His first ascents include: S W Face of the Plan, Grépon traverse (1892), Requin (which he named) (1893) and the first guideless ascent of the Old Brenva Route, Mont Blanc (1894). He accompanied Mummery on the ill-fated Nanga Parbat Expedition (1895).

In 1897 Collie paid his first visit to the Rockies. He repeated his visit in 1898, 1900, 1902, 1910 and 1911. He did a great deal of exploration and made first ascents as follows:

1897	Mt Lefroy, Mt Gordon
1898	Survey Peak, Mt Athabasca, Diadem, Mt Thompson
1900	Goat Peak, Mt Edith
1902–11	Mt Murchison, Freshfield, Forbes, Neptuak and Bees

In 1901, 1903 and 1904 Collie visited the Lofoten Islands where he also made a number of first ascents.

Collie related his experiences in numerous articles for climbing journals and in his book, *Climbing on the Himalaya and Other Mountain Ranges* (1902).

Collie remained a bachelor all his life. He was an acknowledged aesthete: an expert on oriental art, wine, food and cigars. He was a heavy smoker but this did not seem to impede his fitness – he was a very strong man. His crossing of the Mazeno La in the Himalaya is an epic tale of endurance. He was President of the A.C. in 1920–2 and honorary member of the American and Canadian Alpine Clubs.

By profession Collie was a distinguished organic chemist and a professor at University College, London. He discovered the gas neon and made the first practical applications of X-rays.

Collier, Joseph (1855–1905) A Manchester surgeon and pioneer rock-climber (Collier's Exit, Moss Ghyll, 1892; Collier's Climb, 1893; both on Scafell). He climbed in Scotland, Norway and the Caucasus, but his favourite area was the Dolomites, though he does not appear to have made new routes there. His career is poorly documented, but he is known to have been very popular with other climbers of the period and extremely athletic.

Combined tactics It is occasionally necessary in rock-climbing for one climber to assist another by giving him a 'leg up' or 'shoulder'. The second man should, of course, be secured while he does this. Increasingly rare in use; common in pioneer Alpine literature. It was combined tactics that led to the death of ◊ Jones.

Comici, Emilio (1901–40) A notable climber from Trieste; the leading Italian exponent of aid climbing between the wars. He made some 200 new routes in the Dolomites including the first ascent of the Cima Grande N Face (E. Comici, G. Dimai, A. Dimai, 1933): one of the classic north faces of the Alps and regarded at the time as a great breakthrough. He was a proponent of the *direttissima*: 'I wish some day to make a route and from the summit let fall a drop of water and this is where my route will have gone.' Bolting has made this possible today but it is doubtful whether Comici had this in mind: his ideal has perhaps been usurped by technology.

Comici was at one time a caver, holding the world depth record of his day. He died through a silly accident during a training climb.

Commands In rock-climbing it is necessary for easily understood communications to pass along the rope. The climbers may be out of each other's sight, wind and weather may make communication difficult, unusual phrases may be misunderstood. To cope with this a series of commands has evolved.
Leader's instructions to second man
L.: 'Taking in slack!' (pulls in spare rope)
S.M.: 'That's me!' (when all rope has been pulled in)
L.: 'Climb when you're ready!' (S.M. removes his belay and prepares to climb)
S.M.: 'Climbing!'
L.: 'Aye, Aye!' (not always used)
When climbing
'Take in!' (means pull in more rope, it is too slack)
'Slack!' (means give me more rope, it is too tight)
'Tight rope!' (means take the rope in tightly, I expect to come off)
'Ten feet!' (means you are running out of rope – about ten feet left)
'Hold it!' (means stop taking in, I have met an obstruction – e.g. taking off a runner)
'Take in red (white)' (used in double rope techniques when bi-coloured ropes are employed; similarly, 'Slack on red (white)'. 'Take in both', etc.)
General warnings If a stone is knocked off a cliff or stonefall is noticed the general warning shout of 'Below!' is given.

If a climber realizes a fall is imminent he should always shout a warning to his belayer; even a split-second warning improves his chances of a good hold.

Committing move Used somewhat indiscriminately to describe a hard move but it means a move where the climber is forced to commit himself to a technique with the expectation that if he does not succeed he will fall off. Also, a move which is not reversible is a committing move since it commits the climber to finishing the climb – though this is not strictly true since he may be able to ◊ abseil off. In the Alps, an abseil might itself be committing, if it is not possible to climb back up – as on the S Ridge of the Aig. Noire de Peuterey.

Compass An important navigational aid for mountaineers. The heavy prismatic compasses once favoured are now largely replaced by the Silva-type compass developed for orienteering. Local magnetism in the rocks can affect compasses in some areas, for example, Bowfell, Lake District, and the Cuillin of Skye.

Compass party A method of navigating in thick mist over dangerous terrain. The party are roped together (or in a large party stood in line) facing the compass direction required. They move off slowly, the rear member being equipped with a compass and shouting directions to keep the others in line. If the front man also has a compass, the technique is easier.

Competitions Climbing competitions of various sorts have been growing over the last two or three decades, based initially on the East European 'speed climbing' championships which were held on some convenient outcrop. Points were awarded for style and though it gained acceptance in some quarters, especially among young activists, it was resisted by the climbing establishment of the West, led by Britain and the U.S.A.

The increasing sophistication of ◊ climbing walls led to a sudden surge of 'sport climbing' in the late 1980s where the competition is held indoors on a huge climbing wall. Basically the competition is to see who can get highest before a fall. This is still being refined – competitors on the verge of falling off have been known to jump up first, thus gaining a few vital centimetres of competition height! Competitors are protected by a rope.

There is a professional Grand Prix circuit moving round from country to country with competitors accumulating points. In 1990 the men's champion was Jacky Godoffe of France and the women's title was shared by Isabelle Patissier of France and Lynn Hill of the U.S.A. Other leading sports climbers include Jim Karn (U.S.A.), François Legrande (France), Christoph Finkel (Germany), Susi Good (Switzerland) and Luisa Iovane (Italy). Leading British activists include Simon ◊ Nadin, Ben Moon and Jerry Moffatt. Nadin was world champion in 1989.

Compton, Edward Theodore (1849–1921)   A very active climber who lived in Austria and made numerous first ascents, particularly in the Eastern Alps. Notable are: Torre di Brenta and S Face of Cima di Brenta (both 1882). With ◊ Blodig he made the first guideless ascent of Aig. Blanche de Peuterey (1905). His active career spanned over 50 years and he made an ascent of Gross Glockner when he was 70.

Compton was a professional artist, the most famous mountain painter of his day. He exhibited many times at the Royal Academy. His drawings and watercolours illustrate several books and numerous articles written by leading climbers of the time, particularly German climbers (Zsigmondy, Purtscheller etc.). (See D. O. A. V. journals 1883–1912.)

His second son, Harrison Compton, was also a gifted mountain painter, illustrating Reginald Farrer's famous book, *The Dolomites*.

Contouring   Walking across a hillside so as to keep the same height, that is on an imaginary contour line.

Conway, William Martin (1856–1937)   Distinguished art critic, writer and explorer. A romantic, in the manner of Guido ◊ Rey or, later, F. S. ◊ Smythe in his approach to the hills, and a complete contrast to his contemporary, Mummery, whom he greatly admired. From this outlook stem all his major achievements.

In the Alps he made only a few minor new ascents, and is best remembered for his traverse of the Alps from Monte Viso to Gross Glockner, with two Gurkhas and (for part of the time) E. A. ◊ Fitzgerald in 1894. (Wrote *The Alps from End to End*, 1895.)

In 1892 Conway organized the first major climbing expedition to visit the Himalaya, choosing the Karakoram region. The expedition was modelled on Whymper's successful Andean expedition of 1879 and received support from the Royal Society and the Royal Geographical Society. It was the prototype for most subsequent major Himalayan expeditions. The members were: Conway, A. D. McCormick (artist), J. H. Roudebush, O. Eckenstein, Lt. C. G. Bruce, Col. Lloyd-Dickin (naturalist), M. Zurbriggen (guide) and four Gurkhas. They achieved valuable mapping work in the Hispar and Baltoro areas and ascended Pioneer Peak (22,600 ft), the highest point climbed at that date. (Wrote *Climbing and Exploration in the Karakorum Himalayas* [2 vols.], 1894.)

In 1896 and 1897 Conway visited Spitzbergen, climbing and exploring, using skis for travel. (Wrote *The First Crossing of Spitzbergen*, 1897, and *With Ski and Sledges over Arctic Glaciers*, 1898.)

In 1898 he visited the Andes and made the first ascent of Illimani (6,485 m) and the third ascent of Aconcagua (7,035 m). He also tried to climb Mt Sarmiento in Tierra del Fuego, but failed. (Wrote *Climbing and Exploration in the Bolivian Andes* [2 vols.], 1901, and *Aconcagua and Tierra del Fuego*, 1902.)

Early in 1881 Conway had published *The Zermatt Pocket Book*, which was a guide to the climbs in the Pennine Alps and the first real climbing guide as distinct from travellers' guides (◊ Ball). He proposed that the A.C. should publish a whole series of such guides (1886) but this did not happen. He therefore revised his own book (1890) calling it *Pennine Climbing Guide* which became the first of a series known as the Conway and Coolidge Climbers' Guides. Conway had no part in them after the first three. (◊ Guidebooks.)

The romantic nature of his climbing made Conway the leading ex-centrist in the arguments which raged in the A.C. at that time (◊ Centrist and ex-centrist). He gave up climbing in 1901, making his last ascent the Breithorn, as it had also been his first in 1872. He wrote many books and articles on art and climbing, most notably *Mountain Memories* (1920). President of the A.C. 1902–4. Became Lord Conway of Allington, 1931.

Coolidge, William Augustus Brevoort (1850–1926)
An outstanding mountaineer and probably the most accomplished Alpine historian of his, or any other, age.

Coolidge was born near New York. His father died shortly afterwards, and his mother, an invalid, went to live with her sister Miss M. C. Brevoort, to whom fell the task of bringing up the boy. Because he was a delicate child they moved, on doctor's orders, to Paris, and for a short time, to Cannes. In the July of 1865 he climbed the Niesen, the first of his many ascents, and later that year crossed several snow passes.

The part played by Miss Brevoort in Coolidge's career as an Alpinist cannot be over-emphasized. She was herself a mountaineer and encouraged her young nephew to take up the sport. She found a ready disciple: aunt and nephew climbed together until the former's death in 1876. Often, too, they were accompanied by their dog, Tschingel. For the first three seasons they employed as guide François Devouassoud, but when he went to the Caucasus with Freshfield in 1868, Coolidge began his life-long association with Christian ◊ Almer.

Between the Niesen (1865) and his last climb, Ortler (1898), Coolidge did not miss a single Alpine season – 33 years during which he amassed a tremendous practical knowledge of the Alps and made, possibly, more ascents than anyone else (the complete list fills 22 pages of the *Alpine Club Register*). He preferred snow- and ice- to rock-climbing, and in this respect was a little out of his time, for the Golden Age was ending as he began his career and rock-climbing, as exemplified by ◊ Dent and ◊ Mummery, was definitely in. Nevertheless, he made a number of important first ascents, including Piz Badile (1876), Pic Centrale of La Meije, Ailefroide (1870), Agassizhorn (1872) and numerous lesser peaks, especially in the Cottian and Maritime Alps, his favourite districts. In 1874 he made the first winter ascent of Wetterhorn and Jungfrau and, in 1879, Schreckhorn. He made numerous second or third ascents of difficult routes done by the pioneers. In all, he visited every part of the Alps except for Tyrol, Carinthia and Bavaria. He did not climb elsewhere – and had little regard for those who did.

Cornices on the Wildspitze, Tyrol. (*W. Unsworth*)

Meanwhile he had taken double honours at Oxford and become a Fellow of Magdalen (1875). In 1882 he took Holy Orders, but in 1897 left Oxford to live permanently in Grindelwald. From about 1882 he devoted his time almost exclusively to the study of the Alps and he built up an unique Alpine library.

He put his vast knowledge to use in a long series of articles, books and encyclopaedia contributions; 220 by 1912, on his own count. Notable books are: *Josias Simler et les Origines de l'Alpinisme jusqu'en 1600* (1904), *Swiss Travel and Swiss Guidebooks* (1889), *The Alps in Nature and History* (1908) and *Alpine Studies* (1912). His works are informative rather than readable; vital references for Alpinists.

Coolidge's exactitude made him an ideal guidebook writer and editor. He revised Ball's *Western Alps* (1898) and Murray's *Switzerland* (1891, 1904), but his most famous contributions were to the Conway and Coolidge Climbers' Guides (1881–1910), the first practical pocket-sized guidebooks for mountaineers. (◊ Guidebooks.)

From 1880 to 1889 Coolidge was editor of the *Alpine Journal*.

Coolidge was equally famous for his quarrels and stubbornness: he disagreed with almost every climber of note during his lifetime. He resigned from the A.C. in 1899, was elected honorary member in 1904 and resigned from that in 1910. He was re-elected honorary member in 1923. He was called 'the Sage of Grindelwald' and, less politely, 'the Fiery Lamb'. He died at Grindelwald in 1926.

Cordier, Henri (1855–77)   Began climbing in 1874, but it was in 1876 that he made a series of difficult new climbs in several parts of the Alps including routes on Rateau, Piz Roseg and Finsteraarhorn. His best known climb, perhaps, is the Cordier Couloir of Aig. Verte. He also made the first ascents of Les Courtes, Les Droites and Pizzo Bianco. The following year he was killed in the Dauphiné in a glissading accident.

Cornice   A consolidated snow bank projecting over the edge of a ridge, plateau or corrie, and formed by prevailing winds. They may be temporary, as in Scotland, in which case they are likely to avalanche down a gully or face with the onset of thaw, or they may be permanent as are some in the Alps (e.g. Wildspitze, Mont Blanc de Cheilon). On some ridges double cornices are known, that is, extending out on both sides of the ridge. Cornices can be quite large.

Cornices represent a threat to the climber since he may not be aware of their presence and they may collapse beneath him. If they are suspected then careful prodding with the axe may reveal them. It is safer to traverse well below the edge of the ridge on the other side. If there is a cornice at the head of a gully climb and it cannot be avoided, it may have to be tunnelled through.

Corrie (Fr.: cirque; Ga.: coire; W.: cwm)   The head of a hanging valley or glacial hollow (armchair hollow) and one of the most noticeable features of glaciated mountains. Corries often have lakes and are usually ringed with crags. In the Lake District corries are sometimes called combs (e.g. Comb Gill, Borrowdale).

Corsica   A Mediterranean island noted for its fine peaks of which Monte Cinto (2,706 m) is the highest. Other peaks offering fine climbing on perfect granite include: Monte d'Ore (2,389 m), Monte Rotondo (2,622 m), Paglia Orba (2,525 m) and the cirque of Bonifato. May and June are the best months for climbing in Corsica, the high summer months being rather too hot for most tastes. Camping or bivouacking (there are some fine caves) are popular.

The Corsican High Level Route (GR 20) across the mountains from Calenzana to Conca takes 13 days and is reputed to be toughest of all the French Grandes Randonnées.

GUIDEBOOKS Collomb, *Corsica Mountains* (W.C.P.).

Castle, *The Corsican High Level Route* (C.P.).

Couloir (E.: gully)   The French word is invariably used by British climbers in the Alps, and there is a subtle difference in connotation between couloir and gully, hard to define. It perhaps arises from Alpine couloirs being usually that much bigger. Some couloirs are immense (e.g. on the Brenva Face), but most are moderate size. May be snow, ice or rock, depending on the mountains in question. Many are steep, but straightforward, snow slopes.

Couloirs are natural avalanche chutes and are also prone to stonefall, but conditions are local and may be minimal. Where the danger is noticeable, warnings are given in the guidebooks.

Courmayeur   The principal mountaineering centre on the Italian side of the Mont Blanc group. It is connected by road to Aosta and there is a rail-head at Pré St Didier, a few minutes' bus drive away. The Mont Blanc road tunnel connects the village with ♢ Chamonix. At nearby Entrèves is the start of a cable-car system that also connects with Chamonix.

Couzy, Jean (1923–58)   One of the most important climbers in post-war France. From 1947, when he climbed the N Face of Requin (third ascent) until his death he made numerous difficult Alpine ascents, usually an early repeat, e.g. third ascent of the Brandler–Hasse on the Tre Cima Grande, or his own first ascents. These include N Pillar, Droites, 1952; N Ridge of the Noire and N E Face of Olan direct, 1956: E Face of Mont Aiguille, W Face of Pt Bich (Noire), 1957; N Face of Gd Jorasses, Pt Margherita, 1958.

Many of his climbs were done with ◊ Desmaison with whom he was also a pioneer of hard winter routes in the Alps. An example was the West Face of the Dru, up and down, 10–14 March 1957: the longest winter expedition of its time.

In 1950 he was on the ◊ Annapurna expedition and helped discover the best approach to the mountain, then completely unknown. In 1954 he was on the successful reconnaissance of Makalu during which, with ◊ Terray, he crossed into Tibet and climbed Chomo Lonzo (7,790 m). The following year, again with Terray, he climbed Makalu (8,463 m). Both were first ascents.

Couzy was killed by stonefall whilst climbing the S W Face of the Crête des Bergers.

Cowell, John Jermyn (1838–67) Explored the Graian Alps in 1860, making the first ascents of Grand Paradis, Levanna Occidentale and Mont Iseran. In the following year he took part in the first ascent of Nord End (Monte Rosa), after which he visited Italy and there contracted an illness from which he never properly recovered.

Cow's tail A short loop of tape attached in front of a harness or waistband for use in ◊ aid climbing. The climber, standing in his ◊ étrier, can clip the cow's tail into the peg and this will support him, allowing him to use both hands for placing the next peg.

Cox, Anthony David Machell (b. 1913) A leading British rock-climber of the immediate pre-war years, Cox began the development of the Dewerstone in Devon with the C.C. Original and Direct Routes (1935–6) and Vixen Tor on Dartmoor. He then added to his list the popular climbs of Sunset Crack, Clogwyn Du'r Arddu (1937), the Grimmett and Spiral Route, Craig yr Ysfa (1938) and finally one of the great Cloggy classics, Sheaf (1945).

Cox was on the Machapuchare expedition of 1957, but failed to reach the top by about 150 ft. President of the A.C. 1971–3.

Crack (G.: Riss; Fr.: fissure; It.: fessura) A fissure in the rock, not wide enough to be a ◊ chimney. Cracks may be vertical, horizontal or sloping and they play a very important part in rock-climbing. A crack may form the basis for a whole route, or for a ◊ pitch. Smaller cracks may provide convenient holds or useful ◊ protection.

A crack can be climbed using holds on its edge (easiest) but if this is not possible it may be tackled by ◊ jamming or ◊ layback. Cracks are needed for ◊ chocks and ◊ pitons.

Craig Gogarth A line of sea cliffs in Gogarth Bay, between N and S Stacks on Holyhead Island, Anglesey. Discovered as recently as 1964, they have proved to be the finest sea-cliffs for climbing in Britain and the most outstanding discovery of post-war years. The climbs are reasonably long and almost without exception hard. Since their discovery, development has been intense.

The first climb was Gogarth (HVS) on Main Cliff, done by Ingle and Boysen in 1964. There then followed two decades of intense activity in which most of the leading climbers of the day took part. Three routes by Ed Drummond are particularly popular and demonstrate the quality of the cliffs: The Strand, E2, 1967; T Rex, E3, 1968; and Dream of White Horses, HVS, 1968. This latter is a girdle of Wen Zawn and is regarded as one of the great post-war classics of British climbing.

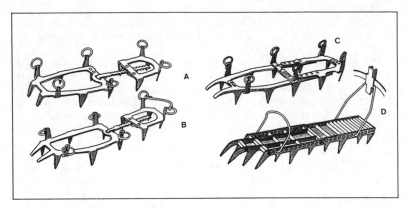

Crampons: **A** 10pt flexible; **B** 12pt flexible; **C** Chouinard rigid; **D** Footfangs (rigid).

More recent classics include:

1975 Position E5,6a free climbed by Sharp
1978 The Cad E5,6a Fawcett, Gibb
1980 The Bells, The Bells E7,6b Redhead, Shorter
1981 Citadel E5,6b Fawcett, Gibb
GUIDEBOOK Pollitt et al., *Gogarth* (C.C.).

Crampons   Used for climbing snow and ice, crampons are steel spikes on frames which fit on to the soles of the boots. They have 10 or 12 points, the front two of which project forward at an angle, for stabbing into steep ice. Most models are adjustable in size and they are fixed on the feet either by straps or clamps. Some crampons have rigid frames, others have a linking bar between heel and sole which acts as a hinge and gives them flexibility. In any case, crampons fit best on boots which have a rigid sole. The French name is universally used nowadays, and the old English terms, 'climbing irons' and 'claws' have long since gone out of use.

Crampons are of great antiquity; specimens from Hallstadt are said to date from 500 B.C. and other early examples have been found near Bad Reichenhall and in Carinthia. The Gauls used them in Roman times and the earliest climbers to visit the Caucasus found the natives fully acquainted with crampons.

Though these early crampons may have been used in crossing icy passes they were probably more commonly used as an aid to balance on steep slopes during haymaking – still to be seen in parts of the Tyrol. Their earliest specific mention in climbing was in 1689 when P. A. Arnod mentioned that his guides used them in an attempt to cross the Col du Géant.

In the nineteenth century crampons were made specifically for climbing by village blacksmiths in the Tyrol, based on those used by peasants. The British engineer, Oscar ◊ Eckenstein, redesigned them and modern crampons stem from his work. Many Alpine pioneers such as Ball, Dent and Raeburn condemned the use of crampons either on the grounds that they were dangerous (improperly used they can be) or on ethical grounds – to use them was cheating. This attitude persisted in some quarters until well after the Second World War, possibly because the great art of step-cutting had become a fetish.

When ◊ Vibram soles replaced nails, crampons became essential even on relatively easy snow and ice. Quite difficult mixed climbing can be done without removing the crampons, as was once the method and in modern high-angle ◊ ice-climbing the use of crampons is a vital part of short axe techniques.

It is common to wear crampons at all times on snow and ice these days; step-cutting is virtually eliminated. The greatest problem is 'balling-up' when soft snow compacts between the spikes. The ball can be removed by a tap from an axe shaft.

Craven, Alfred Eugene (1848–?)   Made the first English ascent of Gross Lohner and the first ascent of the Zahlershorn in 1879. He then joined W. O. ◊ Moseley, an American, in the first traverse from Gross to Kleine Doldenhorn. A few days later they climbed the Matterhorn and Moseley was killed on the descent at the place now called the Moseley Slab.

Crawford, Colin Grant (1890–1959)   Indian civil servant who climbed in Kashmir in 1918 and 1919 and took part in Raeburn's reconnaissance of Kangchenjunga in 1920. Was a member of the Everest expeditions of 1922 and 1933; during the latter he climbed the North Col six times. Made a number of new ascents with Odell and others in the Canadian Selkirks, 1930.

Creagh Dhu Mountaineering Club   Founded in 1930 by A. F. Saunders, the Creagh Dhu had originally 30 members, all from the Glasgow area. Its adventures were chronicled in *Always a Little Further* by A. Borthwick, and this gave rise to numerous legends about the club comparable to those about the ◊ Rock and Ice Club. In the post-war years it was in the forefront of Scottish climbing, with members such as ◊ MacInnes, ◊ Cunningham and Vigano.

Crevasse (G.: Schrund; It.: crepaccio)   A crack in the surface of a ◊ glacier. They can be wide and deep, though this is not always the case. On a dry glacier crevasses can easily be seen and are not usually difficult to avoid. Where this is not the case they can be climbed by the normal ice techniques. Small crevasses are jumped.

Crevasses are much more difficult to detect on a snow-covered glacier. A leader must appraise the general lie of the glacier and estimate the best route. He then probes with his ice axe along the line of march, his companions being constantly alert for a quick belay. The technique is simple but time-consuming and for this reason is too frequently neglected. A good deal depends on the leader's experience.

Some crevasses are spanned by ◊ snow bridges. The crevasse between the glacier and the upper snows of a mountain is called the ◊ bergschrund. F. A. Eschen, a Dane, is the first-known climber to perish in a crevasse (1800, Buet, Switzerland). (◊ Crevasse rescue.)

Crevasse rescue   The techniques employed to get a climber out of a crevasse into which he has fallen. In many cases it is simply a matter of hauling him out on the rope or of him pulling himself out, since very often the victim goes in with only one leg or to waist depth. This is very common. When the victim goes down below the lip of the crevasse it becomes much more serious.

If the victim is tied with a simple waist loop it is first of all necessary for him to take the strain off his loop or he will black out. To do this he should have a prusik loop (◊ Prusiks). He stands in the prusik loop. Then:

Victorian climbers, photographed by George Abraham, tackling crevasses in a dry glacier.

1. *If there is a large party available:* The victim can simply be pulled out.
2. *If the party is smaller:* The middle of a rope is lowered to him, and he passes it through a karabiner at his waist. One end of the rope is secured and the members pull on the other end. The karabiner acts as a pully.
3. *Self-rescue.* Used for a rope of two, possibly three, if the pully method fails. The climber climbs the rope using prusikers. Very tiring.

The active rope is belayed in all the above cases. The belay point should be well back – it has happened that the belayer is also above the crevasse on a snow bridge! Quickness is the essence of good crevasse rescue and the techniques are worth practising.

Crew, Peter (b. 1942)   A leading British rock-climber who, in the early sixties, was Brown's natural successor in the exploration of Clogwyn Du'r Arddu where he made a number of new climbs, usually with B. Ingle. The Great Wall (1962), when the second did not follow, may be mentioned. His explorations on other crags in Wales were also noteworthy; he made some 70 new routes. With Ingle he also made Hiraeth on Dove Crag in Lakeland (1961).

Crew played a leading part in the exploration of Gogarth, with Ingle, J. Brown and others, including the Main Cliff Girdle, The Rat Race, The Red Wall, Central Park (all 1966) and The Spider's Web (1968). In addition, he has made some 50 routes on the local outcrops. He was on the Cerro Torre Expedition of 1967–8.

Crib Goch   A pinnacled ridge leading up to Crib y Ddysgl and forming one arm of the Snowdon Horseshoe. An airy traverse, it is one of the most popular ways of climbing Snowdon, but in a hard winter, when the ridge is coated in snow and ice, it can be a serious proposition.

Below the summit of Crib Goch, on the north side, is a clean 250 buttress which gives a number of climbs, the first and most popular of which is Reade's Route (Reade and Bartrum, 1908).

The name Crib Goch means 'red comb' i.e. a coxcomb.

Croux, Laurent (1864–1938)   A notable Courmayeur guide at the turn of the century, employed by many well-known climbers, particularly the Duke of the ◊ Abruzzi. He made several first ascents, amongst which may be noted:

1897   Mt St Elias (Alaska) with Abruzzi
1898   Aig. de la Brenva, S E Ridge
1899   Aig. Sans Nom, E Ridge
      Pt Croux (named after him)
1902   Mt Mallet, S Face
      Mt Blanc du Tacul, from S
1903   Guide to Queen Margherita on her Spitzbergen expedition; first ascent of Mt Savoie
1909   Traverse of Aig. Blanche de Peuterey
1911   Dôme de Neige des Écrins
      Grandes Jorasses, Hirondelles Ridge (in descent)

In 1916 he was seriously injured by an accident in a saw mill which closed his career.

Crowley, Edward Alexander ('Aleister') (1875–1947)   Aleister Crowley, self-styled Great Beast 666, was a notorious dabbler in black magic and unholy arts during the first part of the present century. At Cefalù Abbey in Sicily and Boleskin House, Foyers, he conducted obscene rituals after the fashion of the eighteenth-century Hellfire Club. A first-class mountebank, many notable people came under his influence.

In earlier years he was a climber of some distinction. He began climbing in 1890. In 1893 he made a new route on Napes Needle and in 1894 climbed on Beachy Head. He visited the Alps each year from 1894 to 1898. Much of his climbing was done with ◊ Eckenstein, the one friend he never betrayed.

In 1900 he visited Mexico and climbed Popacatapetl with Eckenstein. In 1902 he was second-in-command to the latter in the K2 expedition, when Guillarmod and Wesseley reached 21,400 ft – not exceeded until the U.S. expedition of 1938. Nevertheless, Crowley was a neurotic expedition man and it is difficult to see why Guillarmod invited him to lead a Kangchenjunga expedition in 1905. The outcome was disastrous: three porters and a climber were killed and Crowley refused to help in any rescue. The scandal, magnified by a row between Crowley and Guillarmod in the press, and his growing notoriety, ended Crowley's climbing career.

Croz, Michel (1830–65)   The finest Chamonix guide of his generation, born at Le Tour, where he lived all his life. He sprang to prominence when discovered by ◊ Wills in 1859 and took part in the most exciting expeditions of the following five years including the great events of 1864 and 1865 with ◊ Whymper. These include the first ascents of Écrins, Mont Dolent, Aig. de Trélatête, Aig. d'Argentière and Moming Pass (1864), Dent Blanche and Grandes Jorasses (1865). (◊ Almer.)

Croz took part in the first ascent of the Matterhorn (1865) and was killed in the accident on the way down. He was unmarried.

Crux   The hardest part of a climb. One speaks of 'a crux pitch' or 'a crux move'. There may well be more than one: 'first crux', 'second crux'.

Cunningham, Darus Dunlop (1856–96)   A Scottish climber who was an advocate of winter ascents in his own country (with Emile ◊ Rey on Ben Nevis, 1884) and who made the second winter ascent of Mont Blanc (1882). He repeated (often second ascent) a number of the harder Chamonix climbs of the day.

Cunningham is best known as editor with ◊ Abney of *The Pioneers of the Alps* (1887).

Cunningham, John (1927–80)   One of the leading Scottish climbers of the post-war era and one who had a profound effect on mountaineering. With Bill ◊ March Cunningham is generally credited with the invention of the modern ◊ ice-climbing methods.

Amongst his many new routes mention might be made of Guerdon Grooves (1947), the first big wall climb to be done in Scotland, and Bluebell Groove, one of the hardest climbs in the Glencoe area (1955). His ice-craft was demonstrated when he did Point Five Gully, Ben Nevis, in two and a half hours. (First ascent took five days, sieged.)

In 1953 Cunningham and MacInnes formed the two-man Creag Dhu expedition to Everest, which, alas, failed through inadequate financial resources! In 1955–6 he was in South Georgia, where he ascended many ice peaks of *c.* 2,300 m. In 1958 he was on an expedition to Disteghil Sar and in 1959 to Ama Dablam. Between 1960 and 1965, Cunningham was three times in the Antarctic, where he made numerous ascents, including that of Mount

Andrew Jackson (3,505 m), the highest peak in British Antarctica. It involved a dog sled journey of 650 km to base camp.

Cunningham revolutionized modern ice-climbing. The front-pointing techniques that were previously used only applied to slopes up to 70 degrees, but Cunningham showed that with special axes the method could be applied to any angle.

He began his working life in the Glasgow shipyards but later took a P.E. diploma and became a mountaineering instructor. For a while he was a West Scotland wrestling champion. He died trying to rescue a girl student from the sea at Holyhead.

Cust, Arthur (1842–1911)   Whilst a schoolmaster at Rossall, he made with his fellow teachers, Cawood and Colgrove, a number of guideless expeditions which culminated in the first guideless ascent of the Matterhorn (1876). His favourite districts were Arolla and the Lepontine Alps. He made the first known ascent of Mont Brulé (1876) and the Mitre de l'Évêque (1879) in the former area, and numerous first ascents in the little-known Lepontine area. He frequently climbed solo.

Cust's Gully, on Great End, has a remarkable rock arch. Cust led a large A.C. party up the gully in winter, 1880 – almost certainly the first climb done on this popular winter climbing crag.

Cyprus, climbing in   A mountainous island in the Mediterranean. Rock-climbs up to 150 m have been developed, mostly by Service personnel stationed there. The chief areas are Kornos, Pentadtylos and Kantara in the north. The weather is good.

D

Darbellay, Michel (b. 1934) A Swiss guide who made the first solo ascent of the ◊ Eigerwand (1963). He was an early proponent of fast times for hard routes: Noire W Face, 6½ hours (1961); Matterhorn Nordwand (Schmid route), 6 hours (1962). For the Matterhorn Centenary, 1965, he climbed the face again, this time with Hilti von Allmen, for the benefit of T.V.

Davidson, Sir William Edward (1853–1923) One of the leading figures of the second generation of Alpine pioneers, and close contemporary of ◊ Mummery, of whom Davidson had a jealous dislike. Davidson failed on the Grépon and the Charpoua face of the Verte, both expeditions which Mummery accomplished shortly afterwards. There is little doubt that it was Davidson who prevented Mummery's election to the A.C. (1880).

Davidson was a strong climber and his expeditions included most of the difficult climbs then known. His own first ascents were: Mont Maudit (1878), Aig. du Tacul (1880), Wellenkuppe–Gabelhorn traverse (1895), Le Cardinal (1897). He also made many new routes on the Rifelhorn, a peak he is said to have climbed 250 times.

Davidson always climbed with the best of guides in the best of weather. He was a strong socialite and something of a snob. He was Permanent Legal Adviser to the Foreign Office, President of the A.C. 1911–13.

Davies, Rev. John Llewelyn (1826–1916) A leading social reformer of his time, particularly in education. Davies made the first ascents of the Dom (1858) and the Täschhorn (1862). He was an Original Member of the A.C.

Dawes, John Andrew George (b.1964) A leading British rock climber and noted setter of standards for others to try to follow. 1986 was a particularly prolific year with climbs such as Gaia (E8) at Black Rocks and End of the Affair at Curbar, also E8. Another E8 of that year was Quarryman at Twll Mawr, Llanberis, but perhaps the most notable climb was Indian Face (E9,6c) which replaced Jerry Moffatt's Master's Wall of 1983 (E7) on Cloggy. In 1987 Dawes freed The Scoop on Strone Ulladale, Doug Scott's route of 1969. The free grade is E7. The Very Big and The Very Small on Rainbow Slab was done in 1991 and rated E9,7b.

Dawes made the first ascent of the Kame, a 600 m high sea-cliff on Foula, for TV and he has also attempted the EFace of Bhagirathi III in the Himalaya. He has won a number of international awards for his films, including *Stone Monkey*, 1987.

Dead man (snow anchor) A flat alloy plate about six inches square with one edge pointed, and fitted with a wire loop in the centre. Used for belaying in snow. The plate is pushed into the snow at 40° to the surface and a channel cut to take the wire loop, which trails down the slope and to which the climber belays. Some practice is needed in correctly placing dead men, but they are very secure – more so than the traditional axe shaft. There are smaller versions known as 'dead boys'.

Déchy, Maurice de (1851–1917)   A Hungarian mountaineer who made a number of first ascents in the Tyrol, but is best known for his exploration of the Caucasus in the years 1884, 1885, 1886, 1887, 1897, 1898 and 1902. In 1905–7 he published his account of these expeditions in a three-volume work entitled *Kaukasus, Reisen und Forschungen im Kaukasischen Hochgebirge.*

In 1879, with the guide Maurer, he visited Sikkim on what was intended to be a climbing expedition (the first of its kind in the Himalaya) but he was unfortunately taken ill. See *Exploration of the Caucasus*, by D. W. Freshfield.

Dent, Clinton Thomas (1850–1912)   One of the most important of the second generation of Alpine pioneers, Dent was a propagandist for the smaller, harder rock peaks then coming into fashion. In 1870 he began his long association with Alexander ◊ Burgener during which they made the first ascents of Lenzspitze (1870) and Portjengrat (1871), and new routes on Ruinette (1872) and Zinal Rothorn (1872). The partnership culminated with the first ascent of the Dru (1878) after 18 previous attempts by Dent.

He later turned his attention to the Caucasus, which he visited in 1886, 1888, 1889 and 1895. He made the first ascent of Gestola (1886) and Tsiteli (1895) and crossed several new and difficult passes.

Dent was President of the Alpine Club, 1887–9, and head of the committee which produced the Alpine Distress Signal. He was a first-rate photographer and lecturer. His books are *Above the Snowline* and the Badminton Library volume on mountaineering.

In his professional life Dent was an eminent surgeon.

Descendeur   A device made of aluminium alloy and used for belaying and abseiling. There are various types but by far the commonest is the Figure 8, whose name describes its appearance.

Desmaison, René (b. 1930)   Controversial French guide whose new routes include the French Route on Cima Ovest, 1959 and a brilliant series of winter climbs including the N W Face of L'Olan (1960), Central Pillar of Frêney (1967) and the Shroud (1968, with R. Flematti).

In 1966, helped by Mick ◊ Burke, Gary ◊ Hemming and others, Desmaison rescued the German climbers Heinz Ramisch and Hermann Schriddel from the West Face of the Dru, much to the chagrin of the official rescue teams. He was dismissed from the Guides Bureau for this insubordination. In February 1971 he set off with Serge Gousseault to do a new winter route on the Walker Spur of Gd Jorasses. Gousseault died from exposure during a horrific ascent and Desmaison barely survived and had to be rescued. (See R. Desmaison, *Total Alpinism*.)

Destivelle, Catherine (b. 1960)   The modern rock star in every sense!

Born in Oran, Algeria, she later moved with her family to France and she scrambled on the rocks at Fontainebleau (◊ France). At 14 she did her first real climbing on the Saffres rocks near Dijon but was so taken with it that when she was one year older she had climbed at Verdon (◊ France), Freyr and the ◊ Dolomites.

At 16 she made one of the early ascents of La Voie des Enragés at Verdon, a 300 m route that took 20 hours on the first ascent. She climbed it in 7 hours. In 1981 she did the American Direct on the West Face of the ◊ Dru in a similar time. Her climbs in Britain include classics like T. Rex (E3) and Citadel (E5) at ◊ Gogarth.

Kurt Diemberger (left) and Julie Tullis with Walt Unsworth. (*T. Tullis*)

In 1986 she became a full-time professional climber, taking part in competitions, advertising and film making. In June 1991 she made a remarkable solo ascent of a new route on the W Face of the Dru. The ascent took 10 days. She has become a darling of the French media – but still manages to climb 8th grade!

Dibona, Angelo (1879–1956)   A guide from the Dolomites famous for his association with Dr Guido Mayer of Vienna. Climbed the Laliderwand in 1911. In their great 1913 season their new climbs included the Mayer–Dibona Route on the Requin, the Coste-Rouge Ridge of the Ailfroide, and the Aiguille du Pain du Sucre in Dauphiné, later renamed Aig. Dibona.

Dièdre (Fr.) (E.: V-groove)   A large open-book type groove or corner in a crag.

Diemberger, Kurt (b. 1932)   An Austrian mountaineer who is one of the most experienced climbers of the post-war era, with ascents of all the traditional hard Alpine routes such as the Eigerwand etc. It is for his Himalayan exploits, however, that he is best known. He climbed Broad Peak (8,047 m) in 1957 (repeated 1984) and reached 7,150 m on Chogolisa that same year, during which attempt ◊ Buhl was killed. Broad Peak (with M. Schmuck, H. Buhl and F. Wintersteller) was the first 8,000 m peak to be climbed ◊ Alpine fashion – no porters or oxygen.

In 1965 and 1967 Diemberger was in the Hindu Kush and in the latter year he made a new route on the W Face of Tirich Mir (7,706 m) (third ascent) and the first ascent of Tirich Mir West IV (7,338 m) as well as other peaks in the area. He also climbed in Greenland (1966, 1971), Ethiopia (1969) and the Andes (1973).

He has climbed five other 8,000 m peaks: in 1960 he made the first ascent of Dhaulagiri, then came ascents of Everest and Makalu (both 1978), Gasherbrum II, 1979 and K2, 1986. He was one of the survivors from the great ◊ K2 tragedy of 1986 when his companion, Julie ◊ Tullis, died.

During this long period of adventuring he became an excellent photographer and film maker, and a popular lecturer both in Britain and on the Continent. His autobiography, *Summits and Secrets* (1971) is regarded as a modern classic.

Dimai family A well-known guiding family from Cortina in the Dolomites. Fulgenzio Dimai (1821–1904) was with Grohmann on the first ascent of Marmolada (1864) and Monte Cristallo (1865). Angelo and Guiseppe Dimai (1903–46) were with ◊ Comici in 1933 on the first ascent of Cima Grande N Face; one of the seminal climbs of the Alps.

Distress signals The International Alpine Distress Signal (commonly used in Britain) consists of six blasts on a whistle (or flashes on a lamp) in a minute, repeated at minute intervals. If no signal equipment is available then any kind of simple signal can be used, for example a red anorak, waved six times. If a flare gun is carried then a red flare indicates distress.

It is immensely comforting to distressed parties to know that their calls have been seen and a reply such as three flashes on the lamp, or a white flare, will suffice. These should not be used in the course of an actual rescue without the team leader's permission in case they confuse the command signals of the rescue party.

In remote country, distress signals are sometimes laid out so that they can be seen by searching aircraft – usually the letters SOS laid out in stones or coloured clothing.

The International Distress Signal was first proposed by a sub-committee of the Alpine Club in 1894 and subsequently universally adopted.

Dolomite rock Magnesium limestone, the peculiar qualities of which give rise to the towers and pinnacles of the Dolomites. The rock (and area) takes its name from a French geologist, Déodat de Gratet, Marquis de Dolomieu (1750–1801), who visited the Dolomites in 1789 and wrote about the strange quality of the rock. The word 'dolomite' seems to have been established by 1802.

Besides the Dolomites themselves, the rock occurs in several parts of the Alps: Vercors, Royannais, Dévoluy (all near Grenoble) and Pizzo Columbe (near the St Gotthard Pass), the peaks culminating in the Alperschellihorn near the Splügen Pass (the 'Splügen Dolomites'), and the three peaks of the Piz d'Ela group in the Albula Alps. As a dolomite peak, the Piz d'Ela is only exceeded in height by the Marmolata. There are also the Brenta Dolomites, which have the closest affinity with the Dolomites proper.

Dolomite rock is found in England at Brassington, Derbyshire, where it has been well developed for climbing, and in the Cresswell Gorge.

Dolphin, Arthur Rhodes (1924–53) A Yorkshire man who began climbing as a schoolboy at Almscliff in 1939. He soon showed considerable flair and made the crag very much his own. Notable first ascents are: Great Western (1943) and Birdlime Traverse (1946).

Dolphin turned his talents to the Lake District and in 1948 made the first ascent of Kipling's Groove (with J. B. Lockwood) – for long regarded as the hardest climb in Langdale. Other notable climbs were Kneewrecker Chimney (1949), Rubicon Groove (1951), Sword of Damocles (1952) and Dunmail Cracks (1952), all in the Langdale area. The finest ascent of all was that of Deer Bield Buttress (1951, with A. D. Brown) – one of the Lake District's outstanding problems.

The 90 metre Dièdre on the W Face of the Dru. (*R. B. Evans*)

In 1952, having completed his guidebook to Langdale, he turned his attention to the E Buttress of Scafell and put up Hell's Groove and Pegasus.

Though he suffered from mountain sickness at greater heights, he made a solo ascent of the Aig. du Géant in 1953 and was killed in the descent.

Donkin, William Frederick (1845–88)   Visited the Caucasus with ◊ Dent in 1886 and made the first ascent of Gestola. Returned in 1888 with Dent and Fox. After Dent's return, Donkin and Fox continued their tour and were killed in attempting Koshtantau, together with the guides Streich and Fischer.

Donkin was unquestionably one of the finest mountain photographers who ever lived; for his day he was quite outstanding. He was rivalled, but not excelled, by Vittorio ◊ Sella. For examples of his work see the A.C. Centenary volume, 1957. The A.C. have a complete collection of his photographs.

Douglas, Lord Francis William Bouverie (1847–65)   Second son of the Marquess of Queensberry, who died in the Matterhorn tragedy (◊ Whymper). Douglas had two previous seasons in the Alps and had shown himself a good climber. In 1865 he made the first ascent of the Trifthorn,

Unter Gabelhorn and Wellenkuppe and the second ascent of the Gabelhorn (the day after Moore's first ascent).

Du Faur, Freda (d. 1935) An Australian woman climber who made a remarkable series of ascents in the ◊ New Zealand Alps. She paid a chance visit to the Hermitage in 1906 and returned three years later when she persuaded Peter ◊ Graham to teach her climbing. She became the first woman to climb the three greatest New Zealand peaks, Cook, Tasman and Sefton but her finest climb was the first traverse of Mt Cook with P. Graham and D. Thompson in 1913 – possibly the hardest route done by a woman anywhere at that time. She stopped climbing immediately after; possibly influenced by criticism of her on moral grounds, for being alone with men in the mountains! There are uncanny parallels between Miss Du Faur and Peter Graham, and Miss ◊ Bristow and Mummery.

She wrote *The Conquest of Mount Cook and Other Climbs* (1915).

Duhamel, Henri (1853–1917) French climber noted for his Alpine topographical work, especially in the Dauphiné, where he made a number of first ascents. The Pyramide Duhamel on the Meije is named after him.

Dülfer, Hans (1893–1915) A brilliant young rock-climber famous for his ascents in the Kaisergebirge and Dolomites and, like Mummery, a legend in his own lifetime. The ◊ layback is known as 'à la Dulfer', and it was he who first proposed the form of gradings later perfected by ◊ Welzenbach. Dülfer was killed at Arras while serving in the Bavarian army. Among his many new climbs two of the best known are: E Face, Fleischbank, 1912 (with W. Schaarschmidt), W Face, Cima Grande, Dolomites, 1913 (with Wa. von Bernuth).

Dunod, François Henri A Captain in the French army who made the second ascents of the Charmoz and Grépon, and whose use of three ladders on the latter provoked a sly comment from Mummery. Dunod also made the first traverse of the Drus (1887).

Duvet Jackets, trousers, waistcoats and socks made of duvet material are available to mountaineers, but the word by itself when used by climbers refers to the duvet jacket. Duvets are basically heavily quilted anoraks which open down the front like a jacket. They form the best practical insulation against extreme cold. Some are waterproof, but they are usually worn with a ◊ cagoule over the top.

Dyhrenfurth, Gunter Oscar (1886–1975) A geologist and leader of international expeditions to Kangchenjunga (1930), and to the Baltoro region (1934). On the former a number of peaks were climbed, notably Jongsong (7,420 m). Dyhrenfurth was awarded the Olympic Gold Medal for mountaineering achievement, 1936. He wrote a number of books.

Dyhrenfurth, Norman (b. 1919) A Swiss–American who took part in the second Swiss attempt on Everest in the post-monsoon period of 1952, and organized the great American expedition of 1963. He also took part in an expedition to Lhotse in 1955. In 1971 he organized the large international expedition to attempt the S W Face of Everest. The expedition received massive publicity but failed amidst considerable acrimony on the part of the participants. Son of G. O. Dyhrenfurth (above).

E

Eccles, James (1838–1915) A fine climber of the second generation of pioneers, responsible for the first ascents of several peaks and cols in the Mont Blanc area, including Cols Infranchissable, de Toule and des Flambeaux (1870), Aig. du Plan (1871), Aig. de Rochefort (1873), Mont Blanc de Courmayeur (1877), Aig. du Tacul (1880) and Dôme de Rochefort (1881).

Eccles always had as guides the Payot brothers and it was with them that he made his most famous expedition, the ascent of the Peuterey Ridge from near the Col Peuterey to Mont Blanc de Courmayeur (1877). They approached via the Brouillard Glacier and camped below what is now Pic Eccles, site of the Eccles bivouac hut. Next day they crossed a col to the upper Freney Glacier (Col Eccles) and so to the ridge. It was a remarkable expedition, long unrepeated, the first to be done on this difficult face of Mont Blanc.

In 1878 Eccles and Michel Payot visited the Rocky Mountains of Colorado and Utah, where they climbed Wind River Peak and Fremont's Peak. Eccles was an outstanding photographer.

Eckenstein, Oscar Johannes Ludwig (1859–1921) Born in London of a German father and English mother. Eckenstein was an Original Member of the Climbers' Club and played a part in the exploration of Lliwedd with J. M. A. ◊ Thomson. His Alpine career seems to have begun in 1886, when he climbed with Lorria. He later made new routes on the Dom and Dent Blanche, neither of great importance.

In 1892 he was with ◊ Conway in the Karakoram but soon left the party after disagreements with his leader. In 1900 he visited Mexico and climbed Popacatapetl with ◊ Crowley. He organized his own expedition to K2 in 1902, making Crowley second-in-command. Despite numerous troubles (◊ Crowley), two members of the team, Guillarmot and Wesseley, reached 6,520 m.

Eckenstein's greatest contribution to climbing was his application of engineering principles to the sport and its equipment. He redesigned ◊ crampons, introduced the short ice axe, established which knots were strongest and above all preached the virtues of balance climbing.

Eckenstein was an individualist and though he had many friends in the climbing world, his revolutionary outlook and his acquaintance with Crowley made him unpopular with the Establishment.

Ecole Nationale de Ski et d'Alpinisme (E.N.S.A.) Founded as a ski school in 1938 at ◊ Chamonix it became the national training centre for guides and ski teachers in 1943. It is housed in a prestigious modern building in Chamonix.

Edelweiss (Leontopodium alpinum) A flower of the Compositae found between 1,700 m and 3,400 m in the Alps and other mountain ranges. It is the badge of the Austrian Alpine Club and regarded as the archetypal Alpine flower – which it isn't.

'It is not a rarity, but so universally common that you may rely on tramping acres of it on almost any Alpine range above the altitude of 5,500 feet; but it is so far from being a typical and representative high-alpine that it never ascends beyond the fine mountain turf of some 7,000 feet, more or less; and it is so far from being difficult of attainment that on every such slope or final valley under the peaks, or ridge between them, one is treading dense flat lawns of it, in places where a dozen prams could race abreast without imperilling themselves, their conductors, or their inmates. Yet every season the misguided go dropping off precipices on which a few stray tufts have seeded down; not knowing that 200 feet higher, in the soft alpine grass, they could be picking basins-full of blossoms in half an hour's gentle and octogenarian stroll before dinner. So the insane legend still continues, fostered by guides who make a practice, in front of the hotels, of seeming to quest Edelweiss along the face of pathless precipices, where eyelash-hold is of the slightest; and sustained by pompous measures of protection in favour of the commonest and most reproductive and most massively colonising of all mountain plants. Still the reverent inquiry is made in hushed tones, 'And have you ever seen the Edelweiss?' Still maidens grow misty-eyed at the thought of it, and after having tramped the Alps from end to end declare that they would die happy if only they could see the Edelweiss; an aspiration which proves their pedestrianism never to have progressed beyond the highroads of the passes, for, had they anywhere there diverged a hundred yards to right or left it would have been hard luck indeed had they not found themselves upon level lawns of their heart's desire. It is necessary, indeed, to repeat, that in almost every range, be it of lime or granite, you have only to get to the open downs about 2,000 feet above your hotel, to find matted wide carpets everywhere of Flannel-flower, sharing the scant and stony herbage with *Aster alpinus* and *Anemone vernalis*. Go higher, into the grim and stony places where the true high-alpines have their home; Flannel-flower has ceased completely, a species belonging exclusively to the levels of stone and fine poor grass at mid elevations on all the ridges of the world.'   R. FARRER, 1918.

The Edelweiss, like many Alpine flowers, is today a protected species and must not be picked.

Edwards, John Menlove (1910–58)   A Liverpool climber noted for daring escapades and for his exploration of Welsh cliffs which earlier climbers had ignored. Edwards's acceptance of 'bad rock' was a significant breakthrough in British climbing and is best represented by his exploration of the Three Cliffs of Llanberis Pass, Dinas Cromlech, Carreg Wastad and Clogwyn y Grochan, now great favourites with climbers. His most popular routes include: Spiral Stairs (1931), Crackstone Rib, Hazel Groove (1935), Brant and Slape (1940).

His exploration of the Devil's Kitchen cliffs (15 new routes) led to his compiling the Cwm Idwal guidebook for the Climbers' Club (1933). In 1937 he compiled (with Noyce) the guidebook to Tryfan, for which they solved the problem of Soapgut (1936), and made the second (first unaided) ascent of Munich Climb. His last guidebook was Lliwedd (1939), for which he made the first ascent of Central Gully Direct (1938).

Other notable climbs include: first unaided ascent of Flake Crack, Scafell (in nails, 1931), Chimney Route, Clogwyn Du'r Arddu (1931), Western Slabs, Dinas Mot (1931), Bow Shaped Slab, Clogwyn Du'r Arddu (1941).

Increasing disappointment over his work as a psychiatrist led to his suicide in 1958. (See *Menlove* by J. Perrin.)

Eiger (3,970 m)   A mountain in the Bernese Alps overlooking ◊ Grindelwald and easily accessible from Kl. Scheidegg. One of the most publicized mountains in the world, owing to the various attempts on its great N Face (actually N W), the Eigerwand.

The mountain has three principal ridges and faces. The W Ridge and Face, in combination, is fairly easy and was used in the first ascent (C. Barrington with C. Almer and P. Bohren, 1858). It descends directly to Kl. Scheidegg. The S Ridge connects with the Mönch via the Eigerjoch, and the S Face (a difficult climb about which little seems known) overlooks the Fieschergletscher. Running NE from the summit is the long Mittelegi Ridge, descended by M. Kuffner with Burgener, Biener and Kalbermatten in 1885 but not climbed until 1921 by Y. Maki with F. Amatter, F. Steuri and S. Brawand. The N Face proper is on the Grindelwald side of this ridge and is separated from the Eigerwand by a rib (the Lauper Route – H. Lauper, A. Zürcher with J. Knubel and A. Graven, 1932). The Eigerwand itself is a vast triangular concave face.

The first serious attempt at the Eigerwand was in 1935 by M. Seldmayer and K. Mehringer, who were killed by a storm at Death Bivouac. In 1936 came the tragedy of E. Rainer, W. Angerer, A. Hinterstoisser and T. Kurz, who died on the face despite dramatic rescue attempts. It was finally climbed by A. Heckmair, W. Vorg, H. Harrer and F. Kasparek in 1938. This is now known as the Original or 1938 Route and has been climbed many times, including solo. Many climbers have also been killed attempting it. Two more direct routes were made by an international party (Harlin Route, 1966) and a Japanese party (1969) and two routes on the N Pillar (Polish Route, 1968, and Scottish Route, 1970). There are at present 9 routes or variants.

The rock of the Eigerwand is limestone and though there are no pitches technically more difficult than V.S., there is always the danger of stonefall. Almost every part of the 1938 Route has a name: well-known features are: the Difficult Crack, Hinterstoisser Traverse, Swallow's Nest, First Icefield, Ice Hose, Second Icefield, Flatiron, Death Bivouac, Third Icefield, The Ramp, the Ice Bulge, Brittle Ledge, Traverse of the Gods, the Spider and the Exit Cracks. These names give some indication of the route and the problems involved. (See *The White Spider*, by H. Harrer, and *Eiger Direct*, by P. Gillman and D. Haston.)

El Capitan (2,305 m)   A peak in the Yosemite, California, which throws down immense walls to the valley and Merced River below. It stands on the true right bank of the river about 3 km below Yosemite village, and thus, in driving up the valley, it is one of the first cliffs to be encountered. Its startling appearance is more than equalled by the climbing on it: 'El Cap' provides the epitome of Yosemite climbing. All the routes mentioned below are hard; they rank with the most difficult rock climbs in the world.

The impressive profile of the cliff, rising sheer for some 900 m, is formed by the Nose, where the S W and S E Faces meet. Beyond the S W Face is the W Buttress and beyond the S E Face a long wall terminating in the E Buttress. The rock is granite: immense smooth walls and difficult cracks, with many overhangs. Pegging and bolting is essential, though there is hard free climbing too. The routes are multi-day (grade VI) and some bivouacs require hammocks. As in all big Yosemite climbs, water shortage (dehydration) is a major problem. The pegs are removed on each ascent, and this has led to bad scarring of the cracks. Nuts are now being used when possible.

In 1952, A. Steck, W. Siri, W. Dunmire and R. Swift climbed up the E Wall to a pine tree some 400 ft above the ground (El Cap Tree Route), but the

The Eigerwand, most famous of the great north faces. (*W. Unsworth*)

first complete ascent of the cliff took place the following year when Steck and Siri, with W. Unsoeld and W. Long climbed E Buttress in three days. The first big frontal attack took place in 1957–8 with Warren Harding's 18-month siege of the Nose, begun because another party had snatched the N W Face of Half Dome, which he had contemplated climbing himself. With various partners, Harding spent a total of 45 days on the rock, employing 900 m of fixed rope, 675 pegs and 125 bolts. In 1960 the ascent was repeated by J. Fitschen, T. Frost, C. Pratt, R. Robbins in a single seven-day push. The Nose has become the most popular of the El Capitan climbs. It was soloed in 1969 by T. Bauman in six days.

Siege tactics were employed on the first ascent of Dihedral Wall in 1962 by E. Cooper, J. Baldwin and G. Denny, and semi-siege tactics on a few other routes, but generally Royal Robbins's view that siege tactics are unethical has prevailed.

The first breach of the S E Face was North America Wall, climbed in 1964 by Y. Chouinard, T. Frost, R. Robbins and C. Pratt in ten days. Not repeated for four years, it was regarded at the time as a breakthrough in climbing, but has since received less acclaim. More controversial was the ascent by Warren Harding and Dean Caldwell of the Wall of Early Morning Light (Dawn Wall) in 1970 which took 27 days and 300 bolts. It is the longest (time) of any rock-climb in the world. Repeated by Robbins and D. Lauria in 1971 in six days, and soloed by C. Porter (with a variant start) in 1972 in ten days.

The first solo first ascent was of Cosmos by J. Dunn in 1972. The first foreign ascent of any route was the Nose, by two French climbers, J. DuPont and A. Gauci, 1966. The first British ascent was the Nose, by M. Burke, R. Wood, 1968. First woman's ascent was the Nose, by Joanna Marte, 1971, led by Robbins.

Important first ascents:
(W = S W Face or W Buttress; E = S E Face or E Buttress; d = days taken)

1953	E Buttress (E) (3d) – A. Steck, W. Siri, W. Unsoeld, W. Long
1958	The Nose (45d) – W. Harding, W. Merry, G. Whitmore
1961	Salathé Wall (W) (9d) – T. Frost, R. Robbins, C. Pratt
1962	Dihedral Wall (W) (40d) – E. Cooper, J. Baldwin, G. Denny
1963	W Buttress (W) (8d) – L. Kor, S. Roper
1964	North America Wall (E) (10d) – Y. Chouinard, T. Frost, R. Robbins, C. Pratt
1965	Muir Wall (W) (8d) – Y. Chouinard, T. M. Herbert
1967	W Face (W) (5d) – R. Robbins, T. M. Herbert
1970	Heart Route (W) (9d) – S. Davis, C. Kroger
	Wall of Early Morning Light (E) (27d) – W. Harding, D. Caldwell
1971	Aquarius (W) (3d) – K. Schmitz, J. Bridwell
	Son of Heart (W) (10d) – R. Sylvester, C. Wreford-Brown
1972	Magic Mushroom (W) (8d) – H. Burton, S. Sutton
	Cosmos (W) (9d) – J. Dunn (solo)
	The Shield (7d) – C. Porter, G. Bocarde
	Zodiac (E) (7d) – C. Porter (solo)
	New start to W E M L – C. Porter (solo)

GUIDEBOOK Roper, *Climbers' Guide to Yosemite Valley*

Eliminate   A name sometimes given to a direct line up a crag and always of a high standard. The three eliminates of Dow Crag, Lake District, are well known: Eliminate A, Eliminate B and Eliminate C, up A Buttress, B Buttress

El Capitan (*D. Scott*)

and C Buttress respectively. With the modern high standards of climbing, the term is somewhat archaic.

Ellingwood, Albert R. (1888–1934)   A pioneer of Colorado climbing in the early part of the century. He was a professor of Political Science at Colorado College and had been a Rhodes Scholar at Oxford where he had learnt to climb rocks in the Lake District (1910). He introduced the rudimentary belaying of the period to the U.S.A.

With Miss E. S. Davis he climbed Crestone Needle (4,327 m) and Crestone Peak (4,356 m) in 1916; the last of the Colorado ◊ Fourteeners to be climbed. In 1925 they returned to the Needle with S. Hart and M. Warner and climbed a 600 m prow on the N E side, the Ellingwood Ledges (5.7) usually called the Ellingwood Arête. It is regarded today as one of America's classic routes.

In 1920, with J. B. Hoag, Ellingwood climbed the S E Face of Pigeon Peak (4,255 m) and the Lizard Head (3,997 m) still regarded as the most difficult summit in Colorado.

Ellingwood climbed in various parts of the Rockies. In the Tetons, for example, with Miss Davis he made the first ascents of South and Middle Tetons and the fourth of Grand Teton. (All 1923. Miss Davis was the first woman to climb Gd Teton.)

Ellingwood was one of the first to complete all the ◊ Fourteeners.

Elliott, Julius Marshall (1841–69)   The Rev. J. M. Elliott was the first man to climb the Matterhorn from Zermatt after the accident of 1865 (1868). His guides were J. M. Lochmatter and P. Knubel. ◊ Tyndall traversed the mountain next day.

In the Lake District, Elliott took part in the first ascent of the Slab and Notch Route on Pillar (1863) and made one of the earliest 'record' fell-walks,

Nick Estcourt (*centre*) with Peter Boardman (*left*) and Paul Braithwaite. (*W. Unsworth*)

the Head of Wasdale, in eight and a half hours (1864).

Elliott was killed while climbing the Schreckhorn unroped.

Engelhörner   A small range of sharply pointed limestone peaks rising above the hamlet of Rosenlaui in the Bernese Oberland. The nearest town is Meiringen. The Engelhörner peaks are much favoured by rock-climbers. The highest summit is Gross Gstellihorn (2,854 m) but the favourite area is the Semilistock–Kingspitze area. Most climbs are medium to hard in grade. The Engelhörner Hut serves the group.

Guidebook: *Engelhörner and Salbitschijen*, by J. Talbot.

Estcourt, Nicholas John (1942–78)   A computer programmer from Cheshire. Estcourt made a number of fine Alpine climbs, including the first British ascent of the Gervasutti Pillar, Mont Blanc de Tacul (1967), and the first ascent of the N W Face of the Pic Sans Nom (1967). In 1971, with Bonington, he made the first ascent of the White Wizard, on Scafell.

Estcourt's first expedition was to East Greenland in 1963, where he made eight first ascents. He took part in the 1970 Annapurna S Face Expedition and the 1972 Everest S W Face Expedition. In 1973, with Bonington, he reached the summit of Brammah Peak (Kishtwar Himal).

As a member of the successful Everest S W Face expedition of 1975 he partnered Braithwaite on the first ascent of the formidable Rock Band – the key to the climb.

Estcourt was killed by an avalanche while attempting K2.

Ethics of climbing   Because climbing is a sport which has no rules or laws laid down by a governing body (indeed, has no governing body), the *way* in which an ascent is made is left entirely to the climber. To take extreme cases, there is nothing to stop a man bolting his way to the top of Napes Needle and using every protective device known to science, or, on the other hand, attempting Everest naked in winter. In neither case would he get far, of course – in the first instance he would probably be lynched by irate climbers and in the second he would die of exposure. Between these extremes, the right tactics become less certain, and the discussion of these is called the ethics of climbing.

Ethics have concerned climbers since the early days of the sport – take the examples of ◊ Dunod's ladders on the Grépon and the hacking of ◊ Collie's step on Scafell – but they have become more serious since the introduction of modern equipment, particularly the peg, the bolt and the chock. When should these be used for aid, and when merely for protection? Until the 1950s it was generally believed in Britain that no aid should be used at all; if the climb was too difficult for one climber, it should be left until a better man came along. But this policy would deny such climbs as the Kilnsey overhang. Anyway, is not the ancient craft of cutting steps in ice making aids? The trend among the best climbers is to *reduce* the aid used on a route, whether it be bolts or step-cutting.

Another major field of ethics is the employment of ◊ siege tactics. Some of these have aroused great controversy, for instance, ◊ Hardings' ascent of the Nose on El Capitan, Yosemite, and ◊ Maestri's ascent of Cerro Torre.

There is also the question of what constitutes a genuine winter ascent of a route; obviously there are winters when, apart from it being colder, a route may be no different from what it is in summer. Is it a winter ascent, with all that that implies?

It says much for the quality of the sport that despite the many problems and paradoxes, a highly ethical attitude is taken by the vast majority of climbers.

Ethiopia, climbing in   There are nine major ranges in Ethiopia, some like the Batu, with summits over 4,000 m and scarcely known. The highest mountain is Ras Dashan (Dejen) (4,620 m), first ascended by Ferret and Galinier in 1841. The peak stands in the Simien Range near Gondar. There are a number of others over 4,500 m but they are mostly easy to climb, with the exception of some notable pinnacles. Travel is difficult and it is doubtful whether any real climbing has been done.

Étriers (Fr.) (G.: Steigleiter; It.: staffa; Am.: stirrups, tapes)   Small portable steps used in ◊ aid climbing. The two main types are metal étriers and webbing étriers.

Metal étriers have alloy steps about 15 cm long by 3 cm wide, drilled and eyeleted near each end to take 5 mm perlon rope. The étrier will have two or three such steps (individual preference), rarely more. The steps are about 50 cm apart, held in place by a knot *below* the step (it is essential that the step can slide *up* the étrier when needed). There is a loop above the top step for attaching the étrier to a karabiner or ◊ fifi hook and below the bottom step because it is useful to be able to connect one étrier to another, by karabiner. Climbers usually buy the steps and make up their own étriers to suit themselves – a two-step étrier needs about 3 m of rope.

Tape or webbing étriers are simply long lengths of nylon tape, 1½ inches or 2 inches wide, tied off into loops with a tape knot (◊ Knots). The loops are then divided off into steps by overhand knots, with a small loop at the top for the karabiner. Alternatively, they can be purchased ready-made with the steps stitched in place. The advantages of tape étriers are that they do not tangle, are lighter and more comfortable. Their chief disadvantage is that they can be difficult to get one's feet into.

Europe, highest summits in   In 1990 K. Falconer compiled a list of the highest summits in each country in Europe for *Strider Magazine*. Monaco and the Vatican are omitted; Norway, Spitzbergen and Romania each have two contenders. As in more distant regions, spellings and heights vary according to source, so the following is a consensus.

Country	Highest point	Range or region	m	ft
Albania	Korab	Sari Mts	2,751	9,025
Andorra	Pic de Coma Pedrosa	Pyrenees	2,942	9,652
Austria	Grossglockner	Hohe Tauern	3,797	12,457
Belgium	Botrange	Ardennes	694	2,277
Bulgaria	Musala	Rila Mts	2,925	9,596
Cyprus	Mt Olympus	Troodos	1,952	6,404
Czechoslovakia	Gerlach	Tatra Mts	2,655	8,711
Denmark	Yding Skovhoj	10m N of Horsens	173	568
Faroe Islands	Slaettaratindur	Eysturoy Island	882	2,894
Greenland	Gunnbjorns Fjeld	King Christian IX Land	3,700	12,140
Eire	Carrantuohil	Macgillycuddy Reeks	1,041	3,414
Finland	Haltiatunturi	NW Finland	1,324	4,344
France (mainland)	Mt Blanc	Graian Alps	4,807	15,770
Corsica	Cinto	NW Corsica	2,710	8,890
Germany	Zugspitze	Bavarian Alps	2,962	9,718
Gibraltar	The Rock		426	1,398
Greece	Mytikas, Mt Olympus	NE Greece	2,918	9,573
Crete	Melambes	Idhi Oras	2,456	8,058
Hungary	Kekes	Matra Hills	1,015	3,330
Iceland	Hvannadalshnukur	Oraefajokull	2,119	6,952
Italy (mainland)	Mt Blanc de Courmayeur	Graian Alps	4,748	15,577
Elba	Mt Capanne	W Elba	1,019	3,343
Sardinia	Marmora	Mt de Gennargentu	1,834	6,017
Sicily	Mt Etna	E Sicily	3,323	10,902
Liechtenstein	Grauspitze	Rhaetian Alps	2,599	8,527
Luxembourg	Bourgplatz	Ardennes	559	1,834
Malta	Point 3 m S of Rabat		253	830
Netherlands	Vaalserberg	SE Holland	321	1,053
Norway (mainland)	Galdhopiggen	Jotunheimen	2,469	8,100
	Glittertind	Jotunheimen	2,470	8,103
Spitzbergen	Newtontoppen	West Spitzbergen	1,717	5,633
	Perriertoppen	West Spitzbergen	1,717	5,633
Poland	Rysy	Tatra Mts	2,499	8,199
Portugal (mainland)	Malhao da Estrela	Sierra da Estrela	1,991	6,532
Azores	Volcan Pico	Isla Pico	2,351	7,713
Madeira	Puco Ruivo		1,861	6,106

Country	Highest point	Range or region	m	ft
Romania	Negoiul	Transylvanian Alps	2,548	8,359
	Moldoveanu	Transylvanian Alps	2,543	8,343
San Marino	Mt Titano	Apennines	739	2,425
Spain (mainland)	Mulhacen	Sierra Nevada	3,481	11,420
Balearic Islands	Mayor	Majorca	1,445	4,739
Canary Islands	Mt Teide	Tenerife Island	3,716	12,190
Sweden	Kebnekaise	Lapland	2,123	6,965
Switzerland	Monte Rosa Dufourspitze	Pennine Alps	4,634	15,203
Turkey (European)	Mahya	Istranca Mts	1,018	3,340
United Kingdom				
England	Scafell Pike	Lake District	978	3,210
Northern Ireland	Slieve Donard	Mourne Mts	852	2,796
Scotland	Ben Nevis	Lochaber	1,344	4,406
Wales	Snowdon	Snowdonia	1,085	3,560
U.S.S.R. (former)				
Armenia	Mt Aragats	W Armenia	4,095	13,435
Azerbaijan	Bazar-Dyuzi	Caucasus Mts	4,480	14,698
Byelorussia	Dzerzinskaja	Byelorussian Hills	346	1,135
Estonia	Munamagi	Haanja (SE Estonia)	318	1,043
Georgia	Mt Shkhara	Caucasus Mts	5,203	17,070
Latvia	Gaizinakaln	70 m E of Riga	312	1,024
Lithuania	Point 25 m SE Vilnius		293	961
Moldavia	Kodry Hills	50 m W of Kisinev	429	1,407
Russia (European)	Elbrus	Caucasus Mts	5,633	18,480
Ukraine	Mt Goveria	Carpathian Mts	2,061	6,762
Yugoslavia (former)	Triglav	Julian Alps	2,863	9,393

Evans, Sir Robert Charles (b. 1918)   Charles Evans was one of a small group of promising climbers in the immediate post-war years that Tilman was persuaded to take on his Nepal journey of 1950. They attempted Annapurna IV (7,525 m), and Evans, in the first assault, reached a height of about 7,300 m. In 1951 he was in the party which attempted Deo Tibba in Kulu, and in 1952 was with Shipton on Cho Oyu. In 1953 he was Deputy Leader of the successful Everest expedition, and was with Hillary and others in an expedition to the Barun Glacier the following year. In 1955 he was leader of the successful Kangchenjunga expedition.

President of the Alpine Club, 1967–70.

His books are *Eye on Everest* (1955), *On Climbing* (1956) and *Kangchenjunga – The Untrodden Peak* (1956).

Expedition   A journey to attempt some specific objective such as climbing a mountain or surveying a mountain area. The word is used also to refer to the corpus of people involved. In early climbing literature the word was used to describe almost any journey above the snowline, but nowadays it is reserved for journeys to remote areas. Even so, the definition is blurred and vague: with increasing ease of transport it frequently happens today that two or three friends visit some remote area for a climbing holiday, and may even ascend a new peak. Is such a journey an expedition in the modern accepted sense?

Expeditions take a name for themselves usually descriptive of their aims or composition, for example the British–Pakistani Karakoram Expedition. There is a Leader and, usually, Deputy Leader. On a small expedition the rest are known simply as members, though each will have some job allotted to him besides climbing. On large expeditions these jobs usually carry titles – Transport Officer, etc. On a large expedition the Leader may or may not take an actual part in the climbing. Sometimes Himalayan expeditions make the senior Sherpas full members of the expedition, for example, ◊ Tenzing on Everest. The actual number of members can vary – on a very large expedition it can run to dozens, though many will be specialists, and include surveyors, botanists and so on.

The number of people involved depends largely on the objective, though there are divergent philosophies about even large objectives. The vast expeditions such as those of Conway, the Duke of the Abruzzi, and the earlier Everest expeditions, have been challenged in concept by climbers like ◊ Tilman. Both large and small expeditions have an equal record of success and failure.

The organization of an expedition, especially a large one, takes time and money. Sponsorship is necessary, from the media and other sources. In Britain, financial aid may be granted by the ◊ Mount Everest Foundation.

Details showing the organization of a modern expedition can be read in the appendices to Bonington's books: *Annapurna South Face*, and *Everest South-West Face*.

Exposure   1. An exposed climb is one where a sense of space predominates: the 'fly on the wall' syndrome. It is compounded from the steepness and sheerness of the rock and the height above ground level. Difficulty does not enter into it, though the more difficult climbs tend also to be the more exposed climbs. Similarly, one can speak of 'an exposed move'.

2. Hypothermia. A common but serious condition brought on by a loss of deep body heat due to excessive chilling of the skin. Usually caused by bad weather: wind, rain, snowstorms, especially when associated with hard physical effort which itself leads to exhaustion. The symptoms are: unreasonableness, tiredness and coldness, lethargy, failure of vision, slurred speech, excessive shivering, collapsing. Severe cases can lead to death. The treatment is to protect the victim *immediately* from further effort and to insulate the whole body with a sleeping bag to prevent further heat loss. Hot glucose drinks help, but not alcohol. The mountain rescue service should be called out and the victim examined by a doctor as soon as possible.

F

Fall factor   The amount of energy which a given climbing rope can absorb depends upon its active length – the longer the length between the falling climber and the belay, the more energy can be absorbed. Thus, as far as the rope is concerned, it is the ratio of height of fall to length of rope which matters. This is known as the fall factor.

$$\text{Fall factor} = \frac{\text{height of fall}}{\text{length of available rope}}$$

In a 'clean' fall of a leader from above this factor will be 2. A factor of 2 gives a force in excess of 1,000 kgf which puts a heavy strain on the climber, second and belay. This is reduced by rope slip (◊ belay) and by ◊ runners.

Farmer, Sir John Bretland (1867–1944)   One of the pioneers of Lliwedd in Wales, along with Andrews, Eckenstein, Thomson, etc. His best known climb is probably Central Chimney (1908). He was a distinguished botanist.

Farrar, John Percy (1857–1929)   Farrar was one of the strongest climbers in the Alps at the turn of the century. Though his first ascents were minor he completed almost every difficult climb known, often making the second or third ascent. He also climbed in S. Africa, Canada and Japan. He was President of the A.C. 1917–19. Farrar is little heard of today, but his record is outstanding, and during his lifetime he was rightly regarded as one of the greatest living alpinists. He was elected an honorary member of almost every national Alpine club.

Fawcett, Ron (b. 1955)   Born in Embsay in the Yorkshire Dales with gritstone and limestone crags to hand from the earliest times, Fawcett began climbing when he was 14 and is reputed to have done several VS routes on his way to school in the mornings! Very tall, wiry and with a reputation for making rapid ascents in fine style, he was probably the leading British rock-climber of the seventies and eighties, following on from ◊ Livesey.
   His initial first ascent was Mulatto Wall at Malham (E3), made when he was 15 and had been climbing just over a year. He and Livesey dominated Malham in the seventies and in 1975 they virtually freed the formidable Cave Route at Gordale Scar; previously a hard peg climb. In Derbyshire Fawcett's routes include Cream Team Special (1976) and especially, perhaps, Tequila Mocking Bird on Chee Tor (E6 6b) and The Prow, Raven's Tor (E6 6b), both done in 1982. In Wales his routes include The Big Sleep, Atomic Hot Rod and Strawberries – all E6.

Fay, Charles Ernest (1846–1931)   Though he did not begin mountaineering until he was 50 years old, Fay was one of the pioneers of Canadian and American climbing. Between 1895 and 1903 he made 12 first ascents in the Canadian Rockies. It was he who persuaded the Appalachian Club to visit the Rockies and thus spread the idea of greater mountaineering in the U.S.A. He helped to found the American Alpine Club and was its first president.

Ron Fawcett (*J. Beatty*)

Mick Fowler (*M. Fowler*)

Fellenberg, Edmund von (1838–1902) A distinguished archaeologist and mineralogist from Berne. With the exception of a visit to the Tatra in 1860, his climbing was confined to the Bernese Alps, which he visited for geological purposes. His first ascents include: Doldenhorn and Klein Doldenhorn (1862), Silberhorn (1863), Ochs (1864), Lauterbrunnen Breithorn, Gross Grünhorn (1865), Wellhorn (1866), Bietschhorn traverse (1867) and Birghorn (1872). He also made many second and third ascents of famous peaks and crossed many cols.

A member of the A.C. and an Original Member of the S.A.C., of which he was the first secretary.

Fiechtl, Hans (1883–1925) An Austrian guide who was one of the finest rock-climbers of his generation and companion of ◊ Dulfer and ◊ Herzog. In 1913 with Herzog he climbed the Schusselkarspitze South Face, today GrV but then one of the hardest rock climbs of the day. In 1923 with Weinberger he climbed the West Face of Predigstuhl and later in the same year the North Face of Seekarlspitze with E. Schmid; Ypsilon Riss, GrVI/A1, another route of outstanding difficulty.

Fiechtl died as the result of a fall sustained whilst guiding on the Totenkirchl Nord Wandsockel.

Field, Alfred Ernest (1864–1949) Pioneer rock-climber who made the first ascents of Walker's Gully, Pillar Rock with Jones and G. D. Abraham (1898) and Route II, Lliwedd with Abraham and Nettleton (1905). He made a number of good Alpine climbs, including the first traverse of the Sans Nom Ridge to the Verte (1902).

Fifi hook A metal hook fitted to the top of an ◊ étrier so that the latter can be clipped directly into a peg. The fifi has a thin cord attaching it to the climber's harness so that as he steps up, the étrier below him is automatically pulled up too. It makes peg climbing much quicker and also eliminates the chance of dropping an étrier. A griff fifi incorporates a handle and is easier to use.

Filippi, Filippo de (1869–1938)   A surgeon and noted mountaineer who joined the Duke of the ◊ Abruzzi's expedition to Alaska in 1897 and to the Karakoram in 1909. In 1913–14 he conducted his own scientific expedition to the Karakoram: one of the most detailed and painstaking ever carried out. He wrote detailed books about the Duke's expeditions and his own.

Finch, George Ingle (1888–1970)   A climber noted for his icemanship and his advocacy of oxygen equipment for high altitudes.

His notable Alpine routes were: N Face of Castor (1909), S S W Ridge of the Midi (1911), W Ridge of the Bifertenstock (1913), N Face of the Dent d'Hérens (1923). He was chosen for the Everest Expedition of 1921, but failed on medical grounds. He was a member of the 1922 team and made a valiant attempt on the summit with G. Bruce, reaching a record height for the time of 8,300 m. He used primitive oxygen apparatus and was always expounding the advantages it gave him. Critical of the route chosen on Everest, his relationship with the Everest Committee became strained and he took no further part in expeditions.

His active climbing career virtually ended after 1931 when he was involved in an accident on the Jungfrau in which one of his partners was killed. His book, *The Making of a Mountaineer*, was published in 1924. He was President of the A.C. 1959–61.

In private life, Finch was a distinguished scientist.

Firmin, Arthur Herbert (1912–55)   Kenyan mountaineer and photographer of distinction. Firmin made ten expeditions each to Mt Kenya and Kilimanjaro and three to Ruwenzori. Notable ascents include first ascent of the N Face of Batian (1944), first ascent of S Face and S W Ridge of Batian (1946), first descent of the N Face of Batian (1948) and first ascent of the W Face of Nelion (1949). His wife was the first woman to reach the main summit of Mt Kenya and of Alexandra Peak, Ruwenzori. As a professional photographer, Firmin's work was known throughout the world.

First aid   Because of the remoteness of their environment it is essential that climbers should have a good working knowledge of first aid, and the equipment to apply it. They may be required to treat: simple cuts and sprains or other minor illnesses; more serious injuries due to an accident; exposure; frostbite. In certain areas other special hazards may need to be taken into account, snakebites for example. An ability to recognize the seriousness of an injury and its nature is perhaps even more vital than the treatment, especially if rescue is fairly simple.

The steps involved are more complicated than in normal conditions: it may be difficult to reach the patient and the patient may need to be secured against further injury, either by belaying him to the cliff or removing him from a dangerous area, perhaps away from a possible stonefall.

Each climber should carry a small personal first-aid pack to deal with simple emergencies (of all kinds). A typical kit contains Elastoplast strips, wound dressing, burn dressing, triangular bandages, aspirin, insect repellant, poly bag, toilet paper, matches and emergency food. In addition, each party should carry between them extra items such as inflatable splints, flares, small stove and pan, emergency sleeping bag. In both cases, the items will vary according to the conditions and what is being attempted; the time of year, weather, and the difficulties of retreat/rescue should be taken into account.

A comprehensive account of treatments is given in *First Aid*, the official manual of the British Red Cross Society, St John Ambulance Brigade and St Andrew's Ambulance Association. See also *First Aid for Hill Walkers* by Hulse and Renouf. (✧ Accidents; Mountain rescue; Exposure; Frostbite.)

First ascents   The recognized ultimate in achievement on any mountain or climb, and the chief goal of many climbers. Any first ascent counts in this respect, though obviously the harder the climb the greater the achievement. First ascents are usually recorded in the appropriate journal for the district involved, and ultimately in the guidebooks. Failure to report first ascents invariably leads to later confusion and inaccuracy: climbing history is littered with claims and counter-claims. The phrase 'first known ascent' is sometimes used to denote that a climb is suspected of having a previous ascent. There are many instances where first ascents are known to have taken place but where details are lacking.

The historical details of a first ascent usually include the full names of the participants, the exact date of ascent, aid used and, in the case of long climbs (e.g. the Alps), the time taken. A convention is generally employed in guidebooks when noting the names of participants:

A. Smith and B. Jones – means that Smith led the climb
A. Smith and B. Jones (alt. leads) – means that the leading was shared
A. Smith and B. Jones with C. Kaufmann and K. Schmidt – means that Kaufmann and Schmidt were professional guides, Kaufmann being senior
A. Smith and B. Jones, C. Kaufmann and K. Schmidt – means that two ascents were made simultaneously
A. Smith (solo) – means that Smith climbed it alone

The honours attached to a first ascent can be extended considerably, particularly to hard climbs or difficult peaks. The following is a list of ascents usually considered noteworthy:

first ascent of a peak
first traverse of a peak
first ascents of alternate routes
first unaided ascent of pegged routes
first solo ascent
first woman's ascent
first winter ascents of the foregoing
first ascent on skis (or descent in certain cases)
first national ascent (e.g. first British ascent)
first unguided ascent (obsolete)

Fitzgerald, Edward A. (1871–1932)   Perhaps the greatest dilettante of the mountain world. A wealthy man who accompanied Conway (intermittently) on the 'Alps from end to end tour' (✧ Conway) and who, in the same year (1894) visited New Zealand with the objective of climbing Mt Cook, at that time unclimbed. He was beaten to it by local climbers (✧ New Zealand). Nevertheless he and his guide Zurbriggen made several important ascents.

He led a large and expensively equipped expedition to the Andes in 1897 and attempted ✧ Aconcagua. He failed 1,500 ft from the summit, but his guide, Zurbriggen, continued to the top (first ascent). The expedition climbed several other peaks.

On his return, he gave up mountaineering. There was a certain cool rivalry between Fitzgerald and Conway, exemplified in the latter's writings.

Fitzgerald wrote *Climbs in the New Zealand Alps* (1896) and *The Highest Andes* (1899).

Fitzgerald, Gerald (1849–1925) Irish barrister who made the first ascent of Täschhorn from the Domjoch (1878) and of Aig. de Talèfre (1879). He later climbed extensively with ◊ Davidson.

Fixed ropes Are of two kinds: (1) permanent ropes, chains or hawsers fixed to the popular routes of some Alpine peaks, and (2) ropes fixed by climbers during the course of an expedition lasting several weeks, enabling them to pass up and down the mountain quickly.

Fixed ropes appear on a number of peaks in the Eastern Alps but are relatively rare in the Western Alps. The best known examples are probably those on the Hörnli and Italian ridges of the Matterhorn and on the Aig. du Géant in the Mont Blanc range. They make easier what would otherwise be fairly difficult pitches and were originally instituted to help guides get their clients to the summit. Though deprecated by modern climbers there seems little chance that the well-known fixed rope pitches will ever disappear from the climbing scene. There are also fixed ropes of a handrail nature on some of the more hazardous Alpine paths (◊ Via Ferrata).

In the Himalaya fixed ropes are placed between the various camps where necessary to enable porters and climbers to move freely up and down the mountain. On modern Himalayan face climbs this may involve long prusiking pitches using ◊ jumars, but it does enable climbers to retreat to Base Camp for rest periods. The same technique has been used occasionally on hard winter Alpine routes, for example, the Eiger Direct, Harlin Route.

Fixed ropes of all types have been known to break and have been the cause of several notorious accidents.

For fixed rope technique on expeditions see *Eiger Direct*, by D. Haston and P. Gillman, and *Annapurna South Face*, by C. Bonington.

Flake A leaf of rock adhering to a crag. There is an immense one on Scafell Crag giving rise to the famous Flake Crack. Small flakes give rise to 'flake holds' – sometimes brittle.

Foster, George Edward (1839/40–1906) Foster's career is interesting because he made the first ascent of two peaks which subsequently became popular among discerning alpinists: Mont Collon (1866) and Gspaltenhorn (1869). He is also credited with Mont Pleureur and La Singla, but there is serious doubt about the latter. Foster's greatest achievements, however, were in the new routes he put up on established peaks – Midi, Strahlhorn, Dom etc. – thus helping to point the way for future generations. In some respects his career has been seriously overlooked by historians.

In private life Foster was a wealthy banker from Cambridge.

Fourteeners The 54 mountain tops of 14,000 ft (4,267 m) or more in the state of Colorado, U.S.A. Shapely, but mostly easy to climb and several people have climbed them all.

Mountain	Altitude	Range
Mount Elbert	14,431 (4,399 m)	Sawatch
Mount Harvard	14,420 (4,395 m)	Sawatch

Mountain	Altitude	Range
Mount Massive	14,418 (4,394 m)	Sawatch
La Plata Peak	14,340 (4,370 m)	Sawatch
Blanca Peak	14,317 (4,364 m)	Sangre de Cristo
Uncompahgre Peak	14,301 (4,359 m)	San Juan
Crestone Peak	14,291 (4,356 m)	Sangre de Cristo
Mount Lincoln	14,284 (4,354 m)	Mosquito
Grays Peak	14,270 (4,349 m)	Front
Antero Peak	14,269 (4,349 m)	Sawatch
Torreys Peak	14,267 (4,349 m)	Front
Mount Evans	14,264 (4,348 m)	Front
Castle Peak	14,259 (4,346 m)	Elk
Longs Peak	14,256 (4,345 m)	Front
Quandary Peak	14,252 (4,344 m)	Tenmile
Mount Wilson	14,246 (4,342 m)	San Miguel
Shavano Peak	14,229 (4,337 m)	Sawatch
Mount Princeton	14,197 (4,327 m)	Sawatch
Mount Belford	14,197 (4,327 m)	Sawatch
Mount Yale	14,194 (4,326 m)	Sawatch
Crestone Needle	14,191 (4,325 m)	Sangre de Cristo
Mount Bross	14,169 (4,319 m)	Mosquito
El Diente	14,159 (4,316 m)	San Miguel
South Maroon Peak	14,158 (4,315 m)	Elk
Tabeguache Mountain	14,155 (4,314 m)	Sawatch
Mount Oxford	14,153 (4,314 m)	Sawatch
Mount Sneffels	14,150 (4,313 m)	San Juan
Mount Democrat	14,142 (4,310 m)	Mosquito
Capitol Peak	14,137 (4,309 m)	Elk
Mount Lindsey	14,125 (4,305 m)	Sangre de Cristo
Pikes Peak	14,110 (4,301 m)	Front
Kit Carson Peak	14,100 (4,298 m)	Sangre de Cristo
Windom Mountain	14,091 (4,295 m)	Needle
Mount Eolus	14,086 (4,293 m)	Needle
Snowmass Mountain	14,077 (4,291 m)	Elk
Columbia Peak	14,073 (4,289 m)	Sawatch
Culebra Peak	14,069 (4,288 m)	Culebra
Missouri Mountain	14,067 (4,288 m)	Sawatch
Sunlight Peak	14,060 (4,285 m)	Needle
Mount Bierstadt	14,060 (4,285 m)	Front
Redcloud Peak	14,050 (4,282 m)	San Juan
Handies Peak	14,049 (4,282 m)	San Juan
Humboldt Peak	14,044 (4,281 m)	Sangre de Cristo
Little Bear	14,040 (4,279 m)	Sangre de Cristo
Mount Sherman	14,037 (4,278 m)	Mosquito
Stewart Peak	14,032 (4,277 m)	San Juan
Sunshine Peak	14,018 (4,273 m)	San Juan
Wilson Peak	14,017 (4,272 m)	San Miguel
Wetterhorn Peak	14,017 (4,272 m)	San Juan
San Luis Peak	14,014 (4,271 m)	San Juan
Huron Peak	14,005 (4,269 m)	Sawatch
North Maroon Peak	14,000 (4,267 m)	Elk
Pyramid Peak	14,000 (4,267 m)	Elk
Grizzly Mountain	14,000 (4,267 m)	Sawatch

Fowler, Michael (b. 1956) A leading British activist of the last two decades, Mick Fowler has demonstrated a rare breadth of vision combined with high technical skill. Where his contemporaries such as ◊ Livesey and ◊ Fawcett have taken rock-climbing to high standards Fowler has done this but also pushed it into esoteric fields like climbing on ◊ chalk. His best routes are: Linden, Curbar (1976), Stairway to Heaven, Blaven (1977), Heart of Gold, Gogarth (1978), Shield Direct, Ben Nevis (1979), West Central Gully, Ben Eighe (1987) and Sunday Sport, Beachy Head (1990).

He also explored lesser known areas like the Irish cliffs (series of routes, 1990), Corsica (Bonafacio Stack, 1989) and ◊ Kilimanjaro (Western Gully, 1983).

Throughout the eighties he took part in seven expeditions to the greater ranges where his successes included the S Face of Taulliraju, Peru (1982), W Face of Ushba, Caucasus (1986), N W Pillar of Spantink, Pakistan (1987) and N Face of Ak Su in Russian Turkestan (1990). He also climbed the remote Bieluka in the Russian ◊ Altai (1988).

Many of Fowler's routes seem to combine the essence of technical difficulty with remoteness. He has described them in a series of articles in *Mountain*. In a feature in the *Observer* colour supplement, July 1989, Mick Fowler was voted the Mountaineer's Mountaineer by his peers.

Fowler, Robert (1824–97) Irish barrister who made the first ascent of the popular Aig. du Chardonnet (1865) and the Triftjigrat of the Breithorn (1869).

France, climbing in Outside the main mountain areas of the ◊ Alps and ◊ Pyrenees, there are numerous developed crags scattered throughout the country. The most popular of these are limestone, especially in the south-east of the country, though the sandstone boulders of Fontainebleau have a long history of popularity with Parisian climbers. The great gorges of the Verdon and other crags are now popular throughout the European climbing scene – an irresistible combination of sun and rock!

NORTHERN FRANCE

Fontainebleau Near Paris, is a wooded area with numerous sandstone boulders with routes of every shade marked on them. Habitués are known as 'Bleausards'. There are 30 groups of rocks in all, the main ones being L'Elephant and Bas Cuvier. None exceed 13 m in height.
Le Saussois 24 km south of Auxerre. It is a limestone escarpment overlooking the River Yonne with routes of all grades up to 60 m or so.

There are about a dozen other crags in limestone, granite and conglomerate, but just over the border in Belgium are the great buttresses of Freyr with long-established climbing of all grades. They overlook the Meuse near the town of Dinant. Also near the border at Geneva is the Salève, a mountain in its own right and another long-established rock-climbing area.

SOUTHERN FRANCE

This is sun-rock country and there are about 30 crags from which to choose – including some of the most important in world climbing. Pre-eminent is:
Verdon A deep, spectacular gorge near Castellane. The centre for climbing is the hamlet of La Palud. Some of the limestone routes here are well over 300 m but most are half that. All are spectacular and hard.

Other popular places include Buoux, St Victoire, the sea cliffs of the

Calanques near Marseilles and the mountainous rocks of the Vercors.
GUIDEBOOKS Birkett, *French Rock*.
Newcombe, *Rock Climbs in the Verdon*.

Free climbing   As opposed to aid climbing. In Britain a climb is 'free' when
it is climbed without artificial aids such as ◊ pegs and ◊ étriers, though
chockstone runners are allowed. A few climbs (very few) allow for an aided
move such as lassoing a pinnacle or pulling on a jammed chock runner, but
these are always mentioned in the guidebooks. The majority of climbs in
Britain are free. On the Continent a free climb is one which does not involve
étriers.

Freshfield, William Douglas (1845–1934)   One of the greatest of all
mountain explorers, Freshfield travelled and climbed in almost every part of
the world, from the Alps to Japan, from the Pyrenees to the Himalaya. He is
particularly noted for his exploration of the Caucasus (1868, 1887, 1889), and
for his tour round Kangchenjunga (1899). He was President of the A.C.
1893–5, and of the Royal Geographical Society 1914–17, and recipient of
many honours from Alpine and geographical societies throughout the world.

His mother had been a keen mountain traveller and Freshfield as a boy
accompanied her on some of these journeys, which she described in two
books: *Alpine Byways* (1861) and *A Summer Tour in the Grisons and Italian
Valleys of the Bernina* (1862).

His first major ascent was Mont Blanc in 1863. Thereafter he climbed
regularly until 1920 – a career of almost 60 years, spanning every stage in the
development of climbing, except the most recent. His companions included
almost every great mountaineer of the times.

Freshfield's first ascents in the Alps were mostly in the east and included
Presanella, Grosser Mösele, Piz Cengalo, Cima di Brenta and the first
traverse of Piz Palu. In the west he made the first ascent of Tour Ronde and
Tour du Grand St Pierre.

His visit to the Caucasus in 1868 was the first exploration of that region. He
climbed Kasbek and Elbruz (East Peak). In 1887 he climbed Gulba, Tetnuld
and Skoda. His visit of 1889 was to search for ◊ Donkin and Fox who had
mysteriously disappeared, and he found traces of their last bivouac.

With Professor Garwood and the ◊ Sella brothers he made an arduous
circuit of Kangchenjunga in 1899, the first time it had been attempted, and
brought back a detailed description and map of the area.

Freshfield was a considerable author, with an output almost rivalling that of
◊ Coolidge. Unlike the latter, he was a brilliant descriptive writer and his
books were very popular. They are: *From Thonon to Trent* (1865), *Travels in
the Central Caucasus and Bashan* (1869), *Italian Alps* (1875), *The Exploration of the Caucasus* (1896), *Round Kangchenjunga* (1903), *Hannibal Once
More* (1914), *The Life of Horace-Benedict de Saussure* (1920) and *Below the
Snow Line* (1923). He also published two books of verse: *Unto the Hills*
(1914) and *Quips for Cranks* (1923). He was editor of the *A.J.* 1872–80 and
twice Chairman of the Society of Authors.

Friends   A camming device used for protecting rock-climbs in the same way
as nuts, but more flexible. The Friend consists of a shaft to which are attached
4 arc-like heads, toothed. The heads can be manipulated by means of a wire so
that they contract to fit into a crack then expand and jam when the trigger is
released. A tape can be attached to the free end to give protection. There are
various sizes of Friends. They were invented in the 1970s by the American

climber Ray Jardine for use in Yosemite, but have since found universal application.

Frostbite   Is caused by extreme cold, cold winds, or, in the feet, by tight boots being worn for long periods in snow and ice. It affects the extremities: fingers, toes, ears, nose, lips – the affected part turns putty-coloured and goes numb. Frostbite is caused by ice crystals forming between the cells, allied to a constriction of the minor blood vessels – all of which cuts down the supply of oxygen to the cells and leads to their deterioration and infection.

The only effective treatment is to increase the supply of oxygen, and high-altitude oxygen has been used for this on some expeditions. Full treatment can only be given in hospitals with a hyperbaric oxygen tank. The old remedies of rubbing with snow, lashing with ropes and dipping into alternate hot and cold water do not seem effective even as temporary measures. The best emergency treatment is to warm the affected part. The recovery from frostbite is very painful.

Führerbüch (Fr.: livret)   An official notebook issued to Alpine guides in which their patrons can write comments on the guide's performance. It is inspected annually. Führerbücher are of little consequence today, but those of the early guides were highly thought of. There is a collection of early Führerbücher in the Alpine Club library and one or two have been printed in facsimile.

Fyfe, Thomas C. (d. 1947)   One of the self-taught pioneer guides of the New Zealand Alps, and companion of G. Graham and J. Clark on the first ascent of Mt Cook (1894). Fyfe made first ascents of Footstool, De la Beche, Darby, Montgomery, Graham's Saddle, Fyfe's Pass, Minarets, Haidinger N Peak, and first crossing of Lendenfeld Saddle. An injury sustained during the last climb kept him inactive for about ten years but he made a remarkable return to climbing when, in 1906, he joined Peter Graham to guide Turner and Ross on the transverse of Mt Cook.

G

Gabbro An extremely rough rock offering good friction grip and the principal rock of the ◊ Skye Cuillins. Gabbro is found in smaller amounts in other British mountain areas and in the Alps.

Gaiters In winter climbing and Alpine climbing knee-length gaiters of canvas or proofed nylon are worn to prevent snow from getting into the boots. They also keep out small stones, from moraines etc., and give extra warmth to the lower legs. Some mountaineers like to wear gaiters in inclement weather even in summer and on muddy tracks, peat moors and the like.

There are various styles including some which integrate with the boot to form almost a single unit, but the commonest kind usually hook on to the front bootlace and zip up the back or front. There is often a lace or strap which fits under the boot sole to prevent the gaiter riding up.

Small anklets called stop tou were once quite popular but have now largely disappeared, as have the forerunners of gaiters, the puttees. These were long bandages wound round the lower leg and were first used in the Indian army (from the Hindi word 'patti' – a bandage).

Gallet, Julien (1858–1934) Swiss climber noted for his first ascents, particularly in the Oberland. Among his best known routes are the Galletgrat of the Doldenhorn (1899), the E N E Ridge of Lauterbrunnen Breithorn (1896) and the Gallet arête of Mont Blanc de Cheilon (1896). Gallet wrote: *Dans l'Alpe ignoré: Explorations et Souvenirs* (1910) and *Derniers Souvenirs de l'Alpe* (1927).

Galton, Sir Francis (1822–1911) One of the most distinguished scientists of his age, Galton's interests ranged over a wide field. He was largely responsible for the invention of weather maps and stereometric maps, and also for the discovery of finger-printing as a means of identification. Climbed in the Pyrenees with ◊ Packe and ascended Monte Rosa in 1861.

Gangway An inclined ledge on a rock face. A frequent feature of rock-climbs.

Gardening The removal of turf, plants and shrubs from a rock-climb to make the climb cleaner. Gardening often reveals new holds. The process only takes place on first ascents, or on climbs which are fairly new.

Gardiner, Frederick (1850–1919) A Liverpool shipowner, cousin of the ◊ Pilkington brothers. Like the Pilkingtons, he was a keen advocate of guideless climbing and of climbing in Britain (he was with R. ◊ Pendlebury on Pendlebury's Traverse, Pillar, 1872). In the Alps his first ascents were not notable, though he made the first traverse of the Rothorn in 1873 and the first ascent of Elbruz, Caucasus, in 1874.

It was his guideless first ascents, often with the Pilkingtons and ◊ Hulton, which were outstanding for the time. They included Écrins (1878), Meije

(1879), Jungfrau from Wengern Alp (1881) and Finsteraarhorn (1881). Coolidge wrote an account of Gardiner's career which was published privately in 1920.

Garwood, Edmund Johnstone (1864–1949) Geologist and explorer who was with ◊ Conway in Spitzbergen 1896–7 and with ◊ Freshfield during the tour of Kangchenjunga (1899). His map of the latter formed the basis for all subsequent expeditions.

Geiger, Hermann (1914–66) A Swiss flyer known as the 'Gletscherpilot', Geiger was a pioneer of landing light aircraft on glaciers using skis. The system was used for rescue and for supplying ◊ huts. The first landing was at the Mutthorn Hut in the Bernese Alps, 13 July 1952. Geiger made about 23,000 glacier landings, including a number of daring rescues, but the system eventually gave way to helicopters. The idea of rescue by air was first tried by a pilot called Wissel in 1950, but it was Geiger who brought it to perfection. (Autobiography: *Alpine Pilot*, 1956.)

Gendarme (Fr.) (E.: pinnacle; G.: Turm; It.: torre) A free-standing pinnacle on an Alpine ridge. Gendarmes may be quite small or immense. Depending on the route, they are climbed over or avoided by a traverse.

George, Rev. Hereford Brooke (1838–1910) With Stephen, Moore and others, played a considerable part in the exploration of the high Alps. Made a number of difficult passes including the first crossings of the Jungfraujoch and Mischabeljoch (1862) and the Col du Tour Noir (1863, not repeated for 27 years). Took part in the first ascents of Gross Fiescherhorn (1862) and Jungfrau from Wengern Alp (1865).

George was an Original Member of the Climbers' Club. His views on equipment were advanced for the day: he advocated rucksacks instead of knapsacks and an ice axe in preference to the then common alpenstock. Of the latter he said, 'Personally, I would prefer an umbrella.'

He was the founder of the Oxford Alpine Club and the first married don at Oxford. He wrote several books on history.

Germany, climbing in Outside the Alpine zone there are extensive climbing crags in Germany – possibly more than anywhere else in Europe, though they do not rival in height the great ◊ French or ◊ Italian crags. The two main types of rock are limestone and sandstone and on the latter a strict ethical code is enforced. Climbing on the German outcrops (*klettergarten*) dates from the middle of the last century (e.g. Falkenstein near Dresden, 1864).

Swabian Alps 200 km long and 45 km wide the area is the central part of the Jura. There are 120 crags with climbs up to 100 m high, mostly hard. Best known are the Danube valley crags.

Franconian Jura A continuation of the above, from the Danube to Staffelberg. The rock is limestone and there are 700 crags mostly 20–40 m high with some up to 80 m. Highest is the Romerwand at 100 m. Nearly all the routes are hard. In the adjacent Steinwald and Fichtelgebirge there are granite pillars 40 m high, with 300 routes.

Elbsandsteingebirge The most famous outcrop area in Germany, just south of Dresden. The area is 40 km by 25 km and contains about a thousand sandstone crags, some 100 m high. Many are striking pinnacles. There are thousands of routes of all grades. Here is the so-called 'Saxon climbing': very strict ethics regarding how a climb should be done. Transgressors are made unwelcome!

Sudpfalz Another sandstone area; 140 crags and 80 pinnacles in the Vosges forest between Bitsch and Trifels. 1,500 routes of all grades up to 60 m high. Like the Saxons, they are very strict on ethics.

Black Forest There are various rocks, both sandstone and granite, in this popular walking area. Mostly 30–60 m and all grades. Most popular is the Battert, near Baden-Baden, where the sandstone crags are named after Dolomite peaks!

Nordeifel A nature reserve in the Ruhr, near Hausen. The rock is sandstone with quartzite intrusions and there are 600 routes on various crags and pinnacles, 45 m high. All grades. Breidelsley near Blens is the best.

Rotenfels On the north bank of the River Nahe, near Mainz. The rock is a brittle quartz porphyry and the area is noted for hard routes, rotten rocks and several deaths! Bastei Wall is 200 m. Closed to climbing February–May.

Bruchhauser Stein Near Bruchhausen, south of Bremen, are four great rock towers. Made of quartz porphyry they are called Goldstein, Bornstein, Tavenstein and Feldstein and they give 150 routes of 40–90 m. The area is a private nature reserve closed from February to June, and permission to climb is required.

Gervasutti, Giusto (1909–46) An outstanding Italian climber of the immediate pre-war years. With Rene Chabod he attempted the Croz Spur of the Grandes Jorasses in 1934, and might well have made the first ascent of the face had they not retreated in threatening weather – a decision they always later regretted. Both men were very modern in outlook, quoting ◊ Mummery as their mentor (*Alpinismo*, Chabod and Gervasutti, 1935).

Amongst his outstanding first ascents were:

1934   E Face of Tacul
1935   S E Ridge of Pic Gaspard
1936   N W Wall of Ailefroide
       S W Face of Pt Gugliermina
1940   Right Hand Pillar of Frêney

He was killed on the Mont Blanc du Tacul in 1946 attempting what is now called the Gervasutti Pillar.

Gesner, Conrad (1516–65) Professor at Zurich and a keen botanist whose famous declaration that he would 'climb a mountain a year' has caused him to be included among the early alpinists, though whether he ever achieved his aim is quite unknown. He did climb Pilatus in 1555 – not the first ascent and an easy climb. The oft-quoted declaration was in a letter to a friend: 'I have resolved for the future, so long as God suffers me to live, to climb mountains, or at all events to climb one mountain every year, at the season when vegetation is at its best, partly for the sake of studying botany, and partly for the delight of the mind and the proper exercise of the body.'

Ghiglione, Piero (1883–1960) Distinguished Italian climber who is said to have ascended more mountains than anyone else, and in every part of the world. He was in the tradition of Italian climber-writers, fairly wealthy, and absolutely devoted to the mountain world. Made first ascents in the Andes at the age of 70 and led a successful expedition to Api (Himalaya) at 71.

Gibraltar, climbs in A number of routes have been done on this famous rock (limestone), though permission is needed to climb there. The spectacular N Front was climbed by M. Boysen, H. Day and M. Burke in 1971.

Gibson, John Henry (1862–98) A fine and daring rock-climber who made a number of guideless Alpine climbs and some of the first climbs in Scotland. These include the first guideless traverse of Grépon and the first ascent of the Black Shoot of Stob Maol (1892).

Gilbert and Churchill Josiah Gilbert (1814–92) and George Cheetham Churchill (1822–1906) were two friends who 'discovered' the Dolomites. They first saw these mountains in 1856, and explored them between 1860 and 1863. Their actual mountaineering experience was slight, but their book, *The Dolomite Mountains* (1864), became an Alpine classic. Gilbert (a professional artist) wrote most of the narrative and illustrated the work: Churchill contributed scientific notes (he was a leading expert on Alpine flora). The scope of the book is rather wider than a modern interpretation of the title would suggest. The two men later wrote *Knapsack Guide to Tirol* (1867).

Girdlestone, Rev. Arthur Gilbert (1842–1908) The Rev. A. G. Girdlestone was one of the earliest guideless climbers, making a guideless ascent of the Wetterhorn in 1867 (but ◊ Hudson). His experiences, which he related in *The High Alps Without Guides* (1870), caused great controversy and the book probably did much to put back the proper development of guideless ascents. Girdlestone was the sick Englishman that ◊ Whymper visited just before the Matterhorn tragedy. He accompanied Whymper and Lord Francis Douglas to Zermatt and had he been in better health might well have taken part in the Matterhorn ascent.

Gîte An obsolete term for a bivouac. Frequently referred to in early climbing books, such as Whymper's *Scrambles*.
A *gîte d'étape* is a bunkhouse offering simple overnight accommodation. They are found along the major footpaths of France (Grandes Randonnées) and elsewhere. There is cooking provision and sometimes simple meals are provided. They are similar to the *dortoirs* and *matratzenlagers* found throughout the Alps.

Glacier (G.: Gletscher, Ferner; It.: ghiacciaio) The permanent ice associated with high or arctic mountain regions. Glaciers occupy 10 per cent of the earth's surface, but 96 per cent of this is in Antarctica or Greenland. If they all melted they would raise the sea level by 60 m – enough to drown all the major coastal towns of the world.
There are three types of glacier:
Ice-cap or ice-field type Easily in the majority by bulk. Antarctica is virtually one huge ice-cap of 13 million km² and 2,500 m thick, and Greenland Norway, Iceland and Spitzbergen. The well-known Jostedalsbre of Norway (1,300 km²) is of this type.
Valley glaciers The type with which most climbers are best acquainted. Virtually a river of ice trapped between mountain spurs, these are found in the Alps, Andes, Himalaya etc. Large glaciers are known to attain a thickness of 300–900 m. The largest of all is the Beardmore Glacier in Antarctica, which is 190 km long and 120 km wide. The Hubbard Glacier of Alaska is 120 km long, and the Hispar-Biafo of the Karakoram is 122 km long. The Karakoram contains the greatest concentration of large glaciers in the world outside the Antarctic, for example Batura 58 km, Baltoro 58 km, Siachen 72 km. The

longest glacier of the Alps is the Great Aletsch, 22 km long.

Valley glaciers flow down from the upper snows or névé which help to 'feed' them. Fresh powder snow becomes granular ice (firn) which extends to a depth of 30–60 m, gradually losing air as it becomes deeper. The pure ice below this becomes plastic owing to the weight of material above, and flows under gravity. The rate of movement varies from a few centimetres per day to 45 m per day; the former is more common. The centre flows quicker than the edges (hence the curved bands of detritus) and the middle flows quicker than the beginning or terminus.

Because the upper layers are brittle, variations in flow or changes in the underlying rock causes the ice to fracture into crevasses. If there is a large declivity, this may result in an ice-fall.

Piedmont glaciers These spread out laterally at the foot of mountain ranges and are not common. An example is the Bering Glacier of Alaska, 3,900 km².

Since the last Ice Age, glaciers have had periods of advance and retreat. There is evidence to suggest this is fairly consistent on a world-wide basis, but the Alps will serve as an example. During the Middle Ages, the glaciers were not so extensive as they now are; it was possible, for example, to walk from Zermatt to Sion over what is now the icy Col d'Hérens. Their first advance is not recorded but they made substantial advances in 1830–45 and 1875–92. They are now generally in retreat: of 93 Swiss glaciers observed in 1962–3, ten were advancing, six stationary and the rest retreating. The largest advance was the Cambrena Glacier, 93 ft, and the largest retreat was the Ferpècle Glacier, 600 ft. Several were retreating at the rate of about 200 ft per annum.

(✧ Bergschrund; Crevasse; Glacier travel; Hanging glacier; Ice-fall; Moraine; Sérac; Snow bridge.)

Glacier cream A heavily pigmented sun cream made specially for mountaineers, but now largely superseded by modern lotions with a high blocking factor. It should be applied to all exposed parts of the body before venturing above the snow line, especially the nose, neck and ears. It prevents the ravages of solar radiation (ultraviolet rays) which are particularly strong on ✧ glaciers and snowfields due to reflection. It is necessary even in mist or cloud which does not keep out ultraviolet radiation.

Lips are particularly sensitive and special lipsalves (e.g. Labiosan) make the best protection.

All sun protection wears off through perspiration and should be reapplied at periods throughout the day.

Glacier House A famous mountaineering centre in the Selkirk Range of the Canadian Rockies (✧ Canada). When the Canadian Pacific Railroad crossed the Rogers Pass in 1887 they built a small hotel on the Illecillewaet River where passengers could eat, there being no refreshments on the trains at that time. This establishment grew into a rambling wooden building promoted by the railway as a mountaineering centre with imported Alpine guides. Towering over the hotel was Mt Sir Donald, 'the Matterhorn of the Selkirks'.

The Connaught Tunnel below the pass was opened in 1916, so trains no longer passed the hotel and it finally closed in 1925. It was demolished in 1929 and plans to rebuild it never materialized. Present-day climbers use a nearby campsite.

Glacier table A feature of some dry glaciers. A rock, lying on the ice, has protected the underlying ice from the sun's rays. As the surrounding ice melts, the rock is left perched on an ice pedestal, looking somewhat like a mushroom.

Glacier travel   The chief requirements for glacier travel are common sense and a general knowledge of glacier formation. The dangers are real; they should neither be exaggerated nor ignored.

Before embarking on a glacier, even on a dull day, exposed parts of the flesh should be rubbed well with glacier cream, which cuts out ultraviolet rays. Sensitive parts – neck, forearm, tip of nose and ears – should be especially well creamed and the cream should be renewed at intervals during the day. Failure to do this will result in severe glacier burn. Tinted glasses or goggles should also be worn to prevent snow-blindness. An ice axe should be carried at all times.

A glacier which has no powder snow on it is known as a dry glacier. Crevasses on such glaciers are obvious and can be avoided or jumped. If they are not steep, such glaciers do not require a rope (e.g. Mer de Glace).

When crevasses are snow-covered, a rope is essential for safety (◊ Crevasse rescue). Fifteen feet of rope between each pair is enough: the second can carry spare coils in his hand to give the leader more freedom and have the rest of the rope permanently coiled round his shoulders and securely tied off. The leader advances along his chosen route and the second follows, keeping the rope off the snow. Both men should be alert and ready to plunge their axes into the snow for a ◊ belay. Where the leader suspects hidden ◊ crevasses he probes with the axe while his second belays him. He is also belayed while crossing ◊ snow bridges. Crevasse covers are more likely to collapse after several hours of sunshine (hence the early start) and also that a ready beaten track in the snow made by previous parties is no guarantee of safety.

Ice-falls present the danger of unstable ◊ séracs. They should be avoided if this is feasible, or crossed as quickly as possible (e.g. in the Nantillons Glacier, Chamonix). ◊ Moraines are usually laborious but safe, though there is sometimes danger of falling stones (Arolla Glacier for example). On some glaciers surface streams can provide awkward obstacles (for instance, Gorner Glacier).

Glacis   An obsolescent word indicating a gently sloping area of rock which can be walked up without the need for handholds.

Glissading (Fr.: ramasse)   If snow is of a sufficient hardness it is possible to slide down it using the boot soles in the manner of skis. A crouch position is adopted and an ice axe is trailed spike down in the snow to act as brake and rudder. The technique is difficult and many climbers end by sliding down on their rears, but experts can even do ski turns. It is a very quick way down long snow slopes, but also a prime cause of accidents. It is essential that the bottom of the slope should be visible, that the area is crevasse-free, and that the climber knows braking techniques should he get out of control. A rope glissade is very dangerous and is not recommended.

Glover, George Tertius (1870–1953)   Pioneer rock-climber who did much exploration in the far north of Scotland with ◊ Ling and others. Made the first ascent of Engineers' Chimney, Gable, Lake District (1899), and Glover's Chimney, Ben Nevis, 1902. Glover was a railway engineer.

Gloves   Essential for winter climbing in Britain, as well as for Alpine and high-altitude climbing. There are three types: fingerless wool mitts (useful for rock-climbing in cold weather); mitts made of oiled wool or triple-layered with a Gore-tex shell (the general cold-weather glove of the mountaineer); and overmitts of nylon (which are wind and snowproof). In severe conditions all these may be worn in combination.

Despite the intense heat often encountered on Alpine glaciers, gloves should be worn as a protection, especially on a dry glacier where a slip can cause badly lacerated hands if gloves are not worn.

Gobbi, Toni (1914–70)   One of the leading Italian post-war guides and an advocate of advanced winter climbing. First winter ascents of Hirondelles Ridge (1948), S Ridge of the Noire (1949), and Route Major (1953). He made a number of other first ascents in the Dolomites and Mont Blanc areas, the most notable being that with ◊ Bonatti of the Grand Pilier d'Angle (1957). He was a member of the Italian expeditions to Patagonia (1957–8) and Gasherbrum IV (1958). He visited the Caucasus in 1966 and Greenland in 1967 and 1969.

Though a trained lawyer, Gobbi preferred to live at Courmayeur, where his equipment shop became a well-known meeting place for climbers. An expert skier, he was killed by an unfortunate skiing accident in the Dolomites.

Godwin-Austen, Lt.-Col. Henry Haversham (1834–1923)   Military surveyor who did outstanding work in the Himalaya between 1857 and 1877, when he retired. In 1861 he explored the Baltoro Glacier and sighted K2, second highest mountain in the world. For a short time K2 was known unofficially as Mt Godwin-Austen.

Gogna, Allessandro (b. 1946)   An Italian climber who besides repeating many Alpine hard routes has created some two dozen of his own, including the Zmuttnase of the Matterhorn. He is best known for his first winter ascent of the Cassin route on the Piz Badile (1968) and his solo of the Walker Spur of Grandes Jorasses in the same year – also a first.

Golden Age (of Alpinism)   A term used to describe the exploration of the Alps between 1854 (Wills' ascent of the Wetterhorn) and 1865 (Whymper's ascent of the Matterhorn), when almost all the higher peaks and many of the lower ones had their first ascents. The period from 1865 to c. 1914 is sometimes called the Silver Age. Cynics have referred to the period since 1914 as the Iron Age.

Gos, Charles (1885–1949)   A Swiss climber, son of the well-known painter, Albert Gos, and a writer of distinction. In his young days Gos was a keen non-guided man and he made the first unguided ascents of the Petit Dru and the Zmutt Ridge of Matterhorn. Illness brought his climbing career to an early end but he often wrote about mountains. His history of the Matterhorn, *Cervin* (2 vols., 1948), is his major mountain work but his most popular was *Tragédies Alpestres* (1940).

Gosset, Philip Charles (1838–1911)   A Swiss surveyor who made the first ascent of the Klein Doldenhorn (1862). It was during Gosset's winter attempt on the Haut de Cry (1864) that his companion and the guide J. J. ◊ Bennen lost their lives in an avalanche.

Gradings of difficulty   The purpose of grading climbs according to their difficulty is to indicate whether a route is too hard or too easy for a given party. Like guidebooks (with which the growth of the grading system is closely linked), they were at first subject to disapproval. These early objections were quite valid – so much depends upon the temperament and physical make-up of the climber, the weather, the wear and tear on the rocks and other variables, that a correct grading would be impossible. This has proved correct and the story of gradings is one of a continual search for improvement, but climbers have resisted more complex systems in favour of relatively simple ones. Fortunately, these seem to work in practice.

BRITAIN

British mountains are relatively small and there are no gradings for mountain ascents unless they involve ◊ scrambling, ◊ rock-climbing, ◊ snow-climbing or ◊ ice-climbing.

Scrambles are graded in ascending order Gr1, Gr2, Gr3, and Gr3 (S), the latter reserved for particularly serious outings on bad or vegetated rock. Scrambling more or less encompasses the old Easy and Moderate rock-climbing grades.

Rock-climbs were originally graded by O. G. ◊ Jones in 1897 as Easy, Moderate, Difficult and Exceptionally Severe. These have expanded over the years and at present are (colloquial names in brackets): Easy, Moderate (Mod), Difficult (Diff), Very Difficult (V. Diff), Severe, Very Severe (VS) and Extremely Severe (Extreme). The grades can be further subdivided by the prefixes 'Hard' or 'Mild' – thus one can have a Hard V. Diff or Mild Severe, etc. A rather special case is Hard Very Severe (HVS), which is a grade in its own right, due to the wide spectrum of difficulty encompassed by the VS grade. The Extreme grade is similarly very wide, encompassing everything harder than HVS and to overcome the problem this presents as ever harder climbs are done, the grade is numbered in ascending order of difficulty so that E4 is harder than E2 etc. The system is open-ended and at present (1990) the limit lies somewhere about E7, E8 or E9. These are generally referred to as the E grades.

The above grades are for overall impression and may reflect the nature of the rock, the strenuous nature of the climbing etc. They are therefore rather subjective.

In addition, on harder climbs (usually VS and above), a technical grade is given to each pitch reflecting the hardest move on it. These go from 1 to 7 and are subdivided a, b and c in ascending order of difficulty – usually only 4–7 are mentioned, the others being too easy in modern terms to record. Thus a climb described as VS 4a, 4c, 4b, has three pitches of which the middle one is the hardest.

Aid climbs are graded A0–A5 in ascending order of difficulty.

Winter climbs are graded GrI–GrVI in ascending order of difficulty.

Guidebooks sometimes carry graded lists in which all the climbs are graded continuously from the hardest down to the easiest. Accuracy is not a keynote of such lists, but they are good to argue over in the pub. Similarly 'star grading' is open to argument. Certain routes are given from one to three stars for merit (not difficulty) and though three stars should be reserved for the great classics, the system is often abused.

The grading of any climb is done first by the originator, then by the guidebook writer who may or may not take other opinions. Climbs can go up and down in the grades over a period of time, but gradually a consensus will emerge and the climb will settle down until a rockfall or erosion causes a reappraisal.

THE ◊ ALPS

With some variations the Alpine countries use the French system for grading *mountain* climbs, with a numerical system for rock-climbing. The mountain grades are: F (*facile* – easy); PD (*peu difficile* – a little difficult); AD (*assez difficile* – rather difficult); D (*difficile* – difficult); TD (*très difficile* – very difficult); ED (*extrèmement difficile* – extremely difficult). Each can be further refined by a suffix: inf. (*inférieur*) or sup. (*supérieur*), meaning just below or above the grade, e.g. TD inf. means that the climb is not quite TD but is harder than D sup.

These grades cannot be equated with British grades since they are a measure of something quite different.

The numerical rock grades are similar to the British. Other national systems (e.g. the Austrian) seem to be dying out, but there are many local grading systems for boulders such as at Fontainebleau (◊ France), based purely on technical difficulty. The ◊ U.I.A.A. has an international system using roman numerals, but it doesn't seem to be used much.

Just as the British system is an extension of that laid down by Jones, so the Alpine systems are adapted from that laid down by ◊ Welzenbach in 1926.

◊ U.S.A.

The Sierra Club System was introduced into the U.S.A. in 1937. It was purely numerical: 1 – hiking; 2 – off-trail scrambling; 3 – climbing with a rope for beginners; 4 – belayed climbing; 5 – leader uses protection; 6 – aid climbing.

Classes 1–4 are virtually walking and scrambling. In the 1950s at Tahquitz Rock, Gr5 was further divided by decimals, originally 5.0–5.9 but then, by adroit lateral thinking as climbs got harder, to 5.10, 5.11 etc. The upper grades were further divided a–d, and the hardest route currently available is 5.13a. This is known as the Yosemite Decimal System (Y.D.S.) and is the most popular grading system in the U.S.A. The National Climbing Classification System (N.C.C.S.) does not seem to have gained much acceptance. Climbs are graded F1–F13. Other systems such as A.M.C. and Old Teton may be regarded as defunct.

OTHER SYSTEMS

The Australians use an open-ended numerical system, at present from 1 to 33. In ◊ South Africa grades are in ascending order A–E, although recently a modified Australian system has been introduced. In Russia routes are divided into three classes: high-altitude class (above 6,000 m); face ascents class (routes over 75°); and traverse class (across two or more peaks). Difficulty is graded 1–6 with subdivisions A and B; 6A is the maximum.

Because climbers now operate internationally in increasing numbers some sort of standardization seems likely, despite the U.I.A.A.'s apparent failure (see above). The trend seems to be to use the French system for mountain ascents and the Anglo–French numerical systems for rock-climbs.

Graham brothers   Peter Graham (1878–1961) and Alex Graham (b. 1881) were two brothers from Westland who became the leading New Zealand guides during the years 1894 to 1928, and made a number of first ascents in the New Zealand Alps. They were not related to the Graham who made the first ascent of Mt Cook (◊ New Zealand). (See autobiography: *Peter Graham – Mountain Guide*, published posthumously in 1964.)

Graham, William Woodman (c.1859–?)   An experienced mountaineer who made the first ascent of the N E Summit (the highest point, 4,013 m) of the Aig. du Géant in 1882 with the guides A. Payot and A. Cupelin.

In 1883 Graham visited the Himalaya with the expressed intention of climbing 'more for sport and adventures than for the advancement of scientific knowledge'. Since von Déchy's visit of 1879 had failed because of illness, Graham thus became the first climber to specifically visit the Himalaya for purely climbing purposes. He took with him J. Imboden as guide and, when the latter became ill, replaced him with E. Boss and U. Kauffmann.

He first visited Sikkim, crossed two high passes and climbed a peak of about 6,000 m. He next tried to force the Rishi Ganga in Kumaun (not accomplished for another 50 years) and to climb Dunagiri. He reached 6,900 m on Dunagiri before retreating because of bad weather. He then ascended what he thought was Changabang (6,864 m) but was probably some other peak. Returning to Sikkim he climbed Jobonu, explored Pandim and claimed the first ascent of the giant Kabru (7,393 m).

This last has remained one of the great mysteries of Himalayan climbing. Himalayan authorities have argued for and against Graham's claim – all are agreed he climbed *some* big mountain, but was it Kabru? Cooke made the first undisputed ascent in 1935.

Little is known of Graham's later life. He is said to have lost his money and emigrated to the U.S.A., where he became a cowboy.

Grand Capucin (3,838 m)   An impressive pinnacle on the southern slopes of Mont Blanc du Tacul. Though first climbed by a minor route in 1924, it was the ascent of its stupendous E Face by Bonatti and Ghigo in 1951 that attracted attention. It is almost 457 m of aid climbing. Very popular.

Grandes Jorasses (4,208 m)   One of the most important mountains in the Alps. Part of the Mont Blanc group, and on the frontier above Val Ferret. The mountain is a long crest with six summits: Pt Young (3,996 m), Pt Marguerite (4,065 m), Pt Croz (4,110 m), Pt Hélène (4,045 m), Pt Whymper (4,184 m) and Pt Walker (4,208 m). The first ascent of Pt Whymper was made by E. Whymper with M. Croz, C. Almer, F. Biner in 1865 and of Pt Walker by H. Walker with M. Anderegg, J. Jaun, J. Grange, 1868. Both ascents were by the fairly easy S W Face – the only really easy routes on the mountain.

There are four important ridges: the W and E Ridges, and the Tronchey and Pra Sec Ridges running south from the Pt Walker. These were climbed:

1911   W Ridge – G. W. Young, H. O. Jones with J. Knubel
1923   Pra Sec Ridge – F. Ravelli, G. Rivetti, E. Croux
1927   E Ridge (Hirondelles Ridge) – A. Rey, A. Chenoz with G. Gaja, S. Matteoda, F. Ravelli, G. Rivetti
1936   Tronchey arête – T. Gilberti, E. Croux

It is worth noting that in 1911 Young's party descended the Hirondelles Ridge and in 1928 the American Rand Heron's party climbed the Tronchey arête by an indirect variant.

There are four faces: the S W Face (the ordinary route), the S Face (between the Tronchey and Pra Sec ridges), the E Face (between the Tronchey and Hirondelles ridges) and the spectacular N Face, overlooking the Leschaux Glacier. The E Face of Pt Walker was climbed by G. Gervasutti and G. Gagliardone in 1942 and is one of the hardest climbs on the mountain. The S Face of Pt Walker was climbed in 1972 by A. Gogna and G. Machetto. It is one of the largest faces in the Alps, but subject to stonefall.

Left, Grandes Jorasses, Walker Spur. (*C. Bonington*); right, Gritstone at Cratliffe Tor, Derbyshire. (*A. Evans*)

A number of other hard climbs have been done on the south flanks of the mountain, but climbing attention has been mainly focused on the great N Face. This extends along the whole mountain and consists of a series of spurs and couloirs. The first ascent was by the Croz Spur (R. Peters, M. Meier, 1935) but the great prize was the Walker Spur (R. Cassin, L. Esposito, U. Tizzoni, 1938) one of the most famous climbs in the Alps and the subject of numerous attempts in the thirties. It was these attempts that provoked Charlet's comment, '*C'est pas de l'alpinisme, ça, c'est la guerre*'. (First winter ascent: W. Bonatti, C. Zappelli, 1964; first solo ascent: A. Gogna, 1968.)

There are now nine routes on the N Face. Most notable of the rest are:

The Shroud, 1968 – R. Desmaison, R. Flematty, winter; Central Couloir, 1972 – Y. Kanda, Y. Kato, H. Miyazaki, T. Nakano, K. Saito, winter; E Flank of Walker Spur, 1973 – R. Desmaison, G. Bertone, M. Glaret, winter.

Granite An igneous rock of crystalline quality. Granite varies from place to place but is usually sound to climb upon and a great favourite with climbers. There are good granite rocks in Chamonix and Cornwall.

Gray, Dennis Dillon (b. 1935) A gritstone climber who played a large part in re-founding the ◊ Rock and Ice Club. Gray seconded H. Drasdo on the first ascent of N Crag Eliminate, Castle Rock, in 1952. He took part in the first ascents of Grond, Dinas Cromlech (1958), The Scene and Apollyon Ledge, Coire Ardair (1966), Gargoyle Wall, Nevis (1963), winter ascents of last three and various outcrop climbs, including Frisco Bay, Stoney Middleton (1953), and Wombat and Macabre (1964) at Malham. He has made a number of first British ascents in the Alps and climbed in many different parts of the world.

In 1961 Gray attempted Indrasan in Kulu but failed on the W Ridge, though he succeeded in climbing the adjacent two highest Manikaran Spires. He was joint leader of the unsuccessful 1964 Gauri Sankar Expedition, but two years later led the successful first ascent of the N Ridge of Alpamayo in Peru. He was leader of the 1968 Mukar Beh Expedition.

Dennis Gray was the first National Officer to be appointed by the ◊ B.M.C., and later the first General Secretary.

Greasy rock   A term indicating rock which is slippery when wet. Mountain limestone seems to be prone to greasiness. Other rocks are often made greasy by mud from climbers' boots and by lichen.

Great Gable (899 m)   An immensely popular fell of the Lake District rising at the junction of Ennerdale, Borrowdale and Wasdale, and usually approached from the last two valleys. The war memorial tablet of the F.R.C.C. adorns the summit. There are two important groups of crags on the fell: Napes Ridges, overlooking Wasdale and Gable Crag, overlooking Ennerdale.

The Napes are an unusual set of spiky ridges and buttresses which attracted the pioneers, together with the adjacent outcrop of Kern Knotts. ◊ Napes Needle was climbed by ◊ Haskett Smith in 1886 and is the symbol of the birth of rock-climbing as a sport. In fact, Haskett Smith also climbed the ridge above it (Needle Ridge) two years earlier. Other earlier ascents of note are:

1892   Eagle's Nest Ridge Direct – Solly, Slingsby, Baker, Brigg
        Arrowhead Ridge – Slingsby, Waller, Brant, Baker, Brigg
1893   Kern Knotts Chimney – Jones, Fowler, Robinson
1897   Kern Knotts Crack – Jones, Bowen
1921   Innominate Crack – Bower, Beetham, Wilton

Gable Crag has never been popular, though the Central Gully gives a fine winter climb.

Green, William Spotswood (1847–1919)   An Irish clergyman who made some of the earliest explorations of the New Zealand Alps and the Canadian Rockies. In 1882 he made virtually the first ascent of Mt Cook, though he turned back a few feet from the actual summit in order to avoid benightment. In 1888 he visited the Selkirks, making the first ascent of Glacier Crest, Terminal Peak and Mt Bonney. He wrote accounts of his expeditions in *The High Alps of New Zealand* (1883) and *Among the Selkirk Glaciers etc.* (1890). His survey resulted in the first map of the Selkirk Range. There is a Mt Green in both New Zealand and the Selkirks, and Green's Saddle in New Zealand; all commemorate the pioneer.

In his later years he was Government Inspector of Irish Fisheries.

Greenland, climbing in   This vast island consists essentially of a great central ice cap rising to over 3,000 m, surrounded by ranges of mountains. The highest are the Watkins Mountains, on the east coast, south of Cap Brewster, and the highest summit is Gunnbjorn Fjeld (3,700 m, L. R. Wager, 1935). The Watkins Mountains were discovered by Gino Watkins in 1931, but after the thirties they were unvisited until 1969, when both M. Slesser and A. Allen attempted to reach and climb Ejnar Mikkelsen Fjeld (3,261 m), the highest unclimbed peak of the Arctic. Both failed because of bad weather, and the peak was climbed in 1970 by a remarkable small expedition: A. Ross, G. Williams, N. Robinson and P. Lewis.

The Staunings Alps in Scoresby Land (east coast) are lower than 3,000 m (Dansketinde, 2,930 m, J. Haller, W. Diehl, 1954). The peaks are shapely and there have been numerous expeditions in recent years – it is probably the best-known area of Greenland.

Further south on the east coast lie the Alpefjord mountains and other groups, including Mt Forel (3,360 m, 1938) and in the extreme south are the peaks of Cape Farewell. On the west coast are the Sukkertoppen, Umanak Fjord area and the Melville Bay area, which have all attracted at least one expedition. There are many more mountain groups worth exploring.

Gregory, Alfred (b. 1913) Photographer and lecturer. Gregory took part in Shipton's Cho Oyu Expedition of 1952 and the following year was a member of the final assault team on the summit of Everest. At a height of 8,500 m, Gregory, Lowe and Ang Nyima dumped loads for the final camp, leaving Hillary and Tenzing to stay the night and climb to the summit next day (first ascent).

Gregory led a number of other expeditions: Rowaling, Nepal (1955), when 19 first ascents were made, an attempt on Disteghil Sar (1957) and a return to the Everest region in 1958. Wrote: *The Picture of Everest* (1953).

Gréloz, Robert (b. 1905) One of the leading alpinists of the thirties and forties, Gréloz was Swiss and frequently climbed with his countryman, André ◊ Roch. He made the first ascent of Triolet North Face (1931), E Face of Tour Noir (1935), Mummery Pillar of the Brenva Face (1936), West Face of Dent Blanche (1944) and others. He is perhaps best remembered for his descent of the N Face of the ◊ Dru with Roch in 1934 using 235 m of rope. The face was in bad condition and the descent was epic.

Grid reference The Ordnance Survey use a system of imaginary squares covering Britain as a reference for pin-pointing any place with great accuracy. The basic squares are of 100 km size and extend north and east from a point of origin which lies approximately south-west of Cornwall. There are ten such squares northwards and seven eastwards. The coordinates for the square including London, for example, would be 51, meaning the square whose bottom left corner was 500 km east of the point of origin and 100 km north of the point of origin. The eastings are always given first.

On the map scales commonly used by climbers (1:50,000 and 1:25,000) the maps are subdivided into squares of 1 km and these are similarly numbered from bottom left. Thus, on the Lakeland map, Friar's Crag falls in square 26,22. It is possible to estimate by eye further subdivisions into tenths, and Friar's Crag thus becomes 263,222, giving the position to the nearest 100 m. More detailed estimation is only accurate on very large-scale maps. For Friar's Crag, the figure is written 263222, and is known as the normal grid reference. However, since these figures will repeat themselves every 100 km, it may be necessary to give the 100 km square number – in this case, 35. The full grid reference thus becomes 35/263222.

Grid lines are only approximately N–S and E–W, the difference being the grid variation. (◊ Magnetic variation.)

Grill, Johann (1835–1917) Known as 'Der Köderbacher'. Grill came from Berchtesgaden and all his early climbs were done on the peaks of Tyrol where he made the following notable first ascents amongst others:

1868 Traverse of Watzmann's three peaks
1873 Pflerscher Tribulaun
1881 E Face of Watzmann

He made a winter ascent of the W Face of the Weisshorn and expressed a wish to attempt the Eigerwand (1882!).

Grindelwald   A popular tourist and climbing resort in the Bernese Alps, overlooked by the Wetterhorn and ◊ Eiger. It was from here that ◊ Wills made his ascent of the Wetterhorn in 1854, an event often regarded as the beginnings of Alpine sport. The village has always been famous for guides.

Gritstone   The geographical term, millstone grit, is never used by climbers. Gritstone comes in many varieties, all modified sandstones, but with a common abrasiveness which aids friction climbing. Incut holds are not common, which, combined with the usual steepness of the rock, leads to superior technique. Gritstone climbing has a long history, beginning even before J. W. Puttrell, 'the father of gritstone', who started climbing at Wharncliffe in 1885, and continuing with such notables as Herford, Kelly, Kirkus, Longland, Harding, Brown, Whillans, Livesey and Fawcett, all of whom began on gritstone. The transference of gritstone techniques to mountain crags by these and others has led to the continual rise in climbing standards.

Gritstone is found in the Pennines as natural outcrops (edges and tors) and quarries. The most popular is Stanage Edge, near Sheffield. Gritstone climbs seldom exceed 100 ft and are usually shorter.

Grohmann, Paul (1838–1908)   One of the founders of the Austrian Alpine Club (1862). He made a number of the early first ascents in the Dolomites, including Sassolungo and the Cima Grande (both in 1869).

Groove (G.: Verschneidung; Fr.: Dièdre; Am.: dihedral)   A V-shaped fissure in the rock, not deeply incised, but rather flat and varying, from place to place, from a few inches to a few feet in width. The term is used loosely. Rounded grooves are sometimes called 'flutings' and are common on gritstone, for example, Robin Hood's Stride.

Grooves also occur on ice-climbs. In couloirs deep grooves can be caused by avalanche debris – they form natural chutes for falling stones and are best avoided.

Groughs   Erosion channels in the peat surface of a moor. Large groughs can be 15 ft deep and very wide. Groughs sometimes form complex patterns which make walking difficult. The best-known examples are on Bleaklow and Kinder in the ◊ Peak District.

Groupe de Haute Montagne (G.H.M.)   An élitist group of climbers founded in 1919 in France. The standards of entry are very high, but the group is not restricted to French nationals. It issues an annual bulletin of new Alpine climbs and is associated with the C.A.F. in *La Montagne*. It is an influential and highly respected body in the climbing world. The British ◊ Alpine Climbing Group is similar, but of more recent foundation.

Grove, Florence Crauford (1838–1902)   President of the A.C. (1884–6) and one of the best climbers of the period. His first ascents include: Dent d'Hérens, Parrotspitze (1863), Jungfrau from Rottal, Zinal Rothorn (1864), Aig. de Bionnassay (1865) and Elbruz (Caucasus, 1874). In 1867 Grove made the first ascent of the Italian ridge of the Matterhorn by an amateur, which was also the first ascent of the mountain by anybody since the great affair of Whymper and Carrel in 1865. He climbed the mountain again the following year, making the fifth ascent from Zermatt, and was thus the first man to have climbed the Matterhorn by both the routes then known, though ◊ Tyndall had traversed it from Breuil to Zermatt a few weeks earlier.

Grove was with Moore, Gardiner and Walker in the Caucasus in 1874 and wrote an account of their travels in *The Frosty Caucasus* (1875).

Grüber, G. (d. 1899)   An Austrian climber with wide experience of the Alps, who made the second ascent of Mont Blanc via Mont Blanc de Courmayeur (1880) and the third ascent of the Brenva Face (1881). The Rochers Grüber of the Frêney Glacier are named after him.

Gugliermina brothers   Giuseppe F. (1872–1960) and Giovanni Battista (1873–1962) were two Italian brothers from the Val Sesia who made notable new routes on the Monte Rosa and Mont Blanc massifs including the first crossing of the Col Émile Rey (1899), Brouillard Ridge (1901, G. B. with J. Brocherel), Aig. Verte from the Nant Blanc Glacier (1904) and Punta Gugliermina (1914). An account of all their climbs, *Summits*, was compiled by Lampugnani and illustrated by photographs taken by G. F. who usually carried a heavy plate camera. It is suggested that this is why many of their expeditions involved bivouacs. They usually climbed without guides and G. B. led the rope. G. B. made his last ascent at the age of 80 – on the Punta Giordani.

Guide   A professional mountaineer who earns all or part of his living by acting as a paid leader on climbs. It is not a guide's job to instruct, though in fact many do act as instructors on courses. Most Alpine guides are also ski instructors and derive a considerable part of their income from this. Many mountain ◊ huts are looked after by guides or ex-guides.

A guide may be hired for a period of time at a rate agreed between him and the client, though there are minimum charges laid down. The guide provides the rope, but the client must pay his expenses for travel and food. (Guides are not usually charged for overnight accommodation in huts.) The guide's licence extends to all Alpine areas. In a good season, hiring a guide by the week or month is the cheapest method.

A guide may also be hired for a specific climb. Each route is graded by the local association and a fixed charge applies; it is often based on the time taken rather than the difficulty. For difficult climbs a guide will satisfy himself that the client is up to the required standard of competence. Charges are fairly high and because of this some local guides' associations run collective courses in which the guide(s) take a group of clients on a previously advertised route.

The pioneer Alpine guides were local peasants who adapted themselves to the high mountains and saw in the new sport a lucrative supplement to their income. Many of them were poor at their work but the best men were mountaineers in their own right and were skilful; they led most of the early climbs in the Alps. They were lauded by their clients (employers was the current term) and their services eagerly sought. Each guide kept a record book (führerbuch) filled in by his '*herr*', but the best men were so well known, and so often had the same clients for year after year, that these books were somewhat superfluous. For many years it was considered dangerous folly to climb without at least one guide.

◊ Chamonix was the first place to form an official guides' association, owing to its proximity to ◊ Mont Blanc – but the restrictive practices it invoked, including gross overmanning of expeditions, led to many disputes with climbers in the nineteenth century.

Britain had its own mountain guides as early as the mid-eighteenth century – men such as John Morten in Wales and Robin Partridge of the Salutation

Hotel at Ambleside in the Lake District – though because of our smaller mountains they were different from Alpine guides. The first real climbing guide in Britain was probably John ◊ Mackenzie of Skye.

Guides figure prominently in all the early climbing literature and in much of the later literature too. Some guides have written their autobiographies (◊ Klucker, ◊ Kain, ◊ Desmaison etc.) and several are listed in this encyclopaedia, but see also *Pioneers of the Alps* (1887) by ◊ Cunningham and ◊ Abney and *The Early Alpine Guides* (1949) by Clark.

The British Association of Mountain Guides (B.M.G.) was formed in 1975. Together with their counterparts in France, Switzerland, Italy, Austria, Germany, Canada, New Zealand and Norway they form the Union Internationale des Associations de Guides de Montagne (U.I.A.G.M.).

In 1977 the Alpine countries had the following guides: Switzerland 722, France 677, Austria 511, Italy 460 and Germany 140. There are at present (1991) just over 100 British guides.

TRAINING

In Britain anyone may call himself or herself a guide. In some parts of the Continent, however, professional guiding may only be done by properly accredited guides who have undergone rigorous training and bear a U.I.A.G.M. carnet and badge. An accredited guide is not limited to his own country.

Training varies from country to country and in Switzerland, from canton to canton, though they are all fairly similar. In the E.C. countries (Britain, France, Germany, Italy) a uniform training and assessment system operates. The B.M.G. describe the British course thus:

> Before acceptance a candidate has to submit a detailed list of his or her experience, which should be substantial, and an acceptable first aid certificate. There is a summer training course during which the candidate must lead E1 5b grade, use improvised rescue techniques and show ability at teaching novices rock-climbing. There is a summer assessment. A winter course follows, in Scotland, climbing GrIV or above with care of clients in a winter environment, navigation and improvized rescue. This too is assessed.
>
> A successful candidate becomes an Aspirant Guide.
>
> The next stage is an Alpine training course of a week followed by a minimum 30 days with a qualified guide, each day of which is recorded. In winter there is a week's ski-touring in Scotland followed by 10 days ski-touring with a guide.
>
> A successful candidate becomes a qualified guide with badge and carnet. The system normally takes 2 years to complete.

Guidebooks A specialized handbook designed to help climbers achieve their objective. Guidebooks point the way, explain the difficulties, usually give a ◊ grade to a climb, give the time needed (for higher mountains), and facilities such as huts, chairlifts, etc. Some guidebooks give brief notes on climbing history, local geology, flora and fauna. Most give the names of those climbers who made the first ascents. Present-day guidebooks are usually in pocket format and may have a protective plastic cover.

Guidebooks are often published by clubs, either directly or through some agency. The various Alpine clubs publish books on their own areas: in Britain the Fell and Rock Club, Climbers' Club, Scottish Mountaineering Club, Federation of Mountaineering Clubs of Ireland and the Alpine Club, each publish several volumes and various small clubs produce more local guides. In the U.S.A. the American Alpine Club, the Appalachian Club, the Mountaineers and the Sierra Club publish guidebooks.

The principal difficulties with guidebooks are keeping them reasonably up to date and verifying their accuracy. In the Alps and other high mountains, this is especially difficult. Assessment of difficulties is subjective and frequently disputed.

Early Alpinists used ◊ Murray as their guide until it was superseded by ◊ Ball's Alpine Guides (1863–8). The first technical descriptions came with the Conway and Coolidge Guides (1881–1910). The first British climbers' guide was *Climbing in the British Isles* (2 vols.), by W. P. ◊ Haskett Smith (1894–5).

Some guidebooks have had a profound effect on the development of the sport. In Britain notable examples are:

1897   *Rock Climbing in the English Lake District*, by O. G. Jones (the first guide to give a grading system).

1908   *The Island of Skye*, by various authors (published by the Scottish M.C.; the first club guide).

1909   *The Climbs on Lliwedd*, by J. M. A. Thomson and A. W. Andrews (published by the Climbers' Club).

1913   *Some Gritstone Climbs*, by J. Laycock (first guidebook to gritstone climbing).

1922   *Doe Crag and Climbs Around Coniston*, by G. S. Bower (the first Fell and Rock guidebook; start of the 'Red' series).

1950   *Cornwall*, by A. W. Andrews and E. C. Pyatt (first guide to sea cliff climbing).

1955   *Llanberis Pass*, by P. R. J. Harding (contained the supplement recording the new climbs of the Rock and Ice Club and others).

1957   *Further Developments in the Peak District*, by E. Byne and W. B. White (first record of the 'gritstone explosion').

1961   *Rock Climbs on the Mountain Limestone of Derbyshire*, by G. T. W. West (first record of the 'limestone invasion'; the 'Blue Guide').

1968   *Winter Climbs, Ben Nevis and Glencoe*, by Ian Clough (the first guide devoted exclusively to snow- and ice-climbing).

1980   *Scrambles in Snowdonia*, by Steve Ashton (the first guide devoted exclusively to scrambling).

Guideless climbing   A term used well into the present century to denote climbs done in the Alps without professional guides. It was often used censoriously, as guideless climbing was thought to be foolhardy. Guides were always taken on the early expeditions to the Himalaya, Andes and Caucasus. Though guides are still employed by many climbers, guideless climbing is the norm today and the phrase has lost all meaning.

Gully (Fr.: couloir)   The rift between two buttresses caused by erosion. May be very wide or narrow (◊ Chimney) and may contain a stream. They may be so easy that they contain a path, but many are genuine rock-climbs. A gully filled with small stones is known as a 'scree gully' and often forms a quick way down from a crag. In the Lake District a gully is called a 'gill' or 'ghyll'.

Unique features of some gully climbs are chockstones, where the gully is blocked by boulders, and waterfall pitches.

Most gullies are more difficult under ice and snow conditions when even simple summer scrambles can become serious climbs; perversely, *some* gullies become easier if there is a heavy snow layer (for example, Gardyloo Gully, Ben Nevis). Gullies are natural avalanche chutes and winter gullies should not be tackled until the snow has consolidated. Many gullies provide classic winter climbs, especially in Scotland. (◊ Gully epoch; Couloir.)

Gully epoch   A term used to describe the pioneering days of British rock-climbing when the major routes followed the most natural lines, that is, gullies. It ended about the turn of the century: Great Gully, Craig yr Ysfa, 1900; Savage Gully, Pillar Rock, 1901.

Güssfeldt, Paul (1840–1920)   German scientist and Privy Councillor to the Kaiser Wilhelm II, whom he accompanied on numerous journeys, Güssfeldt was also one of the outstanding mountaineers of the nineteenth century. Güssfeldt had very much the same sort of determination as ◊ Whymper and, like Whymper, he employed the best guides – in his case, Burgener, Rey and Klucker.

Among many climbs, two outstanding ones are the first crossing of the Col du Lion from south to north with Burgener (1881) and the first winter ascent of the Grandes Jorasses with Rey (1891).

It was in the Bernina, however, that Güssfeldt first made his name, putting up two fine routes: the Scerscen Eisnase in 1877 and the first complete traverse of the Biancograt of Piz Bernina in 1878.

Later, Mont Blanc became his favourite mountain and he made the fourth ascent of the Brenva Face (1892). In the following year came the traverse of Aig. Blanche de Peuterey (the second ascent) followed by the first complete ascent of the Peuterey Ridge to Mont Blanc de Courmayeur and Mont Blanc, with a return to Courmayeur. The climb lasted 88 hours and the guides were Rey and Klucker. Güssfeldt was 53 years old.

As an explorer, Güssfeldt was less successful. He spent 1873–5 on the West African coast trying to organize an expedition into the interior for the German Africa Company, but misfortune attended his efforts and the whole project ended in a shambles.

In 1876 he spent a month in the Arabian desert with Schweinfurth, but his next major adventure was to the Chilean Andes in 1882–3, where he made the first ascent of Maipo (5,400 m) but failed in two attempts on Aconcagua.

Güssfeldt wrote a number of books, the best known of which are: *In den Hochalpen* (1885) and *Der Mont Blanc* (1894).

H

Habeler, Peter (b. 1942)   An Austrian guide best known for his association with ◊ Messner, 1974–8, when they climbed the Eiger and Matterhorn Nordwands in record times (1974) and climbed Gasherbrum I (8,068 m) in an Alpine-style push (1975). The climax of their partnership came in 1978 when they made the first oxygenless ascent of ◊ Mt Everest, by the S Col route. In descent, climbing solo, Habeler reached the S Col in an hour from the summit. Following the expedition relationships between the two climbers became strained and the partnership broke up.

Hadow, Douglas (1846–65)   The young friend of Charles Hudson whom the latter insisted should join the ◊ Matterhorn party of 1865. It was Hadow's first season and he had made only two minor ascents together with a rapid ascent of Mont Blanc with Hudson. During the descent of the Matterhorn Hadow slipped and fell against ◊ Croz, thus precipitating the famous accident.

Hall, Carl Christian (1848–1908)   A Danish treasury official who, after one season in the Alps (1878), devoted himself to the exploration of Norwegian mountains. Hall was comparable with the much better known Cecil ◊ Slingsby. From 1880 to 1900 he made numerous first ascents, particularly in the Romsdal and Jotenheimen regions, amongst which might be mentioned the first tourist ascent of the Romsdalhorn (1881), his seventh attempt, and the first ascent of Store Trolltind (1882).

Hall, William Edward (1835–95)   A wealthy barrister, traveller and adventurer who made the first ascents of Lyskamm (1861), Dent d'Hérens and Parrotspitze (1863).

Hamel (Dr Hamel's party)   A famous mountaineering accident, and the first on Mont Blanc. In August 1820 a party organized by Dr Hamel, a Russian, set out to climb Mont Blanc. There were 14 men: Hamel, Selligue (Swiss), Joseph Durnford and Gilbert Henderson (Oxford students), and ten guides or porters led by Balmat and Couttet. After waiting a day for bad weather to clear at the Grands Mulets rocks, Selligue and two porters returned to Chamonix while the others attempted the summit. The snow was soft, and some 400 ft up the Ancien Passage, above the Grande Crevasse, it avalanched carrying the party with it. Incredibly, eight survived, but Balmat, Tiarraz and Carrier were buried in the crevasse. Their remains reappeared below the Bossons Glacier forty-one years later.

Hamilton, Arthur Bold (1848–1902)   A barrister whose brief Alpine career was spent exclusively at Arolla, where he made the first travellers' ascent of the Tsa (1870) and first ascents of Dent Perroc and Dents des Bouquetins (1871).

Hammock   Special lightweight hammocks are used for ◊ bivouacs where

Left, Warren Harding who made first ascent of the Nose of El Capitan. (*B. Cropper*); right, Peter Habeler describing climbing Everest without oxygen. (*T. D. Unsworth*)

there are no suitable ledges, on some Yosemite climbs, for instance. The hammocks are slung from pitons or bolts.

Hand traverse A sideways movement across rock where the weight comes mostly on to the hands owing to an absence of footholds. A hand traverse should be carefully assessed and executed quickly. Strenuous, but fairly common.

Hanging glacier A subsidiary glacier set at a higher level than the main glacier or valley. It may be independent and hang over the valley with great ice-cliffs or it may join the main glacier by means of a steep ice-fall.

Harding, Peter Reginald James (b. 1924) One of the greatest climbers of the post-war years in Britain. In partnership with ◊ Moulam and others he raised the standards of rock-climbing to new heights and was the natural forerunner of ◊ Brown and others. His lead of Suicide Wall, Cratcliffe, in 1946 is regarded by some authorities as the beginning of modern high-standard climbing, though this can be no more than a symbol. Like Brown and others who came slightly later, Harding began on gritstone and found full expression in the Llanberis Pass. On Cloggy he only did the West Girdle (1949, G. Dyke). His important new climbs include:

1945   Lean Man's Eliminate, Black Rocks – A. J. J. Moulam
1946   Girdle Traverse, Black Rocks – A. J. J. Moulam
       Suicide Wall, Cratcliffe – Miss V. Lee
       Valkyrie, Roches – B. Black
1947   Spectre, Grochan – E. H. Phillips
       Ivy Sepulchre, Cromlech
       Phoenix, Shining Clough
       Goliath's Groove, Stanage

1948 Trilon, Wastad – N. L. Horsefield
      Girdle, Wastad – P. R. Hodgkinson
      Kaisergebirge Wall, Grochan – A. Disley, A. J. J. Moulam
1949 Unicorn, Wastad – P. R. Hodgkinson, N. G. Hughes
      Lion, Wastad – Moulam
      Halan, Wastad – G. Dyke
      Brant Direct, Grochan
      Green Caterpillar, Cyrn Las – G. Dyke
      Green Necklace, Cyrn Las – G. Dyke
      W Girdle, Clogwyn Du'r Arddu – G. Dyke
      Demon Rib, Black Rocks – A. J. J. Moulam

Almost all of these climbs are now regarded as modern classics. In 1951 he brought out for the Climbers' Club *Llanberis Pass*, a guidebook which had a profound effect on a whole generation. In it two new categories were introduced for the new hard climbs: Extremely Severe and Exceptionally Severe. Known for a time as X. S., they have since been modified.

Harding has been credited with the invention of the modern hand-jam technique and the use of thin slings for runners – now replaced by tape, and essential to modern protection.

With Moulam he produced the guidebook to the *Black Rocks and Cratcliffe* (1949), the first time that the Climbers' Club had sponsored a gritstone guidebook. In private life, Harding is an engineer.

Harding, Warren A leading American rock-climber from Yosemite (◊ U.S.A.). In 1958 he made the first ascent of the Nose of El Capitan – an outstanding achievement, though his ◊ siege tactics did not meet with universal approval. Harding has always adapted his tactics to meet the situation as he sees it. Other routes include:

1964 S Face, Mt Watkins
1970 S Face, Half Dome
      Wall of Early Morning Light (Dawn Wall)

Hard man Someone who climbs at a high standard. Other forms: 'a hard climber', or simply, 'hard'. The phrase returned to vogue in the 1960s but was in use in the nineteenth century when the meaning was slightly different, indicating someone who was a 'good goer' in the Alps.

Hardy, Rev. John Frederick (1826–1888) An Original Member of the A.C. who took part in several of the early Alpine ascents, particularly with E. S. ◊ Kennedy. Amongst his first ascents were: Finsteraarhorn (1857, first English ascent), Piz Bernina (1861, first English ascent) and Lyskamm (1861). With Hudson and others he made the first traverse of the ◊ High Level Route from Zermatt to the Gt St Bernard (1861).

Hardy also climbed Mt Etna and visited Norway. He was an early exponent of guideless climbing.

Harlin, John (1934–66) American climber who founded the International Mountaineering School at Leysin, Switzerland. Harlin made a number of new routes in the Alps including the Harlin–Robbins route on the W Face of the Dru (1965) and the Right Hand Pillar of Brouillard on Mt Blanc (Bonington, Baillie, Robertson, 1965). He was killed when a fixed rope broke during the first ascent of the Eiger Direct. The route was subsequently named the Harlin Route.

Left, John Harlin, killed on first ascent of the Eiger Direct. (*J. Cleare*); right, Heinrich
Harrer on the first ascent of the Eiger, 1938.

Harness (Fr.: baudrier) A device for attaching a climber to a rope so that
in the event of a fall the shock and strain are minimized. There are various
types, all made of webbing, often padded round the waist, and with attachment points for gear to hang. In Britain the best known is the Whillans
harness, which consists of a waist belt and leg loops.

Chest harnesses and all-over body harnesses are popular in the Alps but are
not as handy for difficult climbing.

Swami belts and rope waist lengths are rarely seen today. Harnesses
developed from a combination of these and the rope chest harnesses used in
the Alps.

Harper, Arthur Paul (1865–1955) Co-founder, with G. E. Mannering, of
the New Zealand Alpine Club (1891) and one of the earliest explorers of the
glaciers of Westland. Wrote: *Pioneer Work in the Alps of New Zealand* (1896)
and *Memories of Mountains and Men* (1946).

Harrer, Heinrich (b. 1912) An Austrian climber who was a member of the
team which made the first ascent of the Eigerwand (◊ Eiger) (1938). In 1939
he reconnoitred the Diamirai Face of Nanga Parbat, and was interned in India
at the outbreak of war. He escaped to Tibet where he became friend and
confidant of the Dalai Lama. In 1962 Harrer made the first ascent of the
Carstensz Pyramid, New Guinea. He has also visited S. America.

His books are: *Seven Years in Tibet* (1953), *The White Spider* (1959), and
I Come from the Stone Age (1964).

Hart, Henry Chichester (1847–1908) Irish explorer who was on the
Nares Arctic Expedition (1875–6) and the Hull Expedition to Sinai and
Palestine (1883–4). He made a number of ascents during the latter, including
the Pyramids. Hart was the author of the Irish section of ◊ Haskett Smith's
Climbing in the British Isles (1895).

Hartley brothers James Walker (1852–1932) and Francis Chisholm (1854–98) Hartley were two Liverpool brothers who took part in a number of difficult climbs in the Alps, particularly with ◊ Davidson. J. W. Hartley was with C. T. Dent on the first ascent of the Dru (1878).

Haskett Smith, Walter Parry (1859–1946) Barrister and philologist, regarded as the founder of British rock-climbing.

He first visited the Lake District in 1881, when he spent two months at Wasdale Head with fellow university students from Oxford. Here he met F. H. Bowring, who led the students on fell-walking excursions, which probably included some simple scrambles. In the following year Haskett Smith returned, accompanied by his brother, and began to climb rocks for their own sake: Deep Ghyll, Scafell; West and Central Jordan, Pillar Rock; and Great Gully, Pavey Ark, were climbed, and a brave attempt made on what later became the N Climb, Pillar Rock – an attempt which nearly ended in tragedy, when a loose block came away.

It was Haskett Smith's conception of rock-climbing for its own sake and pursuit of that aim which marks him out as the founder of British climbing, rather than the climbs themselves. There had been earlier climbs, in the Lakes and elsewhere, but usually as a means of achieving a *summit*. Broad Stand on Scafell was climbed early in the nineteenth century and the Old West on Pillar in 1826. Other early routes are N Climb and Mickledore Chimney, both on Scafell (1869), and the Slab and Notch, Pillar Rock (1863). Mention might also be made of Richard ◊ Pendlebury's climbs during the 1870s: Pendlebury Traverse on Pillar Rock, Jack's Rake on Pavey Ark and the gullies of Clogwyn y Person.

It was in 1886 that Haskett Smith made his most famous climb: the first ascent of the striking Napes Needle on Great Gable. He climbed it solo, with 'no ropes or other illegitimate means', to quote his own famous phrase. It was not repeated for three years, but then the fame of the pinnacle spread and became very popular, which it still is. Haskett Smith describes the climb in a classic article written many years after the event (F.R.C.C. Journal 1914).

Haskett Smith climbed with another pioneer, J. W. ◊ Robinson and with the A.C. members who took to rock-climbing in the later 1880s, such as ◊ Slingsby, the ◊ Hopkinsons and ◊ Hastings, making ascents in the Lake District, Wales and Scotland. He visited the Alps and Norway on several occasions and walked in the Pyrenees with ◊ Packe.

In 1894 he published *Climbing in the British Isles – England*, the first volume of a three-part work dealing with climbing in Britain, and the first climbing guide to British crags. The second volume, dealing with Wales and Ireland, followed in 1895, though he was helped considerably in this by O. G. ◊ Jones, Bowring and ◊ Hart; Ellis ◊ Carr drew the diagrams. The Scottish volume never appeared.

Hasler, Gustav Adolf (1877–1952) Wealthy Swiss industrialist and notable Alpinist at the turn of the century. Made many climbs especially in the Oberland and including the first ascent of the Scheidegg Wetterhorn (1901) and the Hasler Rib of the Aletschhorn (1902). His outstanding achievement was the first ascent of the N E Face of the Finsteraarhorn with F. Amatter in 1904: the first great north face to be climbed and still graded TD sup.

Hastings, Geoffrey (1860–1941) A Yorkshire climber, friend of ◊ Slingsby and ◊ Mummery and one of the leading mountaineers of his time. He began climbing with Slingsby in 1885 when they made an unsuccessful attempt on Deep Ghyll, Scafell, a climb they accomplished in the following year (second ascent). In 1889 Hastings made the second ascent of Napes Needle, three years after ◊ Haskett Smith's climb. His importance to Lakeland climbing can be seen from the fact that he took part in the following important first ascents ('L' indicates he led): 1888, Slingsby's Chimney, Scafell and Great Gully, Dow Crag (L); 1890, Shamrock Gully, Pillar Rock (L); 1891, North Climb, Pillar Rock; 1892, Moss Ghyll, Scafell and Great Gully, Screes (L).

He first visited the Alps in 1887, when he made a guideless ascent of the Dru, but it was in 1892–4, with Mummery, that he came to the fore, taking part in the first traverse of Grépon, the first ascent of Requin, first ascent of W Face of the Plan, a new route of Grand Combin (Mummery missed this), first guideless ascent of the Brenva Face of Mont Blanc, second ascent of the Moine Ridge of the Verte, and first traverse of the Col des Courtes.

In 1895, with Mummery, ◊ Collie and ◊ Bruce he made the first exploration of Nanga Parbat in the Himalaya, during which Mummery was killed.

In addition to this Hastings was in the large A.C. party which visited Skye in 1890 (first ascent of Bhastier Gorge) and, with Collie, he made the second descent of Alum Pot in Yorkshire (1893). He visited Norway in 1889, 1897, 1898, 1899 and 1901 with Slingsby, Collier and others, making a number of first ascents. He made a notable early exploration of the Lyngen district during his 1897 visit.

Haston, Dougal (1940–77)   A Scottish climber who sprang to prominence with his ascent of the Eiger Direct in the winter of 1966 (see *Eiger Direct*, by D. Haston and P. Gillman). The following year he made a winter ascent of the Matterhorn Nordwand and was a member of the British ◊ Cerro Torre expedition. In 1969 he made the first winter ascent of the N Face of Argentière, and then in 1970 he took part in the successful S Face of Annapurna expedition. Haston, with Whillans, reached the summit.

He again partnered Whillans in the International Expedition to the S W Face of Everest, 1971, and they reached the highest point yet reached on the face. Though he returned with Bonington's post-monsoon expedition of 1972, the party was defeated by high winds and extreme cold. Returning once more with the Bonington expedition of 1975, Haston partnered D. ◊ Scott on the first ascent. This was the first time any British climbers had reached the summit of Everest. (◊ Mount Everest.)

In 1967, Haston became Director of the International Mountaineering School in Leysin, Switzerland, founded by John Harlin, who was killed during the Eiger Direct assault. Haston's autobiography, *In High Places*, appeared in 1972. He was killed by an avalanche while skiing.

Hawkins, Francis Vaughan (1833–1908)   A London barrister who had a brief but interesting climbing career. He took part in the second ascent of Monte Rosa (1855 – his first Alpine season) and the following year attempted, unsuccessfully, to make new routes on Mont Blanc. In 1859 he reconnoitred the Matterhorn and joined ◊ Tyndall the following year in an attempt on the summit from Breuil. (The third attempt on the mountain; they reached 13,000 ft, the highest point at that date.) Hawkins was an Original Member of the A.C. but resigned in 1861.

Heckmair, Anderl (b. 1906)   One of the leading German climbers of the pre-war era, a member of the so-called 'Munich School'. He began climbing in the Wilder Kaiser in the 1920s, and like many of his companions found plenty of time for climbing because he was out of work. He made the first direct ascent of the Charmoz N Face, and made several attempts on the Walker Spur, but is best known for the first ascent of the Eigerwand (◊ Eiger) (1938) which he led. As a guide in the post-war years, Heckmair has climbed in many parts of the world.

Hector, Sir James (1834–1907) A typical Victorian polymath; medical man who assisted Simpson in anaesthetics and who later turned to geology and meteorology. Noted for his endurance, speed over rough terrain and all-round toughness. He made extensive surveys in the Canadian Rockies and later New Zealand, where he was the first man to set foot on the glaciers (1863). In 1857 in the Palliser Expedition to the Rockies he was injured by a kick from his horse, an incident which gave Kicking Horse Pass to the world.

Hedin, Sven Anders (1865–1952) A Swedish explorer who did a great deal of work in Central Asia. He mapped large areas of the Pamirs and Tibet, but his only attempt at a major ascent was in 1894 when he tried to climb Muztagh Ata and failed at 6,140 m. He wrote many books about his adventures and was honoured by many scientific societies, but his pro-Nazi sympathies in later years damaged his reputation.

Height conversion The heights of mountains are expressed either in metres or feet.

Using the table below the same method can be used to convert feet to metres.

Metres	Feet or Metres	Feet
0·305	1	3·281
0·610	2	6·562
0·914	3	9·842
1·219	4	13·123
1·524	5	16·404
1·829	6	19·685
2·134	7	22·966
2·438	8	26·247
2·743	9	29·528

Example: convert 5,894 m to feet

$$5,000 \text{ m} = 5 \times 1,000 = 16,404 \text{ ft}$$
$$800 \text{ m} = 8 \times 100 = 2,624\cdot7 \text{ ft}$$
$$90 \text{ m} = 9 \times 10 = 295\cdot28 \text{ ft}$$
$$4 \text{ m} = = 13\cdot123 \text{ ft}$$
$$5,894 \text{ m} 19,337\cdot103 \text{ ft} = 19,337 \text{ ft}$$

To make an approximate calculation of metres to feet, multiply by three and add 10 per cent. The result will be high. For instance in the above example: $3 \times 5,894 = 17,682 + 1,768 = 19,450$ ft.

With a calculator, multiply by 3·281 to convert metres to feet and by 0·3048 to convert feet to metres.

Hemming, Gary (1934–69) An outstanding American rock-climber who began his career in the early fifties at Tahquitz Rock, Southern California. Hemming climbed in Yosemite, High Sierra, Tetons and Britain, but his greatest achievements were in the Chamonix area. In 1962, with Kendall, he made the first American ascent of the Walker Spur, Grandes Jorasses and, with ◊ Robbins, a direct start to the W Face of the Dru. In 1963 he climbed the S Face of the Fou with Frost, Harlin and Fulton. These two routes marked the introduction of Yosemite techniques to the Alps – both are extreme rock-climbs. In 1966 he made solo ascents of the Couturier Couloir (Verte) and the N Face of Triolet, and was one of the leaders in a dramatic rescue of two trapped climbers on the Dru W Face.

A moody, temperamental person, Hemming died tragically by committing suicide in 1969.

Herford, Siegfried Wedgwood (1891–1916) A fine rock-climber, who applied his gritstone training to the bigger crags in Lakeland, especially Scafell. He began climbing in the Peak District about 1910 and quickly became the companion of gritstone experts like Laycock, Jeffcoat and A. R. Thomson. Laycock's guidebook to the outcrops, *Some Gritstone Climbs* (1913), was dedicated to Herford.

In 1912 Herford visited Scafell Crag. He made the second ascent of Botterill's Slab and Jones's Direct, completed Hopkinson's Gully, made the first girdle traverse, and finally made a direct ascent to Hopkinson's Cairn – a problem which had baffled experts for years.

In 1914 came the first ascent of the Central Buttress of Scafell, including the famous Flake Crack. The party was Herford, Sansom (who led the upper part of the climb), Gibson and Holland. It remained for many years the most difficult rock-climb in Britain and is still treated with respect.

Herford also climbed in Wales, Scotland, the Alps and the Dolomites. He was killed at Ypres in 1916.

Herzog, Otto (1888–1964) A German climber who is claimed to be the man who first used ◊ karabiners. Amongst a number of very fine first ascents, that of the N Face of Dreizinkenspitze, done in 1921 with G. Haber, was outstanding – probably the first Gr 6+ climb in the Alps.

Hey, Wilson Harold (1882–1956) Distinguished Manchester surgeon and President of the Mountain Rescue Committee from 1939 to 1956. Hey insisted on the need for morphia in the rescue kits and was prosecuted for this, being fined a nominal £10 and costs. The case showed that there was a need for morphia and the authorities eventually gave in to common sense. Hey was a considerable rock-climber and alpinist.

Hiebeler, Toni (1924–84) One of the most influential alpinists of the 1950s, Toni Hiebeler's career ranged from being an *enfant terrible* (falling out with the D.A.V.) to an establishment pundit and prolific author.

Besides repeating several of the hard routes of the time such as the Walker Spur, Hiebeler made over 50 new routes. Best known is his first winter ascent of the Eigerwand (1961) (◊ Eiger) with T. Kinshofer, A. Mannhardt and W. Almberger which extended from 6 to 12 March, with six nights on the face at very low temperatures. Hiebeler had special boots made to avoid frostbite and the party had 200 m of abseil rope in case of retreat. They carried over 20 kg per man and it is probably one of the earliest uses of axe hammers instead of long axes on a major route. Two years later Hiebeler climbed the N W Face of Civetta in winter with I. Piussi and G. Redaelli, which he regarded as the high point of his career. All adventurous sports appealed to Hiebeler; ballooning, skiing, white-water canoeing and sailing.

Meanwhile, in 1957, he wrote his mountaineering book *Abenteur Berg*, the first of many. He edited several magazines over the years but it was as editor of the climbing magazine *Alpinismus* that he set new standards of mountain journalism; it was the definitive magazine of the mid-century.

He died in a helicopter crash near the Julian Alps whilst on a photographic expedition for a new book. His wife died with him as did the famous Yugoslavian mountaineer, Alex Kunaver (1935–84).

High-altitude climbing The term is relative, but is usually reserved for climbing in those ranges which exceed 6,000 m, that is, Himalaya, Andes, Alaska, Pamirs, Tien Shan, Hindu Kush. Much of what follows, however, may well apply to lesser ranges which are nevertheless remote.

The special problems associated with the climbing of big mountains are: transport, logistics, diet, high-altitude equipment, physiology and weather. There may also be problems of human nature brought on by the temperaments of the climbers, the ability of the leader and morale in general. Ultimately, there are the tactics for the actual assault on the peak.

Political restrictions apart, transport to almost any area of the world is now quick and easy, though possibly expensive. Much preliminary work will need to be done over customs clearance, and so on. In the closer approach, animals or human porters will be needed and these are usually hired at the local villages en route. In the Himalaya, Sherpas are used for high-altitude porterage; they take up where the village porters leave off. On a big expedition the Sherpas will include a foreman or Sirdar, a cook, high-altitude Sherpas and ordinary Sherpas. The H. A. Sherpas may take part in the final assault (for example, Tenzing on Everest). In the Muslim areas of the Himalaya, Sherpas are not permitted (Karakoram, for instance) and Hunzas are often used instead (◊ Sherpas). There does not seem to be the equivalent of the Sherpa outside the Himalaya, though local men have from time to time assisted expeditions and gone high.

With a large expedition, radio communication now plays a vital part. There is usually a strong radio link from Base to civilization and from Base to Advance Base. Walkie-talkies are used from the camps to communicate with Advance Base.

The logistic problems increase with the size of the expedition and the remoteness of the peak. Expeditions vary from solo efforts (one climber supported by porters) to vast national and international armies. The problem is pyramidical – the more climbers you need to support at the apex, the more porters you need at the base. In large expeditions there will be specialists for important functions such as supplies, communications, Base Camp management, medicine etc. The leader of such an expedition might be an overall manager and take no part in the climbing. On smaller expeditions, the various tasks are undertaken by the climbers. Every attempt is made to pack the requirements into loads of manageable proportions for the porters (up to 30 kg) and according to how they will be needed en route.

The diet for the climbers must not only be balanced but tempting because there is a general reluctance to face food. Cooking – even the boiling of water – can take a long time and a conscious effort.

High-altitude equipment includes double boots and overboots, down suits, and possibly oxygen. Oxygen increases work rate and also allows proper sleep in the thin atmosphere. Acclimatization helps with this major physiological problem and with proper acclimatization a man may climb up to about 8,200 m without oxygen and stay there for a length of time, but deterioration will set in and probably nobody could do it more than once; recovery takes weeks. However, individuals vary and there have been some considerable feats of endurance in this sphere (◊ Oxygen equipment). Failure to acclimatize properly can result in pulmonary or cerebral oedema.

The climb itself is done from a Base Camp and there may be an Advance Base Camp if the approach to the climb is difficult. As the climb advances further camps are established until one is sufficiently near the top for a summit assault to be made (say, 600 m). The whole business may take several weeks, with climbers and porters moving up and down, ferrying loads, making the route and returning to Base for rest periods. This may be helped by leaving ◊ fixed ropes on the route. The whole art is to get the right two men into the top camp at the right moment for a summit assault. Under favourable conditions the ascent may be repeated by other members of the party and it is not unknown for all members of an expedition to reach the summit. On the return, as much gear as possible is collected and taken down, but quite often considerable amounts are left.

In recent years many high mountains have been climbed without oxygen or expensive logistics; a lightweight Alpine or near-Alpine style.

High Level Route (Fr.: Haute Route) A route from Chamonix to Zermatt originated in 1861 by members of the Alpine Club and utilizing the high mountain passes. The original route was: Chamonix – Col d'Argentière – Val Ferret – Orsières – Bourg St Pierre – Col de Sonadon – Col d'Oren – Praraye – Col de Valpelline – Zermatt.

In 1862 the Col des Planards was discovered and Orsières bypassed, and the route gradually tended further north after the Col de Sonadon as mountain huts were developed. It is usual now to include Arolla in the itinerary.

The route makes an excellent ski tour through some of the grandest scenery in the Alps and this is its principal function today.

In recent years a walkers' High Level Route, avoiding the high cols, has become popular. This follows the route Chamonix – Champex – Mont Fort – Arolla – Moiry – Zinal – Zermatt.

GUIDEBOOKS Roberts, *High Level Route* (W.C.P.).
Reynolds, *Chamonix–Zermatt, Walkers' High Level Route* (C.P.).

Hillary, Sir Edmund Percival (b. 1919) A New Zealand climber who in 1953 was the first man to reach the summit of Everest (with ◊ Tenzing). During an expedition to Garwhal in 1951 Hillary met and joined the Everest Reconnaissance and in the following year he joined Shipton again in the attempt on Cho Oyu. He made further expeditions to the Himalaya in 1954, 1961, 1963 and 1964, when he became involved in providing schoolhouses for the Nepalese children.

In 1956–8 he made a crossing of Antarctica, reaching the South Pole in December 1957.

Hillary has written several books describing his adventures.

His son Peter reached the summit of Everest in 1990, making the first father and son pair to do so.

Hill-walking (fell-walking) The basic mountain craft, hill-walking can cover anything from a simple stroll over the Downs to a winter crossing of the Cairngorms. It involves an ability to walk over rough, hilly country with an economy of effort that does not leave one exhausted at the end. Hill-walkers need good walking boots (not shoes and not climbing boots), protective clothes for bad weather, map and compass. A thorough grasp of the art of navigation is vital.

In winter hill-walking can become part of the greater mountaineering scene, akin to walking in the Alps. Good winter gear and an ice axe are

Ed Hillary (*left*) and Tenzing Norgay after the first ascent of Everest, 1953. (*RGS*)

essential, crampons and rope often useful, and it is important to know how to use these things. On long treks, such as over the Cairngorms, the Carneddau or the Bleaklow–Kinder massifs, it is useful to have an emergency sleeping bag in case of accident or exposure.

The majority of hill-walkers are simply after an enjoyable and not too strenuous day on the hills, but there are some long testing courses for those who wish to extend themselves. Amongst these might be mentioned: the ◊ Welsh 3,000s; the ◊ Scottish 4,000s; the Lakeland 24-hour record; the Lyke Wake Walk; the Four Inns Walk; the Derwent Watershed; and the Yorkshire Three Peaks Walk. There are several others. All these have been done in record times by fell-runners – a specialized and strenuous form of the activity.

Long-distance walks spread over several days (over trails or ways) are fairly common in both America and Britain. They usually have some theme: Offa's Dyke, for example. The best known British walk of this kind is the Pennine Way, which stretches from Edale in Derbyshire to Kirk Yetholm in Scotland, 250 miles.

If we disregard the crossing of glaciers or permanent snow as being outside the scope of hill-walking (and this is arguable) there is still a considerable amount of hill-walking done in the Alps, and especially in the Eastern Alps, where hut to hut tours in the limestone region are commonplace. Walking up to huts in the Western Alps, lunching and then walking down again is a popular pastime.

Himalaya The greatest range of mountains in the world, lying between India in the south and Tibet in the north. The name comes from the Sanskrit words *hima*, snow and *alaya*, abode.

The Himalaya is some 2,400 km long stretching from the Indus in the west to the Brahmaputra in the east and is about 160 km in width. For most of its length it can be divided into three zones: the Siwalik range, rising from the Ganges plain, forested and never more than 900 m high; the complex and wide middle range known as the Lesser Himalaya whose average height is 4,500 m, limestone, and wooded on the lower slopes, with hill stations like Simla and Darjeeling; and finally the Great Himalaya, mostly granite and gneisses, and seldom less than 5,500 m in height. The highest summit is ◊ Mount Everest (8,848 m), the highest mountain in the world. There are fourteen major peaks over 8,000 m, plus several subsidiary tops, and more than 400 over 7,000 m (including adjacent ranges in Asia and China). By far the largest proportion of really high peaks – above 7,500 m – are in the Nepal Himalaya and Karakoram (see lists below).

For most of its length the Himalaya is bounded to the north by the bleak Tibetan plateau, but at the western end there are important trans-Himalayan ranges, the best known of which is the Karakoram.

In 1907 Burrard divided the Himalaya into sections from west to east (revised by Mason, 1955). These are: 1. Punjab Himalaya (sometimes now called Western Himalaya); 2. Trans-Himalaya; 3. Kumaon Himalaya (usually referred to as Garhwal); 4. Nepal Himalaya; 5. Sikkim Himalaya; and 6. Assam Himalaya. Details of these sections are given below.

A group of mountains is usually known as a *himal* or in the Karakoram, a *muztagh*. For example, the Dhaulagiri Himal consists of Dhaulagiri, DII, DIII, DIV and DV – all over 7,600 m – plus several other summits of over 7,000 m.

Politically the range embraces the states of India, Pakistan, Tibet (China), Kashmir (in dispute) and Bhutan. In theory, all these are open to the climber but there are restrictions; Bhutan, for example, allows very limited tourism of any sort on ecological grounds, whilst on the Siachen Glacier of Kashmir there is constant skirmishing between the armies of India and Pakistan. Permits, often quite expensive, are required for mountain ascents, and popular peaks like Everest have to be booked years in advance. Improved roads and internal air services have eased travel throughout the area.

The range is affected by the monsoon rains, more so in the east than the west. The best months for climbing in the Karakoram are June–early August; in the Punjab, June–September but further east, April–June. However, in recent years climbing has taken place all year round and in Nepal, for instance, there are now four recognized seasons which can be 'booked': pre-monsoon, monsoon, post-monsoon and winter. Even Everest can be climbed in winter these days – the first ascent was by L. Cichy and K. Wielicki in 1980, by the S Col route.

Before the coming of the climbers, officers from the Survey of India reached great heights; by 1865 there had been 37 ascents of summits of 6,000 m or more. In that year W. H. Johnson claimed to have climbed E57, now called K5 or Muztagh, in the Kun Lun range, thought to be 7,281 m, though recently downgraded to 6,710 m. His ascent is disputed.

The first climber to make a special visit to the Himalaya was M. ◊ Déchy in 1879, but illness prevented him from doing any climbing. Then in 1883 came W. W. ◊ Graham with the guides J. Imboden and later E. Boss and U. Kauffmann. Graham claimed ascents of Changabang in Garhwal and Kabru in Sikkim, but the former is certainly wrong and the latter is disputed by Mason and others. Apart from Graham, the highest peaks climbed before the First World War were:

Pauhunri   7,128 m – Kellas, 1910
Trisul   7,120 m – Longstaff, 1907
Kun   7,087 m – Piacenza, 1913

Between the wars the highest climbed were:

Nanda Devi   7,816 m – Tilman and Odell, 1936
Kamet   7,756 m – Smythe, 1931

The first of the 14 8,000 m peaks to be climbed was Annapurna in 1950 by Herzog's French expedition. Everest was climbed for the first time by Hunt's British expedition in 1953. (See lists for ascents of 8,000 m peaks.)

The relative success of large expeditions by ◊ Conway in 1892 and the Duke of the ◊ Abruzzi in 1909 (both to the Karakoram), contrasted with the ill-fated small expedition to Nanga Parbat in 1895 during which ◊ Mummery and two Gurkhas were killed, led to the adoption of the large expedition as a norm for big mountains like Everest and ◊ Kangchenjunga. Such expeditions dominated the scene during the inter-war years, often disastrously. At the same time there were plenty of smaller expeditions going on like those of ◊ Shipton, ◊ Tilman, ◊ Smythe, ◊ Hunt and others. Spencer ◊ Chapman and Pasang Dawa climbed Chomolhari (7,315 m) in 1937 – an expedition of two climbers and three Sherpas.

Large expeditions are still common but there are many more smaller ones now, often international in composition. ◊ Sherpas, too, now frequently take part in summit climbs. There have been repeat ascents of many peaks, including new routes of a more challenging nature. Solo ascents sometimes occur and ascents often take place without the oxygen equipment once considered essential.

The impact of cheap air travel on the Himalayan scene can scarcely be over-emphasized. Besides the climbers there are many ◊ trekkers – the Circuit of

Annapurna and Everest Base Camp are two popular walks – and there are even 'trekking peaks', relatively easy summits for which no permit is needed: Island Peak (6,189 m), near Everest is one such. Even so, oedema – severe high-altitude sickness – often strikes and can be fatal. Climbing or walking in the Himalaya is not something to be taken too lightly.

8,000 M PEAKS & TOPS

Peak	Height	Section	1st asc.	Nationality
Everest	8,848 m	Nepal	1953	British
S summit	8,760 m		1953	British
K2	8,611 m	Karakoram	1954	Italian
Kangchenjunga	8,586 m	Sikkim	1955	British
Yalung Kang	8,505 m		1973	Japanese
Central Pk	8,482 m		1978	Polish
S Pk	8,476 m		1978	Polish
Lhotse	8,516 m	Nepal	1956	Swiss
Middle Pk[1]	8,430 m		(no ascent)	
Lhotse Shar	8,400 m		1970	Austrian
Makalu	8,463 m	Nepal	1955	French
S E Pk	8,010 m		1970	Japanese
Cho Oyu	8,201 m	Nepal	1954	Austrian
Dhaulagiri	8,167 m	Nepal	1960	Swiss
Manaslu	8,163 m	Nepal	1956	Japanese
Nanga Parbat	8,125 m	Punjab	1953	German
S Pk	8,042 m		1982	German
Annapurna	8,091 m	Nepal	1950	French
Central Pk	8,051 m		1980	German
E Pk	8,010 m		1974	Spanish
Gasherbrum I[2]	8,068 m	Karakoram	1958	U.S.A.
Broad Peak	8,047 m	Karakoram	1957	Austrian
Central Pk	8,016 m		1975	Polish
Shisha Pangma[3]	8,046 m	Nepal	1964	Chinese
Gasherbrum II	8,035 m	Karakoram	1956	Austrian

1. The highest unclimbed summit in the world (1990)
2. Sometimes known as Hidden Peak
3. Sometimes known as Gosainthan

7,000 M PEAKS & TOPS

There are 415 main and subsidiary summits between 7,000 m and 8,000 m high, though some of these have not been properly surveyed and are probably less. They are all in the Himalaya or the adjacent ranges in Central Asia and China. Of these, 176 have not been climbed (1990).

The highest 7,000 m top is the East Pinnacle of Manaslu, 7,992 m, which has not had an ascent. The highest 7,000 m independent peak is Gasherbrum IV, 7,925 m, climbed by ♢ Bonatti and ♢ Mauri in 1958.

SECTION I PUNJAB HIMALAYA

The westernmost section between the Indus in the west and Sutlej in the east. To the west lies the Hindu Kush and Trans-Himalaya and to the east, Garhwal. At its heart is the beautiful Vale of Kashmir.

Srinagar is the capital and there is excellent trekking from hill towns like Pahalgam and Sonamarg. The treks here are less arduous than in other Himalayan regions, and with less chance of altitude sickness. Gulmarg is a well-known skiing centre – the Davos of Asia!

Around Sonamarg there are numerous good climbing peaks between 4,500 m and 6,000 m; curiously neglected since their development by the wartime Aircrew Mountain Centre. Best known is Kolahoi (5,456 m) (E. F. Neve, K. Mason, 1912).

Further east, in the districts known as Kulu, Lahul and Spiti there are splendid groups of somewhat higher, sharp peaks. Examples are:

Leo Pargial (6,791 m) – M. Pallis, 1933
Papsura (6,451 m) – R. Pettigrew, 1967
Dharmsura (6,446 m) – J. O. M. Roberts, 1941
Indrasan (6,221 m) – Japanese expedition, 1962
Deo Tibba (6,001 m) – J. de V. Graaf, 1952

A good centre for the area is Manali.

There are only two groups of really big peaks in this section: ◊ Nanga Parbat and Nun Kun. The former, seen from the great bend of the Indus or from Gulmarg, is one of the most impressive mountain scenes in the world. The mountain has a notorious fatality rate.

Nanga Parbat (8,124 m) – H. Buhl (solo), 1953
Nun (7,135 m) – P. Vittos, Madame C. Kogan, 1953
Kun (7,087 m) – Count Piacenza, 1913

SECTION 2 TRANS-HIMALAYA (KARAKORAM)

The Karakoram (Karakorum is also acceptable) is a complex system of glaciers and high mountains lying behind and parallel with the Punjab Himalaya at the western end of the great range. It is about 400 km long from the Batura Glacier in the west to Saser Kangri in the east. The Lower Shyok and the Indus separate it from the Punjab Himalaya and the Shaksgam from the Kun Lun range. Within this area the mountains are very complex but can be conveniently divided into the Greater and Lesser Karakoram. The former includes the main crest zone of the system, with all the 8,000 m peaks including ◊ K2, the second highest mountain in the world (8,611 m), whilst the latter lies between the Greater Karakoram and the Indus. It is a shorter range but with some big peaks like Rakaposhi (7,788 m) and Masherbrum (7,821 m).

The Karakoram has the world's longest ◊ glaciers outside polar regions: Hispar-Biafo, 122 km; Siachen, 72 km; Baltoro, 58 km; and Batura, 58 km. Only Nepal can match it for great mountains – bordering the Baltoro glacier alone are ten of the world's thirty highest peaks.

Politically the Karakoram is in Kashmir, but that state is divided between Pakistan and India at the cease-fire line, which leaves most of the great peaks in Pakistan. Sporadic Indo-Pakistani fighting continues on the Siachen Glacier. In addition, China has laid claim to parts of the area.

In 1861 H. H. ◊ Godwin-Austen of the Indian Survey surveyed much of the area including the Baltoro and K2, though the proposal that the latter peak should be named after him never caught on. Mountaineers followed, ◊ Younghusband, ◊ Conway, the ◊ Workmans, ◊ Abruzzi and ◊ Longstaff amongst others. In the early days exploration and survey went hand in hand. None of the peaks over 7,500 m were climbed until after the Second World War; the highest pre-war climb was Sia Kangri (7,422 m), climbed by H. Ertl and A. Hocht in 1934. Post-war ascents are noted below.

The trek to Concordia at the head of the Baltoro is perhaps the most difficult of all the popular Himalayan treks for walkers.

Principal Summits

K2 (8,611 m) – A. Campagnoni, L. Lacedelli, 1954
Gasherbrum I (8,068 m) – P. Schoening, A. Kaufmann, 1958
Broad Peak (8,047 m) – M. Schmuck, H. Buhl, F. Wintersteller, K. Diemberger, 1957
Gasherbrum II (8,035 m) – S. Larch, F. Moravec, H. Willenpart, 1956
Broad Peak Central (8,016 m) – K. Glazek, M. Kesicki, J. Kulis, B. Nowaczyk, A. Sikorski, 1975
Gasherbrum III (7,952 m) – J. Onyskiewicz, A. Chadwick, W. Rutkeiwitcz, K. Zdzitowiecki, 1975
Gasherbrum IV (7,925 m) – W. Bonatti, C. Mauri, 1958
Disteghil Sar (7,885 m) – G. Starker, D. Marchart, 1960
Khungyang Chhiah (7,852 m) – A. Zawada, Z. Heinrich, J. Stryczynski, R. Szafirski, 1971
Masherbrum (7,821 m) – G. Bell, W. Unsoeld, 1960
Masherbrum S W (7,806 m) – Z. Heinrich, M. Maltynski, P. Nowacki, 1981
Batura I (7,795 m) – H. Bleicher, H. Oberhofer, 1976
Rakaposhi (7,788 m) – M. Banks, T. Patey, 1958
Kanjut Sar (7,760 m) – C. Pellissier (solo), 1959
Saltoro Kangri I (7,742 m) – Y. Takamura, A. Saito, Capt. Bashir, 1962
Trivor (7,728 m) – W. Noyce, J. Sadler, 1960
Saser Kangri I (7,672 m) – Dawa Norbu, Da Tenzing, Nima Tenzing, Thondup, 1973
Chogolisa (7,665 m) – G. Ammerer, A. Pressl, 1975
Skyang Kangri (7,544 m) – Y. Fujihoji, H. Nagata, 1976

There are many more peaks of over 7,000 m of which the following may be noted:

Haramosh (7,406 m) – H. Roiss, F. Mandl, S. Pauer, 1958
The Ogre (Baitha Brakk) (7,285 m) – D. Scott, C. Bonington, 1977
Muztagh Tower (7,273 m) – J. Hartog, T. Patey, 1956
Diran (Minapin) (7,257 m) – R. Goschl, R. Pischinger, H. Schell, 1968

SECTION 3 KUMAON HIMALAYA (GARHWAL)

The section of the Himalaya cradled by the great bend of the Sutlej and bounded to the east by the Nepalese border has been a part of India proper since the Gurkha War of 1814–16, when it was ceded by Nepal to the Raj. There were already famous pilgrim shrines at Gaumukh and Badrinath and the British established hill stations at Simla, Chakrata, Mussoorie, Lansdowne, Ranikhet, Almora and Naini Tal. Most important of all, the Survey of India was established at Dehra Dun. It is therefore hardly surprising that this area became relatively easy of access and a prime target for mountaineers in the early days.

The mountains form three ranges here: the Great Himalaya with Nanda Devi (7,816 m), the Lesser Himalaya to the south with peaks less than 7,000 m and joining the Greater Himalaya at Chaukamba (7,138 m), and the northern Zaskar Range which borders Tibet and contains Kamet (7,756 m).

R. and A. Schlagintweit claimed to have reached 6,700 m on Kamet in 1855 but it was probably on Abi Gamin; the two were not readily distinguished in those early days. Similarly W. W. ◊ Graham claimed to have climbed Changabang in 1883 but was certainly mistaken. This was the first climbing expedition, as distinct from exploration, to the Himalaya. In 1907 ◊ Longstaff climbed Trisul (7,120 m), the first 7,000 m peak to be climbed. Much of the climbing before the Second World War concerned Kamet and Nanda

Devi. The latter is guarded by a ring of mountains access to which is via the gorge of the Rishi Ganga, a problem in itself. This was solved by ◊ Shipton and ◊ Tilman in 1934; the mountain was climbed by an Anglo–American expedition in 1936. Kamet was climbed by ◊ Smythe's party in 1931. Both Kamet and Nanda Devi were the highest mountains climbed in their day.

In post-war years the traverse of the ridge from Nanda Devi East to the main peak by an Indo-Japanese party in 1976 was an outstanding feat, as was the ascent of the S W Face of Dunagiri by ◊ Tasker and Renshaw in 1975 and the W Face of Changabang by Tasker and ◊ Boardman in 1976.

This is an area admirably suited for small parties, where many 'smaller' peaks offer exciting climbing. It is also an area where there is extensive trekking for mountain-walkers, including the Valley of the Flowers and the Devi Sanctuary, though conservation sometimes closes both these walks – the position seems to vary. The pilgrim trails mentioned earlier are still very popular.

Principal summits

Nanda Devi (7,816 m) – N. E. Odell, H. W. Tilman, 1936
Kamet (7,756 m) – R. Holdsworth, F. S. Smythe, E. E. Shipton, R. Greene, Lewa, Kesar Singh, 1931
Nanda Devi East (7,434 m) – J. Bujak, J. Klartner, M. Klavouer, 1939
Abi Gamin (7,355 m) – G. Chevalley, R. Dittert, A. Tissieres, 1950

Of the many smaller peaks the following may be noted:

Trisul (7,120 m) – 1907
Santopanth (7,075 m) – 1947
Dunagiri (7,066 m) – 1939
Changabang (6,864 m) – 1974
Shivling (6,543 m) – 1974

SECTION 4 NEPAL HIMALAYA

One of the largest and most important sections of the range, lying between the Kali River in the west and the massif of Kangchenjunga in the east. Nepal is an independent state whose capital is Kathmandu; of the various ethnic groups, two are famous, the Gurkhas and the ◊ Sherpas. Both have played important roles in the history of Himalayan climbing, though for the last half-century or so the Sherpas have been predominant in this respect.

The border with Tibet follows the main watershed and many of the high peaks are on or near it, including Everest, the highest mountain in the world, 8,848 m. The section includes peaks which are politically in Tibet. Eight of the world's fourteen 8,000 m peaks are in this section, plus seven subsidiary tops of this height. There are numerous peaks of between 7,000 m and 8,000 m.

Nepal had a policy of exclusion until 1949, so apart from a few surveyors nobody had explored the mountains. Early attempts on ◊ Mt Everest were made from Tibet and on ◊ Kangchenjunga from Sikkim. In 1949 Nepal was opened to exploration and in the following year ◊ Tilman and ◊ Houston reconnoitred the Khumbu approach to Everest and the French, under Maurice Herzog, climbed ◊ Annapurna (8,078 m) – the first 8,000 m peak to be climbed. Everest was climbed in 1953 by John ◊ Hunt's party and the other high peaks followed shortly thereafter; the last 8,000 m peak to be climbed was Shisha Pangma in 1964 by the Chinese.

There have been many variants made, especially on Everest. Outstanding was the first ascent of the S Face of Annapurna by ◊ Bonington's party in 1970

– the first really big Himalayan wall climb.

Nepal is fine trekking country with many famous walks including Everest Base Camp and the Annapurna Circuit.

Because of its size it is convenient to divide Nepal into three subsections based on the principal rivers. These are (selection of peaks only):

West Nepal (Karnali Section) From the Kali River to the Kali Gandaki.
Dhaulagiri I (8,167 m) – K. Diemberger, P. Diener, E. Forrer,
    A. Schelbert, Nyima Dorje, Nawang Dorje, 1960
Dhaulagiri II (7,751 m) – Austrian, 1971
Dhaulagiri III (7,715 m) – German, 1973
Dhaulagiri IV (7,661 m) – Japanese, 1975
Dhaulagiri V (7,618 m) – Japanese, 1975

Central Nepal (Gandaki Section) From the Kali Gandaki to the Sun Kosi.
Manaslu I (8,156 m) – T. Imanishi, Gyalzen Norbu, 1956
Annapurna I (8,091 m) – M. Herzog, L. Lachenal, 1950
Himalchuli (7,893 m) – Japanese, 1960

East Nepal (Kosi Section) From the Sun Kosi to the Arun River.
Everest (8,848 m) – E. Hillary, Tenzing Norgay, 1953
Lhotse (8,516 m) – E. Reiss, F. Luchsinger, 1956
Makalu (8,463 m) – J. Couzy, L. Terray, 1955
Lhotse Shar (8,400 m) – S. Mayerl, R. Walter, 1970
Cho Oyu (8,201 m) – H. Tichy, J. Jochter, Pasang Dawa Lama, 1954
Gyachung Kang (7,952 m) – Japanese, 1964
Nuptse (7,855 m) – British, 1961
Chomo Lonzo (7,790 m) – French, 1954
Chamlang (7,319 m) – Japanese, 1962
Menlungtse (7,181 m) – unclimbed
Pumori (7,161 m) – German/Swiss, 1962
Gauri Sankar (7,134 m) – U.S.A., 1979
Baruntse (7,129 m) – New Zealand, 1954
Ama Dablam (6,856 m) – British/New Zealand, 1961

SECTION 5 SIKKIM HIMALAYA

Lying between Nepal and Assam, this is the smallest Himalayan section in area, though it has some of the highest peaks in the world, including ◊ Kangchenjunga (8,586 m) which ranks third after Everest and K2. The Kangchenjunga group forms a centrepiece with arms running N–S and E–W. Deep jungle valleys surround the group, then around those are high border ridges with peaks such as Kangchenjau (6,889 m) and Pauhunri (7,128 m). On the Lesser Himalayan range lies the famous hill station of Darjeeling, starting point for the pre-war ◊ Mt Everest and Kangchenjunga expeditions. There are no Siwaliks here and the whole region is one of the most easily accessible in the Himalaya, which accounts for its early exploration.

In 1883 W. W. ◊ Graham came to Sikkim on what was the first climbing expedition to the Himalaya. He claimed to have ascended Kabru (7,395 m), though this is disputed. If true it was the highest summit attained for many years. In 1899 ◊ Freshfield made a classic high-level circuit of Kangchen-junga and in 1905 Guillarmod attempted to climb the peak, aided by the notorious Aleister ◊ Crowley. Two years later the Norwegians Rubenson and Aas made a spirited attack on Kabru. In 1910 ◊ Kellas climbed Pauhunri and Chomiomo.

Between the wars the Germans attempted Kangchenjunga three times

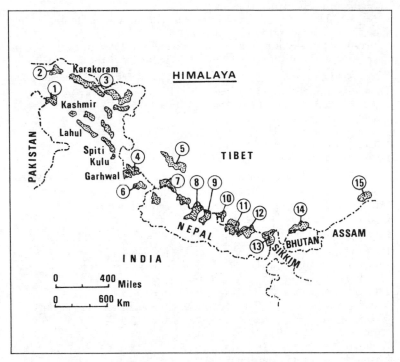

1 Nanga Parbat; 2 Rakaposhi; 3 K2; 4 Kamet; 5 Kailas; 6 Nanda Devi; 7 Gurla Mandhata; 8 Dhaulagiri; 9 Annapurna; 10 Shisha Pangma; 11 Gauri Sankar; 12 Everest; 13 Kangchenjunga; 14 Chomolhari; 15 Namche Barwa.

without success, but they were successful on Siniolchu (6,888 m) and Kirat Chuli (Tent Peak) (7,365 m). In 1935 C. R. Cooke finally climbed Kabru, the first 7,000 m post-monsoon ascent. He reached the summit solo after his companion turned back.

In 1955 J. ♢ Brown and G. C. Band reached the summit of Kangchenjunga. More recently interest has been shown in the attractive but formidable Jannu (7,710 m), first climbed in 1962 by a French team.

Principal peaks
Kangchenjunga (8,586 m) – G. C. Band, J. Brown, 1955
Yalung Kang (8,505 m) – Y. Ageta, T. Matsuda, 1973
Kangchenjunga Central Peak (8,482 m) – W. Branski, Z. Heinrich, K. Olech, 1978
Kangchenjunga South (8,476 m) – W. Wroz, E. Chrobak, 1978
(These are all summits of Kangchenjunga and apart from Nanga Parbat are the only 8,000 m peaks not in Nepal or the Karakoram.)
Kangbachen (7,903 m) – Polish, 1974
Jannu (7,710 m) – French, 1962
Jongsong Peak (7,483 m) – International, 1930
Kirat Chuli (7,365 m) – German, 1939
Kabru (7,338 m) – British, 1883 or 1935
Siniolchu (6,892 m) – German, 1936

SECTION 6 ASSAM HIMALAYA

The most easterly section of the Himalaya, extending from Chomolhari (7,315 m) to Namcha Barwa (7,756 m). The western section extends along the Bhutan–Tibet border and the eastern section along the border between Arunachal Pradesh (India) and Tibet. The whole area is contained within the huge bend of the Tsangpo-Bramaputra river which actually turns back on itself at the Tsangpo Gorge between the great peaks of Namcha Barwa and Gyala Peri (7,150 m – Japanese ascent, 1986). This is usually reckoned to be the eastern extremity of the Himalaya.

The western part is sometimes known as the Bhutan Himalaya and has 27 listed peaks over 6,000 m of which 18 are over 7,000 m. The highest are Kula Kangri (7,554 m) and Gangkar Puensum (7,541 m). None of the range has been properly surveyed; heights, and even some peaks, are speculative. Bhutan has a deliberately restrictive entry policy, but trekkers and explorers report the peaks as looking difficult: the South Ridge of Kula Kangri is a particularly fine challenge. The West Ridge was climbed by a Japanese expedition in 1986. Government policy is to make one peak available to climbers every two years and permits are very expensive – $5,000 for a big peak.

So far very few of the big peaks have been climbed, though Chomolhari was ascended as long ago as 1937 by F. S.◊ Chapman and Pasang Dawa and repeated by the Indians in 1970.

Very little is known of the peaks further east, several of which are over 7,000 m. The whole range now seems one of the most fruitful in the Himalaya for exploration and ascents.

If we discount the lesser tops of other great mountains, then Namcha Barwa is at present (1990) the highest unclimbed mountain in the world.

Himalayan Club   Formed in 1928 by the amalgamation of the original Himalayan Club and the Mountain Club of India, both of which were founded in 1927. The club is based in India and its aim is to encourage Himalayan climbing and exploration. It publishes *The Himalayan Journal* (1929), an authoritative source of Himalayan information.

Hinchcliff, Thomas Woodbine (1825–82)   A leading spirit in the formation of the A.C. of which he was President 1875–7. Hinchcliff's book *Summer Months in the Alps* (1857) was one of those that began the Golden Age of Alpine climbing, though his own achievements were fairly modest: first ascent of Wildstrubel Mittelgipfel, probably first ascent of the Oldenhorn (1857), and first ascent of Alphubel (1860) are the most notable. In 1862 he injured his hand in a gun accident which prevented him from further climbing. The discoverer of Melchior ◊ Anderegg in 1855.

Hindu Kush   An 800 km range of mountains west of the Indus and lying almost entirely within Afghanistan. Much of the range is uninteresting but there is an area of about 2,500 km² centred around the highest summit, Tirich Mir (7,706 m) frequently visited by expeditions. The accessibility of the area, freedom from the monsoon and medium height of most of the peaks makes it an excellent area for small parties.

Principal summits
Tirich Mir (7,706 m) – P. Kvernberg, A. Naess, H. Berg, A. Streather, 1950
Tirich Mir E (7,692 m) – R. Hoibakk, A. Opdal, 1964

Noshaq (7,492 m) – G. Iwatsabo, T. Sakai, 1960
Istor o Nal (7,403 m) – J. Anglada, J. Cerda, E. Civis, J. Pons, 1969
Istor o Nal N (7,373 m) – K. Lapuch, M. Oberegger, 1967
Saraghrar (7,349 m) – F. Alleto, P. Consiglio, 1959
Several other peaks over 7,000 m.

Hoare, Henry Seymour (1848–1930)   Made a number of new routes in the
Alps in the company of Davidson, Hartley, etc. Made the first ascent of the
Gross Engelhorn (1876) and of Mont Maudit (1878). In 1875 he made the
first crossing of the Nantillons Col, which was not repeated for 29 years.

Hoar frost   In conditions of extreme cold, frost crystals grow out from
rocks, especially on exposed ridges. They can achieve remarkable sizes and
look marvellous, but they do little to affect the climbing.

Hodgkinson, Rev. George Christopher (1816–80)   Was with ◊ Hudson
on the first ascents of the Bosses Ridge of Mont Blanc and the Moine Ridge of
the Aig. Verte. Also made the first ascent of the Col de Triolet (1863).

Hoggar Mountains   Sometimes called Ahaggar Mountains. A wide area of
volcanic pinnacles in the Sahara Desert, southern Algeria. Several expeditions have visited the area and many of the pinnacles climbed. The highest is
Tahat (2,918 m).

Hold   A crack or rugosity on which a climber places his hands and feet in the
course of a climb. Holds vary in size and shape and in their relative position to
one another and these factors contribute to the difficulty or otherwise of a
climb. Other factors are the type of rock, its friction and soundness.
   The use of footholds usually offers little choice: one either places the foot
on the hold – possibly just a toe – or, in the case of a suitable crack, jams it into
the hold. There are occasional side-pressure holds suitable for feet.
   Handholds vary considerably. The easiest to use are those incut ones that
the fingers can curl round and afford a pull; these are often called 'jugs' if they
are large. Pressure holds are holds where there is no grip as such and one relies
on the friction of the rock. They may be sideways. There is also the 'pinch
grip', where the rock can be squeezed between fingers. In a jammed hold
(jamming) the hand is jammed into a crack for a pull. An undercut hold is one
that is upside down, but it can be useful. All these holds may vary considerably in size and shape.
   Loose holds occur on some climbs but may have to be used – a hold which
might not bear a pull might bear using as a pressure hold. Some holds are
friable and need gentle handling – thin flakes, for example, or sandstone
flutings. All holds should be tested before use. Nevertheless, holds have been
known to come away for no obvious reason, even on climbs which have been
done many times.
   On ice, handholds may have to be cut with the ice axe. This is usually done
ladder fashion, each hand alternately. The same holds are used for the feet.
Where handholds are not required, the footholds used in snow and ice work
are known as steps. With modern ice tools and techniques this is little used
today.

Holder, Henry William (1851–?)   Made three important visits to the
Caucasus, 1888, 1890 and 1896, during which he made a number of first
ascents including Adai-Khokh (1890).

Holster   A stiff, conical tube attached to a harness for holding a piton hammer or hammer-axe. In modern ice-climbing it is common for the climber to wear two holsters, one for each ice axe.

Holzer, Heini (b. 1945)   An Italian climber best known for his steep ski descents begun in 1970. These include Similaun N Face, Tosa N Couloir, Marmolata N W Face, Ortler N E Couloir, Gran Zebru N E Face, Piz Palu North Face, Biancograt and the Brenva Face of Mont Blanc.

Hong Kong, climbs in   The hills of Hong Kong have been compared with those of the Lake District: a walker's paradise. There are also good climbing areas: Lamtong Island, Kowloon Peak and Lion Rock with routes up to H.V.S.

There are a number of other crags in the region and a long-distance footpath known as the Macleshose Trail through the hills from Sai Kung in the east to Tuen Mun in the west: about 100 km. The highest peak is Tai Mo Shan, 954 m. Lan Tau Peak on the island of the same name is only slightly less – 934 m.

Hopkinson brothers   A distinguished Manchester family related by marriage to the Tribes, Slingsbys, etc., and with them playing an important part in early British climbing. The brothers were: John (1849–98), Alfred (1851–1939), Sir Charles (1854–1920), Edward (1859–1921), Albert (1863–1949). Sir Charles was an M.P. and lawyer, Albert a surgeon, the others engineers – all brilliant.

The Hopkinsons kept few records and much of their climbing is unknown, but they were certainly among the originators of the sport. In 1882 they descended the E Face of Tryfan, four years before Haskett Smith climbed Napes Needle. In 1892 they ascended N E Ridge, Ben Nevis, and descended Tower Ridge, two years before ◊ Collie paid his visit.

Hopkinson's Cairn was erected on the face of Scafell Pinnacle by Edward in 1887, and acted as a magnet to early climbers, who tried to reach it from below (◊ Scafell). It was not climbed until 1912 (Herford).

Either together or singly they took part in several of the famous early ascents, for example, Slingsby's Chimney, Scafell (1888, Edward). Their best-known routes are on Dow Crag: Great Gully Direct (1889), Intermediate Gully (1895) and Hopkinson's Crack (1895).

In the Alps they made a few minor routes, but in 1898 John Hopkinson and three of his children were killed climbing the Petite Dent de Veisivi, Arolla. The other brothers never climbed again.

Hornbein, Thomas F. (b. 1931)   An American doctor who began climbing at the age of 14 when he ascended Signal Mt in Colorado. He was on the Masherbrum expedition of 1960 but not in the summit party. Invited to join the American Everest Expedition for 1963, he was put in charge of oxygen and improved the system. With W. Unsoeld he climbed the W Ridge of Everest (first ascent) and descended the S Ridge (first traverse), bivouacking on the latter at 28,000 ft before reaching Camp 6 next day – one of the most outstanding mountaineering achievements ever accomplished. Wrote: *Everest – the West Ridge* (1966).

Hornby and Philpott   The Rev. James John Hornby (1826–1909) and the Rev. Thomas Henry Philpott (1839–1917) formed a famous partnership which lasted from 1861 to 1866. They crossed a number of difficult passes and made the first traverse of Aletschhorn (1864), the first ascent of Lauterbrunnen Breithorn (1865) (this was technically the second – they arrived about ten minutes after von Fellenberg!) and the N W Face (Ridge) of the Silberhorn (1865). They might well have done the first ascent of the Brenva Route in 1863 had the idea not been vetoed by their guide, ◊ Almer.

Philpott was a student of Hornby's at Durham University. Both men were strong and good athletes, and Hornby was a noted oarsman. The partnership ended in 1866 and Hornby retired from climbing two years later on becoming Headmaster of Eton. Philpott returned after a lapse of 26 years and did a couple of seasons, which included some difficult routes.

Hort, Rev. Fenton John Anthony (1828–92) Distinguished scholar and Professor of Divinity at Cambridge. Hort made two strenuous tours of the Alps in 1854 and 1856 but ill health later confined him to topographical and botanical work. He took an active part in the founding of the A.C.

Houston, Charles S. (b. 1913) American medical professor noted for his contributions to research on high-altitude effects and diseases. Houston began climbing in the Alps in 1925 and had three seasons there. In 1936 he was leader, with Tilman, of the successful team that made the first ascent of Nanda Devi. Two years later he led an American expedition to K2; they reached c.7,900 m. With Tilman again in 1950 he led a small party into Nepal and they were the first to see the south side of Everest and the Western Cwm. Houston was also leader of the American K2 expedition of 1953 which encountered disaster at 7,600 m and in which Gilkey died.

Since 1967 Houston has been director of high-altitude physiology programmes at the laboratory (5,300 m) on Mt Logan, opened every year.

Besides numerous medical contributions to books he is co-author of *Five Miles High* (1939) and *K2, The Savage Mountain* (1954).

Howard, Tony (b. 1940) Played a leading part in the development of the Dovestone area and the limestone dales of Derbyshire in the early 1960s, but is best known for his climbs in Romsdal, Norway, where he made the first ascent of the formidable Troll Wall (1965), said to be the highest rock face in Europe. Besides contributing to several Peakland guides he wrote *Selected Climbs in Romsdal* (1965) and later expanded this to *Walks and Climbs in Romsdal* (1970).

He later developed an affinity for desert country and climbed in Iran and in Jordan, where he played a large part in developing Wadi Rum. (He wrote a guide: *Treks and Climbs in the Mountains of Rum and Petra, Jordan*, 1987.)

Howard is a partner in the well-known equipment manufacturing firm, Troll.

Howard-Bury, Charles Kenneth (1883–1963) An army officer with some experience of exploration in Central Asia (Tien Shan, 1913) and subsequently chosen to lead the first ◊ Mt Everest Expedition in 1921, for which he received the Founder's Medal, R. G. S.

Howgills A compact group of fells above Sedbergh, and dominating the M6 motorway at the Lune Gorge. Popular with fell-walkers, there is no rock-climbing – the gaunt Cautley Crag is too broken to be of use. There are two dramatic waterfalls, Black Force and Cautley Spout: the former is an entertaining scramble, the latter gives a good winter climb on steep ice. The highest top is The Calf (676 m).

Hudson, Rev. Charles (1828–65)   One of the greatest of the early Alpine pioneers, killed in the Matterhorn tragedy of 1865.

Hudson was one of the hardest men of his day. At the age of 17 he averaged 43 km a day on a walking tour of the Lake District, and, according to Whymper, could average 80 km a day in his prime. In 1853 he bivouacked in a sleeping bag at 2,100 m in February when the temperature was 13°F below zero. In the same year he made a solo winter attempt to reach the Aig. du Goûter to reconnoitre a new route up Mont Blanc. He was an early exponent of guideless climbing, making ascents of the Kl. Matterhorn and Breithorn in 1855, and in the same year, the first guideless ascent of Mont Blanc (the first ascent from St Gervais). With E. S. ◊ Kennedy, who accompanied him, he wrote a book about the expedition: *Where There's a Will, There's a Way* (1856).

Not all Hudson's climbs are recorded, but among the most famous are the first ascent of Monte Rosa (1855), first ascent of Mont Blanc by the Bosses Ridge (1859), and the first ascent of the Moine Ridge of the Aig. Verte (1865). (The ascent of the Bosses Ridge claimed by Marie Couttet in 1840 and shown in some guidebooks is now generally discounted.)

In 1865 Hudson, Hadow (a young novice) and their guide, Croz, were to attempt the Matterhorn from Zermatt when they were joined at the last moment by Whymper, Lord Francis Douglas and the Taugwalders, father and son. The combined party reached the summit at 1.40 p.m. on 14 July, but during the descent Hadow slipped, the rope broke and Hudson, Hadow, Croz and Douglas fell to their deaths. (◊ Whymper.)

Amongst his contemporaries, Hudson was held to be the finest mountaineer of all and there is much to support this idea. However, he twice took complete novices on difficult new climbs (◊ Birkbeck) and on both occasions the result was a serious accident.

Hudson had been a Chaplain during the Crimean War (1854–5). At the time of his death he was Vicar of Skillington, Lincolnshire.

Hudson, John Alfred (1838–74)   Took part in the first ascent of Lyskamm and the first traverse of the High Level Route from Zermatt to the Gd St Bernard (1861). Was later a companion of ◊ Girdlestone on the latter's guideless climbs.

Hulton, George Eustace (1842–1909)   A Manchester businessman who made the first ascent of the Arbengrat on the Gabelhorn and of the popular Cresta Rey on Monte Rosa (both 1874). With the Pilkingtons he later became interested in guideless climbing and made with them the first guideless ascents of Piz Kesch, Piz Roseg and Monte della Disgrazia (all 1882).

Hulton was also a pioneer of British climbing and the instigator of regular A.C. meets in Wales and the Lake District, usually in winter. He took part in the first ascent of ◊ Cust's Gully and the first ascent of Deep Ghyll, Scafell (1882). In 1883 he was with Pilkington and Walker in Skye when they made the first ascent of Bidein Druim nan Ramh and the second (or possibly third) ascent of the Inaccessible Pinnacle.

His brother, F. C. Hulton, also did a season in the Alps in 1873, when the two brothers made the 50th ascent of the Matterhorn.

Hunt, John Henry Cecil (b. 1910)   An army officer who led the successful Everest Expedition of 1953, for which he was knighted. Hunt had been on James Waller's spirited attack on Saltoro Kangri in the Karakoram in 1935, but was considered by the medical board not fit enough for the Everest

John Hunt (*A. Gregory*)   Dougal Haston (*C. Bonington*)

Expedition of 1936. In 1937, with Cooke and Mrs Hunt, he explored the approaches to Kangchenjunga from the Zemu side and succeeded in reaching the S W Summit of Nepal Peak (7,144 m).

Hunt played a leading part in the foundation and organization of the Duke of Edinburgh's Award scheme and later in various social inquiries for the government. President of the A.C. 1956–8. Created Baron Hunt of Llanvair Waterdine. Wrote: *The Ascent of Everest, Our Everest Adventure, Life is Meeting*, and, with C. Brasher, *Red Snows*.

Huts (G.: Hutte, Haus; Fr.: refuge, cabane; It.: rifugio, capanna)   A mountain hut is a purpose-built refuge situated at some strategically high place in the mountains so that one or more peaks are readily accessible from it. It may vary from a simple bivouac shelter to something resembling a small hotel in size and facilities.

Huts were built to enable climbers to do away with the bivouacs endured by the pioneers. They mostly belong to the various Alpine Clubs, but there are a few belonging to university clubs and, in Tyrol, even to private families. All huts are open to anyone wishing to use them, though they are cheaper for club members and there are reciprocal rights between the various Continental clubs. There are about 2,000 huts in the Alps.

Huts are cared for by a guardian (G.: *Huttenwart*), who is often a guide or ex-guide. In the larger huts he will have several assistants, often his family. It is unusual for a hut to remain open the whole year, but, with the growth of skiing, many now open for the winter months as well as summer. When a hut is closed, some out-building or separate room is often left open for emergency use. Bivouac huts and some remote huts have no guardian.

There is no standard pattern to the facilities of the huts, even within one area, and the following can only be taken as generalizations:

French Alps: *dortoir*; meals provided; self-catering allowed.

Swiss Alps: *dortoir*; meals provision (except simple soups) not general but increasing; no self-catering – the guardian cooks food brought by the party.

Austrian Alps (including Germany and Italy): *dortoir*, but also small rooms with bunks; meals provided, including a cheap *Bergsteigeressen*.

Dortoir accommodation consists of communal bunks (G.: *Matratzen-lager*). It is usual to sleep fully clothed, ready for a quick start in the morning (often 3 a.m.–4 a.m.), though blankets are provided. In unguardianed huts there are often just the bare necessities, and climbers may have to provide their own fuel for cooking.

Supplies for huts were previously brought up by porters or on mules, but the téléférique or helicopter is more usual today.

The highest mountain hut in the Alps is the Capanna Margherita on the Signalkuppe of Monte Rosa (4,556 m). It holds 25 climbers and is guardianed. The largest hut is probably the Berliner in the Zillertal range, Tyrol. It would be difficult to establish which hut was the oldest but many were established in the 1860s and 1870s.

British mountain huts are usually valley bases, owned by various climbing clubs and available only to club members or those with reciprocal rights from another club. They have no resident guardian. At Glen Brittle, Skye, there is a hut built to commemorate climbers killed in the last war and this is open to members of all clubs affiliated to the British Mountaineering Council.

The Mountain Bothies Association repairs and maintains old shepherds' huts which serve as high-level bivvy huts for climbers.

Hut shoes It is forbidden to wear climbing boots inside Alpine huts. Boots are left in the porch and the climber wears hut shoes. These may be soft chamois leather slippers he has brought up from the valley or wooden soled clogs provided by the huts. Not all huts provide clogs.

I

Ice axe (G.: Pickel; Fr.: piolet; It.: piccozza) An essential piece of equipment wherever ice- and snow-climbing is involved. The axe consists of a head, a shaft and a ferruled spike. The head is of hardened steel with one end fashioned into an adze or blade and the other into a pick. The shaft is straight-grained hickory or ash, though this is now being rapidly ousted by metal shafts or synthetic materials, which are stronger and do not deteriorate. The spike and ferrule are of hardened steel. The axe may or may not be equipped with a wrist strap.

Axe shafts vary in length from 60 to 90 cm – the longer ones are often known as walkers' axes, though in fact they are suitable for all but the very steep ice-climbs (see below). The trend over the years has been for ever shorter ice axes.

More recently, even shorter axes have been developed to cope with the very steep ice encountered in modern ice-climbs and the new techniques of climbing. These often have a hammer head replacing the adze (a hammer axe) and specially curved picks to allow maximum front-pointing techniques.

There are four functions of an axe to be considered and these have changed in emphasis over the years:

1. AS A WALKING STICK. The so-called 'third leg'. Modern short axes often make this impossible and the use has virtually died out. It is still used in the special case of traversing, but otherwise the axe is best carried in a position of braking (below).
2. FOR STEP-CUTTING. Once the main function and still useful for this, though modern crampon techniques have reduced the importance of steps. (◊ Steps.)
3. AS A BELAY. Again, still useful for this, but ice screws and snow anchors are better.
4. AS A BRAKE. The axe can be used as a brake to arrest a slip on snow or snow-ice. The axe is held across the body and if a slip occurs the victim presses the spike gradually into the snow, thus braking. For most climbers this is now the most important function of an axe. The technique needs practice on safe slopes.

Ice axes have been in use from early pioneering days and seem to have originated from peasants' implements. Many climbers designed their own. The axe was contemporary with the ◊ alpenstock but had virtually supplanted the latter by the 1870s.

Early axes were ponderous affairs, very long and heavy, designed for chopping steps by the hundreds. There have been continuous changes and many variations, including axes which unscrewed into sections, so that they could be carried easily when packed.

Ice axes can be dangerous weapons. The spike and head need covering when not in use – this is compulsory on many Continental transport systems.
 (◊◊ Ice tools.)

Ice-climbing The original art in climbing ice was that of step-cutting (◊

Steps), which depended on an ice axe and good nailed boots. Steps were cut using the pick of the axe either straight up the slope, or, where the ice was very steep, in zig-zag fashion with a large bucket step, or turning step, at each bend. The nailed boots gave admirable grip on hard ice though they tended to ball up in snow. Some very difficult climbs were completed in this way, including several of the early north faces. Protection was not possible until ice pegs came into use, about the 1920s.

The greatest single advance in ice equipment was the ◊ crampon, which allowed progress on fairly steep ice which would have otherwise needed steps. Crampons were introduced quite early, but were regarded with suspicion and even hostility by many climbers. They were adopted in the Eastern Alps, however, and by the English climber ◊ Eckenstein who improved their design. With the introduction of the rubber-soled boot in post-war years (pre-war on the Continent) their use became virtually imperative. Many climbers, particularly in Scotland, still preferred nails, and mixed soles of rubbers and nails were used for a time.

As steeper ice-climbs were attempted, particularly in Scotland, the disadvantage of the long axe became obvious and the Scots used slater's picks to cut the hand and footholds necessary. (See *Mountaineering in Scotland*, by W. H. Murray.) By the 1950s, the general advantages of shorter axes were becoming acknowledged in the Alps, and the so-called dagger technique was evolved. In this, a short axe was used in one hand and an ice dagger (often a sharpened piton) in the other. The technique depended upon the front points of the crampons, the 'lobster claws', and consisted of simply stabbing one's way up the face, using axe, dagger and front points alternately. The method was tiring, though quick, and it was usual to cut resting steps at intervals. Belays and runners were provided by ice-screws which came in during the fifties.

Though the early climbers had disdained the use of any attachment to their ice axes, the loss of an axe during a climb is so potentially serious that wrist straps were introduced. It is safe to say that the majority of ice-climbing is still done using a combination of the methods outlined above – that is general cramponing with occasional steps and moderately long axes.

The real change came to ice-climbing when the dagger was replaced by an ◊ ice tool, as was the traditional axe. Climbers such as ◊ Cunningham, ◊ March, ◊ MacInnes and Chouinard were instrumental in developing techniques to maximize the use of these tools and steep ice could be climbed very quickly by the new techniques. The tools are placed in the ice with a swing and pulled up on, using crampon front points for the feet. The tools are then placed higher in turn.

On moderately steep ice it is often possible for two climbers to move together, possibly using runners but not stances. This is quick, but demands a good understanding between the two climbers. Where the ice steepens, one climber cuts a stance and belays to an ice screw (or possibly more than one) while the other climbs. The leader runs out the full length of rope, then he in turn cuts a stance and belays, to bring up the second, and so on.

Belaying on ice is a sensitive business. The best belay is a rock peg, if there is any rock conveniently placed, otherwise a strong ice peg, such as the tubular kind, is needed. If no screws or pegs are carried, a direct belay round the pick of the axe is the only security. Where pegs are used, a normal rock-climbing belay procedure is followed.

Ice-climbs vary from season to season. In Britain the best ice-climbs are found in Scotland in winter, particularly on Ben Nevis and in the Cairngorms and Glen Coe – all popular areas. They are graded in difficulty from the

Left, Ice-climbing on the Eigerwand; right, an ice-fall on the Taschach Glacier, Tyrol. (*W.U.*)

easiest (I) to the hardest (V). South of the border conditions are even less certain, but the Great End gullies in the Lakes, Kinder Downfall and Back Tor in the Pennines, and occasional routes in Wales can give good climbs.

See *Modern Snow and Ice Techniques* by W. March.

Ice-fall When a glacier flows over a steep declivity, the ice fractures into enormous crevasses and pinnacles (⟡ séracs). Such an area is an ice-fall. They sometimes have to be crossed; this is often difficult and always potentially dangerous because the glacier is moving slowly downhill and this causes the séracs to fall. Well-known examples include the Géant ice-fall on the Mer de Glace and the huge two-mile-long ice-fall descending from the Western Cwm of Everest.

Iceland, climbing in Well known for its volcanic scenery of geysers, hot springs and volcanoes, Iceland has an interior which is extremely bleak, with a dozen ice-caps, one of which, Vatnajokull, rises to 2,000 m and has an area of 21,000 km² – the largest in Europe. Travel can be difficult away from the coast roads.

The highest peak is Hvannadalshnukur (2,119 m) in Oraefajokull, a southern arm of the Vatnajokull ice cap. The best base is the National Park Centre at Skaftafell, easily reached by bus from Reykjavik.

There is little in Iceland to interest the rock-climber.

Ice screws Used for protection and belays on ice-climbs.

There are now two major types – those that can be driven in with a hammer and screwed out (snargs) and those that can be screwed in and out by hand. Mostly they are hollow tubes, though there are solid models. The old corkscrew type is little used today.

Ice screws should not be left in place too long in the Alps or other ranges where the sun is hot because the heat is conducted down the metal and the screw works loose. Belays should be repositioned from time to time.

Ice tools   The name usually given to very short ice axes (45–55 cm) used in climbing steep ice. Metal-shafted, they have a spike and an eye to take a tape or krab by which the tool is attached to the harness so that it cannot be dropped accidentally down the ice wall. The pick can be of various shapes and may be removed by the locking nut which allows a new blade to be fitted. Some climbers like to match the type of blade to the ice. Similarly weights can be added to the head to alter the swing of the tool according to the blade in use. A tape wrist loop is attached to the head. One tool of a pair will have a hammer head and the other the traditional adze.

   The system is capable of considerable sophistication and fast times can be achieved on steep ice, but most climbers are content with one type of blade – usually the 'banana' or reversed curve type.

Imseng, Ferdinand (1845–81)   A guide from the Saas valley, though he lived from the age of 20 in Macugnaga. Imseng sprang to fame suddenly when he persuaded the ☿ Pendleburys to attempt the E Face of Monte Rosa in 1872, with great success. A few weeks later he accompanied Passingham and Dent on the first ascent of the Zinal Rothorn from Zermatt, and in 1879 was Penhall's guide in the latter's race with Mummery for the Zmutt Ridge of the Matterhorn. Their route, via the W Face, has seldom been repeated.

   Whilst repeating the Monte Rosa climb with Signor Marinelli in 1881, Imseng and his party were overwhelmed by an avalanche. Marinelli and his two guides were killed; a porter escaped. The climb is now known as the Marinelli Couloir.

Innerkofler, Michael (1848–88)   A member of the pioneer Dolomite guiding family who made a number of first ascents in that region including Zwolferkogel (1875), Elferkogel (1878), Grohmannspitze (1880) and Cima Piccola de Lavaredo (1881). He died in an accident on Monte Cristallo.

Innerkofler, Sepp (1865–1915)   One of the most famous pioneer guides of the Dolomites with numerous first ascents to his credit. Killed making an attack on an Italian observation post on the summit of the Paternkofel.

Iran, climbing in   The borders and coasts of Iran are guarded at almost every point by mountains, many of which are virtually unknown to climbers. Best known, and highest, is the great snow cone of Demavend (5,670 m), first climbed (as far as is known) by Sir W. Taylor Thompson in 1836. Demavend is the summit of the Elburz Mountains of which other interesting peaks are Alam Kuh (4,826 m) and Takht-i-Sulieman (4,619 m). The range has been well explored by British, German and French parties.

   Other mountains explored include Kuh-i-Savalan (Kuhha-ye-Sabalan) in Azerbaijan, whose height of 4,812 m seems in dispute. The same applies to the little-known mountains of the Zagros Range, where Zard Kuh is given the height of 4,200 m and Kuh-i-Dena, 4,432 m.

Ireland, climbing in   Because of heavy rainfall and a reputation for being boggy Irish mountains have never enjoyed the popularity of their English, Welsh or Scottish counterparts. Yet there are fine mountains in every quarter of the island: the quartzite of Connemara, the sandstone of the south and west, the granite of the north and east. The highest point is Carrauntoohil

(1,038 m) in the Macgillicuddy's Reeks of the Inveragh Peninsula in the deep south-west.

The principal mountain groups are (roughly north–south, east–west):

Mournes	Slieve Donard	852 m
Sperrin Mountains	Sawel	683 m
Wicklow Mountains	Lugnaquillia	944 m
Blackstairs Mountains	Mt Leinster	796 m
Silvermine Mountains	Keeper Hill	694 m
Derryveagh Mountains	Errigal	752 m
Blue Stack Mountains	Blue Stack	676 m
Cuilcagh Mountains	Cuilcagh	667 m
Macgillicuddy's Reeks	Carrauntoohil	1,038 m
Brandon Peak	–	953 m
Slieve Mish Mountains	Baurtregaum	852 m
Slieve Miskish Mountains	Maulin	623 m
Caha Mountains	Hungry Hill	686 m
Shehy Mountains	Knockboy	707 m
Galty Mountains	Galtymore	920 m
Knockmealdown Mountains	Knockmealdown	795 m
Comeragh Mountains	Fauscoum	792 m
Murrisk Mountains	Mweelrea	819 m
North Mayo Hills	Nephin	807 m
Twelve Bens	Benbaun	730 m

The Burren, in Co. Clare, though not strictly mountains, is a remarkable area of karst limestone.

There was little rock-climbing in Ireland until after the Second World War, when owing to the efforts of pioneers such as Joss Lynam, W. R. Perrott, P. Kenny, F. Winder, F. Maguire, P. Gribbon and A. Kopczyski numerous climbs of all standards were developed on a variety of cliffs. The Federation of Mountaineering Clubs of Ireland (E.M.C.I.) issues a series of guides, currently including *Burren*, *Donegal*, *Fairhead-Antrim Coast*, *Mourne*, *Twelve Bens* and *Wicklow*.

See also: *Irish Peaks* (J. Lynam) and *Rockclimbing in Ireland* (Torrans and Stelfox).

Irvine, Andrew Comyn (1902–24)   A member of the Oxford Spitzbergen Expedition of 1923, on the strength of which he was chosen to go to Everest on the 1924 Expedition, though his mountaineering qualifications were negligible. Inexplicably, Mallory chose Irvine instead of the experienced Odell as his partner for the summit assault. Both disappeared above Camp VI (8 June 1924).

Irving, Robert Lock Graham (1877–1969)   A Winchester schoolmaster and writer whose pioneering work with pupils in the Alps caused a stir at the turn of the century. His most famous pupil was ◊ Mallory.

Irving's books were popular with a wide public. They are: *La Cime du Mont Blanc* (1933), *Romance of Mountaineering* (1935), *The Mountain Way* (1938), *The Alps* (1939), *Ten Great Mountains* (1940) and *A History of British Mountaineering* (1955).

Isle of Man, climbing in   The highest point of this popular holiday island is Snaefell (620 m). Ten other peaks exceed 450 m, though none reach 600 m. There is a backbone of hills from north-east to south-west across the island

and a number of fell races, including the Manx Mountain Marathon (48 km, Ramsey to Port Erin). There are long-distance walks around the island and across it.

The best rock-climbing is on the coast especially at the Chasms (GR 193633) and Spanish Head (GR 183658). The rock seems to be a sort of slate and all grades are catered for. Some routes reach 60 m, though most are less than half this.

Climbing began with the ascent of the Sugar Loaf sea-stack by Dr A. W. Kelly, solo, in 1933. Post-war development was done by K. R. R. Wilson, W. J. H. West, F. Sharples and J. W. Caine in the fifties, then two decades later by Geoff Gartrell, John Watson, Bill Cheverst, Stu Thomas and R. B. Evans. Later developers include Ron Yuen and Miles Peters, but the island has never found popularity with climbers.

Italy, climbing in   In addition to the major◊ Alpine groups there is a good deal of climbing in Italy. The best known areas are:

Grigne   Near Lecco in northern Italy. Fantastic limestone pinnacles like a miniature Dolomites, and a training ground for climbers such as ◊ Cassin, ◊ Mauri and ◊ Bonatti. There are two main groups, North and South. The North Grigne have routes up to 600 m long but in the South they are 100–200 m. Many hard routes. No English guidebook.

Valle dell' Orco   South of Aosta in Gran Paradiso National Park. The valley has several granite crags of 200 m in height. Mostly hard climbs.

Val di Mello   A beautiful valley with several granite crags, north of Valtellina, in the Alpine foothills. Climbs up to 500 m, mostly hard. Best known is the famous Luna Nascente (Rising Moon), 335 m, E2 5b first climbed by Boscatti, Ghezzi and Milani, 1978.

Valle di Sarca (Arco)   South-west of Trento at the head of Lake Garda. Limestone, with numerous long Dolomite-like routes including some easier grades, up to 600 m on Le Placche Zebrate and also shorter, bolt-protected routes of a harder sort on various crags.

Finale   One of the most popular rock-climbing areas in Italy, at Finale Ligure on the Italian Riviera. Limestone cliffs caused by three rivers cutting into a limestone plateau give climbs up to about 200 m, but mostly shorter. HVS and above.

Corma di Machaby   East of Aosta, near Verres. A huge gneiss cliff with climbs (HVS and above) of 300 m.

In addition to the above there are other developing areas in northern Italy including Valle Susa and Rocca Sbarua, west of Turin; Muzzerone and Monte Proncinto, near La Spezia; Bismantova, west of Bologna; Balmanoslesca, near the Swiss border at Gondo and crags around Lecco.

GUIDEBOOK Churcher, *Italian Rock* (C.P.).

Apennines   A range of mountains running down the length of Italy for more than 1,000 km. The highest peaks are in the central Apennines in the Gran Sasso d'Italia group. The highest summit is Monte Corno (2,921 m) also known as Corno Grande, first climbed in 1794 by Orazio Delfico. (See F. Gribble, *The Early Mountaineers*.)

There are mountain huts provided by the C.A.I. and a good deal of climbing at places such as Monte Morra, Monte Argentario and Monte Leano. The rock is mostly limestone. The climbs seem little known outside Italy and there is no English-language guidebook.

J

Jackson, Mrs Edward Patten (1843–1906)   One of the most outstanding Victorian lady climbers, with about 140 major climbs to her credit. She climbed mainly with her husband until his early death, aged 39, in 1881. She made a new route on the Weissmies (1876) and what seems to be second traverse of the Matterhorn by a woman (1877). In 1884, with Dr K. Schultz, she made a descent of the Ferpècle arête of the Dent Blanche, five years before its first ascent. In 1888 she made the first winter ascents of Gross Lauteraarhorn, Pfaffenstöckli, Gross Viescherhorn and first winter traverse of Jungfrau, all in the space of 12 days. Mrs Jackson's career deserves further research by Alpine historians.

Jackson, Rev. James (1796–1878)   Eccentric vicar of Rivington, Lancashire, who repaired his own church weathercock and was thereafter known as Steeple Jackson. He celebrated this event in one of his many doggerel verses:

> Who has not heard of Steeple Jack
> That lion hearted Saxon?
> Though I'm not he, he was my sire
> For I am Steeple Jackson!

He resigned in 1856 and lived in Cumberland where he made some long walks suitable for a man half his age: 74 km in 14½ hours, followed two days later by 90 km in 18 hours and, a day later, 96 km in under 20 hours. He was then 69.

On 31 May 1875 (aged 79) he climbed Pillar Rock, alone. He called himself Patriarch of the Pillarites. Three years later he tried to repeat the ascent but fell and was killed.

Jackson, James (1845–1926)   A very strong climber noted for carrying out expeditions in a single day, for example, Breuil to Zermatt over Matterhorn (1872), Monch from Wengern Alp, Eiger (first traverse, 1872), etc. In 1876 he made the first ascent of the Mischabelgrat of the Täschhorn.

Jacomb, Frederick William (c.1828–93)   Made the first ascent of Castor and Monte Viso (1861) as well as several cols and minor peaks. Played a large part in establishing the ◊ High Level Route.

James, Ronald (b. 1933)   James was the founder of the Ogwen Cottage Mountain School (1959), the most successful private venture of its type, until it was taken over by an education authority in 1964. He remained as Warden until 1969. During this period he led 350 mountain rescues.

Ron James is perhaps best known for the new Welsh climbs he has originated. These total 80, amongst which might be mentioned: Touch and Go (1957), Mean Feet (1957), Grey Arête (1959), Devil's Nordwand (1959), Connie's Crack (1961), Lavaredo (1961), Meshach (1962), Epitaph (1962), Plum (1964) and Amphitheatre Girdle (1966).

Jamming a crack. (*R. H. Heaton*)

He has made many British first ascents in the Alps, often with his wife, Barbara James.

His books are *Rock Climbing in Wales* (1970) and *Rockface – The Technique of Rock Climbing* (1974).

Jamming An important method of crack climbing where progress is made by wedging one's feet and hands in the crack and relying upon the friction. There are all types of jams: foot-jam, toe-jam, finger-jam, etc. One of the most important is the hand-jam, in which the hand is placed sideways into the crack and then the thumb is brought across the palm, locking the hand into place. Improvements made in jamming techniques have been one of the factors responsible for the advancement of modern rock-climbing.

Jan Mayen Island A small island nearly mid-way between Iceland and Spitzbergen. The Beerenberg (2,341 m) is an extinct volcano, climbed in 1921.

Japan, climbing in The highest mountain in Japan is Fujiyama (3,776 m), the well-known volcano shrine standing isolated and splendid about 50 miles west of Yokohama. It was reputedly first climbed by a monk, Enno Ozuno, in the seventh century. Ski mountaineering has taken place on the peak since 1913.

Most of Japan is mountainous, but the chief climbing interest lies in the Japanese Alps where Kitadake (3,192 m) is the highest point, and the second highest mountain in Japan. The Japanese Alps are divided into three ranges: North, Central and South, with 26 peaks of 3,000 m or more, steep-sided, sharp-ridged and composed of granite. In summer they are bare rock, above the tree line, but in winter they are often deeply snow-covered and temperatures can drop to −20°C. Both summer and winter climbing is popular. The Northern Alps are the most frequented, with splendid peaks like Tsurugidake (2,998 m), Yarigadake (3,180 m) and Hodakadake (3,190 m). There are no permanent glaciers. There are Japanese guidebooks to all the regions. Some winter climbing is also done in the Kurile and Sakhalin Islands.

There are Shinto shrines on the summit of many Japanese mountains and the importance of mountains in their religious beliefs has accustomed the Japanese to the special ambience of mountains, and made modern climbing readily acceptable to them. The Rev. Walter ◊ Weston was the father of Japanese mountaineering, helping to found the Japanese Alpine Club in 1905. It was Weston who first called the Japanese mountains 'alps'. At first the sport was taken up only by students from the privileged classes. With the aid of Swiss guides, Yuko Maki made the first ascent of the Eiger Mittellegigrat in 1921 and Mt Alberta in the Rockies in 1925.

Since those early days, Japanese climbing has developed along familiar lines: increasingly difficult ascents at home, new and hard climbs in the European Alps, and expeditions to the Himalayas and elsewhere. In expeditions, they outnumber every other country – possibly all other countries added together. For instance, in 1965, Japan mounted 53 overseas expeditions. Their successes, and failures, have been in proportion. Outstanding was their first ascent of Manaslu (8,156 m) in 1956. They were the first to attempt the S W Face of Everest (1969) and in 1970 they made the 15th and 16th successful ascent by the S Ridge.

In 1975 Mrs Junko ◊ Tabei became the first woman to climb ◊ Mt Everest.

Jaun, Johann (1843–1921) One of the greatest Oberland guides of the second generation; a pupil of Melchior ◊ Anderegg; intelligent, fast and daring. Jaun was sometimes called Hans or more often Hänserli, to distinguish him from Hans von Bergen, another great Oberland guide who was also a pupil of Melchior.

In 1868 he was with Horace ◊ Walker, Melchior and J. Grange on the first ascent of the ◊ Grandes Jorasses to Pt Walker, the highest summit (4,208 m). In 1874 he met Thomas ◊ Middlemore and there began an extraordinarily daring partnership. They made the dangerous crossing of the Col des Grandes Jorasses that year and the following season, with Lord Wentworth, they tried the Argentière face of the Verte, but without success.

Jaun's greatest season was 1876. A very strong team of Middlemore, ◊ Cordier and ◊ Maund with Jaun, Jakob ◊ Anderegg and Maurer made the first ascent of the Verte from the Argentière glacier by the Cordier Couloir; it was not repeated for many years. They followed this with the first ascents of les Courtes and les Droites: then regarded as 'a tour de force unsurpassed in the history of the Alps'. A few days later, without Maund and Anderegg, they were in the Bernina making the first ascent of the Middlemoregrat on Piz Roseg and Biancograt on Piz Bernina, though they did not follow the latter to the summit.

Jaun was a fine woodcarver, whose work was in much demand, and a keen shot. He went hunting with T. S. ◊ Kennedy in the Himalaya in 1882.

Jerstad, Luther G. (b. 1937)   American University teacher and mountain guide from Oregon who was co-leader of the McArthur–Logan Expedition to Yukon and was on the Mt McKinley Expedition of 1962. In 1963 with Barry ◊ Bishop he made the second American ascent of Everest (S Ridge).

John of Austria, Archduke (1782–1859)   Son of Emperor Leopold II and best known for losing the battle of Hohenlinden (1800). He seems to have climbed Ankogel (3,251 m) and Hochgolling (2,863 m) and sent his physician, Dr Gebhard, to climb Ortler (3,899 m) in 1804. The good doctor failed to reach the top but three guides, J. Pichler, J. Leitner and J. Klausner succeeded in a howling gale.

The Archduke married a postmaster's daughter in 1827 and perhaps stimulated by this, attempted the difficult N W Face of Gross Venediger the following year. Unfortunately his guide, P. Rohregger, was carried away by an avalanche though he survived to take part in the first ascent of the peak 13 years later.

Jones, Owen Glynne (1867–99)   One of the pioneers of British rock-climbing and a close friend of the ◊ Abraham brothers. He began climbing at Cader Idris in 1888 but first visited the Lake District, where he was to make his mark, in 1890, when he climbed on Pillar. He knew none of the climbing fraternity and made many ascents solo, or with chance acquaintances. In 1893 he soloed Moss Ghyll under winter conditions, fell and cracked his ribs, but completed the ascent, and repeated the climb three days later. Apart from Cader Idris, where he had made the first ascent of the Cyfrwy arête (solo), his next first ascent seems to have been the minor East Pisgah Chimney on Pillar (solo).

In 1893 he met J. W. Robinson, with whom he climbed Sergeant Crag Gully and Kern Knotts Chimney – both first ascents. He met the Abrahams in 1895 and climbed frequently with them thereafter; he posing for their photographs and they helping him with his guidebook compilation. (See list of climbs on following page.)

In 1896 he published *Rock Climbing in the English Lake District*, in which he laid out the first system of classification of difficulty (◊ Gradings). These were: Easy, Moderate, Difficult, and Exceptionally Severe.

Jones was not an easy companion and rather abrupt in manner. His climbing was far from elegant – rough and spasmodic was how George Abraham described it – but he was immensely strong. He thought little of his British climbs, hoping to make a name for himself as an alpinist. This he never achieved, though he did many of the standard climbs and made a good winter ascent of the Schreckhorn in 1897. He was killed on the Dent Blanche in 1899 while attempting the Ferpècle arête (sometimes known since then as the Jones arête). His guide, Furrer, fell and pulled off Jones and a second guide, Vuignier. The rope broke between Vuignier and the last man, Hill, who was left to make an incredible solo escape. Jones was buried at Evolene. In private life he was a science teacher.

List of first ascents	Companions
LAKE DISTRICT	
1892 East Pisgah Chimney	
1893 Sergeant Crag Gully	J. W. Robinson
Kern Knotts Chimney	W. H. Fowler, J. W. Robinson
1896 Jones's Direct from Deep Ghyll	Abraham brothers
1897 Central Chimney, Dow	G. Ellis
C. Gully, Screes	H. C. Bowen
Kern Knotts W Chimney	C. W. Patchell
Kern Knotts Crack	H. C. Bowen
1898 Jones's Route, Dow	W. J. Williamson
Jones's Direct from Lords Rake	G. T. Walker
Jones and Collier's Climb, Scafell	–
Pisgah Buttress, Scafell	Abraham brothers
B Chimney, Overbeck	G. Abraham
1899 E. Chimney, Overbeck	G. Abraham, A. E. Field, J. W. F. Forbes
Walker's Gully, Pillar	G. Abraham, A. E. Field
NORTH WALES	
1888 Cyfrwy arête, Cader Idris	
1895 Craig Cau Gullies, Cader Idris	Haskett Smith
1899 North Buttress, Tryfan	Abraham brothers
Terrace Wall Variant, Tryfan	Abraham brothers
Milestone Buttress Ordinary	Abraham brothers
Devil's Staircase, Geifr	G. Abraham
Hanging Garden Gully, Geifr	Abraham brothers

DERBYSHIRE

1897 Boulder Climb, Robin Hood's Stride
    Probably others. Companions probably the Abrahams and Puttrell.

This list is noteworthy in that many of these climbs are still among the most popular in Britain.

Jordan, William Leighton (1837–1922) A widely travelled climber noted for his great strength. He made the first ascent of the Italian Ridge of the Matterhorn by the Maquignaz's variation (1867) and later donated the fixed ladder known as the Échelle Jordan.

Journals   The first mountaineering journal in the world was the ◊ *Alpine Journal* which began in 1863 and has been issued regularly ever since. There are now dozens of journals and magazines world-wide of which the most important are listed below.

BRITAIN   (A = annual; B = bi-monthly; M = monthly)

ALPINE JOURNAL (A)
CLIMBERS' CLUB JOURNAL (A)
FELL & ROCK JOURNAL (A)
SCOTTISH M.C. JOURNAL (A)

CLIMBER & HILLWALKER (M)
HIGH (M)
ON THE EDGE (B)

EUROPE

Alp
Corso Vittorio Emanuele II,
167,10139 Torino, Italy.
Published 12 times a year.
Alpirando
7 Rue de Lille, 75007, Paris.
Published 12 times a year.
Alpin
Ortlerstrasse 8, 8000 München 70,
Germany.
Published 12 times a year.
Der Bergsteiger
Postfach 27, D-8000 München 20,
Germany.
Published 12 times a year.
Desnivel
Diego de León, 27, 1°. izdq. 28006
Madrid, Spain.
Published 11 times a year.
Extrem
Travescra de Dalt 82, 08024
Barcelona, Spain.
Published 6 times a year.
La Montagne
9 rue la Boétie, 75008 Paris,
France.
Published 4 times a year.
Montagnes
1 rue de la Prévachère, 38400 St.
Martin D'Hères, France.
Published 11 times a year.
Norklatt
Postboks 8292 Hammersborg, 0129
Oslo 1, Norway.
Published 4 times a year.
Pyrenaica
Alameda de San Mames, 29-1° izda.
48010 Bilbao, Euskadi, Spain.
Published 4 times a year.
Rivista Della Montagna
Via della Rocca, 29-10123 Torino,
Italy.
Published 4 times a year.

Rotpunkt
Ziegelstrasse 16, 7056 Weinstadt-
Benzach, West Germany.
Published 6 times a year.
Taternik
ul Stanów Zjednoczonych 53 p.
227,04-028 Warsaw, Poland.
Published twice a year.
Vertical
200 avenue de l'Aiguille du Midi,
BP 125, 74400 Chamonix, France.
Published 5 times a year.

U.S.A. & CANADA
American Alpine Journal
113 East 90th St., New York,
N.Y. 10128, U.S.A.
Published once a year.
Canadian Alpine Journal
P.O. Box 1026, Banff, Alberta,
Toloco.
Published once a year.
Climbing
P.O. Box 339, 502 Main Street,
Carbondale, Colorado 81623 U.S.A.
Published 6 times a year.
Rock & Ice
P.O. Box 3595, Boulder, CO 80307,
U.S.A.
Published 6 times a year.

ASIA
The Iwa To Yuki
Yamakei (Publishers) Co. Ltd.,
1-1-33 Shiba Daimon, Minato Ku,
Tokyo. (Contains English language
summary.)
Published 6 times a year.
Indian Mountaineer
Official journal of the Indian
Mountaineering Foundation.
Benito Juarez Road, New
Delhi-110021 (India).
Published twice a year.

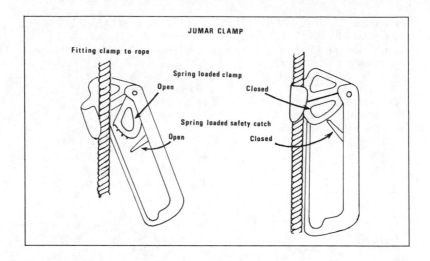

JUMAR CLAMP

Fitting clamp to rope

Spring loaded clamp

Open   Closed

Spring loaded safety catch

Open   Closed

Himalayan Journal
Published by THE HIMALAYAN CLUB,
Contact Oxford University Press,
P.O. Box 31, Oxford House,
Appollo Bunder, Bombay 400001.
Published once a year.
Himavanta
63E Mohanirban Road, Calcutta
700 029, India.

Published 12 times a year.
Wild
P.O. Box 415, Prahran, Victoria
3181, Australia.
Published 4 times a year.
Rock
P.O. Box 415, Prahran, Victoria
3181, Australia.
Published twice a year.

Jumar clamps   A device for ◊ prusiking up ◊ fixed ropes. The most comfortable and effective device for this technique, jumars consist of a clamp fitted with a handle. A jumar can be moved upwards, but will hold a downwards pull unless the locking mechanism is opened. They are less secure when used horizontally, as on a traverse.

Besides their use on fixed ropes, they have obvious uses in crevasse or cliff rescue. The word is frequently used as a verb, 'to jumar', and one speaks of 'jumaring'.

K

K2 (8,611 m)   The second highest mountain in the world. It lies in the Central ◊ Karakoram. The name Mt ◊ Godwin-Austen has never been officially recognized, and is now obsolete; the name Chogori has been suggested by Dyhrenfurth, but the peak is still best known by its original survey number.

K2 rises in splendid apparent isolation at the head of the long Baltoro Glacier, where the latter divides into the Savoie and Godwin-Austen Glaciers. There are six ridges, but only that to the west and that to the north-east join the main line of muztagh and even on these the next big peaks are far enough away to give the mountain its tremendous solitary appeal. Nevertheless, within a fifteen-mile radius there are other stupendous groups, such as Masherbrum, Chogolisa, Gasherbrum and Broad Peak. (◊ Karakoram.)

The head of the Baltoro Glacier was first explored by ◊ Conway in 1899. In 1902, ◊ Eckenstein, who had been with Conway, led the first attempt on the peak: Guillarmod and Wesseley reached a height of about 6,500 m on the N E Ridge. Then followed:

1909   Duke of the Abruzzi's Expedition. Reconnoitred all the southern ridges; reached 6,700 m on the S E (Abruzzi) Ridge, 6,666 m on the N W Ridge.

1938   Houston's Expedition. Houston and Petzoldt reached c.7,950 m on the Abruzzi Ridge.

1939   Wiessner's Expedition. An ill-fated attempt by an American party which ended in the death of D. Wolfe and three Sherpas on the Abruzzi Ridge.

1953   Houston's Second Expedition. Bad weather foiled attempts and in a desperate retreat down the Abruzzi Ridge with the sick Gilkey, five climbers fell simultaneously and were held by P. Schoening – an almost unparalleled feat. Gilkey died.

1954   Desio Expedition. L. Lacedelli and A. Compagnoni reached the summit on 31 August. First ascent, Abruzzi Ridge.

1977   Japanese make second ascent, Abruzzi Ridge.

1978   Nick Escourt killed on W Ridge route: Americans climb N E Ridge.

1979   Messner climbs Abruzzi Ridge.

1982   Japanese climb W Ridge.

1986   A year of stark tragedy for the peak unrivalled in Himalayan climbing since the German expeditions to ◊ Nanga Parbat and ◊ Kangchen-junga in the thirties. Ten teams reached the top, eight by the Abruzzi Ridge, but a Polish team climbed the S Face Central Rib, and a Polish/Czech team climbed the S S W Ridge, the so-called Magic Line.

However, in all this 13 climbers died: John Smolich, Alan Pennington (U.S.A.); Maurice Barrard, Liliane Barrard (French); Renato Casarotto (Italian); Tadeusz Piotrowski, Dobroslawa Wolf, Woiciech Wröz (Polish); Mohammed Ali (Pakistani); Alfred Imitzer, Hannes Wieser (Austrian); Julie Tullis, Alan Rouse (British).

The W Face of K2. (*P. Boardman*)

Kain, Conrad (1883–1934)   An Austrian guide who played a large part in opening up the mountains of Canada. Kain began guiding at the age of 19 and rapidly developed into a skilful and daring climber. He was chosen for expeditions to Spitzbergen in 1901, Egypt in 1902 and the Altai in 1912.

In 1909 Kain visited Canada at the invitation of the Canadian A.C. and it became his home. He crossed the Purcells with Longstaff and Wheeler in 1910, and this was to remain his favourite range. In 1913 he made the first ascent of Mt Robson (3,954 m), the highest peak in the Rockies, with A. H. MacCarthy and W. W. Foster. In 1916 he made the first ascent of the Howser and Bugaboo Spires; the latter was his most difficult climb. (◊ Bugaboos.) Several peaks are named in his honour: Kain, near Robson, Conrad Spire and Glacier in the Purcells, Nasswald Peak after his Austrian home village and Birthday Peak after his birthday.

Kain visited New Zealand several times, acting as a guide at the Hermitage and elsewhere. In 1916 he traversed Mt Cook with Mrs Thompson, a remarkable feat for the time. This brought some criticism and there is no doubt that Kain was regarded by some climbers as too rash.

Kain had a great eye for nature, and told the most amazing tall stories. His autobiography (edited by J. M. Thorington from Kain's notes) appeared shortly after his death: *Where the Clouds Can Go.*

Kammkarte   From the German, *Kamm* (ridge), *Karte* (map). A map on which only ridges are shown, as black lines, with summits indicated by a dot or triangle. Inadequately surveyed country may be indicated thus and the technique is also used for simple maps in books.

Kandersteg   Popular tourist and climbing centre at the western end of the Bernese Alps (Balmhorn, Altels, Wildstrubel, Blumlisalp, etc.). It is connected to Leukerbad by the Gemmi Pass (cable car).

Kangchenjunga N Ridge, looking to upper NE Spur. (*P. Boardman*)

Kangchenjunga (8,586 m) Third highest mountain in the world, being a mere 25 m less than K2. It lies in the Sikkim Himalaya; the central point for two huge ranges which run N–S and E–W. There are thus four faces: N W, approached by the Kangchenjunga Glacier; N E, by the Zemu Glacier; S E, by the Talung Glacier; and S W, by the Yalung Glacier. The supporting ridges contain some fine peaks:

N – Nepal Peak (7,180 m), Kirat Chuli (Tent Peak) (7,365 m), Pathibara (Pyramid Peak) (7,123 m)
E – Zemu Peak (7,780 m), Siniolchu (6,892 m), Simvu (6,816 m)
S – Talung (7,349 m), Kabru (7,395 m)
W – Kangbachen (7,903 m), Jannu (7,710 m)

On the S and N Ridges especially the list could be extended.

The Kangchenjunga region was easy of access and well known to the pioneers. In 1899, ◊ Freshfield made a classic circumnavigation of the mountain (see *Round Kangchenjunga*, by D. Freshfield), and in 1905 Guillarmod made an attempt on the mountain which ended in disaster (◊ Crowley). Pache and three porters were killed. In 1929, P. ◊ Bauer led a German reconnaissance of the Zemu approach and Allwein and Kraus reached 7,400 m; the expedition was an epic of endurance. In 1930, Dyhrenfurth took a large international party to the N W Face, but after the death of a Sherpa, the attempt was abandoned, though ascents were made of other nearby peaks. In 1931, Bauer returned with a second German party to the Zemu Glacier. Schaller and a porter were killed, but a height of 7,700 m was attained before retreat became inevitable. This was another feat of endurance. (See *Himalayan Campaign*, by P. Bauer.)

In 1954 J. Kempe led a reconnaissance of the S W Face and in the following year an expedition led by R. C. ◊ Evans was successful in climbing the mountain; J. ◊ Brown and G. C. Band reached the summit on 25 May, followed next day by H. R. A. Streather and N. Hardie.

There are now four main routes to the summit and several variants. In 1983 P. Beghin (France) soloed the peak via the S W Face without oxygen or support camps. The West Peak (8,505 m) is now called Yalung Kang. It was climbed by a Japanese party in 1973. In 1979 Scott, Boardman and Tasker made the first ascent of the N Ridge without oxygen.

Karabiner (G.) (Fr: mousqueton; E.: snap-link; It.: moschet-tone)   The German word is now used exclusively, often shortened to 'krab'. A karabiner is an oval or D-shaped metal link, one side of which opens by means of a spring clip. It is used for ◊ belays, ◊ runners, ◊ abseiling, ◊ harnesses etc. and is the universal attachment mechanism of climbing. On some karabiners the spring clip (gate) can be locked by a screwed collar (screwgate krab).

Karabiners are made in steel (or steel alloys) or in aluminium alloys. The breaking load should be at least equal to that of the rope and all the leading makes are well above this limit. The screwgate type is recommended for main belays, for tying on and for abseiling, as there are circumstances in which the gate can inadvertently open if not locked. For runners, the non-screwgate is usually preferred because of the speed of handling, and the same goes for ◊ aid climbing. Alloy krabs are only half the weight (or less) of steel ones.

Karabiners need to be examined from time to time: the springs can become faulty and the jaws of the gate do not always lock properly – an incompletely closed karabiner is obviously much weaker than a fully closed one. A little light machine oil should be applied to the spring from time to time.

Karabiners are said to have developed from a pear-shaped clip used by Munich firemen in the early years of this century. They were adapted for climbing by Otto ◊ Herzog.

Kasparek, Fritz (1910–54)   Austrian alpinist who with ◊ Harrer, ◊ Vörg and ◊ Heckmair made the first ascent of the Eigerwand (◊ Eiger) in 1938. He also made the first winter ascent of the Cima Grande N Face in the same year. He fell to his death in the Andes when the summit cornice of Salcantay in Peru gave way.

Kaufmann, Christen (1872–1939)   Grindelwald guide who was with Whymper in the Rockies in 1901. He returned to Canada every summer until 1908, making numerous first ascents. In the winter he climbed in the Oberland. Kaufmann was the guide who led Winston Churchill up the Wetterhorn in 1894.

Kennedy, Edward Shirley (1817–98)   A remarkable Victorian mountaineer who, though wealthy, was an expert on the underworld of his day. He was one of a small group, which included ◊ Hudson, which undertook guideless climbs and was with Hudson on the first guideless ascent of Mont Blanc (1855). Co-author, with Hudson, of *Where There's a Will, There's a Way*. He took part in the first ascent of the Disgrazia (1862) and the first English ascents of the Finsteraarhorn (1857) and Piz Bernina (1861). He may have made the first ascent of the Aig. de l'M in 1854, though this is not certain, and he claimed a guideless ascent of the Täschhorn in a list he made out in 1876, but nothing is known of this.

Kennedy was deeply involved in the founding of the A.C. of which he was President (1860–2). He edited *Peaks, Passes and Glaciers* (2nd series, 1862).

He died relatively poor, having lost his money in a financial crash in 1860.

Kennedy, Thomas Stuart (1841–94) One of the hardest climbers of his day, comparable with ◊ Hudson, with whom he made the first ascent of the Moine Ridge on the Aig. Verte in 1865. (They climbed Mont Blanc *the next day*!)

His most notable first ascents were: Dent Blanche (1862), Aig. de Leschaux (1872) and the N Summit of Aig. de Blaitière (1873).

His record shows he was in many ways ahead of his time, especially in rock-climbing. He made the first ever attempts on peaks such as Lyskamm, Verte and Dru and an incredible winter attempt on the Matterhorn in 1862.

In 1883 he visited the Himalaya but a fever prevented him from making any ascents or attempts.

Kennedy was an all-round athlete and one of the best horsemen and polo-players of his day. His daring was legendary: he once rode the Nile cataracts on a log for fun. Despite this, he was a quiet man; his chief relaxations were mathematics and mechanics.

Kilimanjaro (Kibo, 5,895 m) An extinct volcano on the Tanzania–Kenya border, and the highest mountain in Africa. The three principal peaks are Kibo (5,895 m), Mawenzi (5,148 m) and Shira (4,005 m). The first ascent of Kibo was made by H. Meyer and L. Purtscheller in 1889. Mawenzi was first climbed by E. Oehler and F. Klute in 1912. Shira has no climbing interest.

The ordinary route up Kibo is simple and there are huts *en route*, but there are more serious climbs on the Heim and Kersten Glaciers of the S and S E Faces. Mawenzi provides good rock-climbing of a high standard; the N Face and W Face are 600 m high and the E Face is 1,200 m high:

1958 N Face – Tremonti and Bianchi
1964 E Face – Edwards and Thomson
1972 N Spur – Knowles and Kempson
1972 E Face Variant – Jugoslav team
GUIDEBOOK Savage, *Kilimanjaro Map & Guide*.

King, Sir Henry Seymour (1852–1933) Made a number of first ascents in the Alps, the best known of which are those of the Kingspitze in the Engelhorner (1887) and the Aig. Blanche de Peuterey (1885); the latter a considerable *tour de force* for the time.

Kirkus, Colin (1910–40) A brilliant rock-climber from Liverpool whose most creative period was cut short by a tragedy on Ben Nevis (1934) in which he was seriously injured and his partner, Linnell, killed. He made the first climb on Scafell's E Buttress (Mickledore Grooves, 1930), and played a significant part in the opening up of Clogwyn Du'r Arddu, for which he is said to have coined the name 'Cloggy'. His best known first ascents are: Lot's Groove, Glyder Fach; Central Route, Tryfan; Great Slab, Chimney Route, Pedestal Crack, Birthday Crack, Curving Crack – all on Clogwyn Du'r Arddu; Kirkus's Route, Cwm Silyn; Direct Route, Dinas Mot; Pinnacle Wall, Craig yr Ysfa.

Kirkus expected to be chosen for the 1933 Everest Expedition but was disappointed. Instead he went on Marco Pallis's Gangotri Expedition.

He recovered from the Ben Nevis accident sufficiently to compile the Glyder Fach guidebook (1937). He also compiled a book for novices, *Let's Go Climbing*.

Kirkus was killed when his plane was shot down over Germany during the war.

Kleine Scheidegg   A hotel complex on the col which separates ◊ Grindel-wald and Lauterbrunnen. A mountain railway joins these villages via Kleine Scheidegg and Wengen. The Jungfraujoch Railway starts at Kleine Schei-degg. The col offers superb views of Jungfrau, Mönch and Eiger.

Klotz family   Celebrated Tyrolean guides of the last century. There were two families with the same name and whether they were actually related is not clear. (1) Klotz of Heiligenblut. Martin and his brother (name unknown) were carpenters who acted as guides for ◊ Salm-Reifferscheid on the first ascent of Gross Glockner in 1799 or 1800 – the date is in dispute. At 3,798 m this is the highest peak in Austria. (2) Klotz of Rofen: Nicodemus, Leander and three others – A. Klotz, B. Klotz and G. Klotz (first names not traced). Leander was the star and made several important first ascents in the Otztal, including Wildspitze (3,772 m) in 1848 and Weisskugel (3,739 m) in 1861. As these are respectively the second and third highest peaks, the family seem to have scored a hat trick!

Klucker, Christian (1853–1928)   One of the greatest of all Alpine guides, Klucker came from Sils in the Engadine, where he was schoolmaster and later inspector of schools. Small, thickset and powerful, he was an excellent rock-climber and equally good on ice, as his climbs show. As a guide, his list of *difficult* new climbs has perhaps never been equalled, even by Josef ◊ Knubel.

He made 44 new ascents of peaks and 88 new climbs. His experience ranged from the Dolomites to Dauphiné and he once went to Canada with Whymper (1901). In his own district of Engadine he made the first ascent of many of the popular pinnacles and ridges, for example, Punta Rasica, Ago di Sciora. He was with ◊ Rey and ◊ Güssfeldt on the famous 88-hour traverse of the Peuterey Ridge in 1893.

Klucker's best season was that of 1890 when with ◊ Norman-Neruda he made the following difficult new climbs: N E Face, Lyskamm; N E Face, Piz Roseg; N E Face, Piz Bernina; N W Face, Piz Scerscen; Wellenkuppe–Obergabelhorn traverse.

He climbed until the year of his death. Even in 1927, aged 74, he made a new double traverse of the E arête of Torrione del Ferro. He wrote *Adventures of an Alpine Guide*, published posthumously in 1932.

Knowles, Guy John Fenton (1879–1959)   Friend of ◊ Eckenstein and a member of the ill-starred expedition to K2 in 1902, where he was threatened at pistol point by ◊ Crowley. Engineer and supervisor of the Copyright Agency for the Copyright Libraries.

Knubel, Josef (1881–1961)   Born in St Niklaus, Valais, Knubel came of a guiding family and was himself one of the most important guides of the present century. Small, modest and given to heavy smoking, he was an extremely strong goer and fine climber. His adventures with G. W. ◊ Young are chronicled in the latter's books.

His first climb was the Matterhorn in 1896, when he was aged 15, where he acted as a porter for his father. The same year he climbed the Dom and Monte Rosa. In 1903 he led the American climber, Oliver Perry-Smith, over a number of Zermatt peaks, including the Teufelsgrat of Täschhorn. He gained his guide's certificate the following year.

Among his many first ascents, the following are particularly outstanding. With Young and others: S E Ridge of Requin (and descent), 1906; S W Face of Täschhorn, 1906; Younggrat, Breithorn, 1906; E Face of Zinal Rothorn, 1907; W Ridge of Grandes Jorasses, 1911; Mer de Glace Face of Grépon (via Knubel Crack), 1911; W Ridge of Gspaltenhorn (Rote Zähne), 1914. With ◊ Kurz: first winter ascents of Wellenkuppe, Obergabelhorn, Schallihorn and Täschhorn, all 1920. With Zurcher and others: W Face of Piz Bernina, 1930; Lauper Route, Eiger, 1932.

His great staying power is demonstrated by the following: Charmoz–Grépon–Blaitière (Central and North) in a day: Meije traverse in 6 hr 20 min.: double traverse of Weisshorn in two days.

With ◊ E. Thomas and Zurcher, he climbed all the 4,000 m peaks of the Alps.

Kuffner, Moriz von (1854–1939)   Wealthy Viennese brewer and intellectual who became ◊ Burgener's employer, after Mummery. Von Kuffner climbed most of the 4,000 m peaks of the Alps and made several first ascents, including the first ascent of Lagginhorn from Laggintal (1885), first descent of the Mittelegi Ridge (1885), first ascent of the Frontier Ridge, Mont Blanc (1887), first ascent of the N Ridge of the E Peak, Piz Palu (1899).

In 1938 Von Kuffner lost all his possessions to the Nazis on the invasion of Austria. He fled to Zurich, where he died.

Kugy, Julius (1858–1944)   An Austrian climber noted for his explorations of the Julian Alps, although he also climbed extensively in the Western Alps. Wrote several books, the best known being *Alpine Pilgrimage*.

Kukuczka, Jerzy (1948–89)   A great Polish mountaineer who became the second man (after ◊ Messner) to climb all the 14 8,000 m peaks. Many were new routes done Alpine style, including a new route on the S Face of ◊ K2 during the tragic summer of 1986 when his companion ◊ Piotrowski died in a fall. Kukuczka was killed in a fall attempting the S Face of Lhotse. His autobiography is *My Vertical World*.

Kukuczka's 8,000 m peak ascents

Lhotse: original NW Face route with Czok, Heinrich and Skorek, 1979
Everest: new route on S Face with Czok, 1980
Makalu: new variant on Makalu La and NW Ridge solo, 1981
Broad Peak: original W Spur route with Kurtyka; 17.7.84: new route traversing North and Middle Summits with Kurtyka, 1980
Gasherbrum II: new route on SE Spur with Kurtyka, 1983
Gasherbrum I: new route on SW Face with Kurtyka, 1983
Dhaulagiri: first winter ascent of original NE Spur route with Czok, 1985
Cho Oyu (8,153 m): new route on SE Pillar with Heinrich, after Berbeka and Pawlikowski; first winter ascent of a new route in Himalaya, 1985
Nanga Parbat: new route on SE Pillar with Heinrich, Łobodziński and Carsolio, 1985
Kangchenjunga: first winter ascent of original SW face route with Wielicki, 1986
K2 (8,611 m): new route on S Face with Piotrowski, 1986
Manaslu: new route on NE Face with Hajzer, 1986
Annapurna: first winter ascent of original N Face route with Hajzer, 1987
Shisha Pangma: new route on W Ridge with Hajzer, 1987

Kurz, Marcel Louis (1887–1967)   Noted Swiss topographer and guidebook writer. Though employed initially by the Swiss Federal Institute of Topography, he later worked freelance, and his work on the Mount Olympus area of Greece brought universal recognition (1921). He worked several times with his father on the *Carte de la Chaîne du Mont Blanc* (1910, 1924, 1929).

Kurz was an accomplished winter mountaineer of the old school (first ascent of Grand Combin on ski, 1907). In 1926 he visited New Zealand with H. E. L. Porter where they made the first traverse of Mt Tasman and in 1930 he was on the Dyhrenfurth Kangchenjunga Expedition and took part in the first ascent of Jonsong Peak (7,459 m). (◊ Smythe.) He visited the Himalaya again in 1932 and 1934.

Kurz's guidebooks are models of accuracy and detail. Besides ski guides he wrote guides to Bernina and the Urner Alps and revised his father's guide to the Mont Blanc region. His most famous work, however, was the *Guide des Alps Valaisannes* (4 vols., 1920–37).

In 1934 he wrote *Le Problème Himalayen*, a topic which absorbed the later years of his life and resulted in *Chronique Himalayenne* (1959). Other books are *Le Monte Olympe* (1923) and *Alpinisme Hivernale* (1925). From 1947 to 1953 he was editor of *The Mountain World*.

Kurz, Toni (1913–36)   A German guide from Berchtesgaden who died in one of the most dramatic of mountaineering tragedies, on the ◊ Eiger Nordwand. He had done many difficult climbs in the eastern Alps with his friend Hinterstoisser who also died in the same attempt. Kurz hung from a rope for hours whilst dramatic efforts were made to rescue him, but to no avail.

Kyndwr Club   The first club based on a gritstone tradition; it was founded in 1900 by J. W. Puttrell, E. A. Baker and other Peak District enthusiasts. Its activities included walking and caving as well as climbing. The club explored many of the Peak District rocks, and notes of climbs were included (by Baker) in the Climbers' Club Journal. Baker later published *Moors, Crags and Caves of the High Peak* (1903), the first detailed account of gritstone climbs in book form.

The club dissolved because of a quarrel over the High Tor Gully, Matlock. Baker and his friends attempted this twice without success and denigrated it as a route. Puttrell, Smithard and Bennett climbed it in 1903 and Smithard praised it as a climb. The argument continued for some time and the club broke up. Puttrell and his friends formed the Derbyshire Pennine Club (1907), but Baker had by then moved to the south of England.

L

Lachenal, Louis (1921–55) One of the most important post-war French climbers. Lachenal was a guide and a constant companion of ◊ Terray with whom he made many hard climbs including the second ascent of the Eigerwand (◊ Eiger) in 1947. He was killed in a skiing accident.

Ladakh A mountainous area on the north side of the main Himalayan chain which is crossed by the Zoji La (3,529 m) from Kashmir. The principal town is Leh.

There are four main mountain ranges:

The Zanskar Range: part of the main Himalayan chain with peaks like Nun (7,135 m), Kun (7,087 m), Brahma (6,108 m), and Arjuna (6,280 m). There are also considerable trekking opportunities of an arduous nature.

The Stok Range: above the Indus valley, easily reached from Leh. Stok Kangri (6,121 m), Yan Kangri (6,100 m).

The Ladakh Range: overlooking Leh to the north and of little interest.

The Saser Range: overlooking the Nubra Valley and part of the Karakoram with 5 principal peaks, Saser Kangri I, II, III, IV and V, all around 7,500 m and all ascended in recent years.

Lake District A mountainous area of north-west England famous for its scenic beauty and its literary associations. It contains the highest mountain in England, Scafell Pike (978 m, 3,209 ft). Traditionally, it is also the birthplace of rock-climbing as a sport, though this is open to question. (◊ Haskett Smith.)

Wordsworth likened the mountain ridges to the spokes of a wheel whose hub would be Esk Hause. It is a rough guide at best, but has some truth. Between the ridges are long and lovely valleys (dales) often containing lakes. The lakes are: Windermere, Esthwaite Water, Coniston Water, Wast Water, Ennerdale Water, Buttermere, Crummock Water, Loweswater, Derwent Water, Thirlmere, Elterwater, Ullswater and Haweswater. Of these Windermere is largest and Wast Water deepest. There are numerous smaller lakes called tarns.

The mountains are known as fells, hence fell-walking – a term now widely used beyond the district. Only four fells exceed 3,000 ft (914 m) (cf Snowdonia). In addition to Scafell Pike these are: Scafell (964 m, 3,163 ft); Helvellyn (950 m, 3,117 ft); Skiddaw (931 m, 3,055 ft). The Lake District 3,000s Walk joins these in a single outing, but is not as popular as its Welsh counterpart. The ◊ Lake District Fell Record is a marathon fell-walk, one of the toughest in the world.

The area is a National Park with a park centre at Brockhole, near Windermere. The popularity of the Lake District is immense, both for walkers and others, and there is serious erosion on some paths, though much is being done to restore them.

It is one of the premier climbing areas of Britain, with numerous club huts, many belonging to the long-established Fell and Rock Climbing Club (F.R.C.C.). The principal centres are:

Lake District: Raven Crag and Middlefell Buttress, near head of Langdale. (*W. Unsworth*)

▷ *Wasdale Head*   The pioneers based themselves here for climbs on ▷ Great Gable, ▷ Scafell and ▷ Pillar. Still very popular, with climbs of all standards. The lake is Wast Water, with its celebrated Screes. There is a famous inn, campsite and club hut.

Langdale   Strictly speaking Great Langdale, to distinguish it from the adjacent Little Langdale. The dale stretches west from Ambleside to end in a fine valley head of rocky peaks, including Bowfell, Crinkle Crags and the Langdale Pikes. It contains Elterwater lake.

Langdale is popular with climbers. The principal crags are Gimmer, White Ghyll, Bowfell, Pavey Ark, Raven and Raven Crag Walthwaite. All standards of climbs. Beginners are specially well catered for on Middle Fell Buttress, Scout and Lower Scout Crags and Tarn Crag. The first real climb was Haskett Smith's ascent of Great Gully on Pavey Ark, 1882.

The chief villages are Elterwater and Chapel Stile but climbers prefer to stay near the dale head where there are two famous inns the Old and New Dungeon Ghyll Hotels, a campsite and several climbing huts.

Borrowdale   South of Keswick lies Derwent Water at the far end of which Borrowdale stretches into the fells. At the head of the dale Glaramara is the dominant fell.

Developed late for the Lake District – mainly by Bentley ▷ Beetham – it is now one of the most popular climbing centres. All the crags are easily accessible, several almost on the roadside. Climbs of all standards. The principal crags are: Walla, Lower Falcon, Gowder, Goat, Troutdale Pinnacle, Shepherd's, Great End, Bowderstone, Eagle, Heron, Sergeant's, Raven, Castle, Black, Reecastle, and Grey Knotts. Numerous others, perhaps less popular. The gullies on Great End are the best in the district for winter climbing.

There are half a dozen villages in the dale, with several hotels, club huts and campsites.

Coniston On Coniston Water at the southern end of the district. The one great crag here is Dow Crag (pronounced *'Doe'*). A favourite with the pioneers, it has some long climbs of all standards including hard modern routes. Campsites and huts.

Buttermere A pretty dale with two lakes, Buttermere and Crummock Water, and the village, also Buttermere, between them. Neglected as a climbing centre (it is easily reached from Borrowdale), there are several minor crags and more important ones such as Buckstone How, Grey Crag, High Crag, Dale Head and Miners' Crag. Outstripping all these is Eagle Crag with its classic Eagle Front (VS. Peascod and Beck, 1940).

Eskdale and Duddon Two remote western dales (neither has a lake!) with limited but important crags: Esk Buttress, Heron Crag (in Eskdale) – HS and above – and Wallowbarrow in the Duddon, which has climbs of all standards up to about HVS. The Duddon Valley is also known as Dunnerdale.

Eastern Crags There are crags scattered all over the eastern fells from Longsleddale to Swindale; esoterically fashionable from time to time but mostly neglected. There is no one centre.

Much more popular are the crags near Thirlmere, especially Castle Rock of Triermain and Raven Crag – mostly VS and above, including Overhanging Bastion (VS. Birkett, Wilson, Muscroft, 1939).

Several crags in the small valleys off Patterdale are also well known: Hutaple, Scrubby, Eagle and especially Dove Crag (in Dovedale).

Guidebooks: *Scafell, Dow and Eskdale*; *Pillar Group*; *Langdale*; *Borrowdale*; *Buttermere and Eastern Crags*; *Great Gable* (all F.R.C.C.). *Scrambles in the Lake District I & II* (C.P.), *Winter Climbs in the Lake District* (C.P.).

There are numerous guides to walking in the area but the best known are those of Wainwright – seven area volumes plus Outlying Districts.

Lake District Fell Record 'The aim of these walks is to ascend the greatest possible number of peaks over 2,000 ft and to return to the starting point within twenty-four hours.' (Wakefield.) One of the most arduous tests of endurance in the mountains. There is no set course.

Long Lakeland walks had been recorded by ◊ Elliot, the ◊ Pilkingtons and others in the nineteenth century, but Wakefield's attempt of 1905 gave modern form to the record. He did 59 miles, ascended a total of 23,500 ft and took 22 hr 7 min. E. ◊ Thomas improved on this and in 1932 Bob Graham lifted it to 68 miles and 26,000 ft (42 summits). Graham's record stood for 28 years, and anyone who can match or improve it is entitled to belong to the Bob Graham 24-hour Club.

Graham's record was beaten by Alan Heaton in 1960, who did 42 peaks but in slightly shorter time. In 1961 his brother, Ken Heaton, raised it to 51 peaks in 22 hr 13 min. and in 1963 Eric Beard did 56 peaks in 23 hr 35 min. Joss Naylor in 1975 did 72 peaks in 23 hr 11 min. Mark McDermott later raised this to 76.

The Double Bob Graham was first completed in 1977 by Boyd Millen who crossed 84 peaks, and made 54,000 ft of ascent in 144 miles, with a time of 53 hr. Two years later Roger Baumeister reduced this to 46 hr 34 min. 30 sec.

The standard Bob Graham Round record is at present (1990) held by Billy Bland at 13 hr 50 min.

Lammer and Lorria Eugen Guido Lammer (1863–1945) and August Lorria were two Austrian mountaineers who made a number of very daring ascents during the last two decades of the nineteenth century. Both were advocates of extreme guideless climbing, believing that objective danger, such as stonefall, was all part of the game. Lammer in particular was an advocate of this; he was a follower of Nietzsche, and in his old age an ardent Nazi (see *Jungborn*, by E. G. Lammer). He was a strong advocate of naturalism in climbing, deploring anything that came between the climber and the mountain, and advocated the removal of any man-made structure above the timber line, including climbing huts.

Though constant partners, the two men often did solo climbs as well, and of the highest calibre for the time (for example, Lammer on the N Ridge of Hinterer Brochkogel – first ascent, 1898). They also climbed at night and in bad weather.

In 1887 they attempted Penhall's route on the ◊ Matterhorn and were carried away by an avalanche which they miraculously survived without serious injury. Lammer crawled from the Stokje to Stafel Alp to obtain aid for Lorria.

With ◊ Purtscheller and the ◊ Zsigmondys they represented an approach to climbing totally alien to the traditional, and were heavily criticized for their extremism, and for the 'do or die' attitude it engendered in some Continental climbers during the thirties. With modern equipment (of which Lammer would have disapproved) the argument is now largely academic.

Lorria, with E. A. Martel, was joint author of an unusual and well-illustrated guidebook, *Le Massif de la Bernina* (1894).

Lantern   Because many Alpine climbs begin before dawn it is necessary for climbers to carry a light. This was originally a candle lantern of a folding pattern – incredibly, still in use after the Second World War! Not until long-life batteries became readily available did electric torches come into common use. A head torch, which leaves the hands free, is now the norm.

Lapse rate   The lapse rate is the drop in temperature with altitude. Dependent upon humidity it is approximately 0·6°C per 100 m rise. (◊ Wind-chill factor.)

Larden, Walter (1855–1919)   A well-known climber at the turn of the century, though with few first ascents to his credit; the first complete ascent of the W Ridge of Schreckhorn with ◊ Coolidge is probably his most notable.

Larden did much to popularize Arolla as a climbing centre. He collected together all known routes in the area and made them available in the Mont Collon Hotel (1883). He then brought the information up to date and published it as *Walks and Climbs around Arolla* (1908). His other books are *Recollections of an Old Mountaineer* (1910), *Argentine Plain and Andine Glaciers* (1911) and *Inscriptions from Swiss Chalets* (1913).

Lassoing   Where the rope is thrown over a projection to help the leader. Rope Wall on Tryfan, Wales, is a route on which it is used, or the top block of the Aig. de République at Chamonix. Not very common.

Lauener brothers   Among the best known of the early Oberland guides were Ulrich, Christian, Jakob and Johann Lauener of Lauterbrunnen. Ulrich (1821–1900) was the most famous: he took part in the ascent of the Wetterhorn in 1854 by ◊ Wills and the first ascent of Monte Rosa (1855). Christian (1826–91) was for many years ◊ Tuckett's guide and made the first ascent of Cimon della Pala (1870). The other brothers never achieved the same degree of fame. Johann was killed by an avalanche on Jungfrau in 1853.

Left, laybacking a crack. (*R. H. Heaton*); right, limestone climbing at Trowbarrow Quarry, Lancs. (*W. Unsworth*)

Lauper, Hans (1895–1936) A Zurich dentist and classical scholar who made a series of difficult north face climbs in the Oberland between 1915 and 1932, including the Stockhorn, Kamm, Mönch and Jungfrau. His most famous climb is the Lauper Route on the Eiger (1932), accompanied by Alfred Zurcher and the guides Joseph Knubel and Alexander Graven.

Layback A crack-climbing technique, used for corner cracks or cracks where one edge protrudes more than the other. Feet are placed flat against the protruding edge and hands grip the nearer edge, thus setting up opposing forces. Hands and feet are moved alternately upwards. A difficult and strenuous technique. Alternative methods, e.g. ◊ jamming, are used whenever possible.

The term is said to have been invented by Rice Evans, an American who climbed at Stanage in the twenties. On the Continent it is known as 'à la Dulfer', after the climber of that name.

Leader The first man on a climbing rope. His part in the climb is said to be 'leading' and anyone who has completed a climb as leader is said to have 'led the climb'. Because leading is much more difficult than following, the leader is usually the most experienced member of the rope. In a rope of two, where both may be of equal ability, it is usual for each climber to lead alternate pitches. This is called 'leading through'.

Because the leader goes up first he is not protected by a rope from above as his companions are. He must make his own ◊ protection and the consequences of a fall could be serious on an unprotected pitch. A leader obviously needs considerable experience and judgement: the fate of the party rests in his hands, especially on a long climb.

In descent, the leader comes down last, so that he can protect the party from above. On fairly easy ground the leader may decide to descend first if there are route-finding problems which he judges his companions cannot solve.

On high-altitude expeditions the leader is the man responsible for the expedition as a whole, particularly its strategy. He may or may not take an actual part in the climbing.

Ledge (G.: band; Fr.: vire; It.: cengia) A flat or slightly sloping area on a rock face or mountain side. Ledges often provide resting places, stances and ◊ belays. On the easier rock-climbs, belays are almost always on large ledges. Ledges can be almost any size – some go right across a face. Quite a number of ledges have been given names, for example, The Oval, Scafell.

Lehne, Jorg (1936–69) A leading German post-war climber who, with Brandler, Hasse and Löw, made a famous Direct Route on the Cima Grande; a major advance in aid climbing. He was responsible for a number of winter first ascents in the Eastern Alps but his most famous venture was as leader of the team that made the first ascent of the Eigerwand Direct (Harlin Route) in 1968.

Lehne was killed by stonefall as he was about to start the Walker Spur of Grandes Jorasses.

Letter box A narrow slot or hole in a ridge is sometimes called a letter box. There is a well-known one on Grey Knotts Face, Borrowdale. Rather archaic.

Lightning Can be a hazard in the mountains, especially on exposed ridges and pinnacles, but it can also cause stonefall on faces and in gullies, etc. In Alpine regions particularly, thunderstorms form quickly. Since lightning tends to strike the highest points, it is prudent to keep as low as possible, off the crest of a ridge and away from summits. Ice axes emit a strange humming noise when electrical discharge is near ('singing'). They should not be carried pointing upwards, strapped to a rucksack, but the old idea that they should be abandoned is not always desirable or necessary.

Cracks, gullies, small caves and overhangs should also be avoided in an electrical storm as the lightning can use a damp body as a conductor across the gap.

Limestone A sedimentary rock formed from the compacted remains of tiny marine organisms. The main types of the rock are: chalk, oolitic limestone, carboniferous or mountain limestone, and dolomite or magnesium limestone. Marble is limestone which has undergone a metamorphic change. The rock is noted for containing fossils, minerals and caves.

Limestone is extremely common rock, occurring in many parts of the world. In the Alps it forms much of the Bernese Alps and the Eastern Alps, and in Britain much of the ◊ Pennines.

Mountain limestone is the commonest form of the rock. Despite its popularity in the Alps for many years it was much distrusted in Britain as a suitable rock for climbing until after the last war (though there had been spasmodic climbs made ever since the sport started). This was because of the nature of the rock – heavily fractured and not always sound. Major ascents began in the 1950s, often heavily protected by pegs, but the present tendency is for hard climbs and only a few pegs, if any. All the major ◊ aid routes of Britain are on limestone, a supreme example being the Kilnsey Overhang in

Pat Littlejohn (*C. Howes*)   Peter Livesey (*B. Cropper*)

Yorkshire. Other favourite limestone cliffs include Stoney Middleton, High
Tor and cliffs along the Wye, all in Derbyshire; Malham Cove and Gordale
Scar in Yorkshire; Avon Gorge and Cheddar Gorge in Somerset; Swanage in
Dorset and the Pembroke coast.

Line   (a) The route taken by a climb up a crag. One speaks of 'a good line',
meaning an aesthetically pleasing route following a natural looking line. (b)
The thinnest rope made for climbing. Used for making étriers and prusik
loops. Line ◊ slings have been replaced by tape.

Ling, William Norman (1873–1953)   Companion of ◊ Raeburn and ◊
Glover and one of the outstanding mountaineers at the turn of the century
with first ascents in the Lakes, Scotland, Norway, the Alps and Caucasus.
Ling Chimney (1899) on Gable, Lake District, is named after him.

Littlejohn, Pat (b. 1951)   Director of the International School of Moun-
taineering at Leysin, Pat Littlejohn has for the last 20 years been one of
Britain's most prolific rock-climbers, with a thousand new routes to his credit.
He has been particularly active on the sea cliffs where his routes include Il
Duce E4/6a, Tintagel Head, Cornwall (1972); Pagan E4/5c, Left Hand Wall,
Gogarth (1973); Hunger E5/6b, Main Cliff, Gogarth (1978); Guernica
E6/6b, Carn Gowla, Cornwall (1982); Terminal Twilight E6/6c, Huntsman's
Leap, Pembroke (1984); Above and Beyond E6/6b, Fair Head, Antrim
(1984).
   His rock-climbs overseas include hard new routes in Arizona (Book of
Genesis, Gd. Canyon, 5.11, 1976; Echoes, Cochise Stronghold, 5.10, 1977)
and the Goat Buttress of Yamnuska in the Canadian Rockies, VI+/5b. In the
Alps he made the first free ascents of the Hemming–Robbins on the W Face of
the Dru and the S Face of the Fou (1982), as well as a new hard route on the
S E Face of the Winterstock. In Norway he climbed the N Pillar of Kjerag

E4/6a (1985) with Steve Jones, and in the Karakoram, Raven's Pyramid, which included 1,000 m of ED.

Littlejohn is the author of climbing guides to Pembroke and the South-West.

Liveing, Robert (1834–1919)   A short but notable Alpine career. In 1859 he made the first ascent of the Rimpfischhorn, second ascent of the Dom and second (first English) ascent of Weissmies. In the following year he made the first known ascent of the Oberaarhorn and first ascent of Blümlisalphorn.

Livesey, Michael Peter (b. 1943)   A physical education lecturer who is one of Britain's outstanding rock-climbers. He has made 27 major first ascents in the Lakes, Wales and the outcrops including, for example, Sally Free and Easy (1970), Jenny Wren (1971), Wellington Crack (1974) and Footless Crow (1974).

In Romsdal, Norway, he made the second ascent of the Troll Wall, first ascent of Bispen S Face and first British ascent of Kongen S Face (all 1967). In the Karwendel he made the first British ascent of the Gelbe Kante (1972). Solo ascents include Fleischbank E Face; Rebuffat Route, Aig. du Midi; and Livanos Route, Rocher d'Archaine in the Vercors (first solo).

Further afield, Livesey made first ascents of S Pillar of Kuh-i-Parau, (Zagros Mts, Iran) (1972) and W Face of Tyrokwa, Baffin Island (1975). During several visits to Yosemite he put up climbs such as Clown, Crack a Go Go, Gillette (all 1974) and Moratorium (1975). He made the first free ascents of N Face of Sentinel and E Face of Middle Cathedral and first British ascent of Direct N Buttress on Middle Cathedral, besides numerous second ascents.

Lloyd, Robert Wylie (1868–1958)   A self-made, wealthy businessman from Lancashire, who spent 30 seasons with Josef Pollinger and made a number of good Alpine routes. A supporter of clubs and expeditions, the R. W. Lloyd Hut (Ynys Ettws), Llanberis, is named after him. Lloyd amassed a number of collections in art, stamps, coins, and so on, some of which were internationally renowned.

Lochmatter family   A famous family of guides from St Niklaus, Switzerland, related to the Pollingers and close friends of the Knubels, who were also well-known guiding families.

They first came to notice as three brothers, all guides: Franz (b. 1825), Joseph-Marie (b. 1833) and Alexander (b. 1837). Joseph-Marie, with P. ◊ Knubel, led J. M. Elliott up the Hörnli Ridge of the Matterhorn in 1868 – the first time it had been climbed after the tragedy of 1865. In 1873 he made the first ascent of Le Rateau; in 1879, the first ascent of the W Ridge of Chardonnet; and in 1881 probably the first traverse of the Zinal Rothorn from Zermatt to Zinal. He climbed with many of the best climbers of the day. He was killed in 1882 on the Dent Blanche, together with his eldest son, Alexander. The other brothers had less distinguished careers.

Joseph-Marie Lochmatter had six sons, all good climbers, but especially outstanding were Franz and Joseph who were guides to V. J. E. ◊ Ryan. The E Ridge of the Aig. du Plan (Ryan–Lochmatter Route) (1906), the N W Ridge of the Aig. de Blaitière (1906) and the S Face of the Taschhorn (1906) are perhaps the best known of their ascents. (◊ Young.)

Longland, Sir John Laurence (b. 1905)   One of the best English rock-climbers between the wars. In 1928 he led Birch Tree Wall at the Black Rocks

Jack Longland (*right*) with Anderl Heckmair and his wife. (*T. Tullis*)

of Cromford, and his famous Longland's Climb on the W Buttress of Clogwyn Du'r Arddu. In 1933 Longland was on Everest where, with Wyn Harris, Wager and eight Sherpas, he established Camp VI at 27,400 ft – the highest camp ever at that time. Longland returned leaving Wager and Wyn Harris and during the descent was caught by a storm through which he shepherded the porters to safety. A great feat.

As Director of Education for Derbyshire, Jack Longland was responsible for the establishment of White Hall Outdoors Pursuits Centre in 1951, the first of the many local authority centres in Britain.

Longland has served on various Government inquiries and is well known as a broadcaster. He was knighted in 1970.

Longman, William (1813–77) An Original Member of the A.C. and President 1872–4. Longman was the publisher of many early Alpine classics, including ◊ Ball's *Alpine Guides*, *Peaks, Passes and Glaciers* and the *Alpine Journal* (until 1930). His climbing career was undistinguished.

Longstaff, Tom George (1875–1964) One of the greatest of the early Himalayan climbers and explorers. As a man of private means he was able to indulge his passion for exploration and besides the Alps he visited the Caucasus, the Rockies, the Selkirks, the Arctic (five times) and the Himalaya (six times). He qualified as a doctor but never practised.

In 1903 his Caucasus journey resulted in first ascents of Tiktingen, Latsga, Lakra, Bashiltau and the formidable W Peak of Shkhara. In 1905 he made his first visit to Nanda Devi's 'Ring' and reached the rim of the Sanctuary. He made remarkable but unsuccessful attempts on Nanda Devi E, Nanda Kot and, during a quick visit to Tibet, Gurla Mandhata. In 1907 he returned, failed to force the Rishi Ganga into the Sanctuary, but climbed Trisul (7,120 m). It remained for 21 years the highest peak ever attained.

205

In 1909 he visited the Karakoram, crossed the Saltoro Pass and discovered the great Siachen Glacier. In 1922 he went as technical adviser on the second Everest Expedition. Awarded Gill Memorial (1908) and Founder's Medal (1928) of the R. G. S. President A.C., 1947–9.

His autobiography, *This My Voyage*, was published in 1949.

Longueurs (Fr.)   The dull and uninteresting sections of a hill-walk, or the easy sections of a rock-climb. A climb with too many longueurs is said to be scrappy.

Lunn, Sir Arnold (1888–1974)   One of the great ski mountaineers and the man who, more than most, helped to shape the sport of skiing in its early days. He made many of the first ski and ski-aided ascents in the Alps, including the Dom, the Eiger and the Weisshorn. A world authority on skiing.

Sir Arnold was an honorary member of several famous clubs including the Alpine Club, Dr h. c. of Zurich University and Citoyen d'honneur of Chamonix. Founder of the Oxford M.C. and Alpine Ski Club.

His books on mountaineering are: *The Alps* (1913), *The Alpine Ski Guides* (*Bernese Oberland*, 1920 – the first ski mountaineering guide), *Alpine Skiing at All Heights and Seasons* (1921), *The Mountains of Youth* (1925), *A History of Skiing* (1927), *Mountain Jubilee* (1943), *Zermatt and the Valais* (1955), *Mountains of Memory* (1956), *A Century of Mountaineering* (1957), *The Bernese Oberland* (1963), *Matterhorn Centenary* (1965). He was editor of the *Climbers' Journal* 1912–13, and the journals of the Alpine Ski Club from 1908 to 1974.

M

MacCarthy, Albert H. (1876–1956) Born in the U.S.A. but went to live in British Columbia in 1910, where he and his wife began climbing. Formed partnerships with W. W. Foster and the guide, Conrad ◊ Kain, with whom he made new ascents in the Purcells and elsewhere. Notable first ascents were: Mt Robson from the N (1913), N W Ridge of Mt Sir Donald (1913), Mt Louis (1916), Bugaboo Spire (1916) and first traverse of Mt Assinboine (MacCarthy, Wakefield, Hall, 1920). He was the leader of the expedition to Mt Logan (1924–5), Yukon; the second highest peak in North America. Reached the summit on 23 June 1925. 'Mack' visited the Alps in 1926, doing 101 peaks in 45 days.

MacDonald, Claude Augustus (1859–1949) A sheep farmer from Wagga Wagga who made a number of first ascents in the Alps and New Zealand. His most remarkable exploit was the first ascent of the N W Face of Ebnefluh in 1895, still regarded as a hard climb.

MacDonald, Reginald John Somerled (c. 1840–76) The companion of many of the pioneers. Made first English ascent of Pelvoux with Whymper in 1861, second ascent of Mönch (first English, and now the normal route), first ascent of Dent d'Hérens, first ascent of Parrotspitze (1863), first ascent of Jungfrau from the Rottal (1864) and first ascent of Aig. de Bionnassay.

MacDonald died at the early age of 35 and has perhaps not been given the credit he deserves for his early ascents.

MacInnes, Hamish (b. 1931) One of the most active Scottish mountaineers of the post-war years. His interests have touched on every aspect of the sport and have had a lasting influence.

At home he has climbed many new routes, especially in Glencoe, and often with members of his winter climbing courses. Among his earlier routes the first winter ascent of Raven's Gully, Buachaille Etive Mor (1953, Bonington) and Zero Gully, Ben Nevis (1957, A. G. Nicol, T. W. Patey) are outstanding. Zero Gully, especially, can be regarded as one of the big breakthroughs in British climbing.

In the Alps he made an attempt, with Bonington, on the Eigerwand in 1957, and took part, with Bonington, Whillans and others, in the first British ascent of the Bonatti Pillar of the Dru (1958), when he was seriously injured by stonefall.

MacInnes has climbed in New Zealand, the Caucasus and the Himalaya. He was with ◊ Cunningham in the celebrated Creag Dhu Everest Expedition, which consisted of two men (1953), and in the Yeti-hunting Expedition of 1957 in Lahul. He was also part of the Everest S W Face teams in the two expeditions of 1973 and Deputy Leader of the successful 1975 Expedition. Outstanding among his other climbs is the traverse of Shkhelda, Caucasus, with G. Richie (1961). This was the first major Caucasus traverse by a British party.

Living in Glencoe, he has organized winter climbing courses there for

Hamish MacInnes bivouacking in a snow cave.

many years and been leader of the rescue team in the valley. He was one of the first to advocate the use of dogs in rescue work. He also turned his attention to equipment, developing a new, improved rescue stretcher, and designing the first ice axe to break away from the old pattern – an all-metal axe. Later he developed the inclined pick which has had an influence in modern ice techniques.

MacInnes has been a film cameraman and an adviser on several films and T.V. programmes (*Eiger Sanction*, etc.). Besides autobiographical books he has written guidebooks and books on mountain rescue.

Mackenzie, John (1856–1933)   Best known of the Skye guides during the pioneering days on the island. Made a number of first ascents including Sgurr a'Ghreadaidh, Sgurr Thearlaich and Sgurr Mhic Coinnich (Mackenzie's Peak). Was the constant companion of ◊ Collie, with whom he made the first crossing of the Thearlaich–Dubh Gap and the first ascent of the Cioch. (◊ Skye.)

Mackinder, Sir Halford John (1861–1947)   Distinguished geographer and politician. Mackinder founded geography as a university subject in the 1880s (Oxford). With C. Ollier and J. Borcherel, he made the first ascent of Batian, ◊ Mt Kenya, in 1899. Knighted 1920.

Macnamara, Arthur (1861–90)   Classical scholar and barrister, who, with Slingsby, Barnes and Topham, had a memorable Arolla season in 1887 when he did first ascents of the E Ridge of Mont Blanc de Cheilon and the S Peak of the Aig. Rouges, descending by the celebrated Crête de Coq. He also made the first ascent of the Satarma Pinnacle.

Macnamara was killed descending the Düssistock in 1890.

Cesare Maestri (*T. Tullis*) Pierre Mazeaud

McNaught-Davis, Ian (b. 1929) A leading British post-war climber with various new routes to his credit, including Cioch Grooves, Skye (1951), The Kame, Foula (1972) and Stochastic Groove, Gogarth (1966). He seconded Brown on several other Gogarth climbs.

McNaught-Davis made a number of British first ascents in the Alps and in 1956 was a member of the Muztagh Tower Expedition (first ascent). In 1960 he made the first ascent of Hjornespitze and Bersearkerspitze in Greenland and in 1962 climbed the Peak of Communism in the Pamirs. He visited the Ruwenzori in 1955, Karakoram 1975.

A jovial personality, Mac is well known for his T.V. appearances both as a commentator on climbing programmes and as his alter ego, a computer expert.

Macphee, George Graham (1898–1963) A Scottish doctor who was the first to climb on the Castle Rock of Triermain, Lake District (Yew Tree Climb, 1928), and to investigate Green Gable as a climbing ground. He was with Kirkus on the first ascent of Great Slab, Clogwyn Du'r Arddu (1930). Macphee also made a number of climbs on Ben Nevis and elsewhere in Scotland, and compiled the Ben Nevis guidebooks of 1936 and 1954.

Maestri, Cesare (b. 1929) Italian climber and guide from Trento, notable for his hard Dolomite routes and for his solo exploits. Maestri made the first two ascents of the ◊ Cerro Torre in Patagonia and both ascents aroused controversy.

Magnetic variation The difference between true north and magnetic north, expressed in degrees, e.g. 6°W means that magnetic north is 6° west of true north, and of course, it is to the magnetic north that the compass needle

points. The magnetic variation differs from place to place and changes slowly
year by year (at the moment in Britain it is decreasing from the W by about
⅒° per annum). The relevant information is given at the bottom of all good
maps.

When navigating in the hills, the magnetic variation must be taken into
account. In Britain, where the O.S. maps have the ◊ grid reference, it is easier
to use a false variation calculated by subtracting the grid variation from the
real magnetic variation, and then assuming the grid lines are true north. The
Silva-type compass makes all these calculations very simple (◊ Compass.)

Malczewski, Antoni (1793–1826) A Polish count and noted poet who
climbed the lower (N) summit of the Midi with J. M. Balmat and five
Chamonix guides in 1818 – the first Chamonix aiguille to be climbed. He
ascended Mont Blanc a few days later: 'a pleasurable journey after the sad and
terrible Aiguille du Midi'.

Malkin, Arthur Thomas (1803–88) With his wife was among the earliest
English travellers to the Alps, immediately before the Golden Age. They
were the second English group to visit Saas and Mrs Malkin was the first
Englishwoman to visit the Théodule. They also possibly made the first ascent
of the Eggishorn. (All this in 1840.) Continued to climb for many years after.

Mallory, George Herbert Leigh (1886–1924) An almost legendary figure
in British climbing, whose name is forever associated with Everest. Mallory's
actual total of new climbs in Britain and the Alps was small, and none are of
great importance. Nevertheless he was regarded as the Golden Boy of the
climbing world for some years – ◊ Young called him Sir Galahad, and his
striking features, character and intellectual attitude, as well as his undoubted
ability, made him the centre of the popular Pen y Pass gatherings.

Mallory came from Cheshire, but it was ◊ Irving, who was his schoolmaster
at Winchester, who first took him to the Alps in 1904. He did not climb in
Britain until 1906, when he was at Cambridge, and led a party of undergradu-
ates up Lliwedd. He met Young at this time and became a member of his
circle.

Mallory was a teacher at Charterhouse until the 1921 Everest Expedition
(except for war service). He married in 1914 and had a son and his two
daughters, Clare and Berridge, both became well-known climbers.

Everest became his ruling passion. He was a member of the first three
expeditions and was in the parties which were the first to see the N Face and
reach the N Col. He was also the first to see the Western Cwm, from whence
the success of 1953 was gained; he considered it impracticable.

On 8 June 1924, Mallory, with the inexperienced ◊ Irvine as partner, set
out from Camp VI to climb the last 600 m to the summit. They were seen by
Odell through a break in the cloud, at the first step of the N E Ridge. What
happened after that remains a mystery: they did not return and no trace was
found of them. In 1933 an ice axe belonging to one of them was found at about
8,400 m and it is presumed that an accident occurred at this spot and the two
climbers fell to their deaths. It is unlikely that they reached the summit.

Mallory is famous for two quotations: 'Have we vanquished an enemy?
None but ourselves'; and, in reply to a question as to why he wanted to climb
Mount Everest, 'Because it is there.'

Malta, climbs in The rock of this famous Mediterranean island is a curious
sort of limestone offering in some places climbs of 100 m, though usually

much shorter and in all grades but the very highest. There is room for exploration. Some 200 routes exist, many first developed by the Commandos who were stationed there. No current guidebook.

Mannering, George Edward (1862–1947) One of the founders of the New Zealand Alpine Club. Inspired by W. S. ◊ Green, he attempted Mt Cook five times between 1886 and 1890, reaching a point 43 m from the summit before being forced back. Wrote *With Axe and Rope in the New Zealand Alps* (1891) and *Eighty Years in New Zealand* (1943).

Mannhardt, Anderl (b. 1939) A German guide who completed a number of hard Alpine routes before making the first winter ascent of the Eigerwand (◊ Eiger) (1961). He took part in the second ascent of ◊ Nanga Parbat in the following year by a new route on the Diamir Face.

Mantelshelf A move in rock-climbing to overcome a very high step. The palms are placed on the hold (often a ledge) and a press-up made until one foot can be raised to the same hold. A very delicate movement is then made to stand upright. If there are holds on the facing wall, it is easier, but often it is a question of balance alone. Common on many climbs. One-handed mantelshelves are not unknown, particularly on gritstone.

Maps (G.: Karte; Fr.: carte) Used with the ◊ compass, an indispensable aid to mountain navigation. Apart from the question of accuracy, maps for use in the mountains should be of convenient scale, suitably contoured and contain as much detail as is consistent with clarity. It is essential, too, that the magnetic variation is shown, with date, and the annual increase or decrease. Colour layering and hatching make a relief clearer.

In Britain the maps most commonly used are those of the Ordnance Survey (O.S.). The three series of most interest are *Landranger* 1:50,000, *Outdoor Leisure* and *Pathfinder*, both 1:25,000. *Outdoor Leisure* maps cover popular holiday areas and are much larger sheets than the *Pathfinder*. Commercial maps have no advantages over the O.S.

Alpine maps are on the scales 1:100,000, 1:50,000 and 1:25,000. The first of these is useful for a general picture of an area but the practical maps are the larger scales. Some Alpine maps have ski trails marked. All the popular areas have been resurveyed in recent years and the maps can be relied upon. Older maps show ◊ glaciers much bigger than they now are and omit post-war hydroelectric schemes, roads etc. The main maps are:

FRANCE: Carte de France (I.G.N.); Didier & Richard
SWITZERLAND: Carte National (C.N.) (Landeskarte – L.K.)
GERMANY/AUSTRIA: Alpenvereinskarte (O.A.V.); Freytag-Berndt (F.B.)
ITALY: Touring Club Italiano (T.C.I.); Instituto Geografico Centrale.

Maps of one country invariably overlap into another. Note that German maps usually give the old Austro–Hungarian Empire names for Italian peaks, e.g. Tre Cima becomes Drei Zinnen etc.

In the U.S.A. topographic maps are produced by the U.S. Geological Survey on the scale 1:250,000 and 1:62,500. This latter scale is 15 minutes of longitude and each sheet covers 12 × 18 miles. Recently maps of 1:24,000 have replaced many of the older sheets – these are 6 × 9 miles. (In Alaska the scale, where available, is 1:63,360. Much of Alaska is only covered on the 1:250,000 however.)

Northern Ireland is covered by a 1:50,000 series which extends slightly into the republic, whose own maps are being revised and brought up to date from the existing ½ inch to the mile series.

Nepal is covered by the Schneider maps at 1:50,000 and there is a famous ◊ Mt Everest sheet published by the D.A.V. at 1:25,000. The rest of the ◊ Himalaya and ◊ Karakoram is generally served by U.S. Army maps at 1:250,000, though there is a good trekking map to Kashmir at the same scale, published locally. Obtaining official Indian maps can be difficult as they are restricted.

The situation in the rest of the world varies enormously. Advice on maps is available from the map specialists Edward Stanford Ltd, 12–14 Long Acre, Covent Garden, London WC2E 9LP

Maquignaz, Jean-Joseph (1829–90)   The best known member of a family of guides from Breuil. His career closely parallels that of J.-A. ◊ Carrel, his great rival. Maquignaz was with Carrel on the abortive attempt on the Italian Ridge of Matterhorn in 1865. In 1867, with his brother Jean-Pierre, he succeeded in climbing the ridge direct (Carrel had made a detour near the top). Other members of the party were left at a col below the final peak, named Col Félicité in honour of Félicité Carrel, who was with them. In 1868, the two brothers led ◊ Tyndall on the first traverse of the mountain, and five days later reversed the traverse with another party. He made the first winter traverse with V. ◊ Sella in 1882.

Maquignaz's best work was done with members of the Sella family, for whom he became almost a family retainer (and consequently prosperous). With four of the Sellas he made the first ascent of the Aig. du Géant (1882) – though not to the true top, as it turned out, and with considerable aid from fixed ropes.

Maquignaz disappeared while climbing Mont Blanc in 1890.

March, William Joseph (1941–90)   One of the best known educationist-climbers of his day, Bill March was for a time Deputy at Glenmore Lodge and later (1975–7) Director of the National Mountaineering Centre, Plas y Brenin. He also taught at Pocatello, U.S.A. and at the time of his death was an Assistant Professor at Calgary University.

In 1970–4 he made 35 first ascents in Scotland (rock and ice), including the well-known Chancer, Hells Lum Crag. In the U.S.A. he made several first ascents in the Wind River Range and elsewhere. On the 1974 Dhaulagiri IV expedition he narrowly escaped the avalanche which killed three Sherpas. He led the Canadian ◊ Mt Everest expedition, which though rent by dissension, put two groups on the summit in 1982.

During his time at Glenmore Lodge a fellow instructor was J. ◊ Cunningham and together they developed modern ice techniques. This resulted in *Modern Snow and Ice Techniques* (1973). He later wrote *Modern Rope Techniques in Mountaineering* (1976).

Mason, Alfred Edward Woodley (1865–1948)   Novelist and mountaineer, and one of the few men to write successful mountaineering novels. After Oxford Mason went on the stage for a time but began writing about 1895, describing in articles some adventures in the Tyrol. His first novel was *A Romance of Wasdale*. He had started climbing in 1891 (Wetterhorn) and in the Lake District about the same time. He continued to climb until 1910, doing many of the usual Alpine and British climbs of the period. He was Liberal M.P. for Coventry, 1906–10.

Mason's best-known novel today is probably *The Four Feathers* (1902) but his main climbing novel is *Running Water* (1907), inspired by Mummery's guideless ascent of the Old Brenva on Mont Blanc. It is said that the character of Mr Kenyon is Leslie ◊ Stephen and the villain, Skinner, is an amalgam of ◊ Dent, ◊ Davidson and ◊ Mummery.

Mathews brothers The three Mathews brothers, William (1828–1901), Charles Edward (1834–1905) and George Spencer (1836–1904), were central figures throughout the pioneering days of Alpine climbing. Their experience was vast and they took part in a number of the great first ascents, including Grande Casse, Castor and Monte Viso (William), and Moore's famous ascent of the Brenva Face of Mont Blanc (George Spencer). There was also a cousin, Benjamin St John Attwood-Mathews, who made a number of ascents with William, including the first English ascent of Finsteraarhorn. It was at his father's house that, in 1857, it was finally decided that the ◊ Alpine Club should be formed. William Mathews (together with ◊ Kennedy) was principally responsible for the Club.

C. E. Mathews played a prominent part in the start of Welsh climbing by organizing winter meets at Pen y Gwryd Hotel (including one attended by Melchior ◊ Anderegg in 1888). He formed the ◊ Society of Welsh Rabbits (1870) and the Climbers' Club, of which he was first President (1898–1901).

William was President of the A.C. (1869–71) and C. E. Mathews was President (1878–80).

C. E. Mathews was a solicitor with a strong interest in local politics and a friend of Joseph Chamberlain. The other brothers were in the family business of land agents. The family had great influence in Birmingham and Worcestershire.

Matterhorn (4,477·5 m) (Fr.: Cervin; It.: Cervino) Famous in shape and history; along with Everest, the best known mountain in the world. It stands in a peculiarly isolated position between Breuil (Italy) and Zermatt (Switzerland). In its honour, Breuil has been recently renamed Cervinia; the Swiss have more sense.

The mountain has four distinct ridges and four faces, and the top is a concave crest, about 80 m long, the W end of which forms the true summit and the E end the Italian summit (4,476·4 m). (It is *not* the highest mountain in the Alps (Mont Blanc) nor even in Switzerland [Dom].)

The easiest way up is by the N E Ridge (Hörnli). Long and confusing, sometimes subjected to stonefall from careless parties above, it is mostly rock at an easy angle, with snow to finish. There are fixed ropes at the most difficult part. The ◊ Solvay Hut (emergency only) is at 4,000 m on the ridge.

The S W Ridge (Italian Ridge) is a rock-climb of some difficulty made easier by fixed ropes and ladders. The N W Ridge (Zmutt) is a lovely snow crest which ends in some teeth; the climb then goes to the right of this over slabs to the top. The S E Ridge (Furggen) is the hardest to climb, rising in three big towers to the summit; the final tower is usually avoided on the left.

The N Face is one of the great Grade VI Alpine routes: loose rock, stonefall. The technicalities of this face are not extreme but its seriousness cannot be questioned. The other faces are of minor interest.

A summary of important ascents is given below:

1865 (14 July) First ascent, Hörnli Ridge – Whymper, ◊ Hudson, ◊ Hadow, Douglas, ◊ Croz, Taugwalders, father and son
1865 (17 July) Italian Ridge – ◊ Carrel and ◊ Bich
1867 (13 Sept.) Italian Ridge, present route – ◊ Maquignaz brothers

1868	(27 July) First traverse, Breuil–Zermatt – ◊ Tyndall and Maquignaz brothers
1868	(3 August) First traverse, Zermatt–Breuil – Hoiler, Thoily and Maquignaz brothers
1871	First ascent by a woman – Gardiner, F. Walker and Lucy Walker, with five guides
1874	First double traverse, Breuil to Breuil – J. Birkbeck Jun., Petrus and Bich
1876	First guideless ascent – ◊ Cawood, Colgrove and ◊ Cust
1879	Zmutt Ridge – Mummery, Burgener, Gentinetta, Petrus
1879	W Face – ◊ Penhall, Imseng, Zurbriggen
1911	Furggen Ridge – Piacenza, Carrel and Gaspard
1931	N Face – F. and T. Schmid
1931	S Face – Benedetti, Carrel and Bich
1932	E Face – Benedetti, Mazzotti and four guides
1959	First solo ascent, N Face – Marchart
1962	Direct Ascent, W Face – Ottin and Daguin
1962	First winter ascent, N Face
1965	First ascent of N Face by a woman – Yvette Vaucher and party Direct Route, N Face – W. ◊ Bonatti
1966	All four ridges climbed in a day – two Zermatt guides.
1975	First winter ascent, E Face – R. Arnold, G. Buman, C. Pralong
1989	Zmutt Nose Couloir – Cogna and Cerruti

The Matterhorn has been subjected to various records and stunts. The fastest recorded ascent (Hörnli) is 1 hr 3 min. In 1980 J. M. Boivin skied down the E Face, made a record solo ascent of the N Face (4h 10m) and then hang glided from the summit to base.

It was estimated in 1977 that since 1865 385 people had died on this mountain, including 11 on the N Face.

Maund, John Oakley (1846–1902) Was with Cordier and Middlemore on the first ascent of the Verte from the Argentière Glacier in 1876, and in the same season made the first ascents of Les Courtes and Les Droites. He later made new routes on the Bietschhorn and Lauteraarhorn and twice tried the Mittellegi Ridge (1879, 1881) but without success. In 1878 he was with ◊ Dent for three attempts on the Dru.

Mazeaud, Pierre (b. 1929) One of the best post-war French alpinists. He took part in the terrible retreat from the Central Pillar of Frêney in 1961 when he, ◊ Bonatti and Gallieni were the only survivors of the seven who set out. In 1971 he joined the International Everest Expedition led by Norman ◊ Dyhrenfurth and played a part in the so-called 'Latin Revolt', quitting the expedition early. In 1978 he did climb ◊ Mt Everest by the South Col route and at 49 was the oldest man to do so at that time.

Mazeaud is a politician and one-time government minister.

Meade, Charles Francis (1881–1975) British alpinist noted for his first descent of the N E Ridge of Jungfrau (1902) and for his Himalayan campaigns of 1910, 1912 and 1913 when he attempted to climb Kamet. In 1913 he reached the col between Kamet and Abi Gamin (Meade's Col, 7,138 m) and camped there; until the Everest expeditions this was the highest mountain camp known. The lightweight tent used is named after him. Meade wrote: *Approach to the Hills* (1940) and *High Mountains* (1954).

Reinhold Messner   Willy Merkl

Mer de Glace Perhaps the most famous glacier of the Alps and the longest in the Mont Blanc group (14 km). Its principal feeding ground is the Géant Glacier, which, with the Vallée Blanche, extends from the Aig. du Géant to the Aig. du Midi. The Géant Glacier descends the spectacular Géant Ice-fall to the Tacul Glacier which almost immediately effects a junction with the glaciers of Leschaux and Talèfre to form the Mer de Glace. There are numerous subsidiary feeder glaciers on either bank. The stream issues from the ice above Les Tines and is largely canalized to its junction with the Arve.

The Mer de Glace is usually dry (◊ Glaciers) and though heavily crevassed, is fairly gently inclined and seldom presents difficulties. The chief mode of access is from ◊ Montenvers.

Merkl, Willy (1900–34) A leading climber from the great Munich school of the late 1920s. Merkl made many daring ascents in the Eastern Alps, including the Dolomites, and some first-rate ice-climbs in the Western Alps before visiting the Caucasus in 1929, where the third ascent of the S Peak of Ushba was made, and also the first ascent of the N Ridge of Koshtantau.

In 1932 he adopted ◊ Welzenbach's plans for an attempt on Nanga Parbat and led an expedition which succeeded in finding a practicable way to the top, though had not the resources to carry it out. In 1934 he returned to the attack but the party was overtaken by storm and in a fearful retreat, four Germans and six porters died. Merkl himself died between Camps 7 and 6. His leadership of both expeditions has been strongly criticized.

Merzbacher, Gottfried (1846–1926) Bavarian climber who played a part in the opening of the Dolomites. In 1891 he was with Purtscheller in the Caucasus, then visited the Tien Shan. He later visited the great Bogdo Ola group, though by then his interests had turned to exploring rather than climbing.

Messner, Reinhold (b. 1944) A mountaineer from the Tyrol, well known for his solo ascents of hard climbs, for example, Phillip/Flamm, 1969. An outspoken champion of free climbing. In 1970 Messner, with his brother Gunther, took part in the Nanga Parbat Expedition and both reached the summit by the Rupal Flank (first ascent). Gunther was taken ill and his brother decided they should descend by the little known Diamiri Face. Without even a rope they managed to descend successfully, but Gunther was killed near the foot of the face, presumably by an avalanche.

In 1974 he took part in a new ascent of the S Face of Aconcagua, finishing it solo. In the same year he began a remarkable partnership with Peter ◊ Habeler, climbing the Matterhorn Nordwand in 8 hrs and the Eigerwand in 10 hrs. In 1975 he and Habeler climbed Gasherbrum I (8,068 m) – an outstanding Himalayan 'Alpine-style' push.

In 1976 he made the first ascent of Midnight Sun Wall on Mt McKinley and, returning to the Alps, the West Pillar on Ortler. In 1978 he made the first ascent of Breach Wall on ◊ Kilimanjaro.

In 1978, again with Habeler, he made the first ascent of Everest without supplementary oxygen, by the S Col route. Two years later, by the N Col and a new route on the N Face, he made the first solo ascent of Everest.

Messner's ambition was now to climb all the 8,000 m peaks and he became the first man to do this with his ascent of Lhotse in 1986. He has undoubtedly established himself as one of the greatest mountaineers of all time.

He has written numerous books, some of which have been translated into English, including an autobiography, *Reinhold Messner: Free Spirit*. Best known, perhaps, is *The Seventh Grade* (1974).

Messner's 8,000 m peak ascents

Nanga Parbat 1970, 1978 (solo)	Gasherbrum II 1982, 1984
Manaslu 1972	Broad Peak 1982
Gasherbrum I 1975, 1984	Cho Oyu 1983
Mount Everest 1978, 1980 (solo)	Annapurna 1985
K2 1979	Dhaulagiri 1985
Shisha Pangma 1981	Makalu 1986
Kangchenjunga 1982	Lhotse 1986

Meurer, Julius D. (1838–1924) Founder and first President of the Austrian Alpine Club (1878), but later disagreed with the vogue for guideless climbing and resigned. He was the author of many climbing guidebooks to the Eastern Alps. He made the first ascent of Pala di San Martino (1878).

Mexico, climbing in The highest peaks in Mexico are the three volcanoes, Citlaltepetl (Pico de Orizaba) (5,699 m), Popocatapetl (5,452 m) and Ixtaccihuatl (5,286 m). The famous Popocatapetl was reputedly climbed by the Conquistadores in 1519. The peaks are of little use to mountaineers. Good rock-climbing is reported near Mexico City and Durango.

Meyer family An extraordinary family from Aarau responsible for the first exploration of the Oberland and the mapping of the Swiss Alps. Johann Rudolf Meyer I (1739–1813) founded a prosperous silk mill in Aarau, which enabled him to visit the mountains and sponsor the work of the great mapmakers, J. H. Weiss and J. E. Muller. They climbed Titlis together in 1787. Weiss's Swiss Atlas was published in parts, 1796–1802. For Meyer they constructed a relief model of the Alps, which he sold to Napoleon in 1803.

Meyer had two sons, J.R. II and Heironymus and two grandsons, J.R. III and Gottlieb. In 1811 J.R. II and Heironymus made the first ascent of Jungfrau. In the following year sons and grandsons conducted a six-week Oberland campaign during which J.R. III made the first crossing of the Strahlegg and Gottlieb repeated the Jungfrau. Most remarkable was the first ascent of Finsteraarhorn by J. R. Meyer III and the guides Arnold Abbuhl, Volker, Bortes and Huber. Even today the climb is Gr III with fixed rope, and this has led some historians to dispute the ascent.

Middlemore, Thomas (1842–1923)   In the early 1870s Middlemore was the companion of a number of hard climbers, including Gardiner, T. S. Kennedy and Eccles. In his last season he joined Cordier and Maund on the first ascents of the Verte from Argentière Glacier, Les Courtes and Les Droites. With Cordier he also made the first ascent of Pizzo Bianco and Piz Roseg from the Tschierva Glacier (all in 1876). His passage of the Col des Grandes Jorasses with Kennedy in 1874 (the first) created a fierce controversy as to the moral justification of persuading guides to undertake climbs involving objective dangers.

His brother, S. G. C. Middlemore, also did a few Alpine seasons, but of a less ambitious character.

Midlands, climbing in   Excluding the ◊ Peak District, there are sundry outcrops of rock scattered across the Midland counties. Hangingstones at Woodhouse Eaves in Leicestershire is a natural granite outcrop with some short climbs and a number of quarries have also been developed in the region. In the west there are Llanymynech Quarry and Pontesford Rocks, along with various sandstone outcrops.

GUIDEBOOK Kerr, *Rock Climbs in the West Midlands* (C.P.).

Mixed climbing   A term used in the Alps to indicate a route which involves both rock-climbing and snow- or ice-climbing.

Moffatt, Jerry (b.1963)   One of the outstanding rock-climbers of the 1980s, Moffatt established the E7 grade in the United Kingdom with a string of fierce ascents in the first part of the decade and then helped break the E9 barrier in the latter part after adopting French style. He began climbing at school in North Wales and had soon repeated Fawcett's testpiece Strawberries at the age of only 17 in 1980. Soon after this he took up residence in the Sheffield area, adding Helmut Schmitt (E6) to Stoney Middleton. A regular visitor to the United States, he repeated Genesis in Eldorado in 1982, before returning home to add a string of E7s in 1983 and 1984. Master's Wall on Cloggy, Revelations on Raven Tor and Masterclass on Pen Trwyn stand out. He climbed Germany's first X-, The Face, in 1983 in the southern Franken-jura. In 1985 the immense physical pressures of this standard of climbing took their toll and Moffatt needed surgery and a two year lay-off before returning to the fore, by which time the French ethic had been established. It allowed him to push grades even further with a string of desperate repeats in Buoux, France and the addition of Liquid Amber (E9 7a) to Pen Trwyn. Moffatt was heavily involved in the emerging competition scene with a number of Grand Prix wins, most memorably at Leeds in 1989. A motor-cycle accident prevented him from securing the championship that year.

Monolith   A tall block of rock resting against a crag. The crack or chimney between the monolith and the face often provides a climb, for example, Monolith Crack, Shepherd's Crag, Borrowdale. Perhaps the most famous is the Monolith Crack on the Gribin, Wales, climbed by the ◊ Abraham brothers in 1905.

Montague, Edward Charles (1867–1928)   Author and journalist, some-time acting editor of the *Manchester Guardian*. A keen climber, he is best known for his story *In Hanging Garden Gully* (1923).

Mont Aiguille (2,086 m)   A fantastic limestone peak some 58 km south of Grenoble in the Vercors. It consists of a fine grassy plateau surrounded on all sides by steep limestone walls varying between 150 m and 300 m in height. Its impressive appearance guaranteed its notoriety from medieval days and it is mentioned by English writers as early as 1211, when it was known as Mons Inascensibilis!

In the summer of 1492, Charles VIII of France, on his way to Italy, was so impressed by the peak that he ordered Antoine de Ville, Lord of Domjulien and Beaupré, to attempt its ascent. The noble lord was successful, several men reaching the top by means of ladders and 'subtle engines'. They stayed three days, erecting a hut (surely the first bivouac hut?) and three crosses. Chamois were found on the summit.

Today the mountain offers numerous very hard climbs. There are no easy ways up.

Montandon, Paul (1858–1948)   A Swiss banker who was one of the early exponents of guideless climbing. He made the first guideless ascents of numerous peaks including the Eiger (1878), Schreckhorn (1883), Gspaltenhorn (1885) and the first guideless traverse of the Bietschhorn (1888). One of the earliest skiers in Switzerland. He remained active all his life, and ascended Cevedale at the age of 75.

Mont Blanc (4,807 m)   The highest summit in Western Europe and one of the most important mountains for climbers, not only for its height, but for the variety of climbing it offers. It stands immediately south of ◊ Chamonix on the Italian frontier, though the summit is entirely in France. It forms a distinctive high ridge with the Dôme du Goûter, north-west, and Mont Maudit, north-east, and the latter extends to Mont Blanc du Tacul. From Mont Blanc itself a short ridge runs south to Mt Blanc de Courmayeur. All these peaks are over 4,000 m. The northern face (towards Chamonix) presents great glaciers and snow-fields, well seen from the Brévent on the opposite side of the Chamonix valley, but the south (Italian side) is a complex series of glacier cwms separated by high and often difficult ridges.

The easiest ways to the summit are on the Chamonix side, that via the Goûter Route being the commonest, though the Grands Mulets is also easy. The only really easy route from Italy is via the Dôme Glacier. All three of these routes reach the Col du Dôme and then traverse the Bosses Ridge to Mont Blanc summit. All are fairly lengthy snow/ice-climbs.

The three long high ridges of Brouillard, Innominata and Peuterey are seldom climbed throughout, since their southern ends connect with peaks which are climbs in their own rights. The Peuterey *intégrale* is one of the hardest ridge climbs in the Alps. Between the Brouillard and Innominata Ridges are the important Brouillard Pillars and between the Innominata and Peuterey are the important Frêney Pillars. Beyond the Peuterey is the wide high face of the Brenva terminating in the Brenva Ridge. Strictly speaking, this is the limit of the Italian side of Mont Blanc proper.

The Brenva Face is of particular importance since it contains a number of ridges offering great climbs. These are quite different from the long ridges previously mentioned, being steeper and definitely a part of the face. They face east and are, from the south (Peuterey): Eckpfeiler Buttress (Grand Pilier d'Angle), Pear Route (Via della Pera), Route Major, Sentinelle Rouge and the Brenva Ridge (Old Brenva).

Beyond the Brenva, above the upper bay of the Brenva Glacier, the S E Face of Mt Maudit is an important climbing area and this is limited by the long ridge known as the Frontier Ridge, since the frontier here turns east and follows the ridge to the Tour Ronde. (The correct name of this ridge is the Arête de la Brenva; not to be confused with the Brenva Ridge.) Beyond this again is the glacier bay of the Cirque Maudit, on the far side of which is the Diable Ridge of Mont Blanc du Tacul and the various spectacular pinnacles, of which the best known is the Grand Capucin.

All these climbs, from the Brouillard to the Capucin, are long, remote and fairly difficult. Some are extremely difficult and the area is one of the most important for climbing in the Alps.

In 1760, de ♀ Saussure offered a prize for the first ascent of Mont Blanc. Attempts were made in 1775, 1783, 1784 and 1786, the last two reaching the start of the Bosses Ridge. The summit was finally attained by J. Balmat and M. Paccard on 8 August 1786. The first English ascent was by Col. M. Beaufoy in 1787 and the first woman to reach the top was Maria Paradis in 1808. The first American ascent was by W. Howard and J. Van Rensselaer (1820). (See *The First Ascent of Mont Blanc*, by Brown and de Beer.) Other important first ascents include:

1827	Corridor Route – C. Fellows, W. Hawes with nine guides
c. 1840	Grands Mulets Route – M. Couttet
1861	Goûter Ridge – L. Stephen, F. Tuckett, with M. Anderegg, J. J. Bennen, P. Perren
1865	Brenva Ridge – G. S. Mathews, A. W. Moore, F. and H. Walker with J. and M. Anderegg
1887	Frontier Ridge – M. von Kuffner with A. Burgener, J. Furrer and a porter
1901	Brouillard Ridge – G. B. Gugliermina with J. Brocherel
1919	Innominata Ridge – S. L. Courtauld, E. G. Oliver, with A. Aufdenblatten, A. and H. Rey
1927	Peuterey Ridge – L. Obersteiner, K. Schreiner
1927	Sentinelle Rouge – T. G. Brown, F. S. Smythe
1928	Aigs. du Diable Ridge – Miss M. O'Brien, R. Underhill with A. Charlet, G. Cachet
1928	Route Major – T. G. Brown, F. S. Smythe
1933	Pear Route – T. G. Brown with A. Graven, A. Aufdenblatten
1951	Gervasutti Pillar – P. Fornelli, G. Mauro
1957	Eckpfeiler Buttress – W. Bonatti, T. Gobbi
1961	Central Pillar of Frêney – C. Bonington, D. Whillans, I. Clough, J. Dlugosz
1970	Central Pillar of Brouillard – E. Jones (solo)
1970	Eckpfeiler East Flank – W. Ceccinel, G. Nomine
1982	Super Couloir of Brouillard – P. Gabarrou, A. Steiner
1984	Peuterey Ridge Integrale solo – C. Profit

Mont Blanc, Tour of   One of the finest multi-day walks in the Alps; very popular. It is usual to walk the route in an anti-clockwise direction starting and finishing in the Chamonix valley. Though not particularly arduous it does cross a number of high passes which are sometimes snow-covered early or late in the season. The views are spectacular throughout.

There are a number of variants to the walk and the time taken can vary too, depending on the walker, but a typical itinerary is: Day 1, Les Houches to Les Contamines; 2, Refuge de la Croix de Bonhomme; 3, Rifugio Elisabetta; 4, Courmayeur; 5, Arnuva; 6, La Fouly; 7, Champex; 8, Trient; 9, Le Tour; 10, La Flégère; 11, Les Houches. The route passes through France, Italy and Switzerland to end back in France.

GUIDEBOOK Harper, *Tour of Mont Blanc* (C.P.).

Montenvers   A favourite and historically famous starting point for climbs in the Mont Blanc range. It is a shoulder of alp above Chamonix, on the left bank of the ◊ Mer de Glace near the glacier terminus. There is a hotel, café, bunkhouse, mountain zoo, and (on the glacier) ice grottoes. Plenty of camping space, and the site is easily joined with the extensive Plan de l'Aiguille by a good track. Extremely popular with tourists. It is connected with Chamonix by a rack railway.

Monte Rosa (4,634 m)   A complex mountain mass between Switzerland and Italy. The Swiss side faces Zermatt, the Italian side Macugnaga. It has the third highest summit in the Alps (Dufourspitze, 4,634 m) which is also the highest summit in Switzerland. The other summits are:

4,609 m Nordend	4,436 m Parrotspitze
4,596 m Grenzgipfel	4,341 m Ludwigshohe
4,563 m Zumsteinspitze	4,321 m Corno Nero
4,556 m Signalkuppe	4,215 m Pyramide Vincent
(Punta Gnifetti)	4,046 m Punta Giordani

As the cols between the ridges do not fall below 4,000 m, the mountain as a whole is the largest 4,000 m massif in the Alps.

The mountain is very popular, especially from Zermatt. The ordinary route is long but not very difficult, though rather more so than Mont Blanc. There are rock-climbs, notably the Cresta Rey and Cresta di Santa Caterina, and some famous ice-climbs on the immense E Face, notably the Marinelli Couloir, but generally the mountain offers long mixed traverses from peak to peak. The highest hut in the Alps, Capanna Margherita, is on the summit of the Signalkuppe.

The first ascent (Dufourspitze) was by J. G. and C. Smyth, E. J. Stephenson with U. Lauener, J. and M. Zumtaugwald in 1855. It quickly became one of the most popular climbs in the Alps and certainly the most popular from Zermatt until displaced by the Matterhorn in that respect.

Other notable first ascents include:

1861	Nordend – Buxton brothers, J. Cowell, M. Payot
1872	Marinelli Couloir – Pendlebury brothers, C. Taylor, F. Imseng, G. Spechtenhauser, G. Oberto
1874	Cresta Rey – E. Hulton, P. Rubi, J. Moser
1876	Via Brioschi – L. Brioschi, F. and A. Imseng
1887	Cresta Signal – H. W. Topham, A. Supersaxo, a porter
1906	Cresta di Santa Caterina – V. J. E. Ryan, F. and J. Lochmatter
1931	N E Face, Signalkuppe – J. Lagarde, L. Davies

Moore, Adolphus Warburton (1841–87)   One of the greatest Victorian mountaineers. Moore's career embraced practically all the then known difficult climbs in the Alps: frequently as the second or third ascents. His own first ascents began in 1862 with the Sesia Joch, Jungfraujoch and Gross Fiescherhorn, but his finest seasons were 1864 and 1865. In 1864, mainly with ◊ Whymper and H. ◊ Walker, he made six major first ascents of peaks or cols and several second, third or fourth ascents. In 1865 he raised this to nine first ascents, including Piz Roseg, Obergabelhorn and the Brenva Face of Mont Blanc.

The Brenva climb took place the day following Whymper's ascent of the Matterhorn and, just as Whymper's climb symbolizes the end of the Golden Age, Moore's Brenva endeavour symbolized the birth of a new age of difficult climbing. It is significant, too, that the adverse public reaction to climbing following the Matterhorn tragedy, which threatened the Alpine Club with extinction, was countered by Moore's Secretaryship (1872–4).

In 1866, 1867 and 1869, Moore did some winter climbing in the Alps, including the second ascent of the Brèche de la Meije. In 1868 he visited the Caucasus with Freshfield and Tucker, making first ascents of Kasbek and the E Summit of Elbruz. He paid a second visit in 1874 with Gardiner, Grove and Walker.

In private life Moore was a senior official in the India Office and one-time private secretary to Lord Randolph Churchill. Twice offered the Presidency of the A.C., he declined on the grounds of his official duties.

In 1867 Moore privately published his diary of his great 1864 season: *The Alps in 1864*. An enlarged public edition was published in 1902.

Moraine The detritus of a glacier found at the snout (terminal) and edge (medial). Moraines are formed of boulders, mud and even old ice, crushed together by the grinding action of the glacier's movements. In the Alps, where the glaciers are retreating, the moraines may be extensive. The older ones are usually well compacted and have well trodden paths. New moraine is loose and unpleasant.

Morse, Sir George Henry (1857–1931) Brother-in-law of the ◊ Pasteurs; climbed frequently with them and with ◊ Wicks and ◊ Gibson. He made new routes on the Aig. de Talèfre (1892) and Aig. d'Argentière (1893). He took part in the first guideless ascent of Grépon (1892) and the first traverse of it from south to north (1893). Morse was President of the A.C. (1926–7) and an Original Member of the Climbers' Club. He climbed frequently in Britain. He was knighted for political services in 1923.

Morshead, Frederick (1836–1914) A very active Alpine pioneer who made many early ascents (though no first ascents of great note), especially with ◊ Moore and C. E. ◊ Mathews. With the latter, he was a founder of the Climbers' Club.

Moseley, William Oxnard, Jun. (1848–79) Born in Boston, U.S.A., and a doctor in Massachusetts, Moseley was a keen climber with many ascents in the Alps and Sierra Nevada to his credit. He was killed while descending the Hörnli Ridge of the Matterhorn; a celebrated accident, but one which seems to have been his own fault. His boots were badly nailed and he insisted, against the wishes of his guides and companion (◊ Craven), in unroping too soon. He slipped on the slab which now bears his name, and fell 600 m to his death.

Moulam, Anthony John James (b. 1927) A leading post-war British

Mountain features: **A** Ice-fall; **B** glacier; **C** crevasses; **D** névé; **E** bergschrund; **F** col; **G** ridge; **H** gendarme; **J** couloir; **K** buttress.

rock-climber, and partner to P. R. J. ◊ Harding on many climbs in Llanberis and the Black Rocks, Derbyshire. Moulam's own routes include Mur y Niwl, Ysfa (1952), Ogof Direct, Silyn (1952), Shadrach (1951) and Scratch (1953), both at Tremadoc. (Many others too.) He began climbing at the Black Rocks in 1940 and has climbed in many parts of Britain and the Alps. He has appeared on various television climbing programmes.

Tony Moulam was President of the Climbers' Club, 1970–2, and of the B.M.C., 1971–3. He held the latter Presidency during a period of change and upheaval, initiated many reforms, but finally resigned over policy disagreements.

He compiled a number of post-war guidebooks: *A Guide to Black Rocks and Cratcliffe Tor* (with Harding, 1949. Revised as part of Chatsworth area guide, 1970), *The Carneddau* (1951, 1966), *Tryfan and Glyder Fach* (1956, 1964), *Cwm Idwal* (1958, 1964) and *Snowdon East* (1970).

Mountain An elevated mass of land, circumscribed in area and surrounded by valleys or plains. The highest point is known as the summit and there may be other eminences known as subsidiary summits or tops (e.g. Monte Rosa). These may have separate names or may be given a compass name, e.g. Wildspitze, N Summit, S Summit. Or they may simply be given a spot height e.g., Pt 2,365 m. Where several such summits exist, the highest is known as the Principal Summit.

The sides of the mountain are known as the flanks and are given a compass name or, more rarely, are named after the valley they overlook (e.g. Rupal flank, Nanga Parbat). If the flank is very steep it is called a face or wall. Where the faces meet they form a ridge – often the easiest way up the mountain. Ridges are given compass names or are named after places near-by, people who made the first ascent or attempt, some feature of the ridge, or even some nickname, such as Viereselsgrat, Dent Blanche (Four Asses Ridge).

Some mountains are plateaux, that is, the top is almost equal in area to the bottom and is fairly level, e.g. Kinder Scout, Derbyshire. Not all plateaux are mountains, however. Particularly sharp-pointed mountains are often given special names: Spire, Tower, Aiguille, etc. Mountains formed by special geological processes are also given identifying names – mesa, nunatuk and so on.

Though some mountains exist alone (e.g. Ararat), many are linked by ridges to other mountains. The result is also called a ridge (e.g. Mischabelgrat in Switzerland). A compact group of mountains is known as a massif and a bigger group as a range or chain (obsolete). These last three words are used somewhat indiscriminately: one hears, for example, of the range of Mont Blanc, the chain of Mont Blanc or the Mont Blanc massif. An imaginary line linking the principal summits of a range is known as the crest line, or, because it determines the flow of rivers, the watershed.

The qualities of a mountain which appeal to climbers are the height, the shape of the mountain, and the intrinsic difficulties of an ascent.

In Britain, any peak over 600 m in height is usually regarded as a mountain.

Mountaineering (Am.: mountain climbing; G.: Bergsteigen; F.: alpinisme; It.: alpinismo) The sport of climbing mountains, or, the exploration of high mountains for scientific purposes or simply conquest. The term, like the activity, is capable of wide interpretation, but basic to it is the acknowledgement of some degree of difficulty, only overcome by skill on the part of the mountaineer.

Mountaineering involves four major activities: walking, rock-climbing, snow- or ice-climbing, and navigation. To these may be added: mountain camping, ski-mountaineering, mountain rescue, high-altitude planning. Knowledge of weather, food values, physiological changes and other allied subjects may also be of value in certain circumstances. Physical and mental fitness is required, but probably experience counts for more, for the sport can be continued into old age, and frequently is.

The philosophy of the sport varies according to where it is taking place, in general all the conditions of an ascent must come from within the climber himself, guided by the prevailing opinion. To take an extreme example: any climber found using pitons to help him up the easy Ordinary Route of Milestone Buttress in Wales would be ridiculed, but nobody would complain if he used pegs and bolts on some of the fierce walls of Yosemite, California. Similarly, under present conditions, siege tactics would be ludicrous on the Hörnli Ridge of the Matterhorn, but not on the S Face of Annapurna. There is a thin dividing line between what is acceptable and what is not, and here mountain ◊ ethics play their part. Generally speaking, the best ascent to date is taken as the standard, so that, if a climb *can* be done with four pegs, it is unethical to use more. If someone reduces the number of pegs required to say, two, then that becomes the new standard. In Alpine climbing or winter mountaineering, where snow and ice are involved, these unwritten rules can be blurred by weather and other factors. It must be stressed that all of this is left to the individual conscience.

The aims of mountaineering pass through three phases: to reach the summit; to create a more difficult route; to reduce the aid needed on a difficult route. Each takes precedence in turn over the next. If we examine three areas:
Britain Reaching the summit counts for little. There are only a handful of summits in Britain that cannot be reached by simple walks. The route, and the way in which it is climbed, are both of great importance (see above).
Alps The summit is still of importance, since many are difficult to reach by

any route. The routes, too, are of great importance but the techniques used are more open to debate, though extreme misuse would cause criticism.

Himalaya The summit can still be the prime objective by any route and any technique within reason. A new route on a mountain already climbed is a major event.

Men have been climbing mountains for utilitarian reasons or curiosity since time immemorial. The first sporting ascent is frequently taken as that of Sir Alfred ◊ Wills and his party on the ascent of the Wetterhorn in 1854 – but this is highly debatable.

Mountaineering Association (M.A.) In 1945, the then emergent ◊ British Mountaineering Council was asked to undertake the training of would-be climbers as part of its function. The B.M.C. felt it could not undertake this task and as a result of this decision a group of climbers, led by J. E. B. Wright, a former professional guide, founded the Mountaineering Association in 1946. It was a non-profit-making trust and it quickly established itself as the premier training organization in Britain, with about 1,200 students per year taking its courses. The instructors included many top names in British climbing (e.g. Clough, MacInnes, Scott).

Jerry Wright was Director of Training, and the Association published several books by him and others as well as a popular quarterly. When Wright retired, the organization faltered and came to an end in 1968.

Mountaineering route A phrase used in Britain to indicate a climb of considerable length, where the difficulty is secondary to the fine positions. It is also used by some climbers disparagingly when the lack of difficulty disappoints them.

Mountain flights In the early days of aviation, airframes and engines were pitted against the mountains. Here are some dates of interest:

1910 G. Chavez (Peru) made the first flight over the Alps from Brig to Domodossola via the Simplon. Bleriot monoplane.

1914 H. Parmelin (Switzerland) made the first flight over the summit of Mont Blanc.

1919 Lt. R. Ackermann (Switzerland) made the first glacier landing on the Aletsch Glacier. DH3 machine.

1921 F. Durafour (Switzerland) landed on the Col du Dôme above Chamonix – the first glacier landing above 4,000 m. Caudron G3 biplane. (Built in 1914!)

1931 Sq. Ldr. S. B. Harris (U.K.) led his flight of five Wapiti fighters in the first Himalayan crossing, Risalpur–Gilgit.

1933 Houston Everest Expedition twice flew over the mountain. Westlands with Pegasus supercharged engines.

1935 H. Schreiber (Switzerland) made the first glider crossing of the Alps from Thun to Bellinzona.

1960 H. Giraud (France) landed on the summit of Mont Blanc. Piper Cub Chouca.

1973 M. Harker (U.S.A.) made the first big hang-glider descent in the Alps from top of Zugspitze to Ehrwald – 1,980 m, 12 km, 11.51 min.

1988 J. M. Boivin parapented off summit of Everest.

1991 L. Dickinson ballooned over Everest.

Mountain heights A casual glance at mountain literature or mountain maps will quickly show that there are often discrepancies in the heights attributed to mountains. This is particularly the case of mountains in remote areas. There are good technical reasons for this; survey heights vary from survey to survey. Among the causes are: refraction, earth curvature, vertical deflection caused by unequal gravity, the depth of snow on the summit during observations, and the exact meaning of 'mean sea level', since sea-level is not spheroid. Heights are usually the average of several calculated observations with all possible corrections applied.

Where the peaks have been inadequately surveyed, or not surveyed at all, the heights may be those attributed to the peaks by climbers who have used an aneroid (altimeter) or possibly hypsometer. Variations in temperature and air pressure make these readings highly inaccurate. In some cases the heights given are merely estimates based on climbers' judgements.

National pride has been known to affect published data. This is especially the case when a height approaches a 'magic figure', for example, 6,000 m. If a height is estimated at, say, 5,985 m, the addition of another 20 m seems of little account and makes the peak all the more impressive.

Another source of error is attributable to converting metres to feet and vice versa, and rounding down or up to the nearest unit. For difficulties over Himalayan heights see *Abode of Snow*, by K. Mason. (◊ Height conversion.)

Mountain Leader Training Board (M.L.T.B.) A body responsible to the British Mountaineering Council for overseeing the training of instructors (as distinct from guides). Who should control training – the B.M.C. or the educationists – was the subject of fierce debate in the mid-1970s. Educationists wanted paper qualifications like the Mountain Leadership Certificate (M.L.C.), something mountaineers were opposed to, partly on ideological grounds and partly because it could be used to restrict freedom in the hills. In the end the M.L.C. was scrapped and replaced by a log-book system, recording experience, and an assessment. It is principally for the benefit of teachers taking pupils in the hills. Successful completion leads to recognition as a Mountain Walking Leader. There is no certificate.

The Mountain Instructor's Certificate (M.I.C.) is an advanced qualification principally for instructors working in outdoor pursuits centres. (◊ Guides.)

The M.L.T.B. only covers England. There are separate boards for Scotland, Northern Ireland, Wales and Eire.

Mountain rescue The organization of mountain rescue in Britain is done by the ◊ Mountain Rescue Committee. Teams of volunteers are established in all the mountain areas. There is an experienced leader for each team and the members undergo rigorous training in rescue techniques. Additional volunteers may be co-opted on the spot to assist with arduous procedures such as long carries or sweep and search patterns. The police are often co-opted too and, if necessary, the R.A.F. Mountain Rescue. Each team is fully equipped with the necessary gear, including Land-Rovers and radios. Helicopters are available when required. In addition, the M.R.C. maintain mountain rescue boxes at various strategic places in the hills for immediate use in the event of an accident. There is no charge made for mountain rescue in Britain.

Rescue in the Alps is usually the province of the local guides who call upon such services as they require, including helicopters. The victim has to pay for these services, or in the event of death, his relatives, and the charges can be high. In some parts of the Alps, there are special avalanche rescue teams, mainly concerned with skiing accidents.

In both Britain and the Alps dogs have been trained to take part in search operations: a trained dog is reckoned to be worth 20 searchers.

The procedure for calling out the mountain rescue team in Britain is that a messenger goes from the scene of the accident to the mountain rescue post, or telephones the police, using a 999 call, whichever is quicker. In the case of overdue parties, a contact should be made after a reasonable time, say three hours, and the team leader will then decide whether a search should be started. (◊ Accidents.)

More information is contained in the *International Mountain Rescue Handbook*, by H. MacInnes, and the annual *Mountain and Cave Rescue*, by the M.R.C.

Mountain Rescue Committee The co-ordinating committee for mountain rescue in England and Wales, representing the interests of all those who are concerned with rescue work (climbing clubs, caving clubs, police, R.A.F.). There are separate committees for Scotland and Ireland. It is a voluntary body and charitable trust.

The scope of the M.R.C.'s work is wide. It includes the equipping of rescue posts, assisting in the raising and training of teams, research into improved rescue techniques and facilities, and general fund-raising to promote these activities. Basic equipment is supplied by the N.H.S. through the M.R.C.

The M.R.C. had its origins in the Joint Stretcher Committee of The Rucksack Club and F.R.C.C. formed in 1933 to produce a stretcher suitable for use in the hills (Report 1935, ◊ Thomas, E.). The Committee was widened to include other clubs in 1936 and later. It became the M.R.C. in 1946. (See *Mountain and Cave Rescue*, the annual M.R.C. handbook. This gives current lists of teams and posts throughout Britain.)

Mountain rescue stretchers Specially designed stretchers are necessary for the safe evacuation of injured persons from a mountain. The main types are: Mariner, Thomas, MacInnes and (in emergency) the Pigott rope stretcher. The Thomas and MacInnes are the ones used by British rescue teams.

The Thomas stretcher is issued to M.R. teams in England and Wales. It has long extending handles, yoke straps to distribute weight, and wooden runners to allow it to be slid down suitable slopes. There are two models, the standard and the split two-piece (each half can be carried separately in the latter).

The MacInnes stretcher is used by Scottish teams and the R.A.F. It can be folded, and since it weighs only 15 kg can be carried by one man. The patient is secured by a clever system of straps, and there is a wheel attachment which allows the stretcher to be trundled over easy ground.

The Pigott rope stretcher is only used in emergency. It is difficult to carry and uncomfortable for the patient and it should not be used where there is possible spinal injury. It is made from a normal climbing rope.

Mountain sickness (altitude sickness) The effect on the human system of gaining altitude too rapidly. Though it has been known for at least four centuries, since the Spaniards invaded Peru, it is still not fully understood. Some people are hardly affected, others badly so and there seems no correlation with age, fitness or sex.

In most cases the onset of the illness begins between 3,700 and 4,300 m, but cases have been recorded above and below these limits. The common symptoms are headache, nausea, loss of appetite and inability to sleep.

Severe cases can lead to pulmonary oedema (water on the lungs) or cerebral

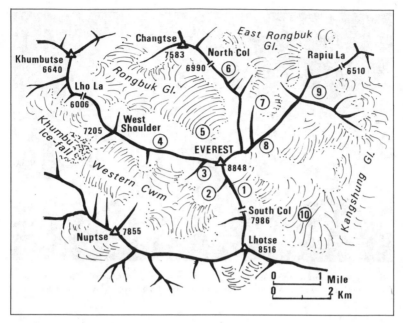

Mount Everest region; **1** SE Ridge; **2** S Pillar; **3** SW Face; **4** W Ridge; **5** N Face; **6** N Ridge; **7** Secondary N Face; **8** NE Ridge; **9** E Ridge; **10** E or Kangshung Face.

oedema (water on the brain). Both are extremely serious and can rapidly cause death. Preventive treatment in the form of diuretic drugs is sometimes employed.

Oxygen masks help reduce the effects of mountain sickness but the only really effective cure is to go down to a lower altitude as quickly as possible. (◇ Acclimatization) (✧ *Mountain Medicine and Physiology*, by Clarke, Ward, Williams.)

Mount Everest (8,848 m)   The highest mountain in the world, lying in the Kosi Section of the Nepal Himalaya. The Chinese call it Chomolungma and the Nepalese Sagarmatha, but the English name given it in 1865 after Sir George Everest, former Surveyor General of India, is the one used by most countries. The mountain lies on the border between Tibet to the north and Nepal to the south. Since the Chinese reopened the northern approaches to Westerners in 1978, all parts of the mountain are now accessible to climbers, though a permit must be obtained and a stiff fee paid by each expedition. Four climbing seasons are recognized: pre-monsoon, monsoon, post-monsoon and winter.

HISTORY

Immediately prior to the First World War, a number of Everest expeditions were mooted but nothing happened until 1921 when political problems were overcome and Lt. Col. Howard Bury led a reconnaissance party through Tibet to the north side of Everest. With minor variations their route was followed by all the pre-war expeditions which were exclusively British.

From a Base Camp at Rongbuk the climbers went up the East Rongbuk

The Everest group with Nuptse in the right foreground, Everest SW Face centre, and the Khumbu Ice-fall, lower left, leading to the Western Cwm. (*W. Unsworth*)

Glacier to Camp III at the foot of the N Col. The steep and avalanche-prone col was climbed and then the north ridge to its junction with the long N E Ridge. Attempts were made either along the ridge over the so-called First and Second Steps or by a traverse across the N Face to the Great Couloir. In 1924 Norton reached 8,573 m on the face route – a height equalled in 1933 by Harris, Wager and Smythe.

The expeditions of 1921, 1922 and 1924 were dominated by G. L. Mallory, who lost his life with his companion Irvine in 1924. Their disappearance is one of the greatest mountain mysteries – some people believe they may have reached the top, though this seems unlikely.

After the war Nepal opened its doors to foreigners and Tibet was closed by the Chinese. In 1950 Tilman and Houston reconnoitred the Khumbu Valley, and in 1951, Shipton led a reconnaissance expedition which overcame the Khumbu Ice-fall and entered the Western Cwm, a glacier bowl surrounded by Everest, Lhotse and Nuptse. This paved the way for a Swiss expedition the following year. Climbing via the S Col, between Everest and Lhotse, Raymond Lambert and Sherpa Tenzing reached 8,595 m on the S E Ridge.

John Hunt's expedition in 1953 went like clockwork and Edmund Hillary and Tenzing reached the summit at 11.30 a.m. on 29 May. This was the first ascent of the mountain.

NOTABLE EXPEDITIONS AND ASCENTS AFTER 1953

1960   First ascent of the N Ridge (Wang Fu-chou, Chu Ying-hua, Konbu) (Chinese)

1963   First ascent of the W Ridge and first traverse (William Unsoeld, Tom Hornbein) (U.S.A.)

1973   First post-monsoon ascent (S E Ridge) (Hisashi Ishiguro, Yasuo Kato) (Japan)

1975   First ascent by a woman (S E Ridge) (Mrs Junko Tabei) (Japan)
1975   First ascent of the S W Face (Dougal Haston, Doug Scott) (U.K.)
1978   First ascent without oxygen equipment (S E Ridge) (Reinhold Mess-
       ner, Peter Habeler) (Italy/Austria)
1979   First ascent of the W Ridge Direct (Jernej Zaplotnik, Andrej Strem-
       felj, Stane Belak, Stipe Bozik, Ang Phu) (Yugoslavia)
1980   First winter ascent (S E Ridge) (Leszek Cichy, Krzysztof Wielicki)
       (Poland)
1980   First ascent of the South Pillar (Andrzej Czok, Jerzy Kukuczka)
       (Poland)
1980   First solo ascent of Everest (by a new route on the N Face) (Reinhold
       Messner) (Italy)
1982   First ascent of Central Rib, S W Face (Eduard Myslovsky, Vladimir
       Balyberdin) (U.S.S.R.)
1983   First ascent E Face (C. Buhler, K. Momb, L. Reichardt) (U.S.A.)
1984   First traverse W Ridge Direct–S E Ridge (Ivan Valchev, Metodi
       Savov, Nikolay Petkov, Kiril Doskov) (Bulgaria)
1984   First ascent of the Great Couloir, N Face (Tim Macartney-Snape,
       Greg Mortimer) (Australia)
1985   Dick Bass, aged 55, climbs Everest and completes all 7 summits of the
       world's continents.
1986   First ascent of the W Ridge from Tibet; first new route by a woman on
       Everest (Sharon Wood, Dwayne Congden) (Canada)
1986   Erhard Loretan, Jean Troillet climb N Face in 31 hours. Descend in
       3½ hours.
1988   Asian Friendship Expedition (China, Japan, Nepal) put 10 climbers
       simultaneously on summit; traverse N–S and S–N; broadcast live
       T.V. from summit.
1988   E Face of S Col (or S E Ridge from Kangshung Glacier) (Stephen
       Venables) (U.K./U.S.A.)
1988   Traverse of the N E Ridge Pinnacles (Harry Taylor, Russell Brice)
       (U.K.)
1988   Marc Batard solos S E Ridge from Base in 22½ hours.
1990   'Peace' expedition via N Col (U.S.A., U.S.S.R., China) puts 20 on
       summit.

STATISTICS (TO 1990)

A total of 289 climbers have reached the top.
There are 36 repeat ascents, so total ascents are 325.
Ten women have climbed Everest.
There have been 266 expeditions, two-thirds of them unsuccessful (1988).
Five ascents have been made by the late Sherpa Sungdare and six by Ang Rita
– in the latter case, without oxygen.
For non-Sherpas, the record is held by the Japanese climbers Yamada and
Kato, with three ascents each. Kato was killed descending from his last climb.
The oldest man to climb Everest is Richard Bass, an American tycoon who
climbed it by the S E Ridge in 1985 when he was 55.
The fastest ascent is that of Marc Batard, 22½ hours from Base Camp to
Summit by the S E Ridge, 29 September 1988.

FATALITIES (TO WINTER 1988/89)

There have been 103 deaths above Base Camp, almost half (46) porters.
Apart from Nepal, Japan has lost most – ten, with Britain losing eight and
India and China six each.

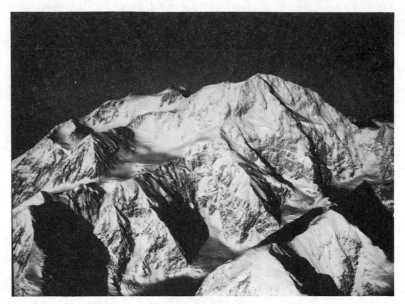

Mount McKinley (Denali). (*B. Washburn*)

Most deaths have occurred in the Khumbu Ice-fall (19).
In the last 20 years someone was killed on Everest every year except 1977.
Most disastrous was 1982, with 11.
Eleven people have died below Base Camp on expeditions.
Fifteen climbers have died descending from summit.
(*Everest* by Walt Unsworth is recognized as the definitive work on the world's highest mountain.)

Mount Everest Foundation   Formed after the 1953 first ascent of the mountain to administer the funds accumulated from book and film rights. The Foundation is jointly controlled by the Alpine Club and the Royal Geographical Society. Grants from the Foundation are made to expeditions. It is necessary for the expedition to show that it has a worthwhile objective (though not necessarily a large one) and that the Leader and other members are competent to undertake the expedition.

Mount Kenya (5,199 m)   An impressive volcanic peak rising from the highlands north of Nairobi. The central core is a volcanic plug forming the twin peaks of Batian (5,199 m) and Nelion (5,188 m), separated by a high col called the Gate of Mists. Other peaks of the core are Lenana (4,985 m), Pt Pigott (4,958 m), Pt John (4,883 m) and Midget Peak (4,700 m), and others of less importance. The former rim of the volcano has also left some high peaks near by, though not such good rock, nor as impressive: Tereri (4,714 m), Sendeyo (4,704 m).

The mountain was discovered by the missionary Krapf in 1849 and was explored by Teleki and Von Hohnel in 1887 and Gregory in 1893. Sir H. Mackinder, with the guides C. Ollier and J. Brocherel, made the first ascent of Batian in 1899. Other notable climbs include:

1929   Nelion first ascent. Batian, second ascent – E. Shipton,
        P. Wynn Harris
1930   Traverse of Nelion and Batian – E. Shipton, W. Tilman
1938   First woman's ascent, Batian – Miss U. Cameron
        First Kenya native ascent, Nelion – Mtu Muthara
1944   N Face – A. Firmin's party
1946   S Face and S W Ridge – A. Firmin, J. W. Howard
1955   W Face – R. A. Caukwell, G. W. Rose
1959   First Kenya native ascent, Batian – Kisoi Munyao
1963   N E Pillar, Nelion – G. B. Cliff, D. Rutowitz
        E Face, Nelion – H. Klier, S. Aeberli, Cliff
1964   Traverse Pt Pigott – Pt John – R. Baillie, T. P. Philips
1973   Diamond Couloir – Y. Laulan, P. Snyder
1975   Diamond Buttress Original Route – I. Howell, J. Temple
1978   Eastern Groove of Nelion – I. Howell, I. Allan
        Forel Glacier – R. Barton, D. Morris

Many other routes have been established, both on the major peaks and the lesser pinnacles. Of the latter, Midget Peak is reputed most difficult. Mention should be made of the attempt to climb the mountain by escaped prisoners of war (see *No Picnic on Mt Kenya*, by F. Benuzzi).

Considerable rock-climbing is done on Lukenya, south of Nairobi, and other rocks.

GUIDEBOOKS Peyron, *Mountains of Kenya*.
Wielochowski/Savage, *Mount Kenya Map & Guide*.

Mount McKinley (6,194 m)   The highest mountain in North America, situated in the Alaska Range of south-central Alaska, was named in 1896 in honour of the American President. But now the original Indian name for the peak, Denali (The Great One), is widespread.

The upper two-thirds of the mountain are covered permanently in snow and ice – a great complex of snow-fields and glaciers. The north side is the more easily accessible, especially since the Denali highway was built. The McKinley area is a National Park.

The first attempt to climb the mountain was by J. Wickersham in 1903, followed by that of F. A. Cook and E. Barrille in 1906. Cook's claim to have reached the top is now discounted. In 1910 came the famous 'Sourdough Expedition' organized by Lloyd and comprising tough local miners and trappers (sourdoughs). Using home-made axes and crampons they attacked the Karstens Ridge, chopping a 1,200 m stairway of ice steps. At last, two of the men, P. Anderson and W. Taylor, carrying a 4 m fir flagpole, made a summit 'dash' of 2,600 m and reached the North Summit (5,934 m). The flagpole was clearly seen by H. P. Karstens, H. Stuck, W. Harper and R. Tatum on the occasion of the first ascent of the S Summit (6,194 m) in 1913.

A series of photographs published by Bradford Washburn in the *American Alpine Journal* in 1947 led to renewed activity, and the peak has been visited frequently since then. Because of the great size of the mountain, the glaciation and terrible weather, all climbing on McKinley is expeditionary in character.

Important ascents include:

1951   W Buttress – Washburn's party
1954   S Buttress and Traverse – Argus, Thayer, Viereck, Wood
        W Ridge of N Peak – Wilson, Beckey
1961   S Face – Cassin, Canali, Alippi, Zucchi, Perego, Airoldi
1963   Wickersham Wall – Gmöser, Prinz, Schwartz

1967   W Buttress – Davidson, Genet, Johnston
1967   S Face Direct – Eberl, Laba, Seidman, Thompson
1976   S Face (Scott-Haston Route) – Haston, Scott

Mount of the Holy Cross   A peak in the Sawatch Range of Colorado which carries snow-filled gullies in the form of a great cross, 370 m high and 150 m wide, brought to public attention by the photograph taken by W. H. Jackson in 1873 and 'hailed by the public that God had blessed America'. The original Mount of the Holy Cross was probably Mt Fletcher, also in Colorado, which has a cross of light-coloured rock, reported by T. J. Farnham in 1839. It is not as obvious as Jackson's cross.

Jackson was accused of retouching the picture and nobody has seen the cross in such perfect shape since. The picture, and Jackson's account of finding it, provoked a poem from H. W. Longfellow, *The Cross of Snow*, 1879.

W. H. Jackson was one of the finest photographers of the pioneering days in the West.

See: P. Hales, *William Henry Jackson* (1984) and W. Naef and J. Wood, *Era of Exploration: The Rise of Landscape Photography in the American West, 1860–1885* (1975).

Mount Olympus (2,917 m)   The fabled home of the Greek gods, and indeed, one of the subsidiary peaks is called the Throne of Zeus (2,909 m). The highest summit, Mitka (the Point), was first reached by D. Baud-Bovy, F. Boissonnas, K. Kakalos in 1913. The ascent is not difficult, but the rock of the area seems rotten. The Greek Alpine Club was inaugurated on the summit of Olympus in 1927.

Mount Robson (3,954 m)   The highest peak in the Canadian Rockies (◊ Canada) towering over the Yellowhead Highway, about 110 km from Jasper. The Cree Indians call it Yuh-hai-has-kun which means 'spiral road mountain', because of the sedimentary stratification.

It was first attempted in 1908 by the Colemans, Kinney and Yates but they were frustrated. The following year G. B. Kinney and D. Phillips reached the summit ice cap by the W Face. Mist and storm drove them back when they were within 18 m of the top. In the same year, L. S. ◊ Amery, G. ◊ Hastings and A. L. ◊ Mumm with M. Inderbinen failed on the E Face but this was climbed and a first ascent made in 1913 by W. W. Foster, A. H. ◊ MacCarthy and C. ◊ Kain. A little later that year an attempt by the S S W ridge reached the summit ice dome but turned back due to bad weather.

Meanwhile another guide on the same meet, Walter Schauffelberger, with Basil Darling and a Mr Prouty, made a spirited attempt on the S W Ridge – the so-called Wishbone Arête. Schauffelberger compared it with the Zmutt on the Matterhorn and they were defeated by storm 150 m from the top in what has been called 'the most dramatic feat of early North American climbing history'. Some 30 parties attempted it before final success came to D. Claunch, M. Sherrick and H. Firestone in 1955. (Now graded 5.6.)

Mount Robson is never easy and tends to be dangerous with avalanches, stonefall and bad weather. In 1930 N. D. Waffl was killed soloing the peak. From 1939 to 1953 the mountain repulsed every party to attempt it! GUIDEBOOK Kuszyna/Putnam, *Climber's Guide to the Rocky Mountains of Canada, North*.

Mumm, Arnold Louis (1859–1927)   A London publisher who liked to

Left, Mallory and Norton without oxygen at 27,000ft on the NE Ridge of Everest, 1922; right, A. F. Mummery and his daughter.

combine climbing with travel. He was with ◊ Freshfield in the Ruwenzori in 1905, and on ◊ Longstaff's Himalayan Expedition in 1907, though he did not reach the summit of Trisul with Longstaff. Mumm took with him some small oxygen cylinders prepared by Siebe Gorman & Co. – the first use of oxygen for high-altitude climbing.

In 1909 Mumm visited the Canadian Rockies for the first time and returned on several later occasions. He made the first ascent of Mumm Peak and Mt Resolution (1910), Mt Hoodoo and Mt Bess (1911) and several minor peaks. He became a member of the American A.C.

He wrote a book about his trip with Longstaff: *Five Months in the Himalaya* (1909), but he is particularly noted for his compilation of *The Alpine Club Register* (3 vols., 1923–8), which gives details of the lives and expeditions of all members of the A.C. elected between 1857 and 1890.

Mumm was a man of immense intellectual capacity (Triple First, Oxford) but shyness and a total lack of ambition prevented him from reaching eminence. He died at sea in 1927.

Mummery, Albert Frederick (1855–95) The foremost climber of the second half of the last century, with justifiable claims to be regarded as the founder of modern Alpinism. His number of first ascents was relatively small, but all were important, as were the climbs he attempted but failed to achieve, such as the Furggengrat of Matterhorn and the N Face of the Plan. In climbing circles he was a legend in his own lifetime with a number of staunch disciples, and not a few enemies, such as ◊ Whymper and ◊ Davidson. Conway called him 'the greatest climber of his, or any other, generation', but Winthrop Young thought his achievements overrated. The truth lies in between, but it cannot be denied that his influence on the development of Alpinism was profound.

Mummery was born in Dover, Kent, in 1855, the son of a successful tannery owner. He was a weak, rather sickly child, and this left him with a permanent deformity and myopic vision. He was never able to carry great loads. His social background, too, was exploited to keep him out of the A.C.;

he was blackballed in 1880 and not elected for another eight years.

His career as a climber can be divided into two parts: first his partnership with the guide Alexander ◊ Burgener, and second his conversion to guideless climbing (about 1890). He began climbing in 1871 but in 1879 met Burgener and his outstanding career really began. His first ascents are:

1879   Fletschhorn (new route), Sonnighorn, Zmutt Arête of Matterhorn

1880   Traverse of Col du Lion, Grands Charmoz, Furggengrat and E Face of Matterhorn (the first time this had been done; they failed on the upper Furggengrat and traversed across the E Face to reach the ordinary Hörnli Ridge)

1881   Charpoua Face of the Verte; Grépon

1887   Täschhorn by the Teufelsgrat – Mrs Mummery also took part

1888   Dychtau (Caucasus) – guide, Zurfluh

His guideless climbing began next year:

1889   Schreckjoch, first crossing – with Petherick, his brother-in-law

1892   First traverse of Grépon – Hastings, Collie, Pasteur

1893   Dent du Requin, first ascent – Slingsby, Hastings, Collie

        W Face of the Plan, first ascent – Slingsby, Hastings, Collie

1894   Col des Courtes, first ascent – Collie, Hastings

        Old Brenva Route, Mont Blanc, first guideless ascent – Collie, Hastings

1895   Died on an expedition to Nanga Parbat

This list includes only the outstanding climbs and takes no account of the enterprising but unsuccessful attempts on other routes, for instance, his attempt on the Hirondelles Ridge of Grandes Jorasses with the guide Émile Rey in 1892. His famous 'easy day for a lady' was a traverse of Grépon in 1893, which he made with Slingsby and Miss ◊ Bristow. The quote comes from the heading of Chapter 6 of his book, which is: *The Grépon. An inaccessible peak – The most difficult climb in the Alps – An easy day for a lady.* These he regarded as the three stages through which all mountains were doomed to pass; the phrase itself was invented by Leslie ◊ Stephen.

Before he left for the Himalayas in 1895, his book *My Climbs in the Alps and Caucasus* was published. It quickly became one of the classics of climbing literature and the final chapter 'The Pleasures and Penalties of Mountaineering', which contains Mummery's climbing philosophy, showed the way the sport had to develop. It had a profound influence, more especially on the Continent.

Mummery went to the Himalayas with Collie and Hastings, and they were joined by ◊ Bruce and two Gurkhas, Raghobir and Goman Singh. They chose Nanga Parbat as their goal because it was reasonably accessible and big, but the area was, of course, largely unknown. It seems likely that they underestimated the scale of the climbing, and particularly Mummery, judging from his letters home – though this may have been deliberate playing down to comfort his wife. After various reconnaissances, and an attempt on the Diamirai Face, the party decided to move to the Rakhiot valley on the other side of the mountain: Collie and Hastings to go round with the porters, Mummery and the two Gurkhas to try a new pass over the intervening ridges. They set off on 24 August 1895, but when Collie and Hastings arrived at Rakhiot, there was no sign of Mummery. Despite intense search, Mummery and the two Gurkhas were never seen again, and it is generally presumed that they were overwhelmed by an avalanche.

Munich School   A name given to the Austro–German climbers of the late twenties and thirties who were putting up hard-face climbs in the Alps. Many, but by no means all, came from the Munich area. The term was coined by British traditionalists as one of disparagement (others were: 'the dangle and whack school', 'the do or die school'). In recent years the term has been revived as one of historical convenience and respect.

Munro Any summit or top of 3,000 ft (914 m) or more in Scotland. The name derives from Munro's Tables, first published by Sir Hugh T. Munro in the S.M.C. Journal of September 1891. This listed 538 tops, of which 283 were regarded as separate mountains. The definition of what constitutes a top – or even a mountain – is somewhat vague, and resurveying has meant revisions of the list from time to time. With the metrication of maps a plea has been made to leave the list as it now stands: 276 mountains and 516 tops.

Collecting all the tops is now a sub-sport called 'Munro bagging', which has many dedicated followers. The first person to do them all was the Rev. A. E. Robertson, in 1901. The first to do them in a continuous excursion was H. M. Brown in 1974. The first woman to complete them was Mrs Hirst in 1947, along with her husband, J. Hirst (ninth and tenth overall). Several people have completed them more than once – H. M. Brown six times. Alas! Munro himself died with two tops still unvisited: the Inaccessible Pinnacle in Skye and Carn Cloichmhuillin, Deeside, which was near his home and which he had been saving for last.

J. Rooke Corbett compiled a list of mountains of 2,500 ft (762 m) (but not Munros), now called Corbetts in his honour. There are 223. Percy Donald similarly compiled a list of 2,000 ft (610 m) mountains which were not Corbetts, divided into 'hills' and 'tops': 87 and 138 respectively, of which 6 hills are in England, in the Cheviots. Both men personally completed their lists.

See *Munro's Tables and Other Tables of Lesser Heights* (S.M.C.) and *Hamish's Mountain Walk* by H. M. Brown.

Murith, Laurent-Joseph (1742–1816) A Canon of the Gt St Bernard Monastery and friend of de ◊ Saussure and ◊ Bourrit. Explored the glaciers of Valsorey, Orny and Otemma and in 1779 made the first ascent of Mont Velan (3,734 m).

Murray, John (1808–92) Publisher, and originator of popular handbooks for travellers, giving detailed information regarding routes, inns, etc. The Alpine volumes were indispensable to the early climbers until superseded by ◊ Ball. John Murray's firm also published Whymper's great books.

Murray, William Hutchison (b. 1913) Scottish climber and author noted for his pre-war ice-climbs, and later for his Himalayan expeditions. While he was a prisoner of war, he wrote *Mountaineering in Scotland* (1947), one of the modern classics of climbing literature. His routes include (winter): Crowberry Ridge by Garrick's Shelf (1937), Deep Cut Chimney, Stob Coire nam Beith (1939), Twisting Gully, Stob Coire nan Lochan (1946) and (summer): Clachaig Gully (1938), Great Gully of Garbh Bheinn of Ardgour (1946). (Numerous others.)

In 1950, Bill Murray led the Scottish Expedition to Garhwal and Almora, and the following year he was Deputy Leader to Shipton on the Everest Reconnaissance. In 1953 he climbed in the Api range. He was awarded the Mungo Park Medal of the R.S.G.S. in 1953 and the O.B.E. in 1966.

N

Nails The early mountaineers nailed their boots with hobs of the common sort. These were later supplemented by special edging nails known as wing nails or clinkers, and the hobs gave way to muggers, which were of soft iron like the hobs and allowed the rock to bite into them. Immediately prior to 1914 a new nail, the tricouni, was invented on the Continent: it had three flattened prongs and was of hard steel – the nail bit into the rock. On all these nails there were many variations.

The ways boots should be nailed – pattern, type and number – were a constant source of discussion. Though nails did lead to a precise sort of climbing they had several disadvantages: they were heavy, they balled up in snow, and they wore away the holds, especially on soft rocks. They were gradually but irrevocably superseded by cleated rubber soles and had practically disappeared by the 1960s.

Naismith, William W. (1856–1935) Scottish alpinist and rock-climber who took part in many of the early Scottish first ascents, such as the Black Shoot of Stob Maol in 1892, King's Chimney and Sgurr Coire an Lochan (1896) and winter ascents of the Castle and South Castle Gully of Ben Nevis (1896). He also climbed in the Alps and Norway.

In January 1889 Naismith wrote a letter to the *Glasgow Herald* proposing the formation of a Scottish Alpine Club: the suggestion resulted in the formation of the Scottish Mountaineering Club a month later. Naismith is best remembered today for his famous 'Rule'. (◊ next entry)

Naismith's Rule A simple rule for determining in advance the time required for a mountain journey, and first formulated by W. W. Naismith. The rule is: allow one hour for every 5 km on the map plus an additional hour for every 610 m of climbing.

The rule does not take into account any halts, nor does it work for very short or very long journeys, but it is fairly satisfactory for an average day. Further refinements can be made (see *Mountain Leadership*, by E. Langmuir), but these spoil the essential simplicity of the calculation.

Nanga Parbat (8,125 m) An impressive mountain standing at the great bend of the Indus in the Punjab Himalaya. As the river is at 1,000 m, Nanga Parbat presents a spectacular 7,000 m face of rock and ice on this side. There are three flanks to the mountain: that to the south, the Rupal Flank, above the Rupal Nullah, long and very steep; the Rakhiot Face, above the Rakhiot Glacier; and the Diamir Face above the Diamir Glacier (see map). All three have been climbed.

Because of its easy accessibility, Nanga Parbat was the first really big Himalayan peak to be attempted (Mummery, 1895). It has a disastrous history of fatalities.

Principal Expeditions

1895 Mummery Expedition – Mummery and two Gurkhas killed

1932 W. Merkl (German) – Rakhiot Peak (23,210 ft) climbed (Aschenbrenner, Kunigk)
1934 W. Merkl (German) – Drexel died of oedema. Merkl, Wieland, Welzenbach and six Sherpas killed
1937 K. Wien (German) – Seven climbers (including Wien) and nine Sherpas buried by avalanche
1938 P. Bauer (German) – Bad weather foiled attempts
1939 P. Aufschnaiter (German) – Reconnoitred Diamir Face
1950 Thornley, Crace, Marsh – Thornley and Crace killed
1953 K. M. Herrligkoffer (German) – Buhl reached summit, solo
1962 K. M. Herrligkoffer (German) – Diamir Face climbed
1970 K. M. Herrligkoffer (German) – Rupal Face climbed and Diamir descended by Messner brothers. G. Messner killed
1978 Messner solos Diamir Face – first ever complete solo of an 8,000 m peak
1985 First women's ascent by five Polish women

Napes Needle A prominent pinnacle, about 18 m high, standing at the foot of the Needle Ridge of the Great Napes, on the Wasdale side of Great Gable (Lake District). It is famous for its first ascent (27 or 30 June 1886) by W. P. ◊ Haskett Smith solo: an event traditionally regarded as the birth of rock-climbing as a sport. Certainly its spectacular appearance in photographs did much to stimulate interest in the sport.

The original route was the Wasdale Crack. The climb was not repeated until 1889, when it was climbed three times:

17 March, G. Hastings
22 June, F. Wellford
12 August, J. W. Robinson

The first lady's ascent was by a Miss Koecher on 31 March 1890. Most ascents (over 600) by J. E. B. Wright (professional guide), who also made the fastest ascent (1930s).

Notable first ascents are:

1892 The Lingmell Crack – O. G. Jones, Mrs Commeline, J. N. Collie
1893 The Crowley Route – E. A. Crowley
1894 The Arête – W. H. Fowler
1912 The Obverse Route – S. W. Herford, W. B. Brunskill
1928 Direct from the Gap – H. G. Knight, H. M. Kelly, W. G. Standring
       The most popular route today is The Arête (Mild Severe).

Neb A jutting gritstone roof, e.g. High Neb, Stanage. It is a north-country term meaning peak, as in peaked cap (neb cap).

Névé (G.: Firn) The snow-slopes on a mountain above the ◊ bergschrund. The névé feeds the glacier with fresh snow or ice.

New Guinea, climbing in The highest and longest island mountain chain in the world extends for 1,800 km along the backbone of this East Indian island. The west of the island is West Irian (Indonesia) and the east is Papua New Guinea. The highest point is Pk Jaya (Carstensz Pyramid) (4,883 m) in the Nassau Range. With Ngga Pulu (4,860 m) and Enggea (Mt Idenburg) (4,717 m), it forms a great mountain horseshoe containing a large glacier enclosed by cliffs more than 3,000 m in height. There are eight other

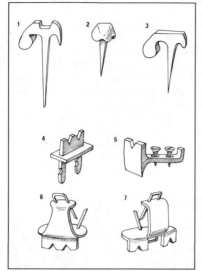 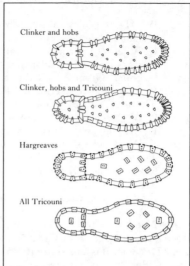

Nails: **1** Clinker; **2** Hob; **3** Clinker (small); **4** Tricouni; **5** Hargreaves; **6** Tricouni; **7** Tricouni.

recognized summits over 4,000 m in this western part of the island.

In Papua New Guinea the highest point is Mt Wilhelm (4,600 m) and there are seven other 4,000 m peaks, including Mt Victoria in the Owen Stanley Range (4,073 m), the first of the high peaks to be climbed – Sir W. MacGregor's expedition of 1888.

The snow peaks of Irian were first discovered by Jan Carstensz in 1623. The first attempt to climb them was made by A. F. R. Wollaston in 1911 and 1913, and though Carstensz Pyramid was reached on the second trip it was not climbed. The approaches are difficult, though now made easier by local airstrips. In 1936 the Dutch climber A. H. Colijn climbed Ngga Pulu, but failed on Carstensz. Philip Temple, a New Zealander, tried in 1961 and was successful on his second attempt (with H. ◊ Harrer) in 1962. (First ascent, Carstensz Pyramid: Temple, Harrer, Kippax, Huizenga.) They also climbed Idenburg and Ngga Pulu.

There have been sundry other expeditions and visits by individual climbers. There is some confusion in West Irian over mountain names and, to a certain extent, heights.

Newmarch, Francis Wells (1853–1918) A civil servant who visited the Caucasus in the three years, 1893–5, with ◊ Cockin, ◊ Solly etc. The expeditions were notable in that they were guideless. Newmarch was a very strong walker.

Newton, Henry Edward (1873–1961) Vicar of Ross, New Zealand, and one of the pioneers of climbing in the island. With the ◊ Graham brothers and others he explored the Fox and La Perouse Glaciers, 1903–6. Made first ascents of La Perouse and David's Dome (1906), Douglas Peak, Glacier Peak, Torres, Lendenfeld, Haast, Bristol Top and Conway (1907). Returned to

England that year but visited New Zealand in 1935, making the first ascent of Mt Eros with Alex Graham.

New Zealand, climbing in   The principal mountains of New Zealand are the Southern Alps and their southward extensions into Fiordland. The highest peak is Mt Cook (3,764 m) and about 17 other peaks exceed 3,000 m, though resurveying keeps altering the number, to the chagrin of the many climbers who claim to have done all the 3,000 m summits. Heavy precipitation ensures a good snow cover and there are numerous glaciers. The Tasman Glacier is 31 km long. Snow- and ice-climbing is the principal attraction because the rock (schists and greywacke), is generally poor.

The Southern Alps extend from Harper Pass in the north to the Hasst Pass in the south. Notable peaks are:

Mt Cook (3,764 m) – 1894, G. Graham, T. Fyfe, J. Clark*
Mt Tasman (3,498 m) – 1894, E. Fitzgerald, M. Zurbriggen
Mt Dampier (3,440 m)
Mt Hicks (3,183 m)
Malte Brun (3,176 m)
Mt Sefton (3,157 m)
Mt Elie de Beaumont (3,109 m)
Mt Douglas (3,081 m)
La Perouse (3,079 m)
Mt Haidinger (3,066 m)
The Minarets (3,055 m)

*In 1882 W. S. ♀ Green made what was virtually the first ascent, stopping a few feet short of the summit to avoid benightment.

The chief centre is the Hermitage, but there are others and there are numerous huts.

South of the Alps, the mountains continue and rise to the Barrier Range, where Mt Aspiring (3,035 m) and Mt Earnshaw (2,819 m) dominate the scene. The former is one of the most dramatic mountains on the island.

South again, in the Fiordland, the mountains continue in complicated ranges, where mention might be made of Mitre Peak (2,621 m).

North of the Alps the mountains extend right across the island in the provinces of Nelson and Marlborough. The Kaikoura Ranges rise to over 2,800 m, the Spenser Range to over 2,000 m and there are several other ranges somewhat less in height.

By contrast, the North Island of New Zealand, though it has peaks between 1,500 and 2,800 m (highest is Ruapehu, 2,797 m), offers little of interest to the climber.

The weather of the New Zealand Alps is often bad, mid-January to the end of March being most favourable. For the main ranges of South Island, an approach from the east is always preferable, often easy, but that from the west can be difficult because of dense forest. The snow-line descends to 6,500 ft in the Southern Alps, and avalanches are common.

By 1894, practically the whole of the New Zealand Alps had been explored by Harper and others, though a lot of detail was unknown. Green's attempt on Mt Cook stimulated others and Fitzgerald and Zurbriggen came out from England for the express purpose of climbing the mountain in 1894, but were forestalled by local enterprise. They climbed Tasman, Sefton, Haidinger, Silberhorn and Sealy – all first ascents. Local climbers such as Mannering, Fyfe and Clark were also active, some as professional guides. The great guides Peter and Alex Graham dominated the New Zealand scene for 25 years.

North-West England: Helsby sandstone. (*W. Unsworth*) North-East England: Crag Lough on the Roman Wall. (*W. Unsworth*)

New Zealand climbers have followed the trend of other areas in attacking the harder ridges and faces of their mountains in recent years, and in sending expeditions overseas. Sir Edmund Hillary, who reached the summit of Everest with Tenzing in 1953, is a New Zealander. The New Zealand Alpine Club was founded in 1891.
GUIDEBOOKS Bishop, *The Mount Aspiring Region*.
Logan, *The Mount Cook Guidebook*.

Niche   A small recess in a rock face, usually with a flat floor where a climber can stand. May offer a stance and ◊ belay. Niches are sometimes difficult to quit. In the Alps the word is sometimes used for a large hollow in a face, e.g. the Niche des Drus.

Nicolson, Alexander (Sheriff Nicolson) (1827–93)   One of the early explorers of the Cuillin, Skye. Descended Nicolson's Chimney, Sgurr nan Gillean, in 1865, and made the first ascent of Sgurr Alasdair, the highest peak of Skye in 1873 (Alexander's Peak). His writings did much to popularize Skye among the members of the Alpine Club. (◊ Skye.)

Norman-Neruda, Ludwig (1864–98)   One of the leading climbers of his day, his outlook was comparable with that of the ◊ Zsigmondys or ◊ Mummery. He climbed with a great guide, ◊ Klucker, or without guides (usually with his wife, May, as companion) or solo (e.g. Dent Blanche, Croda da Lago).
His greatest season was with Klucker in 1890, when they made first ascents of Scerscen N W Face (and descended the same way!), Lyskamm N E Face, Piz Roseg N E Face, and the first traverse of Wellenkuppe–Gabelhorn. They also made an attempt on the N Face of the Dent Blanche and did several other climbs of lesser character. The face climbs were outstandingly difficult for the period and are still highly regarded.

In one sense this early promise (it was his third season) was never fulfilled because he became increasingly involved with the pure rock-climbing of the Dolomites, where he made a number of new climbs. He died of a suspected heart attack while climbing the Schmitt Kamin of the Cinque Dita in 1898.

Norman was his father's surname and Neruda his mother's (later Lady Hallé). He was born in Sweden but lived most of his life in London. An account of his climbs, written in note form by himself and edited by his wife, called *The Climbs of Norman-Neruda*, was published in 1899.

Northern England, climbing in   Outside the major areas of the ◊ Lake District, ◊ North-West England and ◊ the Yorkshire Dales, there are numerous climbing crags, though nothing of major significance.

Northumberland   This is the most important area with over 40 crags on which climbs have been recorded. Best known is Crag Lough, first climbed in about 1912 by M. B. Heywood, G. W. Young and the Trevelyans, who also discovered other rocks like Simonside. Numerous climbs of all standards of hard dolerite. Other good rocks (sandstone) are Bowden Doors, Kyloe Crags, Simonside and the Wanneys.

North York Moors   Various rocks outcrop over the moor, mostly sandstone, of which the best known is the Wainstones, on Hasty Bank. Raven's Scar in the same area is also worth a visit. The limestone of Peak Scar and Whitestone offers longer and generally harder climbs.

Eden Valley   The rocks by the river between Armathwaite and Lazonby have some fine climbs, many hard, on sandstone.

There is actually some Dolomite climbing at Castle Eden Dene, Durham.

GUIDEBOOKS *Northumberland* (N.M.C.).

Rock Climbs on the North York Moors (C.M.C.).

Wilson/Kenyon, *North of England*.

North-West England, climbs in   This above all is the region of the great quarries, of which there are many, and the esoteric art of quarry-climbing, often on gritstone or flagstone that is less than perfect. Some of the best are those near Bolton: Anglezarke, Wilton and Hoghton. Routes are up to 45 m at Hoghton; about half that elsewhere. Among the many fine climbs are Samarkand (VS) and The Golden Tower (E2) at Anglezarke; Cameo (E1) and Constable's Overhang (E4) at Wilton; Rhododendron Buttress (E2) and Mandarin (E2) at Hoghton.

Brownstones, also near Bolton, is a practice quarry with a history of continuous use since the 1920s, making it one of the oldest climbing quarries in the country. The sandstone quarry at Pex Hill near Liverpool is another popular practice place with technical climbs of 10 m on steep walls.

The best limestone quarries are in the far north of the area, particularly Trowbarrow and Warton Main Quarry, in Silverdale. Jean Jeanie (30 m VS) is the best-known climb at Trowbarrow, while Warton Main has Plastic Iceberg (50 m E1) amongst its attractions. Warton must be one of the most awe-inspiring quarries in the country!

As far as natural outcrops are concerned, the only gritstone crag of importance is Cadshaw, near Darwen – mostly easy routes. There is, however, a famous sandstone crag at Helsby, Cheshire, with a long history of climbing. There are routes of all standards including classics like Eliminate 1 (VS). The finest limestone outcrop is the lengthy Chapel Head Scar, near Whitbarrow, South Cumbria. Routes rise to 40 m and are mostly hard. The classic is perhaps Moonchild, 25 m, E3.

The Lancashire quarries and Helsby have been the training grounds for

many of Britain's best climbers, from ◊ Kirkus to ◊ Rouse.
GUIDEBOOK Kelly/Cronshaw, *Lancashire & the North West*. (C.P.)

Norton, Edward Felix (1884–1954)   Leader of the 1924 Everest Expedition. He reached 8,572 m – the highest point on this side of the mountain before the war – subsequently reached by Smythe, Wager and Wyn Harris (1933). Wrote: *The Fight for Everest 1924* (1925). Norton was a grandson of ◊ Wills and related to the ◊ Pasteurs.

Norway, climbing in   The Norwegian coastline is over 1,750 km long (19,000 km if the fjords and islands are counted!) and along much of it rise mountains whose magnificence in Western Europe is only rivalled by the Alps and Pyrenees. In sheer wildness, the Norwegian mountains have the advantage even over these. Though they lack the height of the other two ranges, this is compensated for by the fact that many of them start, literally, at sea level.

Though much of the area is glaciated (the Jodalsbrae is the largest ice-field in Europe), the Norwegian mountains are predominantly rock-climbs on granite, syenite and gabbro. Despite intensive exploration by recent Norwegian climbers, and others, there is so much rock that any number of new ascents can be made. The highest summit is Galdhopiggen (2,469 m) with Glittertind (2,452 m, 2470 m with heavy snow cover) a close second; these are both in the Jotenheimen and are easy snow ascents.

The most popular mountain area is the Jotenheimen (Home of Giants) and particularly the impressive Horungtinder centred on the hotel of Turtegrø. The best known peak is Skagastolstind (2,405 m), one of the many obelisk-type mountains common in Norway. Almost equalling the Jotenheimen in popularity, because of recent explorations, are the mountains around Romsdal, including the Romsdalhorn (1,554 m) and the 1,370 m Troll Wall.

In the far north, the Lyngen Peninsula, the Tys Fjord area, and the islands of the Lofoten have equally good mountains, as indeed have Sunnmöre and Nordmöre. All have been explored, but there is still a lot of virgin rock.

The outstanding figure in early Norwegian climbing was W. C. ◊ Slingsby, who first visited Norway in 1872 and paid 15 subsequent visits, exploring most of the mountain groups. His ascent, solo, of Skagastolstind in 1876 was a considerable achievement. The Danish climber, ◊ Hall, was another notable pioneer, particularly in the Jotenheimen and Romsdal areas. More recently, Norwegian climbers such as A. Naess, A. Randers Heen and R. Hoibakk have put up routes of high quality, though the most famous climb of post-war years is unquestionably the Rimmon Route on the Troll Wall, Romsdal. (J. Amatt, A. Howard, W. Tweedale, 1965.) (◊ Romsdal. Also see *Norway, the Northern Playground*, by W. C. Slingsby.)

Noyce, Cuthbert Wilfrid Frank (1917–62)   Schoolmaster and writer, one of the best known British climbers of the immediate pre-war years and one of the hardest goers the mountains have seen. With Armand Charlet in 1937–8 he did the Mer de Glace face of Grépon in 3¼ hours and the Old Brenva of Mont Blanc in 3½ hours. In the course of a single day in 1942 he did 1,370 m of hard solo rock-climbing in Cwm Idwal and on Tryfan. In 1959, with Sadler and Mortlock, he climbed the Welzenbach Route of Dent d'Hérens, Furggen Direct of Matterhorn, N E Face of Lyskamm and N E Face of Signalkuppe.

In the Himalaya he made the first ascents of Machapuchare and Trivor. He was a member of the 1953 Everest Expedition and forced the passage to the South Col.

He helped ◊ Edwards in the compilation of the guidebooks to Tryfan

(1937) and Lliwedd (1939), making some new routes, including Scars Climb, Soap Gut and the first unaided ascent of Munich Climb.

Noyce wrote a dozen books either by himself or in collaboration with others. Apart from his poems, these were mainly concerned with mountaineering. Best known is *South Col*, his personal account of the successful Everest venture. Noyce was killed with R. Smith during a visit to the Pamirs in 1962.

Nunn, Paul James (b. 1943)   One of the leading post-war British climbers, Nunn sprang to prominence at the age of 16, when he repeated a number of the hard gritstone climbs and began putting up fierce new routes of his own such as Anniversary Arête, Stanage and the Girdle of the Lower Tier at the Roches (both 1959). He has since made some 40 gritstone and 60 limestone new routes and was natural successor to Eric Byne in editing a new series of Peakland guidebooks.

In Wales, Nunn has put up some 50 routes of which might be mentioned Nexus, Llanberis (with Boysen, 1963). In the Lake District his routes include Plagiarism, Falcon Crag; Daedelus, Eagle Crag; and Eyrie, Gillercombe. (He edited a guide to Borrowdale, 1967.)

In Scotland he made a traverse of the Etive Slabs, Thin Red Line (1966), and climbed the Old Man of Stoer (1966) and The Maiden (1970) with Patey and others. It was during the descent of the latter that Patey was fatally injured. He has made a number of hard routes on Foinaven and elsewhere, summer and winter, including the first winter ascent of Emerald Gully, Ben Dearg (1970).

As well as making a number of first British ascents in the Alps, Nunn was a member of the Caucasus Expedition of 1970 which made the first ascent of Pik Shurovski N Face, and in 1972 was in Baffin Island to make the first ascent of N Summit of Asgard, by N E Pillar.

In 1977 Nunn visited the Karakoram and Kishtwar. He made an unsuccessful winter attempt on Everest W Ridge in 1981 and attempted Ogre 2 (6,960 m) the following year.

Nuts   Metal nuts inserted into cracks can be used to protect a leader against a fall. The nut, usually aluminium but sometimes brass, is basically wedge-shaped and carries a swaged wire or in the case of larger sizes, a tape sling, to which a krab can be fixed. The rope is then passed through the krab, and the nut acts as a runner. If the leader falls, the nut will jam in the crack and hold him.

Nuts are a development of natural chockstones. At first ordinary steel engineering nuts were used, their thread machined smooth, but specially designed commercial nuts appeared in the late 1950s. Various designs have appeared: Rocks, RPs and Hexes are currently in vogue but others have come and gone. The nuts come in different sizes and on difficult climbs it is usual to carry various nuts in sets, either on the waistband or on a long sling. They should be arranged ('racked') in a sequence most convenient to the person concerned. (✪ Chockstone, Friends.)

O

Objective Dangers Dangers which cannot be overcome by climbing skill, e.g. stonefall. Routes subjected to objective dangers carry warnings in the guidebooks. Many modern Alpine climbs of the harder sort have objective dangers, e.g. the Eigerwand.

Ogwen Cottage A former guest house that was one of the great pioneering centres of Welsh climbing. The building stands by Llyn Ogwen. The adjacent Idwal Cottage Youth Hostel is also a well-known mountaineering base and figures in Elizabeth Coxhead's novel, *One Green Bottle*.

On sight A climb is said to have been led 'on sight' when the leader has made no previous inspections, such as climbing it on a ◊ top rope. Reserved for hard climbs and new (previously unsolved) problems.

Ordinary route The usual way up a mountain or crag, taken by the majority, usually the easiest, e.g. Hörnli Ridge of the Matterhorn. Sometimes called the Tourist Route if the mountain is popular. On British crags the word is sometimes built into the name, e.g. Milestone Ordinary, Tryfan.

Original route The first route up a mountain or crag. Sometimes so named, as in Original Route, Holly Tree Wall, Idwal.

Ormsby, John (1829–95) Made the first ascent of Grivola in 1859 (the subject of the first lecture paper to the new Alpine Club). Ormsby made interesting excursions into the Atlas Mountains and the Spanish mountains (Picos de Europa, etc.) when they were virtually unknown.

Outcrop Crags which jut out from the flanks of a mountain ('valley crags') were said to be outcrops, for example, Dinas Cromlech, but the term has now come to be exclusively applied to the lesser rocks which appear in many parts of the country, often away from the traditional mountain areas. The Derbyshire edges and the Devon tors are outcrops, as are the limestone cliffs of the Avon Gorge and elsewhere. There are over 400 such crags where climbs have been made in England alone. Quarries may be regarded as outcrops, sea-cliffs are more debatable.

Outram, Sir James (1864–1925) One of the pioneers of Canadian climbing, with Whymper, Collie and others. Climbed a number of peaks for the first time, outstanding being his first ascent of Mt Assiniboine (1901).

Outside route Opposite to ◊ 'through route'. Where a chockstone blocks a chimney, it may be possible to go behind the chockstone (through) or over the front of it – the outside route, more exposed and often more difficult.

Overhang
(*a*) A rock face which is beyond the vertical is said to overhang;

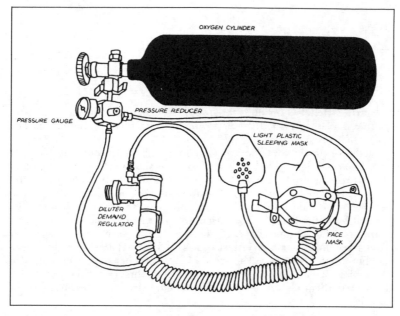

Oxygen equipment: the diluter-demand system used on the 1975 Everest SW Face Expedition.

(b) A sudden jutting out of the rock is called an overhang.

An overhanging wall may be quite short and climbed free; such pitches exist on many climbs. Alternately it may overhang for many feet and only be climbable by ◊ aid techniques.

Similarly, overhangs may be small and easily overcome but some are very big (e.g. Kilnsey Great Overhang, Yorkshire). The underneath of a large overhang is known as a roof.

Oxygen equipment Used to offset the effects of high altitude.

The first use recorded is in 1907 by ◊ Mumm, who took with him some small oxygen cartridges when he went to explore Nanda Devi, but his companions Bruce and Longstaff treated it as a joke. Equipment was developed for use on Everest in 1922, but the early sets were clumsy and their use limited by their weight. There was also strong ethical objection by some of the pioneers.

There are two systems of oxygen apparatus, the closed and the open. In the closed system the oxygen is regenerated by chemicals, but this has never been found entirely satisfactory (though obviously cheaper and easier on porterage). Open systems are used today in which fresh oxygen is supplied in bottles carried by the climber. The rate can be regulated.

Though still used on some large expeditions, oxygen sets are no longer a prerequisite to high-altitude climbing. Even ◊ Mt Everest has been climbed without artificial oxygen.

P

Paccard, Michel-Gabriel (1757–1827) A Chamonix doctor who, with Jacques ◊ Balmat, made the first ascent of Mont Blanc. (Summit reached 6.30 p.m., 8 August 1786.)

Paccard made three attempts on the summit by the Goûter route: in 1775 with Thomas ◊ Blaikie, in 1783 with ◊ Bourrit and in 1784 with two guides. He also reconnoitred the Italian side of the mountain. After his successful climb he prepared a manuscript describing it but this was never published because of the scandalous attack made on him by Bourrit, who claimed that the real hero was Balmat. This began one of the greatest mountaineering controversies of all time. Bourrit's views persisted for many years and only diligent research by modern historians has established Paccard's prime role in the climb. It is believed that Paccard made later climbs and possibly ascended Mont Blanc again. His famous manuscript of the first ascent has never been discovered. (See: *The First Ascent of Mont Blanc*, by T. G. Brown and G. R. de Beer.)

Packe, Charles (1826–96) A devoted explorer of the Pyrenees and a contemporary of ◊ Russell. He paid a brief visit to these mountains in 1853, but it was in 1859 that he began their systematic discovery. Published a guidebook to the area in 1862 (later extended and revised) and in 1893 made a donation to the C.A.F., which went towards the building of the Refuge Packe at the Col de Bugaret.

Packe also visited the Lake District many times. He was an enthusiastic bivouac man and a keen botanist.

Pack frame A lightweight metal frame with a shoulder harness like a rucksack. A bag can be fastened on to the frame. Though the pack frame can be used to carry heavy loads it has been superseded by the modern ergonomically designed rucksack which has a built-in frame.

Pallavicini, Markgraf Alfred (1848–86) This Austrian nobleman is famous for his eponymous couloir between Gross and Kleine Glockner, which he climbed in 1876, one of the most difficult ice-climbs of its day. It is 600 m high and at the crux is 50°. Always regarded as a test-piece in the Eastern Alps the following ascents are notable:

1876 First ascent. Pallavicini, G. Bauerle, J. Kramser, J. Tribusser. Indirect finish
1924 First solo. A. Horeschowsky
1927 First descent. F. Herrmann
1927 First direct to the gap. W. Welzenbach, K. Wein
1961 First ski descent. G. Winter, H. Zakarias

On the first ascent the leading guide, Josef Tribusser, cut the record number of 2,500 steps in seven hours. The climb was repeated only once in the next 45 years.

Pallavicini was killed ten years later by a fall on the Glocknerwand.

Michel-Gabriel Paccard   Tom Patey (*J. Cleare*)

Pamirs   A large area of mountains north of the Hindu Kush in the Tadzhik Republic of the former U.S.S.R. There are two main groups, both east–west orientated, and divided by a headwater of the River Oxus. Both groups contain peaks over 6,400 m and in the northern group (the Trans Alay) is the Peak of Communism (7,495 m), the highest mountain in the U.S.S.R. The Pamirs is a fairly bleak area, and holds some of the world's longest glaciers (◊ Karakoram), including the Fedchenko Glacier, 72 km.

There are three 7,000 m peaks in the Pamirs:

Peak of Communism (7,495 m) – E. Abalakov, solo, 1933
Peak Lenin (Mt. Kaufmann) (7,134 m) – R. Rickmers' party, 1928
Peak Evgenia Korzhenevskaya (7,105 m) – A. Ugarov's party, 1953

These have now been climbed several times by different routes. The Peak of Communism was formerly called Peak Stalin.

Mountaineering has developed rapidly since the thirties, and the Russians have put up some fine face routes and exceedingly long traverses (cf. Caucasus). ◊ Noyce and R. Smith were killed descending Peak Garmo in 1962.

Peaks over 6,500 m include:

Peak Revolution, 6,974 m	Peak Fikker, 6,708 m
Peak Moscow, 6,785 m	Peak Garmo, 6,595 m
Peak October, 6,780 m	Peak Engels, 6,510 m
Peak Karl Marx, 6,726 m	Peak Leningrad, 6,507 m
Peak Dzerzhinsky, 6,713 m	

(It is expected that names of many of these peaks will change).

Papoose carrier   A rucksack type of frame to which is attached a seat for carrying a small child. Often used in British mountains. The child should be firmly secured in the seat.

Paradis, Maria (1786–1838) A serving girl from Chamonix who in 1809 made the first ascent of Mont Blanc by a woman, and the first real mountaineering ascent by a woman anywhere. Leader of the ascent was Jacques ◊ Balmat, accompanied by two sons with the guides M. and V. Tairraz and P.-M. Frasserand. She found the ascent very arduous and when other village women asked her what it was like she advised them to go and find out for themselves! She opened a café at Pélerins where she was known as Maria of Mont Blanc and where, 29 years later, she greeted Henriette d' ◊ Angeville, the second woman to make the ascent.

Parker brothers Charles Stuart Parker (1829–1910), Samuel Sandbach Parker (1837–1905) and Alfred Traill Parker (1837–1900) were three remarkable Liverpool brothers who were pioneers of guideless climbing. They climbed in Skye at a date prior to 1860 (Sgurr nan Gillean) and between 1857 and 1865 made a number of Alpine ascents and crossed several cols. They made the first guideless ascent of the Finsteraarhorn in 1856.

Their chief fame rests on the two guideless attempts they made on the Matterhorn in 1860 and 1861, at a time when even the best guides would not attempt it. They climbed from Zermatt (the first attempt from there) and reached about 11,000 ft in 1860 and somewhat higher the following year. Weather rather than difficulty forced them to retreat and they intended to try again in 1865 but arrived after the accident (◊ Whymper).

C. S. Parker was an M.P. and his brothers were in the family shipping business.

Parson's Nose, the (Clogwyn y Person) The steep end of Crib y Person, a ridge in Cwm Glas, Snowdonia. First climbed by A. H. Stocker about 1884.

Pass The way across a mountain ridge from one valley to another. Open to wide interpretation, but generally of three types:

(a) *motor pass* – accessible to vehicles, e.g. Llanberis Pass, Brenner Pass;
(b) *foot or mule pass* – accessible only to walkers and baggage animals, e.g. Sty Pass, Monte Moro Pass.

The top of these passes is known as the summit, and both types may be blocked during winter.
(c) *climbing pass* – the way over a high ◊ col. In the Alps this may involve steep and serious ice-climbing (e.g. Moming Pass). The making of new passes was regarded almost as highly as the first ascent of a mountain by the pioneers, but is seldom undertaken for its own sake today except in the exploration of new areas.

In pre-climbing days many passes in the Alps had been made for the purposes of trade: Coolidge estimates about 20 before 1600 and about 65 by 1800.

Passingham, George Augustus (1842–1914) A climber noted as the outstanding 'hard man' of his day, with some incredible journeys to his credit, for example, the Dom from Zermatt and back in 17 hours. He took part in the first ascent of the Zinal Rothorn (1872), and made a difficult climb on the W Face of the Weisshorn (1879).

Pasteur family An English family of Swiss ancestry who have maintained a continuous record of mountaineering from 1846 to the present day. The founder was Henri Pasteur (1827–1909), who began with an ascent of the

Buet in 1846 and climbed in the Alps regularly for the next 50 years. His two sons and three daughters were all climbers – the best known being Charles Henry Pasteur (1869–1955), who made the first ascent of L'Évêque (Verte), the first guideless ascent of Grépon, and the first traverse of Grépon, in 1892. Two of his sisters took part in the first of these climbs.

The family was related by marriage to ◊ Morse and ◊ Norton.

Patey, Thomas Walton (1932–70) One of the most outstanding British mountaineers of the post-war era. Patey's climbs revolutionized the game in Scotland, especially in the Cairngorms.

An Aberdonian, Patey tramped the Scottish hills as a schoolboy and began climbing in 1949. In 1950 he made the first winter ascent of the Douglas-Gibson Gully, Lochnagar, a breakthrough in the winter standards at that time. There followed over 70 new routes in the Cairngorms alone, with others on the Ben and in remoter parts of Scotland. His first ascents include:

1952   Tough-Brown Traverse, Lochnagar (winter)
1952   Parallel B Gully, Lochnagar
1953   Eagle Ridge, Lochnagar (winter)
1953   Sticil Face, Shelter Stone Crag
1954   Vertigo Wall, Creag an Dubh Loch
1955   Central Pillar, Creag Meaghaidh (winter)
1956   Parallel Buttress, Lochnagar (winter)
1957   Zero Gully, Ben Nevis (winter)
1957   Cresta Climb, Ben Nevis (winter)
1960   Cioch Nose, Applecross
1962   The Last Post, Creag Meaghaidh (winter)
1964   Diadem, Creag Meaghaidh (winter)
1965   Traverse of the Cuillin Main Ridge (winter)
1966   Old Man of Hoy

After qualifying as a doctor, Patey joined the Royal Marines for a time and then, in 1961, took up a practice at Ullapool. Lack of companions often forced him into solo climbing, though he liked this for its own sake too and he became a leading exponent of the art. His solo routes include The Nose Direct on Fuar Tholl and Gnome Wall, Ben Eighe, but his finest is the winter Girdle of Creag Meaghaidh (1969). South of the border, he played a part in the development of Chudleigh Rocks in Devon.

He first visited the Alps in 1951 doing traditional routes at Chamonix. He returned in 1953 to make the first British ascent of the Sans Nom Arête of the Verte and, in 1955, the first British ascent of the N Face of the Plan. He did not return for eight years, then, with Brown, Bonington and others made first ascents of: W Face of Plan, N W Face of Aig. Sans Nom (1963); S W Ridge of Leschaux, N Face of Pt Migot (1964); W Face of Cardinal (1965); S E Ridge of Aig. Rouge de Rochefort (1968).

Patey was considered for the Everest Expedition of 1953 but was rejected on account of his youth. In 1956 he took part in the first ascent of the Muztagh Tower and in 1958 the first ascent of Rakaposhi. In 1959 and 1960 he made some first winter ascents in Norway.

Patey had made a number of climbs on Scottish sea-stacks and it was while abseiling from one of these, The Maiden, that he was accidentally killed.

Well known as a humorous writer of articles and songs for climbers, the best of this work was published posthumously: *One Man's Mountains*.

Payot, Alphonse (1852–1932) Chamonix guide particularly noted for his association with James ◊ Eccles. They made the first ascent of Mt Blanc from the Brouillard Glacier, and the first ascents of: Mt Blanc de Courmayeur, Aig. du Plan, Aig. du Rochefort, Aig. du Tacul, Dôme de Rochefort, and Aigs. Dorées. In 1882, with the guide A. Cupelin and W. W. ◊ Graham, he made the first ascent of the Aig. du Géant.

Peak District The Peak District embraces the southern limits of the Pennine Chain. The heart of the region is in Derbyshire, but the moors and crags spread themselves into the fringes of the adjacent counties. In effect the district forms a large triangle of open country between the heavily industrialized areas of South Lancashire, South Yorkshire and the Midlands. This alone is enough to ensure its popularity.

The northern part of the district comprises high moors covered in a thick layer of peat in which the weather has eroded a complex of deep channels called ◊ *groughs*. The underlying rock is ◊ gritstone, with outcrops in abundance. The principal summits are Kinder Scout (636 m) and Bleaklow (633 m) (below).

The southern part is more complex. Gritstone moors are to be found east of the River Derwent and west of Buxton, though nothing as high and rugged as those further north. The main central core consists of gentle limestone hills intersected by deep valleys – the famous Derbyshire dales. Even here there are a few small gritstone caps: Stanton Moor and the Black Rocks of Cromford (below), for example.

The difficult nature of the Kinder–Bleaklow massifs lends itself to arduous walking and these moors are well known for long, hard courses such as the Marsden–Edale Walk. By tradition, such walks are usually done in the winter months when the moors are particularly bleak and severe. They require good equipment, stamina and competent navigation. For less ambitious walks Edale is a good centre; it is a tiny hamlet which has also gained some popularity with skiers. By contrast, the limestone area further south, though very beautiful, affords only gentle walks.

Outcrops for climbing are to be found throughout the entire Peak District. The gritstone crags are famous: Stanage Edge, the Roches, Laddow, Black Rocks, Cratcliffe and many others have played a significant part in climbing history. The limestone crags are of more recent development: Stoney Middleton, High Tor, Chee Dale, Miller's Dale, Ravensdale and Willersley are among the best known. In contrast with the relatively low gritstone rocks, the limestone crags provide climbs of a hundred feet or more, mostly of a serious nature. There are also some small outcrops of dolomite near Brassington – the only dolomite climbing in Britain (see below).

Because the crags are widespread, there is no single centre which is suitable for climbing throughout the region. Roads are good, however, and the majority of crags are only a few minutes walk from a road.

Historically, the Peak District has been a womb of English climbing where new techniques have been developed, aided by the superb friction of the gritstone crags. Early pioneers include J. W. ◊ Puttrell, E. A. ◊ Baker and J. Oppenheimer, who took the knowledge gained on gritstone to the higher crags of Scotland and elsewhere. They were followed by S. W. ◊ Herford, who made the first ascent of Scafell's Central Buttress in 1914, and H. M. Kelly, another climber who was to make his mark in the Lakes. The development of the Derwent edges after the last war by J. ◊ Brown, D. ◊ Whillans and others played a significant part in the rise of British climbing standards.

The moors have been the training ground of many outstanding long-

Left, Peak District gritstone: the Roches. (*J. Storah*); right, Pillar Rock, an Abraham photograph.

distance walkers, notably Fred Heardman and E. ◊ Thomas. Among the best known crags are:

GRITSTONE

Kinder Scout   A high plateau in the Peak District, between the Snake Pass on the north and Edale on the south. ◊ Groughs make the going hard, and the walks across the moor are famous, notably the Marsden–Edale and the Pennine Way, which begins at Edale. The moor often holds snow in winter and Edale is a ski centre. There are winter climbs on Kinder Downfall and the near-by Back Tor and Mam Tor. Numerous gritstone crags rim the perimeter of the moor but, except for the Downfall area, none are of much significance.

Bleaklow   A high moor in the Peak District lying between Longdendale in the north and the Snake Pass in the south. It is crossed by the Pennine Way and the Marsden–Edale Walk and is famous for its ◊ groughs. There are a few gritstone crags on the edges of the moor, the only one of note being Shining Clough, above Longdendale, which offers fine climbs of considerable length and difficulty.

Stanage Edge   The most important gritstone crag in Britain. Though not continuous, the edge is about four miles long with climbs up to 23 m or so, though many are only half this. There are almost 500 routes of all grades on excellent Rivelin grit and the crag is immensely popular. The nearest village is Hathersage, Derbyshire.

Climbing began here in 1890 with J. W. ◊ Puttrell and has since seen the development of many noted leaders including Kelly, Piggott, Hargreaves, Linnell, Bridge, Brown, Whillans, John Allen, Drummond and Dawes among many others. The influence of these rocks on the development of British climbing cannot be over-estimated. (See *High Peak*, by E. Byne.)

Derwent Edges   The gritstone outcrops flanking the River Derwent in Derbyshire. They stretch for ten miles from the Ladybower Reservoir to Chatsworth Park on the east bank of the river. They have all been quarried to some extent (even Stanage), but there are some exceptional quarries in the area which may be counted as part of the climbing scene there. Climbs are usually less than 30 m, on excellent Rivelin grit, and are of all standards. The edges are very popular.

From north to south, the principal edges are Stanage, Bamford, Burbage, Higgar Tor, Carl's Wark, Millstone, Lawrencefield, Froggatt, Curbar, Baslow, Gardom's, Birchen's and Chatsworth. Millstone and Lawrencefield are heavily quarried but there are other quarries such as Padley which are worth a visit. Birchen's Edge is one of the finest training grounds for novices in the country.

Sheffield is the natural centre for all these climbs. Other crags in the vicinity are Rivelin, Agden Rocher, Cratcliffe and the Black Rocks, though the last two are further south, in the limestone country.

The history of climbing here is a long one, despite keepering by game wardens and water boards in the past. (See *High Peak*, by E. Byne.)

Roches, the One of the finest of all gritstone crags, forming part of a distinct ridge with Hen Cloud and various lesser rocks, near Upper Hulme, Staffordshire. There are numerous routes of all grades, fairly long.

The crag was visited by the pioneers, and Laycock is reputed to be the first climber benighted on gritstone (Central Climb, Hen Cloud, 1909). The land was once a private zoo, and escaped wallabies still breed here!

Laddow Rocks One of the earliest gritstone outcrops to be developed, Laddow consists of a series of fine buttresses above Crowden Great Brook in the north of Peak District. The best approach is from Longdendale. There are climbs of all standards.

Black Rocks of Cromford One of the earliest developed of the Derbyshire gritstone outcrops; a series of fine buttresses and boulder problems in all grades and longer than usual.

Cratcliffe Tor A gritstone crag near Birchover, Derbyshire, known since pioneering days. All standards of climbs. Robin Hood's Stride is a strange group of pinnacles near by and there are minor rocks at Rowtor and Stanton Moor. The ascent of Suicide Wall, Cratcliffe, by P. J. Harding in 1946, has been hailed as the start of the new era of gritstone climbing which came to fruition at ◊ Stanage.

Dovestones A long edge of gritstone overlooking Greenfield, near Oldham, with many climbs of all standards. On the right of the edge are the two famous Dovestones Quarries where the climbs are mostly long and hard. The development of these quarries, especially Main Quarry, by Brown, West and others, gave impetus to quarry climbing in the 1950s. The Greenfield area has a number of other quarries where climbing takes place, notably Den Lane Quarry near Uppermill.

Wharncliffe Crag In the Don Valley, near Deepcar, Yorkshire. A gritstone crag with numerous climbs of all standards, and the traditional birthplace of gritstone climbing (J. W. Puttrell and W. J. Watson, early 1880s). Strangely enough, it is not true gritstone, but a coarse sandstone. Not very popular today.

LIMESTONE

Stoney Middleton In Derbyshire. One of the most important limestone crags in the country with many fine routes, mostly in the upper grades. No climbs seem to have been done here before 1918–20 when ◊ Puttrell and his companions climbed in Fingal's Cave. The pre-war years also saw the remarkable ascent of Aurora in 1933 (F. Elliott). In 1950, J. ◊ Brown and his companions began the post-war surge with The Golden Gate.

High Tor, Matlock   An impressive limestone crag above the R. Derwent in Derbyshire offering modern, high-grade climbs. The crags extend down the banks of the river as far as Cromford, the principal ones being (besides High Tor) Wild Cat Crags and Willersley Crags.

High Tor Gully (Puttrell, Smithard, Bennett, 1903) led to the dissolution of the famous ◊ Kyndwr Club. The first ascent of the crag's main face was by P. Biven and T. Peck in 1957 (Original Route).

Chee Dale   A Derbyshire dale with many fine limestone climbs. Chee Tor and the Big Plum give climbs of some length and difficulty.

Dovedale (Derbyshire)   Famous beauty spot on Derbyshire–Staffordshire boundary with a number of limestone pinnacles, all yielding climbs. Ilam Rock is best known. In the near-by Manifold Valley are Beeston Tor and Thor's Cave; crags giving long, hard climbs.

Miller's Dale   A Derbyshire dale with a wide selection of limestone climbs. In its middle reaches the dale is known as Water-cum-Jolley, and there is a branch dale, Ravensdale, which also offers fine climbing. Raven's Tor in Miller's Dale is noted for its long, hard climbs.

Brassington   Rainster Rocks and Harborough Rocks near Brassington in Derbyshire provide a number of short climbs on dolomite limestone.

GUIDEBOOKS Whittaker, *Chew Valley*
Milburn, *Kinder & Bleaklow*
Milburn, *Staffordshire Gritstone*
Milburn, *Derwent Gritstone*
Milburn, *Peak Limestone – South*
Milburn, *Peak Limestone – Stoney*
Milburn, *Peak Limestone – Chee Dale*
Milburn, *Moorland Gritstone. Chew Valley*
Milburn, *Stanage*
Ballard/Marshall, *Derwent Valley*

Peck, Annie Smith (1850–1935)   Professor of Latin at Purdue and Smith, ardent American feminist, colourful and flamboyant. Began climbing in her 38th year with an ascent of Mt Shasta in the Cascades. She does not seem to have done any more climbing until she was 45 when she visited the Alps and made a number of ascents including the Matterhorn. In 1900 she visited the Dolomites and was U.S. delegate to the International Congress of Alpinism in Paris. On her return she helped found the American Alpine Club (1902).

In 1897, sponsored by the *New York World*, she climbed Popocatapetl and Orizaba (Citlaltepetl). At 5,699 m Orizaba was the highest peak ever climbed by a woman at that time and Annie was very proud of her record, especially as she was 47 years old. The following year she failed to raise sponsorship for an attempt on Illampu (6,362 m). In 1903 she climbed El Misti and in 1904 reached 5,800 m in the Illampu massif. She also reached the same height on the east side of the unclimbed Huascaran and 5,500 m on the west side.

In 1906 two more attempts on Huascaran failed and in that same year her altitude record fell to her compatriot Mrs Fanny Bullock ◊ Workman, who climbed Pinnacle Peak in the Nun Kun massif (6,957 m). Two years later Miss Peck returned to Huascaran and claimed to have climbed the lower North Peak, which she estimated at 7,300 m. She was 58.

Not to be outdone, Mrs Workman sent a surveyor out to Huascaran at her own expense who measured the North Peak at 6,650 m – thereby robbing Miss Peck of the record again! Moreover, her ascent of the peak began to be questioned, but the evidence, though not conclusive, is heavily in her favour and she is generally credited with the first ascent.

In 1910 she tried to climb the volcano of Coropuna (6,615 m), thought at the time to be higher than ◊ Aconcagua (6,970 m). She reached a couple of the minor summits, on one of which she raised a banner proclaiming VOTES FOR WOMEN. Now in her sixties, she retired from the climbing scene.

Peel   Traditional climbing jargon for a fall; noun or verb. 'I peeled off' or 'I had a peel'.

Peg   A ◊ piton. A peg route is one which relies entirely on pitons, i.e. aid climbing. Using pitons is known as 'pegging' and taking them out is called 'de-pegging'. This English word is gradually replacing the French one in Britain.

Peg hammer   A special hammer for placing and removing ◊ pitons. The head is steel and there are various shapes; the shaft is hickory or metal. Hammers usually have a sling attached as a safety precaution against dropping them. A hammer axe is a very short ice axe in which the blade has been replaced by a hammer face. It is used in steep ice-climbing.

Pendlebury brothers   The two Pendlebury brothers, Richard (1847–1902) and William Martin (1841–1921), were important alpinists during the 1870s. They began in 1870 with a new traverse of the Wildspitze via the Mittelberg Joch: now one of the most popular climbs in the Alps. For most of the following two seasons they confined themselves to the Eastern Alps.

In July 1872, with Ferdinand ◊ Imseng they astonished the Alpine world by making the first ascent of Monte Rosa from Macugnaga by the route now called the Marinelli Couloir. The following year, after some new climbs in the Dauphiné, they made the first real attempt on the Dru, but failed, then the first ascent of Schreckhorn from the Lauteraarsattel. Among other interesting expeditions were first ascents of: S Peak of Aig. de Blaitière (1876), Pic d'Olan (1875), Pic Sans Nom (1877), usually guided by G. Spechtenhauser of Otztal.

Richard can lay claim to being one of the founders of British rock-climbing (◊ Haskett Smith). With his brother and others he climbed the Pendlebury Traverse of Pillar Rock in 1872; also Jack's Rake on Pavey Ark and the Western and Eastern Gullies of Clogwyn y Person (1870s – exact date uncertain).

The brothers came from Liverpool, where William was in business. Richard was a Cambridge mathematician until he retired to Keswick a year before his death.

Pendule (pendulum)   A horizontal ◊ abseil used to change a line of ascent or descent e.g. from one vertical crack to another.

Penhall, William (1858–82)   A medical student noted for his strength and daring during his brief Alpine career. After some new routes with ◊ Conway in 1878 he turned his attention to the unclimbed Zmutt arête of the Matterhorn the following season. After one unsuccessful attempt he returned in an attempt to race ◊ Mummery to the top, and in so doing climbed the great W Face of the mountain, crossing the dangerous Penhall Couloir.

The second ascent was not made until 1929 (Fritz Herrmann, solo) and has seldom been repeated. A few days after his ascent Penhall climbed the Durrenhorn with Mummery – a first ascent, but they mistook it for the Nadelhorn!

Penhall was killed on the Wetterhorn in 1882.

Pennine Hills, the   An extensive range of hills stretching from the upper Tyne valley in the north to Ashbourne in the south and varying in width from about 19 km to 80 km. The chief rocks are limestone and gritstone, though there are some igneous intrusions (e.g. High Cup Nick). The high moors of the north and the ◊ Peak tend to give arduous, boggy walking (habitués are known as 'bogtrotters'), for example, Mickle Fell area, Bleaklow, Kinder, etc., but the limestone regions give easier going (Ingleborough area, the Yorkshire and Derbyshire dales). The highest summit is Cross Fell (893 m).

The Pennines may be divided into convenient distinct groups. These are (north to south): the Northern Moors, the Yorkshire Dales, Forest of Bowland, Rossendale, the High Peak and the Low Peak. There is rock-climbing in all these areas, either on natural limestone and gritstone outcrops or in old quarries (see individual areas).

The Pennines are noted for long-distance walks. The Pennine Way stretches 400 km from Edale to Kirk Yetholm in Scotland (it includes the Cheviots). Other famous walks are: Tan Hill to Cat and Fiddle, Three Peaks (Whernside, Ingleborough, Penyghent), Marsden–Edale, Derwent Watershed and Derwent Edge Walk (Woodhead–Robin Hood).

Pen y Gwryd   An inn in Wales standing at the head of the Nantgwynant valley and famous as one of the great pioneering centres of Welsh climbing.

Pen y Pass (Gorphwysfa Hotel)   A former inn at the summit of Llanberis Pass and the usual starting point for the Pyg Track up Snowdon, or the Crib Goch ridge. Famed as the centre for G. W. ◊ Young's Welsh parties in the early days of this century. The building is now a Youth Hostel.

Peters, Rudolf (b. 1913)   A German guide who with his companion Martin Meier made the first ascent of the Croz Spur of the ◊ Grandes Jorasses in 1935. The previous year he had survived five days and four nights on the spur in a storm during which his partner, Haringer, fell to his death.

Peters made several other first ascents amongst which the first ascent and later, first winter ascent, of the S E Face of Schüsselkarspitze are outstanding (1935, 1936).

Petersen, Theodor (1836–1918)   A German chemist who played an important role in the early days of the D.O.A.V. Petersen made a number of first ascents in the Otztal where the Petersenspitze was named in his honour, though von Déchy made the first ascent in 1874.

Pfann, Hans (1863–1958)   A Nuremberg climber who began climbing in the Kaisergebirge in 1894 and became one of the leading exponents in the Eastern Alps. Climbed guideless and made the first ascent of Pt Walker, Gd. Jorasses by the S Face, first traverse of Les Droites, first traverse Matterhorn – Dent d'Hérens and the first traverse of Ushba (Caucasus) (Pfann, Leuchs, Distel, 1903). Made the first ascent of Illampu (Andes) in 1928. Wrote two books about his climbs: *Führerlose Gipfelfahrten* and *Aus meinem Bergleben*.

Pfannl, Heinrich (1870–1929)   A High Court judge from Vienna with many first ascents in the Eastern Alps to his credit. With Maischberger and Zimmer in 1900 he made the first ascent of the Géant by the N Ridge and N W Face. He also took part in ◊ Eckenstein's expedition to K2 (1902).

Piaz, Giovanni Battista (Tita) (1879–1948)   One of the great Dolomite guides, comparable with ◊ Innerkofler. A somewhat rough personality, he was known as The Devil of the Dolomites. His routes include:

1900   Punta Emma, N E Face (solo)
1907   Vajolet Torre Est, S E Face
1908   Totenkirchl (Kaisergebirge), W Face, Piaz Route
1911   Torre Delago, S W Ridge

Piaz was killed riding a cycle without brakes.

Pichl, Eduard (1872–1955)   An Austrian climber with a number of hard new routes in the eastern Alps. He is best known for his traverse of the three Vajolet Towers with Hans Barth in 1899. The Pichl Crack on the Torre Delago would still be a very serious proposition were it not for numerous pegs. In 1901 Pichl made the first ascent of the Dachstein S Face with E. Gams and F. Zimmer.

Picos de Europa   An important group of karst peaks on the northern edge of the Cantabrian mountains, near Santander. The highest summit is Torre de Cerredo (2,642 m). The unusual name is of unknown derivation, but ancient: Pena de Urrieles is sometimes used instead.

There are three main groups, Western, Eastern and Central: the Eastern is little visited by climbers; the highest point of the Western is Pena Santa de Castilla (2,586 m); but the Central area is the best known. Here is the Cerredo, the Torre de Llambrion (2,639 m) and the strange spire of the Naranjo de Bulnes (2,516 m). (First ascent: P. Pidal, G. Perez, 1904.) The best centre is Arenas de Cabrales.

The whole area consists of narrow gorges and serrated peaks, all closely packed into an area comparable with the Lake District. Travel is extremely difficult and the wildness, combined with the huge rock walls, is the chief attraction.

GUIDEBOOK Walker, *Walks & Climbs in the Picos de Europa* (C.P.).

Pied d'éléphant   A short, down, sleeping bag which covers the legs and hips. Used with a duvet jacket for ◊ bivouacking.

Pigott, Alfred Sefton (1895–1979)   One of the leading British rock-climbers of the years following the First World War. Pigott followed the classical pattern of gritstone training and hard new routes in the greater mountain areas. Between 1920 and 1923 his best known gritstone routes were:

Laddow: Priscilla (shared with Morley Wood), Little Crowberry
Cratcliffe: Giant's Staircase, The Bower Route 1, The Girdle
Black Rocks: Sand Buttress, Lean Man's Climb, Curved Crack
Roches: Batchelor's Buttress, Crack and Corner, Black and Tan's Climb, Via Dolorosa.

With J. Wilding he made his eponymous route on the Comb Buttress of Ben Nevis, 1920; and in 1921 the S Face of Inaccessible Pinnacle, and the Direct Finish to the Crack of Doom, Skye. In 1922 he made the Direct Route, Central Buttress, Ben Eighe.

With Morley Wood, he made the W Route of Eagle Crag, Birkness Combe, 1925, and in 1927 his famous eponymous route on the E Buttress of ◊ Clogwyn Du'r Arddu – the first major breach in that cliff.

Fred Pigott was one of the founders of the ◊ Mountain Rescue Committee in 1933, and Hon. Sec. from its foundation until 1956. Chairman 1956–72; President 1972. Awarded the O.B.E. in 1964.

Pilkington brothers Charles (1850–1918) and Lawrence (1855–1941) Pilkington were of the famous Lancashire glass-making family. Both were strong walkers and Lawrence is sometimes regarded as the founder of the ◊ Lake District Fell Record (1871). With Gardiner and Hulton they were pioneers of guideless Alpine climbing (1878 onwards) and made many first guideless ascents including the Meije and the Guggi route of the Jungfrau. Their influence on guideless climbing was considerable.

They were among the first to climb in Skye (1880), making first ascents of the Inaccessible Pinnacle and the Pinnacle Ridge of Sgurr nan Gillean. Later they made the first ascents of Sgurr Mhic Coinnich, Clach Glas and Sgurr na h-Uamha. Sgurr Thearlaich is so named in honour of Charles (Charles' Peak). Mrs C. Pilkington made the first woman's ascent of Inaccessible Pinnacle (1890).

Lawrence was injured in Piers Ghyll, Lake District, in 1884, and did little climbing thereafter, but Charles climbed regularly until 1911. He was President of the A.C. 1896–8.

Pillar (G.: Pfeiler; Fr.: pilier; It.: pilastro) A tall, narrow column of rock jutting out from the parent mountain to which it is usually attached by a narrow neck. A pillar has its own summit and the word implies that the rock is steep, e.g. Central Pillar of Frêney, Mont Blanc.

Pillar Rock One of the most famous and spectacular crags in Britain with a wide variety of good climbs. The crag stands on the Ennerdale face of Pillar Fell in the Lake District, though it is usually approached from Wasdale Head by a fairly long walk. It is unusual (for Britain) in being an immense free-standing obelisk with two tops, High and Low Man, and two appendages known as Pisgah and the Shamrock. The summit (High Man) can only be reached by climbing, the easiest way being from the foot of East Jordan Gully by simple ledges – very exposed. There are climbs on all the faces and they are of all grades.

The first ascent of the rock was made by J. Atkinson, a local man, in 1826, probably by the Old West Route, though this is not certain. It remained the only way to the top until 1863 when a large party, led by J. W. E. Conybeare, found the present easy way described above. The ◊ Pendlebury brothers and others found the Pendlebury Traverse in 1872, but the first real climb was the West Jordan Climb by ◊ Haskett Smith in 1882. From then on it attracted almost all the leading pioneers. Notable early ascents are:

1890   Shamrock Gully – Hastings, Hopkinson, Robinson
1891   N Climb – Haskett Smith, Hastings, Slingsby
1899   Walker's Gully – Jones, G. Abraham, Field
1901   New W Climb – Abraham brothers, C. Barton, Wigner
       Savage Gully – Barton brothers, Meryon
1906   N W Climb – Botterill brothers, Oppenheimer, Taylor

There was some loss of popularity in post-war years but the rock has more recently been the scene of some new, hard climbs. (◊ Jackson Rev. J., and various pioneers such as Hastings, etc.)

Piotrowski, Tadeusz (1940–86) An outstanding Polish mountaineer particularly known for his hard winter ascents including the Troll Wall in

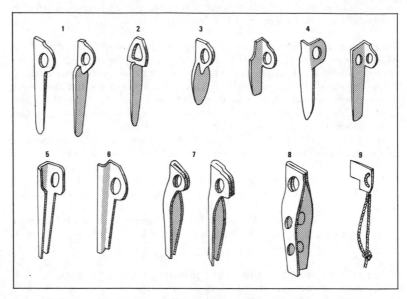

Pegs (Pitons): **1** Blade pitons; **2** Universal; **3** Ace of Spades; **4** Angle pitons; **5** U-section; **6** Z-section; **7** Channel pitons; **8** Bong; **9** RURP (Realised Ultimate Reality Piton)

Norway. In 1973 with ◊ Zawada, he made the first winter ascent of Noshaq (7,392 m) – the first ever for a peak over 7,000 m. In 1983 he made a tough winter ascent of Api (7,132 m).

Piotrowski was killed descending the Abruzzi Ridge of ◊ K2 in 1986 after he and ◊ Kukuczka had made the first ascent of the South Face.

Pitch   The distance between two ◊ belays that a climber has to travel. Thus, two belays may be 6 m apart, but a climber may actually have to move 9 m to get from one to the other: the pitch length is 9 m. Pitches can vary from a few metres to over 30 m. Guidebooks usually indicate the length of rock pitches.

Piton (Fr.) (E.: peg; Am.: pin; G.: Haken; It.: chiodo)   Metal spikes which can be hammered into rock cracks. There is another type designed for use on ice. Pitons have four basic uses: 1. for protection as running belays; 2. for direct aid where the rock is holdless or overhanging; 3. as a belay point where no natural belay exists; 4. as an abseil point where there is no suitable natural feature.

Pitons were rarely used in Britain before the Second World War and are still used sparingly, on the understanding that to place a piton where one is superfluous lowers the grade of the climbing; it is, in fact, cheating. Even on ◊ aid climbs the number of pitons is kept to the minimum. In general, the soundness of this philosophy has been proved in practice many times. Early piton climbs have often been subsequently led free, owing to an improvement in climbing skills and the development of other methods of protection.

In the Alps and the United States there has always been a much freer interpretation of piton use, principally because the climbs there are longer, higher and subject to changes in weather. An Alpine route which is fully pegged is obviously a quicker proposition than the same route where pitons have to be inserted, but to bang in a piton is itself much quicker than searching about for ways to overcome difficulties.

In the Eastern Alps, and to a lesser extent in other places, some routes have permanent pitons cemented into the rock.

With the development of modern bivouac gear, long climbs are often much safer, weatherwise, than they were, and this is leading to a reappraisal of piton usage, especially in the U.S.A.

Pitons of various kinds have been in use throughout climbing history, but their wider use developed in the Eastern Alps during the early decades of this century. Made of mild steel, the essential parts were a blade or spike for inserting in the crack and a ring or hole into which a ♢ karabiner could be clipped. They were basically unchanged until the 1960s when chromolly-steel pitons of specially designed cross-sections were introduced from the United States. These were so superior in every way that they are now almost universally used.

A difficult climb on a big peak may require dozens of pitons, which represent a considerable weight for the climber to carry. There are Russian pitons of titanium, which is strong and very light, and this may well be the piton material of the future but at the moment titanium is far too expensive for commercial use.

USE

Pitons are normally carried in bunches clipped to karabiners and hanging on slings, bandolier fashion, though there are special piton-carrying clips and bags on the market. They are driven in with a piton hammer, usually carried in the hammer pocket of climbing breeches, or the holster of a ♢ harness.

The choice of which piton to use is dictated by the cracks available and the pitons the climber is carrying. The aim is to choose the best combination of the two, bearing in mind the likely direction of strain. Properly placed, even a small piton such as a rurp can take considerable weight.

Placidus à Spescha, Father (1752–1833) 'The monk of Disentis'. Father Placidus was a Benedictine monk born at Truns near Disentis in the Grisons, Switzerland. He served in the Disentis Monastery and in local parishes and explored the local peaks making numerous first ascents: Stockgron (1788), Rheinwaldhorn (1789), Oberalpstock (1792), Piz Urlaun (1793), Piz Aul, Piz Scharboden (1801), Piz Terri (1802), Güferhorn (1806).

He devoted his entire life to the mountains (he attempted Tödi at the age of 72), an interest aroused in him by de ♢ Saussure's books. He met considerable opposition from his brother monks, who thought him mad or a French spy and upon the French invasion of the Grisons his valuable scientific collection was commandeered by the invaders while his manuscripts perished when the monastery was burned.

He was undoubtedly very much in advance of his time; he even suggested the formation of a club for tourists, 'an Alpine club'. Coolidge ranks Father Placidus with de Saussure as one of the founders of alpinism.

Pocket A small hollow in a rock face useful as a handhold. Common on gritstone and sandstone. Sometimes called pigeon holes, for instance, Pigeon Hole Wall, Helsby.

Poly bag A large polythene bag useful as a protective cover in case of benightment, exposure and so on.

Porges, Sigmund   An Austrian climber who made the first ascent of Mönch with Christian ◊ Almer in 1857, and the second ascent of the Eiger (1861).

Porter   A person employed to carry a load either to base camp or on a mountain. The ◊ Sherpas are the best known modern examples. In the pioneer days, porters were used in the Alps, usually to carry firewood, etc., for the ◊ gîte, though some took part in famous ascents. More recently, porters carried provisions to Alpine huts, but this practice seems to have disappeared with the advent of helicopters and téléphériques. They were usually trainee guides.

Portugal, climbing in   In the north of the country, on the Spanish border, is the national park of Peneda-Gerés, an area of granite peaks, not unlike parts of Scotland. It is a remote region with very good walking, often on well-made granite paths, centuries old. There are some crags and a little climbing is reported, but nothing of significance. None of the mountains are named, but the highest points of the ranges are: Serra do Soajo, Pt 1,292 m; and Serra do Gerés, Pt 1,507 m. Arcos de Valdevez is a convenient starting point.

Powell brothers   W. W. R. Powell (b. 1849), L. S. Powell (b. 1855) and C. H. Powell (b. 1857) were three brothers who all made minor first ascents in the Alps in the closing years of the nineteenth century, though they do not seem to have climbed together much. The most important member of the trio was Charles Herbert Powell (Major-General, knighted 1917), who in 1889 joined Dent, Freshfield and Woolley in the Caucasus to search for ◊ Donkin and Fox. Powell spoke Russian and was an experienced Asian traveller.

Pre-Alps   The limestone hills which lap the main Alpine chain to north and south. They are invariably limestone and the Dolomites are the best known, though these are so important they are seldom regarded in this way. For climbers, the most important of the others are: the cliffs of Calanques on the French Mediterranean coast, Vercors and Grande Chartreuse near Grenoble, the Salève near Geneva, the Jura and Vosges on the Swiss–French border, and the Grigne near Lake Como in Italy. Numerous rock-climbs exist in all these areas.

Preuss, Paul (1886–1913)   One of the best Austrian rock-climbers at the turn of the century. Preuss began climbing at the age of 11 with an ascent of the Grosser Bischofsmütze in the Dachstein – one of his favourite areas and where he made a number of first ascents. He climbed numerous new routes in the Gesause, Wilde Kaiser, Wetterstein, Silvretta and Dolomites, many of them solo. His most frequent companions were his sister or Paul Relly. Perhaps his finest ascents came in the last three years of his life: W Face of Totenkirchl (solo), N E Face of Crozzon di Brenta (with Relly), E Face and traverse of Campanile Basso (solo) – all 1911.
    Though noted as a rock-climber, Preuss did a number of hard ice-climbs in the Ortler but did not climb in the Western Alps until 1912, when he met Eckenstein, who taught him additional ice techniques. He made the first ascent of the S E Ridge of the Aig. Blanche de Peuterey and was planning to attempt the Peuterey Ridge *intégrale* in 1914 (not done until 1935). He made many winter climbs.
    Preuss was killed attempting a solo first ascent of N Ridge of Mandlwand in the Gosaukamm. Preuss was a D.Phil. of Munich University, a plant physiologist and a philosopher.

Protection   A term used to indicate protection which a leader can arrange for himself as he climbs, i.e. ◊ runners of various kinds. A well-protected pitch is one where runners can be arranged to safeguard the leader on the hard moves. ◊ Nuts and ◊ Friends have increased the protection on many climbs and have helped to push up standards.

Prusiks (prusik loops)   A system of self-help in crevasse rescue invented by Karl Prusik (1896–1961), a noted Austrian climber during the early part of this century. The climber, when crossing a snow-covered glacier, attaches a loop of thin cord to the main rope, about two feet from his waist, and tucks the other end into his pocket. The knot used for attachment is the Prusik knot which can be slid up the rope but will not slide down if there is pressure on the loop, that is, if a climber stands in it.

If the climber falls into a crevasse, his companion holds him (◊ Crevasse rescue) while he takes the strain off his waist or chest by standing in his prusik loop. He then attaches two more prusik loops to the rope: a short one for under the armpits and another long one for his other foot. By moving each loop in turn up the rope he can raise himself out of the crevasse. This is seldom as simple as it sounds and the method can be very tiring; it is used only as a last resort.

Prusik knots can be awkward to tie and manipulate with gloved hands. A simpler variation using a karabiner was introduced by Bachmann in the 1950s. The 'krab' provides a good handhold. A more recent variation is the Penberthy knot, also claimed to be easier to use than the Prusik knot.

There are at least four mechanical devices intended to make prusiking easier. The best known are jumars. They clamp the rope and replace the prusik knot. They are much less strenuous to operate and are used on expeditions and hard Alpine climbs for climbing ◊ fixed ropes. They can, of course, be used for crevasse rescue as well.

In rock-climbing, prusik loops can be invaluable in relieving the strain on a climber who has parted company with the rock and is hanging free.

Pundits   From 1865 onwards for about three decades native surveyors were trained by the British in Dehra Dun, home of the Indian Survey, and sent incognito to the forbidden territories across the ◊ Himalaya. Working in conditions of extreme difficulty and danger they managed to bring back valuable records, including plans of Lhasa, the course of the upper Oxus and the fact that the Tsangpo of Tibet and Brahmaputra of India were the same river.

The greatest of the Pundits, like Nain Singh, Hari Ram and Kishen Singh ('A.K.') were held in considerable awe by young surveyors. Kipling's Hurree Babu in the novel *Kim* is reputed to be based at least in part on the Pundit Sarat Chandra Das. (See *The Pundits*, by D. Waller.)

Purtscheller, Ludwig (1849–1900)   A noted Austrian alpinist whose list of ascents was said to be second only to that of ◊ Coolidge. Companion of the ◊ Zsigmondy brothers, he was imbued with the same daring; with them he made the first ascent of Kl.Zinne and numerous other climbs in the Eastern Alps. They often climbed solo and almost always guideless, and their assault on the Western Alps in 1884–5 astonished the establishment. They made the first guideless ascent of the Marinelli Couloir of ◊ Monte Rosa, the first guideless traverse of the ◊ Matterhorn, a new route on the S Face of the Bietschhorn and (1885) traversed the Meije from Pic Central to Grand Pic.

Purtscheller went with Hans ◊ Meyer to East Africa in 1889 and they made the first ascent of ◊ Kilimanjaro. In 1891 he visited the ◊ Caucasus. He died from influenza in 1900, his condition weakened by a serious accident he had sustained on the ◊ Dru six months earlier.

Puttrell, James William (1869–1939) A Sheffield man who began climbing on Wharncliffe Crags in 1888 and is indisputably the founder of gritstone climbing. He climbed alone for two years, then was joined by W. J. Watson. In 1900, the growing band of enthusiasts became the ◊ Kyndwr Club.

Puttrell did not visit other mountain areas until 1895 and had no contact with other pioneers. In this respect he was an independent founder of the sport of rock-climbing. Puttrell took part in the first ascents of Crowberry Ridge Direct, Glencoe (1900) and the Chimney of Ben Nuis, Arran (1901), a climb not repeated for 54 years.

Pye, Sir David Randall (1886–1960) Distinguished scientist, friend of Mallory, Young *et al.*, and the originator of three of Britain's best-known climbs: Faith and Charity (Idwal Slabs, Snowdonia, 1916) and The Crack of Doom (Corrie Lagan, Skye, 1918).

Pyrenees A mountain range on the frontier between France and Spain. It is approximately 430 km long and the highest summit is the Pic de Néthou (Aneto), 3,408 m. The topography is very complicated and the rock varies from granite to limestone.

The Pyrenees are different from the Alps in several respects, apart from being generally lower. Glaciers are confined to the north slopes of the central range and the snow-line is about 3,000 m. There are no large lakes, but many streams, and the waterfalls are the highest in Europe outside Norway. Passes are high and scarce. Most notable are the huge cirques heading many of the valleys, of which that at Gavarnie is famous.

Climbing interest is principally in the central part of the range, where there are peaks such as Néthou, Posets (3,375 m), Mont Perdu (3,355 m) and Vignemale (3,298 m) among many others. There are several huts and the centres include Cauterets and Gavarnie in France and the Ordesa National Park in Spain. There are numerous climbs of all grades, including fine modern rock routes.

The high-level traverse of the Pyrenees is a classic and demanding walk, taking about six weeks to complete.

GUIDEBOOKS Reynolds, *Walks & Climbs in the Pyrenees* (C.P.).

Walker, *Rock Climbs in the Pyrenees* (C.P.).

Battagel, *Pyrenees East, West* (2 vols.) (W.C.P.).

Q

Quarry-climbing   Disused quarries frequently offer climbs which are steeper and longer than those of natural outcrops. Best known are the gritstone and limestone quarries of the Pennines, but limestone quarries are also used in other places (e.g. South Wales) and there are granite quarries in Leicestershire and slate quarries at Llanberis. In addition, many of the popular natural outcrops have been quarried to a greater or lesser degree: Stoney Middleton, Helsby and the Avon Gorge among others.

The upsurge in quarry-climbing came in the 1950s with the discovery of Dovestones, in the Pennines, as a superb climbing ground, but a few quarries have a much longer history, notably at Ilkley (1890s) and Brownstones, Bolton (1920s). Many quarries are near to industrial towns and offer good opportunities for a few hours' practice.

Queen Elizabeth Islands   The Arctic islands of Canada, north of ◊ Baffin Island. Climbs have been reported on Ellesmere Island and Axel Heiberg Island, up to 2,590 m. The area is remote and difficult of access.

Quickdraw   A method of extending a running belay so as to make it easy to manipulate. It consists of a tape with a karabiner at each end. One karabiner is clipped into the peg or bolt and the other onto the rope. It is used on steep, hard modern routes where delay in such matters is undesirable. Special karabiners have been developed to make the clipping smoother, with non-snagging gates etc.

R

Raeburn, Harold (1865–1926) One of the greatest figures in Scottish mountaineering. He played a considerable part in developing Scottish crags after the English 'invasion' by ◊ Collie, etc., in 1894. Raeburn's first notable exploit was the climbing of Church Door Buttress on Bidean in 1895, where he led the crux pitch, followed by the Direct Route up the Douglas Boulder on Ben Nevis, 1896.

His name is particularly associated with Ben Nevis, though he climbed in many parts of Scotland. He made 12 new routes on the Ben, including:

1898	The Castle
1901	Observatory Ridge (solo) – also first winter ascent, 1920
1902	Observatory Buttress (solo)
1908	Raeburn's Buttress

Raeburn was also a considerable alpinist. With ◊ Ling and others he made several first British guideless ascents of difficult routes, including the Zmutt Ridge of the Matterhorn (1906). He often climbed solo, both at home and in the Alps, and made the first solo traverse of the Meije (1919).

In 1913 and 1914, Raeburn visited the Caucasus making nine new ascents and in 1920 made an attempt on Kangchenjunga and reached about 6,400 m. He was chosen for the Everest Expedition of 1921 and, though taken ill and evacuated, insisted on rejoining the expedition after his recovery, when he reached 6,700 m. On his return home he had a complete breakdown from which he never recovered. He wrote *Mountaineering Art* (1920).

Rake Used in the Lake District to mean a long, slanting ledge or passage across a crag or mountain, eg. Jack's Rake, Pavey Ark; Lord's Rake, Scafell.

Ramond de Carbonnieres, Baron Louis-François (1755–1827) A native of Alsace who served Cardinal Rohan and Cagliostro and became involved in the Affair of the Diamond Necklace which helped precipitate the French Revolution. Ramond served in the first Revolutionary Parliament but was denounced and imprisoned in Tarbes where he would have been executed except that his enemies forgot about him!

He began his exploration of the Pyrenees in 1787, climbing Pic du Midi de Bigorre and other peaks. His chief fame rests on his attempts on Monte Perdido (3,355 m) which he attempted without success in 1797, but succeeded in climbing in 1802. He was denied a true first ascent, however, because he had sent his guides, Laurens and Rondau, to recce the peak three days earlier and together with a local shepherd they had got to the top!

His career had curious parallels with that of ◊ Placidus à Spescha. Both were pioneers. Carbonnieres described his adventures without any of the hyperbole then common and more like the Victorian literature of more than half a century later. (*Observations faites dans les Pyrenees*, 1789, and *Voyages au Mont Perdu*, 1802.)

Ramsay, Sir Andrew Crombie (1814–91) Eminent nineteenth-century geologist instrumental in solving the geological structure of Snowdonia, and one of the leading protagonists in the great glacier controversy of his day. Took part in the first ascent of Lyskamm (1861).

Ratti, Achille (1857–1939)   An Italian priest who became Pope Pius XI in 1924 and after whom the Achille Ratti climbing club is named. Amongst his ascents was the East Face of ◊ Monte Rosa in 1889. Wrote *Climbs on Alpine Peaks* (1923).

Ravanel, Joseph (1869–1931)   One of the great Chamonix guides noted for his climbs with E. Fontaine. Ravanel was one of the fastest movers ever seen in the Alps. One morning in 1904, he left the Couvercle, climbed the Verte and was back at Montenvers by 8.30 a.m.

Ravanel made many new routes among which were: Aig. du Blaitière, N W arête; Aig. du Fou; Aig. du Moine, N arête; Nom–Verte Traverse; Aigs. Mummery and Ravanel; Crocodile; Ciseaux; Peigne; and the Traverse en Z of the Drus. A typically strong day for Ravanel was his traverse from the Sans Nom over the Verte and down by the Moine (with ◊ Broadrick and ◊ Field, 1902). He was one of the first guides to use skis. Ravanel was nicknamed 'Le Rouge'.

Rébuffat, Gaston (1921–85)   One of the greatest French guides of the post-war era. Born in Marseilles, he learned to climb on the Calanques and became a guide in 1942; accepted by the Chamonix guides' association in 1946. He made early ascents of some of the great north faces such as Eigerwand and Walker Spur and made a number of new climbs in the Mont Blanc area, the most popular being the Rébuffat Route on the Aig. du Midi (1956). He was a member of the Annapurna team in 1950.

Rébuffat made a secondary career as writer and film-maker. His books and films are all about mountaineering; the best known in England is *Starlight and Storm* (1956).

Reciprocal rights   The rights of a club member to use the facilities of another club with whom there is an exchange agreement, particularly for accommodation. When there are full reciprocal rights, a club member can use another club's hut(s) as if he were a member of that club, paying the same charges. Many clubs operate reciprocal rights but usually with some curtailment, e.g. previous notification of hut use, slightly higher charges.

The various alpine clubs generally have complete reciprocal rights with one another, though there are occasional disagreements.

Reverse   To climb down. It may be applied to a single move or a whole climb. The old idea that a climber should not make a move which he cannot reverse is scarcely applicable today (◊ Committing move). When a climb is being reversed, the leader comes down last so as to protect the rest of the party. On very easy rocks and the majority of easier snow- and ice-climbs it is better to come down facing outwards.

Rey, Émile (1846–95)   A guide from Courmayeur, recognized as one of the finest of his day. Rey began guiding at the age of 30 but quickly rose to the top of his profession, being an excellent rock-climber. Perhaps his best-known route is the epic first ascent of the Peuterey Ridge with Güssfeldt (1893), which lasted 88 hours. He made the first ascent of the Aig. Blanche de Peuterey with Seymour King in 1885, and the first descent of the Scerscen

Eisnase with Güssfeldt in 1887.

Rey was intelligent, well read, bi-lingual, and altogether different from most other guides of the times. Klucker perhaps came nearest to matching him and it is interesting they should share the Peuterey Ridge. Rey was immensely popular with his employers, despite the fact that he undoubtedly held a high opinion of himself. He regarded himself as 'lucky'. He died in a fall, unroped, from an easy part of the Aig. du Géant during a descent. There is little doubt that he suffered some sort of stroke or heart attack.

Rey, Guido (1861–1935) Wealthy Italian climber and romantic after whom the Cresta Rey on Monte Rosa was named, though he only made the third ascent. Rey made many fine guideless climbs in his youth but later climbed only with guides following the death of his brother in a guideless climbing accident. Obsessed with the then unclimbed Furggen Ridge of the Matterhorn he made several attempts on it but failed: an ascent was finally achieved with the aid of a rope ladder (1899). The first true ascent was made in 1911.

Rey is best remembered for his great work *The Matterhorn* (1904), the definitive volume on the mountain's early history. In 1914 he published *Peaks and Precipices*, his adventures in the Dolomites and the Chamonix Aiguilles.

Rib (G.: Rippe; Fr.: nervure) A small ridge on a mountain face or a crag. In rock-climbing it is used somewhat indiscriminately and can mean almost any small protuberance.

Richardson, Katherine (1854–1927) One of the finest of the early women climbers. She began in 1871 and her remarkable stamina first showed itself when she made the first traverse of Piz Palu in 1879. In 1885 she was the first woman to climb La Meije – a 'record' later repeated on other peaks. In 1888 she made the first traverse from the Bionnassay to the Dôme de Goûter, long thought impossible, and in the following year made the first ascent of the W Face of the Tsa, and the first traverse, Petit-Grand Dru. Miss Richardson had two of the finest guides of the day: Émile Rey and J. B. Bich.

Rickmers, Willi Rickmer (1873–1965) German mountaineer, explorer and writer who made notable contributions to the knowledge of the Caucasus and Pamirs. Awarded the Patron's Gold Medal, R.G.S., in 1935. Rickmers, of British ancestry, climbed in Britain and the Alps, though he made no new routes. An accomplished skier, he was also noted for his sense of humour; once, posing as a Prof. Dustsucker, he claimed to have discovered Noah's Ark.

Ridge (G.: Grat; Fr.: arête; W.: crib) The crest where two opposing faces of a mountain meet and the feature thus formed. May be broad or narrow, rock or snow. Ridges may be horizontal, gradually sloping, or very steep, and may be interrupted by ◊ gendarmes, gaps, or steps. On a lesser scale, a ridge can also be formed by two faces of a crag, e.g. Crowberry Ridge, Buachaille Etive Mor. In rock-climbing, the term is somewhat loose (◊ Rib, Buttress).

River crossing A number of mountaineers have lost their lives trying to cross swollen mountain torrents; but a procedure to make the crossing as safe as possible has been devised. The leader ties on the middle of the rope and one man stands upstream holding one end of the rope and another man downstream with the other end. The leader wades across facing the current. If he should be swept off his feet the upstream control slackens the rope while the downstream control pulls the leader ashore. It is dangerous to pull against the current as the leader will be towed under. The second man to cross ties on to the two ends of the rope. The leader stands downstream and the third man upstream. The man crosses, the rope acting like an endless belt. Any number can cross in this way. The last man crosses in the same way as the leader, but in reverse.

There are other methods, but the above is the surest. For a wide river ropes can be joined together. It is essential to choose the place where the current is weakest, even though the river might be wider at that point. (See *Mountain Leadership*, by E. Langmuir.)

Robbins, Royal A leading American rock-climber noted particularly for his ascents in Yosemite, some of which are:

1957 N W Face of Half Dome
1961 Salathé Wall
1964 North America Wall

He has made altogether four major routes on Half Dome and three on ◊ El Capitan. Of the six major El Capitan routes first established, Robbins made either the first or second ascent, except for Muir Wall, and in this case he made the first solo ascent (1968). It is regarded as one of the most difficult solo climbs ever made, and took ten days.

Robbins has climbed in Alaska and Britain, and in the Alps he made two very hard variants to the W Face of the Dru (Hemming and Robbins, 1962, Harlin and Robbins, 1965).

Robbins is the exponent of the single push theory of big wall climbing as opposed to ◊ siege tactics.

He has written *Basic Rockcraft* (1971).

Robertson, Robert Augustus (1850–1948) An Original Member of the Climbers' Club and the S.M.C. He was President of both 1907–9. Best known for his first ascent of the S W Ridge of L'Évêque (Arolla), now a popular climb (1894).

Robinson, John Wilson (1853–1907) One of the pioneers of Lakeland climbing. Though he seldom led a climb, Robinson accompanied many parties on first ascents of Lakeland routes, notably Moss Ghyll, Scafell and the Great Gully of the Screes, both in 1892.

Roch, André (b. 1906) Swiss alpinist with many difficult first ascents to his credit in the Mont Blanc and Pennine Alps including Triolet N Face (1931) and Courtes S Pillar (1935). He also has considerable Himalayan experience: E Summit of Baltoro Kangri, 1934; Dunagiri, 1939; Kedarnath, Satopanth and Nanda Ghunti, 1947; and attempts on Dhaulagiri, 1953, and Everest, 1952, when he reached the S Col.

His books are *Climbs of my Youth* (1949), *Everest 1952* (1953) and *On Rock and Ice* (1947).

Rochemelon (3,538 m) A mountain in the Graian Alps climbed in 1358 by Bonifacio Rotario, knight of Asti, and thought to be the first ascent of a high Alpine peak. (1 September 1358.) The Benedictine monks of Novalesa at the foot of the peak had tried an ascent as early as the eleventh century but had not succeeded. There is a small chapel on top, and the ascent is easy in Alpine terms.

Rock and Ice Club   The most celebrated climbing club of the post-war era. It began as a small Manchester group of friends and was formed into a 'club' on 26 September 1951. The original members were: N. Allen, D. Belshaw, J. Brown, D. Chapman, D. Cowan, J. Gill, P. Greenall, R. Greenall, R. Moseley, M. Sorrell, R. White, D. Whillans. Between them they were responsible for a major breakthrough in British climbing, especially with their routes in Derbyshire, Llanberis Pass and Clogwyn du'r Arddu. Most notable were J. ◊ Brown and D. ◊ Whillans.

The Club foundered in 1958 but was reconstituted by N. Allen and D. Gray in February 1959.

Rock-climbing   One of the most important branches of mountaineering. It is the art of climbing steep rocks; of pitting skills, nerves and strength against the obvious dangers of gravity, weather, falling stones and fatigue. It is the acceptance of a challenge according to the climber's judgement of his own skill and endurance. This can vary enormously – a challenge to one man will be no challenge at all to another; some climbers find most satisfaction in taking the challenge to their own limit, whereas others are content to let the challenge be a minor part of the activity and climb well within themselves. In this, rock-climbing is closely allied to other branches of mountaineering (e.g. ice-climbing), but it is capable of finer development and to some it is a sport in its own right.

It is difficult to say where ◊ scrambling ends and real rock-climbing begins; the use of the rope is no criterion because many climbers solo difficult routes which less able climbers would climb roped. Broadly, a climb is one that comes within the system of ◊ gradings used for rock-climbs in the ◊ guidebooks.

Rock-climbing may be treated under four headings: the skills of climbing, route-finding, protection and the psychological barrier. The first includes specific techniques (e.g. bridging) and balance, together with the special techniques associated with ◊ aid climbing. Route-finding can be difficult, especially on long Alpine rock-climbs, and is aided by guidebooks but much more by experience. ◊ Protection includes ◊ belays and ◊ runners. The psychological barrier has many components: doubt as to one's own ability, the worry of exposure, and a general fear of the unknown. Most climbs become easier (in this sense) with familiarity.

There are two common systems of rock-climbing. In the Alps and other high ranges, it is common for the climbers to move together on easy rock or for one to take a simple direct belay while the other climbs. This is for speed. On more difficult routes, the English system is used, whereby one man is belayed by an indirect ◊ belay, while the other climbs, and vice versa. Thus, only one man climbs at a time – if there are three or more in the party, this still applies. It is sometimes called the 'pitch by pitch' system, since the distance between two belays is called a pitch. It is slower but much safer than the other method. Further safeguards are the belays of the stationary climber controlling the rope and the ◊ runners placed by the leader.

Solo climbing is often undertaken, sometimes with complicated rope protection, sometimes with no protection. The extra danger involved is obvious.

Rock-climbing of various sorts has been done since time immemorial for practical reasons such as the collecting of birds' eggs for food (e.g. in the

Hebrides). As a sport, in Britain, it was largely initiated by two men: ◊ Haskett Smith in the Lakes, and ◊ Puttrell in Derbyshire. The ascent of Napes Needle in the ◊ Lake District is often taken as the start of rock-climbing (1886), but this is symbolical rather than historical fact.

DEVELOPMENT

Alpine rock-climbing developed with climbers such as ◊ Dent, ◊ Mummery, the ◊ Zigsmondy brothers and guides like those from the Saastal, led by ◊ Burgener. In the Eastern Alps, the limestone of the region gave rise to fine rock-climbers and in Britain, rock-climbing developed because there were no great mountains and rock provided a sporting outlet to such as O. G. ◊ Jones and the ◊ Abraham brothers. In Britain this pioneering period came to an end with the First World War and the ascent of Central Buttress, Scafell by ◊ Herford.

In between the world wars the British developed a strongly ethical type of rock-climbing which disdained pitons and advocated 'rubbers'; ◊ Longland, ◊ Waller, ◊ Edwards and ◊ Kirkus were amongst the leaders of this time. After the war the challenge was taken up by Peter ◊ Harding and Tony ◊ Moulam and then by Joe ◊ Brown and Don ◊ Whillans, leading an increasing army of activities. Ethical standards were still fairly rigid: as Wilson and Newman put it, 'It is all too easy to forget that it was the British styles of the pre-war and post-war periods that played a key role in preserving the free-climbing, piton-rationing ethic, eschewed bolts, developed nut protection and popularised the P.A., all of which (except the anti-bolt ethic) were to spread out in the seventies to become key elements in the international free-climbing scene we know today.' (*Mountain*, 1987)

RECENT ADVANCES

American rock-climbing developed separately and regionally under Weissner, Durrance, ◊ Robbins and many others. It found its greatest expression in Yosemite (◊ U.S.A.), where the best of the world's climbers tended to congregate on the huge granite walls. This was reinforced in Europe by the limestone of the Verdon.

In Britain the new advances were epitomised by ◊ Livesey and ◊ Fawcett – the former with Footless Crow, Borrowdale and Right Wall of Cenotaph Corner, Llanberis (both E5 6a) and the latter with Tequila Mockingbird and the Prow (both E6 6b) in the Peak.

Protection has advanced, including the sometimes controversial use of bolts. The old adage that a leader simply must not fall is no longer true – falls are taken as part of the attempt, protected by harnesses, Friends and all the other gear.

Many rock-climbers still go on to become all-round mountaineers in the Alps and Himalaya, but others see no pleasure in this and modern rock-climbing can be seen as a separate sport in its own right.

Rognon (Fr.) (G.: Fluh) A rock island in a glacier, usually a safe resting place and frequently used as the site of a mountain hut.

Romsdal The most popular rock-climbing area of Norway, with some of the largest and steepest cliffs in Europe. The centre is Andalsnes, reached by road from Bergen or Alesund or by rail from Oslo.

The Romsdalhorn (1,555 m) is a shapely peak first climbed by local peasants (C. Hoel, H. Bjermeland, 1827). Early explorers included C. ◊ Hall and W. C. ◊ Slingsby. There was intermittent progress over the years, but after the last war this was stepped up by the Norwegian climbers, A. Randers Heen and R. Hoibakk, culminating in the E Pillar of Trollryggen in 1958.

The most spectacular climbs, however, are on the Troll Wall, 1,500 m high, and requiring artificial aid.

Troll Wall (Trollveggen) first ascents:

1965   The Norwegian Route – L. Pettersen, J. Tiegland, O. D. Enersen, O. Eliassen, 11 days

1965   The English (Rimmon) Route – A. Howard, J. Amatt, B. Tweedale, 5½ days

1967   The French Direct Route – Deck, Boussard, Cordier, Brunet, Frehel, 21 days

1972   Arch Wall – E. Drummond, H. Drummond, 20 days

1974   1st Winter ascent (French Route) – Pietrowski, Kesicki, Kurtyka, Kowalewski

There are still many new climbs to be made at Romsdal, particularly in the little-known outer ranges.

Roof (G.: Dach, First; Fr.: toit; It.: tetto)   The underside of a large, sharply jutting overhang.

Rope   (a) The rope used for protection in climbing, or (b) a collective noun for a group of climbers joined together by a rope.

(a) The original climbing rope was hawser-laid hemp and was produced by John Buckingham in London at five pence per yard. It was identified by a thin red line running through it and known as the Alpine Club rope. 18 m was usually carried, though more was not unusual. Silk and cotton ropes also had a vogue, but none of them had the strength of the modern nylon rope. Hemp ropes were often difficult to handle when wet or frozen. They were in use until the 1950s.

Nylon ropes were also hawser-laid at first, but this eventually gave way to the kernmantle construction in which a bunch of strands run the length of the rope and are covered by a woven sheath. Available in various diameters, the most useful are:

9 mm – double rope, ◊ abseiling, ◊ scrambling
11 mm – single climbing rope
They are usually obtained in 45 m or 50 m lengths, though 15 m is enough for a scrambling rope. The best rope is ◊ U.I.A.A. approved and will indicate the number of 'leader falls' it is expected to take – a rough measure at best. Ropes should be examined periodically and abandoned if damaged or after prolonged use. The life of a rope is difficult to determine, but even under favourable circumstances is probably not more than five years. Nevertheless, because they are expensive, climbers tend to use them beyond strict safety limits.

Ropes come in various colours and some are treated with water-repellant.

USE

Single rope   is used for simple rock-climbing and straightforward alpinism. *Double rope*   is used for more technical climbing where there are many ◊ runners, as the ropes can be clipped alternatively, reducing drag. Double ropes also help in technical moves like ◊ pendules. Generally, two different coloured ropes are used because this makes handling easier when passing instructions: 'Slack on red!' etc.

Galen Rowell (*T. D. Unsworth*)   Al Rouse

Scrambling ropes   are meant to give confidence or security on scrambles where some moves are harder than others. A similar rope should be carried by leaders taking novices fell-walking in rough terrain.

(b) The 'rope' means the climbers. The normal climbing rope is two or three persons. In a rope of three, No.1 is called 'the leader', No.2 is 'second' or 'middle-man' and No.3 'last man'. On rock-climbs two is more common these days, and if they are of equal ability, they can 'lead through', i.e. alternate leads. This is more enjoyable and faster. On the easier Alpine climbs, when climbers can move together, 5 m is enough distance between each, the rest of the rope being wrapped around the climbers' shoulders. This also makes for ease of handling and speed, though the rope must have mutual confidence because of ◊ crevasses, ◊ cornices etc.

Long ropes of people are sometimes taken by ◊ guides on easy ◊ glacier tours.

Rope-length   A term used mainly in Alpine guidebooks to describe a distance in the course of the climb. It usually implies easy climbing which is not worth describing in detail, e.g. 'traverse right for three rope-lengths to the foot of a crack'. Often confusing.

Rothschild, Baron Albert de (1844–1911)   Head of the famous banking firm and one of the world's richest men. From 1867 to 1875 he had a very active Alpine career including most of the famous grand courses. He made a minor first ascent – Schwarzhorn, on Monte Rosa (1873).

Rouse, Alan Paul (1951–86)   One of the foremost climbers of recent years with an international reputation, Alan Rouse was born on Merseyside and educated at Cambridge. An erstwhile mathematics teacher, he soon became a full-time professional mountaineer.

He began rock-climbing in 1968 and in his first season was leading climbs such as Vector and Cemetery Gates. Over the next three years he put up a series of hard first ascents including Gemini (Cloggy, 1970), Matrix (Stoney Middleton, 1971) and Beatnik (Helsby, 1971). Beatnik was soloed and Rouse became expert at soloing hard routes, such as Boldest on Cloggy and Suicide Wall at Idwal, both in 1970. In 1972 he turned his attention to Scottish winter climbing, and climbed Kellett's Right Hand Route on the Ben and made the first ascent of South Pillar on Craig Maighaidh.

He first visited the Alps in 1969, and in the next few years did many of the major hard lines such as the Walker Spur, N Face of Triolet, W Face of the Dru etc. He was particularly pleased to rediscover the Lesuer Route on the Drus – a second ascent after years of neglect for a classic climb.

Increasingly his attention was directed beyond Europe. He climbed in the U.S.A., New Zealand and three times in South America, where he made new routes on Rondoy, Yerupaja and other peaks. However, his two attempts at Fitzroy (1973, 1977) came to nothing.

He first visited the Himalaya in 1978 when he made a fine Alpine-style ascent of Jannu, followed the next year with the first ascent of Nuptse N Face from the Western Cwm.

In 1980 he was with ◊ Bonington on the recce of Kongur (7,719 m), which they climbed the following year – an important first ascent of this Chinese peak (Boardman, Tasker, Rouse, Bonington). But he also had a number of failures – a winter attempt on Everest W Ridge in 1981, Ogre 2, Karum Koh, and K2 S Ridge in the next couple of years. However, he did climb Broad Peak in 1983.

In 1986 Alan Rouse became the first British climber to reach the summit of ◊ K2, but too ill to descend, he died in his tent on the ridge – one of many that summer. See *Alan Rouse – A Mountaineer's Life* by G. Birtles et al.

Route (G.: Weg; Fr.: course, voie; It.: via)
(*a*) The directions followed in a mountain journey
(*b*) A climb. The two words are interchangeable, e.g. Murray's Route, Dow Crag.

Route card A card, prepared in advance, giving details of a proposed mountain journey. The information should include bearings for each leg of the journey, estimated time for each leg (◊ Naismith's Rule), bearings for easy ways off, if applicable, names or at least numbers of people taking part.

Route cards are generally used for extremely difficult journeys or, more commonly, by leaders taking large parties into the hills, school parties for example.

Rowell, Galen (b. 1940) An American climber from Berkeley who has taken part in more than a thousand climbs from Yosemite to Alaska and including 10 major Himalayan expeditions. When the Chinese once again allowed access to their mountains Rowell was one of the first to visit them and this resulted in his best known book, *Mountains of the Middle Kingdom* (1985).

As a self-taught photographer Rowell astonished the climbing public with stunning images of action and landscape. His work has appeared in many leading magazines and he has illustrated his own books: *The Vertical World of Yosemite* (1974), *In the Throne Room of the Mountain Gods* (1977), *High and Wild* (1979), *Many People Come, Looking, Looking* (1980) and (with J. MacPhee) *Alaska: Images of the Country* (1981).

Rubbers   Thin, cheap gym-shoes, once popular for difficult climbs but now superseded by rock boots.

Rübenson, Carl Wilhelm (1885–1960)   A Norwegian climber famous for his attempt on Kabru in the Himalaya in 1907. With a fellow countryman, Monrad Aas, he set out determined to make the highest climb then known, though neither were experienced mountaineers. They succeeded in reaching a point within 100 ft of the summit when cold and darkness forced them down to their top camp. They descended by moonlight, Rübenson slipped but was held by Aas and later they found the rope was almost parted.

Rübenson was befriended by ◊ Slingsby, who induced him to make the first ascent of Stedtind (Rübenson, Schjelderup, Bryn, 1910) in Norway. He also made first ascents of Svolvaergjeita, Rorhoptind and Strandatind (Norway) as well as two minor summits in Kashmir. He later became a popular journalist.

Rucksack   A bag, fitted with shoulder straps, used for carrying gear and provisions. Usually made of canvas or nylon.

A framed rucksack, e.g. Bergen type, is usually a commodious bag with outside pockets, used for carrying a fairly large amount of gear. The bag is attached to a metal frame at the back and the shoulder straps are fixed to the frame. At the bottom of the frame is a waistband of canvas or leather. Thus the weight is carried on shoulders and hips. Such a rucksack is inconvenient when climbing because the frame gets in the way and the load is too low on the body.

A pack frame (back pack) is an adaptation of the framed rucksack in which the bag is detachable from the frame. When attached, it sits on a base plate. Pack frames are made so that the load is much higher and consequently more comfortable. Very large loads can be carried this way; useful on expeditions.

Both of the above have now been largely superseded by the rucksack with an internal frame which can be adapted in length and shape to suit a particular body. The straps and waistband are well padded, but the basic principles are the same, i.e. a high load carried on the hips.

A frameless rucksack can be a small affair known as a 'day sack' or the larger 'Alpine sack'. These are the sacks used in climbing. They should have external straps or cords for carrying an ice axe and crampons and a strong metal ring for ◊ sack-hauling. The rucksack should be robust and waterproof and fastened with easily worked buckles. It should also 'sit high' when loaded and carried. There are many varieties: outside pockets which are detachable, extendable sacks and so on.

Runner (running belay)   If a leader came off whilst climbing a ◊ pitch he could fall twice the distance between himself and the second man. To reduce this fall he uses a protective device known as a runner or running belay.

A simple runner consists of a tape ◊ sling hung securely over a spike of rock or threaded round a chockstone. A ◊ karabiner is clipped on to the sling and the main climbing rope is clipped through the karabiner. Provided the runner is secure and the second man understands belaying, the maximum distance the leader can fall is twice the distance between himself and the runner.

If there is no natural attachment then nuts, Friends or pegs may be used. On ice-climbs, ice screws or pegs are used.

Several runners may be employed on a pitch, particularly if it is long and difficult. If there is no means of attaching runners the pitch is said to be 'unprotected'. In many instances the use of pegs for runners is being questioned on ethical and ecological grounds because the repeated use of pegs scars the rock badly. Using runners as handholds, or 'resting' on runners, though sometimes necessary, is generally regarded as unethical.

On a ◊ traverse a runner will also protect the other members of a party besides the leader. On any climb it is the job of the last man to collect the runners as he passes them.

Run-out The length of rope between a leader and second man, as the leader climbs. A full run-out means the ◊ pitch has required all the rope available. It is usual for the second to warn the leader when he is approaching a full run-out by shouting 'ten feet left'. This gives the leader notice to seek a belay.

Ruskin, John (1819–1900) Writer, critic and social reformer; an aesthetic genius who had a profound effect on his times. Mountains, especially the Alps, were the ruling passion of his life and though he made very few real ascents (Buet, Salève, Rifelhorn and various travellers' passes), he knew and understood the mountain world better than most of his contemporaries. Through his writings, he made the world look at mountains in a new, more understanding way.

There is no doubt that Ruskin would have become a mountaineer in the true pioneering spirit of his times had it not been for his parents, and particularly his mother. They were especially possessive and protective, and both lived to a great age. Ruskin could never bring himself to break free from their influence (even his marriage was a failure).

His sensibility over mountain scenery was offended by the activities of the new Alpine Club and in *Sesame and Lilies* (1865) appears his famous stricture:

'The Alps themselves, which your own poets used to love so reverently, you look upon as soaped poles in a bear garden, which you set yourselves to climb and slide down again with shrieks of delight. When you are past shrieking, having no human articulate voice to say you are glad with, you fill the quietude of their valleys with gunpowder blasts, and rush home, red with cutaneous eruption of conceit, and voluble with convulsive hiccough of self-satisfaction.'

The reference to gunpowder comes from the then popular celebration of a successful ascent by firing cannon, especially in Chamonix after an ascent of Mont Blanc. Ruskin was in Chamonix (his favourite Alpine village) when Albert ◊ Smith returned from his celebrated ascent in 1851. Later he wrote, 'true lovers of natural beauty . . . would as soon think of climbing the pillars of the choir at Beauvais for a gymnastic exercise, as making a playground of Alpine snows.' Despite this, he was elected to the Alpine Club in 1869.

He had some training in geology and entered into the glacier controversy with gusto, defending Forbes against Tyndall and Ramsay. His geological training probably helped with his sketching, for, though he refused to recognize himself as an artist, he was a superb draughtsman, especially of mountains. He claimed to have taken the first photograph of the Matterhorn (1849).

Ruskin's eminence as an art critic was unrivalled in his day, though it led him into some stormy waters. His books, in which art and life were blended (particularly the volumes of *Modern Painters*), are outstanding. Later in life he developed theories of socialism and reform much ahead of his time. He was extremely generous and gave away much of his personal fortune – about £200,000. He lived the last 29 years of his life at Brantwood, Coniston, and he is buried in the village churchyard there. His relatives refused the offer of a tomb in Westminster Abbey.

Gaston Rébuffat   Wanda Rutkiewicz

Russell-Killough, Count Henri Patrick Marie (1834–1909)   Born in Toulouse of an Irish father and French mother, Count Henri Russell was, with Charles ◊ Packe, the founder of Pyrenean climbing and exploration. His early life was adventurous, and he travelled in remote parts of the world, but from 1858 he settled down to a detailed exploration of his beloved Pyrenees. He made numerous ascents, including Vignemale, a mountain he was to climb 33 times and on which he built a famous series of refuge-caves. He made only one visit to the Alps, 1867, when he ascended Mont Blanc and Breithorn.

Russell was a big man, very strong and with a pronounced sense of humour. He was one of the founders of the Club Alpin Français.

Rutkiewicz, Wanda (1943–92)   Born in Lithuania, but became a Polish citizen shortly after, living at Wrockaw. Her maiden name was Blaszkiewicz. Graduated M.Sc. in computer science.

She began climbing in 1961 and soon was active in both Eastern and Western Alps doing standard routes like the E Face of Grépon. She also climbed the East Pillar of Troll Wall (GrVI inf) in Norway (1968). Over the next decade her Alpine routes included the second ascent of the N Pillar of ◊ Eiger (1973), the first winter ascent of the ◊ Matterhorn Nordwand by an all-women team (1978), E Face of Capucin and W Face of ◊ Dru (1979).

By this time she had already begun the long series of high-altitude expeditions for which she is best known, beginning with Pic Lenin in the Pamirs in 1970 and Noshaq in the Hindu Kush (1972). In 1975 she led the Polish Women's Karakoram Expedition to Gasherbrum II and III, when Halina Kruger Syrokomska and Anna Okopinska reached the summit of Gasherbrum II and became the first all-women rope to reach an 8,000 m summit. It was done without oxygen. Wanda, with husband and wife team Janusz and Alison Chadwick-Onyszkiewicz and Krzysztof Zdzitowiecki reached the summit of Gasherbrum III, at that time the highest unclimbed mountain in the world at 7,952 m.

After the failure of an attempt on ◊ Nanga Parbat in 1976, she became the first European woman to reach the summit of ◊ Mt Everest (third woman's ascent, 76th overall).

Expeditions continued with attempts on ◊ K2 and Broad Peak. In 1985 she climbed the S Face of ◊ Aconcagua Alpine-style and was in the first all-women's ascent of Nanga Parbat, without oxygen or high-altitude porters. The following year she succeeded in climbing K2, the second highest mountain in the world, and attempted (unsuccessfully) Makalu and ◊ Annapurna. Between 1987–91 she brought her tally of 8,000 m peaks up to eight with Shisha Pangma, Gasherbrum II, Gasherbrum I, Cho Oyu and the South Face of Annapurna. She died at over 8,000 m on Kangchenjunga while attempting the mountain from the north in May 1992. Like her contemporary, Junko ◊ Tabei, she has done great service to the cause of women's mountaineering and was the leading female mountaineer of the present day.

Ruttledge, Hugh (1884–1961) The leader of the 1933 and 1936 Everest Expeditions. He was an Indian civil servant with considerable experience of Himalayan travel but no real mountaineering background, and this led to difficulties and criticism. He wrote *Everest*, 1933 and *Everest, the Unfinished Adventure*.

Ruwenzori A range of East African mountains fabled as Ptolemy's *Lunae Montes* or 'Mountains of the Moon'. They were discovered in 1888 by H. M. Stanley, who gave them their present name, probably derived from the native words *Ru-enzururu* (snow hill). The highest summit, Margherita (5,109 m), was first climbed by the Duke of the Abruzzi, 1906. The area has been thoroughly explored and there are now mountain huts available. The weather is often bad.

Principal summits are:

Mt Stanley (Margherita), 5,109 m	Mt Baker, 4,843 m
(Alexandra), 5,091 m	Mt Emin, 4,798 m
Mt Speke (also called Duwoni),	Mt Gessi, 4,715 m
4,896 m	Mt Luigi di Savoia, 4,627 m

GUIDEBOOKS Wielochowski, *Ruwenzori Map & Guide*.
Osmaston, *Guide to the Ruwenzori*.

Ryan, Valentine John Eustace (1883–1947) One of the most remarkable climbers of the turn of the century. With the Lochmatters, Franz and Josef, he made a series of climbs which were well ahead of their day for the Alps, and joined ◊ Young and ◊ Knubel in others. Their most famous combined ascent was that of the S W Face of the Täschhorn, in 1906, still regarded as one of the most difficult climbs in the Alps.

His climbing career began in 1898 with some small peaks in the St Gotthard area. He missed the following season but was out in the next three (1900–2), although he did nothing out of the ordinary. His army career took him to Malta in 1903 and he climbed on the cliffs there, but in May of that year an early visit to the Alps brought him into contact with the Lochmatter brothers for the first time. In the four seasons, 1903–6, they climbed in many parts of the Alps, including the Dolomites, doing all the hard climbs and making new ones.

In 1904 he did 20 major climbs and made an attempt on the West Ridge of Grandes Jorasses. In 1905, he made 25 ascents, including the second ascent of the Verte from Charpoua, second ascent of the W Face of the Plan, first ascent of the N Face of Charmoz and a number of difficult traverses. He first met Young this year, on the Furggen ridge of the Matterhorn.

In 1906 he made the three routes for which he is best known: the N W Ridge of Blaitière, the Ryan–Lochmatter Route on the Plan and the Cresta di Santa Caterina on Monte Rosa.

Ryan resigned his commission in 1905 and planned to visit the Himalaya (he had been left an estate in Ireland), but instead he married (1906), and returned to the Alps as usual. Young later suggested that the Täschhorn climb might have put Ryan out, and certainly he did not revisit the Alps until 1909, when he did nothing of note. In 1914, however, he (with the Lochmatters) returned with his old ferocity: he made a new route up the Nantillons face of Grépon, various other new climbs and the second ascent of Young's Mer de Glace Face of Grépon, adding the finish which is now the usual one.

But that was the end. He visited the Alps a few times afterwards but did nothing – he lost all interest in the sport, even becoming 'anti-climbing'.

He left Ireland in 1921, during the 'Troubles', and settled in Jersey, which he hated. He was always a difficult person, disliked by many (he failed to gain membership of the A.C.). He never smiled, and drove his guides remorselessly. Some notes he compiled of his great climbs were lost by ◊ Yeld, to whom he had entrusted them and he never bothered to rewrite them. (See *Climbers' Journal*, 1949, for an appreciation of Ryan by Young.)

S

Saas Fee Most important of the hamlets at the head of the Saastal in the Pennine Alps; the others are Saas Grund and Saas Almagell. Popular climbing and ski centre. The climbs are mainly centred on the Weissmies and Mischabel groups.

Sack-hauling On a difficult pitch a leader, and possibly others in the party, may have to do the climb without the encumbrance of a rucksack. Once the leader is up, the sack is tied to the rope by means of the hauling ring, and pulled up. It is essential that the leader have a double rope for this purpose, one strand for hauling, the other to connect him to the rest of the party.

Safety rope A rope held from above to protect novices during ◊ abseiling practice. On a mountain climb which requires abseils, a separate abseil rope is carried and the climbing rope then acts as a safety rope for all the party except the leader, who comes down last. (◊ Top rope.)

Sakashita, Naoe (b. 1948) From Aomori-ken in Japan, though now living in Tokyo, Sakashita was once described as 'climbing like a samurai': he survived a bivouac at 8,300 m on K2. He has many European and American climbing friends and in 1984 attempted an Alpine-style ascent of Tawetse E Face with John Roskelley and Jim Bridwell. He is a member of the strongest Japanese Alpine club, the Sangakudoshikai Club led by Masatsugu Konishi.

His expeditions include: Annapurna II (1973); Jannu (1976), first ascent of N Face; Noshaq (1976), Alpine-style attempt; Kangchenjunga (1980), first ascent of N Face and first Japanese Alpine-style ascent of an 8,000 m peak; Annapurna I (1981), winter solo attempt; K2 (1982) N Ridge, first ascent without oxygen; Tawetse E Face (1984), Alpine-style attempt; Ama Dablam (1984) W Ridge, solo.

Sakashita took part in the Russian Speed Climbing Championships in 1978, when he also climbed the W Face of the Dru, one of the most difficult Alpine grand courses. In 1983 he did some Scottish ice-climbing.

The translator of Choinard's *Climbing Ice*, he is also a mountaineering equipment distributor.

Salathé, John A Swiss-born American who was one of the leading Yosemite climbers of the 1940s with routes to his credit such as the S W Face of Half Dome, Lost Arrow Chimney Route and the N Face of Sentinel Rock (as late as 1956). He was an experienced blacksmith who redesigned pitons, making them from harder steel.

Salm-Reifferscheid, Count Franz Xaver von (d. 1822) Prince-Bishop of Gurk and later a Cardinal, this powerful cleric had a passion for the Gross Glockner (3,798 m), the highest mountain in Austria. He determined to have it climbed and in 1799 got two carpenters from Heiligenblut to make the attempt. These were the ◊ Klotz brothers – the first of a famous family of guides. They failed at first, though they fixed almost 150 m of rope to the

Naoe Sakashita   Doug Scott

steepest parts – presumably to help others to climb it, and probably the first use of ◊ fixed rope.

The Bishop had a hut built as a base for further operations and from it the Klotz brothers took a party to the first summit, Klein Glockner. Whether the two men then continued to the final summit is open to dispute. In the following year a higher hut was built where no fewer than 62 people gathered. Most, including the Bishop, got no further than the hut, but two carpenters, a botanist, two priests and the Klotz brothers reached the Klein Glockner and one of the priests, Fr Horasch, reached the summit with the Klotzes. First ascent 1800? Perhaps, but the Bishop had a medal struck which reads GLOCKNER IN CARINTHIA PRIMUS CONSCENDIT D.25 AUG 1799.

Samivel (b. 1907)   French writer, artist and cartoonist, whose work is highly regarded in France but virtually disregarded elsewhere. In his younger days he was a member of the Groupe de Haute Montagne and made several first ascents in the Trélatête area. An admirer of Dickens, he took the pen-name Samivel from Sam Weller, in *Pickwick Papers*.

Saussure, Horace-Bénédict de (1740–99)   A wealthy scientist of Geneva and one of the earliest mountain explorers. It was de Saussure who offered a prize for the first person to reach the summit of Mont Blanc on his first visit there in 1760. It was not claimed until the Paccard–Balmat ascent of 1786. In 1787 de Saussure himself reached the summit (third ascent). He also climbed the Pizzo Bianco near Macugnaga, and several other minor peaks, and was the first traveller to visit Zermatt (1789).

De Saussure enjoyed wide fame. He was elected F.R.S. in 1768. His book *Voyages dans les Alpes* (1779–96, 4 vols.) contains the first detailed maps of Alpine areas. (See *The First Ascent of Mont Blanc*, by T. G. Brown and G. R. de Beer.)

Scafell Crag and East Buttress   Scafell Crag extends across the Wasdale

Face of Scafell in the Lake District and is one of the largest and most important climbing crags in Britain.

The crag is bounded on the left by Mickledore, a deep gap between Scafell and Scafell Pike. Broad Stand is the route from Mickledore to the summit of Scafell: a popular but dangerous scramble. On the right of the main crag is the easy route of Lord's Rake, also leading to the top, and between Mickledore and the Rake is a tenuous ledge known as Rake's Progress from which most of the climbs start. Three enormous gullies divide the face: from left to right, Moss Ghyll, Steep Ghyll and Deep Ghyll. Beyond the Rake there lies the Shamrock Buttress and other rocks of less interest.

There are climbs of all grades, but they all have an air of seriousness. The E Buttress is on the Eskdale side of Mickledore. It is steep and forbidding and all the climbs are hard. Other crags in the group are: Pike's Crag, on the Wasdale side of Scafell Pike; Esk Buttress and Heron Crag, both on the Eskdale side of the range; Great End, the gullies of which offer good winter climbs.

Various ways up from Mickledore to Scafell were made in the middle of the last century. Deep Ghyll was descended in snow in 1882 by Mumm and King and similar scrambles were accomplished by Haskett Smith in the 1880s, but the first real climb was Slingsby's Chimney (Slingsby, Hastings, E. Hopkinson, Haskett Smith, 1888). Other notable ascents are:

1892   Moss Ghyll – Collie, Hastings, Robinson
1897   Keswick Brothers' Climb – Abraham brothers, Puttrell
1898   Jones's Direct from Lord's Rake – Jones, Walker
1903   Botterill's Slab – Botterill, Williamson, Grant
1912   Hopkinson's Cairn Direct – Herford, Sansom
        Hopkinson's Gully – Herford, Sansom
        Girdle Traverse – Herford, Sansom, Brunskill, Gibson
1914   Central Buttress – Herford, Sansom, Holland
1926   Moss Ghyll Grooves – Kelly, Miss Eden-Smith, Kilshaw
1931   Mickledore Grooves (E) – Kirkus, Waller, Pallis
1932   Great Eastern Route (E) – Linnell, Cross
1938   May Day Climb (E) – Birkett, Hudson, Wilson

Of these the Central Buttress (C.B.) was outstanding for its day and was long regarded as the hardest climb in Britain. It is now graded H.V.S. It contains the well-known Flake Crack. Among the spate of hard post-war climbs the following may be noted (leaders only):

1952   Hell's Groove (E) – Dolphin
1957   Phoenix (E) – Moseley
1959   Centaur (E) – L. Brown
1960   Ichabod (E) – Oliver
1966   Nazgul – L. Brown
1969   Lord of the Rings (E) – Adams/Read
1971   The White Wizard – Bonington
1974   The Cumbrian (Esk) – Valentine, Braithwaite
1976   Lost Horizon (E) – Livesey, Lawrence
1979   Fallout (Esk) – Birkett, Hyslop
1981   The Almighty (E) – Botterill, Lamb
1986   Borderline (E) – Sowden, Berzins
GUIDEBOOK *Scafell, Dow and Eskdale*, Phizacklea.

The most serious *rock-climbing* accident in Britain took place on Scafell Crag when, in 1903, R. W. Broadrick and three companions were killed attempting the slabs below Hopkinson's Cairn.

Schmaderer, Ludwig (1913–45) A leading member of the Munich School who made a number of difficult new climbs in the Alps including the first complete traverse of the Peuterey Ridge (1934 with A. Gottner and F. Krobath).

In 1937 he took part in the second ascent of Siniolchu in Sikkim, was on the unsuccessful ◊ Nanga Parbat expedition of the following year, and in 1939 climbed Tent Peak (7,365 m) in Sikkim (first ascent). Trapped in India by the war he escaped into the mountains, only to be murdered in Spiti in 1945, unaware that the war was over.

Schmid brothers Franz Xaver Schmid (b. 1905) and Toni Schmid (1909–32) were two brothers from the Munich School who did numerous hard climbs, culminating in the first ascent of the ◊ Matterhorn Nordwand in 1931, a significant event in Alpine history. 1931 was Franz's best season – he also did the north faces of Grubenkarspitze and Ortler that year, the first with his brother. Toni was killed attempting the N W Face of Wiesbachhorn in 1932.

At the Olympics of 1932 the brothers were given gold medals for the Matterhorn climb.

Schneider, Erwin (1906–87) An Austrian mountaineer and one of the leading mountain cartographers, best known for his 1:25,000 map of ◊ Mt Everest. Schneider was on the first ascent of Peak Lenin (7,134 m) in the ◊ Pamirs in 1928, along with several other 6,000 m peaks. He was with G. O. ◊ Dyhrenfurth's international ◊ Kangchenjunga expedition of 1930 when they climbed Jongsang (7,483 m) and Nepal Peak (7,180 m). In 1932 he made the first ascent of Huascaran Sur in Peru (6,768 m) along with other peaks and he returned to Peru in 1936 to make a map of Cordillera Huayhuash. He survived the disastrous ◊ Nanga Parbat expedition of 1934 when ◊ Welzenbach and others died.

Apart from the Everest map, he made maps of Alpine areas and ◊ Mt Kenya and was technical director of the German survey in East Nepal 1959–74.

Schubert, Pit (b. 1935) Leading German climber with hard routes to his credit including direct routes on the N Face of Rosengartenspitze and Ciavazes S Face (1961 and 1967). In 1976 with Heinz Baumann he made a dramatic ascent of the S Face of Annapurna IV (7,525 m) and was badly frostbitten. The rest of the expedition gave them up for dead and withdrew from the mountain!

Schubert is a leading member of the ◊ U.I.A.A. Safety Commission, and author of a book on modern alpinism, *Modern Alpine Climbing* (C.P.).

Schuck, Otto An Austrian climber in the second half of the last century who made a number of new routes in the Eastern Alps, particularly the first ascent of the E Face of Watzmann (1881).

Schultz, Karl (1844–1929) A German lawyer who was one of the outstanding climbers of the second half of the nineteenth century. A friend and companion of ◊ Purtscheller and the ◊ Zsigmondys, and something of 'a stormy petrel' (*A.J.*). He attacked ◊ Güssfeldt in print and was himself attacked by ◊ Lammer.

In the Western Alps he made the second ascent of the Biancograt (1883) and a week later the third ascent of the Marinelli Couloir on Monte Rosa, but his outstanding feat was the descent of the Ferpècle Arête of Dent Blanche with Mrs ☿ Jackson, five years before the first ascent. A year later he made the first ascent of Crozzon di Brenta.

In 1885 he was with the Zsigmondys in an attempt on the S Face of Meije, during which Emil Zsigmondy was killed. From then on he climbed exclusively in the Eastern Alps, where he made a number of first ascents.

Schuster, Claud (Lord Schuster) (1869–1956) Mountaineer and skier. Though he made no notable first ascents, Schuster is remembered for three fine books: *Peaks and Pleasant Pastures* (1911), *Men, Women and Mountains* (1931) and *Postscript to Adventure* (1949). President of A.C. 1938–40. He succeeded in abolishing the traditional ballot for new members.

Scoop A rounded niche which may be vertical, or slanting across a rock face. Varies tremendously. A peapod is a scoop shaped like its namesake – there is a famous one at Curbar, Derbyshire.

Scotland, climbing in North and south of the Glasgow–Edinburgh axis Scotland is predominantly mountainous. To the south and the English border are the Southern Uplands and the Galloway Hills. The Merrick (842 m) is the highest summit and there are numerous outcrops on which climbs have been done. Greatest interest, however, centres on the Highlands and Islands among which are:
Northern Highlands This large area lies north of the Dingwall-Kyle of Lochalsh railway. Many of the peaks are not only remote but have attractive shapes and make fine ascents. There is a good deal of metamorphic rock like gneiss and some granite and there is Cambrian quartzite and Old Red Sandstone, but the most striking peaks are Torridonian sandstone: Quinag, Canisp, Stac Pollaidh, An Teallach, Liathach and Ben Alligan are perhaps the best known.

There is rock- and ice-climbing on numerous crags, the best known being Carnmor Crag on Beinn a'Chaisgein Mhor. Routes are VS and above and up to a thousand feet or so. Another popular climbing ground is the impressive buttresses of Coire Mhic Fhearchair on Beinn Eighe – though popular is a relative word in this remote area.

There are impressive sea cliffs near Cape Wrath and two well-known sea-stacks, Am Buachaille in Sandwood Bay and The Old Man of Stoer – both about 60 m high.
Cairngorms The highest part of the Grampian Mountains, between Braemar and the River Spey, Scotland. Glen Avon penetrates into the heart of the group, whose chief summits are Ben Macdhui (1,309 m), Braeriach (1,296 m), Cairn Toul (1,293 m) and Cairn Gorm (1,245 m). There are many other summits only slightly less high. The mountains are rounded, but the corries have magnificent crags. The whole area is barren and wild; the largest area of its kind in Britain. It is a nature reserve.

Lochnagar (1,155 m) is the highest of another group of wild mountains, separated from the Cairngorms by the wide Dee valley. Climbers apply the name 'Cairngorms' to the whole region.

Speyside (Aviemore etc.) and Deeside (Braemar etc.) are the best-known centres, especially the former, which has Glenmore Lodge and the well-known ski hotels. Perhaps more than in most regions, one's base depends on where one is going to climb. There are huts, bothies and so on, but even so, distances tend to be long.

The whole area is very popular with walkers, climbers and skiers. Conditions in winter can be arctic and every precaution is needed to avoid exhaustion and exposure. The vastness of the area has deceived many.

Popular walks (summer) are the four 4,000 ft (1,219 m) peaks (◊ Scottish 4,000s) and the long passes of Lairig Ghru and Lairig an Laoigh.

Climbs in the Cairngorms, particularly on Lochnagar, have been known from an early date, but except in winter the area did not achieve popularity until after the last war, when it began to be extensively developed by Aberdeen climbers such as ◊ Patey and Brooker. The process is continuing and there are now winter and summer climbs of all standards on numerous crags, best known of which are: Garbh Coire, Coire an Dubh Lochain, Coire na Ciche (all on Beinn a'Bhuird); Coire an t'Sneachda, Coire an Lochain (Cairn Gorm); Hell's Lum Crag, Shelter Stone Crag, Carn Etchachan (all above Loch Avon); Coire Etchachan; Coire Sputan Dearg (Ben Macdhui); Coire Bhrochain, Garbh Choire Dhaidh, Garbh Coire Mor (Braeriach-Carn Toul); Sgoran Dubh; Creag an Dubh Loch, Lochnagar (Lochnagar).

Ben Macdhui is reputedly haunted by Ferlas Mhor (the Great Grey Man) (Collie, Kellas and others).

Glencoe A valley in Argyll, scene of the famous Massacre, 1692. In mountaineering terms, it may be said to begin at the Kingshouse Hotel on the edge of Rannoch Moor and run westwards to Glencoe village on Loch Leven, about 23 km. High mountains and crags hem in the valley on both sides. One of the most popular climbing areas in Scotland.

On the N side of the valley the mountains form a simple ridge, the western end of which is the celebrated Aonach Eagach. The S side is more complex with a number of short, steep side valleys running up into the hills, chief of which are Bidean nam Bian (1,150 m), Stob Coire nan Lochan (1,115 m), Stob Coire Sgreamhach (1,072 m) and Stob Dearg of ◊ Buachaille Etive Mor (1,022 m). Below this latter, the long valley of Glen Etive joins Glencoe. Both Glen Etive and Glencoe have motor roads.

The only village is Glencoe, on the shores of Loch Leven. In the valley the accommodation includes the Clachaig and Kingshouse Hotels, Lagangarbh, Black Rock, and other climbers' huts, a private bunk house and a youth hostel.

The winter traverse of Aonach Eagach is a classic, but otherwise the principal climbing, summer and winter, lies on the complex crags of the south flank: Buachaille Etive Mor, Coire Gabhail, Beinn Fhada, Stob Coire Sgreamhach, Lost Valley Buttresses, Gear Aonach, Stob Coire nan Lochan, Aonach Dubh, Coire nam Beith, Bidean nam Bian-Stob Coire nam Beith. The first route made was Collier's Climb, Buachaille Etive Mor (Collie, Collier, Solly 1894).

Central and Western Highlands Apart from Glencoe (above) the chief climbing area of these widespread mountains is the great cirque of ◊ Ben Nevis and Carn Dearg. The Ben offers some of the best winter climbing in Britain as well as numerous summer rock-climbs. Other good climbing crags are Garbh Beinn of Ardgour, with its famous and easy Great Ridge – about 300 m. of V Diff. climbing. There are other and harder routes.

North of the Newtonmore–Spean Bridge road lies Creagh Meaghaidh, where Coire Ardair offers superb winter climbing, rivalling the Ben or Cairngorms.

There are several important outcrops, particularly in Glen Nevis, where Polldubh Crags are popular. All standards up to 90 m.

An area such as this offers endless opportunities for scrambling. The Mamores are well known for this, as is the Forcan Ridge of the Saddle above Glen Sheil further north.

Southern Highlands   South of Rannoch Moor and north of Stirling are some of the most popular areas of the Highlands as far as tourists are concerned. This is Rob Roy country, not to mention the bonny banks of Loch Lomond. It is traversed north–south by the West Highland Way, a long-distance footpath.

The best known rock-climbing is on the Cobbler, the Whangie and Dumbarton Rock. Both the latter are near Dumbarton on the Clyde and are intensely competitive outcrops. The Cobbler climbs are older – genuine mountain peak ascents. Further east, near Balquidder, are the huge Etive Slabs of Beinn Trilleachan. Long routes, VS and above, very popular in the 1960s.

The Islands   Easily the most important island for the mountaineer is ◊ Skye, where there are the Cuillins, the Quirang and the Storr. The Cuillin has a unique place in British climbing.

Adjacent to Skye is Rhum, a nature reserve. Climbing is permitted by authorized parties in the south of the island (highest peak Askival, 810 m). There is a main ridge traverse and rock-climbing which is mostly fairly easy.

After Skye the most important island is Arran, in the Forth of Clyde, where the ridges almost rival those of the Cuillin.

The peaks are in the north-east quarter of the island. They form two roughly parallel ridges joined at their mid-point by a low col known as The Saddle. From The Saddle, Glen Sannox drains north-east to Sannox Bay and Glen Rosa drains south towards Brodick, the principal village of the island.

The so-called Main Ridge is the western one, extending from Ben Nuis (792 m) in the south to Suidhe Fearghas (634 m) in the north. A classic traverse, it includes the celebrated A'Chir (The Comb) and Ceum na Caillich (The Witches' Step). Cir Mhor (798 m), also part of the ridge, has been called 'The Matterhorn of Scotland'.

The eastern ridge is shorter, linking Goat Fell (874 m) to Cioch na h-Oige (661 m). The ascent of Goat Fell, the highest summit in Arran, is by a simple track direct from Brodick, but the rest of the ridge is more difficult. Cioch na h-Oige has one of the largest cliffs in Britain.

There are rock-climbs on most of the peaks, though the rock is a peculiar form of granite. The first ascent of Ben Nuis Chimney in 1901 is one of the classic stories of pioneer days.

On Harris there is the huge bulging crag of Strone Ulladale which was much in vogue in the 1960s, culminating in the ascent of the great overhangs of the Nose (The Scoop: Scott, Lee, Upton, Terry, 1969). More famous, because it featured in a couple of T.V. climbing programmes, is the Old Man of Hoy, a 135 m sea-stack off the island of the same name. The first ascent was by Baillie, Patey and Bonington in 1966; it is now quite popular.

Far out in the Atlantic the island of St Kilda has some huge cliffs. The locals developed considerable climbing skills in the old days as they gathered seabirds' eggs. Some ascents have been made in recent years but the weather is often foul and access is difficult. It is a nature reserve and missile tracking station. The local population was moved to the mainland earlier this century.

Scottish climbing has always developed independently of the rest of Britain. Avoiding the hot-house competition of modern Yorkshire or Peakland climbing, it nevertheless has its own rivalry between the east and west coasts. The country has produced many fine mountaineers: ◊ Raeburn, ◊ Murray, Nimlin, Bell, Kellett, ◊ Cunningham, ◊ Haston and ◊ MacInnes to name just a few. There have also been significant incursions by English climbers from the pioneering days to the present, much to the chagrin of the natives!

GUIDEBOOKS

Handren, *Climber's Guide to Central & Southern Scotland*. (S.M.C.)
Fyffe/Nisbet, *Climber's Guide to the Cairngorms*. (S.M.C.)
Crocket, *Glencoe & Glen Etive*. Rock and Ice Climbs. (S.M.C.)
Marshall, *Ben Nevis*. (S.M.C.)
Stead/Marshall, *Rock & Ice Climbs in Lochaber & Badenoch*. (S.M.C.)
Cuthbertson, *Creag Dubh & Craig-a-Barns*. (S.M.C.)
Wallace, *Arran*. (S.M.C.)
MacKenzie, *Rock & Ice Climbs in Skye*. (S.M.C.)
Fyffe, *Cairngorms Winter Climbs:* Inc. Lochnagar/Creag Meaghaidh. (C.P.)
Kimber, *Winter Climbs: Ben Nevis & Glencoe*. (C.P.)
Crocket/Walker, *A Climbers' Guide to Arran, Arrochar & The Southern Highlands*. (S.M.C.)

There are numerous walking and scrambling guides, especially the S.M.C. District Guides (10 vols.).

Scott, Douglas Keith (b. 1941)   One of the world's leading mountaineers, Scott began climbing at the age of 12. Interested in the concept of big wall climbing, both free and with aid, he tackled some of the great rock routes in ◊ Yosemite, ◊ Norway, and ◊ Baffin Island as well as nearer home at Strone Ulladale and ◊ Anglesey. From 1965 he developed a parallel interest in expeditions, especially to Asia.

He has made 28 expeditions to the high mountains of Asia. He has reached the summit of 25 peaks of which half were first ascents and all were climbed by new routes or for the first time in Alpine style. Apart from his climb up the S W Face of Everest with Dougal Haston during Chris Bonington's expedition of 1975, he has made all his climbs in lightweight or Alpine style without the use of artificial oxygen.

His major expeditions are:

1965   First ascent, Tarso Teiroko, Tibesti Mountains, Sahara
1966   First ascents, Cilo Dag Mountains, S E Turkey
1967   First ascent, S Face Koh-i-Bandaka (6,837 m), Hindu Kush
1971   First British ascent, Salathe Wall, El Capitan, Yosemite
1972   Spring: European Mt Everest Expedition to S W Face
            Summer: First ascent, E Pillar, Mt Asgard, Baffin Island
            Autumn: British Mt Everest Expedition to S W Face
1974   First ascent, S E Spur, P. Lenin (7,189 m), U.S.S.R.
1975   Reached summit of Mt Everest (8,848 m) via S W Face with Dougal Haston as members of the British Everest Expedition (first Britons on summit)
1976   First Alpine-style ascent, S Face, Mt McKinley (6,226 m), Alaska, via new route, British Direct, with Dougal Haston
            First ascent, E Face Direct, Mt Kenya (5,199 m)
1977   First ascent, Ogre (7,330 m), Karakoram
1979   First ascent, N Ridge route, Kangchenjunga (8,593 m), Sikkim/Nepal (without oxygen)
1979   First ascent, N Summit, Kussum Kangguru, Nepal
            First ascent, N Face, Nuptse, Nepal
1980   Alpine-style ascent, Kangchungtse (7,640 m), Nepal
1981   First ascent, E Pillar, Shivling, India
            13 day Alpine-style push, Chamlang N Face to Central Summit, with Reinhold Messner
1982   First ascent, Pungpa Ri (7,445 m), Tibet

First ascent, S Face, Shisha Pangma (8,046 m), Tibet
1983   First ascent, Lobsang Spire, Karakoram
       Ascent, Broad Peak (8,047 m), Karakoram
1984   Ascent, Baruntse (7,143 m), Nepal
       First ascent E Summit, Chamlang (7,287 m), Nepal, and traverse
       over unclimbed Central Summit
       Alpine-style ascent, S E Ridge, Makalu, Nepal, to within 100 m of
       summit
1985   First Alpine-style ascent, Diran (7,260 m), Karakoram
1986   First ascents of rock-climbs, South India
1987   First ascents of rock-climbs, Wadi Rum, Jordan
1988   First ascent, S Face, Jitchudrake (6,793 m), Bhutan, Alpine-style

President Alpine Climbing Group 1976–82.
BOOKS *Big Wall Climbing* (1974); *The Shishapangma Expedition* (with A.
MacIntyre (1984); *Himalayan Climber* (1992).

Scottish 4,000s   Name given to a walk embracing all the 4,000 ft (1,219 m)
peaks in Scotland: four in the ◊ Cairngorms and three in the ◊ Ben Nevis
group. First done by E. Thomas and friends from the Rucksack Club, and
R. S. T. Chorley and friends from the Fell and Rock Club in 1924. Both
groups used a car between the two mountain areas. The first traverse without
car was by F. Williamson in 1954 (158 km, 4,000 m, 50 hours).

Scrambling   In Victorian times this was another term for climbing, as in
Whymper's *Scrambles Amongst the Alps*, but nowadays it refers to ascents
which, though they need the use of hands, are too easy to be regarded as
technical rock-climbs. Famous examples are Crib Goch, Jack's Rake and
Aonach Eagach. The *vie ferratae* of the Dolomites and *klettersteig* of the
German Alps (◊ Alps) are scrambles.
   In the 1980s scrambling became a sub-sport under the influence of a series
of guidebooks published by Cicerone Press (see below), which listed dozens
of virtually unknown routes.
   Although scrambling is technically easier than rock-climbing it has its own
dangers. The exposure can be considerable and the rock is frequently
unsound or well mixed with grass and heather and since scrambling is often
done unroped, great care is needed. In winter conditions many scrambles
become serious climbs.
GUIDEBOOKS *Scrambles in Snowdonia; Scrambles in the Lake District; More
Scrambles in the Lake District; Scrambles in Skye; Scrambles in Lochaber*
(All C.P.)

Scree (Am.: talus; G.: Geröll; F.: éboulis; It.: ghaione)   Rock detritus
from a crag covering the slopes below. In England the most spectacular scree
slopes are those above Wast Water in the Lake District. Scree particles can
vary from boulder-size (sometimes called a boulder slope) to tiny pebbles – it
seems to have an uncanny knack of grading itself. Large scree is always
tiresome and can be dangerous if it lies at a steep angle. It can be crossed by
scree-hopping (leaping lightly from boulder to boulder), but a certain skill is
required to judge those boulders which will not turn over. Loose scree (i.e.
small scree) is tiresome in ascent but often forms a quick way down from a
crag by scree-running, i.e. short hops downhill – again, good judgement is
required. A long slope of loose scree is known as a scree-shoot or stone-shoot,
for example, the Great Stone Shoot of Sgurr Alasdair in Skye.
   Small slopes of scree can lie on ledges, particularly in gullies, and a climber

Sea-cliffs at Jack Scout's Cove. (*W. Unsworth*)

must be careful not to knock them down on those people who may be below. Some gullies are filled with scree from top to bottom and are known as scree gullies.

Scriven, George (1856–1931) Irish doctor who was a companion of ◊ Conway and ◊ Penhall on some of their early Alpine climbs. After 1888 he climbed exclusively in the Eastern Alps, especially the Dolomites. Scriven was a rugby international: Captain of Ireland, 1882.

Sea-cliff climbing A branch of rock-climbing which has become increasingly popular in Britain over the last few years. Though most of the cliffs are easy to reach, the climbs are not always easy of access and to reach the foot of the cliff may involve difficult climbing or abseiling. Tides also present problems, as do occasional rollers (i.e. big waves) which seem to come in sequence. On some cliffs, the top tends to be very loose. Where cliffs are on private land there may be restricted access. Seabirds may be a nuisance because of their slime, or, in Scotland, their aggressiveness. There are also problems of conservation and some cliffs are banned during the nesting season.

The sea-cliff climbing goes back to the early days of the sport when there were climbs done on Sark, St Kilda and Beachy Head. The latter had a certain vogue: Mummery, Crowley and others climbed on the chalk, sometimes cutting steps in it with their ice axes.

The chief development was that in Cornwall, where ◊ Andrews started the cliff-climbing that has grown steadily ever since. The firm, rough granite of Cornwall was a major factor here. The cliffs were also used by the commandos for training, and some of the later explorers were commandos or ex-commandos.

Little seems to have been done on other sea-cliffs until after the last war, though mention might be made of A. W. Kelly's ascent of the Sugar Loaf, a sea-stack off the Isle of Man (1933). The vogue for sea-cliffs really began in the 1950s and gained momentum in the sixties. Mention might be made of Cullernose Point, North Devon, the Gower, Swanage, St Bees, Torbay, Isle of Man, Lundy, Great and Little Ormes, Hoy, Pembroke and, most significant of all, ◊ Craig Gogarth in Anglesey.

Little seems to have been done on Continental sea-cliffs with the exception of the Calanques, on the south coast of France, which have long been popular, though development is now taking place on the Costa Blanca, Spain.

Sella, Vittorio (1859–1943)   Member of the influential Sella family of Biella, Italy; nephew of Quintino Sella; founder of the Italian Alpine Club.

Sella was a distinguished climber, explorer and photographer. He made the first winter traverses of the following: Matterhorn (1882), Monte Rosa (1884), Grand Paradiso, Lyskamm (1885) and Mont Blanc (1888). In 1889 he was with ◊ Dent in the Caucasus, where he returned in 1890 and 1896, making a number of first ascents. In 1897 he was with the Abruzzi Expedition to Alaska and took part in the first ascent of Mt St Elias. He was with Abruzzi again on an expedition to Ruwenzori in 1906 where further first ascents were made (◊ Abruzzi).

Sella paid two visits to the Himalaya. In 1899 he was with ◊ Freshfield on the famous tour of Kangchenjunga, and in 1909 he accompanied Abruzzi on the first real reconnaissance of K2. Sella's photographs of the area played a big part in the successes of later expeditions.

As a mountain photographer, Sella must forever rank amongst the greatest. His expedition pictures contain a wealth of detail and information, are technically brilliant and of the highest artistic quality. They have frequently been reproduced. His Alpine studies, too, are of the highest class; a collection of a hundred of them, *Among the Alps*, was published privately by Samuel Aitken.

Senn, Franz (1831–84)   Known as the *Gletscherpfarrer*, Senn was a priest who opened the Otztal, making many first ascents of the peaks, including Fluchtkogel, Weisseespitze, Vord.Brochkogel etc. He was a founder member of the German Alpine Club.

Sentry box   A large niche in a rock face, sometimes offering a stance and belay. There is a well-known one at the Black Rocks, Derbyshire. Term becoming obsolescent.

Sérac   A pinnacle or tower of ice. Séracs are found in ◊ ice-falls and at the edge of ice-cliffs (e.g. Route Major, Mont Blanc). They can attain an enormous size and because they are unstable are potentially dangerous.

Sherpas   A race of people, Tibetan in origin, who settled in the Sola Khumbu area, south of Everest, and the Walungchung area near Kangchenjunga. They are Mayahana Buddhists and revere the Dalai Lama. Their language is Tibetan and has no written form, though many speak Nepali and some English. Their villages are mostly between 2,100 and 4,200 m above sea level and it is estimated that the Sherpa population is about 100,000. Unlike the Gurkhas, they are totally unwarlike.

It was primarily at the suggestion of ◊ Bruce that Sherpas were used as porters on the first Everest expeditions, and they have been used by every expedition since, except that after the partition of India, they were not allowed into Moslem territories such as the Karakoram. They quickly developed from being mere load-carriers into climbers in their own right and many Sherpas have reached high summits, including ◊ Tenzing on the first ascent of Everest. However, it must not be forgotten that a Sherpa's prime duty is load-carrying, usually between the lower camps. If he goes higher and becomes a high-altitude Sherpa, he regards this as promotion, since it will ensure further expedition work and employment in the lucrative trekking business. The chief Sherpa on an expedition is the Sirdar. A Sherpa often shares in the spoils left over after an expedition too. Many Sherpas now find lucrative employment in the tourist industry, conducting treks.

Shipton, Eric Earle (1907–77) One of the most significant explorer-climbers of the present century. A believer, like ◊ Tilman, who was often his partner, in the small, light expedition.

Shipton lived in Kenya from 1929 to 1932, where he met Tilman, and Wyn Harris. With the latter he climbed Mt Kenya, making the first ascent of Nelion and the second of Batian (1929). The following year he made the first traverse of Nelion–Batian with Tilman.

In 1931 he joined ◊ Smythe's expedition to Kamet and was one of the four men to reach the top – the highest peak climbed at that time. He then took part in the following expeditions:

1933 Everest; reached about 8,400 m
1934 The forcing of the Rishi Ganga, with Tilman
1935 Leader of a monsoon reconnaissance to Everest
1936 Everest; attempts ruined by weather
1937 With Tilman, explored the Shaksgam area of Karakorum
1938 Everest (Tilman's Expedition); ruined by weather
1939 Second Karakoram Expedition, Hispar, Biafo, Panmah, Chogo Lungma areas
1951 Everest reconnaissance; penetrated into the Western Cwm
1952 Leader of the Cho Oyu attempt
1957 Karakoram; third visit
1958–64 Six expeditions to Patagonia, included the N–S crossing of the South Patagonian Ice-cap, 1960–61

Shipton was Consul General in Kashgar, 1940–2 and 1946–8. He held a similar post in Kunming 1949–51. During his second visit to Kashgar he attempted Bogdo Ola (see his *Mountains of Tartary*). He was President of the A.C. 1965–8. His books are: *Nanda Devi* (1936), *Blank on the Map* (1938), *Upon that Mountain* (1948), *The Mountains of Tartary* (1951), *Mount Everest Reconnaissance Expedition, 1951* (1952), *Land of Tempest* (1963), *That Untravelled World* (1969).

Siege tactics A method whereby a mountain or cliff is climbed by making repeated attempts, pushing the route a little further each time and retiring to base in between attempts. ◊ Fixed ropes are left in place so that the previous high point is quickly attainable each time.

The method is extensively used in the Himalayas and has been employed on the first winter ascent of the Eigerwand, the French route on the Troll Wall, Norway, and the ascent of the Nose of El Capitan, Yosemite, among others. The ethics of sieging are much discussed by climbers. It is now generally felt that pure rock-climbs should not be sieged, and there is support growing for the idea that no climbs anywhere should be sieged, though obviously there are severe practical difficulties in the Himalaya.

Simler, Josias (1530–76) A naturalist at Zurich University and one of the first to practise snowcraft. He wrote *Concerning the Difficulties of Alpine Travel and the Means by which they may be Overcome* – almost certainly the first Alpine textbook. It includes the first description of crampons, though these had been in use for many years.

Ski mountaineering A development of ski touring (as distinct from downhill ski running). The techniques and equipment are outside the scope of this book, but it is germane to say that the ski mountaineer, as in all ski touring, faces greater hazards than the man who keeps to a beaten piste. He must recognize the lie of the land, estimate the quality of the snow (which may change considerably during the course of the tour) and be aware of avalanche and crevasse dangers.

It may be possible for the ski mountaineer to make a complete ascent to the summit on his skis, with the possibility of a traverse, or the skis may be left at a convenient col and the final summit ridge ascended on foot.

Skis originated in Norway and the first Englishman to use them is claimed to be W. C. ◊ Slingsby. They quickly spread to the Alps where their popularity was encouraged by ◊ Lunn who made the first ski ascents of many of the big peaks such as Dom, Eiger and Weisshorn. His guidebook to the Oberland was the first ski mountaineering guidebook to be produced (1920). In recent years the ◊ High Level Route from Chamonix to Zermatt has become a popular ski tour. In 1972 there was a British ski traverse of the Alps.

An extreme form of the sport has developed in the descent of steep faces on ski. The following are notable:

1933 F. Rieckh – E Face, Weisskugel; N Face, Zuckerhutl; E Face, Schrankogel (45°)
1935 Kugler and Schlager – N Face, Fuscherkarkopf (50°)
1941 E. Henrich – N E Face, Ruderhofspitze
1960 L. Terray – N Face, Mont Blanc
1964 A. Hörtnagel and H. Wagner – N Face, Hochfernerspitze
1966 K. Lapuch and M. Oberegger – E Face, Göll
1968 Lapuch and Oberegger – N Face, Sonnblick (55°)
      S. Saudan – Whymper Couloir, Verte (55°); Gervasutti Couloir, Tacul (50°)
1969 S. Saudan – Marinelli Couloir, Monte Rosa (45–50°)
      Lapuch and Oberegger – N W Face, Gross Wiesbachhorn (60°); E Face *intégrale*, Monte Rosa (55° plus)
1973 S. Cachat-Rosset – Couturier Couloir, Aig. Verte
      H. Holzer – Brenva Face, Mont Blanc
1988 P. Tardival – Gd Pilier d'Angle (65°)

The second descent of Mont Blanc N Face was made by Giscard d'Estaing, later President of France.

The average angle for a downhill race course is 15°, which gives some idea of the audacity of these routes.

May to July is the best time for this steep skiing, and soft snow is desirable, though it increases the chance of avalanches. Some descents are made roped, pitch by pitch, others solo (e.g. Saudan). Various safety devices are employed though their efficacy is open to doubt.

Another development has been the very short ski (60 cm) called 'snow gliders' or 'ski boards'. These are light enough to be carried on summer ascents and are used to descend snow-fields and glaciers on the return, thus

The Cuillin of Skye from Elgol. (*T. D. Unsworth*)

shortening the day. In 1961 the Austrians Winter and Zakarias used these short skis to descend the Pallavicini Couloir of the Gross Glockner (55°).

Skye Most important of the Inner Hebrides, Scotland. Reached by ferry from Mallaig, Glenelg or (most usual) Kyle of Lochalsh. The principal mountains are the Black Cuillin. Other hills are the Quirang and the Storr, both noted for unusual pinnacles including the Old Man of Storr (first ascent, Whillans, 1955). The rock is bad. Macleod's Maidens are sea-stacks near Loch Bracadale.

In climbing terms 'the Cuillin' means the Black Cuillin, a chain of spiky gabbro and basalt peaks stretching from Sligachan in the north to Loch Scavaig and the neighbouring Marsco–Blaven ridge. The adjacent Red Cuillin are comparatively uninteresting.

The chief centres are: Sligachan Hotel, Loch Scavaig (climbing hut), and, above all, Glenbrittle (hut, Youth Hostel, camp site, accommodation). There are roads to Sligachan and Glen Brittle, but not Scavaig.

The main ridge forms a magnificent horseshoe round Loch Coruisk and its traverse is the best expedition of its kind in Britain. (First traverse: Shadbolt and McLaren, 1911; first winter traverse: Patey, MacInnes, Robertson, Crabbe, 1965; first woman's traverse: Mabel Barker with C. D. Frankland, 1926). A so-called Greater Traverse, including Clach Glas and Blaven, has also been done, but is not popular. A time of 12–15 hours is normal for the traverse, but it has been done in much less (D. Davis, 3 hr, 49 min, 30 sec 12 August 1986). The peaks from S–N (the usual way) are: Gars-bheinn (894 m), Sgurr a Choire Bhig (878 m), Sgurr nan Eag (926 m), Sgurr Dubh na Da Bheinn (935 m), Sgurr Thearlaich (976 m), Sgurr Mhic Coinnich (947 m), An Stac (952 m), Inaccessible Pinnacle (983 m), Sgurr Dearg (977 m), Sgurr na Banachdich (965 m), Sgurr Thormaid (927 m), Sgurr a' Ghreadaidh (965 m), Sgurr a' Mhadaidh (917 m), Bidean Druim nan Ramh (869 m), An Caisteal (832 m), Sgurr na Bhairnich (863 m), Bruach na Frithe (958 m), Sgurr a' Fionn Choire (934 m), Bhasteir Tooth (914 m), Am Bhasteir (936 m), and Sgurr nan Gillean (965 m). (Sgurr Alasdair [1991 m] is the highest summit of the island and is often included on the traverse, though it is off the main ridge.)

Off the main ridge lie: Sgurr Sgumain (946 m), Sgurr Dubh Mor (942 m) and various smaller peaks. Sgurr Coire an Lochain (756 m) was the last peak to be climbed in Britain (1896, Collie, Howell, Naismith, Mackenzie).

Some easy rock-climbing is needed on many parts of the ridge, but the various peaks and corries have many buttresses giving climbs in their own right. Easily most popular are the climbs of Coire Lagan, on the vast crag of Sron na Ciche. Here is the curious pinnacle of The Cioch. There are climbs of all standards.

Skye began to be developed as a climbing area before most other parts of Britain because of its mountaineering qualities as opposed to pure rock-climbing. (◊ Pilkington brothers; Collie.) Notable ascents include:

1836	Sgurr nan Gillean – J. D. Forbes, D. MacIntyre
1873	Sgurr Alasdair – A. Nicolson
1873	Knight's Peak – W. Knight and guide
1874	Sgurr Dubh Mor – A. Nicolson
1880	Inaccessible Pinnacle – C. Pilkington
1883	Bidean Druim nan Ramn – L. Pilkington, Hulton, H. Walker
1887	Sgurr Thearlaich – C. Pilkington, Walker, Heelis
	Sgurr Mhic Coinnich – same party
	Bhasteir Tooth – Collie, King
1891	Thearlaich–Dubh Gap – Collie, King, Mackenzie
1895	Waterpipe Gully – Kelsall, Hallitt
1897	King's Chimney, Mhic Coinnich – King, Naismith, Douglas
1906	The Cioch Ordinary – Collie, Mackenzie
1907	Cioch Direct – A. Abraham, Harland
1918	Crack of Doom – Pye, Shadbolt
1919	Cioch West – Holland, Carr, Miss Pilley
1950	The Fluted Buttress – Dixon, Brooker
1951	The Crack of Dawn – Dixon, Brooker
1960	King Cobra – Bonington, Patey
1962	Trophy Crack – Walsh and party
1968	Purple Haze, Sgumain – Guillard, Irwen
1977	Stairway to Heaven, Bla Bheinn – Fowler, Thomas
1983	Internationale, Kilt Rock – Swindon, Grindley
1983	Killer Whale, Kilt Rock – Birkett, Lyle
1985	Over the Rainbow, Kilt Rock – Birkett, Wightman

Sky hook (Am.: bathook)   A chromolly hook about 7 cm long to which an étrier can be attached. The hooked end has a diameter of about 2 cm and is finished with a squared chisel edge. It can be hooked on to minuscule projections and save the use of a bolt or peg and is secure.

Slab (G.: Platte; Fr.: dalle, plaque; It.: placca)   A flat area of rock inclined approximately between 30° and 75°. May form a pitch of a climb, virtually a whole climb (e.g. Botterill's Slab, Scafell), or be large enough to hold several climbs (e.g. Idwal Slabs).

Sleeping bag   Only good-quality sleeping bags are suitable for mountain environments, especially at high altitudes or under winter conditions. The best are filled with down or a feather/down mix, and are box-quilted to avoid 'cold spots'. A 'mummy' bag is one which is approximately shaped to the body and includes a headpiece. In very cold conditions two bags may be used, an inner and an outer.

For a large party on the hills, especially in winter, a sleeping bag should be carried as an emergency against exposure. (◊ Duvet; Pied d'éléphant.)

Sligachan A lonely inn in Skye at the northern foot of the Cuillins. It was the great pioneering centre in the early days of climbing in the island but most people now prefer Glenbrittle. Prof. J. N. ◊ Collie spent the last years of his life here.

Slings Loops of nylon tape used for ◊ belays, ◊ runners and ◊ abseiling and an important part of a climber's equipment. Although it is possible to make a sling by joining the ends of a tape with a tape knot (◊ knots) it is usual now to buy the slings ready-stitched in loops. No attempt should be made at home stitching! Standard lengths for slings are 1·2 m, 0·6 m and 0·45 m. The tape can vary in width from 15 to 50 mm but 25 mm is most generally useful. It can be flat or tubular. A variety of slings, with associated karabiners, is always useful on a climb.

Nylon or perlon rope should not run over a sling of similar material because the friction causes melting of the fibres. A karabiner should always be interspersed. Rope slings, of nylon or hemp, are little used today.

Slingsby, William Cecil (1849–1929) One of the great central figures of British mountaineering during the closing decades of the last century. A Yorkshire squire and textile manufacturer, Slingsby spent his boyhood in the limestone hills of the Craven area, which aroused in him a passionate interest in climbing and pot-holing that lasted throughout his long life. This was further enhanced by being related to other climbers of the times – the Hopkinsons, Tribes, and later, Winthrop Young, who was his son-in-law.

His greatest affection was for Norway; the mountains and the people. He first visited that country in 1872 and paid 15 subsequent visits, exploring and climbing what was then virtually unknown territory. He made many first ascents, including the formidable-looking Skagastolstind (Jotenheim Mountains) in 1876, which he completed solo when his Norwegian guides refused to continue. He was probably the first Englishman to learn the art of skiing. Wrote: *Norway, the Northern Playground* (1904).

Slingsby's first Alpine season was 1878 and was of little account, but in 1879 he climbed the Weissmies without guides and made traverses of Castor and Pollux, Mont Blanc and Dent d'Hérens. He also climbed the Matterhorn. From then on his summers were divided between the Alps and Norway. In 1887 he made the first ascent of Pt Barnes in the Bouquetins and the first S–N traverse of the Aig. Rouges of Arolla.

In 1892 and 1893 he was one of the élite climbing group centred around A. F. ◊ Mummery and took part in the famous attempt on the N Face of the Plan and the first ascent of the Requin. Slingsby's superb icemanship played a considerable part in both climbs.

He was a passionate propagandist of British rock-climbing and one of the leading pioneers. His many first ascents include Slingsby's Chimney on Scafell (1888) and Eagle's Nest Ridge Direct, Great Gable (1892), where he seconded Solly.

He was a member or honorary member of most British climbing and caving clubs. He died peacefully at his home in 1929.

Smearing Where no foothold exists it is sometimes possible to get upwards pressure from friction between the sole of the rock boot and the rock itself. ◊ Sticky soles help here.

Smith, Albert (1816–60)   A journalist and showman who, after several previous attempts, succeeded in climbing Mont Blanc in 1851. The following year he made his ascent the subject of an 'entertainment' in London, which ran for six years and made Smith a wealthy man. He also wrote an account of his adventures in *The Story of Mont Blanc* (1853).

Smith made no other ascents, but he was genuinely fond of the Alps and his show did much to influence public opinion favourably towards alpinism. He was an Original Member of the Alpine Club and the first of that body to have climbed Mont Blanc.

Smith, Eaglesfield Bradshaw (d. 1881)   One of the Alpine pioneers who made some easy, but popular, first ascents: Dent du Midi (1855), Mittel Gipfel of Wildstrubel (1857) and Oldenhorn (1857).

Smith, Robin (1939–62)   An outstanding Scottish climber who played a significant part in the raising of climbing standards on Scottish mountains. Among many first ascents are Shibboleth, Buachaille Etive Mor (A. Frazer) (1958); The Bat, Carn Dearg (D. Haston) (1959); Yo-Yo, Aonach Dubh (D. Hughes) (1959); Gob, Carnmore Crag (D. Haston) (1960). His skill as an ice-climber is exemplified by his eponymous route on Gardyloo Buttress, Ben Nevis, which he completed with J. R. Marshall in 1960.

Smith was killed with W. ◊ Noyce whilst descending Pic Garmo in the Pamirs.

Smith, William (1827–99)   At the age of 15, with his brother and fellow pupils from Hofwyl School, made the first ascent of the popular Rifelhorn at Zermatt.

Smyth brothers   James Grenville Smyth (1825–1907) and Christopher Smyth (1827–1900) were parsons who, in 1854 and 1855, began the serious exploration of the higher Zermatt peaks. In 1854 they made the first ascent of Strahlhorn and the first English ascent of the Ostspitze of Monte Rosa. In the following year they were with ◊ Hudson and ◊ Ainslie in guideless ascents of Breithorn and Klein Matterhorn and finally, the first ascent of Monte Rosa. Later that season they were with Hudson again on the first guideless ascent of Mont Blanc.

They visited the Alps occasionally after this but did nothing else of note. In 1854 they were accompanied by their brother, Edmund Smyth, who, as an officer in the Indian army, did some early Himalayan exploration.

Smythe, Francis Sydney (1900–49)   A very popular mountaineering writer of the years immediately before the Second World War, and an accomplished mountaineer.

Smythe sprang to Alpine prominence in 1927 when he made the second ascent of the Ryan–Lochmatter route on the Plan (with J. H. B. Bell) and the first ascent, with Graham ◊ Brown, of the Sentinelle Route on the Brenva Face of Mont Blanc. A year later he and Brown climbed Route Major on the same face. These two Brenva climbs were the most important contributions by British alpinists to the inter-war Alpine scene.

In 1930, Smythe was a member of the unsuccessful international Kangchenjunga Expedition. In the following year he led his own expedition to

Kamet (7,756 m) with considerable success; Kamet was the highest summit attained at that time and the first summit over 25,000 ft ever reached.

On the 1933 Everest Expedition Smythe equalled the height record of 8,573 m set by Norton in 1924. He was also a member of the 1936 and 1938 Everest Expeditions. He also climbed in Garhwal and the Canadian Rockies. During the war he acted as an instructor of mountain troops.

In 1927 Smythe abandoned his profession of engineer to become a full-time author. He wrote or edited numerous books on mountaineering which had great vogue at the time, though his somewhat romantic philosophy of climbing is little echoed today. He was a superb photographer.

He was taken ill in India while organizing an expedition in 1949, and, though flown home, had a relapse and died.

Snow blindness   A temporary but painful blindness caused by the glare of the sun from snow and ice over an extended period, for example, during an Alpine climb. Protection is afforded by sun-glasses or snow-goggles: but they should be of good quality. If the glasses are broken, protection may be afforded by an eye mask made from paper or card, with tiny slits to see through. An old remedy for snow blindness was to bathe the eyes in a solution of gunpowder!

Snow bridge   A blockage of snow spanning a ◊ crevasse. Some are quite tenuous and if they have to be crossed require careful testing by the leader. He is securely belayed for this and he in turn belays the next man, and so on. Bridges may well collapse even after two or three people have crossed them. They are often much weaker in the afternoon after several hours of sunshine.

Snow cave (snow hole)   (a) An emergency shelter dug in snow. A bank of firm snow at least 30° and 2·5 m thick is required, usually where the snow has drifted. Two tunnels are dug, 1·5 m apart, into the bank to a depth of about 1·5 m. They are then joined together inside and the cave suitably enlarged. Points to note are: the entrances should be as low as possible to conserve heat; one entrance should be permanently blocked after construction if possible; the other should be blocked with a rucksack as a 'door'; ice axes should be taken into the cave for emergency; an air hole is needed.

The digging of a snow cave takes several hours and should only be undertaken in an extreme emergency.

In the Alps and other ranges, natural crevasses have often been used as shelters from a storm – the main thing is to get out of the wind.

(b) Snow caves are often used in the Himalaya or Andes as an intermediate camp on a ridge, thus dispensing with tents. Light but robust shovels are carried for this purpose.

Snow-climbing   A major part of mountaineering skill, both in the Alps and higher mountain ranges, as well as in Britain during winter conditions. Allied to, but different from, ◊ ice-climbing.

The safe climbing of steep snow slopes depends upon experience, and particularly upon the recognition of the snow quality. This varies enormously: it can be extremely firm and compacted, wet and slushy, powdery, or crusty (when a thin layer of hard snow lies over softer snow). It might be lying over ice or hiding ◊ crevasses. Snow which is quite safe in the early morning may become dangerous later in the day after the sun has been on it.

Steep faces of snow or snow gullies are subject to avalanche. Snow will avalanche at a very low angle given the conditions and there is no certain way of knowing what will and what will not avalanche. As a rule, however, steep slopes should be avoided for about three days after a heavy fall of new snow. (◊ Avalanche.)

◊ Crevasses are dealt with elsewhere. Where thin snow lies over ice, the climb should be treated as an ◊ ice-climb, and crampons worn.

The best snow is compacted snow which allows the climber to kick steps in it. A short sharp kick is given, forming a step which points slightly downwards as it goes in. A steady rhythm is necessary or step-kicking becomes tiring. The second and third man improve the steps by kicking too, and it is possible to change leaders on a long climb and thus share the work. All the climbers move together. It may be necessary to cut the occasional step using the blade of the axe but this is not usual today: if the snow is that hard, it is better to use crampons and treat it as an ice-climb.

It is common practice now to wear crampons on all snow- and ice-climbs, but there are times when the snow is so soft that it balls up the crampons and they become a nuisance, even dangerous.

When long axes were more common, they were used as 'third legs': the axe was shoved into the slope ahead of the climber and used for balance when he stepped up. On normal slopes now, it is usual for the axe to be held across the chest in the position of braking, so as to be ready to hold a slip should one occur. For this, the right hand holds the head of the axe and the left the shaft (or vice versa). If the climber falls, he rolls on to his axe and gradually presses it into the snow. The axe then acts as a brake. This is possibly the most important use of the axe on snow-climbs and the technique should be practised beforehand on short, clear slopes so that it becomes automatic.

Where the climbers are moving together, it is normal to shorten the rope to about 6 m between each man. The spare coils are wrapped round the body and tied off at the waist, and a couple of coils are usually carried in the hand. In the event of a slip the remaining climbers plunge their axes into the snow and whip the coils round to form an emergency belay.

If the snow is very steep, or has been interrupted by an ice pitch or rock pitch, then the rope is run out as in ◊ rock-climbing. If possible, a rock peg provides the best belay, but failing that a ◊ dead man can be used, or the traditional axe shaft. For this the shaft is driven into the snow as far as possible and above the belayer. He ties on to it as in rock-climbing and uses a belay to bring up the next man and so on. This method is invariably used in the Alps where the time taken to place a dead man is too great, though the dead man is safer.

Snow ridges can be very narrow and may be ◊ corniced. In the latter case a line should be chosen well back from the edge, in case the cornice breaks off. If a climber falls from a ridge, his companion should immediately slide the other way as a counterbalance – a frightening but effective device.

In traversing steep snow slopes, the long axe has an advantage since it can be used as a prop against the snow, but balance and the proper kicking of steps is the real answer.

Very soft snow, or crusted snow, is extremely exhausting. On some expeditions to higher ranges, snow shoes (racquets) have been used to overcome this, but they are not common in the Alps or in Britain.

(See *Modern Snow and Ice Techniques*, by W. March.)

Snowdon (1,085 m) The highest summit in Britain south of the Scottish border. It rises as a complex of sharp ridges in the angle formed by the Llanberis and Nantgwynant valleys.

The summit, Yr Wyddfa, has a café and is connected to Llanberis by the

Approaching Snowdon by the Crib Goch ridge. (*T. D. Unsworth*)

only mountain railway in Britain. The other popular ways of ascent are: by track from Llanberis, the Watkin Path from Nantgwynant, the Snowdon Ranger path, the Pyg Track from Pen y Pass, and via the Crib Goch Ridge from Pen y Pass. All are extremely popular.

Important subsidiary summits of the massif are: Crib y Ddysgl (1,065 m), Crib Goch (921 m) and Y Lliwedd (898 m). The Snowdon Horseshoe Walk embraces these as well as Yr Wyddfa: a classic walk.

The ridges enfold a number of small lakes (llyns) including: Llydaw, Glaslyn, Teryn, Glas and Arddu. All the ridges have important north-facing crags, including Lliwedd, Llechog, Clogwyn Du'r Arddu, Dinas Mot, Cyrn Las, Clogwyn y Person and Clogwyn y Ddysgl. Yr Wyddfa itself provides a number of gullies for winter climbing.

Snowdonia The mountains of North Wales surrounding the principal massif of Snowdon (Yr Wyddfa, 1,085 m). The area is bounded to the north by the coastal strip (Bangor, Caernarvon), to the west by the Lleyn Peninsula, to the east by the Vale of Conway and to the south by the Vale of Ffestiniog. Most of this is a National Park.

Major roads penetrate the area, dividing it into easily accessible segments. In the south, the road from Bettws y Coed to Beddgelert cuts off the Moelwyns (Moelwyn Mawr, 770 m) and Moel Siabod (873 m). To the west of the Caernarvon–Beddgelert road lies Moel Hebog (782 m) and east of it lies Snowdon. Then comes the ◊ Llanberis Pass, the Glyders (Glyder Fawr, 999 m), the Vale of ◊ Ogwen and, finally, the Carneddau (Carnedd Llywellyn, 1,062 m). Despite this accessibility, the mountain groups are, within themselves, rugged and wild.

For climbers, the chief villages are Capel Curig, Llanberis, Nant Peris, Bethesda, Beddgelert, Bettws y Coed and Rhyd Ddu – the first three of which are most popular; though there are climbing huts, camp sites, etc. throughout the area in great profusion.

Walking is more rugged than in the Lakes, often involving scrambles, for instance, Bristly Ridge, Crib Goch, Tryfan, Cnicht. Popular walks include the Snowdon Horseshoe, the Glyders, the Carneddau, Moel Siabod and the Moelwyns. The ◊ Welsh 3,000s is one of the most popular long-distance walks in Britain.

Rock-climbing is practised throughout the area, though the main centres are still the traditional ones of Ogwen and Llanberis. The rock is nearly always sound and the climbs are of every length and grade. The first climb was the W Buttress of Lliwedd, done by Stocker and Wall in 1883. Developments since the last war, especially at Llanberis, Clogwyn Du'r Arddu and Gogarth (though the last is not strictly Snowdonia), have put the area well to the front in British climbing. (See individual crags and areas.)

Llanberis Pass A long, sombre valley stretching north-west from Pen y Pass, Snowdonia, to Nant Peris and one of the most popular climbing areas in Britain. It is known simply as 'The Pass'. The nearest centre is Llanberis, but there are climbing huts in the Pass, and a good motor road along its length makes it easily accessible from all parts of the district.

The crags are numerous and their arrangement intricate. On the north side of the road the chief crags are: Craig Ddu, Clogwyn y Grochan, Carreg Wastad, Dinas Cromlech. On the south side they are: Clogwyn y Ddysgl, Cyrn Las, Clogwyn y Person, Crib Goch, Dinas Mot and Dinas Bach. There are others.

◊ Pen y Pass was an early centre of Welsh climbing and notable ascents included:

1897   The Black Cleft, Dinas Mot – J. M. A. Thomson
1898   The Parson's Nose – Kitson, Corbett, Evans, Bedford
1904   Great Gully, Cyrn Las – Thomson, Smith
1906   Schoolmasters' Gully, Cyrn Las – Mitchell, Barker, Drew, Atchison
1908   Reade's Route, Crib Goch – Reade, Bartrum.

All these were on the south side of the Pass. The north side began to be developed in the thirties, chiefly owing to J. M. ◊ Edwards, though there were fine leads elsewhere, most notably Main Wall, Cyrn Las (Roberts, Cooke, 1935), Direct Route and W Rib, Dinas Mot by Kirkus (1930, 1931) and Diagonal Route, Dinas Mot (Birtwistle and Parkinson, 1938).

After the war the Pass, along with Clogwyn Du'r Arddu, played the most significant part in the rise of rock-climbing standards. Those involved included Harding, Moulam, Brown, Whillans and others and the era can be symbolized by the first ascent of Cenotaph Corner, Dinas Cromlech (Brown, Belshaw, 1952).

More recently some of the big slate quarries such as Vivian and Dinorwic have been developed to give hard climbs.

Idwal One of the most popular climbing areas of Snowdonia, it comprises a series of cliffs surrounding Llyn Idwal, a hanging valley above Ogwen. The principal cliffs are: Idwal Slabs, Slabs E Wall, Holly Tree Wall, Gribin Facet (Clogwyn y Tarw), Upper Cliff of Glyder Fawr and the Devil's Kitchen Cliffs (Clogwyn y Geifr). There are a number of minor cliffs, too, and Y Garn usually offers easy snow-climbs in winter.

The Slabs offer mostly easy climbing of some length but without variety: frequently used by novices under instruction. Their E Wall is steep and fierce. The Devil's Kitchen is a deep and striking gully, famous in pioneering days and a trap for the unwary.

The first climb was the Central Gully of Glyder Fawr by J. M. A. ◊ Thomson in 1894. Other notable first ascents include:

1895　Grey Rib, Glyder Fawr – J. M. A. Thomson
　　　 Devil's Kitchen (Twll Du) (winter ascent) – Thomson, Hughes
1897　Slabs Ordinary – Rose, Moss
1898　Devil's Kitchen – Reade, McCulloch
1899　Hanging Garden Gully – O. G. Jones, Abraham brothers
1905　Monolith Crack, Gribin – Abraham brothers
1912　Zig Zag, Gribin – Herford, Laycock, Milligan, Hodgkinson
1915　Hope, Slabs – Mrs Daniell, Richards, Roxburgh, Henderson
1918　Original, Holly Tree Wall – Richards, Holland, Miss Pilley
1919　Tennis Shoe, Slabs – Odell (solo)
1929　Heather Wall – Hicks, Hargreaves, Stewardson
1945　Suicide Wall – Preston, Morsley, Haines
1971　Capital Punishment – Boysen, Alcock
GUIDEBOOK Wilson/Leppert, *Cwm Idwal*.

Glyders and Ogwen　One of the most popular mountain groups in Snowdonia, separating the Ogwen and Llanberis valleys. The principal summits are Elidir Fawr (924 m), Y Garn (946 m), Glyder Fawr (999 m), Glyder Fach (994 m) and Tryfan (917 m). The northern aspect of the chain (for such it is) forms magnificent cwms with fine crags and llyns (lakes) such as Llyn Idwal and Llyn Bochlwyd. The Llanberis flanks are less scenic but have many fine crags near the valley floor.

On the Ogwen side, the chief climbing interest lies in the crags of Cwm Idwal, Tryfan, Glyder Fach and Gallt yr Ogof, though there are many other cliffs as well. On the Llanberis side, there are the well-known ◊ Three Cliffs. Both the Ogwen and Llanberis valleys contain numerous climbing huts. (◊ Tryfan; Ogwen Cottage.)

Craig yr Ysfa　A huge rambling crag in the Carneddau, Snowdonia, with a fine selection of climbs. The nearest centre is Ogwen.

Because of its somewhat isolated situation the crag was fairly late in developing, and Great Gully, one of the finest in Britain, was not climbed until 1900 (J. M. A. Thomson, Simey, Clay). Other notable ascents are:

1905　Ampitheatre Buttress – Abraham Brothers, Leighton, Puttrell
1931　Pinnacle Wall – Kirkus (solo)
1938　The Grimmett – Cox, Beaumont
1952　Mur y Niwl – Moulam, Churchill
1975　Aura – Carrington, Rouse, Hall

In Cwm Eigiau, below the crag, the Rucksack Club established the first climbing hut in Britain (1912).

In the Carneddau, other principal cliffs are Ysgolion Duon (Black Ladders), Llech Ddu, Braich Ty Du and Craig Lloer. There are climbs of all standards. The area is somewhat remote.

Lliwedd (Y Lliwedd) (898 m)　A mountain in the Snowdon massif with a spectacular N Face overlooking Llyn Llydaw. There are actually two summits – West (898 m) and East (896 m). The crag (also Lliwedd) is one of the largest in Wales and offers numerous climbs in the middle grades. Usually approached from ◊ Pen y Pass.

Though not popular today, Lliwedd holds a special place in the history of Welsh climbing. The first ascent of the W Buttress (Stocker, Wall, 1883) marked the start of Welsh climbing and the Girdle Traverse (Thomson and Reynolds, 1907) of the mountain was the first in the world. Almost all the classic lines are of early date when the cliff was dominated by J. M. A. ◊ Thomson. It was regarded as the crag for the expert and consequently many famous names appear among the first ascents. Of the later climbs, only

Central Gully Direct (Dodd, Edwards, 1938) is of note.
Tremadog A name used to denote a series of low-level cliffs close to the Welsh coast, above the village of the same name. Often enjoys better weather than the main Snowdon areas.

The cliffs are Craig y Gesail, Craig y Castell, Craig Pant Ifan and Craig Bwlch y Moch. Routes rarely exceed 90 m.

Tremadog was one of the outstanding post-war discoveries. The first route was Hound's Head Buttress (Craig Pan Ifan) (Moulam and Sutton, 1951) and among many other good climbs, Vector (J. Brown and C. E. Davies, 1960) is perhaps most notable. The crag had tremendous vogue in the sixties and is still popular.

More recent hard routes include:

1975   Void E3,6a – Edwards
1980   Strawberries E6,6b – Fawcett
1981   Psyche'n Burn E6,6c – Moffatt

Moelwyns A group of mountains in the south of Snowdonia whose principal summits are Moelwyn Mawr (770 m), Moelwyn Bach (711 m) and Cnicht (690 m, the 'Matterhorn of Wales'). Immediately east of these are the vast slate quarries of the Blaenau-Ffestiniog region. There are dozens of crags and *llyns* (lakes). Many crags offer climbs, mostly short, the best being those near Llyn Stwlan (The Moelwynion). On the west edge of the area is Carreg Hyll-Drem and on the east is Carreg Alltrem, both popular cliffs with hard climbs.
Cwm Silyn An impressive cwm at the western edge of Snowdonia, just south of Nantlle. The chief crag is Craig yr Ogof with its famous Great Slab (Ordinary Route: Pye, Reade, Elliot, Odell, 1926) but there are several buttresses giving climbs of all standards. Rather remote and so not as popular as it might be. Notable first ascents include:

1931   Kirkus's Route – Kirkus, Macphee
       Outside Edge Route – Edwards, Palmer
       Upper Slab Climb – Kirkus, Hargreaves, Bridge
1952   Ogof Direct – Moulam, Pigott, Bowman
1956   Bourdillon's Climb – Bourdillon, Nicol
1963   Crucible – Ingle, Wilson
1970   Jabberwocky – R. Evans, J. Yates, M. Yates

Nantgwynant A valley in Snowdonia between the ◊ Pen y Gwryd and Beddgelert. On the north side of the road there are three popular valley crags. From east to west these are Clogwyn y Bustach, Clogwyn y Wenallt and Craig y Gelli. Lockwood's Chimney (Bustach) (A. Lockwood, 1909) is an easy old favourite but most of the other routes here are hard. Oxo (Wenallt) (Lees, Roberts, Trench, 1953) was the first of the modern climbs.
Cwellyn The area round the lake of the same name. It lies immediately west of Snowdon and north of Rhy-ddu. Numerous crags of which the most important is Castell Cidwm, quite fierce. The first route was Dwm (Brown, Smith, 1960).

(See also separate entries for: *Clogwyn Du'r Arddu, Craig Gogarth, Snowdon, Tryfan, Wales*)

GUIDEBOOKS
Holliwell, *Carneddau.*
Williams, *Rock Climbing in Snowdonia.*
Campbell/Newton, *Welsh Winter Climbs.*
Pollitt/Haston/Williams/et al., *Gogarth.*
Drasdo, *Lliwedd.*

Williams, *Snowdonia Rock Climbs.*
Pretty/Farrant/Milburn, *Tremadog & Cwm Silyn.*
Williams, *Clogwyn Du'r Arddu.*
Pollitt, *North Wales Limestone.*
Jones, *Lleyn Peninsula Interim Guide.*
Sumner, *Dolgellau Area. Cader/Rhinog.*
Sumner, *Aran-Cader Idris.*
Sumner, *Mid-Wales.*
Williams, *Llanberis.*

Snow plod   A term of disparagement, sometimes used to describe an ascent of an easy snow peak where little technique is called for, e.g. the Strahlhorn, Switzerland.

Society of Welsh Rabbits   An informal club founded by C. E. ◊ Mathews, Adams-Reilly and ◊ Morshead at Pen y Gwryd in January 1870. Its purpose was to explore Snowdonia in winter; most members were also A.C. members.

Socks over boots   On wet, slimy rock better adhesion can often be got by wearing socks over rock boots. Useful in gill scrambles (see R. B. Evans: *Scrambles in the Lake District*).

Solleder, Emil (1899–1931)   Bavarian climber and guide; one of the finest of the inter-war years, and a pioneer of GrVI routes in the Dolomites. His three greatest climbs were:

1925   Furchetta N Face (with F. Wiessner)
1925   Civetta N W Face (with G. Lettenbauer)
1926   Sass Maor E Face (with F. Kummer)

Solleder was killed whilst descending with a client from the Meije. They were unroped and the client was abseiling when the abseil block gave way. The client fell on to a ledge unhurt, but Solleder, perhaps trying to grab the rope, overbalanced and fell 600 m to the Étançons Glacier.

Solly, Godfrey Allan (1858–1942)   A Birkenhead solicitor who had a long and distinguished career in climbing. He was present at, and took an active part in, some of the most significant events of the nineteenth and early twentieth centuries.
Solly began his Alpine career in 1885. He was a keen advocate of guideless climbs; a friend of Carr, Slingsby, Mummery et al. He was with Mummery on his first attempt at the Plan N Face (1892), but his only first ascents were minor ones. In 1893 and 1894 he visited the Caucasus and made a number of new ascents, and in 1909 he was in Canada, climbing in the Lake O'Hara region.
Solly was with ◊ Collie and ◊ Collier on the famous Easter Meet of the S.M.C. at Inveroran, when the first ascent of the crags of Buachaille Etive Mor was made, together with other ascents in Glencoe and the first ascent of Tower Ridge, Ben Nevis (1894). This is regarded as the start of rock-climbing on the Scottish mainland.
In the Lake District he was with Carr on the Hand Traverse of Pillar N Climb (1891) and made the first complete ascent of Arrowhead Ridge on Gable (1893). His most notable achievement, however, was the first ascent of Eagle's Nest Direct, Gable, in 1892.
Solly continued to climb to a great age. He made a guideless traverse of

Grépon, aged 63, ascended Strahlhorn, aged 75 and climbed Pillar at 80. He was President of the S.M.C., 1910 and F.R.C.C., 1920.

Solo climbing   Climbing alone. A safety rope may or may not be used. The additional dangers of solo climbing are obvious, but many expert climbers find great satisfaction in this method of making ascents and indeed the first solo ascent of a given route is recognized as a distinct achievement. Solo climbing has been common since the pioneer days when Lammer, O. G. Jones, Kirkus and others often soloed routes. Many first ascents were done solo, including ◊ Napes Needle. Some of the hardest Alpine climbs of modern times were first done solo, e.g. Matterhorn Nordwand Direct and the Bonatti Pillar of the Dru. (See *On the Heights*, by W. Bonatti.)

Many of the world's highest mountains have been soloed, including Everest (first solo ascent, R. Messner, 1980).

Solvay, Ernest (1838–1922)   Belgian industrialist, inventor of the Solvay process for washing soda, who donated 20,000 Francs to the S.A.C. for the construction of a refuge at 4,000 m on the Hörnli Ridge of the Matterhorn (1906). Opened in 1916, it is known as the Solvay Hut and has played a considerable part in the Matterhorn story. The original structure has been replaced. Solvay himself climbed the Matterhorn at the age of 65.

Southern Africa, climbing in   The numerous mountains of South Africa provide a wide variety of climbs on rock which ranges from the hard sandstone of Table Mountain above Cape Town to the basalts of the Drakensberg and granites of the Spitskop in the deserts of Namibia. The highest peak is in the Drakensberg: Thabantshonyana (various spellings) (3,482 m), which is actually in Lesotho, the Drakensberg forming the boundary between Lesotho and Natal. It was first climbed in 1951 (D. Watkins party), though the ascent is easy. Only then was its height discovered. The highest point strictly in the Republic now seems to be Injasuti (3,459 m), displacing the better-known Champagne Castle (3,377 m), also in the Drakensberg, and climbed in 1888 by A. H. and F. R. Stocker.

There is no permanent snow or ice in South Africa but some such climbing is done during the winter months. Rock-climbing predominates, however, along with hiking on the extensive network of trails. The principal climbing areas are:

Cape Province
Table Mountain. The cradle of South African climbing with hundreds of routes in all grades on good rock.
Elsies Peak. Hard short routes on steep overhanging rock.
Paarl Rock. Hard routes on steep faces and cracks, short.
De Toits Kloof, Hex River and Windhoek. Long climbs, up to 20 pitches, in all grades.
Montagu. Hard, steep crack climbs.
Cedarberg. All grades of climbing – and good backpacking.
Natal
Monteseel. Short steep routes.
Drakensberg. Huge mountain range with many trails and numerous climbs, though the basalt tends to be poor. Impressive peaks include Champagne Castle (3,377 m), Giant's Castle (3,316 m) and Mont Aux Sources (3,282 m).
Transvaal
Magaliesberg. Steep short routes.
Blouberg, Kransberg. Long and sustained routes of quality.

South African ◊ grades are changing at present from an alphabetical system to a numerical open-ended system similar to the Australian. Grades up to 28 are noted in recent literature – probably 6b/c in the British system.

The premier club is the Mountain Club of South Africa, established in 1891. It now has 13 sections with 4,500 members (1990) of which only about 300 are active rock-climbers. There are at present very few Black climbers – about 1 per cent of M.C.S.A. membership.

The M.C.S.A. owns large tracts of South Africa's mountains and is a very strong environmental protection agency.

Southern England, climbs in   In an area just south of Groombridge and Tunbridge Wells there are several outcrops of sandstone of which the best known is Harrison's Rocks, with climbs of all grades. It is owned by the B.M.C. Bowles Rocks, on the other hand, is part of an outdoor centre and only open at a small fee to outsiders.

Climbing began at Harrison's about 1926 with Nea Morin and friends – some of their climbs still retain a 5b grade. The place is very popular.

Eridge Rocks, High Rocks, Bulls Hollow and Stone Farm are other popular crags hereabouts.

In recent years, under the influence mainly of Mick ◊ Fowler, there has been a resurgence of chalk-climbing on the south coast sea cliffs. The pioneers such as ◊ Mummery, and especially ◊ Crowley, climbed here. There are times when the chalk can be treated like ice! (Hence Dry Ice, 55 m IV/V, St Margaret's Bay.) Others can be climbed more traditionally. Most chalk-climbs are in the higher grades.

GUIDEBOOK Turner, *Southern Sandstone* (C.C.)

South Georgia   An island, about 190 km long and averaging 25 km wide, in the sub-Antarctic. A mountain range runs down the middle of the island, the highest point being Mt Paget (2,915 m), with many others of about 2,000 m. D. Carse surveyed the island in the three seasons, 1951–2, 1953–4 and 1955–6, and G. Sutton investigated the climbing in the season 1954–5. The peaks are attractive and a number have been climbed, but the weather is usually very bad.

Mt Paget was first climbed by M. K. Burley's party in 1964.

Expeditions have been made to other islands in the sub-Antarctic: Heard Island, Crozet Islands, Elephant Island, etc., but the weather is nearly always bad, and the attractions are limited.

South-West England, climbs in   John ◊ Tyndall is reputed to have scrambled about the Swanage cliffs in the nineteenth century and Tom ◊ Longstaff climbed Scrattling Crack at Baggy Point on the North Devon Coast in 1898, but with a few exceptions until after the Second World War climbing in South-West England was virtually confined to the Cornish sea cliffs which A. W. ◊ Andrews had opened up as early as 1902. I. B. Prowse ascended the classic Wogs at Chudleigh in 1923 and though A. D. M. ◊ Cox and K. Bere put up Climbers' Club Original at the Dewerstone in 1935 and Fred Balcombe made the Piton Route at Avon during that period, this does not seem to have encouraged others. ◊ Limestone was out of favour and most of the other rock was of dubious parentage.

Limestone began a revival in the 1950s and Avon saw great development by Hugh Banner, Barrie Page, Chris Bonington and others. The Dewerstone, Dartmoor tors, Lundy and eventually Swanage, all saw development in the same decade. In the 1960s Tom Patey drew attention to Chudleigh limestone and by the middle of the decade numerous cliffs large and small had been investigated. Perhaps the Old Redoubt at Berry Head was the most fashionable, with climbs like Moonraker (HVS) by Pat Littlejohn and Peter Biven, 1967. At the end of this period routes such as Pink Void (VS) and Heart of the Sun (Extreme) by A. C. Willmott and M. J. Spring (1969), both at Baggy Point, gave added quality.

After the great surge of the sixties and seventies the area seems to have settled down to steady development, perhaps never quite living up to early expectations.

Principal crags   (Climbing grade needed to make a visit worthwhile. Maximum length – many climbs will be much shorter.)

Avon Gorge (GR562743), Bristol. Limestone, VS+, 75 m
Baggy Point (GR419406), near Ilfracombe. Sandstone, VS+, 100 m
Berry Head (Old Redoubt GR943564), near Brixham. Limestone, VS+, 70 m
Blackchurch (GR300266), near Clovelly. Metamorphic, VS+, 90 m
Bosigran (GR416368), north Cornish coast. Granite, all grades, 70 m
Chair Ladder (GR365216), near Porthgwarra. Granite, all grades, 65 m
Cheddar Gorge (GR472542), near Cheddar. Limestone, VS+, 135 m
Chudleigh Rocks (GR864788), Chudleigh. Limestone, HS+, 50 m
Dewerstone (GR538638), near Plymouth. Granite, all grades, 45 m
Great Zawn (GR415366), north Cornish coast. Granite, VS+, 73 m
Haytor (GR758771), Dartmoor. Granite, all grades, 40 m
Lower Sharpnose (GR195127), near Bude. Metamorphic, VS+, 45 m
Lundy Island (Devil's Slide, GR131468), Bristol Channel. Granite, all grades, 120 m
Swanage (Tilly Whim, 031769 to St Aldhelm's Head, 962754), Swanage. Limestone, S+, 60 m+
Wintour's Leap (GR542958), Wye Valley. Limestone, all grades, 105 m
Wyndcliffe (GR527974), Wye Valley. Limestone, VS+, 45 m

GUIDEBOOKS
Jenkin, *Swanage*.
Jenkin/Oxley/Coe, *Swanage Supplement*.
Smith/Hill, *Jersey and Guernsey*.
Gibson, *Lundy Rock Climbs*.
Littlejohn/O'Sullivan, *South Devon & Dartmoor*.
Willson, *Wye Valley*.
Broomhead, *Cheddar*.
Peters, *North Devon and Cornwall*.

Space blanket   An emergency blanket made out of a silvery foil and used to protect a climber suffering from exposure, or for benightment, etc. There is a heavier cellular model. A ◊ poly bag is probably just as effective.

Spain, climbing in   A good deal of Spain is mountainous and there has been a national mountaineering association (Federation Espanola de Montanismo – F.E.M.) since 1922. There are some 170 clubs and 27 huts in the Gredos, ◊ Pyrenees, ◊ Picos de Europa and Sierra Nevada. These are the principal mountain ranges also.

Sierra Nevada   East of Granada. The highest peak is Mulhacén (3,481 m) – the highest summit in Spain. The Pichacho de la Veleta (3,401 m) carries a permanent snow patch, claimed as the most southerly ◊ glacier in Europe. The area is popular with skiers in winter, but the rock-climbing is of little

South-West England: Doorway Climb, Bosigran. (*T. D. Unsworth*)

account except on the pinnacle called Pulpito de Carnales.

Sierra de Gredos   About 160 km west of Madrid. The highest point is Almanzor (2,592 m), climbed from the Gredos Hut. Rock-climbing on the needles of Los Galayos.

Sierra de Guadarrama   About 50 km north of Madrid. A well-known climbing area is La Pedriza de Manzanares, a collection of granite walls and slabs: El Pajaro, Las Oseras, El Huesco etc., with routes of 100–200 m.

◊ *Picos de Europa*   This important range of limestone mountains in the north of the country, near Santander, is rapidly becoming the most popular climbing area in Spain, though the weather – often wet and misty – militates against it. Good for rock-climbing and hard walking. The most famous peak is Naranjo de Bulnes (Villaviciosa and Perez, 1904).

◊ *Pyrenees*   The mountain range between France and Spain offers a full range of mountaineering on both sides of the border. There is unusual rock-climbing at Los Mallos de Riglos, a collection of conglomerate towers and walls in the foothills near Riglos. Mallo Pison and Mallo Fire are the principal crags. Rabada al Fire (TD, 330 m), (Rabada and Navarro, 1961) is said to be the best climb in Spain!

Montserrat   A mountain some 1,200 m high situated about 55 km inland from Barcelona, and famous for its monastery. The name means the serrated or sawn mountain and it consists of numerous pinnacles of conglomerate, some in excess of 150 m, giving climbs in the upper grades. The best-known pinnacle is the Cavall Bernat (Costa-Boix and Balaguer, 1935).

Costa Blanca   Between Benidorm and Gandia on the Mediterranean coast there are numerous limestone crags where the Sierra de Bernia meets the sea. The principal ones are Puig Campana, Dalle d'Ola, Barranco del Mascarat, Sierra de Toix, Penon de Ifach and Penyaa Rotja de Marxuquera. Routes vary from less than 30 m to over 300 m, mostly HVS or harder. Very popular with British climbers in winter!

Mallorca (Majorca)   The northern part of the island has numerous rocky peaks. The highest is Puig Major (1,450 m) which is a military outpost and prohibited. The walking can be tough and is best done out of the summer season. The best centre is Pollensa. The rock-climbing is being developed slowly, and the potential is enormous.

GUIDEBOOKS

Battagel, *Pyrenees Andorra Cerdagne*. Walking/climbing. (W.C.P.)

Battagel, *Pyrenees West*. Larrau to Gavarnie Cirque. Walking/climbing. (W.C.P.)

Battagel, *Pyrenees Central*. Gedre to the Garonne Gap. Walking/climbing. (W.C.P.)

Collomb, *Gredos Mountains and Sierra Nevada*. Central and Southern Spain. Walking/principal ascents. (W.C.P.)

Craggs, *Costa Blanca Climbs* including *Majorca*. (C.P.)

Parker, *Walking in Mallorca*. (C.P.)

Reynolds, *Walks and Climbs in the Pyrenees*. (C.P.)

Walker, *Walks and Climbs in the Picos de Europa*. (C.P.)

Walker, *Rock Climbs in the Pyrenees*. (C.P.)

Spindrift   Light powder snow blown about by the wind and often seen forming spumes from Alpine crests and summits. A superficial snow slide of powder snow is also called spindrift. It is very uncomfortable since it penetrates clothing by getting up sleeves and down necks.

Eric Shipton (*RGS*)   Sir Leslie Stephen (*AC*)

Spitzbergen (Svalbard)   A group of islands almost mid-way between the North Cape of Norway and the North Pole, and belonging to Norway. West Spitzbergen has mountains rising to just over 1,500 m. The highest summits are: Newtontoppen and Perriertoppen, both 1,717 m. The former was climbed by A. Vassiliev's party in 1900.

The first major expedition was that of Conway in 1896 when he made the first crossing of the island. He returned and climbed a number of peaks the following year. The island has attracted several expeditions since. The peaks, though low, are shapely. The chief difficulty is to reach the inland ice – two or three days through deep mud, dangerous crevasses and thick fog.

Sport Climbing   so called to distinguish it from normal or 'adventure climbing', is now common on French and some other continental crags. The routes are completely bolted and will often end at a 'lower-off point' consisting of a fixed chain and karabiner. The usual protection is by ◊ quickdraws.

It is common to push sports climbs to the limit – falling off is safe (or should be!). Degrees of skill include the 'on sight flash' – an immediate lead, not pulling on bolts; 'flashing' – leading without pre-placed quickdraws but with prior knowledge of the route; 'red pointing' – leading with pre-placed quickdraws; 'dogging' – hanging from bolts as moves are rehearsed.

Stack   A free-standing pinnacle of rock left behind by the erosion of sea-cliffs. They can be of considerable height and may be difficult of access. They are numerous in Scotland, Ireland and elsewhere. Many have been climbed; the islanders of St Kilda once became expert stack-climbers in their search for gulls' eggs. Ball's Pyramid is a 550 m stack, 650 km off the Australian coast (first ascent 1965). Best-known British stack is The Old Man of Hoy (1966, Baillie, Patey, Bonington).

STANCE

Stance (G.: Standplatz; Fr.: relais; It.: punto di sosta)   The top of a ◊ pitch; the place where the climber halts to make a static belay. Usually a ledge, though possibly a very small one. Can be a ◊ chockstone or even a tree. In ◊ aid climbing a stance may be taken in ◊ étriers. Note that the climber may not actually *stand* (though this is common); he may be sitting or even lying down.

Stanig, Valentin (1774–1847)   The earliest amateur mountaineer of the Eastern Alps who took part in the second ascent of Gross Glockner (1800), the first ascent being made by local peasants the previous day. He also made the first ascent of Watzmann (1799 or 1801). Stanig was a cleric and amateur botanist.

Starr, Russell   A Yorkshire climber who made the first ascent of Fussstein, and first English ascent of Olperer, two popular Zillertal peaks, in 1880.

Steinauer, Ludwig (1903–71)   A German guide and member of the ◊ Munich School, who did a number of notable if rather obscure north walls in the thirties including the N Face of Mont Blanc du Cheilon (1938).

Stephen, Sir Leslie (1832–1904)   Biographer, and one of the most eminent literary critics of his day. His first wife was the daughter of Thackeray and his own daughter was the novelist Virginia Woolf.

In his student days Stephen was a keen runner and walker and this stood him in good stead when he began his Alpine career. His first real season (though he visited the Alps previously as a tourist) was in 1858 when E. S. ◊ Kennedy, ◊ Hardy and ◊ Hinchcliff accompanied him on a six weeks' season which included the first traverse of Wildstrubel. It was the start of an astonishing career of first ascents, tabulated below (first ascents unless otherwise noted):

1858	Wildstrubel – first traverse	1862	Jungfraujoch – first crossing
1859	Eigerjoch – first crossing		Fiescherjoch – first crossing
	Bietschhorn		Weisshorn – second ascent
	Weissmies – first English ascent		Pizzo Pioda
			Monte della Disgrazia
	Dom – second ascent	1864	Scherjoch – first crossing
	Rimpfischhorn		Winterlücke – first amateur's crossing
1860	Allalinhorn – second ascent		
	Alphubel		Jungfrau from Rottal
	Oberaarhorn		Lyskamm W summit
	Blumlisalphorn		Zinal Rothorn
1861	Mont Blanc via Goûter – first complete ascent	1869	Cima di Ball – solo
		1871	Mont Mallet
1861	Schreckhorn	1873	Col des Hirondelles – first crossing
		1877	Galenstock – first winter ascent

After his marriage in 1867, he curtailed his climbing at the wish of his wife. In 1871 he published *The Playground of Europe*, a collection of climbing pieces, mostly ones he had contributed to the *A.J.* It is one of the great classics of mountaineering literature. He was President of the A.C. 1866–8.

Stephenson, Tom (1893–1987)   A journalist who first proposed the Pennine Way in an article in the *Daily Herald* in 1935. The idea was inspired by the Appalachian Trail of the United States, but the Pennine Way did not finally come into being until 1965. Stephenson became Secretary to the Ramblers' Association in 1948 and it was his persistent work which opened up long-distance 'trails' in Britain.

Steps   Holds cut or kicked in snow or ice. With the advent of modern crampons and short axe techniques, very little step-cutting is needed today, unlike in the pioneering days when it was regarded as an art and some guides were famous for their prodigious step-cutting abilities.

Crampons sometimes break or get lost and in such cases a knowledge of step-cutting is useful.

Steps should always be kicked in preference to cut with an axe because this saves a lot of time, but on very hard snow and on ice this is not possible. On hard snow, the adze of the ice axe is used to fashion the steps and on ice the pick is used. The ideal is to make a step which will take half a boot width and which slopes slightly inwards.

An expert step-cutter can fashion a step in three blows, even in ice. The weight of the axe head should do most of the work – step-cutting is very tiring. Large steps (usually in snow) are called 'buckets' or 'bucket steps'. When snow lies over ice care should be taken to cut through to the ice.

The direction taken by a line of uphill steps varies according to the nature of the snow or ice and the steepness of the slope. The best and easiest line should be taken. On very steep slopes steps may be fashioned in zig-zag, with a turning step at the end of each line. In all cases it is usual to cut two or three steps ahead.

Sticht plate   A device invented by Fritz Sticht to improve dynamic belaying. Instead of the rope passing round the climber's back for friction, it passes through a metal friction plate, which in the event of a fall by another climber applies a gradual brake to the rope.

Sticky soles   A quality of rubber used as the soles for some rock boots which gives them extra friction and makes them especially suitable for ◊ smearing.

Stogdon, John (1843–1919)   One of the guideless school of alpinists of the early 1870s, but best known for his oft quoted account of a winter crossing of Bowfell in the Lake District, which almost ended in disaster (*A.J.* V).

Stone, James Kent (Father Fidelis) (1840–1921)   Born in Boston, Massachusetts, and educated at Harvard, Stone became a member of the A.C. in 1860 with the best list of qualifications entered up to that date. His only first ascent, however, was of Blumlisalphorn with Stephen and Liveing (1860). In 1869 he became a priest and missionary.

Stonefall   Natural stonefall is due to the processes of erosion and is consequently greatest where erosion is most pronounced. In Britain it is not a serious problem, but it is common in the Alps. Where stonefall is known to be serious, the area should be avoided or, if that is not possible, should be tackled at the time when the stonefall is minimal. This usually means before dawn. Guidebooks are often explicit in this matter. Stonefall occurs on open faces and especially in couloirs and gullies where the confined space makes the danger greater. Ridges are the safest from stonefall.

Though occasional large boulders come down, most stonefall is smaller, though large enough to do serious injury if it strikes a climber. It travels at great speed owing to acceleration under gravity and its ominous whirring can often be heard even when the stones themselves cannot be seen.

Stonefall because of other people on the cliff or mountain is much more common in Britain, and gullies are again the black spots. Every care should be taken not to kick stones down accidentally and, of course, stones should never be thrown down cliffs. If a stone is dislodged a loud warning cry of 'below!' should be shouted. The only protection against stonefall is wearing a climbing helmet.

Stove   There are four main types used by climbers:
(a) liquefied butane (e.g. Gaz); (b) paraffin (e.g. Primus)
(c) petrol; (d) methylated spirits or profol.

Type (a). Uses disposable cartridges. Clean to handle and easy to light. Various sizes. As hot as (b) under laboratory conditions, but the flame seems readily affected by winds. Self sealing cartridges on some models. A special butane/propane mix used for high altitude climbing.

Type (b). Very safe to use but can be fiddling. Needs pre-heating with meths. or profol. Cheap fuel.

Type (c). Probably the hottest type of stove, but the inflammable nature of the fuel and the possibility of leakage make it a little dangerous.

Type (d). Very small and easily portable stoves – 'tommy cookers'. Slow, but useful for bivouacs. Safe and simple.

Straton, Mary Isabella (1838–1918)   One of the pioneer lady climbers, Miss Straton began her Alpine career in 1861 with a visit to the Grands Mulets. She went on to make the first ascent of the Aig. du Moine (1871), Punta Isabella (1875) and Aig. de la Persévérance (1875). In 1876 she made the first winter ascent of Mont Blanc and shortly after she married her guide, Jean Charlet (1840–1925) and the family became Charlet-Straton.

The death of her eldest son, Robert, in the First World War, was a blow from which she never recovered. In happier times he had been the youngest person ever to climb Mont Blanc – 11½ years.

In 1879 Jean Charlet-Straton, piqued that the Dru should have fallen to an outside guide – ◊ Burgener – made the first ascent of the more difficult Petit Dru with two other guides, P. Payot and F. Folliguet.

Streather, Harry Reginald Antony (b. 1926)   A British Army officer who has taken part in a number of important Himalayan expeditions. In 1950 he took part in the Norwegian first ascent of Tirich Mir as a member of the summit party and was with the Americans on K2 in 1953. In 1955, with Hardie, he made the second ascent of Kangchenjunga, following the initial success of Brown and Band.

In 1957, Streather accepted leadership of the Oxford University Haramosh Expedition. The expedition ended in tragedy, but was an epic of endurance and courage on the part of Streather: one of the great stories of modern mountaineering. (See *The Last Blue Mountain*, by R. Barker.)

In 1959 Streather led a British Army expedition to the Karakoram, and made the first ascent of Malubitang East.

Since 1961, Tony Streather has played a considerable part in endeavour training and has led various expeditions to Ethiopia, Kenya, Greenland and the Pindus Mountains of Greece, either for youth groups or the Army. Awarded the M.B.E. He led the successful Army Everest ascent, 1976. President of the A.C., 1990.

Strutt, Edward Lisle (1874–1948)   An accomplished climber and soldier, noted for his rescue of the Austrian Royal Family from a revolutionary mob in 1919. Second-in-command of the 1922 Everest Expedition, though he did not go high.

In the light of history, Strutt's career was blighted by his rigid conservatism over mountaineering detail which was highlighted during his editorship of the *Alpine Journal* in the 1930s and his presidency of the A.C. He undoubtedly weakened the Alpine Club in a changing world and perhaps retarded British (Alpine) climbing by more than a decade.

Studer, Gottlieb (1804–90)   Pioneer alpinist with 643 ascents to his name between 1823 and 1883. Many first ascents, mainly of undistinguished peaks but including Diablerets and Grand Combin. The Studerhorn is named after him. Best known to historians for his book *Uber Eis und Schnee* (4 vols., 1869–83), a history of climbing in the Swiss Alps. Studer came from Berne.

Stutfield, Hugh Edward Millington (1858–1929)   Traveller and game hunter who made a number of first ascents in the Canadian Rockies with Collie, Woolley and Spencer in 1898, 1900 and 1902. The 1898 party discovered the great Columbia Glacier and made the first ascents of: Survey Peak, Dome, Diadem, and Mt Thompson – all guideless. In 1902 the first ascents of: Mt Murchison, Mt Freshfield, Mt Forbes, Howse Peak, Mt Noyes and Mt Neptuak.

Joint author, with J. N. Collie, of *Climbs and Exploration in the Canadian Rockies* (1903).

Summit   The highest point of a mountain or hill. In Britain the summit is generally indicated by a ☖ cairn or a trig-block (☖ Triangulation point). In the Alps a summit may be unmarked, or have a trig-pole, trig-triangle, cross or (very occasionally) some other symbol – even a statue. Many Alpine summits have a book in which to record one's ascent. It is protected by a box.

Sustained   Meaning that the difficulty is sustained throughout the pitch or the climb, whichever is being described. Many climbs have a few pitches which are harder than the rest, and many pitches have a few moves which are harder than the rest, but the use of the word 'sustained' means that the difficulty never relents.

Sweden, climbing in   Kebnekaise (2,117 m) in Arctic Sweden is the highest summit, glaciated, but easy to climb and of little interest. In summer, the whole area is heavily infested with midges.

T

Tabei, Junko (b. 1939)   This Japanese housewife and lecturer was the first woman to climb ◊ Mt Everest (S Col route, 1975). Convinced that given the opportunity, women would make equally good high-altitude climbers as men, she formed the Japanese Ladies Climbing Club in 1969. Their first big success was an ascent of Annapurna III in 1970 – the second ascent of the peak and by a new route from the south. Mrs Tabei, Hiroko Hirakawa and two Sherpas reached the top. After Everest came Shisha Pangma, 1981, the Peak of Communism, 1985 and ◊ Aconcagua, 1987. She climbed the highest points of the five major continents. Mrs Tabei also made notable attempts on Jitchudrake, 1983, and the Chinese side of Pik Pobeda, 1986. On Jitchudrake she reached the S Summit (6,793 m) in what was the first ever attempt on the peak.

Mrs Tabei is a trustee of the Himalaya Adventure Trust established by Sir Edmund ◊ Hillary. She is very influential in the world of Japanese climbing.

Tairraz family   A well-known family of mountain photographers from ◊ Chamonix. The business was founded by Joseph Tairraz (1827–1902), who took the first photographs on the summit of Mont Blanc, about 1860, using a wet plate camera taking 21 × 27 cm plates. Because the sensitivity of the plates was short-lived a special development tent had to be carried to the summit.

Later members of the family became interested in film making. One of the best known films is *Entre Terre et Ciel*, with ◊ Gaston Rébuffat (1961).

Taiwan (Formosa)   An island off the coast of China occupied by the Chinese Nationalist Government. There are some fine mountains rising from the forests of the centre and north-east of the island, many over 3,500 m. The highest is Niitaka (3,997 m), first climbed 1896.

Tardivel, Pierre (b. 1963)   A French extreme skier who has tackled slopes of incredible steepness. Among them are the S E Face of Grande Casse, 1,550 m, 50–55° (1984); Cordier Couloir of Les Courtes, 800 m, 50–55° (1987). His most famous descent is of the N E Face of Grand Pilier d'Angle, 1,000 m, 55–65° (1988). It took him an hour. This is the face that took ◊ Bonatti and Zappelli 18 hours to climb in 1962. The descent involved a 75 m abseil and there was only 5 cm of snow lying on hard ice.

Tasker, Joseph Thomas (1948–1982)   A leading professional mountaineer who made the first British ascents of the N Face of Dent Blanche (1973), Bonatti–Gobbi route, Eckpfeiler (1973) and E Face of ◊ Grandes Jorasses (1974). In the winter of 1975 he made the fourth winter ascent of the ◊ Eigerwand (◊ Eiger). His companion on all these exploits was Dick Renshaw and it was with Renshaw that Tasker made a remarkable Alpine-style ascent of the S Face of Dunagiri (7,066 m) in 1975.

This Himalayan venture led Tasker to concentrate on expeditions and in the following year, his other great partner, Peter ◊ Boardman, and he made the first ascent of Changabang W Wall – one of the most difficult wall climbs

Junko Tabei   Joe Tasker

donc in the Himalaya. In the two years which followed he was unsuccessful on the N Ridge of Nuptse with ◊ Scott and Covington and on the W Ridge of K2 with ◊ Bonington, when ◊ Estcourt was killed by an avalanche.

In 1979, with Scott, Boardman and Bettembourg, Tasker climbed the N Ridge of ◊ Kangchenjunga – an oxygenless ascent of the world's third highest peak. K2 defeated him again in 1980 with Renshaw and Boardman, as did the W Ridge of Everest, tried in winter 1980–1 with ◊ Rouse and Hall.

In 1981 Tasker, Bonington, Rouse and Boardman reached the summit of Kongur (7,719 m) – a first ascent. A year later, with Peter Boardman, Joe Tasker disappeared whilst attempting the N E Ridge of Everest.

HIS BOOKS ARE *Everest, the Cruel Way* (1981) and *Savage Arena* (1982). ◊ Boardman–Tasker Award.

Tatra   The highest mountains between the Alps and Caucasus, lying on the border between Czechoslovakia and Poland. The Tatra are part of the Carpathians, but the rest of that range is wooded and rounded. The best centre is Zakopane in Poland, a well-known ski resort.

The Tatra can be divided into the Low Tatra and High Tatra. The Low Tatra are in the west of the group and are mainly limestone. The High Tatra are granite peaks, shapely, with many fine faces and ridges. The highest summit is Gerlach (2,663 m). The rock faces are usually between 300 and 600 m high and among the hardest climbs are those on the Pulpit Rock, Maly Ganek N Face, Mnich E Face and Lemnica N W Face, though there are many more; the region boasts over two thousand climbs of all standards in an area only 50 km long and 15 km wide. The weather is often poor. There are no glaciers.

Most of the area is covered by the Polish and Czech National Parks, where walking and camping is strictly controlled, though members of alpine clubs have special privileges. There are good huts in all the valleys. Skiing is popular in winter and hard winter ascents are made frequently, too.

Tenzing Norgay (*A. Gregory*)   H. W. Tilman (*J. Perrin*)

Taylor, Charles (1840–1908)   The Rev. Charles Taylor was a companion of the ◊ Pendleburys and with them on the first ascent of Marinelli Couloir.

Teichelmann, Ebenezer (1859–1938)   'The little doctor', one of the famous pioneers of the New Zealand Alps and companion of the ◊ Graham brothers. With Newton and others he made the first ascent of several important peaks including: Douglas, Glacier Peak, Torres, Spencer, Bristol Top, Conway Peak, La Perouse, Tyndall, Malcolm (1902–11). A noted photographer.

Téléphérique (E.: cable car; G.: Seilbahn)   The French word is now in common usage among climbers, probably because of the influence of Chamonix, where téléphériques are common and of considerable importance to the mountaineer. Though téléphériques are built for tourists and skiers, they often help the climber by reducing the time taken to reach a hut, or in some cases a climb itself.

Tenzing Norgay (1914–86)   The Sherpa who, with Edmund ◊ Hillary, was the first man to reach the summit of Everest in 1953. Tenzing served as a porter with British expeditions in 1935, 1936 and 1938, and visited the Karakoram in 1950. In 1951 he was Sirdar to the French party which attempted the traverse between Nanda Devi and Nanda Devi East, when Duplat and Vignes were killed. Tenzing and L. Dubost reached the summit of Nanda Devi (second ascent).

In the following year he was Sirdar and a full member of the Swiss team to attempt Everest, and with R. Lambert reached a height of about 8,600 m on the S Ridge.

Tenzing was awarded the George Medal in 1953. A biography, *Man of Everest* (in America: *Tiger of the Snows*), by J. R. Ullman appeared in 1955, and an autobiography, *After Everest*, in 1977.

Terray, Lionel (1921–65) One of the great French guides of the post-war era. With Lachenal he made the second ascent of the Eigerwand in 1947 and repeated many of the classic hard climbs of the immediate pre-war years. He had an outstanding record on expeditions (all first ascents):

1950 Annapurna
1952 Fitzroy*, Huantsan*, Nevado Pongos*
1954 Chomo Lonzo*, Makalu II*
1956 Nevado Soray*, Nevado Veronica*, Chacaraju West*, Taulliraju*
1962 Jannu*, Chacaraju E*, Nilgiri N*
1964 Alaska – leader of expedition which climbed Huntington*
*indicates Terray reached summit

Terray was killed in a climbing accident at the Vercors.

Thin A climber's expression meaning that the holds are small and scarce and therefore the climbing at that point is delicate and difficult.

Thomas, Eustace (1869–1960) Manchester engineer and designer of the mountain rescue stretcher which bears his name. (◊ Mountain rescue stretcher.)

Thomas did not take up mountaineering until his late thirties, but went on to create some remarkable endurance records for mountain walks, including the first traverse of the ◊ Welsh 3,000s and the Derwent Watershed Walk (Peak District). He made three attempts on the ◊ Lake District Fell Record (1919, 1920, 1922) and was finally successful: 66½ miles, 25,500 ft of ascent and descent within the stipulated 24 hours. In 1924 he made the first traverse of the ◊ Scottish 4,000s, but used a car between Fort William and the Cairngorms, which is no longer allowed.

At the age of 54 he took up Alpine climbing and with the guides Knubel and Lagger climbed 24 major peaks in five weeks. At Knubel's suggestion he later concentrated on peaks of 4,000 m or over and in six years he succeeded in climbing them all: 83 major peaks and 30 smaller ones. He later added minor pinnacles of 4,000 m, including the Aigs. du Diable.

In his sixties he took up gliding and held several records. He then learnt to fly powered aircraft and celebrated his 70th birthday by flying solo to Egypt.

Thomas, Percy William (1854–94) A climber who concentrated on new or difficult expeditions in the Alps during the 1870s. Made the first ascent of Cresta del Naso on Lyskamm (1878) and of the Aig. du Chardonnet W Ridge, now the usual finish to the traverse (1879). Made attempts on the Aig. du Géant and the Mittelegi Ridge of the Eiger (1880), but failed.

In 1890 he visited Colorado and made the first ascent of Mt Wilson in the San Juan Mountains.

Thomson, James Merriman Archer (1863–1912) The most noted pioneer of Welsh rock-climbing. He took a post as a teacher at Bangor in 1884, but his first climb seems to have been in the Lake District (Deep Ghyll, 1890). He did not begin climbing in Wales until 1894, when he quickly established a new school of climbing rivalling that of the Lakes. He raised gully-climbing to new standards and later, with Andrews and Eckenstein, particularly, open-face climbing, especially on Lliwedd.

By 1896 Thomson had made 14 new climbs (there had previously been only 12 climbs in the whole of Snowdonia). These included the Second Pinnacle Rib (1894), Tryfan, and his famous ascent in March 1895 of the Devil's

Kitchen, when it was iced up, using a hatchet from Ogwen Cottage to cut steps. During this period, too, he tackled the gullies of Glyder Fawr.

Two later gullies were also of importance: the Black Cleft of Dinas Mot (1897) – long thought one of the hardest climbs in Wales – and the Great Gully of Craig yr Ysfa (1900).

But it was Lliwedd that drew him most. His first route was the minor one called Intermediate Route (1894). Then came:

1894	Bilberry Terrace Route (the only one he did not lead)	1907	Girdle Traverse; Needle Traverse Climb; The Great Chimney; Avalanche Route; Red Wall Finish; W Wall of Great Chimney
1896	E Gully		
1897	Craig yr Aderyn Route		
1898	Elliptical Route		
1903	Central Route	1908	Rocker Route
1904	Bracket Gully; Route II; Direct Route	1909	Three Pinnacle Route
		1912	Child's Face
1905	The Cracks; Horned Crag Route		

The Girdle Traverse was a new invention in 1907, since copied on almost every cliff. In their day, these Lliwedd climbs were regarded as suitable only for the most advanced experts.

Thomson 'discovered' many of the Welsh cliffs: Idwal Slabs, Glyder Fawr, Craig yr Ysfa, Clogwyn y Person, Cyrn Las, Ysgolion Duon, Pillar of Elidyr. Perhaps because he had such a wide choice, and because his favourite cliff was Lliwedd, relatively few of his climbs are popular today. It is ironical that when the ◊ Abrahams and ◊ Jones visited Wales in 1899, the few routes they put up should remain much more popular than those of Thomson.

The Abrahams came to compile a guidebook, and it was this that convinced Thomson that guidebooks by local experts were needed, though he was originally against the idea. With Andrews he wrote *Climbs on Lliwedd* (1909) and, alone, *Climbing in the Ogwen District* (1910). He refused to use any classification (such as Jones had done), but here again, future events proved him wrong.

Thomson rose to be Headmaster of a Llandudno school. He died suddenl; in 1912.

Thread belay Can be a ◊ runner or a static ◊ belay. The belay loop is threaded behind a chockstone firmly embedded in a crack or some similar opening. For difficult threads a piece of bent wire, known as a threader, might be used to help matters.

Three Cliffs, the An obsolescent name for Clogwyn y Grochan, Carreg Wastad and Dinas Cromlech on the north side of Llanberis Pass, Snowdonia. The name seems to derive from a wartime guidebook published by the Climbers' Club: *Three Cliffs in Llanberis*, by J. E. Q. Barford (1944).

J. M. Edwards began climbing on Dinas Cromlech in 1931 and on the other cliffs in 1935, and all the early routes are his, notably:

1931	Spiral Stairs, Dinas Cromlech; Flying Buttress, Dinas Cromlech
1935	Shadow Wall, Carreg Wastad; Crackstone Rib, Carreg Wastad Hazel Groove, Grochan
1940	Brant, Grochan; Slape, Grochan

It was Edwards's acceptance of the imperfect rock of these cliffs which helped to open the way for post-war developments. The cliffs played the most

One of the famous Three Cliffs of Llanberis, Dinas Cromlech (*W. Unsworth*)

significant part in modern developments of anywhere in Britain, with the possible exception of ◊ Clogwyn Du'r Arddu, and Stanage. Harding, Moulam, Brown and Whillans among others were responsible. Significant routes include:

1947   Spectre – Harding, Phillips
       Ivy Sepulchre – Harding
1948   Kaisergebirge Wall – Harding, Disley, Moulam
       Overlapping Wall, Carreg Wastad – Hughes, solo
1949   Phantom Rib, Grochan – Pigott, Miss Kennedy-Frazer, Stock
       Unicorn, Wastad – Harding, Hodgkinson, Hughes
       Lion, Wastad – Harding, Moulam
       Brant Direct, Grochan – Harding
1951   Hangover, Grochan – Brown, Greenall, Sorrel, Ashton
       Cemetery Gates, Dinas Cromlech – Brown, Whillans
1952   Cenotaph Corner, Dinas Cromlech – Brown, Belshaw
1953   Surplomb, Grochan – Brown, Whillans
       Sickle, Grochan – Brown, Cowan
       Erosion Groove, Carreg Wastad – Whillans, Allen, Cowan, White
1955   Erosion Groove Direct, Carreg Wastad – Whillans, Brown
1956   Cromlech Girdle, Dinas Cromlech – Brown, Whillans
1974   Right Wall, Dinas Cromlech (E5,6a) – Livesey
1979   Lord of the Flies, Dinas Cromlech (E6,6a) – Fawcett, Gibb
1980   Cockblock, Grochan (E5,6b) – Redhead, Shorter, Robinson

Three-point contact The basic rule of balance climbing. Of the four limbs, three should always be in contact with the rock, in other words, only one limb should be moved at a time. Though many climbs can be done strictly in this manner, some demand a more dynamic approach with gymnastic moves; cynics call it the no-point contact.

Through route If a chockstone in a gully or chimney leaves a hole through which a climber can pass, it is known as a through route.

Thrutch A north country expression meaning a hard push, and used to indicate strenuous body cracks or, loosely, any strenuous piece of climbing.

Tibesti A mountainous area in the middle of the Sahara Desert (Chad). The mountains are of volcanic origin, but the rock is said to be very poor for climbing. Visited by several post-war expeditions. The highest summit is Emi Koussi (3,415 m).

Tien Shan A long range of mountains extending some 1,600 km from Tashkent to Urumchi, along the Russo–Chinese border in Central Asia. Beyond Urumchi the peaks rise again as the Bogdo Ola Range, which may be considered an extension.
   The highest peaks are in the central section, and in Russia. There are numerous summits over 6,500 m and some glaciers are said to extend 70 km.
   Called the Celestial Mountains, the Tien Shan have been known since the seventh century, when they were described by a Chinese monk, Hsuan Tsang (whom the Chinese say climbed a 6,000 m peak!). They were rediscovered in 1856 by P. Senyonov, who drew attention to Khan Tengri (6,995 m). Attempted by ◊ Merzbacher in 1902 and ascended by M. T. Pogrebsky's party in 1931, this mountain has since been ascended numerous times.
   In 1943 it was established that Pic Pobeda (7,439 m) was higher than Khan Tengri. It was climbed by ◊ V. M. Abalakov's party in 1956. There have been several ascents since, though the peak has a reputation for deaths – over 60 so far.
   In 1988 one of the longest high-altitude traverses ever done crossed west–east over Vazha Pshavela (6,973 m), Pobeda (7,439 m), Vostochnaya (7,039 m) and Military Surveyors' Summit (6,973 m). Twenty-six Russian climbers took seven days to complete the 20 km route.
   The Bogdo Ola group was examined by Merzbacher in 1908. Sixty kilometres north-east of Urumchi it is a fairly accessible group, though apparently little visited. D. Carruthers visited the region in 1908, and ◊ Shipton came with ◊ Tilman in 1948. They attempted the main peak but were unsuccessful. Bogdo Ola (5,445 m) was climbed by a Japanese party in 1981. They were unsuccessful on the second highest peak, Bogdo Feng (5,362 m).

Tiger A complimentary name once given to someone who is a good climber, though the term is now obsolete.
   The name originated from that given to the 15 Sherpas who were fit enough to go to the North Col and beyond in the 1924 Everest Expedition. Later, a register of Sherpas was formed and those who were particularly distinguished in their work were awarded a Tiger's Badge by the Himalayan Club.

Tilman, Harold William (1898–1977) Explorer, mountaineer, sailor and writer. Bill Tilman was a planter in Kenya between 1919 and 1933, when he visited the main East African mountains and also the Himalaya. His most notable ascent of the period was the first traverse of Nelion–Batian on Mt Kenya, with ◊ Shipton in 1930. In 1934 he and Shipton succeeded in forcing the entrance to the Nanda Devi basin through the Rishi Ganga – a problem which had defeated several strong parties. In 1936, with Odell, Tilman reached the summit of Nanda Devi, the first ascent (7,817 m).
   Like Shipton, Tilman was a strong believer in the small expedition and he

tried this out to a certain degree when he was given command of the 1938 Everest Expedition. Bad weather ruined the attempt and results were inconclusive.

During the Second World War Tilman fought with Balkan partisans, but 1947 found him exploring Sinkiang, where he returned the following year. On the opening of Nepal in 1949 Tilman was quickly on the scene, exploring the headwaters of the Trisuli Gandaki. The following year he led an attempt on Annapurna IV.

Tilman then turned his attention to combining sailing with mountain exploration, particularly in Greenland and Patagonia. In 1956 he made the first traverse of the Southern Patagonian Ice-cap. His converted fishing boat, *Mischief*, became famous through his numerous books on her travels.

Tilman was one of the most popular travel writers. His books are: *Ascent of Nanda Devi* (1937), *Snow on the Equator* (1938), *Mount Everest 1938* (1948), *Two Mountains and a River* (1949), *China to Chitral* (1951), *Nepal Himalaya* (1952) and six *Mischief* books (1957–72).

In November 1977 he set sail from Rio in the cutter *En Avant*, bound for the Falklands, but the boat and her crew disappeared.

Todhunter, Ralph (1867–1926) A fine rock-climber who made a number of first ascents in the Alps and was with H. O. Jones and G. W. Young on the first ascent of the Mer de Glace face of Grépon (1911). One of the first to explore Clogwyn Du'r Arddu (E Gully, with Mallory, 1905).

Topham brothers Harold Ward Topham (1857–1915) was a naturally gifted expert at 'outdoor activities' before such a phrase was known. Sailing, skating, toboganning (three times winner on the Cresta Run) and cyclist, he was also a fine climber with many first ascents of routes which have become classics. These include: Mittaghorn–Egginer Traverse, 1886 (but also accredited to Seymour King, 1882), SW arête of Fletschorn (1887), Cresta Signal of Monte Rosa (1887), E arête of Mont Blanc de Cheilon (1887) and traverse of the Aigs. Rouges d'Arolla (1887).

In 1888, with his brother Edwin, he made the first exploration of the Selkirks, and later, with Williams and Broke, went to Alaska to attempt Mt St Elias. The attempt failed at 11,375 ft on the S Ridge. Two years later (1890) he was back in the Selkirks making the first ascents of Mt Donkin, Mt Fox, Mt Selwyn, Mt Sugarloaf and Mt Purity. Some years later Mt Topham was named in his honour.

Alfred George Topham (1872–1920) made a number of first ascents in the Arolla district including the N Face of Pigne d'Arolla (1889) and the S Peak of the Bouquetins (1894). He also made the first direct ascent of the Arrowhead on Great Gable (1896).

Topo Short for 'topographical picture'. A photograph of a crag or mountain with the routes superimposed on it by means of lines. Used in many guidebooks.

Top rope A rope held from above. A second is naturally on a top rope but the term is reserved for special circumstances:
1. Short climbs where the rope is taken to the top by an easy way, belayed, and the free end lowered, i.e. the climb has not been led. Often used on outcrops for the training of novices since it saves time.
2. A leader in difficulty may call for a top rope from a party above to overcome some pitch. Not common.

Some new climbs and difficult pitches are first led by top rope tactics (e.g. Flake Crack, Scafell), then led 'clean'. The old term was 'inspection on a rope held from above'.

On very short crags, e.g. ◊ Harrison's Rocks, it is possible to pass the rope round a belay such as a tree at the top and handle the rope from the ground.

Tragsitz   A chair-like device used in some mountain rescue situations for lowering injured climbers from a steep rock face. In certain cases of injury (e.g. the spine) a full stretcher will have to be used.

Traverse (G.: Quergang, Überschreitung)   Literally, to cross. To traverse a mountain means to go up by one route and down by another; for example, to traverse the Matterhorn by going up the Hörnli Ridge and down the Italian Ridge. Frequently regarded as the most satisfying method of accomplishing a mountain ascent.

In the course of a climb, to traverse means to make moves leading to the left or right, rather than up. A girdle traverse is a climb which goes from one side of a crag to the other, rather than bottom to top. The first girdle traverse was Lliwedd, Wales (1907).

Travers-Jackson, George Francis (1880–1964)   One of the founders of climbing in South Africa with many first ascents on Table Mountain and elsewhere.

Trekking   The growth of air travel has made possible walking holidays in distant locations such as the Himalaya and the Andes. Multi-day walks, usually with a specific objective like Everest Base Camp or Machu Picchu (the Inca Trail), are known as treks. In Africa they are called safaris and include, for example, the ascent of ◊ Kilimanjaro (5,895 m), a five-day safari. In the Himalaya a number of fairly high mountains have been designated as 'trekking peaks' which means that no special permit or fee is needed to climb them.

Walking the long distance trails of Britain, Europe and North America is not usually called trekking though the activity is basically the same. The chief difference is that most walkers in the greater ranges prefer to have their trip organized for them, with porters and cooks supplied and several companies now specialize in this. All camping gear and food is supplied and the walker need only carry a camera. At high altitude this is a distinct advantage. Permits are often required for treks and trekking companies will provide them – they can take several days to acquire otherwise.

In recent years some climbing expeditions have had accompanying trekkers as far as ◊ Base Camp; a means of raising revenue for the climb.

Trekking can be quite arduous and a degree of fitness is required. In tropical countries, too, hygiene, health and food need careful consideration and trekkers, like climbers, can be subject to altitude sickness in high mountain areas.

Apart from those named above famous treks include the Circuit of ◊ Annapurna, the Milford Trail (New Zealand), the John Muir Trail (U.S.A.), the Tour of ◊ Mont Blanc and the Punta Union (Peru). There are many more. (See Walt Unsworth, *Classic Walks of the World*.)

Trenker, Luis (1892–1990)   Writer and film maker who was also a guide and ski-instructor in earlier days. Better known on the Continent than in the U.K. His many mountain films include *The White Hell of Piz Palu* (1928–9).

Triangulation point (Trig point)   A summit used as a datum point by the Ordnance Survey. Shown on maps as a triangle and identified on the ground as a pillar of concrete or stone with brass fittings on top. In the Alps a similar point may be marked by a wooden pyramid, but this is not universal. (◊ Summit.)

Tribe, Wilberforce Newton (1855–1928)   One of the pioneers of British rock-climbing, friend of the ◊ Hopkinsons. In 1870 he made the first ascent of Sgurr a' Ghreadaidh in Skye, with the 14-year-old John ◊ Mackenzie: one of the first to visit the island for climbing. In 1887 he was with the Hopkinsons on Scafell when they descended the face and erected Hopkinson's Cairn, and in 1893, with C. Hopkinson, he did Hopkinson's and Tribe's Route on the same crag. He also made the first British ascent of the Romsdalhorn. Tribe was President of the Bristol Stock Exchange.

Trog   Colloquialism for a walk – usually implies that it is long or arduous. One hears of 'a hut trog' (the walk to an Alpine hut) and 'just a trog' (an easy ascent). Walking boots are sometimes called trog boots.

Tryfan (917 m)   A fine mountain in Snowdonia, overlooking Llyn Ogwen. Its rocky appearance makes it one of the most impressive peaks in Britain and accounts for its huge popularity. Some easy scrambling is almost essential for an ascent, even on the tourist routes. The summit is marked by two upstanding fingers of rock known as Adam and Eve.

Tryfan is a popular rock-climbing mountain, the principal areas being the E Face and the Milestone Buttress. Most of the routes are in the easier and middle grades of difficulty and are fairly long: a paradise for novices. The first rock-climb on the mountain was South Gully, climbed by R. Williams in 1887. Other notable ascents are:

1894   Second Pinnacle Rib – J. M. A. Thomson and H. Hughes
1899   N. Buttress – O. G. Jones and Abraham brothers
   Terrace Wall Variant – O. G. Jones and Abraham brothers
   Milestone Ordinary – O. G. Jones and Abraham brothers
1902   Gashed Crag – H. B. Buckle and G. Barlow
1911   Grooved Arête – Steeple, Woodhead, Barlow, Bowron, Doughty
1914   Overlapping Rib – Steeple, Barlow, Doughty
1927   Belle Vue Bastion – I. M. Waller and C. H. S. R. Palmer
1936   Munich Climb – Teufel, Seldmayr, Jenkins, Scheuhuber, Reiss and
   Brandt
   Scars Climb – Noyce and Edwards
   Soap Gut – Noyce and Edwards

Tucker, Charles Comyns (1843–1922)   A companion of ◊ Freshfield with whom he made a number of first ascents, including Kasbek and Elbruz in the Caucasus (1868). Tucker later turned his attention to the Dolomites, making the first ascents of the Cima di Brenta (1871), Cima della Vezzana (1872) and the Rosengartenspitze (1874).

Tuckett, Francis Fox (1834–1913)   A Bristol businessman who was one of the foremost explorers of the Alps, rivalling ◊ Ball. He made the first ascent of the Aletschhorn (1859) and was with ◊ Stephen on the first complete ascent of the Goûter route up Mont Blanc (1861). His exploration of the Dauphiné in 1862 opened up this wild area and paved the way for Whymper and others.

He spent many seasons in the Eastern Alps where he made a number of first ascents and where his name is commemorated in the Rif. Tuckett of the Brenta Group.

Tuckett was an inveterate traveller and climbed in many (then) unknown places including Corsica, Greece, Norway, Pyrenees and Algeria. The *A.C. Register* credits him with 269 peaks and 687 passes.

He refused the presidency of the A.C. on business grounds. Though he wrote no books as such, a collection of his papers, entitled *Hochalpenstudien* was published in Germany in 1873, and his diaries and letters of 1856–74 were published in 1920 under the title, *A Pioneer in the High Alps*.

Tullis, Julie (1939–86)   Born in London, she and her husband Terry ran the Festerhaunt, a well-known sports shop and café in Kent, where they also taught climbing, mostly on Harrison's Rocks. At the age of 38 she went to the Andes and later teamed up with ◊ Diemberger to film ascents in the Himalaya. She became the first British woman to climb an 8,000 m peak (Broad Peak, 1984). In 1986 she and Diemberger climbed ◊ K2, a mountain they had visited twice before, but she died in her tent near the summit – one of many that fateful summer.

Turkey, climbing in   The principal mountains of Turkey are: the Taurus, bordering the Mediterranean; the Canik or Pontine Mountains, bordering the Black Sea; Erciyas Dag, near Kayseri; the Cilo Dag and Sat Dag of the Lake Van region; and Ararat, in the extreme east, near the Armenian border. Most of them offer prospects of discovery by modest expeditions, and the Cilo and Sat Dags in particular have a certain popularity in this respect. The heights are 3,500–4,000 m and the rock is sometimes dubious. The highest peaks in each area are:

Cilo Dag, Geliasin (4,170 m)   Erciyas Dag, Erciyas (3,916 m)
Sat Dag, Hendevade (3,810 m)   Taurus, Kaldi Dag (3,734 m)
Canik Mountains, Kackar (3,931 m) Ararat, Ararat (5,165 m)

According to Genesis, the ascent of Ararat was made by Noah – it is certainly the earliest recorded ascent of a high peak, and unusual in that it was made by boat! Expeditions seeking the Ark have been made, and various claims put forward. Sceptics may prefer to believe that the ascent of J. J. F. W. Parrot in 1829 was the first ascent of the mountain.
GUIDEBOOKS Lennon, *Mount Ararat Region*.
Aydingun, *Aladaglar*.
Tüzel, *Ala Dag*. (C.P.)

Turner, Samuel (1869–1929)   A Manchester man who climbed in various parts of the world and recorded his exploits in three books: *My Climbing Adventures in Four Continents*, *Siberia* and *The Conquest of the N.Z. Alps*. His unconventional attitude, especially in ignoring the establishment, caused considerable antagonism and his books were heavily criticized. Turner died in New Zealand.

Tying on   Nowadays it is usual for a climber to wear a ◊ harness to which the rope is tied directly, or in some cases, by means of a karabiner.

The original method of tying on was simply to wrap the rope round the waist and tie it off with a bowline. In the event of a fall this could be quite injurious and it is not possible to hang from a rope like that for more than a few minutes without losing consciousness. In the Alps the chest-tie, either with the main rope or a sling, became popular. In the U.K. and the U.S.A., waist lengths (multiple turnings of light hemp rope) and swami belts (nylon belts) were respectively in vogue for many years after the war. With modern climbing, however, where the ability to hang free is needed, the harness became essential.

Tyndale, Harry Edmund Guise (1888–1948) A member of the Ice Club formed at Winchester School by ◊ Irving, of which the best-known member was ◊ Mallory. Tyndale features in the writings of both these men and was himself translator of several climbing books from German to English, and editor of a series of Alpine classics brought out by Blackwells, as well as the *Alpine Journal*.

Tyndall, John (1820–93) Rose from humble Irish origins to become one of the outstanding scientists of the Victorian age, working with Faraday and finally succeeding him at the Royal Institution. His early Alpine exploits were mostly concerned with glaciers and he was one of the protagonists of the great glacier controversy which raged throughout the latter half of the century. His *Glaciers of the Alps* (1860) was one of the highlights of the argument; his chief opponent was Forbes.

From 1860, he turned to the more competitive element of climbing with an attempt on the Matterhorn, reaching the Great Tower on the Italian Ridge, then the highest point reached. In 1862 he made another attempt and reached the Shoulder, now called Pic Tyndall. Whymper saw in Tyndall a serious rival, but in fact Tyndall did not return to the mountain until 1868 (three years after the first ascent) when he made the first traverse from Breuil to Zermatt via the Italian and Hörnli Ridges.

Meanwhile, in 1861, he made the first ascent of Weisshorn; it was news of this success which made Whymper concentrate on the still unclimbed Matterhorn.

Tyndall was quick to take offence and rouse passions. He resigned from the A.C. (he was Vice-President at the time) over a joke made by Stephen about the place of science in climbing; fell out with Whymper over details of the Matterhorn; and, of course, with Forbes over glaciers. Later in his life he made some disastrous excursions into politics which tarnished his scientific reputation.

Tyndall described his Alpine experiences in *The Glaciers of the Alps* (1860) and *Hours of Exercise in the Alps* (1871).

Tyrolean traverse A sensational way of crossing a deep gap, usually to gain some otherwise inaccessible pinnacle. There are two methods, one for short gaps and one for longer gaps. In both cases the pinnacle has to be lassoed.

1. *Position assise*. A double rope is passed over the pinnacle and the climber sits astride both, pushing them apart. He pulls himself along by his hands.

2. *Position pendue*. For longer gaps. When the rope is secured to the pinnacle the climber hangs from it by his hands and one leg, crooked over the rope. He pulls himself along.

In both cases a safety rope is essential and it is usual for the climber to clip himself by a short line to the Tyrolean rope so that he won't swing if he comes off.

The name comes from the Dolomites (South Tyrol), where the method is used on the Guglia di Amacis, but the technique is uncommon. In Britain it has been used on some sea-stacks.

U

Uemura, Naomi (1942–84) Japanese mountaineer and adventurer who achieved international recognition. Began climbing whilst a student at Meiji University, Tokyo.

His first expedition was to Cho Oyu II in 1964, but it was for his involvement with Mt Everest that he is best known. In 1969 he took part in the Japanese reconnaissance of the S W Face, reaching 8,014 m, and in the following year he climbed the mountain by the S Col route and took part in the ill-fated International Expedition.

Uemura was a keen solo expeditioner. He soloed Mt Blanc, Kilimanjaro, Aconcagua, Mt Sandford (Alaska) and McKinley (twice). His interests went beyond mountaineering, however. He made a solo raft journey down the Amazon and lived for a year with Canadian eskimos. He was particularly attracted by Arctic travel, making solo journeys along Greenland's coast, across the heart of Greenland North–South, Greenland to Alaska, and by dog team to the N Pole.

In 1984 Uemura disappeared whilst descending from a winter solo ascent of McKinley and despite searches his body has never been found.

Uemura was an immensely popular figure in Japan. A dramatized film was made of his life but aroused some controversy in Japanese climbing circles.

Underhill, Miriam (1899–1976) and Robert L. M. (1889–1983) Two of the best known American climbers of the pre-war era. As Miriam O'Brien, before her marriage to Bob Underhill, Mrs Underhill did notable climbs in the New England mountains, the Dolomites and at Chamonix: a number of first ascents and many first ascents by a woman. She was in the first all-women ascent of the Matterhorn and Grépon, and made the first ski traverse of Monte Rosa, Gressoney–Zermatt (1930). In Chamonix she made the first ascent of the Aig. du Roc (A. Couttet, G. Cachat, 1927) and the first traverse of the Aigs. du Diable (R. L. M. Underhill, A. Charlet, G. Cachat, 1928).

As man and wife they climbed together many times in Europe and America. Robert Underhill played a part in founding Yosemite climbing (◊ United States). Miriam Underhill wrote *Give Me the Hills* (1956).

Union Internationale des Associations d'Alpinisme (U.I.A.A.) An international body with representatives from the various countries which have mountaineering clubs. Lays down specifications for climbing equipment standards and discusses all matters of concern to climbers including conservation of mountain areas. Meets annually in various member countries in turn. The ◊ British Mountaineering Council represents Britain.

United States, climbing in The mountains of the United States are so varied in character and so numerous, that they offer the climber a whole spectrum of climbing experience from expeditions of Himalayan size in the remote peaks of Alaska, through the Alpine-style ascents of the Tetons, to the hard rock-climbs of Yosemite and the eastern outcrops. These are dealt with under the relevant sections.

Naomi Uemura being presented with the Award for Valour in Sport in 1979 by the previous year's winner, Kathy Miller. (*T. Tullis*)

In 1876 the Appalachian Mountain Club was formed, followed by the Sierra Club in 1892 and the American Alpine Club in 1902. It is true to say that these mostly followed the pattern of climbing the easier routes up the higher peaks, many of which had been previously climbed by soldiers, surveyors, miners and general adventurers which the West had attracted. At the same time, many Americans went to the European Alps for climbing, including, of course, ◊ Coolidge and Miss Brevoort. The standard began to rise after the First World War, when climbers like R. Underhill and Miriam O'Brien began difficult ascents in the Tetons. In 1931 Underhill taught rock-climbing skills to some Californians who went on to develop the Yosemite. In the 1930s a further boost was added by the arrival of F. Wiessner from Europe, who developed the Shawangunks. Expeditionary climbs to Alaska were done by F. Beckey, Bradford Washburn and others.

In such a large country it was inevitable that much of the climbing was localized. From the late 1930s onwards two Californian groups developed prodigious skills – the Southern Californians at Tahquitz Rock and the Sierrans at Yosemite (see below). These fused in the personality of Royal ◊ Robbins who made the first 5·9 climb at Tahquitz in Open Book, 1952. Under the influence of Robbins, ◊ Harding and other outstanding climbers, Yosemite dominated world climbing for a decade.

In recent years American climbers have shown themselves outstanding expedition climbers as well.

Such is the diversity of the American mountain landscape that every type of mountain activity is encompassed besides pure climbing. There are walking (hiking) trails for backpackers and others, many famous ski resorts such as Aspen and numerous white-water rivers for canoeing and rafting.

The highest mountain in the U.S.A. is Mt McKinley (Denali) in ◊ Alaska (6,194 m).

CASCADES AND OLYMPICS

The Cascades is a long range of high mountains, many volcanic, extending

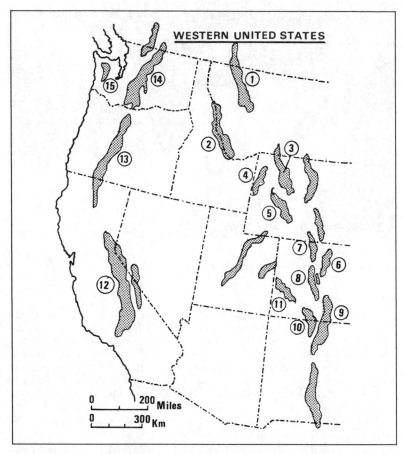

WESTERN UNITED STATES

ROCKY MOUNTAINS: **1** Lewis Range; **2** Bitterroot Range; **3** Absaroka Range; **4** Tetons; **5** Wind River Range; **6** Front Range; **7** Park Range; **8** Sawatch range; **9** Sangre de Cristo/Culebra Ranges; **10** San Miguel/San Juan Ranges; **11** Needle Mountains; **12** SIERRA NEVADA; **13** CASCADES; **14** NORTH CASCADES; **15** OLYMPIC MOUNTAINS.

from the Canadian border down through Washington and Oregon and into California. The highest peak is Mt Rainier (4,392 m). It has 28 glaciers. The first ascent was by H. Stevens and P. B. Van Trump, 1870. Fine ice and mixed routes are found on the north and west faces, including Willis Wall, 1,200 m high (C. Bell, solo, 1961).

There are several other volcanic peaks, two of which are active. The Alpine-style peaks of the North Cascades offer good climbs, including Mount Shuksan, Slesse Mountain (BC), the Picket Range, and in the Cascade Pass region. Liberty Bell has a 365 m granite face which gives a four-day route. Other good climbs are on Mount Stuart and the rock peaks of the Enchantment Lakes area.

In all these areas the chief explorer was Fred Beckey, who made the first ascents of Liberty Bell (1946), Mt Index (1950) and many others.

The Olympic National Park includes Mt Olympus (2,428 m). Plenty of climbing, generally fairly easy. The area has heavy rainfall.

WIND RIVER RANGE

Remote mountains in Wyoming, the Wind River peaks are amongst the most dramatic in the Rockies. They form principally two groups. In the north are 8 summits over 4,100 m, including Gannett Peak (4,207 m) the highest in Wyoming – a state which has several ranges with peaks over 3,500 m, including the Tetons (see below). In the southern part the peaks are slightly smaller, but very rugged. Best known is the Cirque of the Towers, a ridge of 17 peaks, mostly 3,650 m, with numerous climbs. The traverse (R. Robbins, R. McCracken, C. Raymond, 1965) takes two days and is one of the best of its kind. The Wind River mountains have some of the largest ◊ glaciers and icefields of the U.S. Rocky Mountain system. Backpacking is essential to reach the mountains and there are numerous popular trails.

DEVIL'S TOWER

In the north-east corner of Wyoming rises a 275 m basaltic plug, a great columnar monolith which became the first National Monument of the U.S.A. in 1906. It was first climbed by two locals, W. Ripley and W. Rogers, in 1893, using wooden pegs to form a ladder in the cracks. Climbed free in 1937 (F. Wiessner, W. House, L. Coveney). There are now various routes to the top.

The Tower figured in a sensational rescue in 1941 when a parachutist landed on the summit and had to be rescued by Jack Durrance.

TETONS

The Teton range is on the border between Wyoming and Idaho, though mostly in the former state. It rises as granite spires for 1,800–2,100 m above Jackson Hole and the Snake River, which are themselves almost the same height above sea level. The range is some 65 km long and 25 km wide and is part of the Rocky Mountain system. They are very popular.

The highest peaks are:

Grand Teton 4,196 m	S Teton 3,814 m
Mt Owen 3,940 m	Teewinot Mt 3,759 m
Middle Teton 3,903 m	Cloudveil Dome 3,666 m
Mt Moran 3,842 m	Thor Peak 3,663 m

The first ascent of Grand Teton was made by Spaulding and Owen in 1898, although it is possible that there were earlier ascents in 1872 and 1893. There are now some 20 routes, including:
N Ridge – R. Underhill, F. Fryxell, 1931
N Face – P. Petzold, J. Durrance, 1936
The most difficult summit to reach is that of Mt Owen, climbed in 1930 by Underhill, Henderson, Fryxell and Smith.

SIERRA NEVADA (CALIFORNIA)

A range of high mountains, 650 km long and 65 km wide, which includes Mt Whitney (4,418 m), the highest mountain in the U.S.A. outside of Alaska. There is a track to the summit, but the E Face offers good and popular climbs. Other good areas are the Palisades and the Minarets. Undoubtedly the most popular area of the Sierras is Yosemite Valley (see below).

YOSEMITE VALLEY, CALIFORNIA

A valley in the Yosemite National Park of the Sierra Nevada. Though the peaks are fairly low (Half Dome 2,698 m), they rise in sheer walls and spires from the valley, immensely impressive to tourist and climber alike. The post-war climbs at Yosemite have had a profound effect on world rock-climbing, and it is arguably the most important rock-climbing centre in the world.

The rock is a compact granite, glacier-polished and with smooth cracks and flaring chimneys, which tends to give a muscular type of climbing, particularly on the big walls. All the routes tend to be hard, though they vary in length from short 'outcrop' type cracks to major climbs lasting several days. Pegs and bolts are used, but the latter only where strictly necessary, and pegs are removed after use. (It was for use on the hard Yosemite granite that Chouinard developed his special steel pegs which have now become standard in America and Britain.) The ethics at Yosemite are high, and pitches previously bolted have in some cases been repeated with the tiny bat-hooks.

The long multi-day climbs have led to the development of webbing étriers, webbing belay seats, bivvy hammocks and an improvement in the techniques of sack-hauling and various rope manoeuvres.

The best seasons for climbing in Yosemite are spring and autumn when the storms are less frequent than they are in winter. In summer, with temperatures of 38°C plus, dehydration is a serious problem, particularly on the big walls. Even in spring and autumn plenty of water has to be carried.

The principal Yosemite climbs are on the Cathedral Spires, Sentinel Rock, Lost Arrow, Half Dome, El Capitan, Cathedral Rock and Mt Watkins. ◊ El Capitan, with routes of 600–900 m, all hard, is the most famous of these.

Climbing in Yosemite began in 1933 and the following year the Cragmont Climbing Club, inspired by the Easterner R. Underhill, climbed Higher and Lower Cathedral Spires. The ascent of The Lost Arrow by J. Salathé and A. Nelson in 1947 brought this period of development to an end. In 1949 the Sierra Club rationalized ◊ gradings.

The great modern breakthrough came with the first ascent of the Nose of El Capitan by W. Harding, G. Whitmore, W. Merry in 1958. The ascent was by siege tactics – 45 days spread over 18 months. 900 m of fixed rope, 675 pegs and 125 bolts were used. Dihedral Wall of El Capitan (Baldwin, Cooper, Denny, 1962) also involved a 42-day siege, but climbers in the 1960s began to reject siege tactics as unethical. As early as 1960, Fitschen, Robbins, Frost and Pratt repeated the Nose climb in a single push. Other outstanding climbs include:

1957 N W Face, Half Dome – Robbins' party
1960 W Face, Sentinel – Frost, Chouinard
1961 Salathé Wall, El Capitan – Pratt, Frost, Robbins
1964 S Face, Mt Watkins – Harding, Chouinard, Pratt
       North America Wall, El Capitan – Robbins, Pratt, Frost, Chouinard
       N Face, Half Dome – Robbins, McCracken
1966 Muir Wall, El Capitan – Chouinard, Herbert
1968 Muir Wall, El Capitan – Robbins (solo)
1970 S Face, Half Dome – Harding, Rowell
       Wall of Early Morning Light, El Capitan – Caldwell, Harding
1975 Pacific Ocean Wall, El Capitan – Bridwell, Westbay, Fisk, East
       Astro Man, Washington Column – Bachar, Long, Kauk
1977 Phoenix, Cascade Area – Jardine, Lakey (Gr. 5.13a)
1978 Separate Reality, Cookie Area – Kauk

COLORADO ROCKIES

The highest part of the Rocky Mountain system is in Colorado. There are 54 named peaks of 14,000 ft (4,267 m) or more known as the ◊ Fourteeners and more than a thousand summits exceeding 3,000 m. The whole state seems to be one vast complex of mountains but four main areas can be identified:

North Front Range   These mountains are near Denver, the state capital. They include the celebrated Longs Peak, 4,345 m, which has a 550 m E Face including the upper part known as the Diamond – not climbed until 1960 (D. Rearick and R. Kamps). There are several routes on the Diamond now. Longs Peak is in the Rocky Mountain National Park.

Further south, near Boulder, are the rock-climbing centres of Boulder Canyon, Eldorado Canyon and The Flatirons. Further south still and apart from the rest of the Front Ranges is Pikes Peak, once a landmark for pioneers crossing the continent. There is climbing on the peak and on the nearby Garden of the Gods.

The highest of the Front Range peaks is Grays Peak (4,349 m). The ascent is easy.

Central Ranges   Includes the Sawach and Elks Ranges, the latter containing the Maroon Bells. Though high, the Sawach are not difficult. Mt Elbert (4,398 m) is the highest of all the Fourteeners and nine out of the top 20 peaks are in the range. The international ski centre of Aspen is also here. Just south of the ranges lies the Black Canyon of the Gunnison River: granite climbs over 600 m, all hard, in a 30 km gorge – also a GrIV/V river run.

Sangre de Cristo Ranges   These include the Crestone Needle and Crestone Peak, the last of the Fourteeners to be climbed (A. R. Ellingwood and Miss E. S. Davis, 1916). There is also good climbing on Blanca Peak N Face. At 4,378 m, Blanca is fifth highest in the state – Crestone is only 8 m lower and comes seventh.

San Juan Mountains   The San Juans, north of Durango, are a series of complex ranges. Good climbing on Sneffels, Ophir Needles, the Needles, the Grenadiers and Lizard Head – this last is said to be the hardest summit to reach in Colorado (Gr 5.7). It is a rotten rock monolith sitting atop a broad ridge. Spiky ridges, not unlike the ◊ Chamonix aiguilles are characteristic of much of the San Juans – one peak is actually called Jagged Mountain! The Needles and Grenadiers are reached by the romantic and sensational Animas Valley Railroad.

Many Colorado mountains were climbed by miners and surveyors but the chief pioneer climber as such was A. R. ◊ Ellingwood who made the first ascent of Lizard Head, 1920, the Crestones, 1916, and the famous Ellingwood Ledges on Crestone Needle, 1925.

SOUTH-WEST DESERT AREAS

The states of the south-west have some of the most spectacular scenery in the U.S.A., often in the form of giant sandstone pillars or deep canyons. Monument Valley on the Utah–Arizona border is perhaps the best known since it features in films: climbs have been done on the towers but climbing is at present banned by the Navajos in whose tribal territory the Valley lies. It was the ascent of Spider Rock in 1956 – a 240 m pillar – that first alerted climbers to the desert climbs.

Much of the best climbing lies within the Four Corners area where Utah, Arizona, New Mexico and Colorado meet. The nearest is the spectacular volcanic Shiprock; a huge set of walls and pinnacles made of basalt and tuff-breccia. The Indians call it Tsa-Beh-Tai, the Rock with Wings – and that sums it up. First ascent by D. Brower, B. Robinson, R. Bedayn and J. Dyer, 1939. The rock is about 520 m high.

In the La Salle Mountains near Moab, Utah, are the Fisher Towers, 450 m; Titan, 200 m (first ascent 1962); Castleton Tower, 120 m (first ascent 1961); and many similar sandstone pillars, all offering hard climbs.

Some climbing is done in the gigantic Grand Canyon and in Brazos River Canyon, New Mexico, but the best is that in Zion Canyon where there are immense sandstone walls on the Great White Throne (3,056 m) and other peaks.

Further west, in the Californian desert, is Joshua Tree, just 45 minutes drive from Palm Springs. This is a vast area like a super-Brimham, with dozens of granitic outcrops offering short climbs, including many of high standard. The climate is especially agreeable in the winter months and there are over 1,000 routes from which to choose.

THE NORTH-EAST

There are suitable climbing crags in many parts of New England but the major climbing areas of the north-east states are the White Mountains, New Hampshire, and the Shawangunks in New York State. The three main cliffs of the White Mountains are Cannon (over 300 m), White Horse (240 m) and Cathedral (150 m). Called the Yosemite of the north, the rock is good granite and there are many hard routes.

The Shawangunks consist of a series of quartzite conglomerate cliffs extending along a seven-mile ridge on the west rim of the Hudson River valley, about 110 km from New York city. The rocks are 60–90 m high. The Trapps cliff has most routes partly because it is most accessible, though the others are not difficult to reach. The 'Gunks' are extremely popular with climbs of all standards – this place is the Stanage of America!

Other rock-climbing areas include Seneca Rock, West Virginia; Wallface, Chapel Pond and Pokomoonshine in the Adirondacks; and Smugglers Notch in Vermont.

There is no permanent ice and snow in the region but much winter ice-climbing in Vermont, New Hampshire and Maine. The Huntington Ravines on Mt Washington in New Hampshire are the best known; 180–360 m gullies. The mountain is noted for bad weather!

GUIDEBOOKS: There are numerous guidebooks of all types in the U.S.A. The following is a selection. The areas they cover are fairly obvious:

NORTH-WEST

Beckey, *Cascade Alpine Guide I, Columbia River to Stevens Pass*.
Beckey, *Cascade Alpine Guide II, Stevens Pass to Rainy Pass*.
Beckey, *Cascade Alpine Guide III, Rainy Pass to Fraser River*.
Green, *Idaho Rock, Climber's guide to Selkirk Crest and Sandpoint areas*.
Brooks/Whitelaw, *A Climber's Guide to Washington Rock*.
Thomas, *Oregon Rock*.
Climber's Guide to the Olympic Mountains.
Bingham, *City of Rocks–Idaho*.

SOUTH-WEST

Harlin III, *West Coast Rock Climbs*.
Meyers/Reid, *Yosemite Climbs*.
Reid/Falkenstein, *Rock Climbs of Tuolumne Meadows*.
Vogel, *Joshua Tree*. Rock Climbing Guide.
Meytras, *Tahoe Rock Climbing*.
Wheelock/Condon, *Climbing Mount Whitney*.
Roper, *Climber's Guide to Yosemite Valley*.
Secor, *The High Sierra: Peaks, Passes and Trails*.
Urioste, *The Red Rocks of Southern Nevada*.

Wilts, *Tahquitz and Suicide Rocks*.
Steiger, *Climber's Guide to Sabino Canyon and Mount Lemmon Highway*.
(Tucson, Arizona.)
Bjornstad, *Desert Rock*.
Hellweg, *Climber's Guide to Southern California*.
Bartlett/Allen, *The Sierra East Side: Rock Climbs*.
Spencers, *Southern Yosemite Rock Climbs*.
Vogel, *Joshua Tree Select*.
MID-WEST
Piana, *Touch the Sky, The Needles in the Black Hills of South Dakota –
Climber's Guide*. + 2 folding maps.
Gardiner/Guilmette, *Devils Tower National Monument*.
Bagg, *50 Short Climbs in the Midwest*.
Hynek/Landmann, *Prairie Walls*. Minnesota's Blue Mounds State Park.
NORTH-EAST
Harlin III, *East Coast Rock Climbs*.
Williams, *Shawangunk Rock Climbs*.
Ross/Ellms, *A Rock Climber's Guide, Cannon, Cathedral, Humphrey's and
Whitehorse*.
Swain, *The Gunks Guide*.
Mellor, *Climbing in the Adirondacks, Rock and Ice Routes in the Adirondack
Park*.
SOUTH-EAST
Hall, C., *Southern Rock, A Climber's Guide*.
Hackworth, *Stones of Years, A Climber's Guide to Red River Gorge*.
Webster, *Seneca Rocks, West Virginia. Climber's Guide*.
Robinson, *The Illustrated Underground Guide to the Tennessee Wall*.
ROCKIES
Garratt/Martin, *Colorado's High Thirteeners. Climbing and Hiking guide*.
Ament/McCarty, *High Over Boulder*.
Borneman, *Climbing Guide to Colorado's Fourteeners*.
Roach, *Flatiron Classics*.
Kelsey, *Climbing and Hiking in the Wind River Mountains*.
Caffrey, *Climbers' Guide to Montana*.
Harlin III, *Rocky Mountain Rock Climbs*.
Ellison/Smoot, *Wasatch Rock Climbs*.
DuMais, *The High Peaks, Climbing Guide to the Mountain Areas of Rocky
Mountain National Park*.
Kopischka, *Cracks Unlimited, Climbing Guide to Vedauwoo*.
Rosebrough, *San Juan Mountains, Climbing and Hiking Guide*.
Bonney, *Field Book: The Wind River Range, Climbing Routes and Back
Country*.
Also same series, *The Teton Range & The Gros Ventre Range*.
Rossiter, *Boulder Climbs North*.

Unsoeld, William F. (1927–79)   American professor of philosophy and
religion who took part in expeditions to Nilkantha, Garhwal (1949), Makalu
(1954) and Masherbrum (1960). In 1963 with T. F. ◊ Hornbein he made the
first ascent of Everest W Ridge and first traverse of the mountain – an
outstanding feat of mountaineering.

In 1976 he was co-leader of an Indo–American expedition to Nanda Devi
which climbed the N W Face and N Ridge. Tragically his daughter, named
Nanda Devi after the mountain, died of an embolism on the peak at 7,400 m.

Unsoeld was killed by an avalanche on Mt Rainier.

V

Vallot brothers Joseph Vallot (1853–1925) and his brother, Henri, erected an observatory and refuge hut on Mont Blanc at their own expense. The hut figures in many accounts of climbing on Mont Blanc and has probably saved more lives than any other hut, even the Solvay on the ◊ Matterhorn. The brothers spent 40 years on a detailed survey of the region, culminating in the *Carte Vallot*, published posthumously.

Vaucher, Michel (b. 1936) A Swiss guide with wide experience of the hard Alpine routes including the first ascent of the Whymper Pillar on the N Face of Gds Jorasses with ◊ Bonatti in 1964. He is married to Yvette (b. 1929) who also has experience of the hardest routes, making the second women's ascent of the Eigerwand (◊ Eiger) and the first women's ascent of the Matterhorn Nordwand. They were together on the 1971 Everest International Expedition and took part in the so-called 'Latin revolt' against ◊ Dhyrenfurth's leadership.

Venables, Stephen (b. 1954) Read English at Oxford and has become an author and photographer of note, based on his considerable mountain adventures. Tall, bespectacled and slightly academic in appearance, Venables is the modern equivalent of the pioneering Oxbridge mountaineer. Several winter Alpine ascents, the W Face of Jatunhuma in Peru and S E Couloir of Ancohuma in Bolivia. First ascent of Kishtwar-Shivling, 1983; explored Siachen with Indo–British expedition, 1985; first ascent E Face of ◊ Mt Everest by the S Col, 1988.

Author of *Painted Mountains* (1986), *Everest Kangshung Face* (1989), *Island at the Edge of the World* (1991).

Verglas (Fr.) Thin ice lying on rocks and making climbing difficult. May be general in cold conditions, but often, in the Alps, it is a local condition confined to some feature which gets no sun, e.g. a verglassed chimney might occur on an otherwise sunny rock face. Thick verglas can sometimes be tackled in crampons with advantage.

Mountain paths can also become icy and dangerous in cold conditions, even though there may be no snow about. On some crags and many Alpine peaks very cold conditions are an advantage because the ice binds together rock which might otherwise be loose. (◊ Hoar frost.)

Via Ferrata (It.) (G.: Klettersteig) Literally, the Italian means 'iron-road' and the German 'climbing-path' – a combination of the two gives some idea of what is involved. A *via ferrata* is a rock route up or across a mountain involving some scrambling and protected by steel cables to which the climber clips himself for protection. Limestone is particularly well suited because of the ledges and fissures which the 'path' uses: the ledges are joined together by ladders, some of which exceed 30 m. The situations are usually sensationally exposed.

Left, Stephen Venables after climbing Everest Kangshung Face. (*E. Webster*); right, Via Ferrata in the Dolomites. (*W. Unsworth*)

The most famous *vie ferratae* are in the Dolomites, but they are also common in the limestone alps of Austria and Germany.

GUIDEBOOKS Davies, *Via Ferrata, Scrambles in the Dolomites* (C.P.). Pevsner, *Klettersteig, Scrambles in the Limestone Alps* (C.P.).

Vibram soles   Cleated rubber soles were invented by Vitale Bramani of Italy in 1935, and called Vibram in his honour. The name is a registered trade mark and the property of Vibram SpA of Italy who took up the manufacture. They were used on the first ascents of the Walker Spur and N Face of the Dru.

After the war Vibrams (colloquially known at first as 'vibs'), and the similar British marque called Commando, gained immediate acceptance. Nailed soles practically vanished by the late 1950s.

Other cleated soles were later developed including some designed to have less erosion impact, the best known being Klets, designed by Ken Ledward.

Vigne, Godfrey Thomas (b. 1801)   One of the first Europeans to describe the Karakoram. In 1835–8 he made extensive journeys into Baltistan, Ladakh and Kashmir, reaching the snout of the Chogo Lungma Glacier and ascending the Saltoro valley in search of the Saltoro pass. The first to describe ◊ Nanga Parbat.

Vigne was an all-round sportsman and hunter, and played cricket for the M.C.C. His description of his journeys is one of the great classics of Himalayan travel: *Travels in Kashmir, Ladakh and Ishkardoo*.

See also: *When Men and Mountains Meet* by John Keay.

Visser, Philips Christiaan (1882–1955)   Distinguished Dutch diplomat and mountain explorer who, with his wife, Jenny van 't Visser-Hooft, made four journeys to the Karakoram in 1922, 1925, 1929–30, and 1935, which unravelled many of the glacier problems of the region. Mrs Visser-Hooft wrote *Among the Kara-Korum Glaciers* (1926) in English and together they wrote (in German) *Karakorum* (2 vols., 1935, 1938).

Volcano   Any opening in the earth's surface through which magma flows, but here we take the common interpretation of the word to mean a mountain formed by such activity. They are built up of layers of lava and pyroclastic materials (i.e. material ejected by the volcano). The pyroclastic materials can vary in size from bombs or blocks (over 3 cm diameter) to fine ash.

The usual volcanic form is a symmetrical cone, well illustrated by Fujiyama, Japan. If we take their *true* heights, then some volcanoes are among the highest mountains in the world: Mauna Loa, Hawaii, is 9,100 m above its base on the sea bed.

Though there is a well-defined volcano belt around the Pacific, many volcanoes exist outside it, including such well-known mountains as Vesuvius and Kilimanjaro. These, and other volcanoes which are rarely active, such as Cotopaxi, are climbed quite frequently. Attempts are also made to climb active volcanoes (though not during eruptions!). A great many of the world's mountains are originally of volcanic origin.

Voog, Daisy (b. 1932)   Dutch climber who did many difficult routes in the Dolomites and gained considerable fame in 1964 when she became the first woman to climb the Eigerwand (◊ Eiger).

Vörg, Ludwig (1911–41)   One of the famous four who made the first ascent of the Eigerwand (◊ Eiger) in 1938. He had previously been high on the face with Rebitsch in 1937 (see Harrer *The White Spider*). Among his other climbs was the first ascent of Grosser Waxenstein N Face Direct in the Wetterstein Alps and the first ascent of Ushba N Face Direct, in the ◊ Caucasus, both in 1936. Vörg was killed in Poland on the first day of Germany's invasion of Russia.

W

Wager, Lawrence Rickard (1904–65) A member of the 1933 Everest Expedition, when, with Wyn Harris, he equalled the height record for that time of 8,573 m. They also found the famous axe which must have belonged to ◊ Mallory or ◊ Irvine. On the return, Wager climbed to the crest of the N E Ridge and looked over the E Face and into the Karma Valley, the first man known to have done so.

With the exception of 1933, Wager was in Greenland every season from 1930–6 and he returned there in 1953. As a professional geologist, he was in the great tradition of accomplished geologist-mountaineers and received many awards for his work. When he died, he was Professor of Geology at Oxford.

Wainewright, Benjamin (1853–1910) A London eye surgeon noted for his ascents in the Bernina, including the first ascent of Piz Prievalus (1882). A number of his routes on Roseg, Scerscen, Bernina were later added to or improved by other climbers who have subsequently been given the credit.

Wainwright, Alfred (1907–91) The designer of a remarkable series of guidebooks to walking on Lake District mountains (1952–66). The seven volumes are meticulously written by hand and illustrated with unique maps and drawings. In subsequent years he did various other guidebooks, the best known being the Coast to Coast (a walk across the north of England which he invented) and his *Pennine Way Companion* (1968). Other books and T.V. programmes made him a well-known figure. Before retirement he was Borough Treasurer of Kendal. For the Lakeland books he was awarded the M.B.E.

Wakefield, Arthur William (1876–1949) A Keswick doctor who established the ◊ Lake District Fell Record in its present form. He set up a new record in 1904 and improved it a year later: 59 miles, 23,500 ft, 22 hr 7 min. This stood until ◊ Thomas bettered it in 1920 – paced by Wakefield.

Wakefield began climbing with the ◊ Abrahams and took part in a number of first ascents. He left for the Grenfell Mission shortly afterwards, and did not recommence his climbing activities until his return after the First World War. In 1920 he took part with Bower and Masson in the first ascent of the popular Bower's Route on Esk Buttress, Scafell. He took part in the 1922 Everest Expedition and reached the North Col. He also made a number of ascents in the Alps and Canadian Rockies (1908, 1920).

Wales, climbing in Most of Wales is mountainous and even outside ◊ Snowdonia there is plenty of hill-walking and rock-climbing. Similarly ◊ Craig Gogarth is by no means the only sea cliff to be developed.

NORTH AND CENTRAL WALES

Arans Aran Fawddwy (905 m) is the highest summit in Wales outside Snowdonia. There are long climbs of all standards on Craig Cywarch.

Cadair Idris (892 m)   A shapely mountain rising near the coast at Dolgellau, with a long summit ridge and precipitous faces, particularly to the north. This is where the great O. G. Ф Jones began his climbing career, though the crags have never been popular.

Yr Eifl (The Rivals) (564 m)   On the seaward side of these hills in the Lleyn Peninsula is a series of buttresses, Trwyn-y-Gorlech, giving some of the longest climbs in Wales such as Avernus, HS, 245 m, done in 1954. There are a number of other smaller crags and quarries in the peninsula. Climbs of all standards but the area has never been popular.

Eglwyseg Valley   This valley near Llangollen is overlooked by a magnificent limestone escarpment, with a series of high-quality climbing cliffs. On Craig Arthur the climbs are between 35 and 60 m, but shorter on the other rocks. All grades. Numerous small cliffs and quarries throughout Clwyd.

Great and Little Orme's Head   Numerous hard climbs have been done on these well-known limestone headlands at Llandudno. The climb called Separate Elephant, 10·5 m E5, is said to have the largest free-climbed roof in Britain!

Elan Valley   This valley, well known for its reservoirs, has a number of crags with climbs up to 60 m. Best known are: Careg Dhu, Craig y Foel and Cerig Gwynion.

SOUTH WALES

A good deal of popular hillwalking, especially on the Brecon Beacons (Pen y Fan, 886 m). The area is a National Park. Also on the Black Mountains (Waun Fach, 810 m), not to be confused with the Black Mountain (Ban Brycheiniog, 802 m) much further west and not nearly as popular.

There are some inland outcrops such as Taffs Well Quarry, 8 km N W of Cardiff, which has limestone climbs of over 60 m, but the most important climbing is on the coastal cliffs.

The Pembroke Coast   The coast is also a National Park and has one of the best-known long-distance footpaths, from St Dogmaels in the north to Amroth in the south, 291 km. Main areas for climbing are (N–S): Penbwchdy, St David's Head, Stack Rocks, St Govan's Head, Stackpole Head, Lydstep and Giltar Point. All standards and lengths up to 90 m, mostly about half that. The climbing is extremely popular and said to be the best limestone climbing in Britain.

The Gower   Crags lie spread around the Gower Peninsula from Burry Inlet to the Mumbles. Limestone of all grades and up to about 45 m.

Ogmore   Between Ogmore-by-Sea and Southerndown, on the coast near Bridgend is a concentrated set of limestone cliffs with routes in all grades up to about 45 m.

GUIDEBOOKS

Littlejohn/Harber, *Pembroke* (C.C.).

Danford/Penning, *Gower & South East Wales* (S.W.M.C.).

Jones, *Lleyn Peninsula* (C.C.).

Sumner, *Dolgellau Area* (C.C.).

Sumner, *Aran-Cader Idris* (C.C.).

Sumner, *Mid-Wales* (C.C.).

Pollitt, *North Wales Limestone* (C.C.).

Walker, Derek (b. 1936)   The General Secretary of the British Mountaineering Council (B.M.C.), a position he was appointed to on the retirement of D. D. Gray in 1989.

Derek began climbing in 1956 as a member of the R.A.F. Mountain Rescue

The Walker family, with friends and guides. *Back row*: Jacob Anderegg, M. J. Moore, Lucy Walker, Melchior Anderegg; *in front*: Miss Hughes, Frank Walker, Horace Walker, Mrs Frank Walker, A. W. Moore, Johann Jaun. (*AC*)

team in North Wales and has been actively pursuing the sport ever since. He was President of the University of Bristol Mountaineering Club between 1957 and 1960, visiting the Alps for the first time in this period with a trip to Zermatt in 1958.

In 1960–1 he was a member of the first British expedition to Patagonia, doing much to bring the area to the notice of other British climbers. The winter of 1962–3 saw him back in the area with Chris Bonington and Don Whillans, who climbed the Central Tower of Paine. Derek and Ian Clough climbed the North Tower.

Much taken with South America he returned to Chile in 1966 as Headmaster of the British school in Punta Arenas, a job he held until 1970. Whilst there he took part in Ian Clough's expedition to the Fortress in 1967–8 and he attempted the Cathedral in 1970.

He has been a member of the Climbers' Club since 1960 and became President between 1984 and 1987. He is also a member of the Alpine Club and the F.R.C.C. and Chairman of the Don Whillans Memorial Committee.

Walker, Francis (1808–72)   A Liverpool merchant and father of Horace and Lucy Walker (◊ below). Frank Walker did not begin climbing until he was 50. With his family in 1864 he made the first ascent of Balmhorn and the fourth ascent of the Eiger. In 1865, with Lucy, he made the second crossing of the Moming Pass, before joining his son, Moore and G. S. Mathews for their historic first ascent of the Brenva Face of Mont Blanc. In 1871, at the age of 63, he climbed the Matterhorn with Lucy but he was already a sick man and he died the following year.

Walker, Horace (1838–1908) Son of Frank Walker (see above) and brother of Lucy (see below), Horace Walker was one of the most important climbers throughout the Victorian era. He always seemed to have the happy facility of being in the right place at the right time with the right people.

His first ascent was the Vélan at the age of 16 and his last the Pollux at the age of 67. In between he made numerous ascents – the list occupies six pages of the A.C. Register.

His first ascents include: Écrins (1864), Balmhorn (1864), Piz Roseg (1865), Gabelhorn (1865), Pigne d'Arolla (1865), Brenva Face of Mont Blanc (1865), Grandes Jorasses Point Walker (1868), Elbruz (Caucasus 1874) and many new routes on peaks already climbed. He also made numerous second or third ascents and crossed many new cols. He ranged from the Dauphiné to the Tyrol and Dolomites.

Walker was an early advocate of winter climbing (1869, 1879) and, influenced by the Pilkingtons and their friends, began guideless climbing about 1894, including such peaks as Mont Blanc and Piz Bernina.

He was also one of the pioneers of climbing in Skye, where he made several first ascents, and he took enthusiastically to climbing in Snowdonia and the Lake District. In 1892 he made the second ascent of North Climb, Pillar Rock.

Walker was President of the A.C. from 1890–2. He was unmarried.

Walker, Lucy (1835–1916) Daughter of Frank Walker and sister of Horace (see above), Lucy Walker was one of the earliest women climbers. Though she climbed only with her family, guided by the famous ◊ Anderegg cousins, she made several notable ascents including the first ascent of the Balmhorn (1864): the first time in which a woman had taken part in a major first ascent. She also took part in the fourth ascent of the Eiger (1864) and the second crossing of the Moming Pass (1865). In 1871, with her father, she climbed the Matterhorn – the first woman to do so and the nineteenth ascent.

After the death of her father in 1872, Lucy continued to climb with her brother for a few years, but then gave it up and confined herself to valley walks with her life-long companion, Melchior Anderegg. She never married. Her portrait appears in Whymper's well-known engraving, *The Club Room at Zermatt in 1864*.

Waller, Ivan Mark (b. 1906) A daring rock-climber of the inter-war years who took part in a number of first ascents of well-known climbs. In 1927 he made the first ascent of Belle View Bastion, Tryfan, with C. H. S. R. Palmer, and a few weeks later made the second ascent, solo. Later that year he led Fallen Block Crack, Clogwyn y Ddisgl, when the second man failed to follow. In 1931 he seconded ◊ Kirkus on Mickledore Grooves, Scafell, and the West Rib, Dinas Mot. He also took part in the most notable ascents at the Black Rocks, Derbyshire: he was second to Longland on Birch Tree Wall (1928) and to Bridge on Lean Man's Superdirect (1930). In 1928 he made the first ascent, solo, of Lone Tree Groove.

During the Whitsun of 1951, Waller made a remarkable ski descent of the E Face of Helvellyn from the summit to Red Tarn.

Walls (G.: wand) Many of the most important and serious faces in the Alps have a northern aspect. The climbing of these faces is generally associated with the activities of the so-called Munich School in the 1930s (Welzenbach, the Schmids, Harrer and others) and the German word *Nordwand* (north wall) came into general use among climbers. Tied in, as it

Ivan Waller (*left*) and Charles Warren. (*T. D. Unsworth*)

was, with the political climate of the times, the climbing of nordwands and the Munich School in general came in for a good deal of criticism, especially from the conservative elements of British climbing. It is now seen to be an important step forward in the development of the sport.

In fact, the climbing of Alpine faces as distinct from ridges, goes back a good way before the Munich School: one might instance the climbs of Norman-Neruda (N E Face of Lyskamm, 1890), Mummery's attempt on the N Face of the Plan (1892), or the Marinelli Couloir of Monte Rosa (1872). Nor are all the big faces to the north: Monte Rosa and Mont Blanc are cases in point. Even in the thirties, big-face climbing was not an exclusive German affair: the Italians and French were active participants as well.

Nevertheless, the German participation in big-wall climbing has always been large and the mental outlook necessary was cultivated in the nineteenth century by climbers such as Lammer, Lorria, Purtscheller and the Zsigmondys. It certainly reached a climax with Welzenbach and others in the thirties. Outstanding was the Schmids' first ascent of the Matterhorn Nordwand in 1931 and the ascent of the Eigerwand by Harrer, Vorg, Kasparek and Heckmair, 1938. The nordwands still represent the epitome of Alpine climbing and leading climbers are now tackling them in winter, or solo, or making more direct lines up the faces. (See *Big Wall Climbing*, by D. Scott.)

The highest Alpine walls are:

E Face of Monte Rosa, Pennine Alps, 2,400 m; Eiger Nordwand, Bernese Alps, 1,780 m; E Face of Watzmann, Berchtesgadener Alps 1,750 m; Gspaltenhorn Nordwand, Bernese Alps, 1,600 m; Tschingelspitze Nordwand, Bernese Alps, 1,550 m; Hochstadel Nordwand, Lienzer Dolomites, 1,350 m; Triglav Nordwand, Julian Alps, 1,300 m.

There are an estimated 85–90 walls in excess of 1,000 m, mostly in the Western Alps. (List prepared by T. Hiebeler.)

In British rock-climbing the word is more localized. It means rock above approx. 75° i.e. steeper than a slab and possibly overhanging.

Ward, Michael Phelps (b. 1925)　A consulting surgeon who took part in the Mount Everest expeditions of 1951 and 1953. In 1960–1 he climbed a number of peaks in the Everest region, including Ama Dablam (6,865 m). In 1964–5 he explored the little known mountains of Bhutan and made a number of first ascents.

Ward also took part in the first ascent of the E Ridge of Bugaboo Spire (Canada) and in Britain was with Edwards on the first ascent of the Direct Finish to Longland's Climb, Clogwyn Du'r Arddu (1947), and led the first ascent of Angle Groove, Ysfa (1944), Easter Eve, Nevis (1946), and Scimitar Gully, Ben Lui (1972).

In 1980 and 1981 he was leader of expeditions to Kongur, in Chinese Asia, then unclimbed. During the reconnaissance of 1980 he climbed Karatosh (5,440 m) with ◊ Bonington, but the following year concentrated on the medical research aspects of the expedition, whilst the climbing team, led by Bonington, made the first ascent of Kongur.

He is a leading authority on high-altitude medicine and for this and his explorations has been awarded various distinctions by British and American societies. His books are: *Mountaineer's Companion* (ed., 1969), *In This Short Span* (autobiography, 1972), *Man at High Altitude* (1974) and *Mountain Medicine* (1975).

Wasdale Head　A small hamlet with an inn, the Wasdale Head Inn, in the heart of the Lake District. It was the most important centre of rock-climbing during the pioneer days and is still very popular. The principal crags are the Napes, Scafell and Pillar Rock.

Watkins, George H. (1907–32)　Gino Watkins was the dynamic prodigy of Arctic exploration from 1927 until his accidental death in 1932. A good rock-climber he did a number of guideless Alpine climbs while still in his teens and on going up to Cambridge became interested in Arctic exploration. In 1927 he led an expedition to Edge Island, Spitzbergen, and in 1928–9 explored the Quebec–Labrador border.

Watkins considered the possibility of an air route to Canada across the Arctic, learned to fly, and then organized a large-scale expedition to south-east Greenland to survey the route. Among his discoveries was a group of mountains which proved to be the highest in Greenland (Watkins Mountains). For this work Watkins was awarded the Gold Medal of the R.G.S. in 1932. He was then 25.

In 1932 he returned with a smaller expedition to continue his work in Greenland, but was drowned while out hunting in a kayak.

Waymarks　In the Alps popular footpaths are marked with splashes of paint at intervals, the same colour or combination of colours being used throughout. Navigation simply involves following similar marks – though sometimes these are not obvious and have a perverse habit of disappearing just when they are most needed! Sometimes numbers or special symbols are painted in areas where there are a lot of easy walks but usually a stripe suffices. A bent stripe indicates a turn right or left, crossed stripes means you have taken a wrong path.

Wedge　Wooden wedges were formerly used for protection in cracks which were too wide for pitons. They were driven into the crack with a hammer. The wide end had a small hole through which a nylon loop was tied and the rope was attached to this by a karabiner, thus forming a ◊ runner.

Old wedges were always suspect because the wood rotted and they were superseded by American hardware called bongs (because of the noise they made when hit), which were a sort of flared ◊ piton.

Nowadays, camming devices, such as ◊ Friends are used instead.

Welsh 3,000s Name given to a walk embracing all the 14 peaks of 3,000 ft (914 m) or more in Wales. They are all in ◊ Snowdonia and the walk involves about 50 km and 5,500 m of ascent and descent. The route is usually: Y Wyddfa, Crib y Ddysgl, Crib Goch (Snowdon massif), Elidyr Fawr, Y Garn, Glyder Fawr, Glyder Fach, Tryfan (Glyders massif), Pen yr Olewen, Carnedd Dafydd, Yr Elen, Carnedd Llewelyn, Foel Grach, Foel Fras (Carneddau). Time taken is reckoned from summit to summit.

The walk was first done by J. R. Corbett and E. ◊ Thomas in 1919 in a time of 20 hours. Now one of the most popular long-distance walks.

Welzenbach, Willo (1900–34) One of the great school of Munich climbers which arose in the 1920s and of which so many perished on the Alpine nordwands and in the Himalaya. Welzenbach was the supreme prototype: he was the finest climber of his day and one of the best ice-climbers ever. The tragedy is that many of those who followed later did not have his supreme skill.

He began serious climbing in 1921 and between then and 1926, when a diseased elbow made rock-climbing difficult, he made a number of hard climbs in the Eastern Alps. He added 'Gr. VI' to the existing system, elaborated on how the scale should be used and is generally credited with the invention of it, though it originated with Dulfer. (◊ Gradings of difficulty.)

It is for his ice-climbs that he is best remembered. They are still among the most difficult in the Alps:

1924 N W Face of Gross Wiesbachhorn
1925 N Face Direct, Dent d'Hérens
      N Face, Lyskamm E Peak
1926 N W Face of Glockerin
      N Face of Eiskogele
      N Face of Gross Glockner
      N W Face, Zermatt Breithorn
      Pt Welzenbach, S Ridge of Aig. Noire
1930 N Face Direct, Gross Fiescherhorn
1931 N Face, Grands Charmoz
1932 N Face, Grosshorn
      N E Face, Gspaltenhorn
      N W Face, Gletscherhorn
      N Face Direct, Lauterbrunnen Breithorn
1933 N Face, Nesthorn

Ice pitons, invented by his partner F. Rigele, were used for the first time on the Gross Wiesbachhorn.

Welzenbach made plans for an expedition to Nanga Parbat in 1929, but these were frustrated and he did not go out until, against advice, he joined ◊ Merkl as second-in-command of the 1934 attempt on the mountain. In the terrible retreat (◊ Nanga Parbat) he died in Camp 7.

Westmacott, Michael Horatio (b. 1925) A statistician who was a member of the successful Everest team of 1953. Westmacott made the first ascent of Huagaruncho in Peru in 1956 and eight first ascents in the Arrigetch Range of

Don Whillans, with Chris Bonington on the pillion. (*Border TV*)

Alaska, 1964. In 1968 he made the first ascent of Wakhikah Rah in the Hindu Kush.

Weston, Walter (1861–1940)   A clergyman who lived in Japan on three occasions between 1888 and the First World War and who became known as the father of Japanese mountaineering. He made several first ascents in the Japanese Alps and aroused an interest in that country that led to the formation of the Japanese Alpine Club in 1905. He received the Order of the Sacred Treasure from the Emperor and in 1937 Japanese climbers erected a plaque in his honour. Weston also climbed in the Alps, particularly the Oberland, where he made the first unguided crossing of the Eigerjoch (1897). All his life Weston was blind in one eye. He had a commanding personality.

Wheeler, Sir Edward Oliver (1890–1962)   A Canadian from a surveying family who played an important part in the early ascents of the Rockies; climbed Oliver's Peak at age of 12. Joined the Indian Survey and accompanied the first Everest Expedition as surveyor (1921). Discovered the route to the North Col (◊ Mount Everest). Became Surveyor-General of India 1941–7. Knighted 1943.

Wherry, George Edward (1852–1928)   Surgeon and mountaineer, author of one of the strangest climbing books: *Alpine Notes and the Climbing Foot* (1896). Also wrote *Notes from a Knapsack* (1909) in which one chapter is entitled 'Why Both Legs are of Equal Length'.

Whillans, Donald Desbrow (1933–85)   One of the finest mountaineers of post-war Britain, with ascents to his credit ranging from the gritstone outcrops of Derbyshire to the Himalaya. He began climbing at Shining Clough, Derbyshire, in 1950 and was soon leading the hardest climbs of the day. In 1951 he met Joe ◊ Brown and they climbed the Direct Start to Valkyrie at the Roches. Later in the same year they climbed Cemetery Gates, Dinas Cromlech, and Vember, Clogwyn D'ur Arddu. It was the start of one of the most powerful partnerships ever seen in British climbing (for other routes, ◊ Brown). Their last new climb together was Taurus, 1956.

Whillans also climbed with others during this period in Wales, Scotland and the Lakes. New routes include: Slanting Slab, Clogwyn Du'r Arddu (V. Betts, 1955); Strapiombo, Tremadoc (G. J. Sutton, 1955); and the Old Man of Storr (G. J. Sutton, J. Barber, 1955).

In the Alps with Brown, Whillans made a first ascent of the W Face of the Blaitière (1954) and, with Bonington, Clough and Dlugosz, the first ascent of the Central Pillar of Frêney (1961). He took part in several early British ascents of classic routes, including the W Face of the Dru, with Brown (third ascent, first British ascent, 1954). They reduced the time taken from six days to 25 hours.

Whillans's interests veered away from rock-climbing around 1960. Unlike Brown, he has never returned to make concentrated attacks on other new cliffs. Instead he became a leading member of several high-altitude expeditions:

Masherbrum, 1957; Trivor, 1960; Aig. Poincenot, 1962 (first ascent); Central Tower of Paine, 1962 (first ascent); Gauri Sankar, 1964; S Face of Huandoy, 1968; S Face of Annapurna, 1970 (first ascent); S W Face of Everest, 1971 and 1972; Roraima, 1973; Tirich Mir, 1975.

He visited Cerro Torre and Broad Peak in 1983 but without success.

He was a popular lecturer, a fine raconteur and noted wit. Over the years he

343

developed from being 'the little hard man in the flat hat' to a personality of
great character. Few modern climbers have had so much esteem and affection
as Whillans.

See: *Don Whillans – Portrait of a Mountaineer*, by D. Whillans and
A. Ormerod, 1971.

White out An unpleasant phenomenon of snow-scapes, where falling snow
or even mist can merge the land and sky together with complete loss of
horizon. Eerie and dangerous, since it is possible to step over an edge
unknowingly.

Whittaker, James W. (b. 1929) An American mountaineer and guide
from Washington who took part in the Mt McKinley Expedition of 1960. In
1963 with the Sherpa Nawang Gombu he became the first American to ascend
◊ Everest (1 May, S Ridge).

His brother Lou led an expedition to the N Face of Everest in 1982 during
which Marty Hoey was killed. In 1984 Lou and his son Peter returned with an
expedition and again attacked the face. P. Ershler reached the summit.

Whitwell, Edward Robson (1843–1922) A companion of ◊ Tuckett and
making with him the first S–N traverse of Jungfrau and the second traverse of
the Rothorn (1872). In 1974 he made the first ascent of the Aig. de Blaitière.
Whitwell made a couple of attempts at the then unclimbed Dru, but failed.

Whymper, Edward (1840–1911) One of the best-known names in mountaineering, forever associated with the tragic first ascent of the Matterhorn in
which he took part (1865).

Whymper was born in London and became a wood-engraver, like his
father. He showed considerable artistic skill and it was this that prompted W.
◊ Longman, the publisher, to commission from him a series of Alpine
sketches in 1860. It was Whymper's first visit to the Alps, and though he did
little climbing that year, he saw in Alpine climbing a chance to make a name
for himself and a possible chance to realize his ambition of becoming an Arctic
explorer. It was this that led him to concentrate on unclimbed peaks right
from the start (he served no apprenticeship at climbing) and he had as a target
either the Weisshorn or Matterhorn, since they were the highest unclimbed
peaks of the time.

In 1861 he made the first English ascent of Mont Pelvoux in the Dauphiné.
Hearing that ◊ Tyndall had climbed the Weisshorn, he decided to concentrate on the still unclimbed Matterhorn and went to Breuil in order to attempt
the Italian Ridge, the Swiss or Hörnli Ridge being then considered unclimb-
able. At Breuil he met J.-A. ◊ Carrel, a local mason who was to figure
prominently in subsequent attempts on the mountain.

Whymper's attempts on the Matterhorn are summarized in the table (all
attempts on the Italian Ridge except where stated).

Carrel's part in these attempts cannot be overestimated. Whymper was
fascinated by him, though he always did better when Carrel was not present,
and the highest point reached before the final ascent (by Tyndall, 1862) was
made by a party that employed Carrel only as a porter, not a guide. There
seems little doubt that Carrel, a patriot, wanted the mountain climbed by
Italians.

On 11 July 1865 began a series of events that were to end in tragedy. Carrel
had made secret arrangements to attempt the mountain with an Italian party.
Whymper, feeling angry and betrayed, joined Lord Francis Douglas in a

return to Zermatt and there, by a series of coincidences, a large party assembled to attempt the Hörnli Ridge. The members were: Whymper, Douglas, ◊ Hudson and Hadow, with the guides ◊ Croz, Old Peter Taugwalder and Young Peter Taugwalder. Joseph Taugwalder, a younger son of Old Peter, acted as porter for the first day.

The ascent was made without incident (summit reached 1.40 p.m., 14 July) but on the return Hadow, an inexperienced climber, slipped at a difficult passage, knocking over Croz. The two of them pulled Hudson and Douglas off, and though Old Peter and Whymper held the rope tightly, it snapped at the strain, and the four men plunged down the N Face to their deaths. Whymper and the two Taugwalders, shocked at the tragedy, made a dangerous return to Zermatt. The news of the accident stunned the entire civilized world.

More has been written about the Matterhorn tragedy than any other mountaineering event because of the unique circumstances surrounding it. (For details see the *Alpine Journal* and various books on the subject.) The ascent of the Matterhorn is usually recognized as the end of the Golden Age of Alpine climbing.

Whymper made two further ascents of the Matterhorn, in 1874 and 1895.

Though the Matterhorn is the central theme of Whymper's life, his other climbs, before and after, were considerable achievements. They were all first ascents (except where noted):

1861	Pelvoux (first English ascent)	1865	Grand Cornier
1864	Aig. de la Sausse (S Peak, first ascent)		Dent Blanche (third ascent)
	Barre des Écrins		Grandes Jorasses (W Summit, now Pt Whymper)
	Brèche de la Meije		Col Dolent
	Col de Triolet		Aiguille Verte
	Mont Dolent		Col de Talèfre
	Aig. de Trélatête		Ruinette
	Aig. d'Argentière		
	Moming Pass		

After 1865 he did no serious Alpine climbing but became interested in exploration, visiting Greenland in 1867 and 1872, the Andes 1879–80 and the Canadian Rockies 1901, 1904 and 1909. His first ascents include (in the Andes): Chimborazo, Sincholagua, Antisana, Cotopaxi; and (in the Rockies): Mt Mitchell, Mt Whymper, Mt White, Mt Kerr, Mt Marpole, Isolated Peak, Mt des Poilus, Mt Collie, Trolltinder (1901), Crowsnest Mountain (1904).

Besides his own books, Whymper helped to illustrate the following:

Mountaineering in 1861, J. Tyndall (1862).
Dolomite Mountains, Gilbert and Churchill (1864).
Regular Swiss Round, Rev. H. Jones (1865).
Alpine Regions, T. G. Bonney (1868).
Swiss Pictures Drawn with Pen and Pencil, S. Manning (1870).
Frosty Caucasus, F. C. Grove (1875).
Tent Life in Norway, H. Smith Stannier (1876).
Alpine Ascents and Adventures, S. Wilson (frontispiece only, 1878).
Monte Rosa, the Epic of an Alp, S. H. Nichols (1886, U.S.A.).

After six years of meticulous revising and rewriting, Whymper published *Scrambles Amongst the Alps in the Years 1860–9* (1871). It is one of the great classics of climbing literature, universally known simply as

Date		With	Height	Comments
29–30 August	1861	Unknown guide	12,650 ft (3,856 m)	Camped on mountain
7–8 July	1862	Macdonald	12,000 ft (3,658 m)	
9–10 July	1862	Macdonald	12,992 ft (3,960 m)	
18–19 July	1862	Carrel solo	13,400 ft (4,084 m)	Fell on descent
23–24 July	1862	Carrel	13,150 ft (4,008 m)	
25–26 July	1862	Luc Meynet	13,460 ft (4,103 m)	
10–11 August	1863	Carrel	13,280 ft (4,048 m)	
21 June	1865	Croz Almer Biener	11,200 ft (3,414 m)	On the S E Face
13–15 July	1865	(see below)		First ascent. Hörnli Ridge from Zermatt

(The heights given are Whymper's own estimates.)

Scrambles. An abridged version, entitled *The Ascent of the Matterhorn*, appeared in 1880. *Scrambles* has been translated into several languages and there have been several editions.

His second great work, *Travels among the Great Andes of the Equator*, appeared in 1891 with a second volume of scientific data in 1892. In 1891 he also published a pamphlet, *How to Use the Aneroid Barometer*, and, in 1896 and 1897 respectively, his tourist guidebooks to Chamonix and Zermatt. Whymper also wrote many articles for the popular press on mountain affairs, and with the decline of woodcuts in favour of photographs his writings and lectures formed a substantial part of his income.

Whymper did not make friends easily and was not popular with most of his contemporaries. He figures in several long-standing quarrels over mountain matters and his general outlook was austere and severe; a forbidding personality. He married in 1906.

He died suddenly at Chamonix on 16 September 1911.

Wicks, John Herbert (1852–1919) A member of the élite group which concentrated on Chamonix in the late 1880s and 1890s, Wicks made a number of new routes and variants. His usual companions were ◊ Bradby and ◊ Wilson. Among his better-known exploits were: first guideless ascent of Charmoz (the Baton Wicks pinnacle is named after him) (1899); first ascent of S W arête of the Moine (1890); first ascent of the Pic Sans Nom (1890); first traverse S–N of Grépon (1893): and new routes on the Wetterhorn, Aletschhorn, Schreckhorn, Aig. de Talèfre, Aig. de la Brenva, and others of lesser note. In 1904 he made the second guideless ascent of the Old Brenva route.

Edward Whymper (*AC*)   Georg Winkler

Wien, Karl (1906–37)   German scientist and leader of the disastrous Nanga Parbat Expedition of 1937 in which seven climbers (including Wien) and nine Sherpas were killed by an avalanche.

In 1924 he joined the Munich group that included notable climbers such as ◊ Welzenbach and ◊ Bauer. He made three new routes in the Wetterstein in 1925 and in 1926 was with Welzenbach on the first ascents of the Glockerin N W Face, Eiskogele N Face and Gross Glockner N Face. He then began some notable winter climbs (first ascents): Lyskamm, W Peak, and the traverse of Mont Blanc from Géant Glacier to Vallot Hut.

In 1928 he joined ◊ Rickmers' Pamirs Expedition, during which he climbed 26 summits. With Bauer's Kangchenjunga Expedition of 1931, he reached 7,700 m – the highest reached on the expedition (with Hartmann). During 1933–4 he worked in Africa, climbing Mt Meru and attempting Mt Kenya, but in 1936 he returned to the Himalaya with Bauer's Sikkim Expedition, and climbed Siniolchu and Nepal Peak. Siniolchu (6,892 m) is regarded by some authorities as the hardest Himalayan climb achieved before the war.

Wien   edited   *Willo   Welzenbachs   Bergfahrten*   and   Hartmann's *Kantschtagebuch* (Kangchenjunga, 1931).

Wiessner, Fritz Hermann Ernst (1900–88)   German–American chemist who had a considerable effect on the development of climbing in the U.S.A. Wiessner's early career was in the post-First World War arena of the Eastern Alps, where he made numerous early ascents of the hardest routes at that time. Among his own first ascents are:

1919   Totenkirchl W Face (Piazwand) – first solo (but Preuss earlier?)
1925   Fleischbank S E Face with R. Rossi
       Furchetta N Face with E. Solleder

347

1926 Canali W Face with F. Simon
Pala di San Martino, E Face Direct – with F. Simon
1927 Cima dei Lastei S Face – F. Simon, H. Kees
Cima del Coro – Simon and Kees
1928 Sasso d'Ortiga, W Ridge – with H. Kees
Civetta E Face – H. Kees
Marmolata S Face – first solo (Original Route)

Wiessner was a member of Merkl's 1932 Nanga Parbat Expedition and reached the ridge between Rakhiot Peak and Silbersattel; storms then forced the expedition to retreat. In 1939 he led the first American attempt on K2 and with Pasang Dawa reached a height of *c*. 8,300 m, but lack of support caused his lines to be stretched and in a storm three Sherpas and D. Wolfe died. Wiessner was heavily criticized for his handling of the expedition.

Meanwhile he had gone to live in the U.S.A. and began climbing there. He opened up the ◊ Shawangunks in 1935 and by his example generally raised climbing standards, particularly in the east.

In 1935 he made the second ascent of the Grand Teton N Ridge, in 1937 the first free ascent of the Devil's Tower, Wyoming (Coveney, House), and in 1939 the first ascent of Mt Waddington (with W. P. House). Numerous other ascents in the Rockies, etc.

Wiessner climbed in many parts of the world. He completed all the 4,000 m peaks of the Alps and made many ski ascents of the larger Alpine peaks.

Williams, William (1862–1947) An American lawyer who made the first ascent of Piz Bernina by the S W arête (1885). Was with Broke and ◊ Topham on the attempt of the S Ridge of Mt St Elias in Alaska (1888) and lived to hear of the first American ascent 58 years later. Williams had the reputation of being a hard man on mountains.

Willink, George Henry (1851–1938) An amateur artist whose sketches of climbers in action vividly illustrate climbing at the end of the last century. (See the Badminton volume, *Mountaineering*, illustrated by Willink and containing his chapter 'Sketching for Climbers'.)

Wills, Sir Alfred (1828–1912) High Court Judge and one of the best-known pioneers of the Alps. Though he made no notable first ascents it was his description of his ascent of the Wetterhorn in 1854 (fourth ascent), described two years later in his book, *Wanderings Among the High Alps*, that began the ◊ Golden Age (but ✪ Smith, A.).

Wills was a protagonist in the glacier controversy that convulsed climbers and scientists in the latter part of the century, and a strong supporter of Forbes.

An Original Member of the A.C. he was president 1864–5.

He built a famous chalet in the valley of Sixt called 'The Eagle's Nest', where he spent the summer months and where Auguste ◊ Balmat, his guide, was estate manager. He described the chalet and some of his expeditions in a book, *The Eagle's Nest* (1860).

Wills, William Alfred (1862–1924) Son of Sir A. Wills (see above). Wills was associated with the élite party centred on Chamonix at the turn of the century, particularly Bradby, ◊ Wicks and ◊ Wilson. He took part in most of their expeditions. His brother, J. T. Wills, also did some climbing, including a strange circular tour of the Matterhorn (1884).

Wilson, Claude (1860–1937)   One of the outstanding climbers of all time, with a long career beginning in the 1880s. He was one of the Chamonix élite at the end of the last century, contemporary of ◊ Mummery, with whom he was in rivalry for the first ascent of the Requin, then unnamed (it had been provisionally christened Pic C.W. by Wilson's friends).

His first new route was the S Face of the Weissmies (1882), followed by some first ascents in Norway (1885), but from 1889, when he made the first guideless ascent of Charmoz, his record becomes one of continuous success. He made the first guideless ascent of Grépon (1892) and the first guideless traverse of it S–N (1893). In 1904 he made the first traverse of Aig. de la Brenva. His new routes were numerous: ten major ascents other than those mentioned. In all he made 360 major ascents, 238 of which were guideless. His two brothers, Francis Edward and Herbert, accompanied him on some of the early climbs, but his usual companions were Wicks, Bradby, Wills and ◊ Morse.

Wilson was President of the A.C. 1929–31. He wrote *Mountaineering* (1893) and a privately printed account of his climbing career. As a doctor, he was one of the first to use electro-cardiographs.

Wind-chill   The chilling effect of the wind can seriously affect a mountaineer and may lead to ◊ exposure and ◊ frostbite. It is essential to get out of the wind when forced into a ◊ bivouac, for example, and ◊ crevasses have often been used for this purpose. Exposed flesh, especially where it is thin, as in the nose, ears and fingers, is particularly prone to frostbite.

Work has been done on the so-called wind-chill factor symbolized by K. A K factor of 200 is pleasant but at 1,400 exposed flesh freezes. This can be reached, for example, with an air temperature of $-12°C$ and a 29 k.p.h. breeze.

The effect of wind on air temperature is shown below.

Wind	Temperature (Fahrenheit/Celsius)						
0 MPH	30	20	10	0	−10	−20	−30
0 KPH	−1	−7	−12	−18	−23	−29	−34
5 MPH	27	16	7	−6	−15	−26	−35
8 KPH	−3	−9	−14	−21	−26	−32	−37
10 MPH	16	2	−9	−22	−31	−45	−58
16 KPH	−9	−17	−23	−30	−35	−43	−50
15 MPH	11	−6	−18	−33	−45	−60	−70
23 KPH	−12	−21	−28	−36	−43	−51	−57
20 MPH	3	−9	−24	−40	−52	−68	−81
32 KPH	−16	−23	−31	−40	−47	−56	−63
25 MPH	0	−15	−29	−45	−58	−75	−89
40 KPH	−18	−26	−34	−43	−50	−59	−67
30 MPH	−2	−18	−33	−49	−63	−78	−94
48 KPH	−19	−28	−36	−45	−53	−61	−70
35 MPH	−4	−20	−35	−52	−67	−83	−98
56 KPH	−20	−31	−37	−47	−55	−64	−72
40 MPH	−4	−22	−36	−54	−69	−87	−101
64 KPH	−20	−30	−38	−48	−56	−66	−74

Fritz Wiessner   Willo Welzenbach

Winkler, Georg (1869–88)   A Munich climber famous for his solo ascents, including the Winkler Turme in the Vajolet Towers (1887). In the following year he was overwhelmed by an avalanche while soloing the W Face of the Weisshorn. His body reappeared on the Weisshorn Glacier in 1955.

Winkworth, Stephen (1831–86)   A cotton spinner of Bolton who made a number of new passes including Col d'Argentière and Zwillingsjoch. Usually climbed with his wife, Emma, who became the first woman to ascend Aletschhorn and Jungfrau (1863).

Woodmass, Montagu (1834–1917)   In 1863 made the first ascent of Dent d'Hérens and first ascent of Parrotspitze with W. E. ◊ Hall, ◊ Grove and ◊ MacDonald.

Woolley, Hermann (1846–1920)   A Manchester climber of the school of exploration that included ◊ Collie, ◊ Freshfield and ◊ Dent. He made the first ascent of the N W arête of the Gross Fiescherhorn (1887), but it is his climbs in the Caucasus (1888, 1889, 1895, 1896), Lofoten (1897, 1901, 1904) and the Canadian Rockies (1898 and 1902) for which he is remembered. He made first ascents in each of these districts, notably Katuintau, Mishirgitau, Koshtantau, Ailama, Tsitgeli, Sarumbashi and Gumachi (Caucasus) and Mt Athabasca, Dome, Mt Wilcox (solo), Diadem and Mt Thompson (Rockies).

With ◊ Hastings, he made the first exploration of the Lyngen Peninsula (Norway) in 1897, and with Collie and ◊ Stutfield discovered the Columbia Glacier in the Rockies.

A fine photographer, he went to the Alps in winter mainly for the purposes of his hobby, but he made the first winter ascent of Rimpfischhorn (1893). Woolley was an all-round sportsman: champion oarsman, boxer, etc. President of the A.C. 1908–10.

Workmans, the Dr William Hunter Workman (1847–1937) and Mrs Fanny Workman (1859–1925) were a remarkably adventurous couple noted for their explorations in the Karakoram. Both came from Massachusetts and Dr Workman had a practice there until 1889, when bad health forced him to retire. Meanwhile, in 1881, he had married Fanny Bullock (they sometimes used the name Bullock-Workman).

On his retirement they took up cycling and made remarkable journeys by cycle in Europe, N. Africa, the Middle East, Ceylon, Java, Siam and 14,000 miles in India. This took seven years and in the last of their voyages, in 1898, they first saw the Himalaya and were at once attracted.

In 1899 they made their first expedition to the Biafo Glacier of the Karakoram. Then came:

1902–3 Chogo Lungma glacier and the ascent of Pyramis Peak (23,394 ft) – a height record by Dr Workman, then aged 56
1906 Nun Kun Expedition. Mrs Workman, reached about 23,000 ft – woman's height record – then aged 47
1908 Exploration of the Hispar-Biafo glaciers
1911 Siachen glacier exploration
1912 Siachen glacier and over Kaberi Pass to Baltistan

They alternated the leading of the expedition and the scientific work between them trip by trip. They wrote nine books, jointly, and those concerning their Himalayan visits had a certain vogue at the time. They were *In the Ice-World of Himalaya* (1900), *Ice-bound Heights of the Mustagh* (1908), *Peaks and Glaciers of Nun Kun* (1909), *The Call of the Snowy Hispar* (1910) and *Two Summers in the Ice Wilds of the Eastern Karakorum* (1917).

Y

Yamada, Noboru (1950–89)   One of Japan's finest mountaineers whose outstanding ability and personality made him extremely popular in Japan. He climbed nine of the 8,000 m peaks, making the ascent of ◊ Mt Everest no fewer than three times – a winter ascent in 1983, an oxygenless ascent in 1985 and finally traversing the mountain N E Ridge–S E Ridge, 1988. In this last expedition he waited two hours on the summit for others to arrive so that he could share the experience.

That same year Yamada also climbed ◊ Mt McKinley, Shisha Pangma, Cho Oyu, ◊ Aconcagua, ◊ Kilimanjaro and ◊ Mount Blanc. His ambition was to climb the highest summits of the five major continents in winter and he was to go to ◊ Elbruz after making a winter ascent of McKinley in 1989. Unfortunately, like his compatriot Naomi ◊ Uemura five years earlier, he died in the attempt.

His list of ascents include: Dhaulagiri I (S E Ridge, first ascent, 1978), Kangchenjunga (1981), Langtang Ri (7,205 m, first ascent, 1981), Dhaulagiri I (N W Ridge, first ascent, 1982), Manaslu (winter attempt, 1982), Lhotse (1983), Mt Everest (winter, 1983), Mamostong Kangri (7,516 m, first ascent, 1984), Annapurna I (S Face, winter attempt, 1984–5), K2 (without oxygen, 1985), Mt Everest (without oxygen, 1985), Manaslu (winter, Alpine-style, 1985), Trango Tower (attempt, 1986), Makalu (winter, Alpine-style attempt, 1986), Annapurna I (S Face, first winter ascent, 1987–8), Mt Everest (first traverse from N E Ridge to S E Ridge, 1988), McKinley (1988), Shisha Pangma, Cho Oyu (Alpine-style, 1988).

Yeld, George (1845–1938)   A Yorkshire schoolmaster who became the great authority on the Graian Alps, where he made many first ascents. He collaborated with ◊ Coolidge on the guidebook to the area (*The Mountains of Cogne*, 1893) and wrote *Scrambles in the Eastern Graians 1878–1897* (1900). He visited the Eastern Caucasus in 1890 and made the first ascent of Basardjusi. On a visit to the Lipari Islands he climbed Vulcano, Vulcanello and Stromboli (1904). Editor of the *A.J.* 1896–1919 and joint editor 1919–26: a unique record. Expert horticulturist and gold medallist of the R.H.S.

Yorkshire Dales   An area of the Pennines which extends from Sedbergh to Richmond, west to east, and Tan Hill to Skipton, north to south. It consists of a series of long and lovely limestone dales separated by high and often boggy gritstone moors. The gritstone plays relatively little part; here the limestone is everything and it is not surprising that this is the premier caving area of Britain and has many of the finest waterfalls. All the dales have attractive villages; the pubs are outstanding!

The Dales Way traverses the district from Ilkley to Windermere (130 km) but the best-known walk is the Yorkshire Three Peaks round Pen y Ghent (694 m), Whernside (736 m) and Ingleborough (724 m), about 40 km. Popularity has caused serious erosion problems on this walk, though these are now being vigorously tackled.

In many parts of the area there is evidence of former lead mining,

Noboru Yamada   Geoffrey Winthrop Young

particularly at Grassington and Swaledale. Care is needed because of old shafts.

Though much of the area is a National Park, important parts are excluded such as Nidderdale and Ilkley Moor and the exact boundaries of the Dales are obscure.

There are a number of gritstone and limestone crags, the most important of which are listed below. In recent years this area has been a forcing house for standards. Though there are climbs of all grades there are also many very hard ones, especially on limestone.

GRITSTONE

Almscliff One of the most famous gritstone outcrops, well known to the pioneers. The crag is in Lower Wharfedale about five miles from Harrogate and has climbs of all standards, mostly rather short, and numerous boulder problems. The training ground for many famous names – Botterill, Frankland, Dolphin and Austin among them.

Widdop A series of gritstone buttresses on the moors between Burnley and Hebden Bridge, Yorkshire. Mystery Buttress is one of the biggest for this type of rock. At Hebden Bridge there is also Heptonstall Quarry, which has some long climbs, mostly hard.

Ilkley On the edge of the famous moor there are some gritstone outcrops. The three main climbing areas are Cow and Calf Rocks, the Quarry, and Rocky Valley. Fairly short and all standards up to E8. Popular.

Brimham Rocks This is one of the most unusual and fascinating climbing grounds in the country – a collection of huge gritstone boulders scattered round Brimham House, 3 miles east of Pately Bridge. There are at least 20 different rocks with climbs of all standards.

Guisecliff A long line of gritstone crag on the edge of Heyshaw Moor, above Pately Bridge, 300 m above sea level. There are several distinct buttresses, some of which reach 30 m. Climbs of all standards, many in the easier grades.

Crookrise   Two and a half miles north of Skipton, this gritstone crag stands high on the Embsay Moor. Climbs of all standards. Rylstone and Rolling Gate are two other crags on the moor.

LIMESTONE

Development on Yorkshire limestone, especially in the 1980s, has seen some phenomenally difficult climbs. Crags to note for this are Malham, Gordale, Kilnsey and Blue Scar. Some samples of hard routes on these crags are given. Those responsible for earlier developments include A. ♢ Austin, R. B. Evans, F. Wilkinson, M. Bebbington, the Barley brothers and P. ♢ Livesey, whilst later there was R. ♢ Fawcett, P. Gomersall, the Gibson brothers, M. Atkinson, M. Berzins and N. Foster.

Malham Cove   Near the village of the same name; a huge limestone wall, famous as a tourist attraction and geological curiosity. The great Central Wall was first climbed by P. ♢ Biven and T. Peck in 1959, using bolts. It took five days. The wall is now usually divided into Upper and Lower by the Half-Height Ledges.

From the Central Walls, lower wings extend either side. These too have many good climbs, suited to more modest ambitions. Hard routes (up to E9) include New Dawn E6 and King Swing E6/A2.

Gordale Scar   A deep rift in the crags to the east of the Cove; another tourist honeypot and very impressive. Surprisingly, there are quite a number of easier climbs on the shorter walls. The big walls first succumbed in 1954 with West Face Route (D. Farley and N. Rhodes) and 1956 with Face Route (R. Mosely and J. Mortimer) and Cave Route (J. Sumner and E. B. Knox). Hard routes today include Cave Route Left Hand, E6 and Defcon 3, E7.

Blue Scar   In Littondale about half a mile south of Arncliffe, this is a two-tiered crag about 35 m in height. Apart from some minor routes everything is VS or above – usually well above. The Great White E6; Death Wish E7.

Kilnsey   'The steepness, difficulty, and intimidating nature of the climbing make the crag unsuitable for the low-grade or timid climber.' This quote from the guide says it all. A huge mushroom of a crag at the village of the same name in Wharfedale. The big overhangs (which once featured in a T.V. climbing spectacular) are overcome by aid climbing, A2–A4. Hard free routes include Claws E5 and Little Ernie E6.

Attermire Scar   A number of buttresses (with several well-known caves) high above Settle with numerous climbs of all standards to about E3, mostly short.

Twistleton Scars   A long line of low crags on the north side of the valley between Beezleys and Chapel le Dale. Excellent middle-grade climbing with a scattering of harder routes.

There are at least another 20 limestone crags which are climbed on in the Dales.

GUIDEBOOKS Desroy, *Yorkshire Gritstone* and *Yorkshire Limestone* (both Y.M.C.).

Young, Geoffrey Winthrop (1876–1958)   One of the most important figures in British mountaineering. Young was a son of Sir George Young, who made the first ascent of the Jungfrau from Wengern Alp in 1865. In the following year, Sir George's brother was killed while climbing and all mention of mountaineering was forbidden in the Young household, though regular visits were made to Wales for hill walks. Young began rock-climbing in the Lakes as an undergraduate (and on the college spires; he wrote: *The Roof-Climber's Guide to Trinity*, 1900).

His first visit to the Alps was in 1897 (to the Tarentaise) and then followed years in the Oberland and Pennine Alps, making a number of good climbs. In 1905 he met Josef ◊ Knubel, the guide with whom he formed a perfect team and with whom he did most (but not all) his great climbs. He usually climbed with a guide, but he did solo the Grand Cornier and he led an amateur rope on the first ascent of the Nesthorn N E Ridge (Young, Mallory, Robertson, 1909). His best-known routes are:

1905   Weisshorn, S E Face (improved 1906)
1906   Täschhorn, S W Face
       Breithorn, Younggrat
       Dom, S W Face
1907   Zinal Rothorn, E Face
       Weisshorn, Younggrat
1911   Gd. Jorasses, E Ridge (descent)
       Brouillard Ridge of Mt Blanc
       Gd. Jorasses, W Ridge
       Grépon, Mer de Glace Face
1914   Gspaltenhorn, Rote Zähn Ridge

He was a strong climber; he did all the tops of Monte Rosa, Lyskamm, Castor and back to Lyskamm in a day, and Charmoz, Grépon and Blaitière in a day.

During the First World War he served in an ambulance unit and lost his left leg in action. He invented an artificial limb and began climbing again, achieving a number of summits including the Matterhorn. His last ascent was the Zinal Rothorn in 1935. (See his book *Mountains with a Difference*, 1951.)

Young held climbing parties at the Pen y Pass, Snowdonia, from 1900 until well after the war, and these were attended by most of the best climbers of the day. They did much to stimulate the exploration of the district. Young helped to persuade Thomson to publish the first climbers' ◊ guidebooks. As early as 1907 he suggested an association of climbing clubs and in 1919 actually brought about such a thing, though it failed. In 1943 he tried again and the result was the establishment of the ◊ British Mountaineering Council in 1944.

By profession an educationist, Young was also a poet of merit and his poem, *The Cragsman*, is quoted in many anthologies. His textbook, *Mountain Craft* (1920), was for long the standard work. His book *On High Hills* (1927) deals with his early adventures and is a classic of its type.

Young married ◊ Slingsby's daughter Eleanor. He was President of the A.C. 1941–4.

Younghusband, Sir Francis Edward (1863–1942) Noted soldier-explorer. In 1887 he crossed the Gobi Desert from Peking and entered India over the Mustagh Pass, the first crossing by a European. Explored the ◊ Karakoram in 1889 and the Pamirs in 1890. Was head of the famous Mission to Tibet in 1903–4. Wrote *The Heart of a Continent* (1896).

Z

Zawada, Andrzej (b. 1929) Distinguished Polish climber who has specialized particularly in winter ascents. He first came to notice with a three-week winter traverse of the ◊ Tatra, then in 1973 he made the first winter ascent of a 7,000 m peak – Noshaq. In the winter of 1980 he led an expedition which made the first winter ascent of ◊ Mt Everest, which was also the first winter ascent of an 8,000 m peak. A few months later he was also in command of the expedition which made the first ascent of the S Pillar on Everest, a much sought after prize at the time.

In 1974 he tried Lhotse in winter but failed and his winter attempt on K2 in 1988 (when he was 59) also failed. In private life he is a geophysicist.

Zdarsky, Matthäus (d. 1940) One of the early ski-teachers of the Alps and an inveterate inventor of equipment, including the Zdarsky sleeping bag and the first reliable ski-binding. He made the first analysis of ski movements and invented the stem-turn. Zdarsky was badly crushed by an avalanche during the First World War and invented a device to enable him to overcome his disabilities. He has been called the 'Hermit of Lilienfeld' (cf. Coolidge) and the exponents of his ski method were once known as Lilienfelders. He was in his eighties when he died.

Zermatt The principal climbing centre of the Pennine Alps, Switzerland; an international ski resort and tourist village. The view of the Matterhorn from Zermatt is probably the best-known mountain scene in the world.

The village lies at the head of the Mattertal, a branch of the Visptal, and is reached by rail from the Rhône valley. The road is not open to tourist traffic beyond Täsch.

It is the centre for many 4,000 m peaks, including Matterhorn, Weisshorn, Monte Rosa and Dom.

In climbing history only Chamonix can seriously rival Zermatt as a pioneering centre. The Monte Rosa Hotel was practically a club house for the Alpine Club.

Zsigmondy brothers Three Austrian brothers, two of whom, Otto (1860–1918) and Emil (1861–85), were among the leading climbers of the day. With climbers such as ◊ Purtscheller and ◊ Schultz they made ascents which were regarded as outrageously dangerous at that time. They climbed without guides and often solo. Emil was the undoubted leader of the group. Dent said of him: 'He was too dangerous to be imitated.' In fact, the brothers and their friends were merely ahead of their time and the attitude they took to climbing eventually culminated in ◊ Welzenbach and others and ultimately led to the modern concept of Alpinism. Emil was killed trying a new route on the Meije. The Zsigmondyspitze in the Zillertal Alps is named after them.

Zurbriggen, Matthias (1855–1917) Born in ◊ Saas Fee but spent most of his life in Macugnaga, where he became known as 'Lord of the East Face' (of ◊ Monte Rosa), a natural successor to the great ◊ Imseng. He had to fend for himself from an early age and wandering round Europe he had picked up several languages. He came to guiding relatively late, but quickly became accepted as daring and skilful. He also had a fiery temper.

He was a friend of ◊ Eckenstein who introduced him to Martin ◊ Conway who took him to the Karakoram where he climbed Pioneer Peak (6,790 m). He later revisited the region twice with the ◊ Workmans.

In 1894 Zurbriggen went with E. A. ◊ Fitzgerald to ◊ New Zealand where they made the first ascent of Mounts Sefton (3,157 m), Tasman (3,498 m), Silberhorn (3,279 m) and Haidinger (3,066 m). Zurbriggen also made a daring solo ascent of Mt Cook (3,764 m). Three years later he was with Fitzgerald and Vines in South America when he made the first ascent (solo) of ◊ Aconcagua (6,960 m) and (with Vines) Tupungato (6,550 m).

His travels also included the ◊ Tien Shan and at home he made the first *descent* of the Zmutt Ridge with Lily ◊ Bristow (1894). His autobiography *From the Alps to the Andes* appeared in 1899.

Zurbriggen came to a sad end. He left his wife and became a down-and-out drunk in Geneva where in 1917 he hanged himself.

Zurcher, Alfred (1889–1979)   A Swiss mountaineer who started climbing in 1906 and made numerous Alpine ascents, many with Josef ◊ Knubel. His greatest ascents were the first ascent of the N Ridge of Piz Badile (with W. Risch as guide, 1923) and the first ascent of the Lauper Route on the ◊ Eiger, in 1932.

Index

Bold figures indicate a main entry